Excel® 2019

ALL-IN-ONE

by Greg Harvey, PhD

for dummies®

A Wiley Brand

Excel® 2019 All-in-One For Dummies®

Published by: **John Wiley & Sons, Inc.**, 111 River Street, Hoboken, NJ 07030-5774, www.wiley.com

Copyright © 2019 by John Wiley & Sons, Inc., Hoboken, New Jersey

Published simultaneously in Canada

For general information on our other products and services, please contact our Customer Care Department within the U.S. at 877-762-2974, outside the U.S. at 317-572-3993, or fax 317-572-4002. For technical support, please visit https://hub.wiley.com/community/support/dummies.

Wiley publishes in a variety of print and electronic formats and by print-on-demand. Some material included with standard print versions of this book may not be included in e-books or in print-on-demand. If this book refers to media such as a CD or DVD that is not included in the version you purchased, you may download this material at http://booksupport.wiley.com. For more information about Wiley products, visit www.wiley.com.

Library of Congress Control Number: 2018956684

ISBN 978-1-119-51794-8 (pbk); ISBN 978-1-119-51815-0 (ebk); ISBN 978-1-119-51821-1 (ebk)

Manufactured in the United States of America

V10017744_022520

Contents at a Glance

Table of Contents

Introduction

Excel 2019 All-in-One For Dummies brings together plain and simple information on using all aspects of the latest-and-greatest version of Microsoft Excel. It's designed to be of help no matter how much or how little experience you have with the program. As the preeminent spreadsheet and data analysis software for all sorts of computing devices running Windows 10 (desktops, laptops, tablet PCs and even smartphones), Excel 2019 offers its users seemingly unlimited capabilities too often masked in technical jargon and obscured by explanations only a software engineer could love. On top of that, many of the publications that purport to give you the lowdown on using Excel are quite clear on how to use particular features without giving you a clue as to why you would want to go to all the trouble.

Warning: Excel 2019 marks the first version of Microsoft Excel that runs *exclusively* under a home or business version of Windows 10. If your computer runs an earlier version of Windows, such as Windows 7 or 8, you must content yourself with using Excel 2016, which is part of an Office 365 subscription has all the power of Excel 2019 but in a slightly different format. If such is the case, you need to put this book down now and instead pick up the *Excel 2016 All-In-One For Dummies* by Greg Harvey.

The truth is that understanding how to use the abundance of features offered by Excel 2019 is only half the battle, at best. The other half of the battle is to understand how these features can benefit you in your work; in other words, "what's in it for you." I have endeavored to cover both the "how to" and "so what" aspects in all my discussions of Excel features, being as clear as possible and using as little tech-speak as possible.

Fortunately, Excel 2019 is well worth the effort to get to know because it's definitely one of the best data-processing and analysis tools that has ever come along. Its Quick Analysis tool, Office Add-ins, Flash Fill, and Recommended Charts and PivotTables, along with the tried-and-true Live Preview feature and tons of ready-made galleries, make this version of the program the easiest to use ever. In short, Excel 2019 is a blast to use when you know what you're doing, and my great hope is that this "fun" aspect of using the program comes through on every page (or, at least, every other page).

About This Book

As the name states, *Excel 2019 All-in-One For Dummies* is a reference (whether you keep it on your desk or use it to prop up your desk is your business). This means that although the chapters in each book are laid out in a logical order, each stands on its own, ready for you to dig into the information at any point.

As much as possible, I have endeavored to make the topics within each book and chapter stand on their own. When there's just no way around relying on some information that's discussed elsewhere, I include a cross-reference that gives you the chapter and verse (actually the book and chapter) for where you can find that related information if you're of a mind to.

Use the full Table of Contents and Index to look up the topic of the hour and find out exactly where it is in this compilation of Excel information. You'll find that although most topics are introduced in a conversational manner, I don't waste much time cutting to the chase by laying down the main principles at work (usually in bulleted form) followed by the hard reality of how you do the deed (as numbered steps).

Foolish Assumptions

I'm only going to make one foolish assumption about you, and that is that you have some need to use Microsoft Excel 2019 under Windows 10 in your work or studies. If pushed, I further guess that you aren't particularly interested in knowing Excel at an expert level but are terribly motivated to find out how to do the stuff you need to get done. If that's the case, this is definitely the book for you. Fortunately, even if you happen to be one of those newcomers who's highly motivated to become the company's resident spreadsheet guru, you've still come to the right place.

As far as your hardware and software go, I'm assuming that you already have Excel 2019 (usually as part of Microsoft Office 2019) installed on your computing device, using a standard home or business installation running under Windows 10. I'm not assuming, however, that when you're using Excel 2019 that you're sitting in front of a large screen monitor and making cell entries and command selections with a physical keyboard or connected mouse. With the introduction of Microsoft's Surface 4 tablet for Windows 10 and the support for a whole slew of different Windows tablets, you may well be entering data and selecting commands with your finger or stylus using the Windows Touch keyboard and Touch pointer.

To deal with the differences between using Excel 2019 on a standard desktop or laptop computer with access only to a physical keyboard and mouse and a touchscreen tablet or smartphone environment with access only to the virtual Touch keyboard, I've outlined the touchscreen equivalents to common commands you find throughout the text, such as "click," "double-click," "drag," and so forth, in the section that explains selecting by touch in Book 1, Chapter 1.

Warning: This book is intended *only* for users of Microsoft Office Excel 2019! Because of the diversity of the devices that Excel 2019 runs on and the places where its files can be saved and used, if you're using Excel 2007 or Excel 2010 for Windows, much of the file-related information in this book may only confuse and confound you. If you're still using a version prior to Excel 2007, which introduced the Ribbon interface, this edition will be of no use to you because your version of the program works nothing like the 2016 version this book describes.

How This Book Is Organized

Excel 2019 All-in-One For Dummies is actually eight smaller books rolled into one. That way, you can go after the stuff in the particular book that really interests you at the time, putting all the rest of the material aside until you need to have a look at it. Each book in the volume consists of two or more chapters consisting of all the basic information you should need in dealing with that particular component or aspect of Excel.

In case you're the least bit curious, here's the lowdown on each of the eight books and what you can expect to find there.

Book 1: Excel Basics

This book is for those of you who've never had a formal introduction to the program's basic workings. Chapter 1 covers all the orientation material including how to deal with the program's Ribbon user interface. Of special interest may be the section selecting commands by touch if you're using Excel 2019 on a Windows touchscreen device that isn't equipped with either a physical keyboard or mouse.

Chapter 2 is not to be missed, even if you do not consider yourself a beginner by any stretch of the imagination. This chapter covers the many ways to customize Excel and make the program truly your own. It includes information on customizing the Quick Access toolbar as well as great information on how to use and procure add-in programs that can greatly extend Excel's considerable features.

Book 2: Worksheet Design

Book 2 focuses on the crucial issue of designing worksheets in Excel. Chapter 1 takes up the call on how to do basic design and covers all the many ways of doing data entry (a subject that's been made all the more exciting with the addition of voice and handwriting input).

Chapter 2 covers how to make your spreadsheet look professional and read the way you want it through formatting. Excel offers you a wide choice of formatting techniques, from the very simple formatting as a table all the way to the now very sophisticated and super-easy conditional formatting.

Chapter 3 takes up the vital subject of how to edit an existing spreadsheet without disturbing its design or contents. Editing can be intimidating to the new spreadsheet user because most spreadsheets contain not only data entries that you don't want to mess up but also formulas that can go haywire if you make the wrong move.

Chapter 4 looks at the topic of managing the worksheets that contain the spreadsheet applications that you build in Excel. It opens the possibility of going beyond the two-dimensional worksheet with its innumerable columns and rows by organizing data three-dimensionally through the use of multiple worksheets. (Each Excel file already contains three blank worksheets to which you can add more.) This chapter also shows you how to work with and organize multiple worksheets given the limited screen real estate afforded by your monitor and how to combine data from different files and sheets when needed.

Chapter 5 is all about printing your spreadsheets, a topic that ranks only second in importance to knowing how to get the data into a worksheet in the first place. As you expect, you find out not only how to get the raw data to spit out of your printer but also how to gussy it up and make it into a professional report of which anyone would be proud.

Book 3: Formulas and Functions

This book is all about calculations and building the formulas that do them. Chapter 1 covers formula basics from doing the simplest addition to building array formulas and using Excel's built-in functions courtesy of the Function Wizard. It also covers how to use different types of cell references when making formula copies and how to link formulas that span different worksheets.

Chapter 2 takes up the subject of preventing formula errors from occurring and, barring that, how to track them down and eliminate them from the spreadsheet. This chapter also includes information on circular references in formulas and how you can sometimes use them to your advantage.

Chapters 3 through 6 concentrate on how to use different types of built-in functions. Chapter 3 covers the use of date and time functions, not only so you know what day and time it is, but actually put this knowledge to good use in formulas that calculate elapsed time. Chapter 4 takes up the financial functions in Excel and shows you how you can use them to both reveal and determine the monetary health of your business. Chapter 5 is concerned with math and statistical functions (of which there are plenty). Chapter 6 introduces you to the powerful group of lookup, information, and text functions. Here, you find out how to build formulas that automate data entry by returning values from a lookup table, get the lowdown on any cell in the worksheet, and combine your favorite pieces of text.

Book 4: Worksheet Collaboration and Review

Book 4 looks at the ways you can share your spreadsheet data with others. Chapter 1 covers the important issue of security in your spreadsheets. Here, you find out how you can protect your data so that only those to whom you give permission can open or make changes to their contents.

Chapter 2 takes up the subject of building and using hyperlinks in your Excel spreadsheets (the same kind of links that you know and love on web pages on the World Wide Web). This chapter covers how to create hyperlinks for moving from worksheet to worksheet within the same Excel file as well as for opening other documents on your hard drive, or connecting to the Internet and browsing to a favorite web page.

Chapter 3 introduces Excel's sophisticated features for sending out spreadsheets and having a team of people review and make comments on them. It also covers techniques for reviewing and reconciling the suggested changes.

Chapter 4 is concerned with sharing spreadsheet data with other programs that you use. It looks specifically at how you can share data with other Office 2019 programs, such as Microsoft Word, PowerPoint, and Outlook. This chapter also discusses the variety of ways to share your workbooks files online, all the way from inviting people to review or co-author them from your OneDrive or SharePoint site, attaching them to e-mail messages, and adding and sharing comments as an Adobe PDF (Portable Document Format) file, using the AdobePDF Maker add-in.

Book 5: Charts and Graphics

Book 5 focuses on the graphical aspects of Excel. Chapter 1 covers charting your spreadsheet data in some depth. Here, you find out not only how to create great-looking charts but also how to select the right type of chart for the data that you're representing graphically.

Chapter 2 introduces you to all the other kinds of graphics that you can have in your spreadsheets. These include graphic objects that you draw as well as graphic images that you import, including clip art included in Microsoft Office, as well as digital pictures and images imported and created with other hardware and software connected to your computer.

Book 6: Data Management

Book 6 is concerned with the ins and outs of using Excel to maintain large amounts of data in what are known as databases or, more commonly, data lists. Chapter 1 gives you basic information on how to set up a data list and add your data to it. This chapter also gives you information on how to reorganize the data list through sorting and how to total its numerical data with the Subtotal feature.

Chapter 2 is all about how to filter the data and extract just the information you want out of it (a process officially known as *querying* the data). Here, you find out how to perform all sorts of filtering operations from the simplest, which involves relying upon the AutoFilter feature, to the more complex operations that use custom filters and specialized database functions. Finally, you find out how to perform queries on external data sources, such as those maintained with dedicated database management software for Windows, such as Microsoft Access or dBASE, as well as those that run on other operating systems, such as DB2 and Oracle.

Book 7: Data Analysis

Book 7 looks at the subject of data analysis with Excel; essentially how to use the program's computational capabilities to project and predict possible future outcomes. Chapter 1 looks at the various ways to perform what-if scenarios in Excel. These include analyses with one- and two-input variable data tables, doing goal seeking, setting a series of different possible scenarios, and using the Solver add-in.

Chapter 2 is concerned with the topic of creating special data summaries called pivot tables that enable you to analyze large amounts of data in an extremely compact and modifiable format. Here, you find out how to create and manipulate pivot tables as well as build pivot charts that depict the summary information graphically. In addition, you'll get an introduction to using the 3D Maps and Fore-Cast Sheet features as well as the Power Pivot for Excel Add-in to perform more sophisticated types of data analysis on the Data Model that's represented in your Excel pivot table.

Book 8: Macros and VBA

Book 8 introduces the subject of customizing Excel through the use of its programming language called Visual Basic for Applications (VBA for short). Chapter 1 introduces you to the use of the macro recorder to record tasks that you routinely perform in Excel for later automated playback. When you use the macro recorder to record the sequence of routine actions (using the program's familiar menus, toolbars, and dialog boxes), Excel automatically records the sequence in the VBA programming language.

Chapter 2 introduces you to editing VBA code in Excel's programming editor known as the Visual Basic Editor. Here, you find out how to use the Visual Basic Editor to edit macros that you've recorded that need slight modifications as well as how to write new macros from scratch. You also find out how to use the Visual Basic Editor to write custom functions that perform just the calculations you need in your Excel spreadsheets.

Conventions Used in This Book

This book follows a number of different conventions modeled primarily after those used by Microsoft in its various online articles and help materials. These conventions deal primarily with Ribbon command sequences and shortcut or hot key sequences that you encounter.

Excel 2019 is a sophisticated program that uses the Ribbon interface first introduced in Excel 2007. In Chapter 1, I explain all about this Ribbon interface and how to get comfortable with its command structure. Throughout the book, you may find Ribbon command sequences using the shorthand developed by Microsoft whereby the name on the tab on the Ribbon and the command button you select are separated by arrows, as in

Home➪Copy

This is shorthand for the Ribbon command that copies whatever cells or graphics are currently selected to the Windows Clipboard. It means that you click the Home tab on the Ribbon (if it's not already displayed) and then click the Copy button, which sports the traditional side-by-side page icon.

Some of the Ribbon command sequences involve not only selecting a command button on a tab but then also selecting an item on a drop-down menu. In this case, the drop-down menu command follows the name of the tab and command button, all separated by vertical bars, as in

Formulas⇨Calculation Options⇨Manual

This is shorthand for the Ribbon command sequence that turns on manual recalculation in Excel. It says that you click the Formulas tab (if it's not already displayed) and then click the Calculation Options command button followed by the Manual drop-down menu option.

The book occasionally encourages you to type something specific into a specific cell in the worksheet. When I tell you to enter a specific function, the part you should type generally appears in **bold** type. For example, **=SUM(A2:B2)** means that you should type exactly what you see: an equal sign, the word **SUM**, a left parenthesis, the text **A2:B2** (complete with a colon between the letter-number combos), and a right parenthesis. You then, of course, still have to press the Enter key or click the Enter button on the Formula bar to make the entry stick.

When Excel isn't talking to you by popping up message boxes, it displays highly informative messages in the status bar at the bottom of the screen. This book renders messages that you see onscreen like this:

CALCULATE

This is the message that tells you that Excel is in manual recalculation mode (after using the earlier Ribbon command sequence) and that one or more of the formulas in your worksheet are not up to date and are in sore need of recalculation.

Occasionally I give you a *hot key combination* that you can press in order to choose a command from the keyboard rather than clicking buttons on the Ribbon with the mouse. Hot key combinations are written like this: Alt+FS or Ctrl+S. (Both of these hot key combos save workbook changes.)

With the Alt key combos, you press the Alt key until the hot key letters appear in little squares all along the Ribbon. At that point, you can release the Alt key and start typing the hot key letters. (By the way, you type all lowercase hot key letters — I only put them in caps to make them stand out in the text.)

Hot key combos that use the Ctrl key are of an older vintage, and they work a little bit differently because, on a physical keyboard, you have to hold down the Ctrl key as you type the hot key letter. (Again, type only lowercase letters unless you see the Shift key in the sequence as in Ctrl+Shift+C.)

Finally, if you're really observant, you may notice a discrepancy between the capitalization of the names of dialog box options (such as headings, option buttons, and check boxes) as they appear in the book and how they actually appear in Excel on your computer screen. I intentionally use the convention of capitalizing the initial letters of all the main words of a dialog box option to help you differentiate the name of the option from the rest of the text describing its use.

Icons Used in This Book

The following icons are strategically placed in the margins throughout all eight books in this volume. Their purpose is to get your attention, and each has its own way of doing that.

TIP

This icon denotes some really cool information (in my humble opinion) that will pay off by making your work a lot more enjoyable or productive (or both).

REMEMBER

This icon denotes a tidbit that you ought to pay extra attention to; otherwise, you may end up taking a detour that wastes valuable time.

WARNING

This icon denotes a tidbit that you ought to pay extra attention to; otherwise, you'll be sorry. I reserve this icon for those times when you can lose data and otherwise screw up your spreadsheet.

TECHNICAL STUFF

This icon denotes a tidbit that makes free use of (oh no!) technical jargon. You may want to skip these sections (or, at least, read them when no one else is around).

Beyond the Book

In addition to what you're reading right now, this book comes with a free access-anywhere Cheat Sheet. To get this Cheat Sheet, go to www.dummies.com and search for "Excel 2019 All in One For Dummies Cheat Sheet" by using the Search box.

Where to Go from Here

The question of where to go from here couldn't be simpler: Go to Chapter 1 and find out what you're dealing with. Which book you go to after that is a matter of personal interest and need. Just go for the gold and don't forget to have some fun while you're digging!

REMEMBER

Occasionally, Wiley's technology books are updated. If this book has technical updates, they'll be posted at www.dummies.com/go/excel2019aioupdates.

1

Excel Basics

Contents at a Glance

Chapter **1**

The Excel 2019 User Experience

xcel 2019 relies primarily on the onscreen element called the Ribbon, which is the means by which you select the vast majority of Excel commands. In addition, Excel 2019 sports a single toolbar (the Quick Access toolbar), some context-sensitive buttons and command bars in the form of the Quick Analysis tool and mini-bar, along with a number of task panes (such as Clipboard, Research, Thesaurus, and Selection to name a few).

Among the features supported when selecting certain style and formatting commands is the Live Preview, which shows you how your actual worksheet data will appear in a particular font, table formatting, and so on before you actually apply it. Excel also supports an honest-to-goodness Page Layout view that displays rulers and margins along with headers and footers for every worksheet. Page Layout view has a zoom slider at the bottom of the screen that enables you to zoom in and out on the spreadsheet data instantly. The Backstage view attached to the File tab on the Excel Ribbon enables you to get at-a-glance information about your spreadsheet files as well as save, share, preview, and print them. Last but not least, Excel 2019 is full of pop-up galleries that make spreadsheet formatting and charting a real breeze, especially with the program's Live Preview.

Excel 2019's Sleek Look and Feel

If you're coming to Excel 2019 from Excel 2007 or Excel 2010, the first thing you notice about the Excel 2019 user interface is its comparatively flat (as though you've gone from 3-D to 2-D) and decidedly less colorful display. Gone entirely are the contoured command buttons and color-filled Ribbon and pull-down menu graphics along with any hint of the gradients and shading so prevalent in the earlier versions. The Excel 2019 screen is so stark that even its worksheet column and row borders lack any color, and the shading is reserved for only the columns and rows that are currently selected in the worksheet itself.

The look and feel for Excel 2019 (indeed, all the Office 2019 apps) is all part of the Windows 10 user experience. This latest version of the Windows operating system was developed primarily to work across a wide variety of devices from desktop and laptop to tablets and smartphones, devices with much smaller screen sizes and where touch often is the means of selecting and manipulating screen objects. With an eye toward making this touch experience as satisfying as possible on all these devices, Microsoft redesigned the interface of both its new operating system and Office 2019 application programs: It attempted to reduce the graphical complexity of many screen elements as well as make them as responsive as possible on touchscreen devices.

The result is a snappy Excel 2019, regardless of what kind of hardware you run it on. And the new, somewhat plainer and definitely flatter look, while adding to Excel 2019's robustness on any device, takes nothing away from the program's functionality.

REMEMBER

The greatest thing about the look of Office 2019 is that each of its application programs features a different predominant color. Excel 2019 features a green color long associated with the program. Green appears throughout the program's colored screen elements, including the Excel program and file icon, the Status bar, the outline of the cell pointer, the shading of highlighted and selected Ribbon tabs, and menu items. This is in stark contrast to the last few versions of Excel where the screen elements were all predominately blue, the color traditionally associated with Microsoft Word.

Excel's Start Screen

When you first launch Excel 2019, the program welcomes you with an Excel Start screen similar to the one shown in Figure 1-1. This screen is divided into two panes.

The left green navigation pane with the Home icon selected contains New and Open items at the top and Account, Feedback, and Options at the bottom.

The right pane displays a single row of thumbnails showing some of the different templates you can use to create a new workbook at the top with a list of some of the most recently opened workbooks shown below. To see more templates to use in creating a new workbook, you can click the Find More in New link on the right side of the Home screen or the New icon in the navigation pane on the left.

To open an existing Excel workbook not displayed in the Recent list, click the Find More in Open link on the right side of the Home screen or the Open icon in the navigation pane on the left.

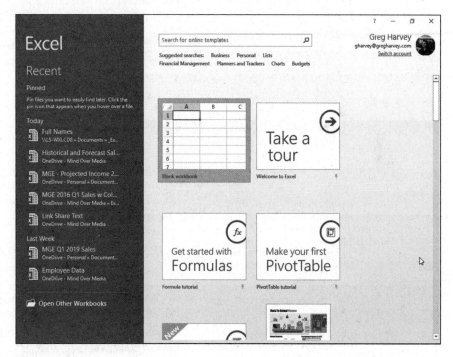

FIGURE 1-1:
The Excel 2019's Start screen with the Home tab selected that appears immediately after launching the program.

The first template thumbnail displayed on the top row of the Home tab on the Start screen is called Blank Workbook, and you select this thumbnail to start a new spreadsheet of your own design. The second thumbnail is called Welcome to Excel, and you select this thumbnail to open a workbook with ten worksheets that enable you to take a tour and play around with several of the nifty new features in Excel 2019.

TIP

I encourage you to take the time to open the Welcome to Excel template and explore its worksheets. When you click the Create button after clicking this thumbnail, Excel opens a new Welcome to Excel1 workbook where you can experiment with using the Flash Fill feature to fill in a series of data entries; the Quick Analysis tool to preview the formatting, charts, totals, pivot tables, and sparklines you can add to a table of data; and the Recommended Charts command to create a new chart, all with a minimum of effort. After you're done experimenting with these features, you can close the workbook by choosing File⇨Close or pressing Ctrl+W and then clicking the Don't Save button in the alert dialog box that asks you whether you want to save your changes.

If none of the Excel templates shown in the Home screen fit the bill, click the Find More in New link to select New in the Navigation pane and display the New screen displaying a whole host of standard templates that you can select to use as the basis for new worksheets. These templates include templates for creating calendars, tracking projects, and creating invoices. (See Book 2, Chapter 1 for more on creating new workbooks from ready-made and custom templates.)

Excel's Ribbon User Interface

When you first open a new, blank workbook by clicking the New Workbook thumbnail in the Home screen, Excel 2019 opens up a single worksheet (with the generic name, Sheet1) in a new workbook file (with the generic filename, Book1) inside a program window such as the one shown in Figure 1-2.

The Excel program window containing this worksheet of the workbook is made up of the following components:

>> **File menu button:** When clicked, Excel opens the Backstage view, which contains a bunch of file-related options including Info, New, Open, Save, Save As, Print, Share, Export, Publish, Close, and Account, as well as Options, which enables you to change Excel's default settings.

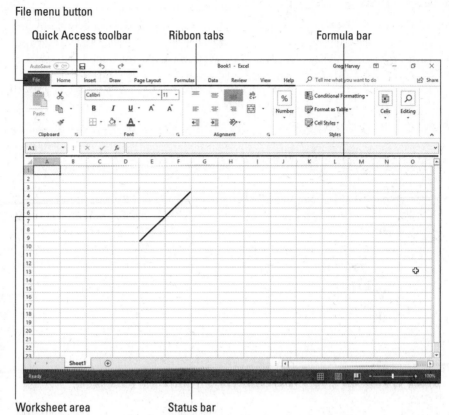

File menu button

Quick Access toolbar   Ribbon tabs   Formula bar

FIGURE 1-2:
The Excel 2019 program window as it appears after first opening a blank workbook when both Ribbon tabs and commands are displayed.

Worksheet area   Status bar

>> **Quick Access toolbar:** This toolbar consists of AutoSave, Save, Undo, and Redo. AutoSave is automatically engaged after you first manually save a workbook to your OneDrive or SharePoint website in the Cloud. You can click the Save, Undo, and Redo buttons to perform common tasks to save your workbook for the first time and save editing changes when AutoSave is not engaged and undo and redo editing changes. You can also click the Customize Quick Access Toolbar button to the immediate right of the Redo button to open a drop-down menu containing additional common commands such as New, Open, Quick Print, and so on, as well as to customize the toolbar, change its position, and minimize the Ribbon.

>> **Ribbon:** Most Excel commands are contained on the Ribbon. They are arranged into a series of tabs ranging from Home through View.

>> **Formula bar:** This displays the address of the current cell along with the contents of that cell.

>> **Worksheet area:** This area contains all the cells of the current worksheet identified by column headings, which use letters along the top, and row headings, which use numbers along the left edge, with tabs for selecting new worksheets. You use a horizontal scroll bar on the bottom to move left and right through the sheet and a vertical scroll bar on the right edge to move up and down through the sheet.

>> **Status bar:** This bar keeps you informed of the program's current mode and any special keys you engage, and it enables you to select a new worksheet view and to zoom in and out on the worksheet.

TIP

When using Excel 2019 on a touchscreen device, the Ribbon Display Options are automatically set to Tabs (so that associated commands appear only when you tap a tab). To make it easier to select Ribbon commands with your finger or a stylus, you can add the Touch/Mouse Mode button to the Quick Access toolbar and simultaneously engage touch mode by tapping the Customize Quick Access Toolbar button before tapping Touch/Mouse Mode option on its drop-down menu. With touch mode engaged, Excel spreads out the tabs and their command buttons on the Ribbon. That way you have a fighting chance of correctly selecting them with your finger or stylus. On a touchscreen tablet such as the Microsoft Surface Pro tablet, Excel automatically adds a Draw tab to the Ribbon containing loads of inking options that enable you to modify settings for drawing with your finger, a stylus, or even the Surface Pen.

Going behind the scenes to Excel's Backstage view

At the top of the Excel 2019 program window, immediately below the AutoSave button to the immediate left of the Save button on the Quick Access toolbar, you find the File menu button (the green one with "File" in white letters to the immediate left of the Home tab).

When you click the File menu button or Alt+F, the Excel Backstage view appears with the Home screen selected. The screen in this view contains a menu of file-related options running down a column on the left side and, depending upon which option is selected, some panels containing both at-a-glance information and further command options.

REMEMBER

At first glance, the File menu button may appear to you like a Ribbon tab — especially in light of its rectangular shape and location immediately left of the Ribbon's initial Home tab. Keep in mind, however, that this important file control is technically a command button that, when clicked, leads directly to a totally new, nonworksheet screen with the Backstage view. This screen has its own menu options but contains no Ribbon command buttons whatsoever.

TIP

After you click the File menu button to switch to the Backstage view, you can then click the Back button (with the left-pointing arrow) that appears above the Info menu item to return to the normal worksheet view or you can simply press the Esc key.

Getting the lowdown on the Info screen

When you click File⇨Info at the top of File menu in the Backstage view, an Info screen similar to the one shown in Figure 1-3 appears.

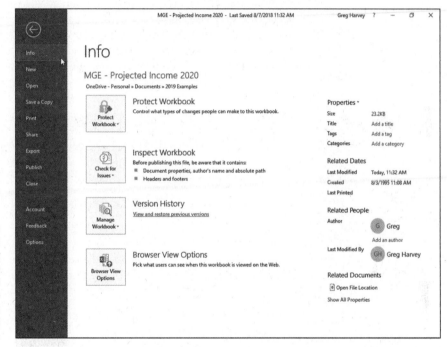

FIGURE 1-3:
The Excel Backstage view displaying the Info screen with permissions, distribution, version commands, and more.

On the left side of this Info screen, you find the following four command buttons:

>> **Protect Workbook** to encrypt the Excel workbook file with a password, protect its contents, or verify the contents of the file with a digital signature (see Book 4, Chapters 1 and 3 for more on protecting and signing your workbooks)

>> **Inspect Workbook** to inspect the document for hidden *metadata* (data about the file) and check the file's accessibility for folks with disabilities and compatibility with earlier versions of Excel (see Book 4, Chapter 3 for details on using this feature)

>> **Manage Workbook** to recover or delete draft versions saved with Excel's AutoRecover feature (see Book 2, Chapter 1 for more on using AutoRecover)

>> **Browser View Options** to control what parts of the Excel workbook can be viewed and edited by users who view it online on the Web

On the right side of the Info screen, you see a list of various and sundry bits of information about the file:

>> **Properties** lists the Size of the file as well as any Title, Tags, and Categories (to help identify the file when doing a search for the workbook) assigned to it. To edit or add to the Title, Tags, or Categories properties, click the appropriate text box and begin typing. To add or change additional file properties, including the Company, Comments, and Status properties, click the Properties drop-down button and then click Show Document Panel or Advanced Properties from its drop-down menu. Click Show Document Panel to open the Document panel in the regular worksheet window where you can edit properties such as Author, Title, Subject, and Keywords and to add comments. Click the Advanced Properties option to open the workbook's Properties dialog box (with its General, Summary, Statistics, Contents, and Custom tabs) to change and review a ton of file properties. If the workbook file is new and you've never saved it on disk, the words "Not Saved Yet" appear after Size.

>> **Related Dates** lists the date the file was Last Modified, Created, and Last Printed.

>> **Related People** lists the name of the workbook's author as well as the name of the person who last modified the file. To add an author to the workbook file, click the Add an Author link that appears beneath the name of the current author.

>> **The Show All Properties link,** when clicked, expands the list of Properties to include text fields for Comments, Template, Status, Categories, Subject, Hyperlink Base, and Company that you can edit.

Sizing up other File menu options

Above the Info option at the very top of the File menu, you find the commands you commonly need for working with Excel workbook files, such as creating new workbook files as well as opening an existing workbook for editing. The New command displays a thumbnail list of all the available spreadsheet templates you can use to create a workbook. (See Book 2, Chapter 1 for more on creating and using workbook templates.)

Immediately below the Info option, you find a Save and Save As command. You generally use the Save command to manually save the changes you make to a workbook. You generally use the Save As command to saves changes in your workbook with a new filename and/or in a new location on your computer or in the Cloud (See Book 2, Chapter 1 for more on saving and closing files and Book 2, Chapter 3 for more on opening them.)

Beneath the Save As command you find the Print option that, when selected, displays a Print screen. This screen contains the document's current print settings (that you can modify) on the left side and a preview area that shows you the pages of the printed worksheet report. (See Book 2, Chapter 5 for more on printing worksheets using the Print Settings panel in the Backstage view.)

Below the Print command you find the Share option, which displays a list of commands for sharing your workbook files online. Beneath this, you find an Export option used to open the Export screen, where you find options for converting your workbooks to other file types as well as controlling the browsing options when the workbook is viewed online in a web browser. (See Book 4, Chapter 4 for more about sharing workbook files online as well as converting them to other file formats.)

The Save as Adobe PDF enables you to save a copy of your workbook in Adobe's open PDF (Portable Document Format) that gives coworkers and clients access to the workbook without having to open it in Excel. (All they need is the free Adobe Reader software on their computer.) The Export option contains an option that enables you to save the workbook in PDF format as well as on for saving the workbook in Microsoft's alternate open file format called XPS (Open XML Paper Specification).

The Publish option enables you to save your Excel workbooks to a folder on your OneDrive for Business account and then publish it to Microsoft's Power BI (Business Information) stand-alone application that enables you to create visual dashboards that highlight and help explain the story behind the worksheet data.

Checking user and product information on the Account screen

At the top of the section below the Close option that is used to close a workbook file (hopefully, after saving all your edits) on the File menu, you find the Account option. You can use this option to review account-related information on the Backstage Account screen. When displayed, the Account screen gives you both user and product information.

On the left side of the Account screen, your user information appears, including all the online services to which you're currently connected. These services include social media sites such as Facebook, Twitter, and LinkedIn, as well as the more corporate services such as your OneDrive, SharePoint team site, and Office 365 account.

To add an online service to this list, click the Add a Service button at the bottom and select the service to add on the Images & Videos, Storage, and Sharing continuation menus. To manage which accounts appear on the list, highlight the name and click the Remove button to take it off the list. To manage the settings for a particular service, click the Manage button and then edit the settings online.

TIP

Use the Office Background drop-down list box that appears between your user information and the Connected Services list on the Account screen to change the pattern that appears in the background of the title bar of all your Office 2019 programs. By default, Office 2019 uses no background. You can change the background by clicking a new pattern from the Office Background drop-down menu on the Excel Account screen (and you can always switch back to have no pattern displayed by clicking No Background from the menu). Below this option, you see the Office Theme selection (White by default) that sets the overall color pattern you use. Just be aware that any change you make here affects the title areas of all the Office 2019 programs you run on your device (not just the Excel 2019 program window).

On the right side of the Account screen, you find the Subscription Product information. Here you can see the activation status of your Office programs as well as review the version number of Excel that is installed on your device. Because many Office 365 licenses allow up to five installations of Office 2019 on different devices (desktop computer, laptop, Windows tablet, and smartphone, for example), you can click the Manage Account link that appears to go online. There, you can check how many Office installations you still have available and, if need be, manage the devices on which Office 2019 is activated. If you need more installations for your company, you can use the Change License button to upgrade to another subscription plan that better fits your needs.

Ripping through the Ribbon

The Ribbon (shown in Figure 1-4) groups related commands together with the goal of showing you all the most commonly used options needed to perform a particular Excel task.

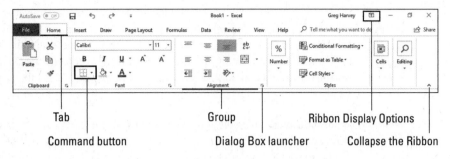

FIGURE 1-4:
Excel's Ribbon consists of a series of tabs containing command buttons arranged into different groups.

Tab

Command button

Group

Dialog Box launcher

Ribbon Display Options

Collapse the Ribbon

The Ribbon is made up of the following components:

>> **Tabs:** Excel's main tasks are brought together and display all the commands commonly needed to perform that core task.

>> **Groups:** Related command buttons can be organized into subtasks normally performed as part of the tab's larger core task.

>> **Command buttons:** Within each group you find command buttons that you can click to perform a particular action or to open a gallery. Note that many command buttons on certain tabs of the Excel Ribbon are organized into mini-toolbars with related settings.

>> **Dialog Box launcher:** This button is located In the lower-right corner of certain groups and opens a dialog box containing a bunch of additional options you can select.

To get more of the Worksheet area displayed in the program window, you can minimize the Ribbon so that only its tabs are displayed. (In fact, this Tabs display option is the default setting for Excel 2019 running on a touchscreen device, such as the Microsoft Surface Pro tablet.)

When the Ribbon is pinned to the Excel program screen, you can minimize it by doing any of the following:

>> **Click** the Collapse the Ribbon button (the button with the caret symbol in the lower-right corner of the Excel Ribbon).

>> **Double-click** a Ribbon tab.

>> **Press** Ctrl+F1 (keep in mind that this is a toggle that can switch from one state to the other collapsing and then expanding the Ribbon each time you depress it).

>> **Right-click** and click the Collapse the Ribbon option the drop-down menu.

TIP

To redisplay the entire Ribbon and keep all the command buttons on the selected tab displayed in the program window, click the tab and then click the Pin the Ribbon button (the one with the push-pin icon that replaces the Collapse the Ribbon button). You can also do this by double-clicking one of the tabs or pressing Ctrl+F1 a second time.

When you work in Excel with the Ribbon minimized, the Ribbon expands each time you click one of its tabs to show its command buttons, but that tab stays open only until you click one of its command buttons. The moment you click a command button, Excel immediately minimizes the Ribbon again so that only the tabs display.

Note, however, that when Excel expands a tab on the collapsed Ribbon, the Ribbon tab overlaps the top of the worksheet, obscuring the header with the column letters as well as the first couple of rows of the worksheet itself. This setup can make it a little harder to work when the Ribbon commands you're selecting pertain to data in these first rows of the worksheet. For example, if you're centering a title entered in cell A1 across several columns to the right with the Merge & Center command button on the Home tab, you can't see the result of selecting the button until you once again minimize the Ribbon by selecting a visible cell in the worksheet. If you then decide you don't like the results or want to further refine the title's formatting, you need to redisplay the Home tab of the Ribbon once again, which obscures the cells in the top two rows all over again! (The workaround for this is to do most of your formatting with the commands on the mini-bar that appears when you right-click a cell selection so that you don't have to open the minimized Ribbon at all. See the section on formatting cells with the mini-bar in Book 2, Chapter 2 for details.)

TIP

If you really want to maximize the worksheet area in Excel 2019, you can use its Auto-Hide Ribbon command to remove the display of the Quick Access toolbar plus the names of the Ribbon's tabs and commands. To do this, click or tap the Ribbon Display Options button (to the immediate left of the Minimize button in the upper-right corner of the screen) and click the Auto-Hide Ribbon command at the top of the drop-down menu. With this mode turned, you simply need to click or tap anywhere in the blank area of the screen above the Formula bar to display the tab names and their commands.

Keeping tabs on the Excel Ribbon

The very first time you launch Excel 2019 and open a new workbook, the Ribbon contains the following seven tabs, proceeding from left to right:

>> **Home:** Use this tab when creating, formatting, and editing a spreadsheet. This tab is arranged into the Clipboard, Font, Alignment, Number, Styles, Cells, and Editing groups.

>> **Insert:** Use this tab when adding particular elements (including graphics, pivot tables, charts, hyperlinks, and headers and footers) to a spreadsheet. This tab is arranged into the Tables, Illustrations, Apps, Charts, Reports, Sparklines, Filter, Links, Text, and Symbol groups.

>> **Page Layout:** Use this tab when preparing a spreadsheet for printing or reordering graphics on the sheet. This tab is arranged into the Themes, Page Setup, Scale to Fit, Sheet Options, and Arrange groups.

>> **Formulas:** Use this tab when adding formulas and functions to a spreadsheet or checking a worksheet for formula errors. This tab is arranged into the Function Library, Defined Names, Formula Auditing, and Calculation groups. Note that this tab also contains a Solutions group when you activate certain add-in programs, such as Conditional Sum and Euro Currency Tools — see Book 1, Chapter 2 for more on Excel Add-ins.

>> **Data:** Use this tab when importing, querying, outlining, and subtotaling the data placed into a worksheet's data list. This tab is arranged into the Get External Data, Connections, Sort & Filter, Data Tools, and Outline groups. Note that this tab also contains an Analysis group if you activate add-ins, such as the Analysis Toolpak and Solver Add-In — see Book 1, Chapter 2 for more on Excel Add-ins.

>> **Review:** Use this tab when proofing, protecting, and marking up a spreadsheet for review by others. This tab is arranged into the Proofing, Language, Comments, and Changes groups. Note that this tab also contains an Ink group with a sole Start Inking button if you're running Excel on a Windows tablet or smartphone or on a laptop or desktop computer that's equipped with some sort of electronic input tablet.

>> **View:** Use this tab when changing the display of the Worksheet area and the data it contains. This tab is arranged into the Workbook Views, Show, Zoom, Window, and Macros groups.

>> **Help:** Use this tab to get online help and training on using Excel as well as give feedback on the program (see "Getting Help" later in this chapter for details).

Note that if you are using Excel 2019 on a touchscreen device, you also have a Draw tab on your Ribbon that enables you to modify inking options when using a drawing device such as Surface Pen. Although these tabs are the standard ones on the Ribbon, they are not the only tabs that can appear in this area. Excel displays contextual tools with their own tab or tabs as long as you're working on a particular object selected in the worksheet, such as a graphic image you've added or a chart or pivot table you've created. The name of the contextual tools for the selected object appears immediately above the tab or tabs associated with the tools.

The moment you deselect the object (usually by clicking somewhere on the sheet outside of its boundaries), the contextual tool for that object and all of its tabs immediately disappears from the Ribbon, leaving only the regular tabs — Home, Insert, Page Layout, Formulas, Data, Review, View, and Help — displayed.

Adding the Developer tab to the Ribbon

If you do a lot of work with macros (see Book 8, Chapter 1) and XML files in Excel, you should add the Developer tab to the Ribbon. This tab contains all the command buttons normally needed to create, play, and edit macros as well as to import and map XML files. To add the Developer tab to the Excel Ribbon, follow these steps:

1. **Click the File menu button followed by the Options item in the Backstage view and then click Customize Ribbon (Alt+FTC) or right-click one of the Ribbon tabs and then click the Customize the Ribbon option on the drop-down menu.**

   The Customize the Ribbon options appear in the Excel Options dialog box open in the worksheet view.

2. **Click the Developer check box under Main Tabs in the Customize the Ribbon list box on the right.**

3. **Click OK to finish.**

Selecting with mouse and keyboard

Because Excel 2019 runs on many different types of devices, the most efficient means of selecting Ribbon commands depends not only on the device on which you're running the program, but on the way that device is equipped as well.

For example, when I use Excel 2019 on my Microsoft Surface Book 2 laptop with its detachable touchscreen with the keyboard and touchpad connected, I select commands from the Excel Ribbon more or less the same way I do when running Excel on my Windows desktop computer equipped with a standalone physical keyboard and mouse or on my Windows 10 laptop computer with its built-in physical keyboard and track pad.

However, when I run Excel 2019 on this device in tablet mode when the touchscreen is disconnected from the keyboard, I'm limited to selecting Ribbon commands directly on the touchscreen with my finger or Surface Pen.

The most direct method for selecting Ribbon commands equipped with a physical keyboard and mouse is to click the tab that contains the command button you want and then click that button in its group. For example, to insert an online image into your spreadsheet, you click the Insert tab and then click the Online Pictures button to open the Online Pictures dialog box.

The easiest method for selecting commands on the Ribbon — if you know your keyboard at all well — is to press the keyboard's Alt key and then type the letter of the hot key that appears on the tab you want to select. Excel then displays all the command button hot keys next to their buttons, along with the hot keys for the Dialog Box launchers in any group on that tab. (See Figure 1-5.) To select a command button or Dialog Box launcher, simply type its hot key letter.

FIGURE 1-5:
When you select a Ribbon tab by pressing Alt plus the hot key assigned to that tab, Excel displays the hot keys for its command buttons.

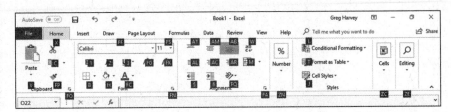

If you know the old Excel shortcut keys from versions prior to Excel 2007, you can still use them. For example, instead of going through the rigmarole of pressing Alt+HCC to copy a cell selection to the Windows Clipboard and then Alt+HVP to paste it elsewhere in the sheet, you can still press Ctrl+C to copy the selection and then press Ctrl+V when you're ready to paste it.

Selecting Ribbon commands by touch

When selecting Ribbon commands on a touchscreen device without access to a physical keyboard and mouse or touchpad, you are limited to selecting commands directly by touch.

Before trying to select Excel Ribbon commands by touch, however, you definitely want to turn on touch mode in Excel 2019. You do this by adding the Touch/ Mouse Mode button to the end of the Quick Access toolbar by selecting the Touch/ Mouse Mode option on the Customize the Quick Access toolbar button's drop-down menu. With touch mode engaged, Excel spreads out the command buttons on the Ribbon tabs by putting more space around them, making it more likely that you'll actually select the command button you're tapping with your finger (or even a more slender stylus or pen tip) instead of the one right next to it. (This is a particular problem with the command buttons in the Font group on the Home tab that enable you to add different attributes to cell entries such as bold, italic, or underlining: They're so close together when touch mode is not on that they're almost impossible to correctly select by touch.)

WHAT "CLICK AND DRAG" MEANS ON YOUR DEVICE

Given all the different choices for selecting stuff in Excel, you need to be aware of a few click-and-drag conventions used throughout this book:

- **When I say "click something"** (a command button, cell, or whatever), this means click the primary mouse button (the left one unless you change it) on a physical mouse or tap the object directly with your finger or stylus.

- **When I say "double-click something,"** this means click the primary button twice in rapid succession on a physical mouse or double-tap the object with your finger or stylus.

- **When I say "right-click,"** this means click with the secondary button (the right button unless you change it) on a physical mouse or tap the item and keep your finger or stylus on the touchscreen until the context menu, pop-up gallery, or whatever appears. When using a digital pen such as the Surface Pen, you need to click the button on the side of the pen as you tap the item.

- **When I say "drag through a cell selection,"** with a physical mouse this means click the first cell and hold down the primary mouse button as you swipe, and then release the button when the selection is made. On a touchscreen, you tap the first cell and then drag one of the selection handles (the circle that appears in the upper-left or lower-right corner of the selected cell) to make the selection.

Adjusting to the Quick Access toolbar

When you first begin using Excel 2019, the Quick Access toolbar contains only the following four buttons:

>> **AutoSave** to automatically save all future edits to a workbook file that you have manually saved at least one time in an online folder on your OneDrive or SharePoint website in the cloud. (This feature does not work on files that are saved in folders on local or network drives.) If you really want to be in charge of when edits are saved to a workbook, you can turn AutoSave off by clicking its On button to change it to Off. Keep in mind that if you do this, you must use the Save command to avoid losing editing changes that you want saved.

>> **Save:** Manually saves any changes made to the current workbook using the same filename, file format, and location when AutoSave is not operational.

>> **Undo:** Undoes the last editing, formatting, or layout change you made.

>> **Redo:** Reapplies the previous editing, formatting, or layout change that you just removed with the Undo button.

The Quick Access toolbar is very customizable because you can easily add any Ribbon command to it. Moreover, you're not restricted to adding buttons for just the commands on the Ribbon; you can add any Excel command you want to the toolbar, even the obscure ones that don't rate an appearance on any of its tabs. (See Book 1, Chapter 2 for details on customizing the Quick Access toolbar.)

By default, the Quick Access toolbar appears above the Ribbon tabs. To display the toolbar beneath the Ribbon above the Formula bar, click the Customize Quick Access Toolbar button (the drop-down button to the direct right of the toolbar with a horizontal bar above a down-pointing triangle) and then select Show Below the Ribbon from its drop-down menu. Doing this helps you avoid crowding out the name of the current workbook that appears to the toolbar's right.

Fooling around with the Formula bar

The Formula bar displays the cell address and the contents of the current cell. The address of this cell is determined by its column letter(s) followed immediately by the row number, as in cell A1, the very first cell of each worksheet at the intersection of column A and row 1, or cell XFD1048576, the very last of each Excel 2019 worksheet at the intersection of column XFD and row 1048576. The contents of the current cell are determined by the type of entry you make there: text or numbers, if you just enter a heading or particular value, and the nuts and bolts of a formula, if you enter a calculation there.

The Formula bar is divided into three sections:

>> **Name box:** The leftmost section displays the address of the current cell address.

>> **Formula bar buttons:** The second, middle section appears as a rather nondescript button displaying only an indented circle on the left (used to narrow or widen the Name box) with the Insert Function button (labeled *fx*) on the right until you start making or editing a cell entry. At that time, its Cancel (an *X*) and its Enter (a check mark) buttons appear in between them.

>> **Cell contents:** The third white area to the immediate right of the Insert Function button takes up the rest of the bar and expands as necessary to display really, really long cell entries that won't fit in the normal area. This area contains a Formula Bar button on the far right that enables you to expand its display to show really long formulas that span more than a single row and then to contract the Cell contents area back to its normal single row.

The Cell contents section of the Formula bar is really important because it *always* shows you the contents of the cell even when the worksheet does not. (When you're dealing with a formula, Excel displays only the calculated result in the cell in the worksheet and not the formula by which that result is derived.) You can edit the contents of the cell in this area at any time. By the same token, when the Cell contents area is blank, you know that the cell is empty as well.

What's up with the Worksheet area?

The Worksheet area is where most of the Excel spreadsheet action takes place because it displays the cells in different sections of the current worksheet. Also, inside the cells is where you do all of your spreadsheet data entry and formatting, not to mention the majority of your editing.

Keep in mind that for you to be able to enter or edit data in a cell, that cell must be current. Excel indicates that a cell is current in three ways:

» The cell cursor or pointer — the dark green border surrounding the cell's entire perimeter — appears in the cell.

» The address of the cell appears in the Name box of the Formula bar.

» The current cell's column letter(s) and row number are shaded (in an orange color on most monitors) in the column headings and row headings that appear at the top and left of the Worksheet area, respectively.

Moving around the worksheet

Each Excel worksheet contains far too many columns and rows for all of its cells to be displayed at one time. (It's true: 17,179,869,184 cell totals equal an illegible black blob, regardless of the size of your monitor.) Excel offers many methods for moving the cell cursor around the worksheet to the cell where you want to enter new data or edit existing data:

>> Click the desired cell — assuming that the cell is displayed within the section of the sheet currently visible in the Worksheet area.

>> Click the Name box, type the address of the desired cell directly into this box, and then press the Enter key.

>> Press Alt+HFDG, Ctrl+G or F5 to open the Go To dialog box, type the address of the desired cell into its Reference text box, and then click OK.

>> Use the cursor keys, as shown in Table 1-1, to move the cell cursor to the desired cell.

>> Use the horizontal and vertical scroll bars at the bottom and right edges of the Worksheet area to move the part of the worksheet that contains the desired cell. Then click the cell to put the cell cursor in it.

TABLE 1-1   **Keystrokes for Moving the Cell Cursor**

Keystroke	Where the Cell Cursor Moves
→ or Tab	Cell to the immediate right.
← or Shift+Tab	Cell to the immediate left.
↑	Cell up one row.
↓	Cell down one row.
Home	Cell in Column A of the current row.
Ctrl+Home	First cell (A1) of the worksheet.
Ctrl+End or End, Home	Cell in the worksheet at the intersection of the last column that has any Home data in it and the last row that has any data in it (that is, the last cell of the so-called active area of the worksheet).
PgUp	Cell one screenful up in the same column.
PgDn	Cell one screenful down in the same column.
Ctrl+→ or End, →	First occupied cell to the right in the same row that is either preceded or followed by a blank cell. If no cell is occupied, the pointer goes to the cell at the very end of the row.
Ctrl+← or End, ←	First occupied cell to the left in the same row that is either preceded or followed by a blank cell. If no cell is occupied, the pointer goes to the cell at the very beginning of the row.

(continued)

TABLE 1-1 *(continued)*

Keystroke	Where the Cell Cursor Moves
Ctrl+↑ or End, ↑	First occupied cell above in the same column that is either preceded or followed by a blank cell. If no cell is occupied, the pointer goes to the cell at the very top of the column.
Ctrl+↓ or End, ↓	First occupied cell below in the same column that is either preceded or followed by a blank cell. If no cell is occupied, the pointer goes to the cell at the very bottom of the column.
Ctrl+Page Down	Last occupied cell in the next worksheet of that workbook.
Ctrl+Page Up	Last occupied cell in the previous worksheet of that workbook.

Note: *In the case of those keystrokes that use arrow keys, you must either use the arrows on the cursor keypad or have the Num Lock key disengaged on the numeric keypad of your keyboard.*

KEYSTROKE SHORTCUTS FOR MOVING THE CELL CURSOR

Excel offers a wide variety of keystrokes for moving the cell cursor to a new cell. When you use one of these keystrokes, the program automatically scrolls a new part of the worksheet into view, if this is required to move the cell pointer. In Table 1-1, I summarize these keystrokes and how far each one moves the cell cursor from its starting position.

The keystrokes that combine the Ctrl or End key with an arrow key (listed in Table 1-1) are among the most helpful for moving quickly from one edge to the other in large tables of cell entries. Moving from table to table in a section of the worksheet that contains many blocks of cells is also much easier.

When you use Ctrl and an arrow key to move from edge to edge in a table or between tables in a worksheet on a physical keyboard, you hold down Ctrl while you press one of the four arrow keys (indicated by the + symbol in keystrokes, such as Ctrl+→). On the Touch keyboard, you tap Ctrl and then tap the appropriate arrow key to accomplish the same thing.

When you use End and an arrow-key alternative, you must press and then release the End key *before* you press the arrow key (indicated by the comma in keystrokes, such as End, →). Pressing and releasing the End key causes the END MODE indicator to appear onscreen in the Status bar. This is your sign that Excel is ready for you to press one of the four arrow keys.

Because you can keep the Ctrl key depressed as you press the different arrow keys that you need to use, the Ctrl-plus-arrow key method provides a more fluid method for navigating blocks of cells on a physical keyboard than the End-then-arrow key method. On the Touch keyboard, there is essentially no difference in technique.

You can use the Scroll Lock key to "freeze" the position of the cell pointer in the worksheet so that you can scroll new areas of the worksheet in view with keystrokes such as PgUp (Page Up) and PgDn (Page Down) without changing the cell pointer's original position (in essence, making these keystrokes work in the same manner as the scroll bars).

After engaging Scroll Lock (often abbreviated ScrLk), when you scroll the worksheet with the keyboard, Excel does not select a new cell while it brings a new section of the worksheet into view. To "unfreeze" the cell pointer when scrolling the worksheet via the keyboard, you just press the Scroll Lock key again.

TIPS ON USING THE SCROLL BARS

To understand how scrolling works in Excel, imagine the worksheet is a humongous papyrus scroll attached to rollers on the left and right. To bring into view a new section of a papyrus worksheet that is hidden on the right, you crank the left roller until the section with the cells that you want to see appears. Likewise, to scroll into view a new section of the worksheet that is hidden on the left, you crank the right roller until that section of cells appears.

You can use the horizontal scroll bar at the bottom of the Worksheet area to scroll back and forth through the columns of a worksheet. Likewise, you can use the vertical scroll bar to scroll up and down through its rows. To scroll one column or a row at a time in a particular direction, click the appropriate scroll arrow at the ends of the scroll bar. To jump immediately back to the originally displayed area of the worksheet after scrolling through single columns or rows in this fashion, simply click the darker area in the scroll bar that now appears in front of or after the scroll bar.

You can resize the horizontal scroll bar, making it wider or narrower, by dragging the button that appears to the immediate left of its left scroll arrow. When working in a workbook that contains a whole bunch of worksheets, in widening the horizontal scroll bar you can end up hiding the display of the workbook's later sheet tabs.

To scroll very quickly through columns or rows of the worksheet, hold down the Shift key and then drag the mouse pointer in the appropriate direction within the scroll bar until the columns or rows that you want to see appear on the screen in the Worksheet area. When you hold down the Shift key as you scroll, the scroll button within the scroll bar becomes really narrow, and a ScreenTip appears next to the scroll bar, keeping you informed of the letter(s) of the columns or the numbers of the rows that you're currently whizzing through.

If your mouse has a wheel, you can use it to scroll directly through the columns and rows of the worksheet without using the horizontal or vertical scroll bars. Simply position the white-cross mouse pointer in the center of the Worksheet area and then hold down the wheel button of the mouse. When the mouse pointer changes to a four-point arrow, drag the mouse pointer in the appropriate direction (left and right to scroll through columns or up and down to scroll through rows) until the desired column or row comes into view in the Worksheet area.

TIP

On a touchscreen, you can scroll the worksheet by swiping the screen with your finger. (Don't use your stylus because pressing it in the worksheet area only results in selecting the cell you touch.) You swipe upward to scroll worksheet rows down and swipe down to scroll the rows up. Likewise, you swipe left to scroll columns right and swipe right to scroll columns left.

REMEMBER

The only disadvantage to using the scroll bars to move around is that the scroll bars bring only new sections of the worksheet into view — they don't actually change the position of the cell cursor. If you want to start making entries in the cells in a new area of the worksheet, you still have to remember to select the cell (by clicking it) or the group of cells (by dragging through them) where you want the data to appear before you begin entering the data.

Surfing the sheets in a workbook

Each new workbook you open in Excel 2019 contains a single blank worksheet, aptly named Sheet1, with 16,384 columns and 1,048,576 rows (giving you a truly staggering total of 51,539,607,552 blank cells!). Should you still need more worksheets in your workbook, you can add them simply by clicking the New Sheet button (the circle with the plus sign in it) that appears to the immediate right of Sheet1 tab.

On the left side of the bottom of the Worksheet area, the Sheet tab scroll buttons appear, followed by the actual tabs for the worksheets in your workbook and the New Sheet button. To activate a worksheet for editing, you select it by clicking its sheet tab. Excel lets you know what sheet is active by displaying the sheet name on its tab in green, boldface type as well as underlining the tab and making the tab appear to be connected to the current worksheet above.

REMEMBER

Don't forget the Ctrl+Page Down and Ctrl+Page Up shortcut keys for selecting the next and previous sheets, respectively, in your workbook. You can also click the Next Sheet and Previous Sheet button marked by the ellipsis (. . .). The Next Sheet button is the one with the ellipsis on the right side of the sheet tabs immediately left of the New Sheet button. The Previous Sheet button is the one with ellipsis on the left side of the sheet tabs to the immediate left of the first visible sheet tab.

If your workbook contains too many sheets for all their tabs to be displayed at the bottom of the Worksheet area, use the Sheet tab scroll buttons to bring new tabs into view (so that you can then click them to activate them). You click the Next Scroll button (the one with the triangle pointing right) to scroll the next hidden sheet tab into view on the right and the Previous Scroll button (the one with the triangle pointing left) to scroll the next hidden sheet into view on the left. You Ctrl+click the Next Scroll button to scroll the last sheet into view and Ctrl+click the Previous Scroll button to scroll the first sheet into view.

TIP

Right-click either Sheet tab scroll button to display the Activate dialog box listing the names of all the worksheets in the workbook in their order from first to last. Then, to scroll to and select a worksheet, double-click its name or click the name followed by the OK button.

Taking a tour of the Status bar

The Status bar is the last component at the very bottom of the Excel program window. (See Figure 1-6.) The Status bar contains the following areas:

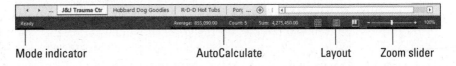

FIGURE 1-6:
The Excel 2019
Status bar.

Mode indicator   AutoCalculate   Layout   Zoom slider

>> **Mode:** This button indicates the current state of the Excel program (READY, ENTER, EDIT, and so on).

>> **Record Macro** button (using an icon with a dot on a tiny worksheet) that you can to record any or all your macros (see Chapter 1 in Book 8 for details)

- » **AutoCalculate:** This indicator displays the AVERAGE, COUNT, and SUM of all the numerical entries in the current cell selection.

- » **Layout:** This selector enables you to select between three layouts for the Worksheet area: Normal, the default view that shows only the worksheet cells with the column and row headings; Page Layout view, which adds rulers and page margins and shows page breaks for the worksheet; and Page Break Preview, which enables you to adjust the paging of a report.

- » **Zoom:** The Zoom slider enables you to zoom in and out on the cells in the Worksheet area by dragging the slider to the right or left, respectively.

TIP

When you begin recording your first macro in Excel 2019 (see Book 8, Chapter 1 for details), the Record Macro button becomes a Stop Recording button (with a square icon) on the Status bar. When you finish recording this macro, the Stop Recording button on the Status bar immediately changes back into a Record Macro button (using an icon with a dot on a tiny worksheet) that you can thereafter use to record any or all your future macros.

Getting Help

In Excel 2019, help is always available to you in two forms:

- » Tell Me help feature that not only shows you the command sequence for the help topic you enter but at times actually initiates and completes the command sequence for you

- » Online Help that contains various help topics that explain Excel's many features

Show-and-tell help with the Tell Me feature

Excel 2019's Tell Me help feature must be from Missouri because it doesn't just tell you what to do; it actually shows you by performing the task for you. This handy little feature is available from the Tell Me What You Want to Do text box located to the immediate right of the last tab of the Excel ribbon. As you enter a help topic into this text box, Excel displays a list of related Excel commands in a drop-down list.

When you then select one of the items displayed on this list, Excel either selects the associated Ribbon command (no matter which Ribbon tab is currently selected) and waits for you to make a selection from the command's submenu or, in some case, just goes ahead and completes the associated command sequence for you.

For example, if you type *print* into the Tell Me What You Want to Do text box, Excel displays a list with the following items:

>> Preview and Print option at the top with a continuation menu that contains Print Preview and Print, Quick Print, and Print Preview Full Screen options

>> Print

>> Print Guidelines

>> Print Preview and Print

>> Print Area

>> Get Help on "Print"

If you select Quick Print on the Preview and Print continuation menu or Print item, Excel immediately sends the current worksheet to the printer. If, however, you select Preview and Print on the continuation menu or on the drop-down list, Excel displays a preview of the printout on the Print Screen in the Backstage view that you can print. If you select the Quick Print item, the program sends the worksheet directly to the printer. But if you select the Print Preview Full Screen item, Excel replaces the Worksheet view with a full screen print preview page from which you can print the worksheet. (See Book 2, Chapter 5 for complete details on previewing and printing your worksheets.)

On the other hand, if you type *underline* in the Tell Me What You Want to Do text box, Excel displays three items: Underline, Get Help on "Underline," and Smart Lookup on "Underline." If you then select the Underline item, you can choose between Underline and Double Underline options, and Excel goes ahead and assigns the kind of underlining font attribute you select to whatever is in the cell that's current in the worksheet. If you choose Smart Lookup on "Underline," Excel opens the Help taskbar showing the definition of underline in various online sources including Wikipedia.

REMEMBER

If you would rather learn how to complete a task in Excel rather than have the program do it for you, select the Get Help on "xyz" item at the end of the list below the Tell Me What You Want to Do text box. This opens an Excel Help window with loads of information about using the commands to accomplish that task (as described in the very next section).

Getting Help from the Help tab on the Ribbon

Excel 2019 offers extensive online help in the Help taskbar that you can make use of anytime while using the program. To display the Excel Help taskbar, you click the Help button the Help tab of the Ribbon (Alt+Y2H) or press function key F1. When you do, an Excel 2019 Help task pane similar to the one shown in Figure 1-7 appears.

FIGURE 1-7:
The Excel 2016 Help window with help topics for on printing worksheets.

TIP

On a device without any access to the function keys, you can display the online Excel 2019 Help window by tapping the Help button on the Help tab of the Ribbon or by using the touch keyboard to enter *help* into the Tell Me What You Want to Do text box and then tapping the Get Help on "help" option in the drop-down list.

At the very top of the Help task pane, you find a search text box with a Search button to the right (with the spyglass icon) below a group of command buttons (Back, Next, Home, Print, and Increase Font). To display a list of related help topics in the Help task pane, type a keyword or name of a category (such as printing, formulas, and so on) and then click the Search button or press Enter. The Excel 2019 Help task pane then displays a list of help topics for that category. To display detailed information about a particular help topic in this list, click its link.

In addition to the Help button, the Help tab of the Excel 2019 ribbon contains these "help"ful command buttons:

>> **Contact Support** to open a Help task pane containing a text box where you can enter a description of your problem with Excel before clicking its Get Help button to display articles that might help you resolve your issue as well as a Talk to Agent button that enables you to get an agent's help with a Live Chat.

>> **Feedback** to open the Feedback screen in the File menu's backstage view where you can send feedback to Microsoft using the I Like Something, I Don't Like Something, and the I Have a Suggestion Option.

>> **Show Training** to open the Help task pane with video tutorials that you can run to learn about features such as designing workbooks, using tables and charts and using formulas and functions.

>> **What's New** to open the Help task pane with a list of new features in the version of Excel 2019 you're running.

>> **Community** to open the Microsoft Excel Community page in your default Web browser with discussions on all sorts of Excel topics where you can post your questions and concerns to the entire Excel Online community.

>> **Blog Site** to open the Excel Blog page in your default Web browser where articles about all sorts of Excel 2019 applications.

>> **Suggest a Feature** to open the Excel Suggestion Box page with your default Web browser where you can give Microsoft your feedback on Excel 2019 as well as suggest new features to be added to future versions.

TIP

When you get familiar enough with Excel 2019 features that you rarely, if ever, consult help, you can remove the Help tab from the Ribbon. Simply open the Excel Options dialog box (File⇨Options), click the Customize Ribbon button on the left, and then click the Help check box under Main Tabs on the right to remove its check mark before you click OK. Note that after removing the display of the Help tab on the ribbon, you still open the Help task pane and get all the Excel help you need by pressing F1 or typing help in the Tell Me text box and then clicking the Get Help option on its drop-down menu.

Launching and Quitting Excel

Excel 2019 runs only under the Windows 10 operating systems. This means that if your PC is running Windows 7 or (heaven forbid) Windows 8, you must upgrade your computer's operating system before you can successfully install and run Excel 2019.

Starting Excel from the Windows 10 Start menu

Windows 10 brings back the good old Start menu that many of you remember from much earlier Windows versions. The Windows 10 Start menu combines the straight up menu from earlier days with the tile icons so prominent in Windows 8 Metro view (which reappears only in Windows 10 on tablets or on touchscreen devices when they are in Tablet mode). To open this menu to launch Excel 2019, click the Windows icon on the taskbar or press the Windows key on your keyboard.

Then, scroll down the alphabetical list of apps installed on your device until you click the Excel icon in the E's, as shown in Figure 1-8.

FIGURE 1-8:
Launching Excel 2019 from the Windows 10 Start screen.

REMEMBER

You can pin the Excel program button to the pinned section of the Windows 10 Start menu so that it's always displayed whenever you open the Windows 10 Start menu. To pin the Excel program button, right-click the Excel icon in the Start menu and then click the Pin to Start item in the displayed context menu. Windows 10 then adds a large Excel program icon to the bottom of the first column of pinned icons. You can then resize the icon (right-click and select Resize followed by Small or Medium) and move it to a more desirable location in pinned section simply by dragging and dropping it.

TIP

After launching Excel 2019 from the Start menu, you can pin the program icon to the Windows 10 taskbar by right-clicking the Excel icon on the taskbar and selecting the Pin to Taskbar item. Thereafter, you can launch Excel from the Windows 10 taskbar by clicking it pinned program icon without having to bother opening the Windows 10 Start menu.

Starting Excel from the Windows 10 Search text box

Instead of opening the Windows 10 Start menu and locating the Excel 2019 item there, you can launch the program by selecting this item from the Windows 10 Search text box (the one that contains the text "Type here to search to the immediate right of the Windows button"). Simply start typing *excel* into this text box until the Excel Desktop app appears at the top of its result list and then click it to launch the program.

Telling Cortana to Start Excel for you

If you want Cortana, the voice-activated online Windows 10 assistant, to launch Excel 2019 for you, click the microphone icon in the Type Here to Search text box and then when she displays the listening prompt, say "Hey Cortana, start Excel." You can also do this by telling her, "launch, Excel" or "open Excel" after getting her attention.

Starting Excel from the Windows 10 Metro view in Tablet mode

TIP

When running Excel 2019 in tablet mode under Windows 10, your Start screen uses tiles in the Metro view first introduced in Windows 8. To start Excel from this Start screen, you simply select the Excel program tile either by clicking it if you have a keyboard and mouse available or tapping it with your finger or stylus.

If you can't locate the Excel program tile among the pinned tiles in the Metro view, you can use the Search feature to find the application and pin it to this Start screen:

1. **From the Start screen, click the Search button on the Windows taskbar (the one with the circle icon between the Back and Task View buttons) and then begin typing** exc **on your physical or virtual keyboard.**

   Windows displays Excel Desktop app in the list under Best Match in the search list.

If you don't have access to a physical or virtual keyboard, you can locate the Excel app by switching the Start screen from the default of displaying just the pinned tiles to all the applications installed on your device. To do this, tap the All Apps button immediately beneath the Pinned Tiles button, the third icon from the top in the upper-left of the Start screen. When you do this, you should see the Excel app button in the E alphabetical listing of all installed applications.

2. **Right-click the Excel app button in the search list to open its pop-up menu.**

   On a touchscreen device, the equivalent to the right-click of the mouse is to tap and hold the Excel menu item with your finger or stylus until the popup menu appears. (With the Microsoft Pen, you hold down the button on the pen's side as you tap the Excel app button with the pen tip.)

3. **Click the Pin to Start option in the pop-up menu.**

After pinning an Excel program tile to the Start screen, you can resize it and then move it by dragging and dropping it in your desired block. If you switched to all apps to find the Excel app, you first need to switch the Metro view back to pinned apps by tapping the Pinned Tiles button before you can do this.

When it's quitting time

When you're ready to call it a day and quit Excel, you have several choices for shutting down the program:

>> Press Alt+FX or Alt+F4 on your physical or Touch keyboard.

>> Select the Close button (the one with the *x*) in the upper-right corner of the Excel program window to close each workbook file you have open.

>> Right-click the Excel program icon on the Windows 10 taskbar and then click the Close Window(s) option on its pop-up menu.

>> Click the Excel program button (the green one with the *x* on a partially opened book to the immediate left of the Save button on the Quick Access toolbar) followed by the Close option on its drop-down menu.

If you try to exit Excel after working on a workbook and you haven't saved your latest changes, the program beeps at you and displays an alert box querying whether you want to save your changes. To save your changes before exiting, click the Yes command button. (For detailed information on saving documents, see Book 1, Chapter 2.) If you've just been playing around in the worksheet and don't want to save your changes, you can abandon the document by clicking the No button.

TIP

QUITTING EXCEL 2019 ON A TOUCHSCREEN DEVICE

If you're running Excel 2019 on a touchscreen device without a physical keyboard (even one with a relatively large screen such as my 10-inch Microsoft Surface 3 tablet), for heaven's sake, don't forget to engage the touch mode on the Quick Launch toolbar as described earlier in this chapter. Turning on Touch mode sufficiently separates the Close button in the very upper-right corner of the Excel screen from the Restore Down button to its immediate left, so that when you tap the Close button, you end up actually exiting Excel rather than just shrinking the Excel program window on the Windows desktop!

Chapter **2**

Customizing Excel 2019

C hances are good that Excel 2019, as it comes when first installed, is *not* always the best fit for the way you use the program. For that reason, Excel offers an amazing variety of ways to customize and configure the program's settings so that they better suit your needs and the way you like to work.

This chapter covers the most important methods for customizing Excel settings and features. The chapter looks at three basic areas where you can tailor the program to your individual needs:

» The first place ripe for customization is the Quick Access toolbar. Not only can you control which Excel command buttons (on and off of the Ribbon) appear on this toolbar, but you can also assign macros you create to this toolbar, making them instantly accessible.

» The second place where you may want to make extensive modifications is to the default settings (also referred to as options) that control any number of program assumptions and basic behaviors.

» The third place where you can customize Excel is in the world of add-ins, those small, specialized utilities (sometimes called *applets*) that extend the built-in Excel features by attaching themselves to the main Excel program. Excel Add-ins provide a wide variety of functions and are available from a wide variety of sources, including the original Excel 2019 program, the Microsoft Office website, and various and sundry third-party vendors.

Tailoring the Quick Access Toolbar to Your Tastes

Excel 2019 enables you to easily make modifications to the Quick Access toolbar, the sole toolbar of the program. When you first launch Excel, this toolbar appears on the left side of the screen right above the Ribbon with the four most commonly used command buttons: AutoSave, Save, Undo, and Redo.

To add other commonly used commands to the Quick Access toolbar, such as New, Open, E-mail, Quick Print, and the like, simply click the Customize Quick Access toolbar button and click the command to be added from the drop-down menu.

TIP

If you use Excel 2019 on a touchscreen device (such as the Microsoft Surface Tablet), you will want to add the Touch/Mouse Mode button to the Quick Access toolbar by selecting the Touch/Mouse Mode option on this menu. This button enables you to switch Excel in and out of touch mode (engaged by default). Touch mode puts more space between the command buttons on each tab of the Excel 2019 Ribbon, thus making it a whole lot easier to select the correct command with either your finger or stylus. Even when running Excel on a computer without any touch capabilities, you can still add the Touch/Mouse Mode button to the Quick Access toolbar and use touch mode to make it easier to select Tab commands with your mouse.

Adding Ribbon commands to the Quick Access toolbar

Excel 2019 makes it super-easy to add a command from any tab on the Ribbon to the Quick Access toolbar. To add a Ribbon command, simply right-click its command button on the Ribbon and then click Add to Quick Access Toolbar from its shortcut menu. Excel immediately adds the command button to the very end of the Quick Access toolbar, immediately in front of the Customize Quick Access Toolbar button.

If you want to move the command button to a new location on the Quick Access toolbar or group it with other buttons on the toolbar, you need to click the Customize Quick Access Toolbar button and then click More Commands from its drop-down menu.

Excel then opens the Excel Options dialog box with the Quick Access Toolbar tab selected (similar to the one shown in Figure 2-1). Here, Excel shows all the buttons currently added to the Quick Access toolbar in the order in which they appear from left to right on the toolbar corresponding to their top-down order in the list box on the right side of the dialog box.

Move Up

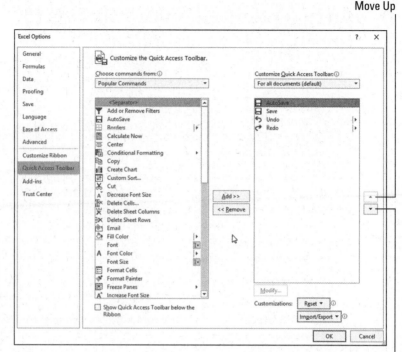

Move Down

FIGURE 2-1:
Use the buttons
on the Quick
Access Toolbar
tab of the Excel
Options dialog
box to customize
the appearance
of the Quick
Access toolbar.

To reposition a particular button on the bar, click it in the list box on the right and then click either the Move Up button (the one with the black triangle pointing upward) or the Move Down button (the one with the black triangle pointing downward) until the button is promoted or demoted to the desired position on the toolbar.

REMEMBER

You can add separators to the toolbar to group related buttons. To do this, click the <Separator> selection in the list box on the left and then click the Add button twice to add two. Then, click the Move Up or Move Down button to position one of the two separators at the beginning of the group and the other at the end. Also keep in mind that you can always return the Quick Access toolbar to its default state with its three buttons (Save, Undo, and Redo) by selecting the Reset Only Quick Access Toolbar option from the Reset drop-down list.

TIP

If you've added too many buttons to the Quick Access toolbar and can no longer read the workbook name, you can reposition it so that it appears beneath the Ribbon immediately on top of the Formula bar. To do this, click the Customize Quick Access Toolbar button at the end of the toolbar and then click Show Below the Ribbon from the drop-down menu.

Customizing Excel 2019

Adding non-Ribbon commands to the Quick Access toolbar

You can also use the options on the Quick Access Toolbar tab of the Excel Options dialog box (refer to Figure 2-1) to add a button for any Excel command even if it's not one of those displayed on the tabs of the Ribbon:

1. **Select the type of command you want to add to the Quick Access toolbar from the Choose Commands From drop-down list box.**

   The types of commands include the default Popular Commands, Commands Not in the Ribbon, All Commands, and Macros, as well as each of the standard and contextual tabs that can appear on the Ribbon. To display only the commands not displayed on the Ribbon, click Commands Not in the Ribbon near the top of the drop-down list. To display a complete list of all the Excel commands, click All Commands near the bottom of the drop-down list.

2. **Click the command option whose button you want to add to the Quick Access toolbar in the Choose Commands From list box on the left.**

3. **Click the Add button to add the command button to the bottom of the list box on the right.**

4. **(Optional) To reposition the newly added command button so that it's not the last one on the toolbar, click the Move Up button until it's in the desired position.**

5. **Click the OK button to close the Excel Options dialog box.**

ADDING COMMANDS LOST FROM EARLIER EXCEL VERSIONS TO THE QUICK ACCESS TOOLBAR

TIP

Although certain commands from earlier versions of Excel, such as Data⇨Form and View⇨Web Page Preview, did not make it to the Ribbon in Excel 2019, this does not mean that they were entirely eliminated from the program. The only way, however, to revive these commands is to add their command buttons to the Quick Access toolbar after clicking the Commands Not in the Ribbon category from the Choose Commands From drop-down list on the Customization tab of the Excel Options dialog box.

Adding macros to the Quick Access toolbar

If you've created favorite macros (see Book 8, Chapter 1) that you routinely use and want to be able to run directly from the Quick Access toolbar, click Macros from the Choose Commands From drop-down list box and then click the name of the macro to add in the Choose Commands From list box followed by the Add button.

REMEMBER

Excel 2019 then adds a custom macro command button to the end of the Quick Access toolbar whose generic icon displays the branching of a programming diagram. This means that if you add several favorite macros to the Quick Access toolbar, the only way to tell them apart is by their ScreenTips, each of which displays the location and name of the macro attached to the particular custom button when you highlight the button by passing the mouse pointer over it.

Exercising Your Options

Each time you open a new workbook, Excel makes a whole bunch of assumptions about how you want the spreadsheet and chart information that you enter into it to appear onscreen and in print. These assumptions may or may not fit the way you work and the kinds of spreadsheets and charts you need to create.

In the following five sections, you get a quick rundown on how to change the most important default or *preference* settings in the Excel Options dialog box. This is the biggest dialog box in Excel, with a billion tabs (12 actually). From the Excel Options dialog box, you can see what things appear onscreen and how they appear, as well as when and how Excel 2019 calculates worksheets.

TIP

Nothing discussed in the following five sections is critical to your being able to operate Excel. Just remember the Excel Options dialog box if you find yourself futzing with the same setting over and over again in most of the workbooks you create. In such a situation, it's high time to get into the Excel Options dialog box and modify that setting so that you won't waste any more time tinkering with the same setting in future workbooks.

Changing some of the more universal settings on the General tab

The General tab (shown in Figure 2-2) is the first tab in the Excel Options dialog box. This tab is automatically selected whenever you first open this dialog box by clicking File➪Options or by pressing Alt+FT.

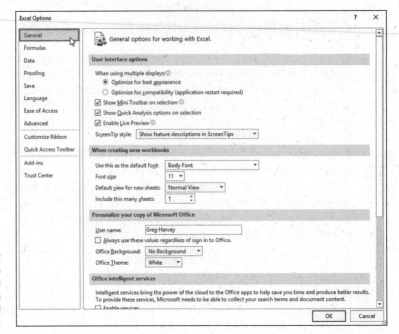

FIGURE 2-2:
The General tab's
options enable
you to change
many universal
Excel settings.

The options on the General tab are arranged into four groups: User Interface Options, When Creating New Workbooks, Personalize Your Copy of Microsoft Office, and Start Up Options.

The User Interface Options group

The User Interface Options group contains the following check boxes and buttons:

» **When Using Multiple Displays:** Enables you to select the Optimize for Best Appearance setting rather than the default setting of Optimize for Compatibility so that you can have the Excel program window plus whatever other windows you have open on the connected display screens look their very best.

» **Show Mini Toolbar on Selection:** Disables or re-enables the display of the mini-toolbar, which contains essential formatting buttons from the Home tab, above a cell selection or other object's shortcut menu when you right-click it.

» **Show Quick Analysis Options on Selection:** Disables or re-enables the appearance of the new Quick Access toolbar in the lower-right corner of a cell selection. The Quick Analysis toolbar contains options for applying formatting to the selection as well as creating new charts and pivot tables using its data.

» **Enable Live Preview:** Disables or re-enables the Live Preview feature whereby Excel previews the data in the current cell selection using the font or style you highlight in a drop-down list or gallery before you actually apply the formatting.

>> **ScreenTip Style:** Changes the way ScreenTips (which display information about the command buttons you highlight with the mouse) are displayed onscreen. Click Don't Show Feature Descriptions in ScreenTips from the ScreenTip Style drop-down list to display a minimum amount of description in the ScreenTip and eliminate all links to online help, or click Don't Show ScreenTips to completely remove the display of ScreenTips from the screen (potentially confusing if you add macros to the toolbar that all use the same icon).

The When Creating New Workbooks group

The options in the When Creating New Workbooks section of the Popular tab of the Excel Options dialog box include only these four combo and text boxes:

>> **Use This as the Default Font:** Select a new default font to use in all cells of new worksheets by entering the font name in the combo box or clicking its name in the drop-down list (Body Font, which is actually Microsoft's Calibri font).

>> **Font Size:** Select a new default size to use in all cells of new worksheets (11 points is the default size) by entering the value in the box or by clicking this new point value by in the drop-down list.

>> **Default View for New Sheets:** Select either Page Break Preview (displaying page breaks that you can adjust) or Page Layout (displaying page breaks, rulers, and margins) as the default view (rather than Normal) for all new worksheets.

>> **Include This Many Sheets:** Increase or decrease the default number of worksheets in each new workbook (1 being the default) by entering a number between 2 and 225 or select this new number by clicking the spinner buttons.

Personalize Your Copy of Microsoft Office section

The Personalize Your Copy of Microsoft Office section contains the following three options:

>> **UserName:** This text box enables you to change the username that's used as the default author for new workbooks created with Excel 2019.

>> **Office Background:** This drop-down list enables you to select a faint, background pattern to be displayed on the right side of the Excel program window where your name, the Ribbon Display Options, and Minimize,

Restore, and Close buttons all appear. To switch back to the default of no pattern in this area of the screen after selecting one the available background patterns, you click the No Background option at the top of this drop-down list.

» **Office Theme:** This drop-down list enables you to select between three different tint options — Colorful, Light Gray, and White — that are applied to the borders of the Excel screen, creating a kind of background color for the Ribbon tabs, column letter and row number indicators on the worksheet frame, and the Status bar.

REMEMBER

Remember that when you click the Always Use These Values Regardless of Sign In to Office check box in the Personalize Your Copy of Microsoft Office section, the username, background pattern, and theme you select for the UserName, Office Background, and Office Theme options are applied to all the Office 2019 application programs that you use, such as Word 2019, PowerPoint 2019, and so on.

The Office Intelligent Services and LinkedIn Features options in their respective sections of the General tab of the Excel Options dialog box are both enabled by default. The Office Intelligent Services setting is responsible for bringing in such features as the data Insights (on the Insert menu), Tell Me, translation, and smart lookup into Excel 2019. The LinkedIn Features is really used more in Office programs such as Outlook 2019 and Word 2019 to keep you better connected to the people in your network.

Start Up Options section

The final section, Start Up Options, contains the following three options:

» **Choose the Extensions You Want Excel to Open by Default:** The Default Programs button, when clicked, opens a Set Associations for Program dialog box that enables you to select all the types of application files that you want associated with Excel 2019. Once associated with Excel, double-clicking any file carrying its extension automatically launches Excel 2019 for viewing and editing.

» **Tell Me if Microsoft Excel Isn't the Default Program for Viewing and Editing Spreadsheets:** This check box determines whether or not you're informed should another Spreadsheet program or viewer on your computer other than Excel 2019 be associated with opening Excel workbook files.

» **Show the Start Screen When This Application Starts:** This check box determines whether or not the Start screen (described in detail in Book 1, Chapter 1) appears when you launch Excel 2019.

TIP

If you deselect the Show the Start Screen When This Application Starts check box, whenever you launch Excel 2019, the program immediately opens a new, blank workbook file in the worksheet view, skipping entirely the Excel Backstage view. Excel 2019 then works just like Excel 2010 and 2007 on startup.

Changing common calculation options on the Formulas tab

The options on the Formulas tab (see Figure 2-3) of the Excel Options dialog box (File➪Options➪Formulas or Alt+FTF) are divided into Calculation Options, Working with Formulas, Error Checking, and Error Checking Rules.

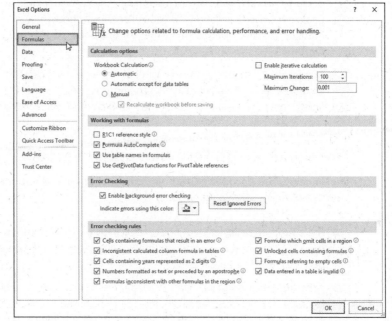

FIGURE 2-3:
The Formulas tab's options enable you to change how formulas in the spreadsheet are recalculated.

The Calculation Options group

The Calculation Options enable you to change when formulas in your workbook are recalculated and how a formula that Excel cannot solve on the first try (such as one with a circular reference) is recalculated. Choose from the following items:

>> **Automatic** option button (the default) to have Excel recalculate all formulas immediately after you modify any of the values on which their calculation depends.

- >> **Automatic Except for Data Tables** option button to have Excel automatically recalculate all formulas except for those entered into what-if data tables you create. (See Book 7, Chapter 1.) To update these formulas, you must click the Calculate Now (F9) or the Calculate Sheet (Shift+F9) command button on the Formulas tab of the Ribbon.

- >> **Manual** option button to switch to total manual recalculation, whereby formulas that need updating are recalculated only when you click the Calculate Now (F9) or the Calculate Sheet (Shift+F9) command button on the Formulas tab of the Ribbon.

- >> **Enable Iterative Calculation** check box to enable or disable iterative calculations for formulas that Excel finds that it cannot solve on the first try.

- >> **Maximum Iterations** text box to change the number of times (100 is the default) that Excel recalculates a seemingly insolvable formula when the Enable Iterative Calculation check box contains a check mark by entering a number between 1 and 32767 in the text box or by clicking the spinner buttons.

- >> **Maximum Change** text box to change the amount by which Excel increments the guess value it applies each time the program recalculates the formula in an attempt to solve it by entering the new increment value in the text box.

The Working with Formulas options group

The Working with Formulas group contains four check box options that determine a variety of formula-related options:

- >> **R1C1 Reference Style** check box (unchecked by default) to enable or disable the R1C1 cell reference system whereby both columns and rows are numbered as in R45C2 for cell B45.

- >> **Formula AutoComplete** check box (checked by default) to disable or re-enable the Formula AutoComplete feature whereby Excel attempts to complete the formula or function you're manually building in the current cell.

- >> **Use Table Names in Formulas** check box (checked by default) to disable and re-enable the feature whereby Excel automatically applies all range names you've created in a table of data to all formulas that refer to their cells. (See Book 3, Chapter 1.)

- >> **Use GetPivotData Functions for PivotTable References** check box (checked by default) to disable and re-enable the GetPivotTable function that Excel uses to extract data from various fields in a data source when placing them in various fields of a pivot table summary report you're creating. (See Book 7, Chapter 2 for details.)

The Error Checking and Error Checking Rules groups

The remaining options on the Formulas tab of the Excel Options dialog box enable you to control error-checking for formulas.

In the Error Checking section, the sole check box, Enable Background Error Checking, which enables error-checking in the background while you're working in Excel, is checked.

In the Error Checking Rules, all of the check boxes are checked, with the exception of the Formulas Referring to Empty Cells check box, which indicates a formula error when a formula refers to a blank cell.

REMEMBER

To disable background error checking, click the Enable Background Error Checking check box in the Error Checking section to remove its check mark. To change the color used to indicate formula errors in cells of the worksheet (when background error checking is engaged), click the Indicate Errors Using This Color drop-down button and click a new color square on its drop-down color palette. To remove the color from all cells in the worksheet where formula errors are currently indicated, click the Reset Ignore Errors button. To disable other error-checking rules, click their check boxes to remove the check marks

Digging the options on the Data tab

The Data Options group on the Data tab of the Excel Options dialog box contains four check box options. These options control the way that Excel 2019 handles huge amounts of data that you can access in Excel through external data queries discussed in Book 6, Chapter 2 or through Excel's pivot table feature (especially when using the Power Pivot add-in) discussed Book 7, Chapter 2.

By default, Excel 2019 disables the undo feature when refreshing data in a pivot table created from external data that has more than 300,000 source rows (also called *records*) to significantly reduce the data refresh time. To modify the minimum number of source rows at which the Undo Refresh feature is disabled, enter a new number (representing thousands of records) in the text box containing the default value of 300 under the Disable Undo for Large PivotTable Refresh Operations check box or select the new value with the spinner buttons. To enable the undo feature for all refresh operations in your large pivot tables (regardless of how long the refresh operation takes), simply deselect the Disable Undo for Large PivotTable Refresh Operations check box.

Excel 2019 also automatically disables the Undo feature for Excel data lists that are created from related external database tables (referred to in Excel as a *data model*) that exceed 64MB in size. To change the minimum size at which the Undo feature is disabled, enter a new number (representing megabytes) in the text box containing the default value of 64 under the Disable Undo for Large Data Model Operations check box or select this new value with the spinner buttons. To enable the Undo feature for all operations involving data lists created from an external data model (regardless of how long the undo operation takes), simply deselect the Disable Undo for Large Data Model Operations check box.

TIP

If you want Excel to automatically assume that any external data used in creating new pivot tables or imported into data lists from external data queries involve a data model so that Excel automatically looks for the fields that are related in the various files you designate, select the Prefer the Excel Data Model When Creating PivotTables, Query Tables, and Data Connections check box.

In addition to Data Options, the Data tab contains a Show Legacy Data Import Wizards section with a number of unselected check boxes for each of the various Wizards that earlier versions of Excel used in order to import particular types of data, such as tables from Microsoft Access databases, web page queries, or text files.

TIP

As Excel 2019 has greatly improved its data import capabilities for automatically recognizing and parsing data imported into one of its worksheets, selecting any of these so-called Legacy Import Wizards is unnecessary unless you have extensive experience with these older import engines *and* find that Excel 2019's data intelligence capabilities are having trouble properly importing data from one of these external sources on which your work depends.

Changing correction options on the Proofing tab

The options on the Proofing tab (see Figure 2-4) of the Excel Options dialog box (File⇨Options⇨Proofing or Alt+FTP) are divided into two sections: AutoCorrect Options and When Correcting Spelling in Microsoft Office Programs.

The AutoCorrect Options group

Click the AutoCorrect Options button to open the AutoCorrect dialog box for the primary language used in Microsoft Office 2019. This dialog box contains the following four tabs:

>> **AutoCorrect** with check box options that control what corrections Excel automatically makes, an Exceptions button that enables you to indicate what words or abbreviations are not to be capitalized in the AutoCorrect Exceptions dialog box, and text boxes where you can define custom replacements that Excel makes as you type.

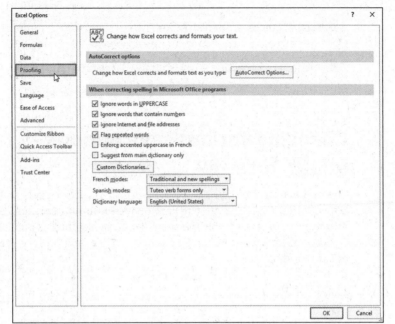

FIGURE 2-4:
The Proofing tab's options enable you to change AutoCorrect and spell-checking options.

>> **AutoFormat As You Type** with check box options that control whether to replace Internet addresses and network paths with hyperlinks, and to automatically insert new rows and columns to cell ranges defined as tables and copy formulas in calculated fields to new rows of a data list.

>> **Actions** with an Enable Additional Actions in the Right-Click Menu check box and Available Actions list box that let you activate a date or financial symbol context menu that appears when you enter certain date and financial text in cells.

>> **Math AutoCorrect** with Replace and With text boxes that enable you to replace certain text with math symbols that are needed in your worksheets.

The When Correcting Spelling in Microsoft Office Programs group

The options in the When Correcting Spelling in Microsoft Office Programs group of the Proofing tab control what types of errors Excel flags as possible misspellings when you use the Spell Check feature. (See Book 2, Chapter 3.) This section also contains the following buttons:

>> **Custom Dictionaries,** which opens the Custom Dictionaries dialog box, where you can specify a new custom dictionary to use in spell checking the worksheet, define a new dictionary, and edit its word list.

>> **French Modes** or **Spanish Modes,** which specify which forms of the respective language to use in proofing spreadsheet text.

>> **Dictionary Language,** which specifies by language and country which dictionary to use in proofing spreadsheet text.

Changing various save options on the Save tab

The options on the Save tab (see Figure 2-5) of the Excel Options dialog box (File⇨Options⇨Save or Alt+FTS) are divided into four sections: Save Workbooks, AutoRecover Exceptions for the current workbook (such as Book1), Offline Editing Options for Document Management Server Files, and Preserve Visual Appearance of the Workbook.

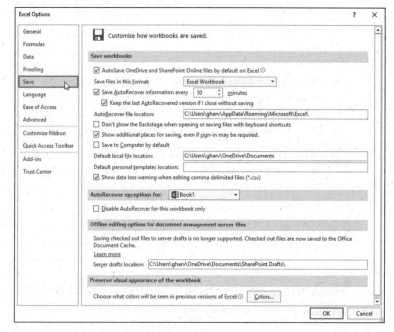

FIGURE 2-5:
The Save tab's options enable you to change the automatic save and backup and recovery options.

The first option in the Save Workbooks section is the AutoSave OneDrive and SharePoint Online Files by Default on Excel. With this option selected, Excel 2019 automatically saves all editing changes in all workbook files that you initially save in the cloud in a folder on your OneDrive or SharePoint site. Note that using the AutoSave feature gives you the benefit of seeing the editing changes made by others who are also working on the same workbook saved in the cloud in real time.

The default setting for the Saves Files in this Format drop-down list box at the top of the Saves Workbooks section is Excel Workbook, the XML-based file format first introduced in Excel 2007 that appends the .xlsx suffix to the filename. If you want Excel 2019 to automatically save your new workbook files in another file format (such as the old Excel workbook file format that uses the *.xls suffix), select the Excel 97-2013 menu option in this drop-down list box.

The settings in the Save Workbooks section on this tab also include the program's AutoRecover settings. The AutoRecover feature enables Excel to save copies of your entire Excel workbook at the interval displayed in the Minutes text box (10 by default). You tell Excel where to save these copies in the AutoRecover File Location text box by specifying a drive, a folder, and maybe even a subfolder.

If your computer should crash or you suddenly lose power, the next time you start Excel, the program automatically displays an AutoRecover pane on the left side of the worksheet area. From this pane, you can open a copy of the workbook file that you were working on when this crash or power loss occurred. If this recovered workbook (saved at the time of the last AutoRecover) contains information that isn't saved in the original copy (the copy you saved the last time you used the Save command before the crash or power loss), you can then use the recovered copy rather than manually reconstructing and re-entering the otherwise lost information.

You may also use the recovered copy of a workbook should the original copy of the workbook file become corrupted in such a way that Excel can no longer open it. (This happens very rarely, but it *does* happen.)

WARNING

Don't disable the AutoRecover feature by removing the check mark from the Keep the Last AutoRecovered Version If I Close without Saving check box on the Save tab even if you have a battery backup system for your computer that gives you plenty of time to manually save your Excel workbook during any power outage. Disabling AutoRecover in no way protects you from data loss if your workbook file becomes corrupted or you hit the computer's power switch by mistake.

Beneath the AutoRecover File Location text box, you find the following Save Workbook options:

>> **Don't Show the Backstage when Opening or Saving Files:** Normally, Excel 2019 shows the Open screen in the Backstage view whenever you press Ctrl+O to open a file for editing and the Save As screen when you press Ctrl+S or click the Save button on the Quick Access toolbar to save a new workbook. Click this check box if you want Excel to display the Open and Save Dialog box in the Worksheet area (as was the case in previous versions of Excel) instead.

- » **Show Additional Places for Saving, Even If Sign-in May Be Required:** When Excel 2019 opens the Save As screen in the Backstage view, the program automatically displays the text boxes for logging into online services, such as your SkyDrive or the SharePoint team site, on this screen. If you do not save your files to the cloud or don't have access to a SkyDrive, you can deselect this check box to remove such log-in options from the Save As screen.

- » **Save to Computer by Default:** If you prefer to save your workbook files locally on your computer's hard drive or a virtual drive on a local area network to which you have access, click this check box.

- » **Default Local File Location:** This text box contains the path to the local folder where Excel 2019 saves new workbook files by default when you click the Save to Computer by Default check box as described in the preceding bullet item.

- » **Default Personal Templates Location:** If the templates that you commonly use in creating new Excel workbooks are located in a local folder on your computer's hard drive or a network drive to which you have access, enter the folder's entire pathname in this text box after clicking the Save to Computer by Default check box as described earlier.

- » **Show Data Loss Warning When Editing Comma Delimited Files (*.csv):** When this option is selected, if you try to directly open a text file containing data fields separated by commas and saved in the .csv (Comma Separated Values) file format, Excel displays an alert dialog box indicating that the file may be corrupted or unsafe. If you go ahead and click Yes to try top to open the text file anyway, another alert appears where you can click OK to have Excel try to import the text file into an Excel Workbook using the old Text Import Wizard (see Chapter 2 of Book 6 for more on importing text files into Excel workbooks).

If your company enables you to share the editing of certain Excel workbooks through the Excel Services offered as part of SharePoint Services software, you can change the location where Excel saves drafts of the workbook files you check out for editing. By default, Excel saves the drafts of these checked-out workbook files locally on your computer's hard drive inside a SharePoint Drafts folder in the Documents or My Documents folder. If your company or IT department prefers that you save these draft files on the web server that contains the SharePoint software, click the Office Document Cache option button to deselect The Server Drafts Location on This Computer option button and then enter the network path in the Server Drafts Location text box. Alternatively, click the Browse button and locate the network drive and folder in the Browse dialog box.

TIP

If you share your Excel 2019 workbooks with workers who are still using older versions (97–2003) of Excel, use the Colors command button to determine which color in the Excel 2019 worksheet to preserve in formatted tables and other graphics when you save the workbook file for them using the Excel 97–2003 file format option. (See Book 2, Chapter 1.)

Changing the Office 2019 language preferences

The options on the Language tab of the Excel Options dialog box enable you to add editing languages in the Choose Editing Languages section at the top of the dialog box. When you add a new language, Office 2019 incorporates the sorting, grammar checking, and spelling dictionaries necessary to proof your workbooks in that language. The program will prompt you to download the necessary files for this new language if they aren't already available to Office on your computer, as long as the Let Me Know When I Should Download Additional Proofing Tools check box remains selected.

To add a language, simply click the language in the Add Additional Editing Languages drop-down list box and then click the Add button to its right to add its name to the list box above.

Besides adding proofing tools to your Office programs such as Excel 2019 for a new language on the Language tab, you can also change the priority of the Office program's display and the language used when you ask for online help in Excel (see Chapter 1 of Book 1 for details). In the Set the Language Priority Order for the Buttons, Tabs, and Help section of Language tab, Excel shows all the display and help languages installed for Microsoft Office in their respective list boxes. To boost the usage of a particular language, simply click the Promote button (with the triangle pointing upward) in either or both the Display Language and Help Language list boxes.

TIP

To get additional Language Packs that cover both the display and help languages for Office 2019 to use in Excel, click the How Do I Get More Display and Help Languages from Office.com link that you find at the very bottom of the Language tab in the Excel Options dialog box. Doing this opens a Language Packs page on the Office.com website in your default web browser where you can get information on the Language Packs available for Office 2019 as well as purchase them.

Changing a whole lot of other common options on the Advanced tab

The options on the Advanced tab (see Figure 2-6) of the Excel Options dialog box (File⇨Options⇨Advanced or Alt+FTA) are divided into the 14 sections listed in the following table:

Option	What It Does
Editing Options	Changes the way you edit the worksheets you create
Cut, Copy, and Paste	Changes the way worksheet editing that involves cutting, copying, and pasting to and from the Clipboard works
Pen	If you're using Excel on a tablet or other touchscreen device, this option makes digital ink (as when making entries with the Windows 10 touch keyboard) the default
Image Size and Quality	Controls how an image's data is used in a worksheet
Print	Controls whether high or regular quality is used for the graphic images in the printed worksheet
Chart	Controls how Excel deals with the charts you add to a worksheet
Display	Determines how various elements (from recently used workbooks in the Backstage view to ruler units, the presence of the Formula bar, ScreenTips, and comments in the worksheet) appear onscreen
Display Options for This Workbook	Sets display options for the current workbook open in Excel
Display Options for This Worksheet	Sets display options for the currently selected worksheet in the workbook open in Excel
Formulas	Determines how Excel deals with calculating sophisticated formulas in the worksheets in your workbook
When Calculating This Workbook	Sets calculation parameters for the workbook open in Excel
General	Controls various all-purpose options, including such diverse options as the workbook files that you want opened when Excel launches, how your workbooks appear on the web, and the creation of custom AutoFill lists
Lotus Compatibility	Sets general Lotus 1-2-3 compatibility in Excel 2019
Lotus Compatibility Settings	Sets Lotus 1-2-3 compatibility for a particular worksheet in the workbook open in Excel

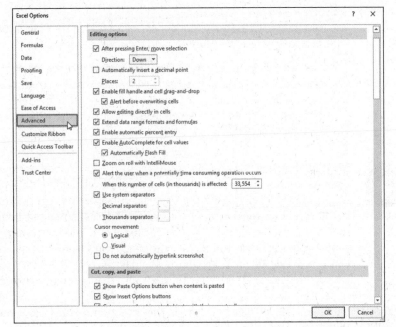

FIGURE 2-6:
The Editing and Cut, Copy, and Paste options on the Advanced tab control how Excel behaves during editing.

The various and sundry options in these 14 sections of the Advanced tab actually fall into 4 somewhat distinct areas: options for editing in the worksheet; options controlling the screen display; a potpourri area of formulas, calculating, and general options; and Lotus compatibility options for old Lotus 1-2-3 users (assuming that there are still some of you left) who are just now upgrading to Excel to make the transition easier.

Working the worksheet editing options

As you can see in Figure 2-6, the options in the Editing Options and Cut, Copy, and Paste sections on the Advanced tab control what happens when you edit the contents of an Excel worksheet.

When you first open the Advanced tab of the Excel Options dialog box, all of the check box options in the Editing Options and Cut, Copy, and Paste sections are checked with the exception of these three:

>> **Automatically Insert a Decimal Point** to have Excel add a decimal point during data entry of all values in each worksheet using the number of places in the Places text box. (See Book 2, Chapter 1 for details.)

>> **Zoom on Roll with IntelliMouse** to have Excel increase or decrease the screen magnification percentage by 15 percent on each roll forward and back of the center wheel of a mouse that supports Microsoft's IntelliMouse

technology. When this option is not checked, Excel scrolls the worksheet up and down on each roll forward and back of the center wheel.

>> **Do Not Automatically Hyperlink Screenshot** to prevent Excel from automatically creating hyperlinks to any screenshots that you take of the Windows desktop using the Screen Clipping option on the Take a Screenshot button in the Illustrations group on the Insert tab of the Ribbon. (See Book 5, Chapter 2 for details.)

REMEMBER

Most of the time, you'll want to keep all the check box options in the Editing Options and Cut, Copy, and Paste sections checked. The only one of these you might want to disengage is the Use System Separators check box when you routinely create spreadsheets with financial figures expressed in foreign currency that don't use the period (.) as the decimal point and the comma (,) as the thousands separator. After you remove the check mark from the Use System Separators check box, the Decimal Separator and Thousands Separator text boxes become active, and you can then enter the appropriate punctuation into these two boxes.

TIP

By default, Excel selects Down as the Direction setting when the After Pressing Enter, Move Selection check box option is checked. If you want Excel to automatically advance the cell cursor in another direction (Right, Up, or Left), select the direction from its drop-down list. If you don't want Excel to move the cell cursor outside of the active cell upon completion of the entry (the same as clicking the Enter button on the Formula bar), click the After Pressing Enter, Move Selection check box to remove its check mark.

Playing around with the display options

The display options in the middle of the Advanced tab of the Excel Options dialog box (see Figure 2-7) fall into three categories: general Display options that affect the Excel program; Display Options for This Workbook that affect the current workbook; and Display Options for This Worksheet that affect the active sheet in the workbook.

Most of the options in these three categories are self-explanatory as they either turn off or on the display of particular screen elements, such as the Formula bar, ScreenTips, scroll bars, sheet tabs, column and row headers, page breaks, (cell) gridlines, and the like.

REMEMBER

When using these display options to control the display of various Excel screen elements, keep the following things in mind:

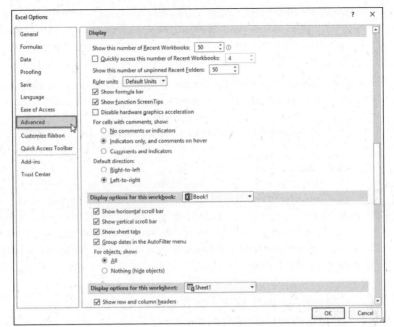

FIGURE 2-7:
The various display options in the center of the Advanced tab control what's shown on the screen.

>> The Ruler Units drop-down list box automatically uses the Default Units for your version of Microsoft Office (Inches in the U.S. and Centimeters in Europe). These default units (or those you specifically select from the drop-down list: Inches, Centimeters, or Millimeters) are then displayed on both the horizontal and vertical rulers that appear above and to the left of the column and row headings only when you put the Worksheet area display into Page Layout view (Alt+WP).

>> Click the Comments and Indicators option button under the For Cells with Comments, Show heading when you want Excel to display the text boxes with the comments you add to cells at all times in the worksheet. (See Book 4, Chapter 3.)

>> Click the Nothing (Hide Objects) option button under the For Objects, Show heading when you want Excel to hide the display of all graphic objects in the worksheet, including embedded charts, clip art, imported pictures, and all graphics that you generate in the worksheet. (See Book 5, Chapters 1 and 2 for details.)

>> Click the Show Page Breaks check box to remove its check mark whenever you need to remove the dotted lines indicating page breaks in Normal (Alt+WN) view after viewing the Worksheet area in either Page Break Preview (Alt+WI) or Page Layout view (Alt+WP).

>> Instead of going to the trouble of clicking the Show Formulas in Cells Instead of Their Calculated Results check box to display formulas in the cells of the worksheet, simply press Ctrl+' (apostrophe) or click the Show Formulas button on the Formulas tab of the Ribbon. Both the keystroke shortcut and the button are

toggles so that you can return the Worksheet area to its normal display showing the calculated results rather than the formulas by pressing the Ctrl+' shortcut keys again or clicking the Show Formulas button.

>> Instead of going to the trouble of removing the check mark from the Show Gridlines check box whenever you want to remove the column and row lines that define the cells in the Worksheet area, click the Gridlines check box in the Show/Hide group on the View tab or the View check box in the Gridlines column of the Sheet Options group on the Page Layout tab to remove their check marks.

TIP

Use the Gridline Color drop-down list button immediately below the Show Gridlines check box to change the color of the Worksheet gridlines (when they're displayed, of course) by clicking a new color on the color palette that appears when you click its drop-down list button. (I find that navy blue makes the cell boundaries stand out particularly well and gives the screen a hint of the old paper green-sheet look.)

Caring about the Formulas, Calculating, and General options

At the bottom of the Advanced tab of the Excel Options dialog box (see Figure 2-8), you find a regular mix of options in five sections. The first three sections, Formulas, When Calculating This Workbook, and General, contain a veritable potpourri of options.

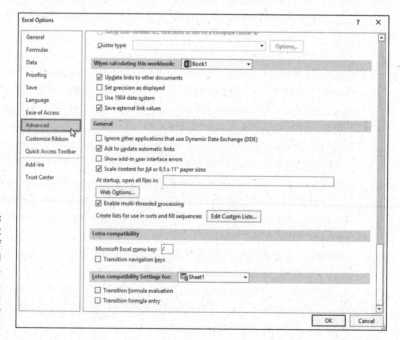

FIGURE 2-8:
The options at the bottom of the Advanced tab control various calculation, general, data, and 1-2-3 compatibility settings.

The settings of most of the options in these three sections won't need changing. In rare cases, you may find that you have to activate the following options or make modifications to some of their settings:

>> **Set Precision as Displayed:** Click this check box *only* when you want to permanently change the calculated values in the worksheet to the number of places currently shown in their cells as the result of the number format applied to them.

>> **Use 1904 Date System:** Click this check box when you're dealing with a worksheet created with an earlier Macintosh version of Excel that used 1904 rather than 1900 as date serial number 1.

>> **Web Options:** Click this command button to display the Web Options dialog box, where you can modify the options that control how your Excel data appears when viewed with a web browser, such as Edge and Internet Explorer.

>> **Edit Custom Lists:** Click this command button to create or edit custom lists with the Fill handle. (See Book 2, Chapter 1.)

Click the Prefer the Excel Data Model When Creating PivotTables, QueryTables and Data Connections check box to select it in the Data section on the Advanced tab of the Excel Options dialog box.

Laying on the Lotus 1-2-3 compatibility

The last two sections on the Advanced tab, Lotus Compatibility and Lotus Compatibility Settings For, are only of interest to Lotus 1-2-3 users who are just now coming to use Microsoft Excel as their spreadsheet program.

TIP

If you're a dyed-in-the-wool 1-2-3 user, you'll definitely want to put a check mark in all three check boxes, Transition Navigation Keys, Transition Formula Evaluation, and Transition Formula Entry, in both the Lotus Compatibility and Lotus Compatibility Settings For sections. That way, you'll be able to start formulas with built-in functions with the @ symbol — which Excel dutifully converts to an equal sign (=) — as well as use all the keys for navigating the worksheet to which you've become so accustomed.

REMEMBER

Keep in mind that you can activate the hot keys on the Excel Ribbon by pressing the forward slash (/) key even when none of the Lotus compatibility options are selected. When I want to use the program's hot keys to select an Excel command from the Ribbon, I find pressing the forward slash, which activated the pull-down menus in Lotus 1-2-3, to be much easier than pressing the Alt key — this is because / is part of the QWERTY keyboard. This means that whenever you see a keyboard shortcut such as Alt+WP in the book, you can just press /WP (which in this particular case puts the Worksheet display area into Page Layout view).

Customizing the Excel 2019 Ribbon

The options on the Customize Ribbon tab (see Figure 2-9) of the Excel Options dialog box (File⇨Options⇨Customize Ribbon or Alt+FTC) enable you to modify which tabs appear on the Excel Ribbon and the order in which they appear, as well as to change which groups of command buttons appear on each of these displayed tabs. You can even use its options to create brand-new tabs for the Ribbon as well as create custom groups of command buttons within any of the displayed tabs.

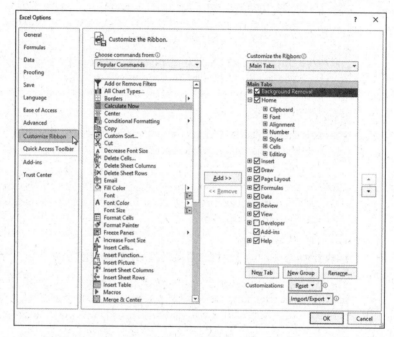

FIGURE 2-9:
The Customize Ribbon tab options enable you to control which tabs are displayed on the Ribbon and which groups of command buttons they contain.

Customizing the Ribbon's tabs

If you find that the default arrangement of main tabs and groups on the Excel Ribbon is not entirely to your liking, you can simplify or rearrange them to suit the way you routinely work:

>> **Hide tabs on the Ribbon** by deselecting their check boxes in the Main Tabs list box on the right side of the Excel Options dialog box. (To later redisplay a hidden tab, you simply click its check box to select it.)

>> **Modify tab order on the Ribbon** by selecting the tab to move and then click either the Move Up button (with the triangle pointing up) or Move Down button (the triangle pointing down) until the name of the tab appears in the desired position in the list shown in the Main Tabs list box.

» **Modify group order on a tab** by first expanding the tab to display the groups by clicking the Expand button (with the plus sign) in front of the tab name in the Main Tabs list box. Next click the name of the group you want to reposition and click either the Move Up or Move Down button until it appears in the desired position in the list.

» **Remove a group from a tab** by selecting its name in the expanded Main Tabs list and then clicking the Remove command button (under the Add button between the two list boxes that now appear in the main section of the Excel Options dialog box).

In addition to the main tabs of the Ribbon, you can control which groups of command buttons appear on its various contextual tabs (such as the Drawing Tools or Chart Tools contextual tabs that automatically appear when you're working on an Excel table of data or chart):

» **Display the groups to be modified on a contextual tab** by clicking the Tool Tabs option on the Customize the Ribbon drop-down list and then clicking the Expand button in front of the contextual tab whose groups you want to modify.

» **Modify the group order on a contextual tab** by clicking the group name and then clicking the Move Up or Move Down buttons to move it into its new position.

» **Remove a group from a contextual tab** by clicking its group name and then clicking the Remove command button.

TIP

To restore the original groups to a particular tab you've modified, click the tab in the Customize the Ribbon list box on the right side of the Excel Options dialog box and then click the Reset drop-down button beneath this list box before you click the Reset Only Selected Ribbon Tab option.

WARNING

If you want to restore all the tabs and groups on the Ribbon to their original default arrangement, you can click the Reset drop-down button and then click the Reset All Customizations option from its drop-down list. Just be aware that clicking this option not only restores the Ribbon's default settings but also negates all changes you've made to the Quick Access toolbar at the same time. If you don't want this to happen, restore the tabs of the Ribbon individually by using the Reset Only Selected Ribbon tab option described in the preceding tip.

Adding custom tabs to the Ribbon

The Customize Ribbon tab of the Excel Options dialog box not only lets you customize the existing Ribbon tabs but also lets you add ones of your own. This is great news for you if you want Ribbon access to Excel commands you routinely rely on that didn't make it to the default Ribbon.

To add a brand-new tab to the Ribbon, follow these steps:

1. **Open the Customize Ribbon tab of the Excel Options dialog box (File⇨Options⇨Customize Ribbon or Alt+FTC).**

   Excel opens the Customize Ribbon tab with the Main Tabs selected in the Customize the Ribbon list box on the right.

2. **Under Main Tabs in this list box, click the tab that you want to come before the new tab you're about to insert.**

   By default, Excel inserts the new tab after the one that's currently selected in the Customize the Ribbon list box. This means that if you want your new custom tab to precede the Home tab, you must put it ahead of the Home tab with the Move Up button after first creating the new tab behind it.

3. **Click the New Tab command button below Main Tabs in the Customize the Ribbon list box.**

   Excel inserts a tab called New Tab (custom) with the single group called New Group (Custom) displayed and selected. This New Tab (Custom) is placed immediately after the currently selected tab.

4. **Add all the commands you want in this group on the custom tab by clicking them in the Choose Commands From list box and then clicking the Add Command button.**

   When adding commands, you can select them from any of the categories: Popular Commands, Commands Not in the Ribbon, All Commands, Macros, File Tab, All Tabs, Main Tabs, Tool Tabs, and Custom Tabs and Groups (which lists all custom tabs and groups you've previously created).

   As you add each command from these categories, Excel displays the button's icon and name in the list beneath New Group (Custom) in the left-to-right order in which they'll appear. (See Figure 2-10.) To change the order of these command buttons in the new group on the custom tab, click the Move Up and/or Move Down buttons.

5. **Rename the new group by clicking the Rename button under the Customize the Ribbon list box and then typing the new name in the Display Name text box of the Rename dialog box before clicking OK.**

6. **(Optional) To add other groups to the same custom tab, click the New Group button under the Customize the Ribbon list box and then add all its command buttons before renaming it. (Refer to Steps 4 and 5.)**

To add any additional groups of commands to be included on the new custom tab, simply repeat Step 6. Use the Move Up and Move Down buttons if you need to reposition any groups on the custom tab.

7. **Rename the custom tab by clicking the New Tab (Custom) in the Customize the Ribbon list box. Then, click the Rename button and type the name for the tab in the Display Name text box of the Rename dialog box before you click OK.**

    To add additional custom tabs to the Ribbon, repeat Steps 2 through 7. After you finish all your custom tabs to the Ribbon, you're ready to close the Excel Options dialog box and return to the worksheet.

8. **Click the OK button in the Excel Options dialog box.**

    When Excel closes this dialog box and returns you to the worksheet, the new custom tab appears in the Ribbon at the position where you placed it.

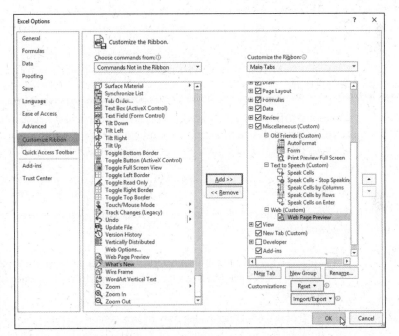

FIGURE 2-10:
Adding forgotten Excel commands to a custom group on a brand new Ribbon tab.

Figure 2-11 shows you the Excel Ribbon on my computer after I added a Miscellaneous tab between the Review and View tab. As you can see, when this new tab is clicked, it contains three custom groups: Old Friends (Custom) with AutoFormat, Form, and Print Preview Full Screen; Text to Speech (Custom) with the Speak Cells, Stop Speaking, and On Enter buttons; and Web (Custom) with its Web Page Preview button.

FIGURE 2-11:
Excel Ribbon
after selecting a
Miscellaneous tab
with its command
buttons clustered
in three custom
groups.

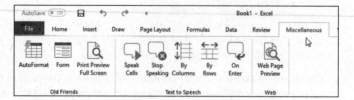

REMEMBER

If you use shortcut keys to access Ribbon commands, keep in mind that Excel automatically assigns hot-key letters to each of the custom tabs and commands you add to the Ribbon. To display the custom tabs' hot keys, press the Alt key. To display the hot keys assigned to the commands on a particular custom tab, type its specific hot-key letter.

Using Office Add-ins

Excel 2019 supports the use of Office Add-ins to help you build your worksheets. *Office Add-ins* are small application programs that run within specific Office 2019 programs, such as Excel, and increase particular functionality to promote greater productivity.

There are Office Add-ins to help you learn about Excel's features, look up words in the *Merriam-Webster* dictionary, and even enter dates into your spreadsheet by clicking them on a calendar. Many of the Office Add-ins for Excel 2019 are available free of charge, whereas others are offered for a trial period after which you may purchase them from the Office Store for a small price.

To use any of these Office Add-ins in Excel 2019, you first need to install them by following these steps:

1. **Click the My Add-ins option on the Add-ins button on the Insert tab of the Ribbon; then, click the See All option on the drop-down menu (or press Alt+NAPS).**

   Excel opens the Office dialog Add-ins box containing the My Add-ins and Store buttons, along with thumbnails of all the Office Add-ins already installed and ready to insert into the current Excel workbook (see Figure 2-12).

2. **To install new Office Add-ins, click the Store button in the Office Add-ins dialog box.**

   Excel connects to the Office Store. Your Office Add-ins dialog box displays a list add-ins for Excel along with a brief description of the add-in's functionality, its current rating by users (one to five stars), and price if it's not free (these usually have Free Trial Available) or May Require Additional Purchase alert if a limited version of the add-in is downloadable for free but a more complete and robust version requires a purchase. These add-ins are organized by particular categories ranging from All (the default) to Utilities that you can select in a column on the left side of the dialog box.

To display more information about a particular add-in of interest, click its description. Excel then displays thumbnails of an Excel worksheet using the add-in, a more extensive description of its operation, a few sample reviews and stats on its current version, when it was first released, and whether or not the add-in can make changes to your worksheet and send data over the Internet.

3. **(Optional) To restrict the display of Office Add-ins to a particular category, such as Visualization, Document Review, or Editor's Picks, click its category in the column on the left side of the Office Add-ins dialog box.**

4. **When you find an add-in that you may want to install in any one of the categories, click its green Add button.**

   After you click the Add button for a free Office Add-in, Excel closes the Office Add-ins dialog box and downloads the add-in in the current worksheet for you to use while usually opening a taskbar for the new add-in in the current worksheet that enables you to start using it right away.

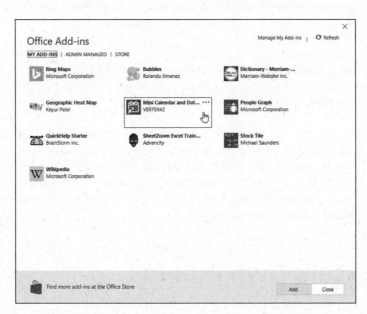

FIGURE 2-12:
Inserting the Excel Mini Calendar and Date Picker add-in into an Excel worksheet.

It also adds the Office Add-in to the list of installed Office Add-ins on the My Add-ins tab of the Office Add-ins dialog box. After initially installing an add-in, you can thereafter insert the Office Add-in you want to use into any open worksheet that you're working on by following these steps:

1. **If the Office Add-ins dialog box is not currently open in Excel, open it by clicking Insert⇨Add-ins⇨My Add-ins⇨See All or press Alt+NAPS.**

   Excel displays all the Office Add-ins currently installed in Excel 2019 in the My Add-ins tab of the Office Add-ins dialog box.

2. **Click the Office Add-in you want to use in your worksheet to select it and then click the Add button or press Enter.**

   Excel then inserts the Office Add-in into your current worksheet so that you can start using its features.

Many Office Add-ins, such as *Merriam-Webster Dictionary* and Wikipedia, open in task panes docked on the right side of the worksheet window. Others, such as Bing Maps and the Mini Calendar, open as graphic objects that float above the worksheet.

To close Office Add-ins that open in docked task panes, you simply click the pane's Close button. To close Office Add-ins that open as floating graphic objects, you need to select the graphic and then press the Delete key (don't worry — doing this only closes the app without uninstalling it).

Note that after you start using various Office Add-ins in Excel, they're added to the Recently Used Add-ins section of the My Add-ins button's drop-down menu. You can then quickly re-open any closed Office add-in that appears on this menu simply by clicking it.

TIP

If an Office Add-in you've installed doesn't appear on the My Add-in tab of the Office Add-ins dialog box, click the Refresh link to refresh the list. Use the Manage My Apps link in this dialog box to keep tabs on all the Office Add-ins you've installed for Office 2019 and SharePoint. If you want to delete an Office Add-in you're no longer using, right-click its icon on the My Add-ins tab and then click Remove on its pop-up menu.

Using Excel's Own Add-ins

Office Add-ins aren't the only ones that you can use to extend Excel's features. You can also use built-in add-ins created by Microsoft or third-party Excel Add-ins that you can purchase from a wide variety of vendors. Before you can use any

Excel Add-in program, the add-in must be installed in the proper folder on your hard drive, and then you must click the add-in in the Add-Ins dialog box.

There are two different types of Excel Add-in programs immediately available that you can use to extend the features in Excel 2019:

>> **Excel Add-ins:** This group of add-ins (also known as automation add-ins) is designed to extend the data analysis capabilities of Excel. These include Analysis ToolPak, Euro Currency Tools, and Solver.

>> **COM Add-ins:** COM (Component Object Model) add-ins are designed to extend Excel's capability to deal with and analyze large amounts of data in data models (collections of related database tables). These include Inquire, Microsoft Office PowerPivot for Excel, and Power View.

When you first install Excel 2019, the add-in programs included with Excel are not loaded and therefore are not yet ready to use. To load any or all of these add-in programs, you follow these steps:

1. **Click the File menu button, click Excel Options or press Alt+FT to open the Excel Options dialog box, and then click the Add-Ins tab.**

   The Add-Ins tab lists all the names, locations, and types of the add ins to which you have access.

2. **(Optional) In the Manage drop-down list box at the bottom, Excel Add-Ins is selected by default. If you want to activate one or more of your COM add-ins, click COM Add-Ins from the Manage drop-down list.**

3. **Click the Go button.**

   If Excel Add-Ins was selected in the Manage drop-down list box, Excel opens the Add-Ins dialog box (similar to the one shown in Figure 2-13), showing all the names of the built-in add-in programs you can load. If COM Add-Ins was clicked, the COM Add-Ins dialog box appears instead.

4. **Click the check boxes for each add-in program that you want loaded in the Add-Ins or COM Add-Ins dialog box.**

   Click the name of the add-in in the Add-Ins Available list box to display a brief description of its function at the bottom of this dialog box.

5. **Click the OK button to close the Add-Ins or COM Add-Ins dialog box.**

TIP

When you first install Excel 2019, all four add-ins (Analysis ToolPak, Analysis ToolPak - VBA, Euro Currency Tools, and Solver Add-In) are available in the Add-Ins dialog box. All you have to do to activate them is click their respective check boxes to select them before clicking OK. (For more about these add-ins, see the following section, "Managing Excel Add-ins.") The tools in the two Analysis ToolPaks are added as special functions to the Function Library group and the Euro Currency tools to a Solutions group on the Formulas tab. The Solver add-in appears in the Analysis group on the Data tab.

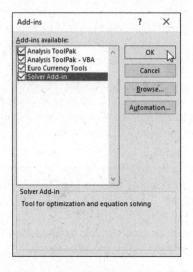

FIGURE 2-13:
Activating built-in
Excel Add-ins
in the Add-Ins
dialog box.

Excel Add-in programs are saved in a special file format identified with the .XLL or .XLAM (for Excel Add-in) filename extension. These files are normally saved inside the Library folder (sometimes in their own subfolders) that is located in the Office16 folder. The Office16 folder, in turn, is located in your Microsoft Office folder inside the Program Files folder on your hard drive (often designated as the C:\ drive). In other words, the path is

```
c:\Program Files\Microsoft Office\Office16\Library
```

After an add-in program has been installed in the Library folder, its name then appears in the list box of the Add-Ins dialog box.

TIP

If you ever copy an XLAM add-in program to a folder other than the Library folder in the Office19 folder on your hard drive, its name won't appear in the Add-Ins Available list box when you open the Add-Ins dialog box. You can, however, activate the add-in by clicking the Browse button in this dialog box and then clicking the add-in file in its folder in the Browse dialog box before you click OK.

Managing the standard Excel Add-ins

Whether you know it or not, you already have a group of Excel Add-in programs included when you install Excel 2019:

>> **Analysis ToolPak:** Adds extra financial, statistical, and engineering functions to Excel's pool of built-in functions.

>> **Analysis ToolPak - VBA:** Enables VBA programmers to publish their own financial, statistical, and engineering functions for Excel.

>> **Euro Currency Tools:** Enables you to format worksheet values as euro currency and adds a EUROCONVERT function for converting other currencies into euros. To use these tools, click the Euro Conversion or Euro Formatting buttons that appear on the Ribbon in the Solutions group at the end of the Formulas tab.

>> **Solver Add-In:** Calculates solutions to what-if scenarios based on cells that both adjust and constrain the range of values. (See Book 7, Chapter 1.) To use the Solver add-in, click the Solver button that appears on the Ribbon in the Analysis group at the end of the Data tab.

REMEMBER

To use one of the additional statistical or financial functions added as part of the Analysis ToolPak add-in, you don't access the Add-Ins tab. Instead, click the Insert Function button on the Formula bar, click either Financial or Statistical from the Select a Category drop-down list, and then locate the function to use in the Select a Function list box below.

Managing Excel COM add-ins

The following COM add-in programs are included when you install Excel 2019:

>> **Acrobat PDFMaker Office COM Add-in:** Enables coworkers and clients to view PDFs on the their devices with in the free PDF viewer. (See Book 2, Chapter 1.) Note that this is the only COM add-in automatically installed with Excel 2019 that enables you to save your Excel workbook file in the Adobe PDF (Portable Document Format)

>> **Microsoft Power Map for Excel**: Enables you to map geographic data on an interactive 3D globe (see Book 7, Chapter 2).

>> **Microsoft Power Pivot for Excel:** Enables you to build complex data models using large amounts of data. It also facilitates data queries using DAX (Data Analysis Expressions) functions. (See Book 7, Chapter 2.)

REMEMBER

Keep in mind that you readily manage your COM add-ins using the COM Add-Ins button in the Add-Ins group on the Developer tab. (To display the Developer tab in Excel 2019, click File⇨Options⇨Customize Ribbon [Alt+FTC] and then click the check box in front of Developer in the Main Tabs list box to select it before you click OK.) When you click the COM Add-Ins button, Excel opens the COM Add-Ins dialog box that shows all of the COM add-ins that are installed and activated. Here, you can activate and deactivate individual add-ins as needed.

Purchasing third-party add-ins

The add-ins included with Excel are not the only Excel Add-ins that you can lay your hands on. Many third-party vendors sell Excel Add-ins that you can often purchase online and then immediately download onto your hard drive.

To find third-party vendors and get information on their add-ins, open your web browser and search for *Excel Add-ins.*

Even before you do a web search, you may want to visit the Add-Ins.com website at www.add-ins.com.

This online outfit offers a wide variety of useful Excel Add-ins. One example is the Spreadsheet Assistant (its most popular Excel Add-in) that adds an Assistants tab to your Excel Ribbon with a whole of assistant command buttons designed to streamline working with Excel worksheets.

Note that you can expect to pay Add-Ins.com between $25 and $50 for add-in programs such as these (really reasonably priced if you consider how many hours it would take to split up names into separate cells in huge worksheets).

2

Worksheet Design

Contents at a Glance

IN THIS CHAPTER

» **Creating a spreadsheet from a template**

» **Designing a spreadsheet from scratch**

» **Understanding the different types of cell entries**

» **Knowing the different ways of entering data in the worksheet**

» **Using Data Validation to restrict the data entries in cells**

» **Saving worksheets**

Chapter **1**

Building Worksheets

B efore you can begin building a new spreadsheet in Excel, you must have the design in mind. As it turns out, the design aspect of the creative process is often the easiest part because you can borrow the design from other work-books that you've already created or from special workbook files, called *templates*, which provide you with the new spreadsheet's form along with some of the standard, or *boilerplate*, data entries.

After you've settled upon the design of your new spreadsheet, you're ready to begin entering its data. In doing the data entry in a new worksheet, you have several choices regarding the method to use. For this reason, this chapter not only covers all the methods for entering data — from the most basic to the most sophisticated — but also includes hints on when each is the most appropriate. Note, however, that this chapter doesn't include information on building formulas, which comprises a major part of the data entry task in creating a new spreadsheet. Because this task is so specialized and so extensive, you find the information on formula building covered in Book 3, Chapter 1.

Designer Spreadsheets

Anytime you launch Excel (without also opening an existing workbook file), the Excel Start screen in the Backstage view presents you with a choice between

>> Opening a new workbook (with the generic filename, Book1), consisting of a single totally blank worksheet (with the generic worksheet name, Sheet1) by clicking the Blank Workbook template

>> Opening a new workbook based on the design in one of the other templates displayed in the Start screen or available in the New screen opened by clicking the Find More in New link or New button in its navigation pane

If you select the Blank Workbook template, you can start laying out and building your new spreadsheet in the blank worksheet. If you select one of the other designed templates, you can start by customizing the workbook file's design as well as entering the data for your new spreadsheet.

Take it from a template

Spreadsheet templates are the way to go if you can find one that uses the design of the spreadsheet that you want to build. There are many templates to choose from when you initially launch Excel and then click the New option in the navigation pane. (See Figure 1-1.) The templates displayed on the New screen in the Backstage view run the gamut from budgets and schedules to profit and loss statements, invoices, sales reports, and calendars.

If none of the templates displayed on the New screen fit the bill, you can then search for templates. This screen contains links to common suggested searches: Business, Personal, Lists, Industry, Small Business, Calculator, Finance-Management, Charts, and Calculator.

When you click one of these links, the New screen displays your choices in that particular category. Figure 1-2 shows you the first part of New screen that appears when you click the Financial Management link in the Suggested Searches. As you can see in this figure, the template choices in this category include a variety of financial planners, trackers, calculators, logs, and lists, to name a few.

TIP

If the type of template you're looking for doesn't fit any of the categories listed in the Suggested Searches area of the New screen, you conduct your own template search. Simply click the Search for Online Templates text box, type in keywords describing the type of template (such as **expense report**), and then click the Start Searching button (the one with the magnifying glass icon).

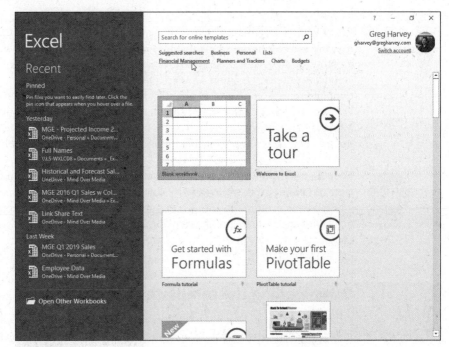

FIGURE 1-1:
Selecting a template from which to generate a new workbook in the Excel New screen.

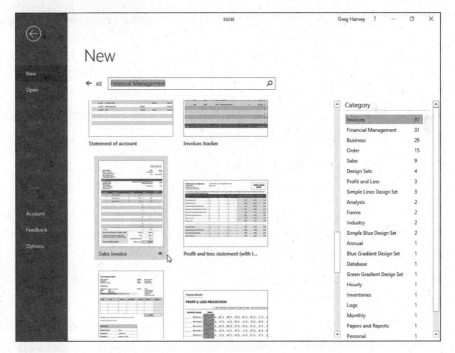

FIGURE 1-2:
Searching for an Invoice template using the Financial Management link in Suggested Searches on the Start screen.

When you do any kind of template search, suggested or one of your own making, the New screen not only displays examples of templates that match but also a listing of other subcategories of available templates that might fit the bill in a scrollable Category column on the right side of the screen. To further refine your template search, you have only to click the name of the category shown in this list. For example, in the New screen shown in Figure 1-2 with the results of a Financial Managements suggested search, I can limit the limit the display to the 19 available budget templates simply by clicking Budgets in the Category column.

REMEMBER

Keep in mind that instead of using ready-made templates, you can create your own templates from your favorite Excel workbooks. After you save a copy of a workbook as a template file, Excel automatically generates a copy of the workbook whenever you open the template file. This way, you can safely customize the contents of the new workbook without any danger of inadvertently modifying the original template.

Downloading the template to use

When you locate a template whose design can be adapted to your spreadsheet needs, you can download it. Simply click its thumbnail in the Excel or New screen. Excel then opens a dialog box similar to the one shown in Figure 1-3, containing a more extensive description of the template and its download file size. To download the template and create a new Excel workbook from it, you simply click the Create button.

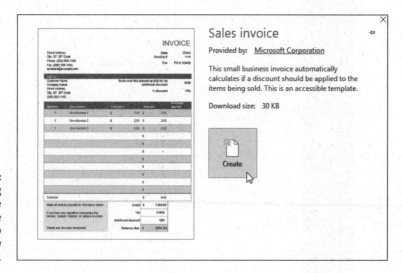

FIGURE 1-3:
Downloading a Sales Invoice financial template from which to generate a new workbook.

Figure 1-4 shows the Invoice with Finance Charge1 workbook in the Excel worksheet area created from the Invoice with Finance Charge template after you click the Create button. As you can see on the Excel window title bar in this figure, when Excel generated this first workbook from the original template file, the program also gave it the temporary filename Sales Invoice. If you were to then create a second copy of this report by once again opening the Sales Invoice template, the program would name that copy Sales Invoice2. This way, you don't have to worry about one copy overwriting another, and you never risk mistakenly saving changes to the original template file itself (which actually uses a completely different filename extension — .xltx for an Excel template as opposed to .xlsx for an Excel worksheet).

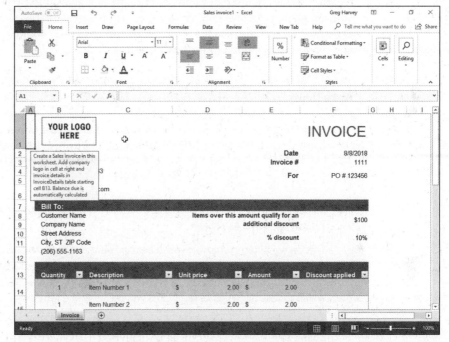

FIGURE 1-4:
The new Sales Invoice1 workbook in the Excel worksheet area generated from the template by the same name.

To customize a spreadsheet generated from one of the installed templates, you replace the placeholder entries in the new invoice worksheet with your own data. You might begin by replacing the Company Name placeholder in cell B2 with the actual name of your company, after which you could replace the *company slogan* placeholder directly below it in cell B3, with your own company's catchphrase or motto (assuming that your company has one). Then, you would start filling in the company contact info and replace the placeholder invoice number, date and customer ID with your number, dates and customer IDs. For strategies on entering your labels and values into the cells of a worksheet, see "It Takes All Kinds (of Cell Entries)" later in this chapter.

Note that when filling in or replacing the data a spreadsheet generated from one of these ready-made templates, you have access to all the cells in the worksheet: those that contain standard headings as well as those that require personalized data entry.

After you finish filling in the personalized data, save the workbook just as you would a workbook that you had created from scratch. (See the "Saving the Data" section at the end of this chapter for details on saving workbook files.)

Saving changes to your customized templates

You can save the customization you do to the templates you download to make the workbooks you create from them easier to use and quicker to fill out. For example, you can make your own custom Invoice with Finance Charge template from one generated by the downloaded template by filling in your company name, slogan, and contact information in the top section.

To save your changes to a downloaded template as a new template file, follow these steps:

1. **Click the Save button on the Quick Access toolbar (the one with the disk icon), or click File⇨Save from the File menu button, or press Ctrl+S.**

The Save As screen opens where you select the location where the customized template file is to be saved.

2. **Select the drive and folder where you store all your personal template files in the Save As screen.**

This personal templates folder can be local on your OneDrive. However, you need to mark its location (because later on you need to enter its pathname in the Excel Options dialog box), and you need to designate it as the place in which to save all personal templates you create in the future.

As soon as you select the folder and drive in which to save your template, Excel opens the Save As dialog box, where you need to change the file type from a regular Microsoft Excel Workbook (*.xlsx) to ExcelTemplate (*.xltx) in the Save as Type drop-down list box.

3. **Click the Save as Type drop-down button and then click Excel Template from the drop-down list.**

If you need your new template file to be compatible with earlier versions of Excel (versions 97 through 2003), click Excel 97–2003 Template (*.xlt) rather than Excel Template (*.xltx) from the Save as Type drop-down list. When you do this, Excel saves the new template file in the older binary file format (rather than the newer XML file format) with the old .xlt filename extension instead of the newer `.xltx` filename extension. If your template contains macros that you want the user to be able to run when creating the worksheet, click Excel Macro-Enabled Template (*.xltm).

Note that Excel will suggest saving this new template in the folder listed as computer's Default Personal Template Location in the Excel Options dialog boxlocal drive as soon as you change the file type from Excel Workbook to Excel Template (if you did not already select this folder in Step 2). You can override this suggestion and save it in another folder but if you do, you need to inform Excel of this new folder location as described in the section following Step 5.

4. **Click in the File Name text box and then modify the default filename as needed before you click the Save button to close the Save As dialog box and save your customized template in the Templates folder.**

After the Save As dialog box closes, you still need to close the customized template file in the Excel work area.

5. **Click File⇨Close, or press Alt+FC, or press Ctrl+W to close the customized template file.**

If you saved your customized template file in any folder other than the one currently listed as the Default Personal Template Location in the Excel Options dialog box, you need to tell Excel about this folder and where it is by following these steps:

1. **Click File⇨Options⇨Save (Alt+FTS).**

Excel opens the Excel Options dialog box and selects the Save tab.

2. **Click the Default Personal Templates Location text box and enter the complete filename path for the folder where you saved your initial personal template file.**

For example, if I created a Templates folder within the Documents folder on my personal OneDrive where I save all my personal Excel template files, I would enter the following pathname in the Default Personal Templates Location text box:

```
C:\Users\Greg\OneDrive\Documents\Templates
```

3. **Click OK to close the Excel Options dialog box.**

After designating the location of your personal templates folder as described in the preceding steps, the next time you open the Excel New screen in the Excel Backstage, three links, Business, Personal, and Lists now appear under the Suggested Searches headings (see Figure 1-1). To generate a new workbook from one of your custom spreadsheet templates, you click the Personal link to display thumbnails for all the templates saved in the designated personal templates folder. To open a new Excel workbook from one of its custom templates, you simply click its thumbnail image.

Creating your own spreadsheet templates

You certainly don't have to rely on spreadsheet templates created by other people. Indeed, many times you simply can't do this because, even though other people may generate the type of spreadsheet that you need, their design doesn't incorporate and represent the data in the manner that you prefer or that your company or clients require.

When you can't find a ready-made template that fits the bill or that you can easily customize to suit your needs, create your own templates from sample workbooks that you've created or that your company has on hand. The easiest way to create your own template is to first create an actual workbook prototype, complete with all the text, data, formulas, graphics, and macros that it requires to function.

When readying the prototype workbook, make sure that you remove all headings, miscellaneous text, and numbers that are specific to the prototype and not generic enough to appear in the spreadsheet template. You may also want to protect all generic data, including the formulas that calculate the values that you or your users input into the worksheets generated from the template and headings that never require editing. (See Book 4, Chapter 1 for information on how to protect certain parts of a worksheet from changes.)

After making sure that both the layout and content of the boilerplate data are hunky-dory, save the workbook in the template file format (.xltx) in your personal templates folder so that you can then generate new workbooks from it. (For details on how to do this, refer to the steps in the previous section, "Saving changes to your customized templates.")

As you may have noticed when looking through the sample templates included in Excel (refer to Figure 1-4, for example) or browsing through the templates that you can download from the Microsoft Office.com website found at http://office.microsoft.com, many spreadsheet templates abandon the familiar worksheet grid of cells, preferring a look very close to that of a paper form instead. When converting a sample workbook into a template, you can also remove the grid, use cell borders to underscore or outline key groups of cells, and color different cell groups to make them stand out. (For information on how to do this kind of stuff, refer to Book 2, Chapter 2.)

Keep in mind that you can add online comments to parts of the template that instruct coworkers on how to properly fill in and save the data. These comments are helpful if your coworkers are unfamiliar with the template and may be less skilled in using Excel. (See Book 4, Chapter 3 for details about adding comments to worksheets.)

Designing a workbook from scratch

Not all worksheets come from templates. Many times, you need to create rather unique spreadsheets that aren't intended to function as standard models from which certain types of workbooks are generated. In fact, most of the spreadsheets that you create in Excel may be of this kind, especially if your business doesn't rely on the use of highly standardized financial statements and forms.

Planning your workbook

When creating a new workbook from scratch, you need to start by considering the layout and design of the data. When doing this mental planning, you may want to ask yourself some of the following questions:

>> Does the layout of the spreadsheet require the use of data tables (with both column and row headings) or lists (with column headings only)?

>> Do these data tables and lists need to be laid out on a single worksheet, or can they be placed in the same relative position on multiple worksheets of the workbook (like pages of a book)?

>> Do the data tables in the spreadsheet use the same type of formulas?

>> Do some of the columns in the data lists in the spreadsheet get their input from formula calculation, or do they get their input from other lists (called *lookup tables*) in the workbook?

>> Will any of the data in the spreadsheet be graphed, and will these charts appear in the same worksheet (referred to as *embedded charts*), or will they appear on separate worksheets in the workbook (called *chart sheets*)?

>> Does any of the data in the spreadsheet come from worksheets in separate workbook files?

>> How often will the data in the spreadsheet be updated or added to?

>> How much data will the spreadsheet ultimately hold?

>> Will the data in the spreadsheet be shared primarily in printed or online form?

All these questions are an attempt to get you to consider the basic purpose and function of the new spreadsheet before you start building it, so that you can come up with a design that is both economical and fully functional.

ECONOMY

Economy is an important consideration because when you open a workbook, all its data is loaded into your computer's dynamic memory (known simply as *memory*). This may not pose any problems if the device you're running Excel 2019 on is one of the latest generation of PCs with more memory than you can conceive of using at one time, but it can pose quite a problem if you're running Excel on a small Windows tablet with a minimum of memory or smartphone with limited memory or share the workbook file with someone whose computer is not so well equipped. Also, depending on just how much data you cram into the workbook, you may even come to see Excel creep and crawl the more you work with it.

To help guard against this problem, make sure that you don't pad the data tables and lists in your workbook with extra empty "spacer" cells. Keep the tables as close together as possible on the same worksheet (with no more than a single blank column or row as a separator, which you can adjust to make as wide or high as you like) or — if the design allows — keep them in the same region of consecutive worksheets.

FUNCTIONALITY

Along with economy, you must pay attention to the functionality of the spreadsheet. This means that you need to allow for future growth when selecting the placement of its data tables, lists, and charts. This is especially important in the case of data lists because they have a tendency to grow longer and longer as you continue to add data, requiring more and more rows of the same few columns in the worksheet. This means that you should usually consider all the rows of the columns used in a data list as "off limits." In fact, always position charts and other supporting tables to the right of the list rather than somewhere below the last used row. This way, you can continue to add data to your list without ever having to stop and first move some unrelated element out of the way.

This spatial concern is not the same when placing a data table that will total the values both down the rows and across the columns table — for example, a sales table that sums your monthly sales by item with formulas that calculate monthly totals in the last row of the table and formulas that calculate item totals in the last column. In this table, you don't worry about having to move other elements, such as embedded charts or other supporting or unrelated data tables, because you use Excel's capability of expanding the rows and columns of the table from within. As the table expands or contracts, surrounding elements move in relation to and with the table expansion and contraction. You do this kind of editing to the table because inserting new table rows and columns ahead of the formulas ensures that they can be included in the totaling calculations. In this way, the row and column of formulas in the data table acts as a boundary that floats with the expansion or contraction of its data but that keeps all other elements at bay.

Finalizing your workbook design

After you've more or less planned out where everything goes in your new spreadsheet, you're ready to start establishing the new tables and lists. Here are a few general pointers on how to set up a new data table that includes simple totaling calculations:

>> Enter the title of the data table in the first cell, which forms the left and top edges of the table.

>> Enter the row of column headings in the row below this cell, starting in the same column as the cell with the title of the table.

>> Enter the row headings down the first column of the table, starting in the first row that will contain data. (Doing this leaves a blank cell where the column of row headings intersects the row of column headings.)

>> Construct the first formula that sums columns of (still empty) cell entries in the last row of the table, and then copy that formula across all the rest of the table columns.

>> Construct the first formula that sums the rows of (still empty) cell entries in the last column of the table, and then copy that formula down the rest of the table rows.

>> Format the cells to hold the table values and then enter them in their cells, or enter the values to be calculated and then format their cells. (This is really your choice.)

When setting up a new data list in a new worksheet, enter the list name in the first cell of the table and then enter the row of column headings in the row below. Then, enter the first row of data beneath the appropriate column headings. (See Book 6, Chapter 1 for details on designing a data list and inputting data into it.)

Opening new blank workbooks

Although you can open a new workbook from the Excel screen in the Backstage view when you first start the program that you can use in building a new spreadsheet from scratch, you will encounter occasions when you need to open your own blank workbook from within the Worksheet area itself. For example, if you launch Excel by opening an existing workbook that needs editing and then move on to building an entirely new spreadsheet, you'll need to open a blank workbook (which you can do before or after closing the workbook with which you started Excel).

The easiest way to open a blank workbook is to press Ctrl+N. Excel responds by opening a new workbook, which is given a generic Book name with the next unused number (Book2, if you opened Excel with a blank Book1). You can also do the same thing in Backstage view by clicking File⇨New and then clicking the Blank Workbook thumbnail.

As soon as you open a blank workbook, Excel makes its document window active. To then return to another workbook that you have open (which you would do if you wanted to copy and paste some of its data into one of the blank work-sheets), click its button on the Windows taskbar or press Alt+Tab until its file icon is selected in the dialog box that appears in the middle of the screen.

TIP

If you ever open a blank workbook by mistake, you can just close it right away by pressing Ctrl+W, clicking File⇨Close, or pressing Alt+FC. Excel then closes its document window and automatically returns you to the workbook window that was originally open at the time you mistakenly opened the blank workbook.

It Takes All Kinds (Of Cell Entries)

Before covering the many methods for getting data into the cells of your new spreadsheet, you need to understand which type of data you're entering. To Excel, everything that you enter in any worksheet cell is either one of two types of data: *text* (also known as a *label*) or a *number* (also known as a *value* or *numeric entry*).

The reason that you should care about what type of data you're entering into the cells of your worksheet is that Excel treats your entry differently, depending on what type of data it thinks you've entered.

>> **Text** entries are automatically left-aligned in their cells, and if they consist of more characters than fit within the column's current width, the extra charac-ters spill over and are displayed in blank cells in columns on the right. (If these cells are not blank, Excel cuts off the display of any characters that don't fit within the cell borders until you widen its column.)

>> **Numbers** are automatically right-aligned in their cells, and if they consist of more characters (including numbers and any formatting characters that you add) than fit within the column's current width, Excel displays a string of number signs across the cell (######), telling you to widen the column. (In some cases, such as decimal numbers, Excel truncates the decimal places shown in the cell instead of displaying the number-sign overflow indicators.)

So, now all you have to know is how Excel differentiates text data entries from numeric data entries.

What's in a label?

Here's the deal with text entries:

>> All data entries beginning with a letter of the alphabet or a punctuation mark are considered text.

>> All data entries that mix letters (A–Z) and numbers are considered text, even when the entry begins with a number.

>> All numeric data entries that contain punctuation other than commas (,), periods (.), and forward slashes (/) are considered text, even when they begin with a number.

This means that in addition to regular text, such as *First Quarter Earnings* and *John Smith*, nonstandard data entries, including *C123, 666-45-0034,* and *123C*, are also considered text entries.

However, a problem exists with numbers that are separated by hyphens (also known as *dashes*): If the numbers that are separated by dashes correspond to a valid date, Excel converts it into a date (which is most definitely a kind of numeric data entry — see the "Dates and times" section in this chapter for details). For example, if you enter *1-6-16* in a cell, Excel thinks that you want to enter the date January 6, 2016, in the cell, and the program automatically converts the entry into a date number (displayed as 1/6/2016 in the cell).

TIP

If you want to enter a number as text in a cell, you must preface its first digit with an apostrophe ('). For example, if you're entering a part number that consists of all numbers, such as 12-30-19, and you don't want Excel to convert it into the date December 30, 2019, you need to preface the entry with an apostrophe by entering into the cell:

'12-30-19

Likewise, if you want to enter 3/4 in a cell, meaning three out of four rather than the date March 4, you enter

'3/4

(Note that if you want to designate the fraction, three-fourths, you need to input =3/4, in which case Excel displays the value 0.75 in the cell display.)

When you complete an entry with an initial apostrophe that Excel would normally consider a value, such as the 12-30-19 date example, the apostrophe is not displayed in the cell. (It does appear, however, on the Formula bar.) Instead, a tiny green triangle appears in the upper-left corner of the cell, and an alert symbol appears to the immediate left (as long as the cell cursor is in this cell). When you position the mouse pointer on this alert indicator, a drop-down button appears to its right (shown in the left margin). When you click this drop-down button, a drop-down menu similar to the one shown in Figure 1-5 appears. In this example, the first option indicates that the number is currently stored as Text Date with 2-Digit Year, and the second and third options enable you to convert this text back into a twentieth or twenty-first century date (by removing the apostrophe).

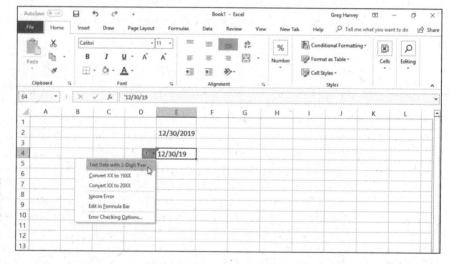

FIGURE 1-5:
Opening the drop-down menu attached to the Number Stored as Text alert.

WARNING

If you start a cell entry with the equal sign (=) or the at symbol (@) followed by other characters that aren't part of a formula, Excel displays an error dialog box as soon as you try to complete the data entry. Excel uses the equal sign to indicate the use of a formula, and what you have entered is not a valid formula. The program knows that Lotus 1-2-3 used the @ symbol to indicate the use of a built-in function, and what you have entered is not a valid built-in function. This means that you must preface any data entry beginning with the equal sign and @ symbol that isn't a valid formula with an apostrophe in order to get it into the cell.

What's the value?

In a typical spreadsheet, numbers (or numeric data entries) can be as prevalent as the text entries — if not more so. This is because traditionally, spreadsheets were developed to keep financial records, which included plenty of extended item totals, subtotals, averages, percentages, and grand totals. Of course, you can create spreadsheets that are full of numbers that have nothing to do with debits, credits, income statements, invoices, quarterly sales, and dollars and cents.

Number entries that you make in your spreadsheet can be divided into three categories:

>> **Numbers that you input** directly into a cell. (You can do this with the keyboard, your voice if you use the Speech Recognition feature, or even by handwriting if your keyboard is equipped with a writing tablet.)

>> **Date and time numbers** that are also input directly into a cell but are automatically displayed with the default Date and Time number formats and are stored behind the scenes as special date serial and hour decimal numbers.

>> **Numbers calculated by formulas** that you build yourself by using simple arithmetical operators and/or Excel's sophisticated built-in functions.

Inputting numbers

Numbers that you input directly into the cells of the worksheet — whether they are positive, negative, percentages, or decimal values representing dollars and cents, widgets in stock, workers in the Human Resources department, or potential clients — don't change unless you specifically change them, either by editing their values or replacing them with other values. This is quite unlike formulas with values that change whenever the worksheet is recalculated and Excel finds that the values upon which they depend have been modified.

When inputting numbers, you can mix the digits 0–9 with the following keyboard characters:

```
+ - ( ) $ . , %
```

You use these characters in the numbers you input as follows:

>> Preface the digits of the number with a plus sign (+) when you want to explicitly designate the number as positive, as in +(53) to convert negative 53 into positive 53. Excel considers all numbers to be positive unless you designate them as negative.

>> Preface the digits of the number with – or enclose them in a pair of parentheses to indicate that the number is a negative number, as in –53 or (53).

>> Preface the digits of the number with a dollar sign ($), as in $500, to format the number with the Currency style format as you enter it. (You can also apply this format after it's entered.)

>> Input a period (.) in the digits of the number to indicate the position of the decimal point in the number, as in 500.25. (Note that you don't have to bother entering trailing zeros after the decimal point because the General number format automatically drops them, even if you type them in.)

>> Input commas (,) between the digits of a number to indicate the position of thousands, hundred thousands, millions, billions, and the like, and to assign the Comma style number format to the number, as in 642,153. (You can also have Excel add the commas by assigning the Comma format to the number after you input the number.)

>> Append the percent sign (%) to the digits of a number to convert the number into a percentage and assign the Percent number style to it, as in 12%.

The most important thing to remember about the numbers that you input is that they inherit the type of number formatting currently assigned to the cells in which they're entered. When you first open a blank workbook, the number format appropriately called General (which some have called the equivalent of no number formatting because it doesn't add any special format characters, such as a constant number of decimal places or thousands separators) is applied to each cell of the worksheet. You can override the General format by adding your own formatting characters as you input the number in a cell or, later, by selecting the cell and then assigning a different number format to it. (See Book 2, Chapter 2 for details.)

Dates and times

Excel stores dates and times that you input into a spreadsheet as special values. Dates are stored as serial numbers, and times are stored as decimal fractions. Excel supports two date systems: the 1900 date system used by Excel for Windows (also used by Lotus 1-2-3), which uses January 1, 1900, as serial number 1, and the 1904 system used by Excel for the Macintosh, which uses January 2, 1904, as serial number 1.

REMEMBER

If you use Excel on the Windows PCs and Macintosh OS computers in your office, you can switch from the default 1900 date system to the 1904 date system for those worksheets that you create in the Windows version and then transfer to the Macintosh version. To switch to the 1904 date system, click the Advanced tab of the Excel Options dialog box (File⇨Excel Options or Alt+FT) and then click the Use 1904 Date System check box in the When Calculating This Workbook section.

By storing dates as serial numbers representing the number of days that have elapsed from a particular date (January 1, 1900, or January 2, 1904), Excel can perform arithmetic between dates. For example, you can find out how many days there are between February 15, 1949, and February 15, 2019, by entering 2/15/19 in one cell and 2/15/49 in the cell below, and then creating a formula in the cell below that one that subtracts the cell with 2/15/49 from the one containing 2/15/19. Because Excel stores the date 2/15/19 as the serial number 43511 and the date 2/15/49 as the serial number 17944, it can calculate the difference and return the result of 25567 (days, which is equal to 70 years).

TIP

When you type a date directly into a formula that performs date arithmetic (as opposed to constructing a formula using references to cells that contain date entries), you must enclose the date in quotation marks. So, for example, if you type the dates in a formula that calculates the number of days between February 15, 1949, and February 15, 2019, in the cell you have to type the following formula:

```
="2/15/19"-"2/15/49"
```

Times of the day are stored as decimal numbers that represent the fraction of the 24-hour period starting with 0.0 for 12:00 midnight through 0.999 for 11:59:59 p.m. By storing times as decimal fractions, Excel enables you to perform time calculations such as those that return the elapsed time (in minutes) between any two times of the day.

INPUTTING DATES AND TIMES USING RECOGNIZED FORMATS

Although Excel stores dates as serial numbers and times as decimal fractions, luckily you don't have to use these numbers to enter dates or times of the day into cells of the worksheet. You simply enter dates by using any of the recognized Date number formats that are used by Excel, and you enter times by using any of the recognized Time number formats. Excel then assigns and stores the appropriate serial number or decimal fraction at the same time the program assigns the date or time format that you used for this value. Table 1-1 shows you typical date and time entries that you can use as examples when entering dates and times in the cells of a worksheet.

TABLE 1-1

Common Ways to Enter Dates and Times

What You Enter in the Cell	Date or Time Recognized by Excel (As Displayed on the Formula Bar)
1/6/2019	January 6, 2019
1/6/19	January 6, 2019
1-6-19	January 6, 2019
6-Jan-19	January 6, 2019
6-Jan	January 6
Jan-16	January 2019
1/6/19 5:25	1/6/2016 5:25 a.m.
5:25	5:25:00 AM
5:25 P	5:25:00 PM
17:25	5:25:00 PM
17:25:33	5:25:33 PM

UNDERSTANDING HOW EXCEL TREATS TWO-DIGIT YEARS

The only thing that's a tad bit tricky about inputting dates in a spreadsheet comes in knowing when you have to input all four digits of the year and when you can get away with entering only two. As Table 1-1 shows, if you input the date 1/6/19 in a cell, Excel recognizes the date as 1/6/2019 and not as 1/6/1919. In fact, if you enter the date January 6, 1919, in a spreadsheet, you must enter all four digits of the year (1919).

Here's how Excel decides whether a year for which you enter only the last two digits belongs to the 20th or 21st century:

>> 00 through 29 belong to the 21st century, so Excels interprets 7/30/29 as July 30, 2029.

>> 30 through 99 belong to the 20th century, so Excel interprets 7/30/30 as July 30, 1930.

This means that you don't have to enter the four digits of the year for dates in the years 2000 through 2029, or for dates in the years 1930 through 1999.

Of course, if you can't remember these cutoffs and are just generally confused about when to enter two digits versus four digits, just go ahead and enter all four digits of the year. Excel never misunderstands which century the date belongs to when you spell out all four digits of the year.

Numeric formulas

Many numeric entries in a typical spreadsheet are not input directly but are returned as the result of a calculation by a formula. The numeric formulas that you build can do anything from simple arithmetic calculations to complex ANOVA statistical analyses. (See Book 3 for complete coverage of all types of numeric formulas.) Most spreadsheet formulas use numbers that are input into other cells of the worksheet in their calculations. Because these formulas refer to the address of the cell containing the input number rather than the number itself, Excel is able to automatically recalculate the formula and return a new result anytime you change the values in the original cell.

The most important thing to remember about numeric formulas is that their calculated values are displayed in their cells in the worksheet, whereas the contents of the formulas (that indicate how the calculation is done) are displayed on the Formula bar whenever its cell contains the cell cursor. All numbers returned by formulas inherit the nondescript General number format. The only way to get these calculated numbers to appear the way you want them in the worksheet is to select them and apply a new, more appropriate number format to them. (See Book 2, Chapter 2 for details.)

Data Entry 101

I want to pass on a few basic rules of data entry:

>> You must select the cell where you want to make the data entry before you can make the entry in that cell.

>> Any entry that you make in a cell that already contains data replaces the original entry.

>> Every data entry that you make in any cell must be completed with some sort of action, such as clicking the Enter button on the Formula bar (the button with the check mark that appears when you start entering data), pressing the Enter key, or clicking a new cell before the entry is officially entered in that cell.

Building Worksheets

I know that the first rule sounds so obvious that it should go without saying, but you'd be surprised how many times you look at the cell where you intend to add new data and then just start entering that data without realizing that you haven't yet moved the cell cursor to that cell. As a result, the data entry that you're making is not destined to go into the cell that you intended. In fact, you're in the process of making the entry in whatever cell currently contains the cell cursor, and if that cell is already occupied, you're in the process of replacing its entry with the one you meant to go somewhere else!

REMEMBER

This is why the third rule is so important: Even if you're in the process of messing up your spreadsheet by entering data in the wrong cell (and, if that cell is occupied, you're destroying a perfectly good entry), you haven't done it until you take the action that completes the entry (such as clicking the Enter button on the Formula bar or pressing the Enter key). This means that you can recover simply by clicking the Cancel button on the Formula bar or by pressing the Escape key on your keyboard. As soon as you do that, the errant data entry disappears from the Formula bar (and the original data entry — if it exists — returns), and you're then free to move the cell cursor to the desired cell and redo the entry there.

Data entry keyboard style

The only trick to entering data from the keyboard is to figure out the most efficient way to complete the entry in the current cell (and Excel gives you many choices in this regard). You can, of course, complete any data entry by clicking the Enter button on the Formula bar (presumably this is what Microsoft intended; otherwise, why have the button?), but clicking this button is not at all efficient when the mouse pointer isn't close to it.

You should know of another potential drawback to clicking the Enter button on the Formula bar to complete an entry: When you do this, Excel doesn't move the cell cursor but keeps it right in the cell with the new data entry. This means that you still have to move the cell cursor before you can safely make your next data entry. You're better off pressing the Enter key because doing this not only completes the entry in the cell, but also moves the cell cursor down to the cell in the next row.

Of course, pressing the Enter key is efficient only if you're doing the data entry for a table or list down each row across the succeeding columns. If you want to enter the data across each column of the table or list down succeeding rows, pressing Enter doesn't work to your advantage. Instead, you'd be better off pressing the → key or the Tab key to complete each entry (at least until you get to the cell in the last column of the table) because pressing these keys completes the entry and moves the cell cursor to the next cell on the right.

Take a look at Table 1-2 to get an idea of the keys that you commonly use to complete data entries. Keep in mind, however, that any key combination that moves the cell cursor (see Table 1-1 in Book 1, Chapter 1, for a review of these keystrokes) also completes the data entry that you're making, as does clicking another cell in the worksheet.

TABLE 1-2

Keys Used in Completing Data Entry

Press Key	To Have Cell Pointer Move
Enter	Down one row
↓	Down one row
Tab	Right one column
→	Right one column
Shift+Tab	Left one column
←	Left one column
↑	Up one row

TIP

If you have more than one cell selected (see Book 2, Chapter 2 for more on this) and then press Ctrl+Enter to complete the data entry that you're making in the active cell of this selected range, Excel simultaneously enters that data entry into all the cells in the selection. You can use this technique to enter a single label or value in many places in a worksheet at one time.

If you have more than one worksheet selected (see Book 2, Chapter 4) at the time that you make an entry in the current cell, Excel makes that entry in the corresponding cells of all the selected worksheets. For example, if you enter the heading *Cost Analysis* in cell C3 of Sheet1 when Sheet1 through Sheet3 are selected, Excel enters *Cost Analysis* in cell C3 of Sheet2 and Sheet3 as well.

Doing data entry with the Touch keyboard

TIP

If you're running Excel 2019 on a touchscreen device that lacks any kind of physical keyboard, such as a Surface Pro tablet without the optional Type Cover, you need to open the Windows 10 Touch keyboard and use it to input your spreadsheet data. To open the Touch keyboard, simply tap the Touch Keyboard button that appears on the right side of the Windows 10 taskbar. Doing this displays the standard Touch keyboard docked at the bottom of the Excel program window.

Building Worksheets

To undock the standard Touch keyboard beneath the Excel 2019 program window or select one of the other styles of Touch keyboard, tap the Keyboard Settings button (the one with the cog on top of the keyboard icon) to the left of the Microphone icon on the left side and then tap the Float Keyboard button (the rightmost white icon on the second row of the pop-up menu). Figure 1-6 shows you how your touchscreen looks after undocking the Windows 10 standard Touch keyboard and dragging it up away from the Excel Status bar.

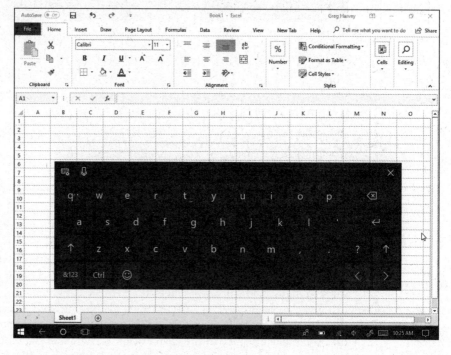

FIGURE 1-6:
A Windows 10 touchscreen after displaying and undocking the standard Touch keyboard so it floats in the middle of the Excel 2019 program window.

As shown in this figure, when undocked, the Windows 10 standard Touch keyboard remains completely separate from the Excel program window so that you can reposition it so that you still have access to most of the cells in the current worksheet when doing your data entry. The standard Touch keyboard is limited mostly to letter keys above a spacebar with a few punctuation symbols (apostrophe, comma, period, and question mark). This standard keyboard also sports the following special keys:

>> **Backspace** key (marked with the *x* in the shape pointing left) to delete characters to the immediate left when entering or editing a cell entry

>> **Enter** key (with the bent arrow) to complete an entry in the current cell and move the cursor down one row in the same column

- » **Shift** key (with arrows pointing upward) to enter capital letters in a cell entry

- » **Numeric** key (with &123) to switch to the Touch keyboard so that it displays a numeric keyboard with a Tab key and extensive punctuation used in entering numeric data in a cell (tap the &123 key a second time to return to the standard QWERTY letter arrangement)

- » **Ctrl** key to run macros to which you've assigned letter keys (see Book 8, Chapter 1 for details) or to combine with the left arrow or right arrow key to jump the cursor to the cell in the last and first column of the current row, respectively

- » **Emoticon** key (with that awful smiley face icon) to switch to a bunch of emoticons that you can enter into a cell entry (tap the Emoticon key a second time to return to standard QWERTY letter arrangement)

- » **Left** arrow (with the < symbol) to move the cell cursor one cell to the immediate right and complete any cell entry in progress

- » **Right** arrow (with the > symbol) to move the cell cursor one cell to the immediate left and complete any cell entry in progress

TIP

Windows 10 also supports a much smaller version (called a mobile Touch keyboard) of the standard Touch keyboard. This is ideal when running Excel on a smaller tablet. To switch from the standard to the mobile Touch keyboard, tap the Keyboard Settings button followed by the Mobile Keyboard button (the white keyboard icon in the very middle of the first row of the pop-up menu, three icons from the left or right).

If you want to have access to a fully functional Touch keyboard when working in Excel, you need to switch to the expanded Touch keyboard by tapping the Keyboard Settings button followed by the Expanded Keyboard button (the rightmost white keyboard icon at the end of the first row of the pop-up menu). The expanded version of the Windows 10 Touch keyboard includes these special keys in addition all to those listed earlier for the standard Touch keyboard:

- » **Esc** key to abandon incorrect cell entries and close dialog boxes without making any changes

- » **Tab** key to move the cell cursor one cell to the right like the → key

- » **Caps** key to caps lock on when you want to shift all the letters to capitals for a cell entry

- » **Del** key to clear a cell of its current entry

- » **Windows** key to open the Windows 10 Start screen with the Metro tiles from Windows 8

- » **Fn** key to replace the top row of numbers, minus, and equals keys with the Excel function keys F1 through F12 to use their shortcuts

- » **Alt** key to tap out keyboard shortcuts, such as Alt+NF, to open the Online Pictures dialog box in order to select and import an online graphic into your worksheet

- » **Up** arrow (with the ^ symbol) to move the cell cursor one row up in the current column

- » **Down** arrow (with the ^ symbol facing downward) to move the cell cursor one row down in the current column

Window10 supports a split-keyboard arrangement of the Touch keyboard that enables you to see more of the cells in your worksheet as you enter your text and numbers in the worksheet from separated banks of keys on the left and right side of the worksheet area. To switch to this arrangement, tap the Keyboard Settings button followed by the Split Keyboard button (the white keyboard icon second from the left in the first row of the pop-up menu). Excel then displays the split keyboard with the QWERTY letter keys separated into a left and right bank.

You can also switch to an Inking keyboard (the white keyboard icon second from the right with a stylus sticking out of it on the first row of the Keyboard Settings pop-up menu) where you can make cell entries by writing your entries in the keyboard area with your finger, stylus, or digital pen and then inserting them into the worksheet by tapping its Insert button.

TIP

If you've enabled Windows speech services on your device, you can just dictate your entry for the current cell in your worksheet. You do this by tapping the Microphone button (to the immediate right of the Keyboard Settings button in whatever style of touch keyboard you're using) and then dictate the text or value you wanted entered when the Listening prompt appears. Excel then enters what you dictated into the current worksheet cell when you pause and promptly turns the microphone off.

When you finish entering your worksheet data with your Windows Touch keyboard, you can close it and return to the normal full screen view of the Excel program window by tapping the Close button.

You AutoComplete this for me

Excel automatically makes use of a feature called AutoComplete, which attempts to automate completely textual data entries (that is, entries that don't mix text and numbers). AutoComplete works this way: If you start a new text entry that begins with the same letter or letters as an entry that you've made recently in the same region of the worksheet, Excel completes the new text entry with the characters from the previous text entry that began with those letters.

For example, if you type the spreadsheet title *Sales Invoice* in cell A1 of a new worksheet and then, after completing the entry by pressing the ↓, start entering the table title *Summary* in cell A2, as soon as you type *S* in cell A2, Excel completes the new text entry so that it also states *Sales Invoice* by adding the letters *ales Invoice*.

When the AutoComplete feature completes the new text entry, the letters that it adds to the initial letter or letters that you type are automatically selected (indicated by highlighting). This way, if you don't want to repeat the original text entry in the new cell, you can replace the characters that Excel adds just by typing the next letter in the new (and different) entry. In the previous example, in which Sales Invoice was repeated in the cell where you want to input *Summary,* the *ales Invoice* text appended to the *S* that you type disappears the moment you type *u* in *Summary.*

Note that when you have two different entries that begin with the same first letter but have different second letters, typing the second letter of one entry causes Excel to complete the typing of that entry, leaving you free to insert its text in the cell by pressing the Enter key or using any of the other methods for completing a cell entry.

To make use of automatic text completion rather than override it as in the previous example, simply press a key (such as Enter, Tab, or an arrow key), click the Enter button on the Formula bar, or click another cell to complete the completed input in that cell. For example, say you're building a sales table in which you're inputting sales for three different account representatives — George, Jean, and Alice. After entering each name manually in the appropriate row of the Account Representative column, you need to type in only their first initial (*G* to get George, *J* to get Jean, and *A* to get Alice) in subsequent cells and then press the ↓ or Enter key to move down to the next row of that column. Of course, in a case like this, AutoComplete is more like automatic typing, and it makes filling in the Account Representative names for this table extremely quick and easy.

TIP

If the AutoComplete feature starts to bug you when building a particular spreadsheet, you can temporarily turn it off; simply click the Enable AutoComplete for Cell Values check box in the Editing Options section, and remove the check mark on the Advanced tab of the Excel Options dialog box (File⇨Options or Alt+FTA).

Note that disabling AutoComplete in this manner also disables the Flash Fill feature as well. (See "Flash Fill to the rescue" later in this chapter for details.)

You AutoCorrect this right now!

Along with AutoComplete, Excel has an AutoCorrect feature that automatically fixes certain typos that you make in the text entries as soon as you complete them. For example, if you forget to capitalize a day of the week, AutoCorrect does this for you (turning *friday* into *Friday* in a cell as soon as you complete the entry). Likewise, if you mistakenly enter a word with two initial capital letters, AutoCorrect automatically lowercases the second capital letter (so that *QUarter* typed into a cell becomes *Quarter* upon completion of the cell entry).

In addition to these types of obvious capitalization errors, AutoCorrect also automatically takes care of common typos, such as changing *hsi* to *his* (an obvious transposition of two letters) or *inthe* to *in the* (an obvious case of a missing space between letters). In addition to the errors already recognized by AutoCorrect, you can add your own particular mistakes to the list of automatic replacements.

To do this, open the AutoCorrect dialog box and then add your own replacements in the Replace and With text boxes located on the AutoCorrect tab, shown in Figure 1-7. Here's how:

1. **Click File ⇨ Options and then click the Proofing tab (Alt+FTP) followed by the AutoCorrect Options button.**

   The AutoCorrect dialog box opens for your language, such as English (U.S.).

2. **If the AutoCorrect options aren't already displayed in the dialog box, click the AutoCorrect tab to display them.**

3. **Click the Replace text box and then enter the typo exactly as you usually make it.**

4. **Click the With text box and enter the replacement that AutoCorrect should make (with no typos in it, please!).**

   Check the typo that you've entered in the Replace text box and the replacement that you've entered in the With text box. If everything checks out, go on to Step 5.

5. **Click the Add button to add your new AutoCorrect replacement to the list of automated replacements.**

6. **Click the OK button to close the AutoCorrect dialog box.**

TIP

You can use the AutoCorrect feature to automatically replace favorite abbreviations with full text, as well as to clean up all your personal typing mistakes. For example, if you have a client with the name Great Lakes Securities, and you enter this client's name in countless spreadsheets that you create, you can make an AutoCorrect entry so that Excel automatically replaces the abbreviation *gls* with *Great Lakes Securities*. Of course, after you use AutoCorrect to enter Great Lakes Securities in your first cell by typing *gls*, the AutoComplete feature kicks in, so the next time you type the *g* of *gls* to enter the client's name in another cell, it fills in the rest of the name, leaving you with nothing to do but complete the entry.

REMEMBER

Keep in mind that AutoCorrect is not a replacement for Excel's spelling checker. You should still spell check your spreadsheet before sending it out because the spelling checker finds all those uncommon typos that haven't been automatically corrected for you. (See Book 2, Chapter 3 for details.)

Constraining data entry to a cell range

One of the most efficient ways to enter data into a new table in your spreadsheet is to preselect the empty cells where the data entries need to be made and then enter the data into the selected range. Of course, this trick only works if you know ahead of time how many columns and rows the new table requires.

The reason that preselecting the cells works so well is that doing this constrains the cell cursor to that range, provided that you press *only* the keystrokes shown in Table 1-3. This means that if you're using the Enter key to move down the column as you enter data, Excel automatically positions the cell cursor at the beginning of the next column as soon as you complete the last entry in that column. Likewise, when using the Tab key to move the cell cursor across a row as you enter data,

Excel automatically positions the cell cursor at the beginning of the next row in the table as soon as you complete the last entry in that row.

TABLE 1-3

Keystrokes for Moving Within a Selection

Keystrokes	Movement
Enter	Moves the cell pointer down one cell in the selection (moves one cell to the right when the selection consists of a single row)
Shift+Enter	Moves the cell pointer up one cell in the selection (moves one cell to the left when the selection consists of a single row)
Tab	Moves the cell pointer one cell to the right in the selection (moves one cell down when the selection consists of a single column)
Shift+Tab	Moves the cell pointer one cell to the left in the selection (moves one cell up when the selection consists of a single column)
Ctrl+period (.)	Moves the cell pointer from corner to corner of the cell selection

That way you don't have to concentrate on repositioning the cell cursor at all when entering the table data; you can keep your attention on the printed copy from which you're taking the data.

TIP

You can't very well use this preselection method on data lists because they're usually open-ended affairs to which you continually append new rows of data. The most efficient way to add new data to a new or existing data list is to format it as a table. (See Book 2, Chapter 2.)

Getting Excel to put in the decimal point

Of course, if your keyboard has a ten-key entry pad, you'll want to use it rather than the numbers on the top row of the keyboard to make your numeric entries in the spreadsheet. (Make sure that the Num Lock key is engaged, or you'll end up moving the cell cursor rather than entering numbers.) If you have a lot of decimal numbers (suppose that you're building a financial spreadsheet with loads of dollars and cents entries), you may also want to use Excel's Fixed Decimal Places feature so that Excel places a decimal point in all the numbers that you enter in the worksheet.

To turn on this feature, click the Automatically Insert a Decimal Point check box in the Editing Options section of the Advanced tab of the Excel Options dialog box (Alt+FTA) to put a check mark in it. When you do this, the Places text box immediately below it determines the number of decimal places that the program is to add to each number entry. You can then specify the number of places by changing its value (2 is, of course, the default) either by entering a new value or selecting one with its spinner buttons.

After turning on the Automatically Insert a Decimal Point option, Excel adds a decimal point to the number of places that you specified to every numeric data entry that you make at the time you complete its entry. For example, if you type the digits 56789 in a cell, Excel changes this to 567.89 at the time you complete the entry.

Note that when this feature is turned on and you want to enter a number without a decimal point, you need to type a period at the end of the value. For example, if you want to enter the number 56789 in a cell and *not* have Excel change it to 567.89, you need to type

```
56789.
```

Ending the number in a period prevents Excel from adding its own decimal point to the value when Fixed Decimal Places is turned on. Of course, you need to turn this feature off after you finish making the group of entries that require the same number of decimal places. To do this, deselect the Automatically Insert a Decimal Point check box on the Advanced tab of the Excel Options dialog box (Alt+FTA).

You AutoFill it in

Few Excel features are more helpful than the AutoFill feature, which enables you to fill out a series of entries in a data table or list — all by entering only the first item in the series in the spreadsheet. You can sometimes use the AutoFill feature to quickly input row and column headings for a new data table or to number the records in a data list. For example, when you need a row of column headings that list the 12 months for a sales table, you can enter *January* or *Jan.* in the first column and then have AutoFill input the other 11 months for you in the cells in columns to the right. Likewise, when you need to create a column of row headings at the start of a table with successive part numbers that start at L505-120 and proceed to L505-128, you enter L505-120 in the first row and then use AutoFill to copy the part numbers down to L505-128 in the cells below.

The key to using AutoFill is the Fill handle, which is the small black square that appears in the lower-right corner of whatever cell contains the cell cursor. When you position the mouse or Touch pointer on the Fill handle, it changes from the normal thick, white-cross pointer to a thin, black-cross pointer. This change in shape is your signal that when you drag the Fill handle in a single direction, either down or to the right, Excel will either copy the current cell entry to all the cells that you select or use it as the first entry in a consecutive series, whose successive entries are then automatically entered in the selected cells.

Note that you can immediately tell whether Excel will simply copy the cell entry or use it as the first in a series to fill out by the ScreenTips that appear to the right of the mouse pointer. As you drag through subsequent cells, the ScreenTip indicates which entry will be made if you release the mouse button (or remove your finger or stylus from a touchscreen) at that point. If the ScreenTip shows the same entry as you drag, you know Excel didn't recognize the entry as part of a consecutive series and is copying the entry verbatim. If, instead, the ScreenTips continue to change as you drag through cells showing you successive entries for the series, you know that Excel has recognized the original entry as part of a consecutive series.

Figures 1-8 and 1-9 illustrate how AutoFill works. In Figure 1-8, I entered January as the first column heading in cell B2 (using the Enter button on the Formula bar so as to keep the cell cursor in B2, ready for AutoFill). Next, I positioned the mouse pointer on the AutoFill handle in the lower-right corner of B2 before dragging the Fill handle to the right until I reached cell G2 (and the ScreenTip stated June).

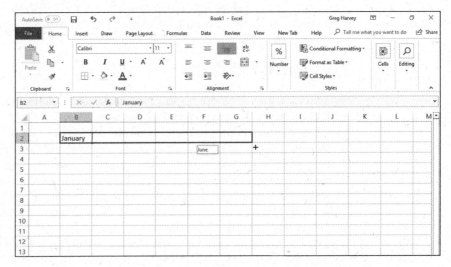

FIGURE 1-8:
Dragging the Fill handle to fill in a series with the first six months of the year.

Figure 1-9 shows the series that was entered in the cell range B2:G2 when I released the mouse button with cell G2 selected. For this figure, I also clicked the drop-down button attached to the Auto Fill Options button that automatically appears whenever you use the Fill handle to copy entries or fill in a series to show you the items on this drop-down menu. This menu contains a Copy Cells option button that enables you to override Excel's decision to fill in the series and have it copy the original entry (January, in this case) to all the selected cells.

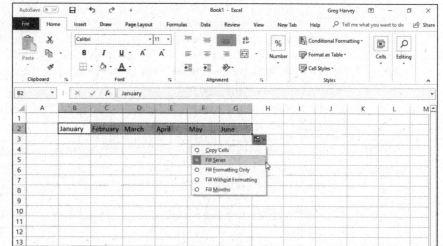

FIGURE 1-9:
The series of
monthly column
headings with the
AutoFill Options
drop-down menu.

Note that you can also override Excel's natural decision to fill in a series or copy an entry before you drag the Fill handle. To do so, simply hold down the Ctrl key (which adds a tiny plus sign to the upper-right corner of the Fill handle). Continue to depress the Ctrl key as you drag the Fill handle and notice that the ScreenTip now shows that Excel is no longer filling in the series or copying the entry as expected.

TIP

When you need to consecutively number the cells in a range, use the Ctrl key to override Excel's natural tendency to copy the number to all the cells you select. For example, if you want to number rows of a list, enter the starting number (1 or 100, it doesn't matter) in the first row and then press Ctrl to have Excel fill in the rest of the numbers for successive rows in the list (2, 3, 4, and the like, or 102, 103, 104, and so on). If you forget to hold down the Ctrl key and end up with a whole range of cells with the same starting number, click the Auto Fill Options drop-down button and then click the Fill Series option button to rectify the mistake by converting the copied numbers to a consecutively numbered series.

When using AutoFill to fill in a data series, you don't have to start with the first entry in that particular series. For example, if you want to enter a row of column headings with the last six months of the year (June through December), you enter *June* first and then drag down or to the right until the mouse pointer selects the cell where you enter *December* (indicated by the December ScreenTip). Note also that you can reverse-enter a data series by dragging the Fill handle up or left. In the June-to-December column headings example, if you drag up or left, Excel enters June to January in reverse order.

REMEMBER

Keep in mind that you can also use AutoFill to copy an original formula across rows and down columns of data tables and lists. When you drag the Fill handle in a cell that contains a formula, Excel automatically adjusts its cell references to suit the new row or column position of each copy. (See Book 3, Chapter 1 for details on copying formulas with AutoFill.)

AutoFill on a Touchscreen

TIP

To fill out a data series using your finger or stylus when using Excel on a touch-screen tablet without access to a mouse or touchpad, you use the AutoFill button that appears on the touchscreen mini-toolbar as follows:

1. **Tap the cell containing the initial value in the series you want AutoFill to extend.**

   Excel selects the cell and displays selection handles (with circles) in the upper-left and lower-right corners.

2. **Tap and hold the cell until the mini-toolbar appears.**

   When summoned by touch, the mini-toolbar appears as a single row of command buttons, Paste to AutoFill, terminated by a Show Context Menu button (with a black triangle pointing downward).

3. **Tap the AutoFill button on the mini-toolbar.**

   Excel closes the mini-toolbar and adds an AutoFill button to the currently selected cell (with a blue downward-pointing arrow in the square).

4. **Drag the AutoFill button through the blank cells in the same column or row into which the data series sequence is to be filled.**

   When you release your finger or stylus after selecting the last blank cell to be filled, Excel fills out the data series in the selected range.

AutoFill via the Fill button on the Ribbon

Instead of using the Fill handle or AutoFill button on the mini-toolbar, you can also fill out a series using the Fill button on the Excel 2019 Ribbon. To use the Fill button on the Home tab of the Ribbon to accomplish your AutoFill operations, you follow these steps:

1. **Enter the first entry (or entries) upon which the series is to be based in the first cell(s) to hold the new data series in your worksheet.**

2. **Select the cell range where the series is to be created, across a row or down a column, being sure to include the cell with the initial entry or entries in this range.**

3. **Click the Fill button on the Home tab and then tap Series on its drop-down menu.**

The Fill button is located in the Editing group right below the AutoSum button (the one with the Greek sigma). When you click the Series option, Excel opens the Series dialog box.

4. **Click the AutoFill option button in the Type column followed by the OK button in the Series dialog box.**

Excel enters a series of data based on the initial value(s) in your selected cell range just as though you'd selected the range with the fill handle.

Note that the Series dialog box contains a bunch of options that you can use to further refine and control the data series that Excel creates. In a linear data series, if you want the series to increment more than one step value at a time, you can increase it in the Step Value text box. Likewise, if you want your linear or AutoFill series to stop when it reaches a particular value, you enter that into the Stop Value text box.

REMEMBER

When you're entering a series of dates with AutoFill that increment on anything other than the day, remember the Date Unit options in the Series dialog box enable you to specify other parts of the initial date to increment in the series. Your choices include Weekday, Month, or Year.

AutoFill series with increments other than one

Normally, when you drag the Fill handle to fill in a series of data entries, Excel increases or decreases each entry in the series by a single unit (a day, month, hour, or whatever). You can, however, get AutoFill to fill out a series of data entries that uses some other increment, such as every other day, every third month, or every hour-and-a-half.

Figure 1-10 illustrates a number of series all created with AutoFill that use increments other than one unit. The first example in row 2 shows a series of different times all 45 minutes apart, starting with 8:00 a.m. in cell A3 and extending to 2:00 p.m. in cell I3. The second example in row 4 contains a series of weekdays consisting of every other day of the week, starting on Monday in cell A4 and extending to Saturday in cell G4. The third example in row 6 shows a series of numbers, each of which increases by 15, that starts with 35 in cell A6 and increases to 155 in cell I6. The last example in row 8 shows a series with every other month, starting with Jan. in cell A8 and ending with Nov. in cell F8.

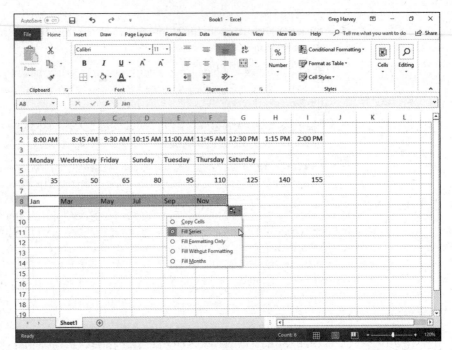

FIGURE 1-10:
Various series created with AutoFill by using different increments.

To create a series that uses an increment other than one unit, follow these four general steps:

1. **Enter the first two entries in the series in consecutive cells above one another in a column or side by side in a row.**

   Enter the entries one above the other when you intend to drag the Fill handle down the column to extend the series. Enter them side by side when you intend to drag the Fill handle to the right across the row.

2. **Position the cell pointer in the cell with the first entry in the series and drag through the second entry.**

   Both entries must be selected (indicated by being enclosed within the expanded cell cursor) before you use the Fill handle to extend the series. Excel analyzes the difference between the two entries and uses its increment in filling out the data series.

3. **Drag the Fill handle down the column or across the row to extend the series by using the increment other than one unit.**

   Check the ScreenTips to make sure that Excel is using the correct increment in filling out your data series.

4. Release the mouse button when you reach the desired end of the series (indicated by the entry shown in the ScreenTip appearing next to the black-cross mouse pointer).

Creating custom AutoFill lists

Just as you can use AutoFill to fill out a series with increments different from one unit, you can also get it to fill out custom lists of your own design. For example, suppose that you often have to enter a standard series of city locations as the column or row headings in new spreadsheets that you build. Instead of copying the list of cities from one workbook to another, you can create a custom list containing all the cities in the order in which they normally appear in your spreadsheets. After you create a custom list in Excel, you can then enter all or part of the entries in the series simply by entering the first item in a cell and then using the Fill handle to extend out the series either down a column or across a row.

To create a custom series, you can either enter the list of entries in the custom series in successive cells of a worksheet before you open the Custom Lists dialog box, or you can type the sequence of entries for the custom series in the List Entries list box located on the right side of the Custom Lists tab in this dialog box, as shown in Figure 1-11.

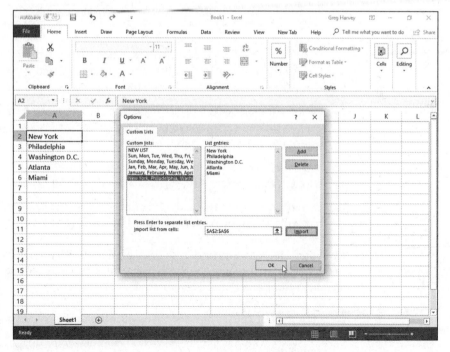

FIGURE 1-11:
Creating a custom list of cities for AutoFill.

If you already have the data series for your custom list entered in a range of cells somewhere in a worksheet, follow these steps to create the custom list:

1. **Click the cell with the first entry in the custom series and then drag the mouse or Touch pointer through the range until all the cells with entries are selected.**

   The expanded cell cursor should now include all the cells with entries for the custom list.

2. **Click File⇨Options⇨Advanced (Alt+FTA) and then scroll down and click the Edit Custom Lists button located in the General section.**

   The Custom Lists dialog box opens with its Custom Lists tab, where you now should check the accuracy of the cell range listed in the Import List from Cells text box. (The range in this box lists the first cell and last cell in the current selected range separated by a colon — you can ignore the dollar signs following each part of the cell address.) To check that the cell range listed in the Import List from Cells text box includes all the entries for the custom list, click the Collapse Dialog Box button, located to the right of the Import List from Cells text box. When you click this button, Excel collapses the Custom Lists dialog box down to the Import List from Cells text box and puts a marquee (the so-called marching ants) around the cell range.

   If this marquee includes all the entries for your custom list, you can expand the Custom Lists dialog box by clicking the Expand Dialog box button (which replaces the Collapse Dialog Box button) and proceed to Step 3. If this marquee doesn't include all the entries, click the cell with the first entry and then drag through until all the other cells are enclosed in the marquee. Then, click the Expand Dialog box button and go to Step 3.

3. **Click the Import button to add the entries in the selected cell range to the List Entries box on the right and to the Custom Lists box on the left side of the Custom Lists tab.**

   As soon as you click the Import button, Excel adds the data entries in the selected cell range to both the List Entries and the Custom Lists boxes.

4. **Click the OK button twice, the first time to close the Custom Lists dialog box and the second to close the Excel Options dialog box.**

If you don't have the entries for your custom list entered anywhere in the worksheet, you have to follow the second and third steps listed previously and then take these three additional steps instead:

1. **Click the List Entries box and then type each of the entries for the custom list in the order in which they are to be entered in successive cells of a worksheet.**

Press the Enter key after typing each entry for the custom list so that each entry appears on its own line in the List Entries box, or separate each entry with a comma.

2. **Click the Add button to add the entries that you've typed into the List Entries box on the right to the Custom Lists box, located on the left side of the Custom Lists tab.**

Note that when Excel adds the custom list that you just typed to the Custom Lists box, it automatically adds commas between each entry in the list — even if you pressed the Enter key after making each entry. It also automatically separates each entry on a separate line in the List Entries box — even if you separated them with commas instead of carriage returns.

3. **Click the OK button twice to close both the Custom Lists box and Excel Options dialog box.**

After you've created a custom list by using one of these two methods, you can fill in the entire data series by entering the first entry of the list in a cell and then dragging the Fill handle to fill in the rest of the entries. If you ever decide that you no longer need a custom list that you've created, you can delete it by clicking the list in the Custom Lists box in the Custom Lists dialog box and then clicking the Delete button. Excel then displays an alert box indicating that the list will be permanently deleted when you click OK. Note that you can't delete any of the built-in lists that appear in this list box when you first open the Custom Lists dialog box.

REMEMBER

Keep in mind that you can also fill in any part of the series by simply entering any one of the entries in the custom list and then dragging the Fill handle in the appropriate direction (down and to the right to enter succeeding entries in the list or up and to the left to enter preceding entries).

Flash Fill to the rescue

Excel 2019's handy Flash Fill feature gives you the ability to take a part of the data entered into one column of a worksheet table and enter just that data in a new table column using only a few keystrokes. The series of entries appear in the new column, literally in a flash (thus, the name *Flash Fill*), the moment Excel detects a pattern in your initial data entry that enables it to figure out the data you want to copy. The beauty is that all this happens without the need for you to construct or copy any kind of formula.

The best way to understand Flash Fill is to see it in action. Figure 1-12 contains a new data table consisting of four columns. The first column already contains the full names of clients (first, middle, and last). The second, third, and fourth columns need to have just the first, middle, and surnames, respectively, entered into them (so that particular parts of the clients' names can be used in the greetings of form e-mails and letters as in, "Hello Keith," or "Dear Mr. Harper,").

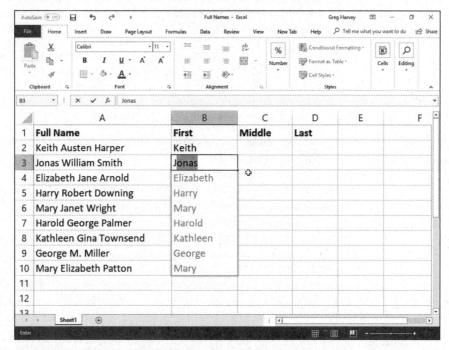

FIGURE 1-12:
New data table containing full names that need to be split up in separate columns with Flash Fill.

Rather than manually entering the first, middle, or last names in the respective columns (or attempting to copy the entire client name from column A and then editing out the parts not needed in the First Name, Middle Name, and Last Name columns), you can use Flash Fill to quickly and effectively do the job. And here's how you do it:

1. **Type** Keith **in cell B2 and complete the entry with the ↓ or Enter key.**

When you complete this entry with the ↓ key or Enter key on your keyboard, Excel moves the cell pointer to cell B3, where you have to type only the first letter of the next name for Flash Fill to get the picture.

2. **In Cell B3, type only** J**, the first letter of Jonas, the second client's first name.**

Flash Fill immediately does an AutoFill type maneuver by suggesting the rest of the second client's first name, Jonas, as the text to enter in this cell. At the same time, Flash Fill suggests entering all the remaining first names from the full names in column A in column B. (See Figure 1-12.)

3. **Complete the entry of Jonas in cell B3 by clicking the Enter button or pressing an arrow key.**

> The moment you complete the data entry in cell B3, the First Name column is done: Excel enters all the other first names in column B at the same time!

To complete this example name table by entering the middle and last names in columns C and D, respectively, you simply repeat these steps in those columns. You enter the first middle name, **Austen,** from cell A2 in cell C2 and then type **W** in cell C3. Complete the entry in cell C3 and the middle name entries in that column are done. Likewise, you enter the first last name, **Harper,** from cell A2 in cell D2 and then type **S** in cell D3. Complete the entry in cell D3, and the last name entries for column D are done, finishing the entire data table.

By my count, completing the data entry in this Client Name table required me to make a total of 26 keystrokes, 20 of which were for typing in the first, middle, and last name of the first client along with the initial letters of the first, middle, and last name of the second client and the other six to complete these entries. If Column A of this Client Name table contains the full names of hundreds or even thousands of clients, this 26 keystrokes is insignificant compared to the number that would be required to manually enter their first, middle, and last names in their separate First Name, Middle Name, and Last Name columns or even to edit down copies of the full names in each of them.

REMEMBER

Keep in mind that Flash Fill works perfectly at extracting parts of longer data entries in a column provided that all the entries follow the same pattern and use same type of separators (spaces, commas, dashes, and the like). For example, in Figure 1-12, there's an anomaly in the full name entries in cell A9 where only the middle initial with a period is entered instead of the full middle. In this case, Flash Fill simply enters M in cell C9, and you have to manually edit its entry to add the necessary period. Also, remember that Flash Fill's usefulness isn't restricted to all-text entries as in my example Client Name table. It can also extract parts of entries that mix text and numbers, such as ID numbers (AJ-1234, RW-8007, and so forth).

Limiting data entry with Data Validation

The Data Validation feature in Excel can be a real timesaver when you're doing repetitive data entry, and can also go a long way in preventing incorrect entries in your spreadsheets. When you use Data Validation in a cell, you indicate what type of data entry is allowed in the cell. As part of restricting a data entry to a number (which can be a whole number, decimal, date, or time), you also specify the permissible values for that type of number (a whole number between 10 and 100 or a date between January 1, 2019, and December 31, 2019, for example).

When you restrict the data entry to text, you can specify the range of the minimum and maximum text length (in characters) or, even better, a list of permissible text entries that you can choose from a pop-up menu (opened by clicking a pop-up button that appears to the right of the cell whenever it contains the cell cursor).

When using Data Validation to restrict the type of data entry and its range of acceptable values in a cell, you can also specify an input message that is automatically displayed next to the cell when you select it and/or an error alert message that is displayed if you try to input the wrong type of entry or a number outside the permissible range.

To use the Data Validation feature, put the cell cursor in the cell where you want to restrict the type of data entry that you can make there and then click the Data Validation button on the Data tab of the Ribbon (or press Alt+AVV). The Data Validation dialog box opens with the Settings tab selected (similar to the one shown in Figure 1-13).

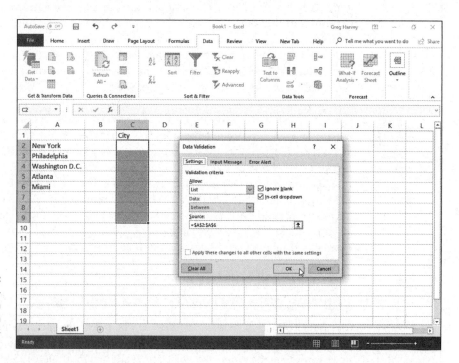

FIGURE 1-13:
Creating a custom drop-down list in the Data Validation dialog box.

You then click the drop-down button attached to the Allow drop-down list box and select among the following items:

>> **Any Value** to remove any previous restrictions thereby canceling data validation and once again enabling the user to enter anything he wishes into the cell

>> **Whole Number** to restrict the entry to a whole number that falls within a certain range or adheres to particular parameters that you specify

>> **Decimal** to restrict the entry to a decimal number that falls within a certain range or adheres to particular parameters that you specify

>> **List** to restrict the entry to one of several text entries that you specify in a list that is then displayed by clicking a pop-up button that appears to the right of the cell whenever it contains the cell cursor

>> **Date** to restrict the entry to a date that falls within a certain range or on or before a particular date

>> **Time** to restrict the entry to a time that falls within a certain range or on or before a particular time of the day

>> **Text Length** to restrict a text entry so that its length in characters doesn't fall below or go above a certain number or falls within a range that you specify

>> **Custom** to restrict the entry to the parameters specified by a particular formula entered in another cell of the worksheet

To specify an input message after selecting all the items on the Settings tab, click the Input Message tab of the Data Validation dialog box, where you enter a short title for the input message (such as *List Entry*) in the Title text box, and then enter the text of your message in the Input Message list box below.

To specify an alert message, click the Error Alert tab of the Data Validation dialog box, where you can select the kind of warning from the Style drop-down list: Stop (the default, which uses a red button with a cross in it), Warning (which uses a yellow triangle with an exclamation point in it), or Information (which uses a balloon with a blue *I* in it). After selecting the type of alert, you then enter the title for its dialog box in its Title text box and enter the text of the alert message in the Error Message list box.

TIP

To apply the restriction you're defining in the Data Validation dialog box to all the other cells that are formatted the same way as in a cell range formatted as a table (see Book 2, Chapter 2 for details), click the Apply These Changes to All Other Cells with the Same Settings check box before you click OK. To copy the restriction to a range that is not formatted as a table, use the Data Validation feature to set up the type of entry and permitted range in the first cell and then use the Fill handle to copy that cell's Data Validation settings to subsequent cells in the same column or row.

By far, the most popular use of the Data Validation feature is to create a drop-down menu from which you or someone who uses your spreadsheet can select the appropriate data entry. Figures 1-13 and 1-14 illustrate this type of usage.

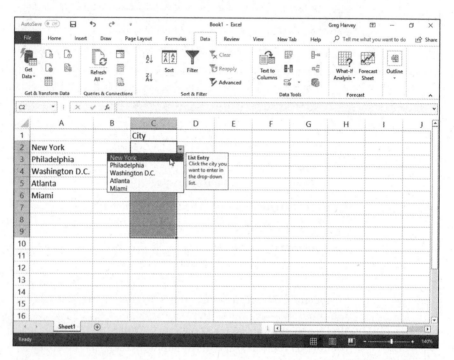

FIGURE 1-14:
Selecting a city from the custom drop-down list.

As Figure 1-13 shows, on the Settings tab of the Data Validation dialog box, I chose List from the Allow drop-down list box and then in the Source text box, I designated the cell range A2:A6, which just happens to contain the list of allowable entries. (You can type them in the Source text box separated by commas if the list doesn't already exist someplace on the worksheet.) Notice in this figure that, as soon as you select List in the Allow combo box, a check box appears. Keep this check box selected because it tells Excel to create a drop-down list (or pop-up menu, as it's also called) containing only the entries specified in the Source text box.

Figure 1-14 shows you what happens in the spreadsheet after you close the Data Validation dialog box. Here, you see the pop-up menu (with a list of cities taken from the cell range A2:A6) as it appears when you click the cell's new pop-up button. In this figure, you can also see the input List Entry message box that I created for this cell by using the options on the Input Message tab of the Data Validation dialog box. Note that you can reposition this message box (officially known as a *Comment box*) so that it's close to the cell but doesn't get in the way of selecting an entry — simply drag the Comment box with the mouse pointer.

Figure 1-15 demonstrates what happens if you try to input an entry that isn't on the drop-down list. For this figure, I deliberately disregarded the input instructions and typed *Boston* as the location. As soon as I clicked the Enter button on the Formula bar, the custom alert dialog box (which I named *Invalid Entry*) appears. I created this alert dialog box by using the options located on the Error Alert tab of the Data Validation dialog box.

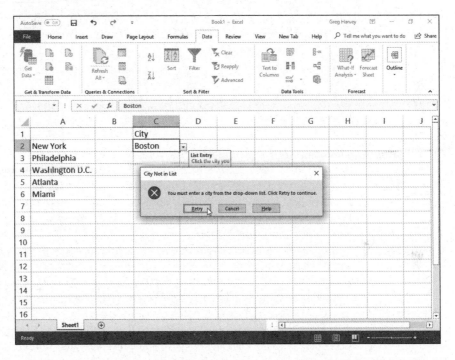

FIGURE 1-15:
Getting an error message after trying to input a city that's not on the list.

To find cells to which Data Validation has been applied, open the Go To dialog box (Ctrl+G or F5), then click the Special button, and then click the Data Validation option button in the Go To Special dialog box. Click the Same option button under Data Validation to have Excel go to the next cell that uses the same Data Validation settings as the active cell. Leave the All option button under Data Validation selected to go to the next cell that uses any kind of Data Validation setting.

To get rid of Data Validation settings assigned to a particular cell or cell range, select the cell or range, open the Data Validation dialog box (Alt+AVV), and then click the Clear All button before you click OK.

REMEMBER

Although Data Validation is most often used to restrict new data entries in a spreadsheet, you can also use it to quickly identify values that are outside desired parameters in ranges of existing numeric data entries — see Book 2, Chapter 3 for details.

Saving the Data

One of the most important tasks you ever perform when building your spreadsheet is *saving your work!* Excel offers three different ways to invoke the Save command:

>> Click the Save button on the Quick Access toolbar (the one with the disk icon).

>> Press Ctrl+S or F12.

>> Click File⇨Save.

TIP

To encourage frequent saving on your part after you first save your workbook file on a local drive such as your computer's hard disk, Excel provides you with a Save button on the Quick Access toolbar (the one with the picture of a floppy disk, the very first on the toolbar). You don't even have to take the time and trouble to use the Save command from the File pull-down menu or even press Ctrl+S; you can simply click this button whenever you want to save new work on disk. If you're saving your workbook file in an online location such as a folder on your OneDrive or SharePoint site, Excel 2019 goes one further by activating its Auto-Save feature that automatically saves any further editing changes you make to the workbook without you having to bother with the Save button!

When you click the Save button, press Ctrl+S, or click File⇨Save for the first time, Excel displays the Save As screen in the Backstage view similar to the one shown in Figure 1-16. By default, Excel 2019 selects the Documents folder on your One-Drive as the place to which to save the new workbook.

To save the file locally instead — on your computer's hard drive or a virtual drive on your company's local area network — select the Browse button at the bottom of the Other Locations section. The Save As dialog box opens with the default location for saving workbook files from which you can select the drive and folder where the new workbook should be stored (see Figure 1-17). Use this dialog box to replace the temporary document name (Book1, Book2, and so forth) with a more descriptive filename in the File Name text box; to select a new file format from the Save As Type drop-down list box; and, if necessary, to select a new folder where it's to be stored before you save the workbook.

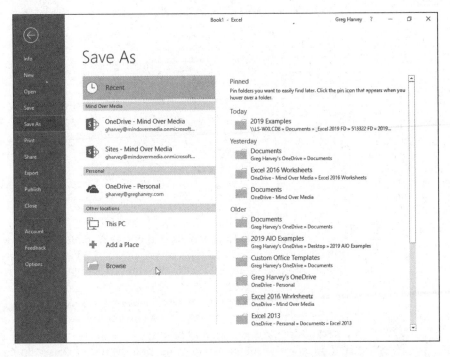

FIGURE 1-16:
Specifying the place to save a new workbook file on the Save As screen.

TECHNICAL STUFF

WHAT'S UP WITH THE OneDrive?

You've undoubtedly heard of the *cloud* (sometimes called the "almighty Cloud"), but your understanding of it may yet be as nebulous as its name. OneDrive (once known as SkyDrive) is the current name that Microsoft's storage space in the cloud that it lends to its users with a Windows account The great thing about saving a workbook file in a folder on your OneDrive is that you then can open it for further editing and printing from any device running Excel 2019 that has Internet access. For example, if you save a workbook file that you create in Excel on your office desktop computer, you can then open it for more editing on your laptop at home or even your Windows tablet or smartphone at the local coffee shop. For more information on OneDrive and to set it up on your computer, open the Excel Save As screen and click the Learn More link under Get OneDrive for Windows and Take Your Files with You Anywhere.

Building Worksheets

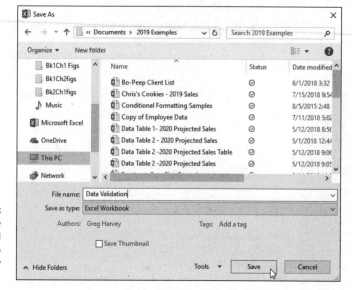

FIGURE 1-17:
Specifying the
folder and
filename prior to
saving the new
workbook file.

When you finish making changes in the Save As dialog box, click the Save button or press Enter to have Excel 2019 save your work. When Excel saves your workbook file, the program saves all the information in every worksheet in your workbook (including the last position of the cell cursor) in the designated folder and drive.

REMEMBER

You don't have to fool with the Save As dialog box ever again after initially saving a workbook unless you want to save a copy of the workbook under a new filename and/or in a new folder. If you want to do either of these things, you must click File ⇨ Save As or press Alt+FA to click the Save As command rather than click the Save button on the Quick Access toolbar or press Ctrl+S. Then, select the folder where you want the new version of the file saved if it's different from the current folder, and you can edit the workbook's filename if you also want to rename the workbook file.

TIP

The Save As dialog box enables you to change the author or add a title and/or tags to the new workbook file by clicking the Authors or Add a Tag link. You can then use any or all of these pieces of information you add to the file when later searching for the workbook. Click the Save Thumbnail check box to have Excel save a preview of the workbook's initial worksheet that can be displayed in the Preview pane of the Open dialog box or when viewing the workbook files with the Large Icons or Extra Large Icons settings. (See Book 2, Chapter 3 for details.)

Saving workbooks in other commonly used file formats

When you click the Save As Type drop-down button in the Save As dialog box, Excel displays a long laundry list of file formats that you can choose from when saving the workbook file. You can use these file format options to instantly convert your worksheet data into another file format for use with applications other than Excel 2019.

TIP

Before saving a new workbook file in a non-Excel file format for use with another type of program (such as Web Page for the Internet, or PDF for the Adobe reader), be sure that you've first saved the spreadsheet data in a regular Excel Workbook file. That way, you continue to have ready access to the data in Excel 2019 for the purposes of further editing, printing, and so forth without having to convert the new file back into a native Excel Workbook file format.

The most commonly used file format options include the following:

» **Excel Workbook:** Saves the workbook in the default Excel 2019 `.xlsx` file format.

» **Excel Macro-Enabled Workbook:** Saves the workbook in the default `.xlsm` file format with all macros (see Book 8, Chapter 1) it contains enabled.

» **Excel Binary Workbook:** Saves the workbook in the binary file format optimized that enables faster loading of really large workbooks with tons of data.

» **Excel 97–2003 Workbook:** Saves the workbook in the `.xls` file format used by earlier versions of Excel 97 through Excel 2003 — note that an alert dialog box appears if Excel finds any features used in the workbook that aren't supported in this file format.

» **XML Data:** Saves the workbook in an XML (Extensible Markup Language) format (using the `.xml` filename extension) often used to exchange lists of data over the Internet.

» **Single File Web Page:** Saves the workbook in an MIME HTML (Multipurpose Internet Mail Extension Hypertext Markup Language) with the `.mhtm` or `.mhtml` file extension. This special HTML format is used by some web browsers (mainly Internet Explorer) to mimic the worksheets in the original workbook through the use of tabbed pages in the resulting web page.

» **Web Page:** Saves the workbook in an HTML (Hypertext Markup Language) used to render all the data on all worksheets in the workbook in a single continuous web page with the `.htm` or `.html` filename extension.

- » **Excel Template:** Saves the workbook in the `.xltx` file format as an Excel template file that you can use to generate new workbooks containing the same layout and content as the template.

- » **Excel Macro-Enabled Template:** Saves the workbook in the `.xltx` template file format with all the macros (see Book 8, Chapter 1) it contains enabled.

- » **PDF:** Saves the workbook in an Adobe PDF (Portable Document File) format with the `.pdf` filename extension that can be opened with the free Adobe Reader program.

- » **XPS Document:** Saves the workbook in an XPS (XML Paper Specification) file with the `.xps` filename extension used by many printers to render the data in a document, including Microsoft Office programs.

- » **OpenDocument Spreadsheet:** Saves the workbook in ODF (OpenDocument Format) with an `.ods` filename extension that's used by other Office suites of programs, particularly Sun Microsystems's StarOffice suite.

REMEMBER

Although less frequently needed, don't forget that the Save As options include a number of text file conversions that you can use when your spreadsheet contains lists of data that you need to make available to programs that can deal with strings of text data. The major difference between the various text file formats is what character they use to separate the data in each worksheet cell. So, the various Text (`.txt`) formats use tabs, the various comma-separated value (or CSV, `.csv`) formats use commas, and the various text (`.txt`) formats use spaces.

Changing the default file location

Whenever you click the This PC button under Locations on the Save As screen in the Backstage view to save a new workbook file locally (as opposed to in the cloud on a SharePoint site or your OneDrive), Excel 2019 automatically selects the folder listed in the Default File Location text box on the Save tab of the Excel Options dialog box (File➪Options➪Save or Alt+FTS).

TIP

If you don't have a OneDrive or don't ever save workbook files in the cloud, you can prevent Excel 2019 from asking you to sign into your OneDrive location when saving a new workbook by clicking the Show Additional Places for Saving, Even If Sign-In May Be Required check box on the Save tab of the Excel Options dialog box to deselect it. Also, if you prefer selecting the drive and folder into which to save your workbook files directly in the Save As dialog box, you can prevent Excel 2019 from initially displaying the Save As screen by clicking the Don't Show the Backstage When Opening or Saving Files check box to select it on this same tab of the Excel Options dialog box.

The very generic Documents folder may not be the place on your hard drive where you want all the new workbooks you create automatically saved. To change the default file location to another folder on your computer, follow these steps:

1. **Click File⇨Options⇨Save or press Alt+FTS to open the Save tab of the Excel Options dialog box.**

   The Default File Location text box displays the directory path to the current default folder.

2. **Click the Default File Location text box to select the current directory path.**

   When you click the Default File Location text box, Excel selects the entire directory path so that if you begin typing, the characters you type replace the entire path. To edit part of the path (such as the Documents folder name after your username), click the mouse or Touch pointer at that place in the path to set the Insertion point.

3. **Edit the existing path or replace it with the path to another existing folder in which you want all future workbooks to automatically be saved.**

4. **Click OK to close the Excel Options dialog box.**

Saving a new workbook in the old file format

Excel 2019 automatically saves each new workbook file in a Microsoft version of the XML-based file format, which carries the filename extension .xlsx. The problem with this XML file format is that it's not one that versions of Excel prior to Excel 2007 can open. This means that if everybody who needs to work with the workbook you've just created hasn't yet upgraded to Excel 2007 or 2010, you need to save the new workbook in the earlier file format used in versions 97 through 2003 with the old .xls filename extension.

To save a new workbook in the old binary Excel file format for back compatibility, be sure to click the Save as Type drop-down button and then select Excel 97–2003 Workbook from the drop-down list.

WARNING

Excel automatically displays the Excel Compatibility Checker dialog box whenever you try to save a workbook file containing Excel 2019 features that aren't supported in earlier versions of the program from Excel 97–2003. This dialog box lists each incompatible feature in the workbook and gives you details on what will happen to the feature if you go ahead and save the workbook file in the older file format. To ignore these warnings and go ahead and save your workbook in the 97–2003 binary format, click the Continue button in the Excel Compatibility Checker dialog box.

TIP

If you still want to have access to all the features in the Excel 2019 workbook but you still need to create a backwardly compatible version of the workbook file (even if it has less fidelity), first save the workbook in the XML file format with the .xlsx file extension. Then, save a copy in old 97-2003 binary file format with the .xls file extension by opening the Save As dialog box (File⇨Save As or Alt+FA) and then selecting Excel 97-2003 from the Save as Type drop-down list before clicking the Save button.

REMEMBER

Keep in mind that filename extensions such as .xlsx and .xls do not appear as part of the filename (even though they are appended) in the File Name text box in the Save As dialog box unless you click the File Name Extensions check box found on the View tab⇨ in the Windows 10 File Explorer window to select it.

Document Recovery to the Rescue

Excel 2019 offers a document recovery feature that can help you in the event of a computer crash because of a power failure or some sort of operating system freeze or shutdown. The AutoRecover feature saves your workbooks at regular intervals. In the event of a computer crash, Excel displays a Document Recovery task pane the next time you start Excel after rebooting the computer.

TIP

When you first start using Excel 2019, the AutoRecover feature is set to automatically save changes to your workbook (provided that the file has already been saved) every ten minutes. You can shorten or lengthen this interval as you see fit. Click File⇨Options⇨Save or press Alt+FTS to open the Excel Options dialog box with the Save tab selected. Use the spinner buttons or enter a new automatic save interval into the Save AutoRecover Information Every 10 Minutes text box before clicking OK.

The Document Recovery Task pane shows the available versions of the workbook files that were open at the time of the computer crash. It identifies the original version of the workbook file and when it was saved, along with the recovered version of the file and when it was saved. To open the recovered version of a workbook (to see how much of the work it contains that was unsaved at the time of the crash), position the mouse pointer over the AutoRecover version. Then click its drop-down menu button and click Open on its pop-up menu. After you open the recovered version, you can (if you choose) then save its changes by clicking the Save button on the Quick Access toolbar or by clicking File⇨Save.

You then have these choices:

>> To save the recovered version of a workbook without bothering to first open it, place your mouse over the recovered version, click its drop-down button, and click the Save As option on the pop-up menu.

>> To permanently abandon the recovered version (leaving you with *only* the data in the original version), click the Close button at the bottom of the Document Recovery Task pane. When you click the Close button, an alert dialog box appears, giving you the chance to retain the recovered versions of the file for later viewing.

>> To retain the files for later viewing, select the Yes (I Want to View These Files Later) radio button before clicking OK.

>> To retain only the original versions of the files shown in the Task pane, select the No (Remove These Files. I Have Saved the Files I Need) radio button instead.

WARNING

The AutoRecover feature only works on Excel workbooks that have been saved at least one time (as explained in the earlier section "Saving the Data"). In other words, if you build a new workbook and don't bother to save and rename it prior to experiencing a computer crash, the AutoRecover feature will not bring back any part of it. For this reason, it's really important that you get into the habit of saving new workbooks with the Save button on the Quick Access toolbar very shortly after beginning to work on a worksheet. Or you can use the trusty keyboard shortcut Ctrl+S.

IN THIS CHAPTER

» Selecting cell ranges and adjusting column widths and row heights

» Formatting cell ranges as tables

» Assigning number formats

» Making alignment, font, border, and pattern changes

» Using the Format Painter to quickly copy formatting

» Formatting cell ranges with Cell Styles

» Applying conditional formatting

Chapter **2**

Formatting Worksheets

ormatting — the subject of this chapter — is the process by which you determine the final appearance of the worksheet and the data that it contains. Excel's formatting features give you a great deal of control over the way the data appears in your worksheet.

For all types of cell entries, you can assign a new font, font size, font style (such as bold, italics, underlining, or strikethrough), or color. You can also change the alignment of entries in the cells in a variety of ways, including the horizontal alignment, the vertical alignment, or the orientation; you can also wrap text entries in the cell or center them across the selection. For numerical values, dates, and times, you can assign one of the many built-in number formats or apply a custom format that you design. For the cells that hold your entries, you can apply different kinds of borders, patterns, and colors. And to the worksheet grid itself, you can assign the most suitable column widths and row heights so that the data in the formatted worksheet is displayed at its best.

A RANGE BY ANY OTHER NAME

TECHNICAL STUFF

Cell ranges are always noted in formulas by the first and last cell that you select, separated by a colon (:); therefore, if you select cell A1 as the first cell and cell H10 as the last cell and then use the range in a formula, the cell range appears as A1:H10. This same block of cells can just as well be noted as H10:A1 if you selected cell H10 before cell A1. Likewise, the same range can be equally noted as H1:A10 or A10:H1, depending upon which corner cell you select first and which opposite corner you select last. Keep in mind that despite the various range notations that you can use (A1:H10, H10:A1, H1:A10, and A10:H1), you are working with the same block of cells, the main difference being that each has a different active cell whose address appears in the Name box on the Formula bar (A1, H10, H1, and A10, respectively).

With the FORMATTING and TABLES options on the Quick Analysis tool and the readily available mini-bar with its commonly used formatting buttons, formatting selected data tables in an Excel worksheet has never been easier or quicker. If those features are not enough, you still have access to the Table Styles and Cell Styles galleries and all the command buttons in the Font, Alignment, and Number groups on the Home tab of the Ribbon to get your spreadsheet data looking just right.

This is because Excel's Live Preview feature enables you to see how a new font, font size, or table or cell style would look on your selected data before you actually apply it (saving you tons of time otherwise wasted applying format after format until you finally select the right one). And thanks to having buttons for all the most commonly used formatting commands right up front on the Home tab, you can now readily fine-tune the formatting of a cell in a worksheet by making almost all needed changes right from the Ribbon.

Making Cell Selections

Although you have to select the cells of the worksheet that you want to work with before you can accomplish many tasks used in building and editing a typical spreadsheet, perhaps no task requires cell selection like that of formatting. With the exception of the special Format as Table feature (which automatically selects the table to which its multiple formats are applied), selecting the cells whose appearance you want to enhance or modify is always your first step in their formatting.

In Excel, you can select a single cell, a block of cells (known as a *cell range*), or various discontinuous cell ranges (also known as a *nonadjacent selection*). Figure 2-1 shows a nonadjacent selection that consists of several different cell ranges (the smallest range is the single cell I9).

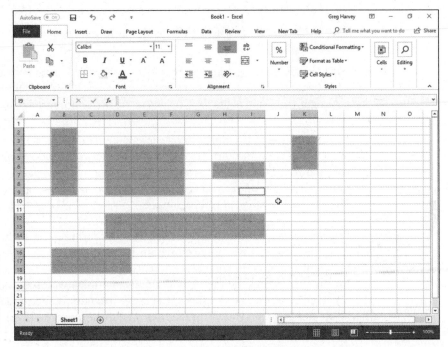

FIGURE 2-1:
Worksheet with a nonadjacent cell selection made up of several different sized ranges.

REMEMBER

Note that a simple cell selection consisting of a single cell range is denoted in the worksheet both by highlighting the selected cells in a light blue color as well as by extending the border of the cell cursor so that it encompasses all the highlighted cells. In a nonadjacent cell selection, however, all selected cells are highlighted but only the active cell (the one whose address is displayed in the Name Box on the Formula bar) contains the cell cursor (whose borders are quite thin when compared to the regular cell cursor).

Selecting cells with the mouse

Excel offers several methods for selecting cells with the mouse. With each method, you start by selecting one of the cells that occupies the corner of the range that you want to select. The first corner cell that you click becomes the *active cell* (indicated by its cell reference in the Formula bar), and the cell range that you then select becomes anchored on this cell.

Formatting Worksheets

After you select the active cell in the range, drag the pointer to extend the selection until you have highlighted all the cells that you want to include. Here are some tips:

>> To extend a range in a block that spans several columns, drag left or right from the active cell.

>> To extend a range in a block that spans several rows, drag up or down from the active cell.

>> To extend a range in a block that spans several columns and rows, drag diagonally from the active cell in the most logical directions (up and to the right, down and to the right, up and to the left, or down and to the left).

If you ever extend the range too far in one direction, you can always reduce it by dragging in the other direction. If you've already released the mouse button and you find that the range is incorrect, click the active cell again. (Clicking any cell in the worksheet deselects a selected range and activates the cell that you click.) Then select the range of cells again.

TIP

You can always tell which cell is the active cell forming the anchor point of a cell range because it is the only cell within the range that you've selected that isn't highlighted and is the only cell reference listed in the Name box on the Formula bar. As you extend the range by dragging the thick white-cross mouse pointer, Excel indicates the current size of the range in columns and rows in the Name box (as in 5R x 2C when you've highlighted a range of five rows long and two columns wide). However, as soon as you release the mouse button, Excel replaces this row and column notation with the address of the active cell.

You can also use the following shortcuts when selecting cells with the mouse:

>> To select a single-cell range, click the thick white-cross mouse pointer somewhere inside the cell.

>> To select all cells in an entire column, position the mouse pointer on the column letter in the column header and then click the mouse button. To select several adjacent columns, drag through their column letters in the column header.

>> To select all cells in an entire row, position the mouse pointer on the row number in the row header and then click the mouse button. To select several adjacent rows, drag through the row numbers in the row header.

>> To select all the cells in the worksheet, click the box in the upper-left corner of the worksheet at the intersection of row and column headers with the triangle in the lower-right corner that makes it look like the corner of a dog-eared or folded down book page. (You can also do this from the keyboard by pressing Ctrl+A.)

- » To select a cell range composed of partial columns and rows without dragging, click the cell where you want to anchor the range, hold down the Shift key, and then click the last cell in the range and release the Shift key. (Excel selects all the cells in between the first and the last cell that you click.) If the range that you want to mark is a block that spans several columns and rows, the last cell is the one diagonally opposite the active cell. When using this Shift+click technique to mark a range that extends beyond the screen, use the scroll bars to display the last cell in the range. (Just make sure that you don't release the Shift key until after you've clicked this last cell.)

- » To select a nonadjacent selection comprised of several discontinuous cell ranges, drag through the first cell range and then hold down the Ctrl key as you drag through the other ranges. After you have marked all the cell ranges to be included in the nonadjacent selection, you can release the Ctrl key.

TIP

The Ctrl key can work with the mouse like an *add* or *subtract* key in Excel 2019. As an add key, you use it to include non-neighboring objects in the current worksheet. See the section "Nonadjacent cell selections with the keyboard," later in this chapter. By using the Ctrl key, you can add to the selection of cells in a worksheet or to the document names in a list without having to deselect those already selected. To use the Ctrl key to deselect a range of cells within the current cell selection, hold down the Ctrl and drag through the range that you want to deselect (subtract from the selected range) before releasing the mouse button and Ctrl key.

Selecting cells by touch

TIP

If you're running Excel 2019 on a touchscreen device such as a Windows tablet or smartphone without the benefit of a mouse or physical keyboard, you can use your finger or stylus to make your cell selections:

- » To use your finger, tap the first cell in the selection (the equivalent of clicking with a mouse). Selection handles (with the circle icons) appear in the upper-left and lower-right corner of the selected cell. Simply drag or swipe one of the selection handles through the rest of the adjacent cells to extend the cell selection and select the entire range.

- » To use your finger or tablet's stylus, tap the first cell and then drag the white-cross pointer to the last cell in the selection.

Selecting cells with the keyboard

Excel also makes it easy for you to select cell ranges with a physical or Touch keyboard by using a technique known as *extending a selection*. To use this technique, you move the cell cursor to the active cell of the range; then press F8 to turn on

Extend Selection mode (indicated by Extend Selection on the Status bar) and use the direction keys to move the pointer to the last cell in the range. Excel selects all the cells that the cell cursor moves through until you turn off Extend Selection mode (by pressing F8 again).

You can use the mouse as well as the keyboard to extend a selection when Excel is in Extend Selection mode. All you do is click the active cell, press F8, and then click the last cell to mark the range.

You can also select a cell range with the keyboard without turning on Extend Selection mode. Here, you use a variation of the Shift+click method by moving the cell pointer to the active cell in the range, holding down the Shift key, and then using the direction keys to extend the range. After you've highlighted all the cells that you want to include, release the Shift key.

To mark a nonadjacent selection of cells with the keyboard, you need to combine the use of Extend Selection mode with that of Add to Selection mode. To turn on Add to Selection mode (indicated by Add to Selection on the status bar), you press Shift+F8. To mark a nonadjacent selection by using Extend Selection and Add to Selection modes, follow these steps:

1. Move the cell cursor to the first cell of the first range you want to select.

2. Press F8 to turn on Extend Selection mode.

3. Use the arrow keys to extend the cell range until you've highlighted all its cells.

4. Press Shift+F8 to turn off Extend Selection mode and turn on Add to Selection mode instead.

5. Move the cell cursor to the first cell of the next cell range you want to add to the selection.

6. Press F8 to turn off Add to Selection mode and turn Extend Selection mode back on.

7. Use the arrow keys to extend the range until all cells are highlighted.

8. Repeat Steps 4 through 7 until you've selected all the ranges that you want included in the nonadjacent selection.

9. Press F8 to turn off Extend Selection mode.

You AutoSelect that range!

Excel's AutoSelect feature provides a particularly efficient way to select all or part of the cells in a large table of data. AutoSelect automatically extends a selection in a single direction from the active cell to the first nonblank cell that Excel encounters in that direction.

You can use the AutoSelect feature with the mouse and a physical keyboard. The general steps for using AutoSelect to select a table of data with the mouse are as follows:

1. **Click the first cell to which you want to anchor the range that you are about to select.**

In a typical data table, this cell may be the blank cell at the intersection of the row of column headings and the column of row headings.

2. **Position the mouse pointer on the edge of the cell in the direction you want to extend the range.**

To extend the range up to the first blank cell to the right, position the mouse or Touch pointer on the right edge of the cell. To extend the range left to the first blank cell, position the pointer on the left edge of the cell. To extend the range down to the first blank cell, position the pointer on the bottom edge of the cell. And to extend the range up to the first blank cell, position the pointer on the top edge of the cell.

3. **When the pointer changes shape from a cross to an arrowhead, hold down the Shift key and then double-click the mouse.**

As soon as you double-click the mouse or Touch pointer, Excel extends the selection to the first occupied cell that is adjacent to a blank cell in the direction of the edge that you double-clicked.

To get an idea of how AutoSelect works, consider how you use it to select all the data in the table (cell range A3:J8) shown in Figures 2-2 and 2-3. With the cell cursor in cell A3 at the intersection of the row with the Date column headings and the column with the Part row headings, you can use the AutoSelect feature to select all the cells in the table in two operations:

» In the first operation, hold down the Shift key and then double-click the bottom edge of cell A2 to highlight the cells down to A6, selecting the range A2:A6. (See Figure 2-2.)

» In the second operation, hold down the Shift key and then double-click the right edge of cell range A2:A6 to extend the selection to the last column in the table (selecting the entire table with the cell range A2:J6, as shown in Figure 2-3).

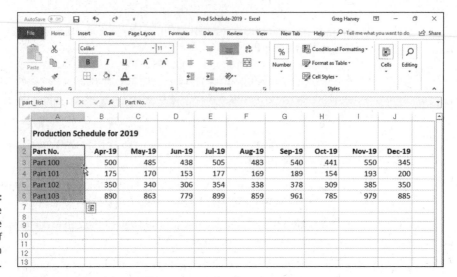

FIGURE 2-2:
Selecting the cells in the first column of the table with AutoSelect.

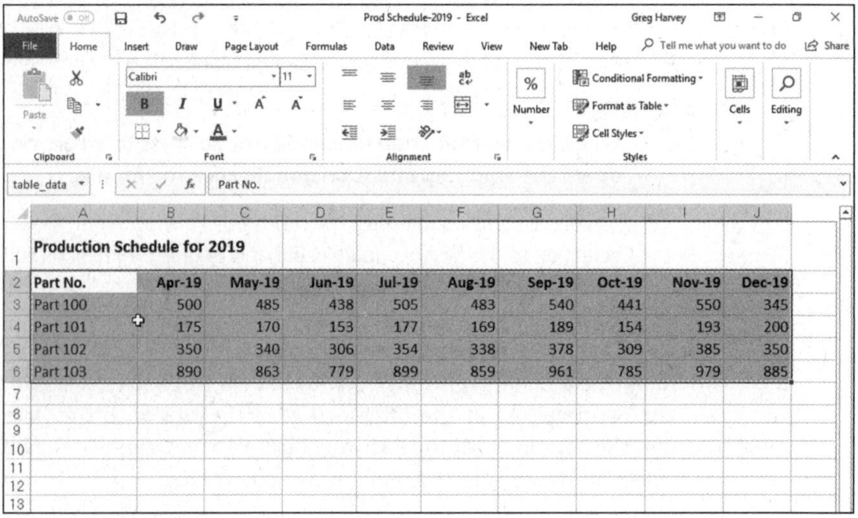

FIGURE 2-3:
Selecting all the remaining columns of the table with AutoSelect.

If you select the cells in the first row of the table (range A2:J2) in the first operation, you can then extend this range down the remaining rows of the table by double-clicking the bottom edge of one of the selected cells. (It doesn't matter which one.)

To use the AutoSelect feature with the keyboard, press the End key and one of the four arrow keys as you hold down the Shift key. When you hold down Shift and press End and an arrow key, Excel extends the selection in the direction of the arrow key to the first cell containing a value that is bordered by a blank cell.

In terms of selecting the table of data shown in Figures 2-2 and 2-3, this means that you would have to complete four separate operations to select all of its cells:

1. **With A2 as the active cell, hold down Shift and press End+↓ to select the range A2:A6.**

   Excel stops at A6 because this is the last occupied cell in that column. At this point, the cell range A2:A6 is selected.

2. **Hold down Shift and then press End+→.**

   Excel extends the range all the way to column J (because the cells in column J contain entries bordered by blank cells). Now all the cells in the table (the cell range A2:J6) are selected.

Selecting cells with Go To

Although you usually use the Go To feature to move the cell cursor to a new cell in the worksheet, you can also use this feature to select a range of cells. When you click the Go To option from the Find & Select button's drop-down menu on the Home tab of the Ribbon (or press Ctrl+G or F5), Excel displays a Go To dialog box similar to the one shown in Figure 2-4. To move the cell cursor to a particular cell, enter the cell address in the Reference text box and click OK. (Excel automatically lists the addresses of the last four cells or cell ranges that you specified in the Go To list box.)

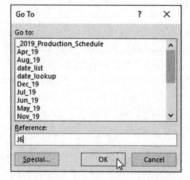

FIGURE 2-4:
Selecting a cell range with the Go To dialog box.

Instead of just moving to a new section of the worksheet with the Go To feature, you can select a range of cells by taking these steps:

1. **Select the first cell of the range.**

   This becomes the active cell to which the cell range is anchored.

2. **On the Ribbon, click the Find & Select command button in the Editing group on the Home tab and then click Go To from its drop-down menu or press Alt+HFDG, Ctrl+G or F5.**

   The Go To dialog box opens.

3. **Type the cell address of the last cell in the range in the Reference text box.**

   If this address is already listed in the Go To list box, you can enter this address in the text box by clicking it in the list box.

4. **Hold down the Shift key as you click OK or press Enter to close the Go To dialog box.**

   By holding down Shift as you click OK or press Enter, you select the range between the active cell and the cell whose address you specified in the Reference text box.

TIP

Instead of selecting the anchor cell and then specifying the last cell of a range in the Reference text box of the Go To dialog box, you can also select a range simply by typing the address of the cell range in the Reference text box. Remember that when you type a range address, you enter the cell reference of the first (active) cell and the last cell in the range separated by a colon. For example, to select the cell range that extends from cell B2 to G10 in the worksheet, you would type the range address **B2:G10** in the Reference text box before clicking OK or pressing Enter.

Name that range!

One of the easiest ways to select a range of data is to assign a name to it and then click that name on the pop-up menu attached to the Name box on the Formula bar or in the Go To list box in the Go To dialog box. Of course, you reserve this technique for cell ranges that you work with on a somewhat regular basis; for example, ranges with data that you print regularly, consult often, or have to refer to in formula calculations. It's probably not worth your while to name a range of data that doesn't carry any special importance in the spreadsheet.

To name a cell range, follow three simple steps:

1. **Select all the cells in the range that you intend to name.**

   You can use any of the cell selection techniques that you prefer. When selecting the cells for the named range, be sure to include all the cells that you want selected each time you select its range name.

2. **Click the Name box on the Formula bar.**

   Excel automatically highlights the address of the active cell in the selected range.

3. **Type the range name in the Name box and then press Enter.**

As soon as you start typing, Excel replaces the address of the active cell with the range name that you're assigning. As soon as you press the Enter key, the name appears in the Name box instead of the cell address of the active cell in the range.

When naming a cell range, however, you *must* observe the following naming conventions:

» Begin the range name with a letter of the alphabet rather than a number or punctuation mark.

» Don't use spaces in the range name; instead, use an underscore between words in a range name (as in Qtr_1).

» Make sure that the range name doesn't duplicate any cell reference in the worksheet by using either the standard A1 or R1C1 notation system.

» Make sure that the range name is unique in the worksheet.

After you've assigned a name to a cell range, you can select all its cells simply by clicking the name on the pop-up menu attached to the Name box on the Formula bar. The beauty of this method is that you can use it from anywhere in the same sheet or a different worksheet in the workbook because as soon as you click its name on the Name box pop-up menu, Excel takes you directly to the range, while at the same time automatically selecting all its cells.

REMEMBER

Range names are also very useful when building formulas in your spreadsheet. For more on creating and using range names, see Book 3, Chapter 1.

TIP

If you're using a touchscreen device without access to a mouse or physical keyboard, I can't recommend highly enough naming cell ranges that you regularly select for editing or printing in Excel 2019. Tapping the range name on the Name box's drop-down menu to select a large and distant cell range in a worksheet on the normally very small and cramped screen of a Windows tablet is so far superior to futzing with the cell's selection handles to select the range that it's just not funny!

Adjusting Columns and Rows

Along with knowing how to select cells for formatting, you really also have to know how to adjust the width of your columns and the heights of your rows. Why? Because often in the course of assigning different formatting to certain cell ranges (such as new font and font size in boldface type), you may find that data entries that previously fit within the original widths of their column no longer do and that the rows that they occupy seem to have changed height all on their own.

In a blank worksheet, all the columns and rows are the same standard width and height. The actual number of characters or pixels depends upon the aspect ratio of the device upon which you're running Excel 2019. On most computer monitors, all Excel 2019 worksheet columns start out 8.47 characters wide (or 136 pixels at a 3240 x 2160 display resolution), and all rows start out 14.30 points high (or 38 pixels). On a smaller touchscreen such as the Microsoft Surface 4 tablet, Excel worksheet columns start out at 8.09 characters wide (or 96 pixels, given their distinctive aspect ratio) with rows at 13.50 characters or 27 pixels high.

As you build your spreadsheet, you end up with all sorts of data entries that can't fit within these default settings. This is especially true as you start adding formatting to their cells to enhance and clarify their contents.

Most of the time, you don't need to be concerned with the heights of the rows in your worksheet because Excel automatically adjusts them up or down to accommodate the largest font size used in a cell in the row and the number of text lines (in some cells, you may wrap their text on several lines). Instead, you'll spend a lot more time adjusting the column widths to suit the entries for the formatting that you assign to them.

REMEMBER

Remember what happens when you put a text entry in a cell whose current width isn't long enough to accommodate all its characters. If the cells in columns to the right are empty, Excel lets the display of the extra characters spill over into the empty cells. If these cells are already occupied, however, Excel cuts off the display of the extra characters until you widen the column sufficiently. Likewise, remember that if you add formatting to a number so that its value and formatting can't both be displayed in the cell, those nasty overflow indicators appear in the cell as a string of pound signs (#####) until you widen the column adequately.

You AutoFit the column to its contents

The easiest way to adjust the width of a column to suit its longest entry is to use the AutoFit feature. AutoFit determines the best fit for the column or columns selected at that time, given their longest entries.

>> **To use AutoFit on a single column:** Position the mouse pointer on the right edge of that column in the column header and then, when the pointer changes to a double-headed arrow, double-click the mouse or double-tap your finger or stylus.

>> **To use AutoFit on multiple columns at one time:** Select the columns by dragging through them in the column header or by Ctrl+clicking the column letters and then double-clicking the right edge of one of the selected columns when the pointer changes to a double-headed arrow.

These AutoFit techniques work well for adjusting all columns except for those that contain really long headings (such as the spreadsheet title that often spills over several blank columns in row 1), in which case AutoFit makes the columns far too wide for the bulk of the cell entries.

For those situations, use the AutoFit Selection command, which adjusts the column width to suit only the entries in the cells of the column that you have selected. This way, you can select all the cells except for any really long ones in the column that purposely spill over to empty cells on the right, and then have Excel adjust the width to suit. After you've selected the cells in the column that you want the new width to fit, click the Format button in the Cells group on the Home tab and then click AutoFit Selection from the drop-down menu.

Adjusting columns the old fashioned way

AutoFit is nothing if not quick and easy. If you need more precision in adjusting your column widths, you have to do this manually either by dragging its border with the mouse or by entering new values in the Column Width dialog box.

>> **To manually adjust a column width with the mouse:** Drag the right edge of that column onto the Column header to the left (to narrow) or to the right (to widen) as required. As you drag the column border, a ScreenTip appears above the mouse pointer indicating the current width in both characters and pixels. When you have the column adjusted to the desired width, release the mouse button to set it.

>> **To manually adjust a column width by touch:** Tap the right edge of the column header with your finger or stylus to select the column and make the black, double-header pointer appear. Then swipe the pointer left or right as needed. As you swipe, the Name box on the Formula bar indicates the current width in characters and pixels. When you have the column adjusted to the desired width, remove your finger or stylus from the touchscreen.

TIP

To make this operation easier, remember that you can instantly zoom in on the column border by stretching your forefinger and thumb on the touchscreen — doing this makes the column letter area larger, making it a lot easier to tap and swipe the border left and right with your finger or stylus.

>> **To adjust a column width in the Column Width dialog box:** Position the cell pointer in any one of the cells in the column that you want to adjust, click the Format button in the Cells group on the Home tab of the Ribbon, and then click Column Width on the drop-down menu to open the Column Width dialog box. Here, you enter the new width (in the number of characters between 0 and 255) in the Column Width text box before clicking OK.

TIP

You can apply a new column width that you set in the Column Width dialog box to more than a single column by selecting the columns (either by dragging through their letters on the Column header or holding down Ctrl as you click them) before you open the Column Width dialog box.

Setting a new standard width

You can use the Default Standard Width command to set all the columns in a worksheet to a new uniform width (other than the default 8.43 or 8.09 characters). To do so, simply click the Format button in the Cells group on the Home tab of the Ribbon and then click Default Width from the drop-down menu (Alt+HOD). Doing this opens the Standard Width dialog box where you can replace the default value in the Standard Column Width text box with your new width (in characters) and then click OK or press Enter.

REMEMBER

Note that when you set a new standard width for the columns of your worksheet, this new width doesn't affect any columns whose width you've previously adjusted either with AutoFit or in the Column Width dialog box.

Hiding out a column or two

You can use the Hide command to temporarily remove columns of data from the worksheet display. When you hide a column, you're essentially setting the column width to 0 (and thus making it so narrow that, for all intents and purposes, the sucker's gone). Hiding columns enables you to remove the display of sensitive or supporting data that needs to be in the spreadsheet but may not be appropriate in printouts that you distribute (keeping in mind that only columns and rows that are displayed in the worksheet get printed).

To hide a column, put the cell pointer in a cell in that column, click the Format button in the Cells group on the Home tab and then click Hide & Unhide ➪ Hide Columns from the drop-down menu (or you can just press Alt+HOUC).

To hide more than one column at a time, select the columns either by dragging through their letters on the Column header or by holding down Ctrl as you click them before you choose this command sequence.

Excel lets you know that certain columns are missing from the worksheet by removing their column letters from the Column header so that if, for example, you hide columns D and E in the worksheet, column C is followed by column F on the Column header.

To restore hidden columns to view, select the visible columns on either side of the hidden one(s) — indicated by the missing letter(s) on the column headings — and then click the Format button in the Cells group on the Home tab. Then click Hide & Unhide⇨Unhide Columns from the drop-down menu (or you can just press Alt+HOUL).

Because Excel also automatically selects all the redisplayed columns, you need to deselect the selected columns before you select any more formatting or editing commands that will affect all their cells. You can do this by clicking a single cell anywhere in the worksheet or by dragging through a particular cell range that you want to work with.

REMEMBER

Keep in mind that when you hide a column, the data in the cells in all its rows (1 through 1,048,576) are hidden (not just the ones you can see on your computer screen). This means that if you have some data in rows of a column that need printing and some in other rows of that same column that need concealing, you can't use the Hide command to remove their display until you've moved the cells with the data to be printed into a different column. (See Book 2, Chapter 5 for details.)

Rambling rows

The controls for adjusting the height of the rows in your worksheet parallel those that you use to adjust its columns. The big difference is that Excel always applies AutoFit to the height of each row so that even though you find an AutoFit Row Height option under Cell size on the Format button's drop-down menu, you won't find much use for it. (Personally, I've never had any reason to use it.)

Instead, you'll probably end up manually adjusting the heights of rows with the mouse or by entering new height values in the Row Height dialog box (opened by choosing Row Height from the Format button's drop-down menu on the Home tab) and occasionally hiding rows with sensitive or potentially confusing data. Follow these instructions for each type of action:

>> **To adjust the height of a row with the mouse:** Position the mouse on the lower edge of the row's border in the Row header and then drag up or down when the mouse pointer changes to a double-headed, vertical arrow. As you drag, a ScreenTip appears to the side of the pointer, keeping you informed

of the height in characters and also in pixels. (Remember that 14.3 points or 38 pixels is the default height of all rows in a new worksheet at a 3240 x 2160 display resolution.)

» **To manually adjust the height of a row by touch:** Tap the lower edge of the row border with your finger or stylus to select the row and make the black, double-header pointer appear. Then swipe the pointer up or down as needed. As you swipe, the Name box on the Formula bar indicates the current row height in characters and pixels. When you have the row adjusted to the desired height, remove your finger or stylus from the touchscreen.

TIP

To make this operation easier, remember that you can instantly zoom in on the row border by stretching your forefinger and thumb on the touchscreen — doing this makes the row number area larger, making it a lot easier to tap and swipe the border up and down with your finger or stylus.

» **To change the height of a row in the Row Height dialog box:** Click Row Height from the Format button's drop-down menu in the Cells group of the Ribbon's Home tab and then enter the value for the new row height in the Row Height text box before you click OK or press Enter.

» **To hide a row:** Position the cell cursor in any one of the cells in that row and then click the Format button in the Cells group on the Home tab before you click Hide & Unhide ⇨ Hide Rows from the drop-down menu (or press Alt+HOUR). To then restore the rows that you currently have hidden in the worksheet, click the Format button and then click Hide & Unhide ⇨ Unhide Rows from the drop-down menu (or just press Alt+HOUO instead).

REMEMBER

As with adjusting columns, you can change the height of more than one row and hide multiple rows at the same time by selecting the rows before you drag one of their lower borders, open the Row Height dialog box, or click Format ⇨ Hide & Unhide ⇨ Hide Rows on the Home tab, or press Alt+HOUR.

Formatting Tables from the Ribbon

Excel 2019's Format as Table feature enables you to both define an entire range of data as a table and format all its data all in one operation. After you define a cell range as a table, you can completely modify its formatting simply by clicking a new style thumbnail in the Table Styles gallery. Excel also automatically extends this table definition — and consequently its table formatting — to all the new rows you insert within the table and add at the bottom as well as any new columns you insert within the table or add to either the table's left or right end.

The Format as Table feature is so automatic that, to use it, you only need to position the cell pointer somewhere within the table of data prior to clicking the Format as Table command button on the Ribbon's Home tab. Clicking the Format as Table command button opens its rather extensive Table Styles gallery with the formatting thumbnails divided into three sections — Light, Medium, and Dark — each of which describes the intensity of the colors used by its various formats. (See Figure 2-5.)

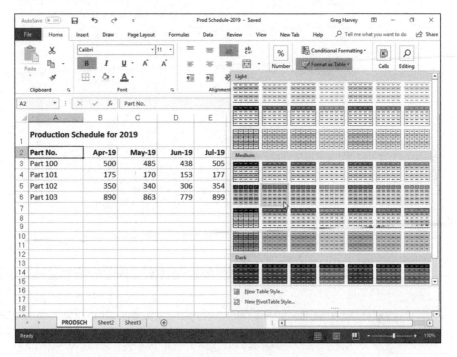

FIGURE 2-5:
Selecting a format
for the new data
table in the Table
Styles gallery.

As soon as you click one of the table formatting thumbnails in this Table Styles gallery, Excel makes its best guess as to the cell range of the data table to apply it to (indicated by the marquee around its perimeter), and the Format As Table dialog box similar to the one shown in Figure 2-6 appears.

This dialog box contains a Where Is the Data for Your Table? text box that shows the address of the cell range currently selected by the marquee and a My Table Has Headers check box (selected by default).

If Excel does not correctly guess the range of the data table you want to format, drag through the cell range to adjust the marquee and the range address in the Where Is the Data for Your Table? text box. If your data table doesn't use column

Formatting Worksheets

headers, click the My Table Has Headers check box to deselect it before you click the OK button — Excel will then add its own column headings (Column1, Column2, Column3, and so forth) as the top row of the new table.

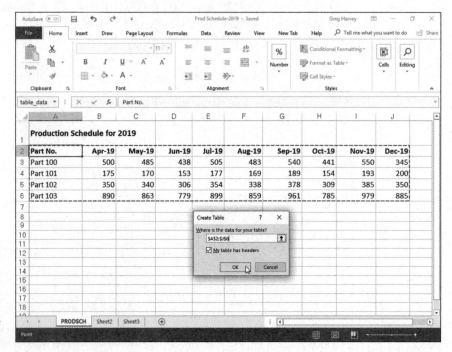

FIGURE 2-6:
Indicating the range of the table in the Format As Table dialog box after selecting the style of table format.

Keep in mind that the table formats in the Table Styles gallery are not available if you select multiple nonadjacent cells before you click the Format as Table command button on the Home tab. You can convert only one range of cell data into a table at a time.

After you click the OK button in the Format As Table dialog box, Excel applies the format of the thumbnail you clicked in the gallery to the data table, and the command buttons on the Design tab of the Table Tools contextual tab appear on the Ribbon. (See Figure 2-7.)

REMEMBER

As you can see in Figure 2-7, when Excel defines a range as a table, it automatically adds AutoFilter drop-down buttons to each of the column headings (the little buttons with a triangle pointing downward in the lower-right corner of the cells with the column labels). To hide these AutoFilter buttons, click the Filter button on the Data tab or press Alt+AT. (You can always redisplay them by clicking the Filter button on the Data tab or by pressing Alt+AT a second time.)

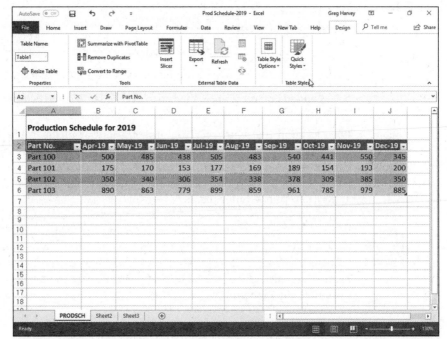

FIGURE 2-7:
After you select an initial table format, the Design tab under Table Tools appears.

The Design contextual tab enables you to use the Live Preview feature to see how your table data would appear in other table styles. Simply click the Quick Styles button and then highlight any of the format thumbnails in the Table Style group with the mouse or Touch pointer to see the data in your table appear in that table format, using the vertical scroll bar to scroll the styles in the Dark section into view in the gallery.

In addition to enabling you to select a new format from the Table gallery in the Table Styles group, the Design tab contains a Table Style Options group you can use to further customize the look of the selected format. The Table Style Options group contains the following check boxes:

» **Header Row:** Add Filter buttons to each of the column headings in the first row of the table.

» **Total Row:** Add a Total row to the bottom of the table that displays the sum of the last column of the table (assuming that it contains values). To apply a Statistical function other than Sum to the values in a particular column of the new Total row, click the cell in that column's Total row. Doing this displays a drop-down list — None, Average, Count, Count Numbers, Max, Min, Sum, StdDev (Standard Deviation), or Var (Variation) — on which you click the new function to use.

- **»** **Banded Rows:** Apply shading to every other row in the table.

- **»** **First Column:** Display the row headings in the first row of the table in bold.

- **»** **Last Column:** Display the row headings in the last row of the table in bold.

- **»** **Banded Columns:** Apply shading to every other column in the table.

REMEMBER

Keep in mind that whenever you assign a format in the Table Styles gallery to one of the data tables in your workbook, Excel automatically assigns that table a generic range name (Table1, Table2, and so on). You can use the Table Name text box in the Properties group on the Design tab to rename the data table by giving it a more descriptive range name.

TIP

When you finish selecting and/or customizing the formatting of your data table, click a cell outside of the table to remove the Design contextual tab from the Ribbon. If you later decide that you want to further experiment with the table's formatting, click any of the table's cells to redisplay the Design contextual tab at the end of the Ribbon.

Formatting Tables with the Quick Analysis Tool

You can use Excel's handy Quick Analysis tool to quickly format your data as a new table. Simply select all the cells in the table, including the cells in the first row with the column headings. As soon as you do, the Quick Analysis tool appears in the lower-right corner of the cell selection (the outlined button with the lightning bolt striking the selected data icon). When you click this tool, the Quick Analysis options palette appears with five tabs (Formatting, Charts, Totals, Tables, and Sparklines).

Click the Tables tab in the Quick Analysis tool's option palette to display its Table and Pivot Table buttons. When you highlight the Table button on the Tables tab, Excel's Live Preview shows you how the selected data will appear formatted as a table. (See Figure 2-8.) To apply this previewed formatting and format the selected cell range as a table, you have only to click the Table button.

As soon as you click the Table button, the Quick Analysis options palette disappears, and the Design contextual table appears on the Ribbon. You can then use its Table Styles drop-down gallery to select a different formatting style for your table. (The Tables button on the Quick Analysis tool's Tables tab offers only the one blue medium style shown in the Live Preview.)

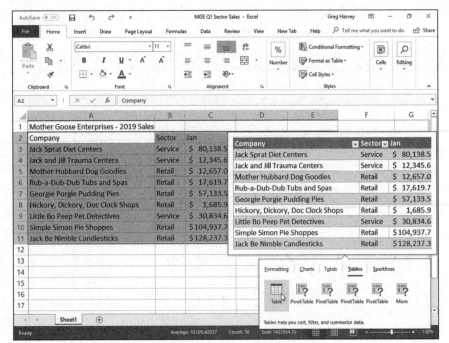

Mother Goose Enterprises - 2019 Sales

Company	Sector	Jan
Jack Sprat Diet Centers	Service	$ 80,138.5
Jack and Jill Trauma Centers	Service	$ 12,345.6
Mother Hubbard Dog Goodies	Retail	$ 12,657.0
Rub-a-Dub-Dub Tubs and Spas	Retail	$ 17,619.7
Georgie Porgie Pudding Pies	Retail	$ 57,133.5
Hickory, Dickory, Doc Clock Shops	Retail	$ 1,685.9
Little Bo Peep Pet Detectives	Service	$ 30,834.6
Simple Simon Pie Shoppes	Retail	$104,937.7
Jack Be Nimble Candlesticks	Retail	$128,237.3

FIGURE 2-8:
Previewing the selected data formatted as a table with the Quick Analysis tool.

Formatting Cells from the Ribbon

Some spreadsheet tables require a lighter touch than formatting as a table offers. For example, you may have a data table where the only emphasis you want to add is to make the column headings bold at the top of the table and to underline the row of totals at the bottom (done by drawing a borderline along the bottom of the cells).

The formatting buttons that appear in the Font, Alignment, and Number groups on the Home tab enable you to accomplish just this kind of targeted cell formatting. See Table 2-1 for a complete rundown on the use of each of these formatting buttons.

REMEMBER

Don't forget about the shortcut keys: Ctrl+B for toggling on and off bold in the cell selection, Ctrl+I for toggling on and off italics, and Ctrl+U for toggling on and off underlining for quickly adding or removing these attributes from the entries in the cell selection.

TABLE 2-1 **The Formatting Command Buttons in the Font, Alignment, and Number Groups on the Home Tab**

Group	Button Name	Function	Hot Keys
Font			
	Font	Displays a Font drop-down menu from which you can assign a new font for the entries in your cell selection.	Alt+HFF
	Font Size	Displays a Font Size drop-down menu from which you can assign a new font size to the entries in your cell selection. Click the Font Size text box and enter the desired point size if it doesn't appear on the drop-down menu.	Alt+HFS
	Increase Font Size	Increases by one point the font size of the entries in your cell selection.	Alt+HFG
	Decrease Font Size	Decreases by one point the font size of the entries in your cell selection.	Alt+HFK
	Bold	Applies and removes boldface in the entries in your cell selection.	Alt+H1
	Italic	Applies and removes italics in the entries in your cell selection.	Alt+H2
	Underline	Applies and removes underlining in the entries in your cell selection.	Alt+H3U (single) or Alt+H3D (for double)
	Borders	Opens a Borders drop-down menu from which you can assign a new border style to or remove an existing border style from your cell selection.	Alt+HB
	Fill Color	Opens a drop-down Color palette from which you can assign a new background color for your cell selection.	Alt+HH
	Font Color	Opens a drop-down Color palette from which you can assign a new font color for the entries in your cell selection.	Alt+HFC
Alignment			
	Top Align	Aligns the entries in your cell selection with the top border of their cells.	Alt+HAT
	Middle Align	Vertically centers the entries in your cell selection between the top and bottom borders of their cells.	Alt+HAM

Group	Button Name	Function	Hot Keys
	Bottom Align	Aligns the entries in your cell selection with the bottom border of their cells.	Alt+HAB
	Orientation	Opens a drop-down menu with options for changing the angle and direction of the entries in your cell selection.	Alt+HFQ
	Wrap Text	Wraps all entries In your cell selection that spill over their right borders onto multiple lines within the current column width	Alt+HW
	Align Text Left	Aligns all the entries in your cell selection with the left edge of their cells	Alt+HAL
	Center	Centers all the entries in your cell selection within their cells.	Alt+HAC
	Align Right	Aligns all the entries in your cell selection with the right edge of their cells.	Alt+HAR
	Decrease Indent	Decreases the margin between entries in your cell selection and their left cell borders by one tab stop.	Alt+H5 or Ctrl+Alt+Shift+Tab
	Increase Indent	Increases the margin between the entries in your cell selection and their left cell borders by one tab stop.	Alt+H6 or Ctrl+Alt+Tab
	Merge & Center	Merges your cell selection into a single cell and then centers the combined entry in the first cell between its new left and right borders. Click the Merge and Center drop-down button to display a menu of options that enable you to merge the cell selection into a single cell without centering the entries, as well as to split up a merged cell back into its original individual cells.	Alt+HMC
Number			
	Number Format	Displays the number format applied to the active cell in your cell selection. Click its drop-down button to open a drop-down menu where you can assign one of Excel's major Number formats to the cell selection.	Alt+HN

(continued)

TABLE 2-1 *(continued)*

Group	Button Name	Function	Hot Keys
	Accounting Number Format	Opens a drop-down menu from which you can select the currency symbol to be used in the Accounting number format. When you select the $ English (U.S) option, this format adds a dollar sign, uses commas to separate thousands, displays two decimal places, and encloses negative values in a closed pair of parentheses. Click the More Accounting Formats option to open the Number tab of the Format Cells dialog box where you can customize the number of decimal places and/or currency symbol used.	Alt+HAN
	Percent Style	Formats your cell selection using the Percent Style number format, which multiplies the values by 100 and adds a percent sign with no decimal places.	Alt+HP
	Comma Style	Formats your cell selection with the Comma Style Number format, which uses commas to separate thousands, displays two decimal places, and encloses negative values in a closed pair of parentheses.	Alt+HK
	Increase Decimal	Adds a decimal place to the values in your cell selection.	Alt+H0 (zero)
	Decrease Decimal	Removes a decimal place from the values in your cell selection.	Alt+H9

Formatting Cell Ranges with the Mini-Toolbar

Excel 2019 makes it easy to apply common formatting changes to a cell selection right within the Worksheet area thanks to its mini-toolbar feature — nicknamed the *mini-bar.*

To display the mini-toolbar, select the cells that need formatting and then right-click somewhere in the cell selection. The mini-toolbar then appears immediately below or above the cell selection's shortcut menu. (See Figure 2-9.)

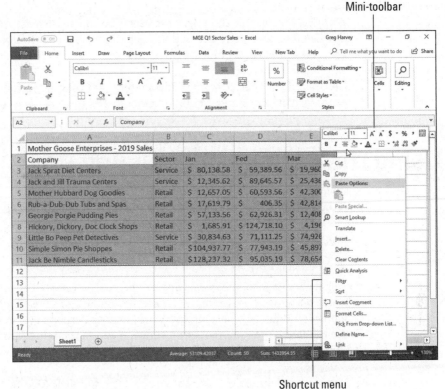

Mini-toolbar

Shortcut menu

FIGURE 2-9:
Right-click your
cell selection
to display its
shortcut menu
along with the
mini-bar, whose
buttons you can
use to format
the selection.

The mini-toolbar contains most of the buttons from the Font group of the Home tab (with the exception of the Underline button). It also contains the Center & Merge and Center buttons from the Alignment group (see "Altering the alignment" later in this chapter) and the Accounting Number Format, Percent Style, Comma Style, Increase Decimal, and Decrease Decimal buttons from the Number group. Simply click these buttons to apply their formatting to the current cell selection.

In addition, the mini-toolbar contains the Format Painter button from the Clipboard group of the Home tab, which you can use to copy the formatting in the active cell to a cell selection you make. (See "Hiring Out the Format Painter" later in this chapter for details.)

TIP

To display the mini-toolbar on a touchscreen device, tap and hold any cell in the selected range with your finger. Note that the mini-toolbar that appears is a little different from the one you see when you right-click a cell selection with a physical mouse. This one contains a single row of command buttons that combine editing and formatting functions — Paste, Cut, Copy, Clear, Fill Color, Font Color, and AutoFill followed by a Show Context Menu button (with a black triangle pointing

Formatting Worksheets

downward). Tap the Show Context Menu button to display a pop-up menu of other editing and formatting options. Tap the Format Cells button on this menu to get access to all sorts of formatting options (see section that follows for details).

Note that if your device has a stylus, tapping and holding a cell in the selected cell range displays the standard mini-toolbar just as though you were using a mouse.

Using the Format Cells Dialog Box

Although the command buttons in the Font, Alignment, and Number groups on the Home tab give you immediate access to the most commonly used formatting commands, they do not represent all of Excel's formatting commands by any stretch of the imagination.

To have access to all the formatting commands, you need to open the Format Cells dialog box either by clicking the Dialog Box launcher in the Number group on the Ribbon's Home tab, choosing the More Number Formats option at the bottom of the Number Format button's drop-down menu in the same Number group, or by simply pressing Ctrl+1.

The Format Cells dialog box contains six tabs: Number, Alignment, Font, Border, Fill, and Protection. (In this chapter, I show you how to use them all except the Protection tab; for information on that tab, see Book 4, Chapter 1.)

TIP

The keystroke shortcut that opens the Format Cells dialog box — Ctrl+1 — is one worth knowing. Just keep in mind that the keyboard shortcut is pressing the Ctrl key plus the *number* 1 key, and not the *function key* F1.

Assigning number formats

When you enter numbers in a cell or a formula that returns a number, Excel automatically applies the General number format to your entry. The General format displays numeric entries more or less as you enter them. However, the General format does make the following changes to your numeric entries:

>> Drops any trailing zeros from decimal fractions so that **4.5** appears when you enter **4.500** in a cell.

>> Drops any leading zeros in whole numbers so that **4567** appears when you enter **04567** in a cell.

>> Inserts a zero before the decimal point in any decimal fraction without a whole number so that **0.123** appears when you enter **.123** in a cell.

>> Truncates decimal places in a number to display the whole numbers in a cell when the number contains too many digits to be displayed in the current column width. It also converts the number to scientific notation when the column width is too narrow to display all integers in the whole number.

Remember that you can always override the General number format when you enter a number by entering the characters used in recognized number formats. For example, to enter the value 2500 and assign it the Currency number format that displays two decimal places, you enter **$2,500.00** in the cell.

Note that although you can override the General number format and assign one of the others to any numeric value that you enter into a cell, you can't do this when you enter a formula into a cell. To apply another format to a calculated result, select its cell and then assign the Currency number format that displays two decimal places by clicking Accounting Number Format in the Number group on the Ribbon's Home tab or by selecting Currency or Accounting on the Number tab of the Format Cells dialog box (Ctrl+1).

Using one of the predefined number formats

Any time you apply a number format to a cell selection (even if you do so with a command button in the Number group on the Ribbon's Home tab instead of selecting the format from the Number tab of the Format Cells dialog box), you're telling Excel to apply a particular group of format codes to those cells.

TECHNICAL STUFF

WHAT YOU SEE IS NOT ALWAYS WHAT YOU GET

The number format that you assign to cells with numeric entries in the worksheet affects *only* the way they are displayed in their cells and not their underlying values. For example, if a formula returns the value 3.456789 in a cell and you apply a number format that displays only two decimal places, Excel will display the value 3.46 in the cell. If you then refer to the cell in a formula that multiplies its value by 2, Excel returns the result 6.913578 instead of the result 6.92, which would be the result if Excel was actually multiplying 3.46 by 2. If you want to modify the underlying value in a cell, you use the ROUND function. (See Book 3, Chapter 5 for details.)

When you first open the Format Cells dialog box with a range of newly entered data selected, the General category of number formats is highlighted in the Category list box with the words "General format cells have no specific number format" showing in the area to the right. Directly above this cryptic message (which is Excel-speak for "We don't care what you've put in your cell; we're not changing it!") is the Sample area. This area shows how the number in the active cell appears in whatever format you choose. (This is blank if the active cell is blank or if it contains text instead of a number.)

When you click the Number, Currency, Accounting, or Percentage category in the Category list box, more options appear in the area just to the right of the Category list box in the form of different check boxes, list boxes, and spinner buttons. (Figure 2-10 shows the Format Cells dialog box when Currency is selected in the Category list box.) These options determine how you want items such as decimal places, dollar signs, comma separators, and negative numbers to be used in the format category that you've chosen.

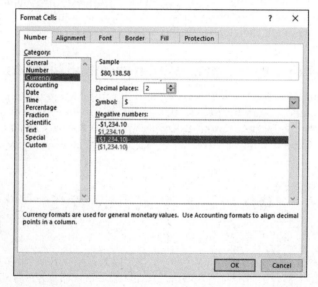

FIGURE 2-10:
Options for customizing the formatting assigned by the Currency number format.

When you choose the Date, Time, Fraction, Special, or Custom category, a large Type list box appears that contains handfuls of predefined category types, which you can apply to your value to change its appearance. Just like when you're selecting different formatting categories, the Sample area of the Format Cells dialog box shows you how the various category *types* will affect your selection.

I should note here that Excel always tries to choose an appropriate format category in the Category list box based on the way you entered your value in the selected cell. If you enter 3:00 in a cell and then open the Number tab of the Format Cells dialog box (Ctrl+1), Excel highlights the h:mm time format in the Custom category in the Type list box.

Deciphering the Custom number formats

You probably noticed while playing around selecting different formats in the Category list box that, for the most part, the different categories and their types are pretty easy — if not a breeze — to comprehend. For most people, that self-assured feeling goes right out the window as soon as they click the Custom category and get a load of its accompanying Type list box, shown in Figure 2-11. It starts off with the nice word *General*, then 0, then 0.00, and after that, all hell breaks loose! Codes with 0s and #s (and other junk) start to appear, and it only goes downhill from there.

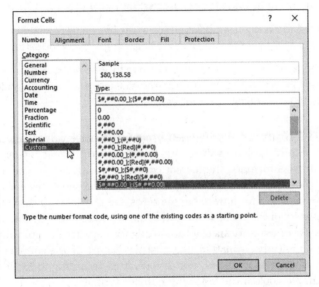

FIGURE 2-11: Creating your own number format using the Custom category in the Format Cells dialog box.

As you move down the list, the longer codes are divided into sections separated by semicolons and enclosed within square brackets. Although at first glance these codes appear as gibberish, you'll actually find that they're quite understandable. (Well, would you believe *useful*, then?)

And these codes *can* be useful, especially after you understand them. You can use them to create number formats of your own design. The basic keys to understanding number format codes are as follows:

>> Excel number formats use a combination of 0, ?, and # symbols with such punctuation as dollar signs, percent signs, and commas to stand for the formatted digits in the numbers that you format.

>> The 0 is used to indicate how many decimal places (if any) are allowed in the format. The format code 0.00 indicates that two decimal places are used in the number. The format code 0 alone indicates that no decimal places appear. (The display of all values is rounded up to whole numbers.)

>> The ? is used like the 0 except that it inserts spaces at the end as needed to make sure that values line up on the decimal point. For example, by entering the number format 0.??, such values as 10.5 and 24.71 line up with each other in their cells because Excel adds an extra space after the 5 to push it over to the left so that it's in line with the 7 of 71. If you used the number format 0.00 instead, these two values would not line up on the decimal point when they are right-aligned in their cells.

>> The # symbol is used with a comma to indicate that you want thousands, hundred thousands, millions, zillions, and so on in your numbers, with each group of three digits to be separated with a comma.

>> The $ (dollar sign) symbol is added to the beginning of a number format if you want dollar signs to appear at the beginning of every formatted number.

>> The % (percent sign) symbol is added to the end of the number format if you want Excel to actually transform the value into a percentage (multiplying it by 100 and adding a percent sign).

Number formats can specify one format for positive values, another for negative values, a third for zero values, and even a fourth format for text in the cells. In such complex formats, the format codes for positive values come first, followed by the codes for negative values, and a semicolon separates each group of codes. Any format codes for how to handle zeros and text in a cell come third and fourth, respectively, in the number format, again separated by semicolons. If the number format doesn't specify special formatting for negative or zero values, these values are automatically formatted like positive values. If the number format doesn't specify what to do with text, text is formatted according to Excel's default values. For example, look at the following number format:

```
#,##0_);(#,##0)
```

This particular number format specifies how to format positive values (the codes in front of the semicolon) and negative values (the codes after the semicolon). Because no further groups of codes exist, zeros are formatted like positive values, and no special formatting is applied to text.

If a number format puts negative values inside parentheses, the positive number format portion often pads the positive values with a space that is the same width as a right parenthesis. To indicate this, you add an underscore (by pressing Shift and the hyphen key) followed immediately by a closed parenthesis symbol.

By padding positive numbers with a space equivalent to a right parenthesis, you ensure that digits of both positive and negative values line up in a column of cells.

You can assign different colors to a number format. For example, you can create a format that displays the values in green (the color of money!) by adding the code [GREEN] at the beginning of the format. A more common use of color is to display just the negative numbers in red (ergo the saying "in the red") by inserting the code [RED] right after the semicolon separating the format for positive numbers from the one for negative numbers. Color codes include [BLACK], [BLUE], [CYAN], [GREEN], [MAGENTA], [RED], [WHITE], and [YELLOW].

Date number formats use a series of abbreviations for month, day, and year that are separated by characters, such as a dash (—) or a slash (/). The code m inserts the month as a number; mmm inserts the month as a three-letter abbreviation, such as Apr or Oct; and mmmm spells out the entire month, such as April or October. The code d inserts the date as a number; dd inserts the date as a number with a leading zero, such as 04 or 07; ddd inserts the date as a three-letter abbreviation of the day of the week, such as Mon or Tue; and dddd inserts the full name of the day of the week, such as Monday or Tuesday. The code yy inserts the last two digits of the year, such as 05 or 07; yyyy inserts all four digits of the year, such as 2005, 2007, and so on.

Time number formats use a series of abbreviations for the hour, minutes, and seconds. The code h inserts the number of the hour; hh inserts the number of the hour with leading zeros, such as 02 or 06. The code m inserts the minutes; the code mm inserts the minutes with leading zeros, such as 01 or 09. The code s inserts the number of seconds; ss inserts the seconds with leading zeros, such as 03 or 08. Add AM/PM or am/pm to have Excel tell time on a 12-hour clock, and add either AM (or am) or PM (or pm) to the time number depending on whether the date is before or after noon. Without these AM/PM codes, Excel displays the time number on a 24-hour clock, just like the military does. (For example, 2:00 PM on a 12-hour clock is expressed as 14:00 on a 24-hour clock.)

So that's all you really need to know about making some sense of all those strange format codes that you see when you select the Custom category on the Number tab of the Format Cells dialog box.

Designing your own number formats

Armed with a little knowledge on the whys and wherefores of interpreting Excel number format codes, you are ready to see how to use these codes to create your own custom number formats. The reason for going through all that code business is that, in order to create a custom number format, you have to type in your own codes.

To create a custom format, follow this series of steps:

1. **Open a worksheet and enter a sample of the values or text to which you will be applying the custom format.**

   If possible, apply the closest existing format to the sample value as you enter it in its cell. (For example, if you're creating a derivative of a Currency format, enter it with the dollar sign, commas, and decimal points that you know you'll want in the custom format.)

2. **Open the Format Cells dialog box and use its categories to apply the closest existing number format to the sample cell.**

3. **Click Custom in the Category list box and then edit the codes applied by the existing number format that you chose in the Type list box until the value in the Sample section appears exactly as you want it.**

What could be simpler? Ah, but Step 3, there's the rub: editing weird format codes and getting them just right so that they produce exactly the kind of number formatting that you're looking for!

Actually, creating your own number format isn't as bad as it first sounds, because you "cheat" by selecting a number format that uses as many of the codes as possible that you need in the new custom number that you're creating. Then you use the Sample area to keep a careful eye on the results as you edit the codes in the existing number format. For example, suppose that you want to create a custom date format to use on the current date that you enter with Excel's built-in NOW() function. (See Book 3, Chapter 3 for details.) You want this date format to display the full name of the current month (January, February, and so on), followed by two digits for the date and four digits for the year, such as November 06, 2019.

To do this, use the Insert Function button on the Formula bar to insert the NOW() function into a blank worksheet cell; then with this cell selected, open the Format Cells dialog box and scroll down through the Custom category Type list box on the Number tab until you see the date codes m/d/yyyy h:mm. Highlight these codes and then edit them as follows in the Type text box directly above:

```
mmmm dd, yyyy
```

The mmmm format code inserts the full name of the month in the custom format; dd inserts two digits for the day (including a leading zero, like 02 and 03); the yyyy code inserts the year. The other elements in this custom format are the space between the mmmm and dd codes and a comma and a space between the dd and yyyy codes (these being purely "punctuational" considerations in the custom format).

What if you want to do something even fancier and create a custom format that tells you something like "Today is Sunday, November 06, 2016" when you format a cell containing the NOW function? Well, you select your first custom format and add a little bit to the front of it, as follows:

```
"Today is" dddd, mmmm dd, yyyy
```

In this custom format, you've added two more elements: *Today is* and *dddd*. The Today is code tells Excel to enter the text between the quotation marks verbatim; the dddd code tells the program to insert the whole name of the day of the week. And you thought this was going to be a hard section!

Next, suppose that you want to create a really colorful number format — one that displays positive values in blue, negative values in red (what else?), zero values in green, and text in cyan. Further suppose that you want commas to separate groups of thousands in the values, no decimal places to appear (whole numbers only, please), and negative values to appear inside parentheses (instead of using that tiny little minus sign at the start). Sound complex? Hah, this is a piece of cake.

1. **In four blank cells in a new worksheet, enter** 1200 **in the first cell,** -8000 **in the second cell,** 0 **in the third cell, and the text** Hello There! **in the fourth cell.**

2. **Select all four cells as a range (starting with the one containing 1200 as the first cell of the range).**

3. **Open the Format Cells dialog box and select the Number tab and Number in the Category list.**

4. **Click the #,##0_);[Red](#,##0) code in the Custom category Type list box (it's the eighth set down from the top of the list box) and then edit it as follows:** [Blue]#,##0_);[Red](#,##0);[Green];[Cyan].

5. **Click OK.**

That's all there is to that. When you return to the worksheet, the cell with 1200 appears in blue as 1,200, the -8000 appears in red as (8,000), the 0 appears in green, and the text "Hello There!" appears in a lovely cyan.

Before you move on, you should know about a particular custom format because it can come in really handy from time to time. I'm referring to the custom format that hides whatever has been entered in the cells. You can use this custom format to temporarily mask the display of confidential information used in calculating the worksheet before you print and distribute the worksheet. This custom format provides an easy way to avoid distributing confidential and sensitive information while protecting the integrity of the worksheet calculations at the same time.

To create a custom format that masks the display of the data in a cell selection, you simply create an "empty" format that contains just the semicolon separators in a row:

```
;;;
```

This is one custom format that you can probably type by yourself!

After creating this format, you can blank out a range of cells simply by selecting them and then selecting this three-semicolon custom format in the Format Cells dialog box. To bring back a cell range that's been blanked out with this custom format, simply select what now looks like blank cells and then select one of the other (visible) formats that are available. If the cell range contains text and values that normally should use a variety of different formats, first use General to make them visible. After the contents are back on display, format the cells in smaller groups or individually, as required.

Altering the alignment

You can use Excel's Alignment options by using command buttons in the Alignment group of the Ribbon's Home tab and by using options on the Alignment tab of the Format Cells dialog box to change the way cell entries are displayed within their cells.

Alignment refers to both the horizontal and vertical placement of the characters in an entry with regard to its cell boundaries as well as the orientation of the characters and how they are read. Horizontally, Excel automatically right-aligns all numeric entries and left-aligns all text entries in their cells (referred to as General alignment). Vertically, Excel aligns all types of cell entries with the bottom of their cells.

In the Horizontal drop-down list on the Alignment tab of the Format Cells dialog box, Excel offers you the following horizontal text alignment choices:

>> **General** (the default) right-aligns a numeric entry and left-aligns a text entry in its cell.

>> **Left (Indent)** left-aligns the entry in its cell and indents the characters from the left edge of the cell by the number of characters entered in the Indent combo box (which is 0 by default).

>> **Center** centers any type of cell entry in its cell.

>> **Right (Indent)** right-aligns the entry in its cell and indents the characters from the right edge of the cell by the number of characters entered in the Indent combo box (which is 0 by default).

- >> **Fill** repeats the entry until its characters fill the entire cell display. When you use this option, Excel automatically increases or decreases the repetitions of the characters in the cell as you adjust the width of its column.

- >> **Justify** spreads out a text entry with spaces so that the text is aligned with the left and right edges of its cell. If necessary to justify the text, Excel automatically wraps the text onto more than one line in the cell and increases the height of its row. If you use the Justify option on numbers, Excel left-aligns the values in their cells just as if you had selected the Left align option.

- >> **Center Across Selection** centers a text entry over selected blank cells in columns to the right of the cell entry.

- >> **Distributed (Indent)** indents the text in from the left and right cell margins by the amount you enter in the Indent text box or select with its spinner buttons (which appear when you select this option from the Horizontal drop-down list) and then distributes the text evenly in the space in between.

For text entries in the worksheet, you can also add the Wrap Text check box option to any of the horizontal alignment choices. (Note that you can also access this option by clicking the Wrap Text button in the Alignment group of the Home tab on the Ribbon.) When you select the Wrap Text option, Excel automatically wraps the text entry to multiple lines within its cells while maintaining the type of alignment that you've selected (something that automatically happens when you select the Justify alignment option).

Instead of wrapping text that naturally increases the row height to accommodate the additional lines, you can use the Shrink to Fit check box option on the Alignment tab of the Format Cells dialog box to have Excel reduce the size of the text in the cell sufficiently so that all its characters fit within their current column widths.

In addition, Excel offers the following vertical text alignment options from the Vertical drop-down list:

- >> **Top** (the default) aligns any type of cell entry with the top edge of its cell.

- >> **Center** centers any type of cell entry between the top and bottom edges of its cell.

- >> **Bottom** aligns any type of cell entry with the bottom edge of its cell.

- >> **Justify** wraps the text of a cell entry on different lines spread out with blank space so that they are vertically aligned between the top and bottom edges of the cell.

- >> **Distributed** wraps the text of the cell entry on different lines distributed evenly between the top and bottom edges of its cell.

Formatting Worksheets

Finally, as part of its alignment options, Excel lets you alter the *orientation* (the angle of the characters in an entry in its cell) and *text direction* (the way the characters are read). The direction is left-to-right for European languages and right-to-left for some languages, such as Hebrew and Arabic. (Chinese characters can also sometimes be read from right to left, as well.)

Wrapping text entries to new lines in their cells

You can use the Wrap Text button on the Ribbon's Home tab or the Wrap Text check box in the Text Control section of the Alignment tab to have Excel create a multi-line entry from a long text entry that would otherwise spill over to blank cells to the right. In creating a multi-line entry in a cell, the program also automatically increases the height of its row if that is required to display all the text.

To get an idea of how text wrap works in cells, compare Figures 2-12 and 2-13. Figure 2-12 shows you a row of long text entries that spill over to succeeding blank cells in columns to the right. Figure 2-13 shows you these same entries after they have been formatted with the Wrap Text option. The first long text entry is in cell A8 and the last in cell I8. They all use General alignment (same as Left for text) with the Wrap Text option.

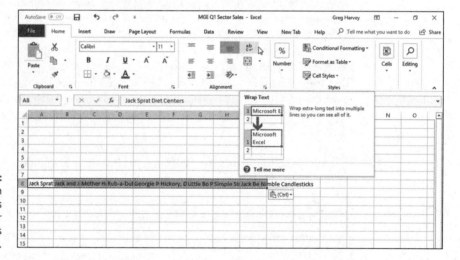

FIGURE 2-12: Worksheet with long text entries that spill over into blank cells on the right.

When you create multi-line text entries with the Wrap Text option, you can decide where each line breaks by inserting a new paragraph. To do this, you put Excel in Edit mode by clicking the insertion point in the Formula bar at the place where a new line should start and pressing Alt+Enter. When you press the Enter key to return to Ready mode, Excel inserts an invisible paragraph marker at the insertion point that starts a new line both on the Formula bar and within the cell with the wrapped text.

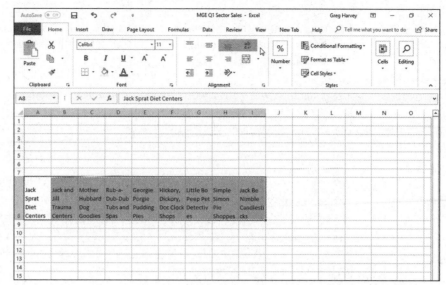

FIGURE 2-13:
Worksheet after wrapping long text entries in their cells, increasing the height of their rows.

TIP

If you ever want to remove the paragraph marker and rejoin text split on different lines, click the insertion point at the beginning of the line that you want to join on the Formula bar and press the Backspace key.

Reorienting your entries

Excel makes it easy to change the *orientation* (that is, the angle of the baseline on which the characters rest) of the characters in a cell entry by rotating up or down the baseline of the characters.

The Orientation command button in the Alignment group on the Ribbon's Home tab contains the following options on its drop-down menu:

>> **Angle Counterclockwise** rotates the text in the cell selection up 45 degrees from the baseline.

>> **Angle Clockwise** rotates the text in the cell selection down 45 degrees from the baseline.

>> **Vertical Text** aligns the text in the cell selection in a column where one letter appears over the other.

>> **Rotate Text Up** rotates the text in the cell selection up 90 degrees from the baseline.

>> **Rotate Text Down** rotates the text in the cell selection down 90 degrees from the baseline.

>> **Format Cell Alignment** opens the Alignment tab on the Format Cells dialog box.

You can also alter the orientation of text in the cell selection on the Alignment tab of the Format Cells dialog box (Ctrl+1) using the following options in its Orientation area:

>> Enter the value of the angle of rotation for the new orientation in the Degrees text box or click the spinner buttons to select this angle. Enter a positive value (such as 45) to have the characters angled above the normal 90-degree line of orientation and a negative value (such as –45) to have them angled above this line.

>> Click the point on the sample Text box on the right side of the Orientation area that corresponds to the angle of rotation that you want for the characters in the selected cells.

>> Click the sample Text box on the left side of the Orientation area to have the characters stacked one on top of the other (as shown in the orientation of the word "Text" in this sample box).

After changing the orientation of entries in a selection, Excel automatically adjusts the height of the rows in the cell selection to accommodate the rotation up or down of the cell entries. Figure 2-14 shows the top part of a worksheet after rotating the column headings for a new data table up 90 degrees. Note how Excel increased the height of row 10 to accommodate this change.

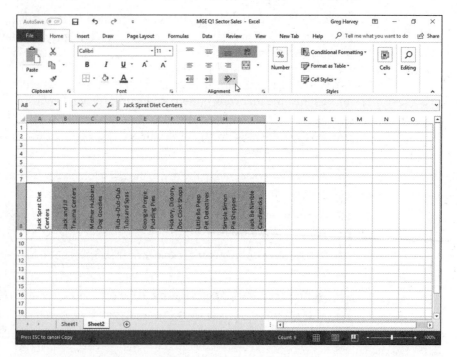

FIGURE 2-14: Worksheet after rotating a table's column headings up 90 degrees.

Fancy fonts and colors

You can assign any of the fonts that you've installed for your printer to cells in a worksheet. Along with selecting a new *font* (also known as a *typeface*), you can choose a new font size (in points), assign a font style (such as bold, italic, under–line, or strikethrough), as well as change the color of the font.

TIP

Note that you can always tell the font and font size of the cell entry in the active cell by looking at the font name displayed in the Font combo box and the point size displayed in the Font Size combo box in the Font group on the Home tab of the Ribbon. You can also tell which, if any, text attributes are assigned to the entry by looking at the Bold, Italic, and Underline buttons in this group. Excel indicates which of these attributes have been assigned to the cell by highlighting the **B**, *I*, or U button in the standard beige highlight color.

Selecting fonts and colors from the Ribbon

You can change the font, font size, font style, and font color using the command buttons in the Font group on the Home tab of the Ribbon. The only aspects you can't change or assign are the type of the underlining (besides single or double) and special font styles including strikethrough, superscript, and subscript.

To change the font with the command buttons in the Font group on the Ribbon's Home tab, select the cell, cell range, or nonadjacent selection to which you want to assign the new font, size, style, or color, and then do one of the following:

» To assign a new font to the selection, click the Font drop-down button and then select the font from the drop-down list.

» To assign a new point size to the selection, click the Font Size drop-down button and then select the size from the drop-down list. (You can also do this by clicking the Font text box, typing the point size, and pressing Enter.)

» To increase the font size a single point at a time, click the Increase Font Size button.

» To decrease the font size a single point at a time, click the Decrease Font Size button.

» To assign a new font style to a selection, click the appropriate tool in the Formatting toolbar: Click the Bold button (the one with **B**) to bold the selection, the Italic button (the one with *I*) to italicize the selection, and the Underline button (the one with the U) to underline the selection. To assign double underlining to the cell selection, click the drop-down button attached to the Underline button and then click Double Underline from its drop-down menu.

» To assign a new font color, click the Font Color pop-up button and then click the new color in the drop-down palette.

REMEMBER

Live Preview enables you to see how the cell selection looks in a font or font size that you highlight on the Font or Font Size drop-down list — provided, of course, that the selection in the columns and rows is not obscured when these drop-down lists are displayed.

TIP

Note that you can immediately remove any font change that you make by clicking the Undo button on the Quick Access toolbar (or by pressing Ctrl+Z). You can also remove boldface, italics, and underlining assigned to a cell selection by clicking the appropriate button (Bold, Italic, and Underline) on the Formatting toolbar. This action removes the shading that outlines the button's **B,** *I,* or U icon.

Selecting fonts and colors in the Format Cells dialog box

You can also select a new font, font size, font style, and font color for your selection on the Font tab of the Format Cells dialog box (Ctrl+1). Figure 2-15 shows the Font tab of the Format Cells dialog box that appears when an empty cell that uses the Normal style is active. In this figure, the current Font is Calibri (Body), the Font Style is Regular, the Font Size is 11 (points), the Underline is None, and the Color is Automatic.

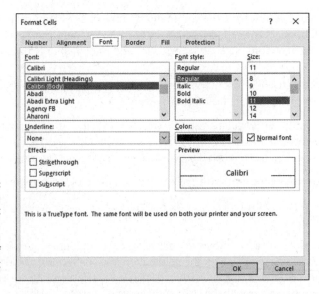

FIGURE 2-15:
You can assign new fonts, font sizes, attributes, and colors on the Font tab of the Format Cells dialog box.

To select a new font color from the Font Color drop-down palette in the Font group on the Ribbon's Home tab or from the Color drop-down palette on the Font tab of the Format Cells dialog box, click its drop-down button. Both drop-down palettes contain color swatches arranged in two groups: Theme colors to select one of the colors used in Excel's themes (see Book 5, Chapter 2) and Standard colors to select one of the primary Windows colors. To select a font color from either of these two groups, click its color swatch.

If none of the preset colors will do, click the More Colors option at the bottom of the drop-down palette to open the Colors dialog box. This dialog box contains a Standard tab where you can select a new color by clicking its hexagram swatch in the color honeycomb or shade of gray hexagram below. The Custom tab enables you to select a custom color by changing the RGB (Red, Green, and Blue) or HSL (Hue, Saturation, and Luminosity) values. You can do this either by dragging through the color grid and tint slider at the top of the Custom tab or by entering new values in the Red, Green, and Blue (when the RGB Color Model is selected) or the Hue, Sat, and Lum (when the HSL Color Model is selected) text boxes below or by selecting them with their spinner buttons.

REMEMBER

Note that Excel adds a swatch for each custom color you select or define to a Recent Colors section that then appears on both the Font Color and Fill Color buttons' drop-down palettes, making it easy to apply these custom colors to the text and fills of other cells in the worksheet.

Basic borders, fills, and patterns

Excel makes it easy to add borders as well as to assign new background fill colors, gradients, and shading patterns to cells in the worksheet. You can use the borders to outline tables of data — particularly important cells — or to underscore rows of key data. You can also apply various color gradients and shading patterns to cells to draw attention to significant aspects of the spreadsheet.

TIP

When adding borders and shading, you can make your job a great deal easier by removing the gridlines used in the Worksheet area to indicate the borders of the cells in the worksheet. To remove these gridlines, deselect the Gridlines check box on the View tab of the Ribbon (or press Alt+WVG) to remove its check mark. After you've dispensed with a worksheet's gridlines, you can immediately tell whether you've added the kind of borders that you want and better judge the effect of the color and shading changes that you make.

REMEMBER

Note that removing the display of the gridlines in the Workbook window has no effect on the appearance of gridlines in a printed copy of the spreadsheet. If you turn on gridlines for a printout in the Page Setup dialog box (Alt+PSP) by select-ing the Gridlines check under the Print heading on the Sheet tab, Excel prints these lines on the printed version of the worksheet even when they do not appear onscreen.

Right on the borderline

When applying borderlines to a cell selection, you have a choice between using the options on the drop-down menu that's attached to the Borders button in the Font group on the Home tab and using the options on the Border tab of the Format Cells dialog box. You can compare the options offered by each in Figures 2-16 and 2-17. Figure 2-16 shows the border options on the drop-down menu, and Figure 2-17 shows the options on the Border tab of the Format Cells dialog box.

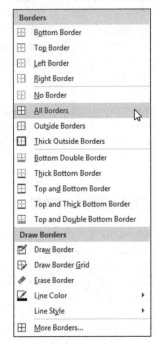

FIGURE 2-16:
The border options available on the Home tab's Borders button's drop-down menu.

To apply borders to the cell selection by using the options on the Borders button's drop-down menu, choose the option on the menu with the type of border you want drawn. To remove a borderline that you select in error, simply click the No Border option at the top of this drop-down menu.

While defining the borderlines to apply in the Border tab, you can select a new style for the borderlines by clicking the Line style in the Style sample area. To select a new color (besides boring old black) for the borderlines that you're about to apply, click the swatch of the new color you want to use in the Color drop-down palette.

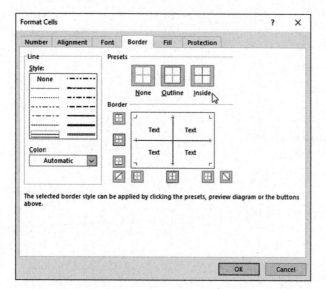

FIGURE 2-17:
The border options available on the Border tab of the Format Cells dialog box.

When using the Borders palettes to assign borderlines to a cell selection, your options are limited to just the Border buttons displayed on the palette. This means that you don't have as much choice in terms of line style and type of borderlines. (In other words, you can't be applying any dashed diagonal borderlines from this palette.) You also can't change the color of the borderlines from the Borders palette.

REMEMBER

Keep in mind that the Borders button's drop-down menu includes a couple of options that enable you to literally draw borders around a cell selection in your worksheet by dragging the mouse pointer through the cells. Click the Draw Border option to draw a border just outlining the cells you select or Draw Border Grid to draw borders around each and every cell you select with the mouse.

TIP

To get rid of borderlines that you've added to a cell range, no matter which method you used to add them, select the range and then click the No Border option from the Borders button's drop-down menu. Fun fills, great-looking gradients, and pretty patterns

In Excel 2019, you can not only select new background colors (referred to as fill colors) for the cell selection, but you can also assign gradients (fills that gradually go from one color to another) and new dotted and crosshatched patterns to them.

When simply assigning a new fill color to the current cell selection, you can do this either by clicking a new color swatch on the Fill Color button's drop-down palette (located in the Font group on the Ribbon's Home tab) or by clicking the swatch in the Background Color area of the Fill tab in the Format Cells dialog box (Ctrl+1) shown in Figure 2-18.

Formatting Worksheets

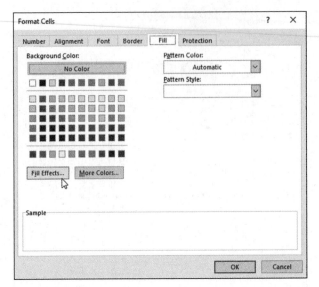

FIGURE 2-18:
Using the options
on the Fill tab to
select a new fill
color, gradient,
or shading
pattern for your
cell selection.

» To assign a gradient to the cell selection, click the Fill Effects button to open the Fill Effects dialog box. (See Figure 2-19.) Select the beginning gradient color by clicking its swatch on the Color 1 drop-down color palette and the ending gradient color by clicking its swatch on the Color 2 drop-down palette. Note that you can then further refine the gradient by selecting a new shading style option button that determines the direction of the gradient pattern before you click OK.

» To add a dotted or crosshatched shading pattern to the cell selection (instead of a gradient — they don't go together), click the pattern square on the Pattern Style's drop-down palette. To change the color of the shading pattern (which is by default the black Automatic color), click a color swatch on the Pattern Color's drop-down palette.

REMEMBER

Check the Sample area at the bottom of the Fill tab of the Format Cells dialog box to check out the shading pattern and make sure that it's the one you want to use before you click OK to apply it to the cell selection. If you don't like the effect after you've applied it to the cell selection, click the Undo button on the Quick Access toolbar or press Ctrl+Z immediately to remove it.

TIP

To get rid of all fill colors, gradients, and shading patterns used in a cell selection, click the No Fill option at the bottom of the Fill Color button's drop-down palette on the Home tab.

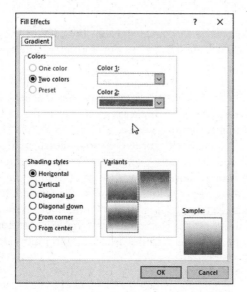

FIGURE 2-19:
Selecting a new
gradient for your
cell selection in
the Fill Effects
dialog box.

Hiring Out the Format Painter

The Format Painter button (with paintbrush icon) in the Clipboard group of the Home tab takes formatting from the current cell and applies it to cells that you "paint" by dragging its special thick-white cross-plus-paintbrush mouse pointer through them. This tool, therefore, provides a quick-and-easy way to take a bunch of different formats (such as a new font, font size, bold, and italics) that you applied individually to a cell in the spreadsheet and then turn around and use them as the guide for formatting a new range of cells.

To use the Format Painter, follow these steps:

1. **Position the cell cursor in a cell that contains the formatting that you want copied to another range of cells in the spreadsheet.**

    This cell becomes the sample cell whose formatting is taken up by Format Painter and copied in the cells that "paint" with its special mouse pointer.

2. **Click the Format Painter button (with the paintbrush icon) in the Clipboard group on the Home tab of the Ribbon.**

    As soon as you click this button, Excel adds a paintbrush icon to the standard thick white-cross mouse pointer, indicating that the Format Painter is ready to copy the formatting from the sample cell.

3. **Drag the mouse pointer through the range of cells that you want format- ted identically to the sample cell.**

Formatting Worksheets

The moment that you release the mouse button, the cells in the range that you just selected with the Format Painter become formatted the same way as the sample cell.

TIP

Normally, using the Format Painter is a one-shot deal because as soon as you release the mouse button after selecting a range of cells with the Format Painter, it turns off, and the mouse pointer reverts back to its normal function of just selecting cells in the worksheet (indicated by the return of the regular thick white-cross icon). If you ever want to keep the Format Painter turned on so that you can use it to format more than one range of cells in the worksheet, you need to double-click the Format Painter button on the Home tab instead of just single-clicking it. When you do this, the Format Painter button remains depressed (indicated by the shading) on the Home tab until you click its command button again. During this time, you can "paint" as many different cell ranges in the worksheet as you desire.

Using Cell Styles

Cell styles combine a number of different formatting aspects that can include number format, text alignment, font and font size, borders, fills, and protection status. (See Book 4, Chapter 1.)

In Excel 2019, cell styles really come alive in the form of the Cell Styles gallery that you open by clicking the Cell Styles button in the Styles group on the Ribbon's Home tab.

The Cell Styles gallery contains loads of ready-made styles you can immediately apply to the current cell selection. These predefined cell styles are arranged into various sections: Good, Bad, and Neutral; Data and Model; Titles and Headings; Themed Cell Styles; and Number Format. (See Figure 2-20.)

To apply one of the styles on the Cell Styles gallery, simply click the thumbnail of the desired style in the gallery after using the Live Preview feature to determine which style looks best on the data in your cell selection.

Using the Number Format cell styles

The Number Format section near the bottom of the Cell Styles gallery (see Figure 2-20) contains the following five predefined styles that you can use to format the values entered into the cell selection as follows:

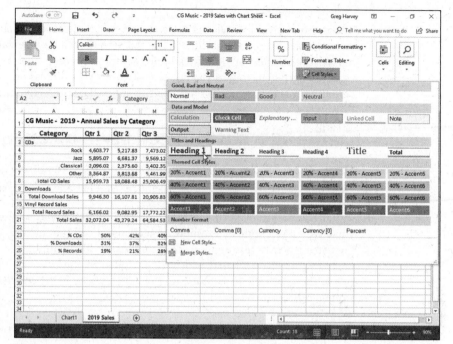

FIGURE 2-20:
Selecting a new style for a cell selection from the Cell Styles gallery.

>> **Comma** sets the number format to the Comma Style (same as clicking the Comma Style command button in the Number group of the Home tab).

>> **Comma (0)** sets the number format to the Comma Style format without any decimal places.

>> **Currency** sets the number format to the Currency style format (same as clicking the Accounting Number Format command button in the Number group of the Home tab).

>> **Currency (0)** sets the number format to the Currency style format without any decimal places (making your financial figures all dollars and no cents).

>> **Percent** sets the number format to Percent style (same as clicking the Percent Style command button in the Number group of the Home tab).

REMEMBER

You can combine the number formatting assigned from one of the Number Format cell styles with the other cell formatting assigned by the cell styles in the other three cell style groups: the Good, Bad, and Neutral (except for Normal, which applies the General number format); Data and Model; and Themed Cell Styles. To do this, however, assign the number formatting by clicking its style in the Number Format section of the Cell Styles gallery before you assign the other formatting by clicking its style in one of the other three sections of the Cell Styles gallery.

Click Normal, the first style in the Good, Bad, and Neutral section, in the Cell Styles gallery to return the formatting in the cell selection to its original state: General number format, left or right (depending on the contents), horizontal and bottom vertical alignment, Calibri (body), 11-point font size (unless you've changed the default font and size), no borders, no fill, and locked protection status.

Defining a custom cell style by example

You don't have to live with just the predefined styles that Excel gives you on the Cell Styles gallery because you can readily create custom cell styles of your own.

By far the easiest way to create a new custom cell style is by example. When you create a cell style by example, you choose a cell that already displays all the formatting attributes (applied separately using the techniques discussed previously in this chapter) that you want included in the new cell style. Then, you follow these simple steps to create the new style by using the formatting in the sample cell:

1. **Position the cell pointer in the cell with the formatting that you want in the new style.**

2. **Click the New Cell Style option at the bottom of the Cell Styles drop-down gallery (opened by clicking the Cell Styles button in the Styles group on the Ribbon's Home tab).**

    This action opens the Style dialog box with a generic style name (Style 1, Style 2, and so on), and the formatting attributes applied to the cell are listed in the Style Includes (By Example) section of the dialog box.

3. **Type the name for the new style in the Style Name text box (replacing the Style 1, Style 2, generic style name).**

4. **Click OK to close the Style dialog box.**

When defining a style by example, select only one cell that you know contains all the formatting characteristics that you want in the new style. This way, you avoid the potential problem of selecting cells that don't share the same formatting. If you select cells that use different formatting when defining a style by example, the new style will contain only the formatting that all cells share in common.

After you close the Style dialog box, Excel adds a thumbnail for the new style to a Custom section at the top of the Cell Styles gallery. To apply this new custom cell style to other cell selections in the worksheet, all you have to do is click its thumbnail in the Custom section of the gallery.

Creating a new cell style from scratch

You can also create a custom cell style from scratch by defining each of its formatting characteristics in the Style dialog box as follows:

1. **Position the cell pointer in a cell that doesn't have only the Excel default formatting applied to it and then click the New Cell Style option at the bottom of the Cell Styles drop-down gallery (opened by clicking the Cell Styles button in the Styles group on the Ribbon's Home tab).**

   This action opens the Style dialog box with a generic style name (Style 1, Style 2, and so on), and with the attributes for the Normal style listed in the Style Includes (By Example) section of the dialog box.

2. **Type a name for the new style that you are defining in the Style Name text box (replacing Style 1, Style 2, generic style name).**

   Now you need to select the formatting settings for the new style.

3. **(Optional) Remove the check mark from the check box for any attribute (Number, Alignment, Font, Border, Fill, or Protection) that you don't want included in the new style.**

   They are all selected by default.

4. **Click the Format button in the Style dialog box.**

   This action opens the standard Format Cells dialog box, where you can use the options on its six tabs (Number, Alignment, Font, Border, Fill, and Protection) to select all the formatting attributes that you do want used when you apply the new style to a cell selection.

5. **After you finish assigning the formatting attributes that you want in the new style in the Format Cells dialog box, click OK to return to the Style dialog box.**

   The Style Includes (By Example) section now lists all the attributes that you assigned in the Format Cells dialog box.

6. **Click OK to close the Style dialog box.**

As soon as you click OK, Excel applies the formatting in your newly defined custom style to the current cell and adds the new style to the Custom section of the Cell Styles gallery. To apply this new custom cell style to other cell selections in the worksheet, all you have to do is click its thumbnail in the Custom section of the gallery.

REMEMBER

To remove a custom style from the Cell Styles gallery that you've defined by example or from scratch, you have to right-click its thumbnail in the gallery and then click Delete on its shortcut menu.

Formatting Worksheets

Merging styles into other workbooks

All custom cell styles that you create are saved, along with the data and formatting in the worksheet, when you save the file. The only styles, however, that are available when you begin a new worksheet are those predefined styles provided by Excel.

If you've created custom styles in another workbook that you want to use in a new workbook or in an existing one that you've opened for editing, you have to merge them into that workbook as follows:

1. **Open the workbook file containing the custom styles that you want to copy and use.**

   You must have the workbook containing the custom styles to merge open, along with the workbook into which these custom styles will be copied.

2. **Click the button on the Windows taskbar for the workbook file into which the custom styles will be merged.**

   This action makes the workbook into which the custom styles are to be copied the active one.

3. **Click the Merge Styles option at the bottom of the Cell Styles drop-down gallery (opened by clicking the Cell Styles button in the Styles group on the Ribbon's Home tab).**

   Excel opens the Merge Styles dialog box with a list box that displays the filenames of the all the workbooks that currently open in the program.

4. **Click the name of the workbook that contains the custom styles you want merged into the active workbook and then click OK.**

   This action closes the Merge Styles dialog box. If the worksheet file that you selected contains custom styles with the same names as the custom styles defined in the active worksheet, Excel displays an alert box that asks whether you want to merge the styles that have the same names. Click Yes to replace all styles in the active workbook with those that have the same name in the workbook file that you're copying from. Click No if you don't want the styles in the active workbook to be overwritten, in which case Excel merges the styles with unique names from the other worksheet.

After merging styles from another open workbook, you can close that workbook by clicking its button on the Windows taskbar and then clicking its Close Window. You can then begin applying the merged custom styles, which now appear in the Custom section at the top of the Cell Styles gallery, to cell selections by clicking their thumbnails in the gallery.

Conditional Formatting

Excel 2019's Conditional Formatting feature enables you to format a range of values so that unusual or unwanted values, or values outside certain limits, are automatically formatted in such a way as to call attention to them.

When you click the Conditional Formatting button in the Styles group on the Ribbon's Home tab, a drop-down menu appears with the following options:

>> **Highlight Cells Rules** opens a continuation menu with various options for defining formatting rules that highlight the cells in the cell selection that contain certain values, text, or dates, or that have values greater or less than a particular value, or that fall within a certain ranges of values.

>> **Top/Bottom Rules** opens a continuation menu with various options for defining formatting rules that highlight the top and bottom values, percentages, and above and below average values in the cell selection.

>> **Data Bars** opens a palette with different color data bars that you can apply to the cell selection to indicate their values relative to each other by clicking the data bar thumbnail.

>> **Color Scales** opens a palette with different three- and two-colored scales that you can apply to the cell selection to indicate their values relative to each other by clicking the color scale thumbnail.

>> **Icon Sets** opens a palette with different sets of icons that you can apply to the cell selection to indicate their values relative to each other by clicking the icon set.

>> **New Rule** opens the New Formatting Rule dialog box, where you define a custom conditional formatting rule to apply to the cell selection.

>> **Clear Rules** opens a continuation menu, where you can remove conditional formatting rules for the cell selection by clicking the Selected Cells option, for the entire worksheet by clicking the Entire Sheet option, or for just the current data table by clicking the This Table option.

>> **Manage Rules** opens the Conditional Formatting Rules Manager dialog box, where you edit and delete particular rules as well as adjust their rule precedence by moving them up or down in the Rules list box.

Graphical conditional formatting

Perhaps the coolest (and certainly easiest) conditional formatting that you can apply to a cell range is with the sets of graphical markers pop-up palettes attached to the Data Bars, Color Scales, and Icon Sets options on the Conditional Formatting button's drop-down menu:

>> **Data Bars** represents the relative values in the cell selection by the length of the color bar in each cell — data bars are a great way to quickly pinpoint the lower and higher values within a large range of data.

>> **Color Scales** classify the relative values in a cell selection with a color gradation using a one-, two-, or three-color scale — color scales are great for identifying the distribution of values across a large range of data.

>> **Icon Sets** classify the values in the cell selection into three to five categories and each icon within the set represents a range of values that go from high to low — icon sets are great for quickly identifying the different ranges of values in a range of data.

Figure 2-21 shows how the initial Color Scales option and Directional Icon Set appear when applied to two cell selections that both contain a simple series of whole numbers, ranging from 6 to 1 and 1 to 6. The cell range A2:A12 is formatted with Color Scales, and Live Preview shows how these values in cell range B2:B12 appear when formatted with the first Directional Icon Set.

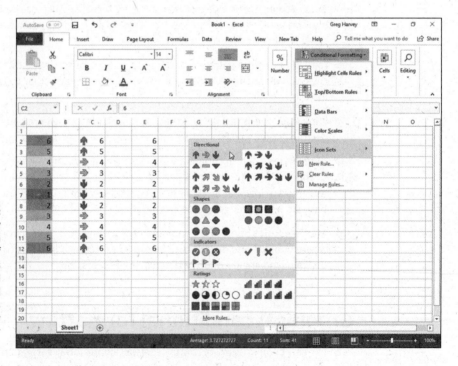

FIGURE 2-21: Conditionally formatting a sequence of numeric entries with the initial color scales and directional icons that graphically indicate their relative values.

TIP

If you want to hide the values in a cell range and only display a type of graphical conditional formatting, apply the desired graphical conditional formatting to the range of numeric entries and then hide the underlying values by formatting the same cell range with the custom numeric format that masks the numeric entries (;;;), as described in "Designing your own number formats," earlier in this chapter.

Formatting with the Quick Analysis tool

Excel 2019's Quick Analysis tool enables you to apply various types of conditional formatting to selected cell ranges. Figure 2-22 illustrates how this works. For this figure, I selected the cell range E3:E13 containing a copy of the range of values from 6 to 1 and 1 to 6 before clicking the Quick Analysis tool that routinely appears in the lower-right below the last selected cell.

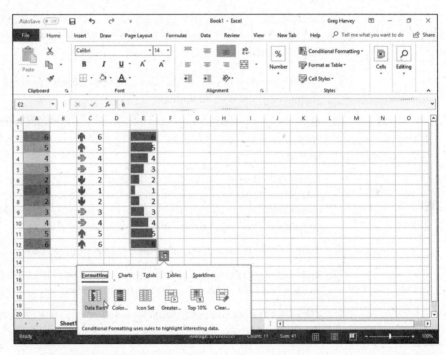

FIGURE 2-22: Using the Formatting tab's options on the Quick Analysis tool's palette to preview conditional formatting applied to a cell selection.

As soon as you select the Quick Analysis tool, the Formatting tab is automatically selected with its conditional formatting option buttons (Data Bars, Color Scale, Icon Set, Greater Than, Top 10%, and Clear Format) displayed. You can then use Live Preview to sample how the selected data would appear in different conditional formats. When you see one you like, you can then apply it by clicking the particular conditional formatting option button.

Identifying particular values or text entries in a cell range

The options attached to the Highlight Cell Rules and Top/Bottom Rules items on the Conditional Formatting button's drop-down menu enable you to specify a particular type of formatting when certain conditions are met.

The rules that you set up for meeting these formatting conditions can vary widely. You can set up a rule whereby a particular type of formatting is applied when a cell in the range contains a certain text entry (such as Fixed or Variable). You set up a rule whereby a particular type of formatting is applied when a cell in the range is exactly a particular value or exceeds or falls below a particular value. So too, you can set up a rule whereby a particular type of formatting is applied when the value is one of the top ten in the range, is below the average value in the range, or falls into the lower ten percent.

For example, to set up the rule that Excel formats any cell within a range with a light red fill color and dark red font color whenever it contains the word *Fixed*, you follow these steps:

1. **Select the range of cells in the worksheet to which this conditional formatting rule is to be applied.**

2. **Click the Conditional Formatting button on the Ribbon's Home tab and then click Highlight Cell Rules ⇨ Text That Contains from the drop-down menu.**

Excel opens the Text That Contains dialog box with a text box on the left where you enter or select in the worksheet the text that tells Excel when to apply the conditional formatting and a drop-down list box on the right where you select or define the conditional formatting the program is to apply.

3. **Type** Fixed **in the Format Cells That Contain the Text box.**

In this case, you don't have to change the formatting in the drop-down list box, as Light Red Fill with Dark Red Text is the default formatting.

4. **Click OK to apply the conditional formatting rule to the selected cell range.**

Say you wanted to apply three different types of conditional formatting to the cells in a single range of the worksheet: one type of formatting whenever a cell in the range contains a target value, another when it exceeds this target value, and third when it falls below the target value.

Here are the steps for setting up the rules to apply a yellow fill with a dark yellow font to cells in a range when they contain 100,000, a green fill with dark green text when they're greater than 100,000, and a light red fill with dark red text when they're less than 100,000:

1. **Select the range of cells in the worksheet to which the three conditional formatting rules are to be applied.**

   Start by defining the rule that applies yellow fill with dark yellow font to all values in the range that are equal to 100,000.

2. **Click the Conditional Formatting button on the Home tab and then click Highlight Cell Rules ⇨ Equal To from the drop-down menu.**

   Excel opens the Equal To dialog box, where you define the formatting rule when a cell contains 100,000.

3. **Type** 100,000 **in the Format Cells That Are EQUAL TO text box and then select Yellow Fill with Dark Yellow Text from the drop-down list box to the right before you click OK.**

   Next, you define the rule that applies green fill with dark green font to all values that are greater than 100,000.

4. **Click the Conditional Formatting button on the Home tab and then click Highlight Cell Rules ⇨ Greater Than from the drop-down menu.**

   Excel opens the Greater Than dialog box, where you define the formatting rule when a cell contains a value higher than 100,000.

5. **Type** 100,000 **in the Format Cells That Are GREATER THAN text box and then click Green Fill with Dark Green Text in the drop-down list box to the right before you click OK.**

   Finally, you define the rule that applies red fill with dark red font to all values that are less than 100,000.

6. **Click the Conditional Formatting button on the Home tab and then click Highlight Cell Rules ⇨ Less Than from the drop-down menu**

   Excel opens the Less Than dialog box, where you define the formatting rule when a cell contains a value below 100,000.

7. **Type** 100,000 **in the Format Cells That Are LESS THAN text box and then leave the default Light Red Fill with Dark Red Text selected in the drop-down list box to the right when you click OK.**

As you define the three rules, Excel applies them to the range selected in the worksheet. If the cell range is blank at the time you set up these three rules, all the blank cells in the range are given a red fill. As you enter values into the cells, their text takes on the color assigned to their values: dark red font for values below 100,000, dark yellow for all values of 100,000, and dark green for all values above

100,000. In addition, when the values are equal to 100,000, Excel fills the cell with a light yellow background color and when values are above 100,000, a light green background color.

Finally, here are the steps you'd follow to create a rule that formats all values in a cell range that are below the average value in the range with a custom conditional format that applies bold italic to the font and a bright yellow fill color:

1. **Select the range of cells in the worksheet to which this conditional formatting rule is to be applied.**

2. **Click the Conditional Formatting button on the Home tab and then click Top/Bottom Rules ⇨ Below Average from the drop-down menu.**

   Excel opens the Below Average dialog box that contains a single drop-down list box where you define the formatting to be used when a value is below the calculated average for the cell range.

3. **Select Custom Format at the bottom of the Format Cells That Are BELOW AVERAGE drop-down list box.**

   Excel opens the Format Cells dialog box where you define all the attributes to be part of the custom conditional formatting.

4. **Click the Font tab in the Format Cells dialog box and then click Bold Italic in the Font Style list box.**

5. **Click the Fill tab in the Format Cells dialog box and then click the bright yellow swatch in the Background Color section before you click OK.**

   Excel closes the Format Cells dialog box, returning you to the Below Average dialog box, which now displays Custom Format in the Format Cells That Are BELOW AVERAGE drop-down list box.

6. **Click OK to close the Below Average dialog box.**

Excel then applies the custom formatting of bold italic text with bright yellow fill color to all values in the cell selection that are below the calculated average (displayed after the Average heading on the status bar at the bottom of the Excel program window).

Highlighting duplicate values in a cell range

The Duplicate Values option on the Highlight Cell Rules continuation menu enables you to highlight duplicate values within a selected cell range.

To highlight duplicate values in a cell range, follow these steps:

1. **Select the range of cells in the worksheet where you want duplicates formatted in a special way.**

2. **Click the Conditional Formatting button in the Styles group of the Home tab of the Ribbon; then click Highlight Cell Rules ⇨ Duplicate Values from the drop-down menu.**

   Excel opens the Duplicate Values Columns dialog box containing two drop-down lists: the first where you indicate whether Excel is to format identical values (Duplicate, the default) in the range or the standalone values (Unique) in the range, and the second where you indicate the type of formatting applied to either the duplicates or one-of-a-kind values.

3. **Click the type of preset formatting (Red Fill with Dark Red Text, Yellow Fill with Dark Yellow Text, Green Fill with Dark Green Text, and so forth) or click the Custom Format option and select the custom formatting in the Format Cells dialog box.**

   If you define a custom format rather than select one of the preset formats, use the options on the Number, Font, Border, and Fill tabs of the Format Cells dialog box to designate all the formatting to be applied, and then click OK to close the Format Cells dialog box and return to the Compare Columns dialog box (where Custom Format appears in the third drop-down list box).

4. **Click OK to close the Duplicate Values dialog box.**

Excel then formats all the cells in the selected cell range whose values are exact duplicates with the conditional formatting you selected.

Creating your own conditional formatting rules

Although Excel 2019 gives you a ton of ready-made Highlight Cell Rules and Top/Bottom Rules to define, you may still find that you need to create your own rules for conditional formatting. To do this, you choose the New Rule option near the bottom of the Conditional Formatting button's drop-down menu or you click the New Rule button in the Conditional Formatting Rules Manager dialog box. (See the "Managing conditional formatting rules" section that immediately follows.)

Figure 2-23 shows you the New Formatting Rule dialog box as it first appears after clicking the New Rule option or button. To create a new conditional formatting rule, you first click the type of rule to create in the Select a Rule Type list box and then specify the criteria and define the formatting using the various options that appear in the Edit the Rule Description section below — note that these options vary greatly depending on the type of rule you click in the Select a Rule Type list box above.

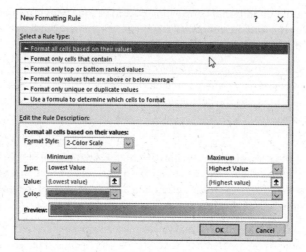

FIGURE 2-23:
Define a new conditional formatting rule using the options in the New Formatting Rule dialog box.

TIP

Select the Use a Formula to Determine Which Cells to Format rule type when you want to build a formula as the rule that determines when a particular type of conditional formatting is applied. Note that this formula can refer to cells outside the current cell selection to which the conditional formatting is applied, but it must be a logical formula, meaning that it uses comparison operators (see Book 3, Chapter 1) and/or Logical functions (see Book 3, Chapter 2) that when calculated return either a logical TRUE or FALSE value.

Managing conditional formatting rules

The Conditional Formatting Rules Manager dialog box, which you open by choosing the Manage Rules option at the very bottom of the Conditional Formatting button's drop-down menu, enables you to do all of the following:

» Create new rules by clicking the New Rule button to open the New Formatting Rule dialog box. (See the "Creating your own conditional formatting rules" section immediately preceding.)

» Edit existing rules by selecting the rule in the Rule list box and clicking the Edit Rule button in the Editing Formatting Rule dialog box (which looks just like the New Formatting Rule dialog box except it contains the rule type, criteria, and formatting for the particular rule you selected).

>> Delete rules by clicking the rule in the Rule list box and then clicking the Delete Rule button — click the Apply button to remove formatting from the worksheet that was applied to the rule you just deleted.

>> Change the order of precedence in which multiple conditional formatting rules assigned to the same cell selection or table are applied by promoting or demoting individual rules in the Rule list box by clicking the rules and then clicking either the Move Up button (with the thick arrow pointing upward) or Move Down button (with the thick arrow pointing downward) until the rules appear in the desired order of precedence.

TIP

By default, the Conditional Formatting Rules Manager dialog box shows all the rules assigned only to the current cell selection or table. To see all the conditional formatting rules in a particular worksheet or table, select its name from the Show Formatting Rules For drop-down list at the top of the dialog box.

REMEMBER

A rule that appears higher in the Rule list box of the Conditional Formatting Rules Manager dialog box has a higher precedence and is therefore applied before one lower in the list. When more than one rule is true, what happens depends on whether or not the formatting applied by those rules conflict. When they don't conflict (as when one rule formats the cells in bold italic and the other formats the cells with a light red fill), both formats are applied. However, when the formats conflict (as when one rule formats the cells with black fill and bright yellow text and the other formats the cells with yellow fill and black text), the rule with the higher precedence wins, and only its conditional formatting is applied.

Formatting Worksheets

Chapter **3**

Editing and Proofing Worksheets

reating a spreadsheet is seldom a one-time experience. In fact, some of the spreadsheets that you create with Excel require routine changes on a regular basis, whereas others require more radical changes only once in a while. Regardless of the extent of the changes and their frequency, you can be sure that sooner or later, most of the spreadsheets you create in Excel will require editing.

In this chapter, you find out how to make simple editing changes in a worksheet by modifying the contents of a cell as well as how to do more complex editing in your worksheets. These techniques include how to use the Undo and Redo features, zoom in and out on data, move and copy data, delete data entries and insert new ones, search and replace data entries, and proof the contents of the final worksheet.

However, before you can use any of these fine editing techniques, you have to open the workbook whose contents require editing. So, with that in mind, this chapter starts out by giving you the lowdown on finding and opening workbooks in Excel.

Opening a Workbook

One of the simplest ways to open a workbook for editing in Excel is to open its folder in Windows Explorer and then double-click the workbook file icon. If you haven't yet started Excel 2019 at the time you open the workbook, Windows automatically launches Excel at the same time that it opens the file.

REMEMBER

Keep in mind that Excel automatically saves workbook files in your Documents folder on your OneDrive unless you specifically select another folder or you save your workbooks locally on hard drive or network drive connected to your device. Under Windows 10, you can type the name of the workbook file in the Type Here to Search text box, or you can use Cortana to locate the file by saying to her "Find . . ." followed by the name of the workbook file.

If you can't remember where you saved the workbook that you need to edit (a common occurrence), you can browse for the workbook file from the Open screen or use the Search Documents text box in the Open dialog box to locate the file. See the "Finding misplaced workbooks" section later in this chapter for details.

Using the Open screen in the Backstage view

If Excel 2019 is already running and you want to open a workbook file for editing from within Excel, you can click File ⇨ Open or press Alt+FO or Ctrl+O to launch the Open screen in the Backstage view and locate and open the file.

When Excel displays the Open screen (similar to the one shown in Figure 3-1), the program selects Recent Workbooks under Places on the left, while listing recently opened workbook files on the right. If the workbook file you want to edit is listed there, you can open the file simply by clicking its name in the list. If the Excel file you want to edit is not in the list of workbooks but in one of the folders in which you routinely save your workbooks, click the Folders link to the immediate right of the Workbooks to switch to a list of folders from which you've recently retrieved workbooks. When you locate the folder with the file you need, double-click it and then double-click its file icon to open the workbook in Excel 2019.

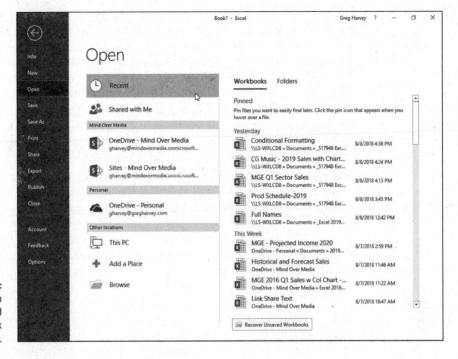

Editing and Proofing
Worksheets

FIGURE 3-1:
Use the Open
screen to find and
open a workbook
for editing.

If the workbook file is not among those in the Recent Workbooks list, you need to select its location under Places:

» **Shared with Me** to display a list of workbooks that your coworkers or clients have shared with you (see Book 4 Chapter 3 for more on sharing Excel workbooks)

» **OneDrive** to find a workbook saved in a folder online on your OneDrive

» **This PC** to find a workbook file saved in folder on a local drive, which includes your computer's hard drive or a network drive to which you have access or even a removable storage device connected to your computer or tablet PC

» **Add a Place** to a folder on your OneDrive or SharePoint website to the list of places in the Open screen for easy access

» **Browse** to open the Open dialog box where you can search for misplaced workbook files or open a folder not listed in the Open screen

REMEMBER

Keep in mind that if your company maintains a SharePoint Team website where you save Excel workbook files and you've added it as a place (with the Add a Place link), its name will also appear under the Places heading on the Excel Open screen. In Figure 3-1, for example, Mind Over Media is the name of my SharePoint Team site, and I select this link when I need to open a workbook saved on the website for editing.

Click the Recover Unsaved Workbook button at the bottom of the Open screen if you ever need to open an workbook that you inadvertently didn't save on one of your computer's local drives before you closed the file. Excel opens an Open dialog box showing the contents of an UnsavedFiles folder, containing a list of any workbook files that the program automatically saved there before closing the Excel program window. Unfortunately, the filenames in this list, as in Book1((Unsaved 30683148768452)), are pretty nondescript, and there are with no worksheet previews available (because the files never got saved, so no previews got created). This means that you need to rely on the date and time listed in the Date Modified column of the Open dialog box to help you identify the file you want to open for editing. When you click the filename of the unsaved file to open followed by the Open button, Excel opens it in the program window in Read Only mode with an alert appearing beneath the Ribbon indicating that this is a recovered file. You can then click the Save As button at the end of the alert text to open the Save As dialog box where you can properly name and save the file, thus enabling you to edit it contents.

As soon as you select the place containing your workbook file, the Excel Open screen displays links to all the folders you've recently visited. (See Figure 3-2.) You can click one of these links to select its folder and display its files in the Open dialog box that is then automatically displayed. If none of the recently visited folders hold the workbook you want to open, you can select the Browse button to peruse the folders and files on the selected location in the ensuing Open dialog box.

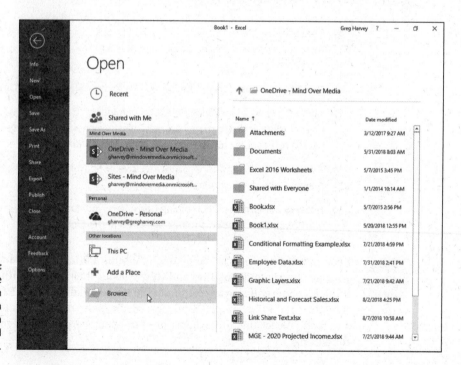

FIGURE 3-2:
Selecting the Browse button in the Excel Open screen to open a workbook saved on my OneDrive.

When the Open dialog box is displayed, the contents of the selected location or recently visited folder are listed in its main pane. (See Figure 3-3.) If you see the name of the workbook you want to edit in this list, click it, followed by the Open button (or double-click it) to open the workbook in Excel. To open a workbook in another folder, click its link in the left pane of the Open dialog box.

Show the Preview Pane

Directory Path List box   Change Your View

FIGURE 3-3:
Selecting the workbook file to open for editing in the Open dialog box.

Places pane   Folder and File List box   Open options

REMEMBER

If you open a new folder and it appears empty of all files (and you know that it's not an empty folder), this just means the folder doesn't contain any of the types of files that Excel can open directly, such as workbooks, template files, and macro sheets. To display all the files, whether or not Excel can open them directly (meaning without some sort of conversion), click the drop-down button that says All Excel Files and then select the All Files option at the top of its drop-down menu.

Note that you can change the way folder and file icons appear in the dialog box. To do so, use the slider attached to the Change Your View drop-down list button located on the right side of the toolbar at the top of the Open dialog box. When you select Large Icons or Extra Large Icons on this slider (or anywhere in between), the Excel workbook icons actually show data in the upper-left corner of the first worksheet. This applies to all Excel 2019 workbooks saved with the Save

Thumbnail check box selected and Excel 97 through 2003 workbooks saved with the Save Preview Picture check box on the Summary tab of the workbook's Properties dialog box selected. This preview of part of the first sheet helps you quickly identify the workbook you want to open for editing or printing.

TIP

If you're comfortable opening workbook files directly from the Open dialog box, you can completely bypass the Open screen by clicking the Don't Show the Backstage When Opening or Saving Files check box on the Save tab of the Excel Options dialog box (Alt+FTS) to select it. Just be aware that when you select this check box, Excel 2019 not only immediately displays the Open dialog box anytime you click the File⇨Open command to open a workbook file for editing but also displays the Save As dialog box anytime you click the File⇨Save option (or any of its equivalents) to save a new workbook file. This means that you must be comfortable in using the Save As dialog box to select the place to save a new file as you are in using the Open dialog box to select the place containing the file to edit.

Using the Open dialog box

The Open dialog box that appears after you select a folder in the Excel 2019 Open screen is divided into two sections: a Places pane on the left and a Folder and File list box on the right. (See Figure 3-3.)

When you can't find the filename you're looking for in the list box, check to make sure that you're looking in the right folder — because if you're not, you're never going to find the missing file. To tell which folder is currently open, check the Look In drop-down list box at the top of the Open dialog box.

The Directory Path list box displays the full path of the folder currently displayed in the Folder and File list box. If the folder that is currently open is not the one that has the workbook file you need to use, you then need to open the folder that does contain the file. To back up a level in the file path, click the Back button (with the left arrow) that appears to the left of the Look In list box that contains the complete pathname.

For example, say the path to the Excel 2019 folder within the Documents folder on my OneDrive is displayed in the Directory Path list box as

```
Greg Harvey⇨OneDrive⇨Excel 2019
```

However, I realize that the Excel workbook I want to open and edit is in the Examples 2019 folder on my OneDrive, and this folder is not within the Excel 2019 folder but back on the same level as this folder. To get back up a level to the Documents folder, I simply click the Back button one time (Alt+←) or the Up To button

(Alt+↑) to the immediate left of the Directory Path text. The Directory Path list box now contains the following pathname:

```
Greg ⟳ OneDrive
```

Below, in the center section of the Open dialog box (referred to as the Folders and Files list box), I now see the Examples 2019 folder displayed along with the Excel 2019 folder. To open the Examples 2019 folder and display the workbook files stored there in the Folders and Files list box, I simply click Examples 2019 followed by the Open button (or double-click the Samples folder icon).

If you realize the workbook file you want is on another drive entirely from the one currently displayed, use the buttons in the Places pane on the left side of the Open dialog box (normally Desktop or Documents under Quick Access, Microsoft Excel, OneDrive, This PC, and Network) to easily open any folders associated with these buttons that contain workbook files:

>> **Desktop:** Click this to display folders and folder and file shortcuts saved directly on the Windows desktop of your computing device.

>> **Documents:** Click this button to display folders and workbook files saved in the Personal folder on the Windows hard drive.

>> **Microsoft Excel**: Click this button to display any Excel-related files, such as Add-ins or templates saved in the folder containing the Excel 2019 program file

>> **OneDrive:** Click this button to display a list of folder and files online on your OneDrive.

>> **This PC:** Click this button to display a list of local and network drives as well as devices with removable storage that are connected with your computing device.

>> **Network:** Click this button to display a list of networked drives you've mapped on your computer.

REMEMBER

Keep in mind that you can click Preview from the Views button's drop-down menu. Doing so displays a preview pane on the right side of the Open dialog box. This dialog box shows data in the upper-left corner of the first worksheet for all Excel 2019 workbooks saved with the Save Thumbnail check box selected and all Excel 97 through 2003 workbooks saved with the Save Preview Picture check box on the Summary tab of the workbook's Properties dialog box selected. This preview of the first part of the initial worksheet can really help you quickly identify the workbook you want to open for editing or printing.

Opening more than one workbook at a time

If you know that you need to edit worksheets saved in multiple workbook files, you can open them all up in Excel at the same time by selecting all their files in the Folder and File List in the Open dialog box before you select the Open button.

REMEMBER

Remember that in order to select multiple files that appear sequentially in the Open dialog box, you click the first filename and then hold down the Shift key while you click the last filename. To select files that are not listed sequentially, you need to hold down the Ctrl key while you click the various filenames.

After the workbook files are open in Excel, you can then switch documents by selecting their filename buttons on the Windows taskbar or by using the Flip feature (Alt+Tab) to select the workbook's thumbnail. (See Book 2, Chapter 4 for more information on working on more than one worksheet at a time.)

Finding misplaced workbooks

Everything's hunky-dory as long as you correctly remember the folder containing the workbook file or files you need to edit. But what about those times when they seem to have mysteriously migrated and are now nowhere to be found? For those rare occasions, you simply use the Search Documents text box in the Open dialog box (see Figure 3-3) that enables you to search for missing notebooks right from within the dialog box.

To use this search feature to find a workbook, click the Search Documents text box in the upper-right corner of the Open dialog box and then begin typing search characters used in the workbook's filename or contained in the workbook itself.

As Windows finds any matches for the characters you type, the names of the workbook files (and other Excel files such as templates and macro sheets as well) appear in the Open dialog box. As soon as the workbook you want to open is listed, you can open it by clicking its icon and filename followed by the Open button or by double-clicking it.

Using the other Open options

The drop-down menu attached to the Open button in the Open dialog box enables you to open the selected workbook file(s) in special ways. These ways include

>> **Open Read-Only:** Opens the files you select in the Open dialog box's list box in a read-only state, which means that you can look but you can't touch. (Actually,

you can touch; you just can't save your changes.) To save changes in a read-only file, you must use the File ⇨ Save As command from the Excel menu bar and give the workbook file a new filename.

>> **Open as Copy:** Opens a copy of the files you select in the Open dialog box. Use this method of file opening as a safety net: If you mess up the copies, you always have the originals to fall back on.

>> **Open in Browser:** Opens workbook files you save as web pages in your favorite web browser (which would normally be Microsoft Internet Explorer). Note that this command is not available unless the program identifies that the selected file or files were saved as web pages rather than plain, old Excel worksheet files.

>> **Open in Protected View:** Opens the selected workbook in Protected View, which prevents you from making any editing changes to its worksheets until you click the Enable Editing button that appears in the red Protected View panel at the top of the worksheet area.

>> **Open and Repair:** Attempts to repair corrupted workbook files before opening them in Excel. When you select this command, a dialog box appears, giving you a choice between attempting to repair the corrupted file or opening the recovered version, extracting the data out of the corrupted file, and placing it in a new workbook (which you can save with the Save command). Click the Repair button to attempt to recover and open the file. Click the Extract Data button if you previously tried unsuccessfully to have Excel repair the file.

>> **Show Previous Versions:** Displays a list of various versions of the workbook file automatically saved by Excel's AutoRecover feature and given filenames that describe when the file and under what circumstances the version was saved.

Cell Editing 101

The biggest thing to remember about basic cell editing is that you have to put the cell pointer (also known as the cell cursor) in the cell whose contents you want to modify. When modifying a cell's contents, you can replace the entry entirely, delete characters from the entry, and/or insert new characters into the entry:

>> **To replace a cell's contents,** position the cell pointer in the cell and just start inputting your new entry over it. (Remember you can do this by typing from the keyboard or on a touchscreen, writing it by hand using the Windows Inking virtual keyboard.) The moment you start inputting the new entry, the

first characters that are input entirely replace the existing data entry. To finish replacing the original entry, complete the new cell entry by using whatever technique you like (such as pressing an arrow key or Enter or clicking the Enter button on the Formula bar). To abort the replacement and restore the original cell entry, click the Cancel button on the Formula bar or press the Escape key on your keyboard.

>> **To delete characters in a cell entry,** click the insertion point in the entry on the Formula bar, press F2, or double-click the mouse in the cell to get Excel into Edit mode (indicated by EDIT on the status bar). Then, use the Home, End, or ← and → keys to move the insertion point to a proper place in the entry and use the Backspace and Delete keys to remove unnecessary or incorrect characters. (Backspace deletes characters to the left of the insertion point, and Delete removes characters to the right of the insertion point.)

>> **To insert new characters in a cell entry,** click the insertion point in the entry on the Formula bar, press F2, or double-click the mouse in the cell to get Excel into Edit mode (indicated by EDIT on the status bar). Then, use the Home, End, or ← and → keys to move the insertion point to the place in the entry where the new characters are needed and start inputting the new characters. Excel automatically inserts the new characters at the insertion point, thus pushing existing text to the right. If Excel replaces existing characters instead, you need to press the Insert key to get out of overtype mode (in which the new characters you input eat up the existing ones on the right) before you start inputting.

When you edit the contents of a cell by inserting and/or deleting characters in it, you need to remember to click the Enter button on the Formula bar or press the Enter key to complete the editing change and switch the program from Edit back to Ready mode (indicated by the reappearance of READY on the status bar). If you're editing a cell with a simple text or number entry, you can also do this by clicking the mouse pointer in another cell to make it current. (This doesn't work, however, when you're editing a formula because Excel just includes the address of the cell that you click as part of the edited formula.) Also, you can't use any of the keystrokes that normally complete a new cell entry except for the Tab and Shift+Tab keystrokes for moving to the next and previous columns in the worksheet. (All the rest, including the arrow keys, Home, and End, just move the insertion point within the cell entry.)

Undo and Redo

Excel supports multiple levels of undo that you can use to recover from potentially costly editing mistakes that would require data re-entry or extensive repair operations. The most important thing to remember about the Undo command is that it is cumulative, meaning that you may have to select it multiple times to reverse several actions that you've taken before you get to the one that sets your spreadsheet right again.

You can select the Undo command either by clicking the Undo button on the Quick Access toolbar or by pressing Alt+Backspace or Ctrl+Z. Excel will then reverse the effect of the last edit you made in the worksheet. For example, if you edit a cell entry and erase some of its text in error, clicking Undo restores the characters that you just erased to the entry. Likewise, if you delete a group of cells by mistake, clicking Undo restores both their contents and formatting to the worksheet.

On the Quick Access toolbar, you can click the drop-down button attached to the Undo command button to display a brief menu of the actions that you've recently taken in the spreadsheet. Instead of undoing one action at a time, you undo multiple actions by dragging through them in the drop-down menu. As soon as you release the mouse button, Excel then restores the spreadsheet to the state that it was in before you took all the actions that you chose from this drop-down menu.

When you make an editing change in a spreadsheet, the Undo item on the Undo button's drop-down menu actually changes to reflect the action that you just took. For example, if you delete a group of cells by pressing the Delete key and then open the Undo button's drop-down menu, the first item on the Undo menu appears as follows:

```
Clear
```

If you then apply new formatting to a cell selection, such as assigning a new center alignment, and then open the Undo drop-down menu, the first item on the Undo menu now appears as follows:

```
Center Alignment
```

WARNING

The Undo feature works by storing a "snapshot" of the worksheet in the memory of your computer at each stage in its editing. Sometimes, if you attempt a large-scale edit in a worksheet, Excel will determine that sufficient free memory doesn't exist to hold a snapshot of the worksheet in its current state and complete the planned editing change as well. For example, this can happen if you try to cut and paste a really large range in a big worksheet. In such a case, Excel displays an Alert dialog box that indicates a lack of enough memory and asks whether you want to continue without Undo. If you then select the Yes option, Excel completes the planned edit but without the possibility of you being able to reverse its effects with Undo. Before you take such an action, consider how much time and effort would be required to manually restore the worksheet to its previous state if you make a mistake in carrying out your editing change.

After you use the Undo feature to reverse an editing change, the Redo button on the Quick Access toolbar becomes active. The Redo command item on the Redo button's drop-down menu has the name of the latest type of editing that you just reversed with the Undo button, such as Redo Clear when the last action you took was to restore a cell entry that you just deleted.

You use the Redo command to restore the worksheet to the condition that it was in before you last clicked the Undo command. As with using the Undo button on the Quick Access toolbar, when you click the drop-down button attached to the Redo button, you can drag through a series of actions that you want repeated (assuming that you used the Undo command multiple times). You can also restore edits that you've undone one at a time by pressing Ctrl+Y.

TIP

You can use Undo and Redo to toggle between a Before and After view of your spreadsheet. For example, suppose that you update an entry in a cell that was used in formulas throughout a data table. As soon as you enter the new number in this cell, Excel recalculates the table and displays the new results. To once again view the original version of the table before you make this latest change, you use Undo (Ctrl+Z). After checking some values in the original table, you then restore the latest change to its numbers by clicking the Redo command (Ctrl+Y). You can then continue in this manner as long as you want, switching between Before and After versions by holding down the Ctrl key as you type Z and then type Y, alternating between Undo and then Redo.

TIP

EDITING IN THE CELL VERSUS ON THE FORMULA BAR

When doing simple editing to a cell's contents, the question arises as to whether it's better to edit the contents in the cell directly or edit the contents on the Formula bar. When editing short entries that fit entirely within the current column width, it really is a matter of personal choice. Some people prefer editing on the Formula bar because it's out of the way of other cells in the same region of the worksheet. Other people prefer editing on the Formula bar because they find it easier to click the insertion point with the I-beam mouse pointer at precisely the place in the entry that needs editing. (When you press F2 to edit in the cell, Excel always positions the insertion point at the very end of the entry, and when you double-click the thick white mouse pointer in the cell, you really can't tell exactly where you're putting the insertion point until you finish double-clicking, at which time you see the flashing insertion point.)

When it comes to editing longer cell entries (that is, text entries that spill over into empty neighboring cells, and numbers that, if their digits weren't truncated by the number format assigned, wouldn't fit within the current cell width), you probably will want to edit their contents on the Formula bar. You can click the Formula Bar button (the carat symbol turned downward) to display the entire contents of the cell without obscuring any of the cells of the worksheet.

Get that out of here!

Sometimes you need to delete an entry that you made in a cell of the spreadsheet without replacing it with any other contents. Excel refers to this kind of deletion as *clearing* the cell. This is actually more correct than referring to it as "emptying" the cell because although the cell may appear empty when you delete its contents, it may still retain the formatting assigned to it, and therefore it will not truly be empty.

For this reason, clicking the Clear button (the one with the eraser icon) in the Editing group on the far right of the Home tab (or pressing Alt+HE) opens a drop-down menu with these options:

>> **Clear All:** Use this to get rid of both the contents and the formatting assigned to the current cell selection.

>> **Clear Formats:** Use this to get rid of just the formatting assigned to the current cell selection without getting rid of the contents.

>> **Clear Contents:** Use this to get rid of just the contents in the current cell selection without getting rid of the formatting assigned to it. (This is the equivalent of pressing the Delete key.)

>> **Clear Comments:** Use this to get rid of just the comments assigned to the cells in the selection without touching either the contents or the formatting.

>> **Clear Hyperlinks:** Use this to remove hyperlinks from the cells in the selection without also removing their formatting.

>> **Remove Hyperlinks**: Use this to remove only the hyperlink from the cells without affecting the contents or the formatting.

The Clear All option is great when you need to truly empty a cell of all formatting and contents while at the same time retaining that empty cell in the worksheet. However, what about when you need to get rid of the cell as well as all its contents? For example, suppose that you entered a column of numbers that you've totaled with a summing formula only to discover that midway in the list, you entered the same number twice, in one cell above the other. You don't want to just delete the duplicate number in one of the two cells, thus leaving a single empty cell in the middle of your list of values. Having an empty cell in the middle of the list won't skew the total, but it won't look professional!

In this case, you want to delete both the duplicate entry and remove the newly emptied cell while at the same time pulling up the cells with the rest of the numbers in the list below along with the cell at the end that contains the formula that sums the values together. Excel offers just such a command on the Home tab in the form of the Delete button and its drop-down menu. When you click Delete

Cells from the Delete button's drop-down menu (or press Alt+HDD), a Delete dialog box appears, similar to the one shown in Figure 3-4. This dialog box lets you choose how you want the remaining cells to be shifted when the selected cell (or cells) is removed from the worksheet.

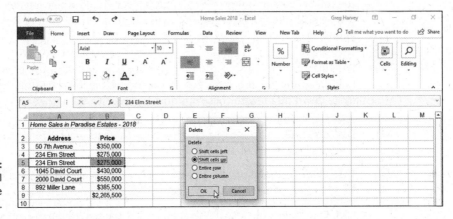

FIGURE 3-4:
Deleting a cell with a duplicate entry.

REMEMBER

Keep in mind that when you use the Delete Cells option, Excel zaps everything, including the contents, formatting, and any and all attached comments. Don't forget about the Undo button on the Quick Access toolbar or Ctrl+Z in case you ever zap something you shouldn't have!

Figures 3-4 and 3-5 illustrate how Delete works in the example where a duplicate entry has been mistakenly entered in a column of numbers that is totaled by a summing formula. In Figure 3-4, I selected cells A5:B5, which contain duplicate entries, before clicking the Delete button's drop-down button and then clicking Delete Cells from its drop-down menu to display the Delete dialog box.

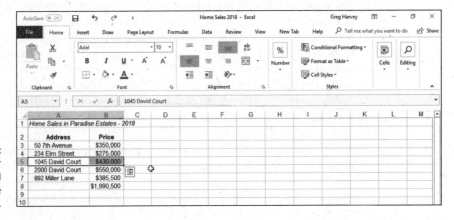

FIGURE 3-5:
Worksheet after deleting the cell with the duplicate entry.

As this figure shows, when the Delete dialog box opens, the Shift Cells Up option button is automatically selected. Figure 3-5 shows the same worksheet after clicking the OK button in the Delete dialog box. Notice how Excel pulled up the entries in the cells below when it deleted the duplicate in cell B5, while at the same time automatically recalculating the summing formula to reflect the total of the remaining entries.

WARNING

Don't confuse the use of the Delete key and the Delete Cells command. When you press the Delete key, Excel automatically deletes just the contents of the cells that are selected (keeping whatever formatting is used intact), leaving seemingly blank cells in the worksheet. When you click Delete Cells from the Delete button's drop-down menu, Excel displays the Delete dialog box, which deletes the selected cells and then shifts the remaining cells in the direction that you designate (up or to the left) to fill in what would otherwise be blank cells.

TIP

If you know that you want to use the Shift Cells Up option when deleting the current cell selection, you don't have to bother with opening the Delete dialog box at all: Simply click the Delete button (rather than its drop-down button), and Excel instantly deletes the selection and pulls all remaining cells up.

Can I just squeeze this in here?

The Insert command button in the Editing group of the Ribbon's Home tab is set very much like the Delete button immediately below it. You click the Insert button's drop-down button and then its Insert Cells option (or press Alt+HII) to open an Insert dialog box, where you indicate how Excel is to deal with existing cell entries in order to accommodate the blank cells you need to squeeze in.

For example, suppose that you discover that you've left out three numbers from a column of summed numbers and that these values should have appeared in the middle of the column. To make this edit, position the cell cursor in the first cell of those cells whose values need to be shifted down to make room for the three missing entries and then drag the cell cursor down two rows so that you have selected the three cells with entries that you want to retain but also need to have moved down.

Figures 3-6 and 3-7 illustrate this situation. In Figure 3-6, I selected the cell range A5:B7, where cells for the six missing entries are to be inserted. I then clicked the drop-down button on the Insert button followed by Insert Cells on its drop-down menu. This action opened the Insert dialog box with the Shift Cells Right option button selected. Because I needed to have the cells in the selected range moved down to make room for the missing entries, I then simply selected the Shift Cells Down option before clicking OK.

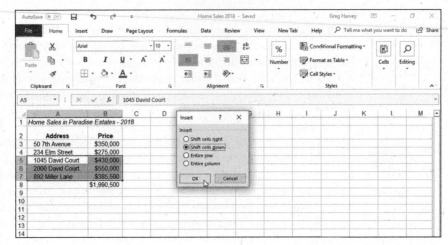

FIGURE 3-6:
Inserting six blank cells for missing entries in two columns of a table while shifting the existing entries down.

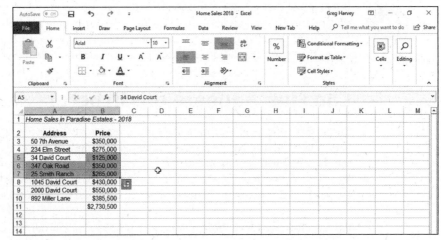

FIGURE 3-7:
The worksheet table after entering the missing entries in the newly inserted blank cells.

After clicking OK in the Insert dialog box, Excel moves down the existing entries as follows:

>> 2000 David Court and $550,000 previously in cells A5 and B5 to A8 and B8, respectively

>> 892 Miller Lane and $385,500 previously in cells A6 and B6 to A9 and B9; respectively

>> The total of $1,560,500 previously in cell B7 to B10.

This leaves the previously occupied range A5:B7 with six blank cells, where I can enter the following values:

>> 34 6th Avenue and $125,000 in new blank cells A5 and B5, respectively

>> 347 Oak Road and $350,000 in new blank cells A6 and B6, respectively

>> 25 Smith Ranch and $285,000 in new blank cells A7 and B7, respectively

As you can see, the sum formula in the last cell in this column, cell B10, has automatically been recalculated so that the total reflects the addition of the missing values that I entered in the newly inserted cells.

TIP

If you know that you want to move existing cells down with the Shift Cells Down option when inserting new cells in the current cell selection, you don't have to bother with opening the Insert dialog box at all: Simply click the Insert button (rather than its drop-down button), and Excel instantly inserts new cells while moving the existing ones down.

A Spreadsheet with a View

The biggest problem with editing is finding and getting to the place in the worksheet that needs modification and then keeping your place in the worksheet as you make the changes. This problem is exacerbated by the fact that you probably often work with really large spreadsheets, only a small portion of which can be displayed at any one time on your screen.

Excel provides a number of features that can help you find your way and keep your place in the spreadsheet that needs editing. Among these are its Zoom feature, which enables you to increase or decrease the magnification of the worksheet window, thus making it possible to switch from a really up-close view to a really far-away view in seconds, and its Freeze Panes feature, which enables you to keep pertinent information, such as column and row headings, on the worksheet window as you scroll other columns and rows of data into view.

"Zoom, zoom, zoom"

Excel 2019 makes it really easy to see more data in the active worksheet window with its Zoom slider feature on the Status bar in the lower-right corner of the window. The Zoom slider contains two buttons on either end: a Zoom Out button on the left side that reduces the Worksheet area's magnification percentage by 10 percent each time you click it and a Zoom In button on the right side that increases the Worksheet area's magnification percentage by 10 percent each time you click it. You can also quickly change the Worksheet area's magnification percentage (and thus zoom out and in on the data) by dragging the slider's button to the left or right.

Note that the Zoom slider button is always located in the very center of the Zoom slider, putting the Worksheet area magnification at 100% (the normal screen, depending upon your computer monitor's screen resolution) when you first open the worksheet. As you click the Zoom Out or Zoom In button or drag the slider button, Excel keeps you informed of the current magnification percentage by displaying it to the immediate left of the Zoom Out button on the status bar. Note too, that 10% is the lowest percentage you can select by dragging the button all the way to the left on the slider, and 400% is the highest percentage you can select by dragging the button all the way to the right.

On a touchscreen device, you can use your fingers to zoom in and out on a worksheet. Simply stretch your forefinger and thumb out to zoom in on the cells and pinch them together to zoom out. As you do, the Zoom slider on the Status bar shows you the currently selected zoom percentage and moves the slider right or left to follow your stretch or pinch gesture.

Although the Zoom slider is always available on the Status bar in any worksheet you have open, you can change the Worksheet area's magnification percentage by clicking the Zoom button on the Ribbon's View tab or by pressing Alt+WQ. Doing this opens the Zoom dialog box, where you can select preset magnification percentages 200%, 100%, 75%, 50%, and 25% by clicking its option button before you click OK. In addition, you may enter any magnification percentage between a minimum of 10% and a maximum of 400% by clicking its Custom options button and entering the percentage in its text box before you click OK.

You can also have Excel change the magnification to suit the cell range that you've selected. To do this, select your cell range, click the Zoom to Selection button on the View tab, or press Alt+WG. Note that you can also do this same thing by clicking the Fit Selection option button when the Zoom dialog box is open before you click OK.

If the device you're running Excel 2019 on is equipped with a physical mouse with a wheel in between the two mouse buttons (sometimes referred to as an IntelliMouse), you can set it up in Excel so that rolling the wheel back and forth zooms out and in on the current worksheet. To do this, click the Zoom on Roll with IntelliMouse check box in the Editing Options section of the Advanced tab of the Excel Options dialog box (File ⇨ Options ⇨ Advanced or Alt+FTA). After you select this check box, instead of scrolling up the rows of the worksheet, rolling the wheel forward increases the magnification (by 15% until you reach the maximum 400%). Instead of scrolling down the rows of the sheet, rolling the wheel backward decreases the magnification (by 15% until you reach the minimum 10% value).

Figures 3-8 and 3-9 illustrate how you can use the Zoom feature to first zoom out to locate a region in a large spreadsheet that needs editing and then zoom in on the region to do the editing. In Figure 3-8, I zoomed out on the Income Analysis to display all its data by selecting a 50% magnification setting. (I actually did this by dragging the Zoom slider button to the left until 50% appeared on the status bar to the left of the Zoom Out button.) At the 50% setting, I could just barely make out the headings and read the numbers in the cells. I then located the cells that needed editing and selected their cell range (J20:L25) in the worksheet.

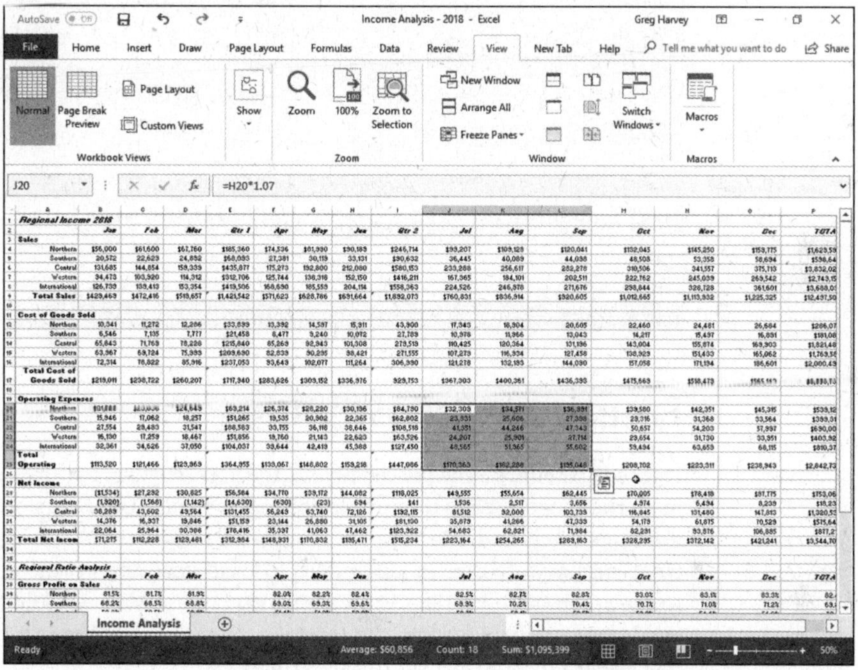

FIGURE 3-8:
The Income Analysis worksheet after zooming out to a 50% magnification setting.

After selecting the range of cells to be edited, I then clicked the Zoom to Selection command button on the View tab. You can see the result in Figure 3-9. As you can see on the Status bar, Excel boosted the magnification from 50% up to 371% the moment I clicked the Zoom to Selection button: a comfortable size for editing these cells on even one of the smaller computer monitors.

TIP

Because Excel immediately puts the slider button at whatever point you click, you can instantly return the magnification percentage to the normal 100% after selecting any other magnification. Simply click the line at the midpoint in the Zoom slider on the Status bar.

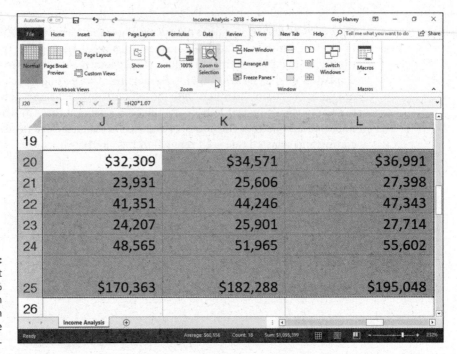

FIGURE 3-9:
Worksheet at 232% magnification after zooming in on the cell range J20:L25.

Freezing window panes

Figure 3-9 could be the poster boy for the Freeze Panes feature. Although zooming in on the range of cells that needs editing has made their data entries easy to read, it has also removed all the column and row headings that give you any clue as to what kind of data you're looking at. If I had used the Freeze Panes command to freeze column A with the row headings and row 2 with the column headings, they would remain displayed on the screen — regardless of the magnification settings that I select or how I scroll through the cells.

To use the Freeze Panes feature in this manner, you first position the cell pointer in the cell that's located to the immediate right of the column or columns that you want to freeze and immediately beneath the row or rows that you want to freeze before you click the Freeze Panes button on the Ribbon's View tab followed by Freeze Panes on the button's drop-down menu. (You can also do this by pressing Alt+WF and pressing the Enter key to click the Freeze Pane option from the drop-down menu.)

TIP

To freeze the top row of the worksheet (assuming that it contains column headings) from anywhere in the worksheet (it doesn't matter where the cell cursor is), click the Freeze Top Row option from the Freeze Panes button's drop-down menu. If you want to freeze the first column (assuming that it contains row headings) from anywhere in the worksheet, click the Freeze First Column option from the Freeze Panes button's drop-down menu instead.

Figures 3-10 and 3-11 illustrate how this works. Figure 3-10 shows the Income Analysis spreadsheet after freezing column A and rows 1 and 2. To do this, I positioned the cell cursor in cell B3 before choosing Freeze Panes from the Freeze Panes button's drop-down menu. Notice the thin black line that runs down column A and across row 2, marking which column and rows of the worksheet are frozen on the display and that will now remain in view — regardless of how far you scroll to the right to new columns or scroll down to new rows.

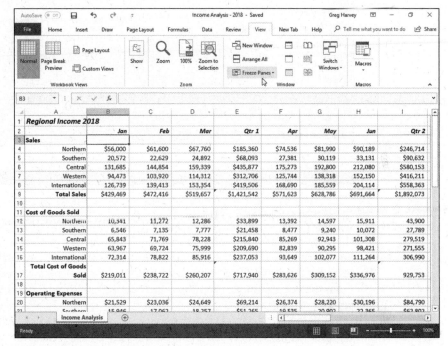

FIGURE 3-10:
The income worksheet after freezing column A and rows 1:2 in the worksheet display.

As Figure 3-11 shows, frozen panes stay on the screen even when you zoom in and out on the worksheet. For Figure 3-11, I repeated the steps I took in changing the magnification for Figures 3-8 and 3-9 (only this time with the frozen panes in place). First, I zoomed out on the Income Analysis spreadsheet by dialing the 50% magnification setting on the Zoom slider; second, I selected the range J20:L25 and then clicked the Zoom to Selection button on the View tab.

Figure 3-11 shows the result. Note that with the frozen panes in place, this time Excel only selected a 276% magnification setting instead of the original 371% setting. This lower magnification setting is worth it because of all the important information that has been added to the cell range.

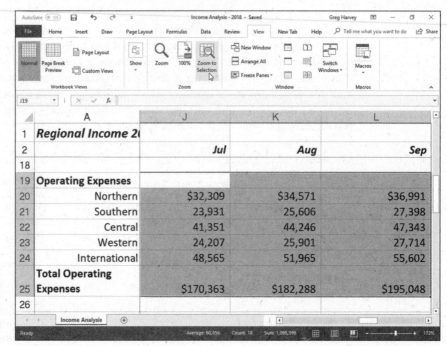

	A	J	K	L
1	**Regional Income 2(**			
2		*Jul*	*Aug*	*Sep*
18				
19	**Operating Expenses**			
20	Northern	$32,309	$34,571	$36,991
21	Southern	23,931	25,606	27,398
22	Central	41,351	44,246	47,343
23	Western	24,207	25,901	27,714
24	International	48,565	51,965	55,602
25	**Total Operating Expenses**	$170,363	$182,288	$195,048
26				

FIGURE 3-11:
The income worksheet after zooming in on the cell range J20:L25 after freezing panes.

TIP

When you press the Ctrl+Home shortcut key after you've frozen panes in a worksheet, instead of positioning the cell cursor in cell A1 as normal, Excel positions the cell cursor in the first unfrozen cell. In the example illustrated in Figure 3-10, pressing Ctrl+Home from anywhere in the worksheet puts the cell cursor in B3. From there, you can position the cell cursor in A1 either by clicking the cell or by pressing the arrow keys.

To unfreeze the panes after you've finished editing, click the Unfreeze Panes option on the Freeze Panes button's drop-down menu. (This option replaces Freeze Panes at the top of the menu.)

REMEMBER

Freeze Panes in the worksheet display have a parallel feature when printing a spreadsheet called Print Titles. When you use Print Titles in a report, the columns and rows that you define as the titles are printed at the top and to the left of all data on each page of the report. (See Book 2, Chapter 5 for details.)

Saving custom views

In the course of creating and editing a worksheet, you may find that you need to modify the worksheet display many times as you work with the document. For example, you may find at some point that you need to reduce the magnification of the worksheet display to 75% magnification. At another point, you may need to return to 100% magnification and hide different columns in the worksheet. At some later point, you may have to redisplay the hidden columns and then freeze panes in the worksheet.

Excel's Custom Views feature enables you to save any of these types of changes to the worksheet display. This way, instead of taking the time to manually set up the worksheet display that you want, you can have Excel re-create it for you simply by selecting the view. When you create a view, Excel can save any of the following settings: the current cell selection, print settings (including different page setups), column widths and row heights (including hidden columns), display settings on the Advanced tab of the Excel Options dialog box, as well as the current position and size of the document window and the window pane arrangement (including frozen panes).

To create a custom view of your worksheet, follow these steps:

1. **Make all the necessary changes to the worksheet display so that the worksheet window appears exactly as you want it to appear each time you select the view. Also select all the print settings on the Page Layout tab that you want used in printing the view. (See Book 2, Chapter 5 for details.)**

2. **Click the Custom Views command button in the Workbook Views group at the beginning of the View tab or press Alt+WC.**

   This action opens the Custom Views dialog box, similar to the one shown in Figure 3-12, where you add the view that you've just set up in the worksheet.

3. **Click the Add button.**

   This action opens the Add View dialog box, where you type a name for your new view.

4. **Enter a unique descriptive name for your view in the Name text box.**

   Make sure that the name you give the view reflects all its pertinent settings.

5. **To include print settings and hidden columns and rows in your view, leave the Print Settings and Hidden Rows, Columns and Filter Settings check boxes selected when you click the OK button. If you don't want to include these settings, clear the check mark from either one or both of these check boxes before you click OK.**

   When you click OK, Excel closes the Custom Views dialog box. When you next open this dialog box, the name of your new view appears in the Views list box.

6. Click the Close button to close the Custom Views dialog box.

Custom views are saved as part of the workbook file. To be able to use them whenever you open the spreadsheet for editing, you need to save the workbook with the new view.

7. Click the Save button on the Quick Access toolbar or press Ctrl+S to save the new view as part of the workbook file.

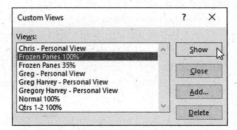

After you create your views, you can display the worksheet in that view at any time while working with the spreadsheet. To display a view, follow these steps:

1. Click the Custom Views command button in the Workbook Views group on the View tab or press Alt+WC.

2. Double-click the name of the view that you want to use in displaying your worksheet in the Views list box or click the name and then click the Show button.

TIP

Always start by defining a Normal 100% view in the Custom Views dialog box that represents the standard view of the worksheet before you go about defining custom views that hide columns, freeze panes, and mess with the worksheet's magnification. This way, you can recover from a special view (especially one that you only use in printing part of the spreadsheet but never use when editing it) simply by double-clicking Normal 100% in the Views list box of the Custom Views dialog box.

Copying and Moving Stuff Around

Moving and copying worksheet data are among the most common editing tasks that you perform when editing a typical spreadsheet. Excel offers two basic methods for moving and copying a cell selection in a worksheet: First, you can use drag-and-drop to drag the cells to a new location, or second, you can cut or copy the contents to the Clipboard and then paste them into the desired area. Moving and copying data to new areas in a spreadsheet are basically very straightforward procedures. You need to keep a few things in mind, however, when rearranging cell entries in a worksheet:

>> When you move or copy a cell, Excel moves everything in the cell, including the contents, formatting, and any comment assigned to the cell. (See Book 4, Chapter 3, for information on adding comments to cells.)

>> If you move or copy a cell so that it overlays an existing entry, Excel replaces the existing entry with the contents and formatting of the cell that you're moving or copying. This means that you can replace existing data in a range without having to clear the range before moving or copying the replacement entries. It also means that you must be careful not to overlay any part of an existing range that you don't want replaced with the relocated or copied cell entries.

>> When you move cells referred to in formulas in a worksheet, Excel automatically adjusts the cell references in the formulas to reflect their new locations in the worksheet.

>> When you copy formulas that contain cell references, Excel automatically adjusts the cell references in the copies relative to the change in their position in the worksheet. (See Book 3, Chapter 1 for details on copying formulas in a spreadsheet.)

REMEMBER

For situations in which you need to copy only a single data entry to cells in a single row or to cells in a single column of the worksheet, keep in mind that you can use AutoFill to extend the selection left or right or up or down by dragging the Fill handle. (See Book 2, Chapter 1 for information about using AutoFill to extend and copy a cell entry.)

Doing it with drag-and-drop

Drag-and-drop provides the most direct way to move or copy a range of cells in a single worksheet. To move a range, simply select the cells, position the pointer on any one of the edges of the range, and then drag the range to its new position in the worksheet and release the mouse button.

REMEMBER

Note that it can be a real drag to use drag-and-drop to copy or move a cell selection when the first cell of the range into which the cells are being copied or moved is far away in an unseen part of the Excel worksheet area. To make it easier, set up windows in the Excel worksheet area that display both the cells that you're moving or copying and the cells into which they're being moved or copied. (See Book 2, Chapter 4 for information on setting up windows that enable this.) Use the cut-and-paste method (as described in the later section, "Carried away with cut-and-paste") to move and copy cell selections beyond the current worksheet when you don't have such windows set up.

TIP

You can use drag-and-drop with a stylus on your touchscreen device if it's so equipped. If you're using your finger, however, you must tap the cell selection and then use the Cut or Copy option followed by the Paste option on the mini-toolbar that appears (see "Carried away with cut-and-paste," later in this chapter).

When you use drag-and-drop with a stylus, Excel displays a pop-up menu when you release the rectangular outline indicating where the range is to be moved or copied in a new area of the worksheet by removing the stylus' pointer from the touchscreen. You then select between the Move Here and Copy Here options on this pop-up menu to complete the move or copy operation.

Moving cells with drag-and-drop

The only thing that you need to be mindful of when using drag-and-drop is that you must position the mouse (or stylus) pointer on one of the edges of the cell range and *wait* until the pointer's cursor changes shape from a thick white cross to an outlined arrowhead pointing to the center of a black cross, before you begin dragging the range to its new position in the worksheet. Also, when positioning the pointer on an edge of the range, avoid the lower-right corner because locating the pointer there transforms it into the Fill handle (a simple black cross) used by the AutoFill feature to extend the cell range rather than move the range.

As you drag a cell range using drag-and-drop, Excel displays only the outline of the range with a ScreenTip that keeps you informed of its new cell or range address. After you've positioned the outline of the selected range so that the outline surrounds the appropriate cells in a new area of the worksheet, simply release the mouse button or your finger or stylus from the touchscreen. Excel moves the selected cells (including the entries, formatting, and comments) to this area.

If the outline of the cell selection that you're dropping encloses any cells with existing data entries, Excel displays an Alert dialog box asking whether you want to replace the contents of the destination cells. If you click OK in this dialog box, the overlaid data entries are completely zapped when they're replaced by the incoming entries.

Copying cells with drag-and-drop

You can use drag-and-drop to copy cell ranges as well as to move them. To modify drag-and-drop so that the feature copies the selected cells rather than relocating them, hold down the Ctrl key when you position the mouse pointer on one of the edges of the selected range. Excel indicates that drag-and-drop is ready to copy rather than move the cell selection by changing the mouse pointer to an outline pointer with a small plus sign in the upper-right. When the pointer assumes this shape, you simply drag the outline of the selected cell range to the desired position and release both the Ctrl key and mouse button.

Carried away with cut-and-paste

Given the convenience of using drag-and-drop, you may still prefer to use the more traditional cut-and-paste method when moving or copying cells in a worksheet. This is especially true when running Excel 2019 on a touchscreen device that doesn't have access to a mouse. Cut-and-paste uses the Clipboard (a special area of memory shared by all Windows programs), which provides a temporary storage area for the data in your cell selection until you paste the selection into its new position in the worksheet.

To move a cell selection, click the Cut command button (the one with the scissors icon) in the Clipboard group at the beginning of the Ribbon's Home tab (or press the shortcuts, Alt+HX, Ctrl+X, or Shift+Delete). To copy the selection, click the Copy command button (with the two sheets of paper side by side immediately beneath the Cut button) on the Home tab (or press the shortcuts, Alt+HC, Ctrl+C, or Ctrl+Insert).

When you cut or copy a selection to the Clipboard, Excel displays a marquee around the cell selection (sometimes called *marching ants*), and the following message appears on the status bar:

```
Select destination and press ENTER or choose Paste
```

To complete the move or copy operation, simply select the first cell in the range where you want the relocated or copied selection to appear and then press the Enter key, click the Paste button on the Home tab, or press the shortcuts Alt+HV, Ctrl+V, or Shift+Insert. Excel then completes the move or copy operation, pasting the range as required, starting with the active cell. When selecting the first cell of a paste range, be sure that you have sufficient blank cells below and to the right of the active cell so that the range you're pasting doesn't overlay any existing data that you don't want Excel to replace.

WARNING

Unlike when moving and copying a cell selection with drag-and-drop, the cut-and-paste method doesn't warn you when it's about to replace existing cell entries in cells that are overlaid by the incoming cell range — it just goes ahead and replaces them with nary a beep or an alert! If you find that you moved the selection to the wrong area or replaced cells in error, immediately click the Undo button on the Quick Access toolbar or press Ctrl+Z to restore the range to its previous position in the worksheet.

"Paste it again, Sam"

When you complete a copy operation with cut-and-paste by clicking the Paste button in the Clipboard group at the beginning of the Ribbon's Home tab instead of pressing the Enter key, Excel copies the selected cell range to the paste area in the worksheet without removing the marquee from the original range. You can continue to paste the selection to other areas in the worksheet without having to open the Clipboard task pane to recopy the cell range to the Clipboard. If you don't need to paste the cell range in any other place in the worksheet, you can press Enter to complete the copy operation. If you don't need to make further copies after using the Paste command, you can remove the marquee from the original selection simply by pressing the Escape or the Enter key.

Also, when you paste a cell selection that you've copied to the Clipboard (this doesn't apply when pasting cells that you've cut to the Clipboard), Excel displays the Paste Options button in the lower-right corner of the cell selection (marked with the word Ctrl). When you position the mouse pointer over this Paste Options button (or press the Ctrl key), a palette of buttons divided into three sections (Paste, Paste Values, and Other Paste Options) appears as shown in Figure 3-13.

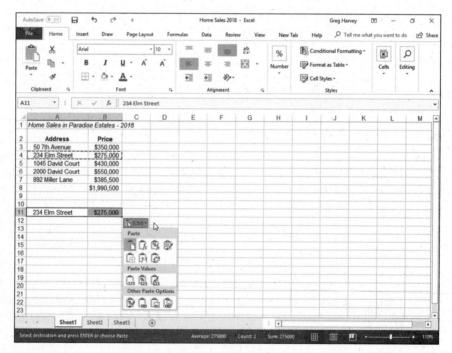

FIGURE 3-13: The Paste Option button's palette with the option buttons that commonly appear after pasting a cell selection that's been copied to the Clipboard.

The buttons in these three sections of the Paste Options palette offer you the following choices for refining your paste operation. The seven buttons that appear in the Paste section include

>> **Paste (P):** Excel pastes everything in the cell selection (text, values, formulas, and cell formatting).

>> **Formulas (F):** Excel pastes all the text, numbers, and formulas in the current cell selection without their formatting.

>> **Formulas & Number Formatting (O):** Excel pastes the number formats assigned to the copied values along with their formulas.

>> **Keep Source Formatting (K):** Excel copies the formatting from the original cells and pastes this into the destination cells (along with the copied entries).

>> **No Borders (B):** Excel pastes everything in the cell selection without copying any borders applied to its cell range.

>> **Keep Source Column Widths (W):** Excel makes the width of the columns in the destination range the same as those in the source range when it copies their cell entries.

>> **Transpose (T):** Excel changes the orientation of the pasted entries. For example, if the original cell entries run down the rows of a single column of the worksheet, the transposed pasted entries will run across the columns of a single row.

The three buttons that appear in the Paste Values section of the Paste Options palette include

>> **Values (V):** Excel pastes only the calculated results of any formulas in the source cell range.

>> **Values & Number Formatting (A):** Excel pastes the calculated results of any formulas along with all the formatting assigned to the labels, values, and formulas in the source cell range into the destination range. This means that all the labels and values in the destination range appear formatted just like the source range even though all the original formulas are lost and only the calculated values are retained.

>> **Values & Source Formatting (E):** Excel pastes the calculated results of all formulas along with formatting assigned to source cell range.

The four buttons that may appear in the Other Paste Options section of the Paste Options palette include

>> **Formatting (R):** Excel pastes only the formatting (and not the entries) copied from the source cell range to the destination range.

>> **Paste Link (N):** Excel creates linking formulas in the destination range so that any changes that you make to the entries in cells in the source range are immediately brought forward and reflected in the corresponding cells of the destination range.

>> **Picture (U):** Excel pastes only the pictures in the copied cell selection.

>> **Linked Picture (I):** Excel pastes a link to the pictures in the copied cell selection.

Taking it out of the Clipboard task pane

Excel puts the contents of all cell selections that you copy and paste (using the Copy and Paste command buttons or their keyboard equivalents) into the Office Clipboard. In fact, as you edit your spreadsheet in this manner, the Clipboard stores the contents of up to the last 24 copied-and-pasted cell selections (before replacing them with new copied-and-pasted selections). Up to that time, you can examine the contents of the Clipboard and even paste your cell selections in other places in your spreadsheet or in documents open in other programs that you're running. (See Book 4, Chapter 4 for information about pasting Excel data from the Clipboard into other applications.)

To open the Clipboard task pane on the left side of the Excel program window, click the Dialog Box launcher in the Clipboard group on the Ribbon's Home tab (the button in the lower-right corner of the Clipboard group with an arrow pointing downward at a diagonal 45-degree angle).

When the Clipboard task pane is displayed, it shows all the individual copied-and-pasted items that have been placed there (up to a maximum of 24). While this pane is open, Excel also places there all selections that you cut or copy in the worksheet, even those that you paste by pressing the Enter key as well as those you don't paste elsewhere.

REMEMBER

If you want Excel to place all selections that you cut and copy in the worksheet into the Office Clipboard even when the Clipboard task pane is not open, click the Collect Without Showing Office Clipboard item on the Options button's pop-up menu at the bottom of the Clipboard pane.

To paste an item on the Clipboard into a cell of one of your worksheets, click the cell and then position the mouse pointer over the item in the Clipboard task pane. When the item's pop-up button appears, click it and then click Paste from the pop-up menu, shown in Figure 3-13.

TIP

If you're doing a lot of cut-and-paste work in a spreadsheet using the Clipboard, you can have Excel automatically display the Clipboard task pane as you do the editing. Simply open the Clipboard task pane, click the Options button at the very bottom, and then click the Show Office Clipboard Automatically option from its pop-up menu to select this setting. When this setting is selected, Excel automatically opens the Clipboard task pane if you put more than two items in the Clipboard during your work session. To have Excel display the Clipboard task pane when you press Ctrl+C twice in a row (Ctrl+CC), click the Show Clipboard When Ctrl+C Pressed Twice option from this menu.

Inserting rather than replacing copied cells

When you use cut-and-paste to move or copy a cell selection, you can have Excel paste the data into the worksheet without replacing existing entries in overlaid cells by choosing the Insert Cut Cells or Insert Copied Cells from the Insert button's drop-down menu (depending on whether you cut or copied the cells to the Clipboard) on the Ribbon's Home tab instead of clicking the normal Paste command button. Excel then displays the Insert Paste dialog box, where you can choose between a Shift Cells Right and a Shift Cells Down option button. Select Shift Cells Right to have existing cells moved to columns on the right to make room for the moved or copied cells. Select Shift Cells Down to have the existing cells moved to lower rows to make room for them.

TIP

If you want to shift existing cells down to make room for the ones you've cut or copied to the Clipboard, you can simply click the Insert button on the Home tab rather than bothering to click the Insert Cut Cells or Insert Copied Cells option on the button's drop-down menu.

Pasting just the good parts with Paste Special

Normally, when you paste worksheet data from the Clipboard, Excel pastes all the information (entries, formatting, and comments) from the cell selection into the designated paste area, thus replacing any existing entries in the cells that are overlaid. You can, however, use the options on the Paste button's drop-down menu or use the options in the Paste Special dialog box (by choosing Paste Special from this drop-down menu or pressing Alt+HVS) to control what information is pasted into the paste range.

If you open the Paste Special dialog box (see Figure 3-14), you also have access to options that perform simple mathematical computations (Add, Subtract, Multiply, and Divide) between the number of cell entries that overlay each other. (See Table 3-1.)

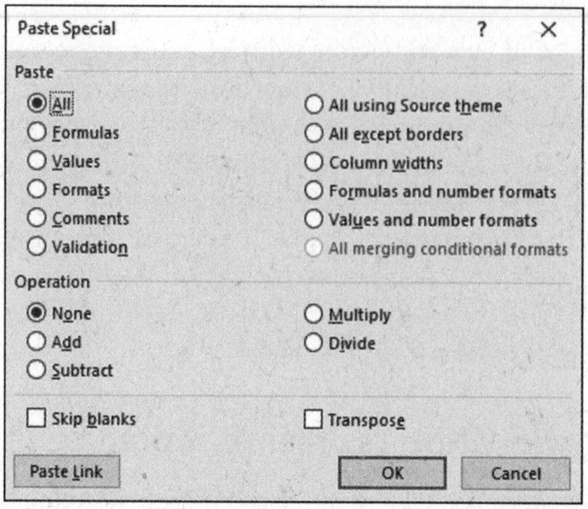

FIGURE 3-14:
The paste options in the Paste Special dialog box give you control over how a cell selection on the Clipboard is pasted into your worksheet.

TABLE 3-1   **The Paste Special Dialog Box Options**

Option	What It Does
All	Pastes all types of entries (numbers, formulas, and text), their formats, and comments from the selection in the paste area
Formulas	Pastes only the entries (numbers, formulas, and text) from the selection in the paste area
Values	Pastes only numbers and text from the selection in the paste area, converting all formulas to their current calculated values so they're pasted into the worksheet as numbers
Formats	Pastes only the formats from the selection into the paste area
Comments	Pastes only the comments from the selection into the paste area
Validation	Pastes only the Data Validation settings from the selection into the paste area (see Book 2, Chapter 1 for info on Data Validation)
All Using Source Theme	Pastes all types of entries (numbers, formulas, and text), their formats, and comments from the selection in the paste area and uses the colors, fonts, and graphic effects in the theme assigned to their source worksheet (see Book 5, Chapter 2)
All Except Borders	Pastes everything but the borders assigned to the cell selection into the paste area
Column Widths	Pastes everything into the paste area and adjusts the column widths in this area to match those of the original cell selection
Formulas and Number Formats	Pastes only the formulas and number formatting (omitting all text and numeric entries) from the cell selection into the paste area
Values and Number Formats	Pastes only the numbers and number formatting (omitting all text and converting all formulas to their calculated values) from the cell selection into the paste area

Option	What It Does
All Merging Conditional Formats	Pastes only the numbers and number formatting that meets the conditions specified by conditional formatting in the cell selection (see Book 2, Chapter 2)
None	Performs no mathematical operation between the values in the cell selection placed on the Clipboard and those in the destination range in the worksheet (the default)
Add	Adds the values in the cell selection placed on the Clipboard to those in the destination range in the worksheet
Subtract	Subtracts the values in the cell selection placed on the Clipboard from those in the destination range in the worksheet
Multiply	Multiplies the values in the cell selection placed on the Clipboard with those in the destination range in the worksheet
Divide	Divides the values in the cell selection placed on the Clipboard by those in the destination range in the worksheet
Skip Blanks	Does not replace existing entries in the worksheet with any overlaying blank cells placed on the Clipboard as part of the cut or copied cell selection
Transpose	Switches the orientation of the entries in the cell selection placed on the Clipboard so that data that originally ran across the rows now runs down the columns in the new area of the worksheet and the data that ran down columns now runs across rows
Paste Link	Pastes links to the original cell selection placed on the Clipboard

The options in the Paste Special dialog box are divided into two areas: Paste and Operation. The Paste option buttons (some of which duplicate the options on the drop-down menu on the Ribbon and the Paste Option's palette in the worksheet) enable you to specify which components of the copied cell selection you want copied; see Table 3-1 for a list of options.

The Operation option buttons in the Paste Special dialog box enable you to specify which mathematical operation, if any, should be performed between the overlaying values in copy and paste ranges. Click the Skip Blanks check box to select it when you don't want Excel to replace existing entries in the paste range with overlaying blank cells in the copy range.

The Transpose option, which appears on the Paste button's drop-down menu and the Paste Options button (also duplicated by the Transpose check box in the Paste Special dialog box), is particularly helpful when you have a row of column headings that you want to convert into a column of row headings or when you have a column of row headings that you want to convert into a row of column headings. You can also use this option to pivot an entire table of data so that the data that runs across the rows now runs down the columns, and vice versa.

Figure 3-15 illustrates just such a situation. Here, I selected the production schedule table (including the column headings) in the cell range A2:J6, clicked the Copy button on the Home tab of the Ribbon, and then moved the cell cursor to cell A8. After that, I chose the Transpose option from the Paste button's drop-down menu. Excel's Live Preview feature then shows how this transposition would appear in the cell range A8:E17 in Figure 3-15.

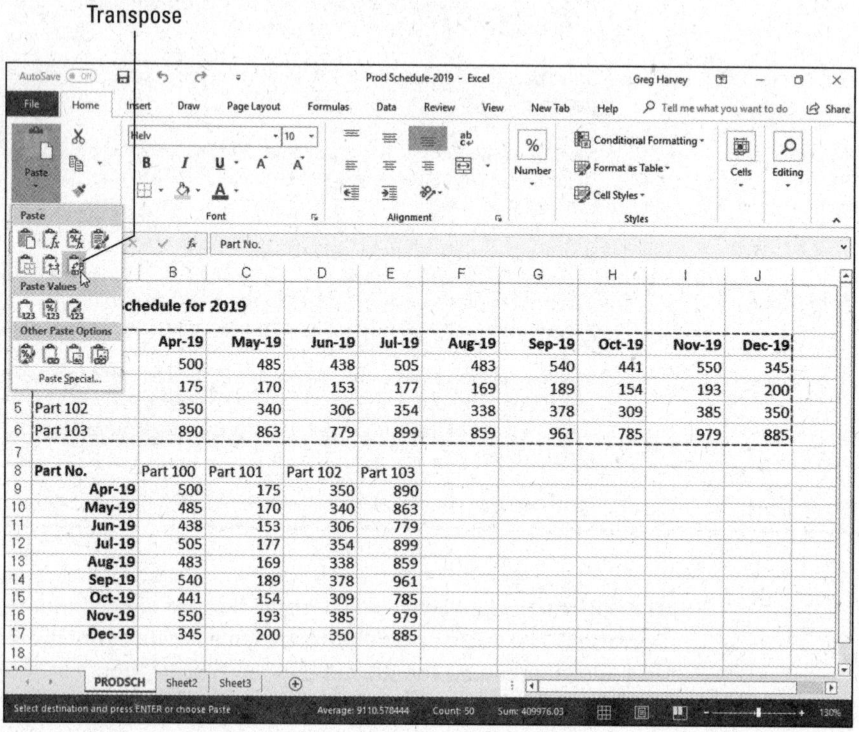

FIGURE 3-15:
Transposing a copy of the production schedule table so that dates now form the row headings and the part numbers now form the column headings.

In the transposed table, the original row headings are now the column headings just as the original column headings are now the row headings. Note, too, that in transposing the table, Excel retained the formulas that total the units produced each month, although now they appear in the last column of the table instead of the last row.

TIP

To convert a cell range that contains formulas to its calculated values (as though you had input them as numbers), select the cell range, click the Copy button on the Home tab, and then click the Paste Values option from the Paste button's drop-down menu *without* moving the cell cursor. This causes Excel to paste the calculated values on top of the formulas that created them, thus zapping the overlaid formulas and leaving you with only the computed values!

Find and Replace This Disgrace!

No discussion of spreadsheet editing would be complete without including the Find and Replace features in Excel. You can use the Find feature to quickly locate each and every occurrence of a specific *string* (a series of characters) in a worksheet. You can use the Replace feature to have Excel actually update the cells that it finds with new text or numbers.

Both the Find and the Replace features share the same dialog box (aptly called the Find and Replace dialog box). If you only want to find a cell's particular contents, you just use the options on the Find tab. (The Find tab is automatically selected when you open the Find and Replace dialog box by clicking the Find option on the Find & Select button's drop-down menu on the Home tab of the Ribbon, or when you press Alt+HFDF or simply Ctrl+F.) If you want to update the contents of some or all of the cells that you find, use the options on the Replace tab (which is automatically selected when you open the Find and Replace dialog box by choosing the Replace option from the Find & Select button's drop-down menu, or when you press Alt+HFDR or simply Ctrl+H).

The Find and Replace tabs in the Find and Replace dialog box contain a bunch of search options that you can use in finding and replacing stuff in your spreadsheet. The only problem is that these options are hidden when you first open the Find and Replace dialog box. To expand the Find and Replace dialog box to display the extra search options on the Find and Replace tab, click the Options button.

Finding stuff

To use the Find command to locate information in your worksheet, follow these steps:

1. **To search the entire worksheet, select a single cell. To restrict the search to a specific cell range or nonadjacent selection, select all the cells to be searched.**

2. **Choose the Find option from the Find & Select button's drop-down menu on the Ribbon's Home tab or press Ctrl+F.**

   Excel opens the Find and Replace dialog box with the Find tab selected.

3. **Type the search string that you want to locate in the Find What combo box.**

   When entering the search string, you can use the question mark (?) or asterisk (*) wildcards to stand in for any characters that you're unsure of. Use the question mark to stand for a single character, as in *Sm?th*, which will match either *Smith* or *Smyth*. Use the asterisk to stand for multiple characters as in *9*1*, which will locate *91, 94901*, or even *9553 1st Street*. To search with the asterisk as a wildcard character, precede the character with a tilde (~), as in ~*2.5, to locate formulas that are multiplied by the number 2.5. (The asterisk is the multiplication operator in Excel.)

If the cell holding the search string that you're looking for is formatted in a particular way, you can narrow the search by specifying what formatting to search for.

4. **Click the Options button and then click the Format drop-down button to specify the formatting to search for in addition to your search string. Click the Format button to select the formatting from the Find Format dialog box or click Choose Format from Cell to select the formatting directly from a cell in the worksheet.**

When you click the Format button, Excel opens a Find Format dialog box with the same tabs and options as the standard Format Cells dialog box. You then select the formatting that you want to search for in this dialog box and click OK.

When you choose the Choose Format from Cell item from the Format button's drop-down menu, the Find and Replace dialog box temporarily disappears until you click the cell in the worksheet that contains the formatting that you want to search for with the thick, white-cross mouse pointer with eyedropper icon.

Note that when using the Find feature to locate a search string, by default, Excel searches only the current worksheet for your search string. If you want Excel to search all the cells of all worksheets in the workbook, you need to follow Step 5.

5. **Choose the Workbook option from the Within drop-down menu to have Excel search all worksheets in the workbook.**

If the Within drop-down list box doesn't appear at the bottom of your Find and Replace dialog box, click the Options button to expand it and add the Within, Search, and Look In drop-down lists along with the Match Case and Match Entire Cell Contents check boxes.

By default, Excel searches across the rows in the worksheet or current selection (that is, to the right and then down from the active cell). If you want to have the program search down the columns and then across the rows, you need to follow Step 6.

6. **Choose the By Columns option from the Search drop-down menu to have Excel search down the columns (that is, down and then to the right from the active cell).**

By default, Excel locates the search string in the contents of each cell as entered on the Formula bar. This means that if you're looking for a cell that contains 1,250 and the spreadsheet contains the formula =750+500, whose calculated value as displayed in the cell is 1,250, Excel won't consider this cell to be a match because in searching the Formula bar, it finds =750+500 instead of 1,250.

To have Excel search the contents of each cell (and thus, consider a cell that displays your value to be a match even when its contents on the Formula bar don't contain the search string), you need to change the Look In setting from Formulas to Values. If you want Excel to search for the search string in the comments you've added to cells, you need to change the Look In setting to Comments.

7. **Choose Values from the Look In drop-down menu to have Excel locate the search string in the contents of each cell as it's displayed in the worksheet. Choose Comments from this drop-down menu instead to have Excel locate the search string in the comments that you've added to cells.**

Note that when you select Comments to search the comments you've added to the spreadsheet, you can't specify any formatting to search for because the Format button in the Find and Replace dialog box becomes grayed out.

By default, Excel ignores case differences between the search string and the content of the cells being searched so that *Assets, ASSETS,* and *assets* all match the search string, *Assets.* To find only exact matches, follow Step 8.

8. **Select the Match Case check box to find occurrences of the search string when it matches the case that you entered.**

By default, Excel considers any occurrence of the search string to be a match — even when it occurs as part of another part of the cell entry. So when the search string is 25, cells containing 25, 15.25, 25 Main Street, and 250,000 are all considered matches. To find only complete occurrences of your search string in a cell, follow Step 9.

9. **Select the Match Entire Cell Contents check box to find occurrences of the search string only when it's the entire cell entry.**

After you've entered the search string and search options as you want them, you're ready to start searching the spreadsheet.

10. **Click the Find All button to find all occurrences of the search string. Click the Find Next button to find just the first occurrence of the search string.**

When you click Find All, Excel lists all the cells containing the search string in a list box at the bottom of the Find and Replace dialog box, as shown in Figure 3-16. You can then have Excel select the cell with a particular occurrence by clicking its link in this list box. You may have to drag the Find and Replace dialog box out of the way to see the selected cell.

When you click Find Next, Excel selects the next cell in the spreadsheet (using the designated search direction). To find subsequent occurrences of the search string, you need to continue to click Find Next until you reach the cell that you're looking for. Again, you may have to drag the Find and Replace dialog box out of the way to see the cell that Excel has located and selected in the worksheet.

11. **After you finish searching the spreadsheet for the search string, click the Close button.**

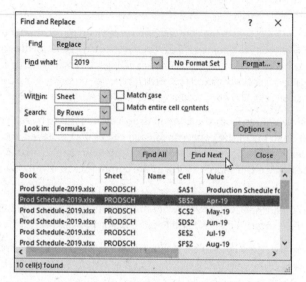

Note that Excel retains your search string and search option conditions even after closing the Find and Replace dialog box. To repeat a search, just press Ctrl+F and then click Find All or Find Next. You can also reinstate a search string that you used earlier in your work session by choosing it from the Find What drop-down menu.

Finding and replacing stuff

The Find feature is sufficient if all you want to do is locate an occurrence of a search string in your worksheet. Many times, however, you will also want to change some or all of the cells that match the search string. For those situations, you use the Replace feature to locate the search string and replace it with some other string.

To search and replace information in your worksheet, follow these steps:

1. **To search and replace the entire worksheet, select a single cell. To restrict the search and replace operation to a specific cell, range, or nonadjacent selection, select all the cells to be searched.**

2. **Choose the Replace option from the Find & Select button's drop-down menu on the Ribbon's Home tab or press Ctrl+H.**

   Excel opens the Find and Replace dialog box with the Replace tab selected (similar to the one shown in Figure 3-17). Note that if the Find and Replace dialog box is already open from choosing the Find option from the Find & Select button's drop-down menu or pressing Ctrl+F, all you have to do is click the Replace tab.

3. **Type the search string that you want to locate in the Find What combo box and specify any formatting to be searched by using its Format button.**

Refer to the previous steps on finding a search string for details on specifying the search string in the Find What combo box and specifying the formatting to be searched for.

4. **Type the replacement string in the Replace With combo box.**

Enter this string *exactly* as you want it to appear in the cells of the worksheet. Use uppercase letters where uppercase is to appear, lowercase letters where lowercase is to appear, and the question mark and asterisk only where they are to appear. (They don't act as wildcard characters in a replacement string.)

5. **Click the Options button and then click the Format drop-down button and click Format to select the formatting to be added to your replacement string from the Find Format dialog box. Or click Choose Format from Cell and select the formatting directly from a cell in the worksheet.**

When you click the Format item, Excel opens a Find Format dialog box with the same tabs and options as the standard Format Cells dialog box. You may then select the formatting that you want the replacement string to have in this dialog box and then click OK.

When you click the Choose Format from Cell item on the Format button drop-down menu, the Find and Replace dialog box temporarily disappears until you click the cell in the worksheet that contains the formatting that you want the replacement string to have with the thick, white-cross mouse pointer with eyedropper icon.

6. **Make any necessary changes to the Within, Search, Look In, Match Case, and Match Entire Cell Contents options for the search string.**

These options work just as they do on the Find tab. If these options aren't displayed on the Replace tab of your Find and Replace dialog box, click its Options button to expand the dialog box.

7. **Click the Find Next button to locate the first occurrence of the search string. Then, click the Replace button to replace the first occurrence with the replacement string or click the Find Next button again to skip this occurrence.**

Using the Find Next and Replace buttons to search and replace on a case-by-case basis is by far the safest way to use the Find and Replace feature. If you're certain (really certain) that you won't mess up anything by replacing all occurrences throughout the spreadsheet, you can click the Replace All button to have Excel make the replacements globally without stopping to show you which cells are updated.

8. **When you finish replacing entries on a case-by-case basis, click the Close button.**

This action abandons the Find and Replace operation and closes the Find and Replace dialog box. When you globally replace the search string, Excel automatically closes the Find and Replace dialog box after replacing the last search string match.

FIGURE 3-17: Updating dates in a worksheet using the Find and Replace feature.

Remember that you can click the Undo button on the Quick Access toolbar or press Ctrl+Z to restore any replacements that you made in error.

REMEMBER

Spell Checking Heaven

You can use Excel's Spell Check feature to catch all the spelling mistakes that AutoCorrect lets slip through. To spell check your spreadsheet, click the Spelling button at the beginning of the Ribbon's Review tab or press Alt+RS or, simply, F7.

When you spell check a spreadsheet, Excel looks up each word in the Excel Dictionary. If the word is not found (as is often the case with less-common last names, abbreviations, acronyms, and technical terms), Excel selects the cell with the unknown spelling and then displays a Spelling dialog box showing the unknown word in the Not in Dictionary text box with suggested correct spellings shown in a Suggestions list box below, which is similar to the one shown in Figure 3-18.

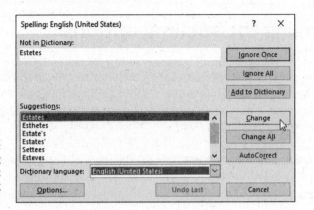

FIGURE 3-18:
Spell checking a worksheet with the Spelling dialog box.

You can then take any of the following actions to take care of the unknown word:

>> Click one of the words in the Suggestions list box and then click the Change button to have Excel replace the unknown word with the selected suggestion and continue spell checking the rest of the spreadsheet.

>> Click one of the words in the Suggestions list box and then click the Change All button to have Excel replace all occurrences of the unknown word with the selected suggestion throughout the entire spreadsheet and then continue spell checking.

>> Click the Ignore Once button to let the misspelling slide just this once and continue spell checking the rest of the spreadsheet.

>> Click the Ignore All button to ignore all occurrences of the unknown word in the spreadsheet and continue spell checking.

>> Click the Add to Dictionary button to add the unknown word to a custom dictionary so that Excel will know the word the next time you spell- check the worksheet.

>> Click the AutoCorrect button to have Excel add the unknown word to the AutoCorrect list with the selected suggestion as its automatic replacement.

REMEMBER

Keep in mind that Excel checks the spelling of the cells only in the current worksheet (and not all the sheets in the workbook). If you want Excel to spell check another worksheet, you need to click its sheet tab to make it active and then click the Spelling button on the Review tab (or press F7). If you want to spell check just a portion of the worksheet, select the range or nonadjacent cell selection before you start the spell check.

When Excel finishes checking the current worksheet or cell selection, the program displays an alert dialog box that indicates that the spell checking has been completed.

Changing the spelling options

When you use the Spell Check feature, you can change certain spelling options to better suit the spreadsheet that you're checking. To change the spelling options, click the Options button at the bottom of the Spelling dialog box. This action opens the Proofing tab of the Excel Options dialog box with the following options in the When Correcting Spelling in Microsoft Office Programs section:

>> **Ignore Words in UPPERCASE:** Remove the check mark from the check box so that Excel marks acronyms and other words entered in all uppercase letters as misspellings.

>> **Ignore Words That Contain Numbers:** Remove the check mark from the check box so that Excel marks words such as B52 that contain letters and numbers as misspellings.

>> **Ignore Internet and File Addresses**: Remove the check mark from the check box so that Excel marks web URL addresses such as www.dummies.com and file pathnames such as c:\documents\finance as misspellings.

>> **Flag Repeated Words:** Remove the check mark so that Excel no longer marks repeated words such as Bora Bora as misspellings.

>> **Enforce Accented Uppercase in French:** Add a check mark so that Excel marks uppercase French words that don't have the proper accent marks as misspellings.

>> **Suggest from Main Dictionary Only:** Have Excel use only the main dictionary when doing a spell check (thus, ignoring all words that you've added to a custom dictionary).

>> **Custom Dictionaries:** Open the Custom Dictionaries dialog box where you can edit the words in a custom dictionary or add a new custom dictionary to be used in spell checking. (See "Adding words to the custom dictionary" that follows.)

>> **French Modes or Spanish Modes:** Choose between the traditional or more modern spellings of French or Spanish words, respectively.

>> **Dictionary Language:** Specify the language and country of the dictionary to use when spell checking the worksheet.

Adding words to the custom dictionary

You use the Add to Dictionary button in the Spelling dialog box to add unknown words to a custom dictionary. By default, Excel adds words to a custom dictionary file named Custom.dic. This file is located in the UProof folder, which is located within the Microsoft folder inside the AppData folder. The Application Data folder is either inside the Windows User folder on your Local Disk (C:) drive or, if you're on a network, this file may be located in your username folder inside the Profiles folder that lies within the Windows folder on your C: drive. To locate it on your device, simply search for **custom.dic** in the Windows 10 File Explorer.

If you want, you can create other custom dictionaries to use when spell checking your worksheets. To create a new custom dictionary, follow these steps:

1. **Click the Custom Dictionaries button in the When Correcting Spelling in Microsoft Office Programs section of the Proofing tab.**

   Excel opens the Custom Dictionaries dialog box, where you can create a new custom dictionary to use.

2. **Click the New button in the Custom Dictionaries dialog box.**

   Excel opens the Create Custom Dictionary dialog box.

3. **Type the name for your new custom dictionary and then click the Save button.**

   After the Create Custom Dictionary dialog box closes, the name of the custom dictionary you created appears underneath CUSTOM.DIC (Default) in the Dictionary list box.

4. **(Optional) To restrict the language of a custom dictionary, select the language from the Dictionary Language drop-down list after clicking the dictionary's name in the Dictionary list box to select it.**

5. **To make the new custom dictionary the default dictionary into which new words are saved, click the dictionary's name in the Dictionary list box to select it and then click the Change Default button.**

6. **Click OK to close the Custom Dictionaries dialog box and then click OK again to close the Excel Options dialog box.**

   Excel returns you to the Spelling dialog box.

7. **Click the Add to Dictionary button to add the unknown word to the new default custom dictionary and then continue spell checking your spreadsheet.**

Note that Excel continues to add all unknown words to your new custom dictionary until you change the default back to the original custom dictionary (or to another custom one that you've created). To change back and start adding unknown words to the original custom dictionary, select the RoamingCustom.dic file in the Custom Dictionaries dialog box and then click the Change Default button.

TIP

You can directly edit the words that you add to your custom dictionary. Click the Custom Dictionaries button on the Proofing tab of the Excel Options dialog box (File ⇨ Options ⇨ Proofing or Alt+FTP) and then click the Edit Word List command button. Excel then opens a dialog box with the default dictionary's name that contains a Word(s) text box where you can enter new words to add to the custom dictionary and a Dictionary list box below that lists all the words added to the dictionary in alphabetical order. To add a new word to the dictionary, type it in the Word(s) text box (carefully, you don't want to add a misspelling to the dictionary) and then click the Add button. To remove a word, click it in the Dictionary list box and then click the Delete button.

Looking Up and Translating Stuff

In addition to the very useful Spelling button (discussed in the previous section), the Proofing, Insights, and Language groups on the Review tab contains three other command buttons that can come in handy from time to time:

» **Thesaurus** opens the Thesaurus task pane with the Thesaurus option selected. Here you can look up synonyms for a particular term that you enter into the Search For text box or for the contents of the current cell automatically entered into this text box.

» **Smart Lookup** opens the Smart Lookup task pane where you can find a definition and more online information about the entry that's in the active cell when you click it.

» **Translate** opens the Translator task pane. Here you can look up a translation for a particular term that you enter into the Select Text from the Document or Enter Text Here to Translate text box under the From drop-down button and then select the language into it is to be translated in the To drop-down button's list located right below it. The first time you select this option, Excel displays an Use Intelligent Services dialog box where you click the Turn On button to make this service operational.

REMEMBER

When the Smart Lookup task pane is first opened by clicking the Smart Lookup button, the Explore tab is selected, enabling you to explore the term that's in the active cell using Wikipedia, Bing Image search, and a general web search. If you want a dictionary definition for the entry that's in the current cell, click the Define tab at the top of the Insights task pane.

Marking Invalid Data

In addition to using the Data Validation feature to restrict what kind of data can be entered into cell ranges of a worksheet as described in Book 2, Chapter 1, you can use it to mark all the data (by circling their cells) that are outside of expected or allowable parameters.

To use the Data Validation feature in this way, you follow this general procedure:

» Select the cell range(s) in the worksheet that need to be validated and marked.

» Open the Data Validation dialog box by clicking the Data Validation button on the Data tab of the Ribbon or by pressing Alt+AVV, and then use its options to set up the validation criteria that determine which values in the selected cell range are out of bounds. (See Book 2, Chapter 1 for details.)

» Choose the Circle Invalid Data option from the Data Validation button's drop-down menu on the Data tab of the Ribbon.

Figure 3-19 shows an example of how you might use Data Validation to mark entries that are below a certain threshold. In this case, I set it up for Excel to mark all subtotal monthly sales cells entries in the range D4:D15 in the 2019 Sales worksheet that are above $50,000 by drawing a red circle around their cells.

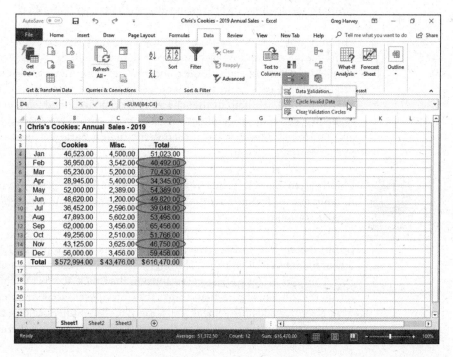

FIGURE 3-19: Using Data Validation to mark unexpected entries (monthly sales above $50K) in a data table.

To set this up in the 2019 Sales worksheet, I followed these three steps:

>> Selected the cell range (D4:D15) with monthly sales data for the year.

>> Opened the Data Validation dialog box (Alt+AVV) and then on the Settings tab selected Decimal in the Allow drop-down list and Greater Than in the Data drop-down list, and entered 50000 in the Minimum text box before clicking OK.

>> Chose the Circle Invalid Data option from the Data Validation button's drop-down menu on the Data tab. (You can also press Alt+AVI.)

REMEMBER

To remove the circles from the cells marked as invalid, choose the Clear Validation Circles option from the Data Validation button's drop-down menu or press Alt+AVR. To clear the validation settings from the cells, select the range and then open the Data Validation dialog box and click its Clear All button before you click OK.

Eliminating Errors with Text to Speech

Find and Replace is a great tool for eliminating errors that you've flagged in the worksheet. Likewise, the Spell Check feature is great for eliminating input errors that result from typos. Unfortunately, neither of these features can help you to identify data input errors that result from actions, such as mistyping the entry (without misspelling it) or transposing one entry with another.

The only way that you can flag and then correct these errors is by checking and verifying the accuracy of each and every data entry in the worksheet. Usually, you do this by checking the columns and rows of data in a spreadsheet against the original documents from which you generated the spreadsheet. Excel's Text to Speech feature can help in this checking by reading aloud each entry that's been made in a selected range of cells or data table within the worksheet. As the data entries are read aloud, you can then verify their accuracy against documents used in the original data entry.

REMEMBER

The Text to Speech translation feature requires no prior training or special microphones: All that's required is a pair of speakers or headphones connected to your computer.

Unfortunately, the various Text to Speech command buttons are not available from any of the tabs on the Ribbon. The only way to access them is by adding their command buttons either as custom buttons on the Quick Access toolbar or to a custom tab on the Ribbon. Figure 3-20 shows the Quick Access toolbar on my copy of Excel 2019 after I've added the Speak Cells, Speak Cells - Stop Speaking Cells, and Speak Cells on Enter buttons needed to check cell entries by having them read aloud.

Speak Cells by Rows

Speak Cells - Stop Speaking   Speak Cells on Enter

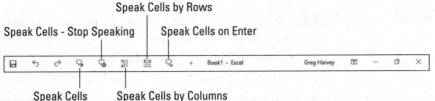

Speak Cells   Speak Cells by Columns

To add the Speak Cells, Speak Cells - Stop Speaking Cells, and Speak Cells on Enter command buttons to the Quick Access Toolbar, follow these steps:

1. **Click the Customize Quick Access Toolbar drop-down button and then choose the More Commands option from its drop-down menu.**

   Doing this opens the Quick Access Toolbar tab of the Excel Options dialog box.

2. **Choose Commands Not in the Ribbon from the Choose Commands From drop-down menu.**

   The Text to Speech command buttons include Speak Cells, Speak Cells - Stop Speaking Cells, Speak Cells by Columns, Speak Cells by Rows, and Speaks Cells on Enter.

3. **Click the Speak Cells button in the Choose Commands From list box on the left and then click the Add button to add it to the bottom of the Customize Quick Access Toolbar list box on the right.**

4. **Repeat the process outlined in Step 3, this time adding the Speak Cells - Stop Speaking Cells and Speak Cells on Enter buttons.**

   If you want to reposition the Text to Speech buttons on the Quick Access toolbar, select each button in the Customize Quick Access Toolbar list box and then move it left on the bar by clicking the Move Up button or right by clicking Move Down. If you want to set off the Text to Speech buttons as a separate group on the Quick Access toolbar, add a <Separator> icon ahead of the Speak Cells command button (and following the Speak Cells on Enter button if you have buttons not related to the Text to Speech function that follow on the Quick Access toolbar).

5. **Click the OK button to close the Excel Options dialog box.**

After adding the Text to Speech buttons to the Quick Access toolbar, you can use them to corroborate spreadsheet entries and catch those hard-to-spot errors as follows:

1. **Select the cells in the worksheet whose contents you want read aloud by Text to Speech.**

   If you want to check a table of data, simply position the cell cursor in the first cell, and Excel will then automatically select the entire table when you click the Speak Cells button.

2. **Click the Speak Cells button to have your Windows device begin reading back the entries in the selected cells.**

   The Text to Speech feature reads the contents of each cell in the cell selection by first reading down each column and then across the rows.

3. **To pause the Text to Speech feature when you locate a discrepancy between what you're reading and what you're hearing, click the Speak Cells - Stop Speaking Cells button.**

REMEMBER

Keep in mind that you can click the Speak Cells on Enter button to have your computer speak each new entry that you make as you complete it by pressing the Enter key. Excel also moves the cell cursor down one row.

Chapter **4**

Managing Worksheets

B eing able to manage and reorganize the information in your spreadsheet is almost as important as being able to input data and edit it. As part of these skills, you need to know how to manipulate the columns and rows of a single worksheet, the various worksheets within a single workbook, and, at times, other workbooks that contain supporting or relevant data.

This chapter examines how to reorganize information in a single worksheet by inserting and deleting columns and rows, as well as how to apply outlining to data tables that enables you to expand and collapse details by showing and hiding columns and rows. It also covers how to reorganize and manipulate the actual worksheets in a workbook and discusses strategies for visually comparing and transferring data between the different workbooks that you have open for editing.

Reorganizing the Worksheet

Every Excel 2019 worksheet that you work with has 16,384 columns and 1,048,576 rows — no more, no less, regardless of how many or how few of its cells you use. As your spreadsheet grows, you may find it beneficial to rearrange the data so that it doesn't creep. Many times, this involves deleting unnecessary columns and rows to bring the various data tables and lists in closer proximity to each other. At other times, you may need to insert new columns and rows in the worksheet so as to put a minimum of space between the groups of data.

Within the confines of this humongous worksheet space, your main challenge is often keeping tabs on all the information spread out throughout the sheet. At times, you may find that you need to split the worksheet window into panes so that you can view two disparate regions of the spreadsheet together in the same window and compare their data. For large data tables and lists, you may want to outline the worksheet data so that you can immediately collapse the information down to the summary or essential data and then just as quickly expand the information to show some or all of the supporting data.

Inserting and deleting columns and rows

The first thing to keep in mind when inserting or deleting columns and rows in a worksheet is that these operations affect all 1,048,576 rows in those columns and all 16,384 columns in those rows. As a result, you have to be sure that you're not about to adversely affect data in unseen rows and columns of the sheet before you undertake these operations. Note that, in this regard, inserting columns or rows can be almost as detrimental as deleting them if, by inserting them, you split apart existing data tables or lists whose data should always remain together.

One way to guard against inadvertently deleting existing data or splitting apart a single range is to use the Zoom slider on the Status bar to zoom out on the sheet and then check visually for intersecting groups of data in the hinterlands of the worksheet. You can do this quickly by dragging the Zoom slider button to the left to the 25% setting. Of course, even at the smallest zoom setting of 10%, you can see neither all the columns nor all the rows in the worksheet, and because everything's so tiny at that setting, you can't always tell whether or not the column or row you intend to fiddle with intersects those data ranges that you can identify.

Another way to check is to press End+→ or End+↓ to move the cell pointer from data range to data range across the column or row affected by your column or row deletion. Remember that pressing End plus an arrow key when the cell pointer is in a blank cell jumps the cell pointer to the next occupied cell in its row or column. That means if you press End+→ when the cell pointer is in row 52 and the pointer jumps to cell XFD52 (the end of the worksheet in that row), you know that there isn't any data in that row that would be eliminated by your deleting that row or shifted up or down by your inserting a new row. So too, if you press End+↓ when the cell pointer is in column D and the cell pointer jumps down to cell D1048576, you're assured that no data is about to be purged or shifted left or right by that column's deletion or a new column's insertion at that point.

When you're sure that you aren't about to make any problems for yourself in other, unseen parts of the worksheet by deleting or inserting columns, you're ready to make these structural changes to the worksheet.

Eradicating columns and rows

To delete columns or rows of the worksheet, select them by clicking their column letters or row numbers in the column or row header and then click the Delete button in the Cells group on the Ribbon's Home tab. Remember that you can select groups of columns and rows by dragging through their letters and numbers in the column or row header. You can also select nonadjacent columns and rows by holding down the Ctrl key as you click them.

When you delete a column, all the data entries within the cells of that column are immediately zapped. At the same time, all remaining data entries in succeeding columns to the right move left to fill the blank left by the now-missing column. When you delete a row, all the data entries within the cells of that row are immediately eliminated, and the remaining data entries in rows below move up to fill in the gap left by the missing row.

TIP

You can also delete rows and columns of the worksheet corresponding to those that are a part of the current cell selection in the worksheet by clicking the drop-down button attached to the Delete command button on the Home tab of the Ribbon and then clicking the Delete Sheet Rows or Delete Sheet Columns option, respectively, from its drop-down menu. If you find you can't safely delete an entire column or row, delete the cells you need to get rid of in the particular region of the worksheet instead by selecting them and then clicking the Delete Cells option from the Delete button's drop-down menu. (See Book 2, Chapter 3 for details.)

REMEMBER

Remember that pressing the Delete key is *not* the same as clicking the Delete button on the Home tab of the Ribbon. When you press the Delete key after selecting columns or rows in the worksheet, Excel simply clears the data entries in their cells without adjusting any of the existing data entries in neighboring columns and rows. Click the Delete command button on the Home tab when your purpose is *both* to delete the data in the selected columns or rows *and* to fill in the gap by adjusting the position of entries to the right and below the ones you eliminate.

Should your row or column deletions remove data entries referenced in formulas, the #REF! error value replaces the calculated values in the cells of the formulas affected by the elimination of the original cell references. You must then either restore the deleted rows or columns or re-create the original formula and then recopy it to get rid of these nasty formula errors. (See Book 3, Chapter 2 for more on error values in formulas.)

Adding new columns and rows

To insert a new column or row into the worksheet, you select the column or row where you want the new blank column or row to appear (again by clicking its column letter or row number in the column or row header) and then click the Insert command button in the Cells group of the Ribbon's Home tab or right-click and select Insert on the pop-up menu.

When you insert a blank column, Excel moves the existing data in the selected column to the column to the immediate right, while simultaneously moving any other columns of data on the right over one. When you insert the blank row, Excel moves the existing data in the selected row down to the row immediately underneath, while simultaneously adjusting any other rows of existing data that fall below it down by one.

To insert multiple columns or rows at one time in the worksheet, select the columns or rows where you want the new blank columns or rows to appear (by dragging through their column letters and row numbers in the column and row header) before you click the Insert command button on the Home tab of the Ribbon.

You can also insert new rows and columns of the worksheet corresponding to those that are a part of the current cell selection in the worksheet by clicking the drop-down button attached to the Insert command button on the Home tab and then clicking the Insert Sheet Rows or Insert Sheet Columns option, respectively, from its drop-down menu. If you find that you can't safely insert an entire column or row, insert the blank cells you need in the particular region of the worksheet instead by selecting their cells and then clicking the Insert Cells option from the Insert command button's drop-down menu. (See Book 2, Chapter 3 for details.)

Whenever your column or row insertions reposition data entries that are referenced in other formulas in the worksheet, Excel automatically adjusts the cell references in the formulas affected to reflect the movement of their columns left or right, or rows up or down.

Splitting the worksheet into panes

Excel enables you to split the active worksheet window into two or four panes. After splitting up the window into panes, you can use the Excel workbook's horizontal and vertical scroll bars to bring different parts of the same worksheet into view. This is great for comparing the data in different sections of a table that would otherwise not be legible if you zoomed out far enough to have both sections displayed in the worksheet window.

To split the worksheet window into two horizontal panes, position the cell pointer in column A of the worksheet in the cell whose top border marks the place where you want the horizontal division to take place before clicking the Split button on the View tab of the Ribbon (or pressing Alt+WS). Excel then splits the window into two horizontal panes with the cell pointer in the upper-left corner of the lower pane. (See Figure 4-1.)

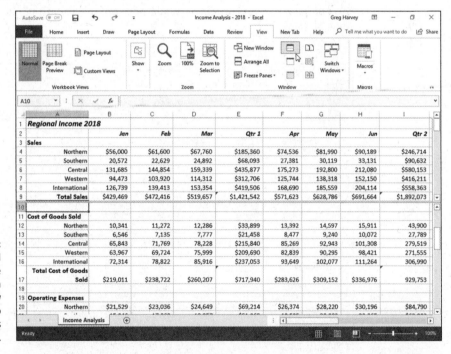

FIGURE 4-1:
The Regional Income worksheet with the window divided into two horizontal panes at row 10.

REMEMBER

To split the window into two vertical panes, you put the cell pointer in the first row of the column where the split is to occur. To split the window into four panes, you place the cell pointer in the cell in the column to the right of the vertical dividing line and the row below the horizontal dividing line so that the cell pointer will be in the upper-left corner of the lower-right pane when the split occurs (as shown in Figure 4-3).

Excel displays the borders of the window panes you create in the document window with a bar that ends with the vertical or horizontal split bar. To modify the size of a pane, you position the white-cross pointer on the appropriate dividing bar. Then as soon as the pointer changes to a double-headed arrow, drag the bar until the pane is the correct size and release the mouse button.

When you split a window into panes, Excel automatically synchronizes the scrolling, depending on how you split the worksheet. When you split a window into two horizontal panes, as shown in Figure 4-1, the worksheet window contains a single horizontal scroll bar and two separate vertical scroll bars. This means that all horizontal scrolling of the two panes is synchronized, while the vertical scrolling of each pane remains independent.

When you split a window into two vertical panes, as shown in Figure 4-2, the situation is reversed. The worksheet window contains a single vertical scroll bar and two separate horizontal scroll bars. This means that all vertical scrolling of the two panes is synchronized, while horizontal scrolling of each pane remains independent.

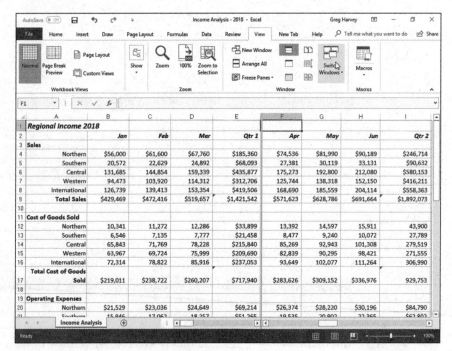

FIGURE 4-2:
The Regional Income worksheet with the window divided into two vertical panes at column F.

When you split a window into two horizontal and two vertical panes, as shown in Figure 4-3, the worksheet window contains two horizontal scroll bars and two separate vertical scroll bars. This means that vertical scrolling is synchronized in the top two window panes when you use the top vertical scroll bar and synchronized for the bottom two window panes when you use the bottom vertical scroll bar. Likewise, horizontal scrolling is synchronized for the left two window panes when you use the horizontal scroll bar on the left, and it's synchronized for the right two window panes when you use the horizontal scroll bar on the right.

FIGURE 4-3:
Splitting the worksheet window into four panes: two horizontal and two vertical at cell F10.

	A	B	C	D	E	F	G	H	I
1	Regional Income 2018								
2		Jan	Feb	Mar	Qtr 1	Apr	May	Jun	Qtr 2
3	Sales								
4	Northern	$56,000	$61,600	$67,760	$185,360	$74,536	$81,990	$90,189	$246,714
5	Southern	20,572	22,629	24,892	$68,093	27,381	30,119	33,131	$90,632
6	Central	131,685	144,854	159,339	$435,877	175,273	192,800	212,080	$580,153
7	Western	94,473	103,920	114,312	$312,706	125,744	138,318	152,150	$416,211
8	International	126,739	139,413	153,354	$419,506	168,690	185,559	204,114	$558,363
9	Total Sales	$429,469	$472,416	$519,657	$1,421,542	$571,623	$628,786	$691.664	$1,892,073
10									
11	Cost of Goods Sold								
12	Northern	10,341	11,272	12,286	$33,899	13,392	14,597	15,911	43,900
13	Southern	6,546	7,135	7,777	$21,458	8,477	9,240	10,072	27,789
14	Central	65,843	71,769	78,228	$215,840	85,269	92,943	101,308	279,519
15	Western	63,967	69,724	75,999	$209,690	82,839	90,295	98,421	271,555
16	International	72,314	78,822	85,916	$237,053	93,649	102,077	111,264	306,990
17	Total Cost of Goods Sold	$219,011	$238,722	$260,207	$717,940	$283,626	$309,152	$336,976	929,753
18									
19	Operating Expenses								
20	Northern	$21,529	$23,036	$24,649	$69,214	$26,374	$28,220	$30,196	$84,790

To remove all panes from a window when you no longer need them, you simply click the Split button on the View tab of the Ribbon, press Alt+WS, or drag the dividing bar (with the black double-headed split arrow cursor) either for the horizontal or vertical pane until you reach one of the edges of the worksheet window. You can also remove a pane by positioning the mouse pointer on a pane-dividing bar and then, when it changes to a double-headed split arrow, double-clicking it.

TIP

Remember that on a touchscreen, you can also remove the panes in a worksheet by directly double-tapping the pane-dividing bar with your finger or stylus.

Keep in mind that you can freeze panes in the window so that information in the upper pane and/or in the leftmost pane remains in the worksheet window at all times, no matter what other columns and rows you scroll to or how much you zoom in and out on the data. (See Book 2, Chapter 3 for more on freezing panes.)

Outlining worksheets

The Outline feature enables you to control the level of detail displayed in a data table or list in a worksheet. To be able to outline a table or list, the data must use a uniform layout with a row of column headings identifying each column of data and summary rows that subtotal and total the data in rows above (like the CG Media Sales table shown in Figure 4-4).

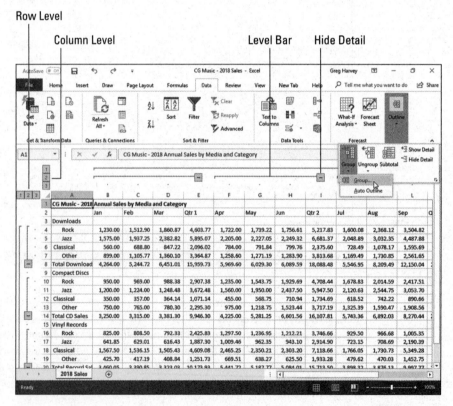

FIGURE 4-4: Automatic outline applied to the CG Music sales table with three levels of detail displayed.

After outlining a table or list, you can condense the table's display when you want to use only certain levels of summary information, and you can just as easily expand the outlined table or list to display various levels of detail data as needed. Being able to control which outline level is displayed in the worksheet makes it easy to print summary reports with various levels of data (see Book 2, Chapter 5) as well as to chart just the summary data (see Book 5, Chapter 1).

Spreadsheet outlines are a little different from the outlines you created in high school and college. In those outlines, you placed the headings at the highest level (I.) at the top of the outline with the intermediate headings indented below. Most worksheet outlines, however, seem backward in the sense that the highest level summary row and column are located at the bottom and far right of the table or list of data, with the columns and rows of intermediate supporting data located above and to the left of the summary row and column.

The reason that worksheet outlines often seem "backward" when compared to word-processing outlines is that, most often, to calculate your summary totals in the worksheet, you naturally place the detail levels of data above the summary rows and to the left of the summary columns that total them. When creating a word-processing outline, however, you place the major headings above subordinate headings, while at the same time indenting each subordinate level, reflecting the way we read words from left to right and down the page.

Outlines for data tables (as opposed to data lists) are also different from regular word-processing outlines because they outline the data in not one, but two hierarchies: a vertical hierarchy that summarizes the row data, and a horizontal hierarchy that summarizes the column data. (You don't get much of that in your regular term paper!)

Creating the outline

To create an outline from a table of data, position the cell pointer in the table or list containing the data to be outlined and then click the Auto Outline option on the Group command button's drop-down menu on the Data tab on the Ribbon (or press Alt+AGA).

By default, Excel assumes that summary rows in the selected data table are below their detail data, and summary columns are to the right of their detail data, which is normally the case. If, however, the summary rows are above the detail data, and summary columns are to the left of the detail data, Excel can still build the outline.

Simply start by clicking the Dialog Box launcher in the lower-right corner of the Outline group on the Data tab of the Ribbon to open the Settings dialog box. In the Settings dialog box, clear the check marks from the Summary Rows below Detail and/or Summary Columns to Right of Detail check boxes in the Direction section. Also, you can have Excel automatically apply styles to different levels of the outline by clicking the Automatic Styles check box. (For more information on these styles, see the "Applying outline styles" section, later in this chapter.) To have Excel create the outline, click the Create button — if you click the OK button, the program simply closes the dialog box without outlining the selected worksheet data.

Figure 4-4 shows you the first part of the outline created by Excel for the CG Music 2018 Sales worksheet. Note the various outline symbols that Excel added to the worksheet when it created the outline. Figure 4-4 identifies most of these outline symbols (the Show Detail button with the plus sign is not displayed in this figure), and Table 4-1 explains their functions.

TABLE 4-1   ## Outline Buttons

Button	Function
Row Level (1-8) and Column Level (1-8)	Displays a desired level of detail throughout the outline (1, 2, 3, and so on up to 8). When you click an outline's level bar rather than a numbered Row Level or Column Level button, Excel hides only that level in the worksheet display, the same as clicking the Hide Detail button (explained below).
Show Detail (+)	Expands the display to show the detail rows or columns that have been collapsed.
Hide Detail (–)	Condenses the display to hide the detail rows or columns that are included in its row or column level bar.

TIP

If you don't see any of the outline doodads identified in Figure 4-4 and Table 4-1, this means that the Show Outline Symbols If an Outline Is Applied check box in the Displays Options for This Worksheet section of the Advanced tab in the Excel Options dialog box (Alt+FTA) is not checked. All you have to do is press Ctrl+8 to display the outline symbols. Keep in mind that Ctrl+8 is a toggle that you can press again to hide the outline symbols.

REMEMBER

You can have only one outline per worksheet. If you've already outlined one table and then try to outline another table on the same worksheet, Excel will display the Modify Existing Outline alert box when you click the Outline command. If you click OK, Excel adds the outlining for the new table to the existing outline for the first table (even though the tables are nonadjacent). To create separate outlines for different data tables, you need to place each table on a different worksheet of the workbook.

Applying outline styles

You can apply predefined row and column outline styles to the table or list data. To apply these styles when creating the outline, be sure to select the Automatic Styles check box in the Settings dialog box before you click its Create button, opened by clicking the Dialog Box launcher in the Outline group on the Data tab of the Ribbon. If you didn't select this check box in the Settings dialog box before you created the outline, you can do so afterwards by selecting all the cells in the outlined table of data, opening the Settings dialog box, clicking the Automatic Styles check box to put a check mark in it, and then clicking the Apply Styles button before you click OK.

Figure 4-5 shows you the sample CG Music Sales table after I applied the automatic row and column styles to the outlined table data. In this example, Excel applied two row styles (RowLevel_1 and RowLevel_2) and two column styles (ColLevel_1 and ColLevel_2) to the worksheet table.

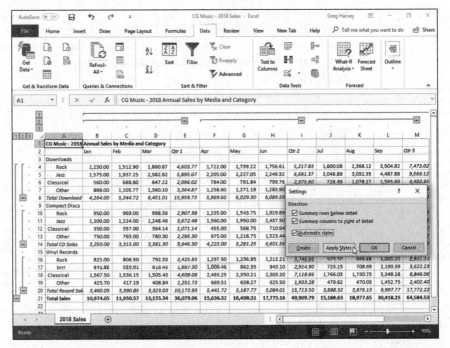

FIGURE 4-5:
Worksheet
outline after
applying
automatic styles
with the Settings
dialog box.

The RowLevel_1 style is applied to the entries in the first-level summary row (row 21) and makes the font appear in bold. The ColLevel_1 style is applied to the data in the first-level summary column (column R, which isn't shown in the figure), and it, too, simply makes the font bold. The RowLevel_2 style is applied to the data in the second-level rows (rows 8 and 20), and this style adds italics to the font. The ColLevel_2 style is applied to all second-level summary columns (columns E, I, M, and Q), and it also italicizes the font. (Note that columns M and Q are also not visible in Figure 4-5.)

TIP

Sometimes Excel can get a little finicky about applying styles to an existing outline. If, in the Settings dialog box, you click the Automatic Styles check box, click the Apply Styles button, and nothing happens to your outline, simply click the OK button to close the Settings dialog box. Then, re-create the outline by selecting the Auto Outline option on the Group drop-down list on the Data tab. Excel displays an alert dialog box asking you to confirm that you want to modify the existing outline. As soon as you click OK, Excel redisplays your outline, this time with the automatic styles applied.

Displaying and hiding different outline levels

The real effectiveness of outlining worksheet data becomes apparent as soon as you start using the various outline symbols to change the way the table data are displayed in the worksheet. By clicking the appropriate row or column level symbol, you can immediately hide detail rows and columns to display just the summary information in the table. For example, Figure 4-6 shows you the CG Music Sales table after clicking the number 2 Row Level button and number 2 Column Level button. Here, you see only the first- and second-level summary information, that is, the totals for the quarterly and annual totals for the three types of music sales.

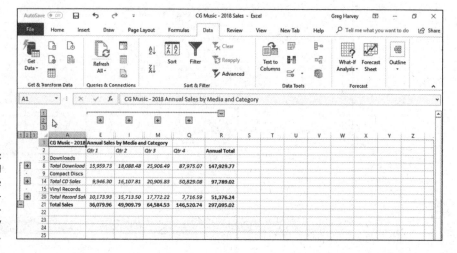

TIP

You can also hide and display levels of the outlined data by positioning the cell cursor in the column or row and then clicking the Hide Detail (the one with the red minus sign) or the Show Detail button (the one with the green minus sign) in the Outline group of the Data tab of the Ribbon. Or you can press the hot keys, Alt+AH, to hide an outline level, and Alt+AJ to redisplay the level. The great thing about using these command buttons or their hot key equivalents is that they work even when the outline symbols are not displayed in the worksheet.

Figure 4-7 shows you the same table, this time after clicking the number 1 Row Level button and number 1 Column Level button. Here, you see only the first-level summary for the column and the row, that is, the grand total of the annual CG Music sales. To expand this view horizontally to see the total sales for each quarter, you would simply click the number 2 Column Level button. To expand this view even further horizontally to display each monthly total in the worksheet, you would click the number 3 Column Level button. So too, to expand the outline vertically to see totals for each type of media, you would click the number 2 Row

Level button. To expand the outline one more level vertically so that you can see the sales for each type of music as well as each type of media, you would click the number 3 Row Level button.

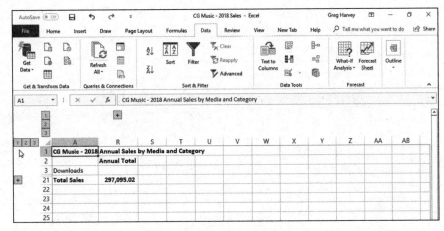

FIGURE 4-7:
Totally collapsed worksheet outline showing only the first-level summary information.

When displaying different levels of detail in a worksheet outline, you can use the Hide Detail and Show Detail buttons along with the Row Level and Column Level buttons. For example, Figure 4-8 shows you another view of the CG Music outlined sales table. Here, in the horizontal dimension, you see all three column levels have been expanded, including the monthly detail columns for each quarter. In the vertical dimension, however, only the detail rows for the Download sales have been expanded. The detail rows for the CD and Vinyl Record sales are still collapsed.

To create this view of the outline, you simply click the number 2 Column Level and Row Level buttons, and then click only the Show Detail (+) button located to the left of the Total Download Sales row heading. When you want to view only the summary-level rows for each media type, you can click the Hide Detail (–) button to the left of the Total Download Sales heading, or you can click its level bar (drawn from the collapse symbol up to the first music type to indicate all the detail rows included in that level).

REMEMBER

Excel adjusts the outline levels displayed on the screen by hiding and redisplaying entire columns and rows in the worksheet. Therefore, keep in mind that changes that you make that reduce the number of levels displayed in the outlined table also hide the display of all data outside of the outlined table that are in the affected rows and columns.

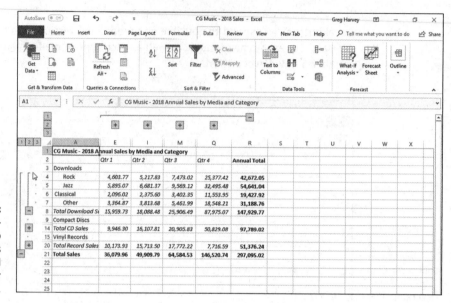

FIGURE 4-8:
Worksheet outline expanded to show only details for Download sales for all four quarters.

TIP

After selecting the rows and columns you want displayed, you can then remove the outline symbols from the worksheet display to maximize the amount of data displayed onscreen. To do this, simply press Ctrl+8.

Manually adjusting the outline levels

Most of the time, Excel's Auto Outline feature correctly outlines the data in your table. Every once in a while, however, you will have to manually adjust one or more of the outline levels so that the outline's summary rows and columns include the right detail rows and columns. To adjust levels of a worksheet outline, you must select the rows or columns that you want to promote to a higher level (that is, one with a lower level number) in the outline and then click the Group button on the far right side of the Data tab of the Ribbon. If you want to demote selected rows or columns to a lower level in the outline, select the rows or columns with a higher level number and then click the Ungroup button on the Data tab.

Before you use the Group and Ungroup buttons to change an outline level, you must select the rows or columns that you want to promote or demote. To select a particular outline level and all the rows and columns included in that level, you need to display the outline symbols (Ctrl+8), and then hold down the Shift key as you click its collapse or expand symbol. Note that when you click an expand symbol, Excel selects not only the rows or columns visible at that level, but all the hidden rows and columns included in that level as well. If you want to select only a particular detail or summary row or column in the outline, you can click that row number or column letter in the worksheet window, or you can hold down the Shift key and click the dot (period) to the left of the row number or above the column letter in the outline symbols area.

If you select only a range of cells in the rows or columns (as opposed to entire rows and columns) before you click the Group and Ungroup command buttons, Excel displays the Group or Ungroup dialog box, which contains a Rows and Columns option button (with the Rows button selected by default). To promote or demote columns instead of rows, click the Columns option button before you click OK. To close the dialog box without promoting or demoting any part of the outline, click Cancel.

To see how you can use the Group and Ungroup command buttons on the Data tab of the Ribbon to adjust outline levels, consider once again the CG Music 2018 Annual Sales table outline. When Excel created this outline, the program did not include row 3 (which contains only the row heading, Downloads) in the outline. As a result, when you collapse the rows by selecting the number 1 Row Level button to display only the first-level Total Sales summary row (refer to Figure 4-7), this Download row heading remains visible in the table, even though it should have been included and thereby hidden along with the other summary and detail rows.

You can use the Group command button to move this row (3) down a level so that it is included in the first level of the outline. You simply click the row number 3 to select the row and then click the Group command button on the Data tab (or press Alt+AGG). Figure 4-9 shows you the result of doing this. Notice how the outside level bar (for level 1) now includes this row. Now, when you collapse the outline by clicking the number 1 row level button, the heading in row 3 is hidden as well. (See Figure 4-10.)

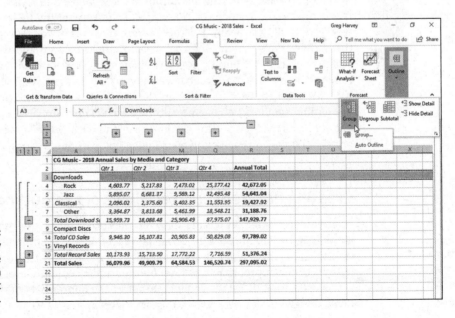

FIGURE 4-9: Manually adjusting the level 1 rows in the worksheet outline.

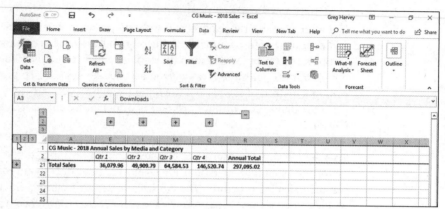

FIGURE 4-10:
Collapsing
the adjusted
worksheet
outline to the first
level summary
information.

Removing an outline

To delete an outline from your worksheet, you click the drop-down button attached to the Ungroup button on the Data tab of the Ribbon and then click the Clear Outline option from its drop-down menu (or you press Alt+AUC). Note that removing the outline does not affect the data in any way — Excel merely removes the outline structure. Also note that it doesn't matter what state the outline is in at the time you select this command. If the outline is partially or totally collapsed, deleting the outline automatically displays all the hidden rows and columns in the data table or list.

REMEMBER

Keep in mind that restoring an outline that you've deleted is not one of the commands that you can undo (Ctrl+Z). If you delete an outline by mistake, you must re-create it all over again. For this reason, most often you'll want to expand all the outline levels (by clicking the lowest number column and row level button) and then hide all the outline symbols by pressing Ctrl+8 rather than permanently remove the outline. Note that if you press Ctrl+8 when your spreadsheet table isn't yet outlined, Excel displays an alert dialog box indicating that it can't show the outline symbols because no outline exists. This alert also asks you whether you want to create an outline. To go ahead and outline the spreadsheet, click OK or press Enter. To remove the alert dialog box without creating an outline, click Cancel.

Creating different custom views of the outline

After you've created an outline for your worksheet table, you can create custom views that display the table in various levels of detail. Then, instead of having to display the outline symbols and manually click the Show Detail and Hide Detail buttons or the appropriate row level buttons and/or column level buttons to view a particular level of detail, you simply select the appropriate outline view in the Custom Views dialog box (View ⇨ Custom Views or Alt+WCV).

When creating custom views of outlined worksheet data, be sure that you leave the Hidden Rows, Columns, and Filter Settings check box selected in the Include in View section of the Add View dialog box. (See Book 2, Chapter 3 for details on creating and using custom views in a worksheet.)

Reorganizing the Workbook

Any new workbook that you open already comes with a single blank worksheet. Although most of the spreadsheets you create and work with may never wander beyond the confines of this one worksheet, you do need to know how to organize your spreadsheet information three-dimensionally for those rare occasions when spreading all the information out in one humongous worksheet is not practical. However, the normal, everyday problems related to keeping on top of the information in a single worksheet can easily go off the scale when you begin to use multiple worksheets in a workbook. For this reason, you need to be sure that you are fully versed in the basics of using more than one worksheet in a workbook.

REMEMBER

To move between the sheets in a workbook, you can click the sheet tab for that worksheet or press Ctrl+PgDn (next sheet) or Ctrl+PgUp (preceding sheet) until the sheet is selected. If the sheet tab for the worksheet you want is not displayed on the scroll bar at the bottom of the document window, use the tab scrolling buttons (the buttons with the left- and right-pointing triangles) to bring it into view.

To use the tab scrolling buttons, click the one with the right-pointing triangle to bring the next sheet into view and click the one with the left-pointing triangle to bring the preceding sheet into view. Ctrl-click the tab scrolling buttons with the directional triangles to display the very first or very last group of sheet tabs in a workbook. Ctrl-clicking the button with the triangle pointing left to a vertical line brings the first group of sheet tabs into view; Ctrl-clicking the button with the triangle pointing right to a vertical line brings the last group of sheet tabs into view. When you scroll sheet tabs to find the one you're looking for, for heaven's sake, don't forget to click the desired sheet tab to make the worksheet current.

REMEMBER

Excel 2019 indicates that there are more worksheets in a workbook whose tabs are not visible by adding a continuation button (indicated by an *ellipsis,* that is, three dots in row) either immediately following the last visible tab on the right or the first visible tab on the left. Keep in mind that you can also scroll the next or previously hidden sheet tab into view by clicking the continuation button on the right of the last visible sheet tab or left of the first visible tab, respectively.

Renaming sheets

The sheet tabs shown at the bottom of each workbook are the keys to keeping your place in a workbook. To tell which sheet is current, you have only to look at which sheet tab appears on the top, matches the background of the other cells in the worksheet, and has its name displayed in bold type and underlined.

When you add new worksheets to a new workbook, the sheet tabs are all the same width because they all have the default sheet names (Sheet1, Sheet2, and so on). As you assign your own names to the sheets, the tabs appear either longer or shorter, depending on the length of the sheet tab name. Just keep in mind that the longer the sheet tabs, the fewer you can see at one time, and the more sheet tab scrolling you'll have to do to find the worksheet you want.

To rename a worksheet, you take these steps:

1. **Press Ctrl+PgDn until the sheet you want to rename is active, or click its sheet tab if it's displayed at the bottom of the workbook window.**

   Don't forget that you have to select and activate the sheet you want to rename, or you end up renaming whatever sheet happens to be current at the time you perform the next step.

2. **Choose Rename Sheet from the Format button's drop-down menu on the Home tab, press Alt+HOR, or right-click the sheet tab and then click Rename from its shortcut menu.**

   When you choose this command, Excel selects the current name of the tab and positions the insertion point at the end of the name.

3. **Replace or edit the name on the sheet tab and then press the Enter key.**

When you rename a worksheet in this manner, keep in mind that Excel then uses that sheet name in any formulas that refer to cells in that worksheet. So, for instance, if you rename Sheet2 to 2019 Sales and then create a formula in cell A10 of Sheet1 that adds its cell B10 to cell C34 in Sheet2, the formula in cell A10 becomes

```
=B10+'2019 Sales'!C34
```

This is in place of the more obscure =B10+Sheet2!C34. For this reason, keep your sheet names short and to the point so that you can easily and quickly identify the sheet and its data without creating excessively long formula references.

TIP

Right-click either of the two tab scrolling buttons to display the Activate dialog box. This dialog box displays the names of all the worksheets in the current workbook in their current order. You can then scroll to and activate any of the sheets simply by selecting them followed by OK or by double-clicking them.

Designer sheets

Excel 2019 makes it easy to color-code the worksheets in your workbook. This makes it possible to create a color scheme that helps either identify or prioritize the sheets and the information they contain (as you might with different colored folder tabs in a filing cabinet).

REMEMBER

When you color a sheet tab, note that the tab appears in that color only when it's not the active sheet. The moment you select a color-coded sheet tab, it becomes white with just a bar of the assigned color appearing under the sheet name. Note, too, that when you assign darker colors to a sheet tab, Excel automatically reverses out the sheet name text to white when the worksheet is not active.

Color coding sheet tabs

To assign a new color to a sheet tab, follow these three steps:

1. **Press Ctrl+PgDn until the sheet whose tab you want to color is active, or click its sheet tab if it's displayed at the bottom of the workbook window.**

    Don't forget that you have to select and activate the sheet whose tab you want to color, or you end up coloring the tab of whatever sheet happens to be current at the time you perform the next step.

2. **Click the Format button on the Home tab and then highlight Tab Color, press Alt+HOT, or right-click the tab and then highlight Tab Color on the shortcut menu to display its pop-up color palette.**

3. **Click the color swatch in the color palette with the color and shade you want to assign to the current sheet tab.**

REMEMBER

To remove color-coding from a sheet tab, click the No Color option at the bottom of the pop-up color palette (Alt+HOT) after selecting it to make the worksheet active.

Assigning a graphic image as the sheet background

If coloring the sheet tabs isn't enough for you, you can also assign a graphic image to be used as the background for all the cells in the entire worksheet. Just be aware that the background image must either be very light in color or use a greatly reduced opacity in order for your worksheet data to be read over the image. This probably makes most graphics that you have readily available unusable as worksheet background images. It can, however, be quite effective if you have a special corporate watermark graphic (as with the company's logo at extremely low opacity) that adds just a hint of a background without obscuring the data being presented in its cells.

To add a local graphic file as the background for your worksheet, take these steps:

1. **Press Ctrl+PgDn until the sheet to which you want to assign the graphic as the background is active, or click its sheet tab if it's displayed at the bottom of the workbook window.**

   Don't forget that you have to select and activate the sheet to which the graphic file will act as the background, or you end up assigning the file to whatever sheet happens to be current at the time you perform the following steps.

2. **Click the Background command button in the Page Setup group of the Page Layout tab or press Alt+PG.**

   Doing this opens the Insert Picture dialog box, where you select the graphics file whose image is to become the worksheet background.

3. **Click the Browse button to the right of the From a File link.**

   Excel opens the Sheet Background dialog box, where you select the file containing the graphic image you want to use.

4. **Open the folder that contains the image you want to use and then click its graphic file icon before you click the Insert button.**

   As soon as you click the Insert button, Excel closes the Sheet Background dialog box, and the image in the selected file becomes the background image for all cells in the current worksheet. (Usually, the program does this by stretching the graphic so that it takes up all the cells that are visible in the Workbook window. In the case of some smaller images, the program does this by tiling the image so that it's duplicated across and down the viewing area.)

REMEMBER

Keep in mind that a graphic image that you assign as the worksheet background doesn't appear in the printout, unlike the pattern and background colors that you assign to ranges of cells in the sheet.

To remove a background image, you simply click the Delete Background command button on the Page Layout tab of the Ribbon (which replaces the Background button the moment you assign a background image to a worksheet) or press Alt+PSB again, and Excel immediately clears the image from the entire worksheet.

TIP

You can also turn online graphics into worksheet backgrounds. Simply select the Bing Image Search text box (to insert a web graphic). Then, perform a search for the image you want to use. (See Book 5, Chapter 2 for details.) When you locate the online graphic you want to use, double-click its thumbnail to download the image and insert it into the current worksheet as the sheet's background.

Adding and deleting sheets

You can add as many worksheets to the single Sheet1 that comes as part of every new workbook as you need in building your spreadsheet model. To add a new worksheet, click the New Sheet button, which always appears on its own tab immediately after the last sheet tab in the workbook (with the plus inside a circle icon).

Excel then inserts a new sheet at the back of the default Sheet1 worksheet in the workbook (and immediately in front of the tab with the New Sheet button), and the program assigns it the next available sheet number (as in Sheet2, Sheet3, Sheet4, and so on).

REMEMBER
You can also insert a new sheet (and not necessarily a blank worksheet) into the workbook by right-clicking a sheet tab and then clicking Insert at the top of the tab's shortcut menu. Excel opens the Insert dialog box containing different file icons that you can select — Chart, MS Excel 4.0 Macro, and MS Excel 5.0 Dialog, along with a variety of different worksheet templates — to insert a specialized chart sheet (see Book 5, Chapter 1), macro sheet (Book 8, Chapter 1), or worksheet following a template design (Book 2, Chapter 1). Note that when you insert a new sheet using the Insert dialog box, Excel inserts the new sheet *in front* of the worksheet that's active (and not at the end of the workbook as when you insert a worksheet by clicking the New Sheet button).

TIP
If you find that a single worksheet just never seems sufficient for the kind of spreadsheets you normally create, you can change the default number of sheets that are automatically available in all new workbook files that you open. To do this, open the General tab of the Excel Options dialog box (File ⇨ Options or Alt+FT), and then enter a number in the Include This Many Sheets text box or select the number with the spinner buttons (from 2 up to a maximum of 255). You can't go lower than 1 because a workbook with no worksheet is no workbook at all.

To remove a worksheet, make the sheet active and then click the drop-down button attached to the Delete button on the Home tab of the Ribbon and choose Delete Sheet from its drop-down menu — you can also press Alt+HDS or right-click its tab and then click Delete from its shortcut menu. If Excel detects that the worksheet contains some data, the program then displays an alert dialog box cautioning you that data may exist in the worksheet you're just about to zap. To go ahead and delete the sheet (data and all), you click the Delete button. To preserve the worksheet, click Cancel or press the Escape key.

WARNING
Deleting a sheet is one of those actions that you can't undo with the Undo button on the Quick Access toolbar. This means that after you click the Delete button, you've kissed your worksheet goodbye, so please don't do this unless you're *certain* that you aren't dumping needed data. Also, keep in mind that you can't delete a worksheet

if that sheet is the only one in the workbook until you've inserted another blank worksheet: Excel won't allow a workbook file to be completely sheetless.

Changing the sheets

Excel makes it easy to rearrange the order of the sheets in your workbook. To move a sheet, click its sheet tab and drag it to the new position in the row of tabs. As you drag, the pointer changes shape to an arrowhead on a dog-eared piece of paper, and you see a black triangle pointing downward above the sheet tabs. When this triangle is positioned over the tab of the sheet that is to follow the one you're moving, release the mouse button.

If you need to copy a worksheet to another position in the workbook, hold down the Ctrl key as you click and drag the sheet tab. When you release the mouse button, Excel creates a copy with a new sheet tab name based on the number of the copy and the original sheet name. For example, if you copy Sheet1 to a new place in the workbook, the copy is renamed Sheet1 (2). You can then rename the worksheet whatever you want.

You can also rearrange the sheets in your workbook using the Move or Copy dialog box opened by right-clicking a sheet tab and then choosing the Move or Copy command from the shortcut menu. Then, click the name of the worksheet that you want the currently active worksheet to now precede in the Before Sheet list box and clicking OK.

Group editing

One of the nice things about a workbook is that it enables you to edit more than one worksheet at a time. Of course, you should be concerned with group editing only when you're working on a bunch of worksheets that share essentially the same layout and require the same type of formatting.

For example, suppose that you have a workbook that contains annual sales worksheets (named YTD16, YTD17, and YTD18) for three consecutive years. The worksheets share the same layout (with months across the columns and quarterly and annual totals, locations, and types of sales down the rows) but lack standard formatting.

To format any part of these three worksheets in a single operation, you simply resort to group editing, which requires selecting the three sales worksheets. Simply click the YTD16, YTD17, and YTD18 sheet tabs as you hold down the Ctrl key, or you can click the YTD16 tab and then hold down the Shift key as you click the YTD18 tab.

After you select the last sheet, the message [Group] appears in the title bar of the active document window (with the YTD16 worksheet, in this case).

The [Group] indicator lets you know that any editing change you make to the current worksheet will affect all the sheets that are currently selected. For example, if you select a row of column headings and add bold and italics to the headings in the current worksheet, the same formatting is applied to the same cell selection in all three sales sheets. All headings in the same cell range in the other worksheets are now in bold and italics. Keep in mind that you can apply not only formatting changes to a cell range, but also editing changes, such as replacing a cell entry, deleting a cell's contents, or moving a cell selection to a new place in the worksheet. These changes also affect all the worksheets you have selected as long as they're grouped together.

After you are finished making editing changes that affect all the grouped worksheets, you can break up the group by right-clicking one of the sheet tabs and then clicking Ungroup Sheets at the top of the shortcut menu. As soon as you break up the group, the [Group] indicator disappears from the title bar, and thereafter, any editing changes that you make affect only the cells in the active worksheet.

TIP

To select all the worksheets in the workbook for group editing in one operation, right-click the tab of the sheet where you want to make the editing changes that affect all the other sheets, and then choose Select All Sheets from its shortcut menu.

"Now you see them; now you don't"

Another technique that comes in handy when working with multiple worksheets is hiding particular worksheets in the workbook. Just as you can hide particular columns, rows, and cell ranges in a worksheet, you can also hide particular worksheets in the workbook. For example, you may want to hide a worksheet that contains sensitive (for-your-eyes-only) material, such as the one with all the employee salaries in the company or the one that contains all the macros used in the workbook.

As with hiding columns and rows, hiding worksheets enables you to print the contents of the workbook without the data in worksheets that you consider either unnecessary in the report or too classified for widespread distribution but which, nonetheless, are required in the workbook. Then after the report is printed, you can redisplay the worksheets by unhiding them.

To hide a worksheet, make it active by selecting its sheet tab, then click the Format command button on the Home tab of the Ribbon and click Hide & Unhide ➪ Hide Sheet from its drop-down menu (or press Alt+HOUS). Excel removes this sheet's tab from the row of sheet tabs, making it impossible for anyone to select and display the worksheet in the document window.

To redisplay any of the sheets you've hidden, click the Format command button on the Home tab and click Hide & Unhide ⇨ Unhide Sheet from its drop-down menu (or press Alt+HOUH) to display the Unhide dialog box.

In the Unhide Sheet list box, click the name of the sheet that you want to display once again in the workbook. As soon as you click OK, Excel redisplays the sheet tab of the previously hidden worksheet — as simple as that! Unfortunately, although you can hide multiple worksheets in one hide operation, you can select only one sheet at a time to redisplay with the Unhide command.

Opening windows on different sheets

The biggest problem with keeping your spreadsheet data on different worksheets rather than keeping it all together on the same sheet is being able to compare the information on the different sheets. When you use a single worksheet, you can split the workbook window into horizontal or vertical panes and then scroll different sections of the sheet into view. The only way to do this when the spreadsheet data are located on different worksheets is to open a second window on a second worksheet and then arrange the windows with the different worksheets so that data from both desired regions are displayed on the screen. The easiest way to do this is to use Excel's View Side by Side command to tile the windows one above the other and automatically synchronize the scrolling between them.

Comparing worksheet windows side by side

Figure 4-11 helps illustrate how the View Side by Side feature works. This figure contains two windows showing parts of two different worksheets (2015 Sales and 2016 Sales) in the same workbook (CG Music 2015 - 2017 Sales.xlsx). These windows are arranged horizontally so that they fit one above the other and in order to show more data, I have unpinned the Ribbon in both windows so that only the row of tabs are visible.

As you can see, the top window shows the upper-left portion of the first worksheet with the 2015 sales data, while the lower window shows the upper-left portion of the second worksheet with the 2016 sales data. Note that both windows contain the same sheet tabs (although different tabs are active in the different windows) but that only the top, active window is equipped with a set of horizontal and vertical scroll bars. However, because Excel automatically synchronizes the scrolling between the windows, you can use the single set of scroll bars to bring different sections of the two sheets into view.

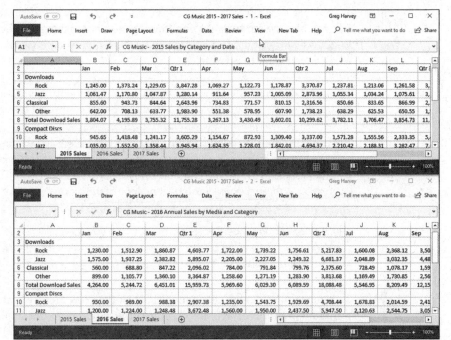

FIGURE 4-11:
Using windows
to compare data
stored on two
different sheets
in the same
workbook.

Here is the procedure I followed to create and arrange these windows in the CG Music 2015 – 2017 Sales.xlsx workbook:

1. **Open the workbook file for editing and then create a new window by clicking the New Window command button on the View tab of the Ribbon — you can also do this by pressing Alt+WN.**

   Excel appends the number 2 to the workbook's filename displayed at the top of the screen (as in CG Music 2015 – 2017 Sales.xlsx – 2) to indicate that a new window has been added to the workbook.

2. **Arrange the windows one on top of the other by clicking the View Side by Side command button (the one with the pages side by side to the immediate right of the Split button) in the Window group of the View tab or by pressing Alt+WB.**

3. **Click the lower window (indicated by the – 2 after the filename on its title bar) to activate the window and then click the 2013 Sales sheet tab to activate it and the Unpin the Ribbon button to display only Ribbon tabs in the first window.**

4. **Click the upper window (indicated by the – 1 following the filename on its title bar) to activate the window and then click its Collapse the Ribbon button to display only Ribbon tabs in the second window.**

Managing Worksheets

You can also switch between windows open in a workbook by clicking the Switch Windows button on the View tab followed by the name (with number) of the window you want to activate.

Immediately below the View Side by Side command button in the Windows group on the View tab of the Ribbon, you find these two command buttons:

>> **Synchronous Scrolling:** When this button is selected, any scrolling that you do in the worksheet in the active window is mirrored and synchronized in the worksheet in the inactive window beneath it. To be able to scroll the worksheet in the active window independently of the inactive window, click the Synchronous Scrolling button to deactivate it.

>> **Reset Window Position:** Click this button if you manually resize the active window (by dragging its size box) and then want to restore the two windows to their previous side-by-side arrangement.

To remove the side-by-side windows, click the View Side by Side command button again or press Alt+WB. Excel returns the windows to the display arrangement selected (see "Window arrangements" that follows for details) before clicking the View Side by Side command button the first time. If you haven't previously selected a display option in the Arrange Windows dialog box, Excel displays the active window full size.

Note that you can use the View Side by Side feature when you have more than two windows open on a single workbook. When three or more windows are open at the time you click the View Side by Side command button, Excel opens the Compare Side by Side dialog box. This dialog box displays a list of all the other open windows with which you can compare the active one. When you click the name of this window and click OK in the Compare Side by Side dialog box, Excel places the active window above the one you just selected (using the arrangement shown in Figure 4-11).

Note, too, that you can use Excel's View Side by Side feature to compare worksheets in different workbooks just as well as different sheets in the same workbook. (See "Comparing windows on different workbooks" later in this chapter.)

Window arrangements

After creating one or more additional windows for a workbook (by clicking the New Window command button on the View tab), you can then vary their arrangement by selecting different arrangement options in the Arrange Windows dialog box, opened by clicking the Arrange All button on the View tab (or by pressing

Alt+WA). The Arrange Windows dialog box contains the following four Arrange options:

>> **Tiled:** Select this option button to have Excel arrange and size the windows so that they all fit side by side on the screen in the order in which you open them (when only two windows are open, selecting the Tiled or Vertical option results in the same side-by-side arrangement).

>> **Horizontal:** Select this option button to have Excel size the windows equally and then place them one above the other (this is the default arrangement option that Excel uses when you click the View Side by Side command button).

>> **Vertical:** Select this option button to have Excel size the windows equally and then place them next to one other, vertically from left to right.

>> **Cascade:** Select this option button to have Excel arrange and size the windows so that they overlap one another with only their title bars visible.

After arranging your windows, you can then select different sheets to display in either window by clicking their sheet tabs, and you can select different parts of the sheet to display by using the window's scroll bars.

TIP

To activate different windows on the workbook so that you can activate a different worksheet by selecting its sheet tab and/or use the scroll bars to bring new data into view, click the window's title bar or press Ctrl+F6 until its title bar is selected.

When you want to resume normal, full-screen viewing in the workbook window, click the Maximize button in one of the windows. To get rid of a second window, click its button on the taskbar and then click its Close Window button on the far right side of the menu bar (the one with the X). (Be sure that you don't click the Close button on the far-right of the Excel title bar, because doing this closes your workbook file and exits you from Excel!)

Working with Multiple Workbooks

Working with more than one worksheet in a single workbook is bad enough, but working with worksheets in different workbooks can be really wicked. The key to doing this successfully is just keeping track of "who's on first"; you do this by opening and using windows on the individual workbook files you have open.

With the different workbook windows in place, you can then compare the data in different workbooks, use the drag-and-drop method to copy or move data between workbooks, or even copy or move entire worksheets.

Comparing windows on different workbooks

To work with sheets from different workbook files you have open, you manually arrange their workbook windows in the Excel Work area, or you click the View Side by Side command button on the View tab of the Ribbon or press Alt+WB. If you have only two workbooks open when you do this, Excel places the active workbook that you last opened above the one that opened earlier (with their active worksheets displayed). If you have more than two workbooks open, Excel displays the Compare Side by Side dialog box where you click the name of the workbook that you want to compare with the active one.

If you need to compare more than two workbooks on the same screen, instead of clicking the View Side by Side button on the View tab, you click the Arrange All button and then select the desired Arrange option (Tiled, Horizontal, Vertical, or Cascading) in the Arrange Windows dialog box. Just make sure when selecting this option that the Windows of Active Workbook check box is *not* selected in the Arrange Windows dialog box.

Transferring data between open windows

After the windows on your different workbooks are arranged onscreen the way you want them, you can compare or transfer information between them. To compare data in different workbooks, you switch between the different windows, activating and bringing the regions of the different worksheets you want to compare into view.

To move data between workbook windows, arrange the worksheets in these windows so that both the cells with the data entries you want to move and the cell range into which you want to move them are both displayed in their respective windows. Then, select the cell selection to be moved, drag it to the other worksheet window, drag it to the first cell of the range where it is to be moved to, and release the mouse button. To copy data between workbooks, you follow the exact same procedure, except that you hold down the Ctrl key as you drag the selected range from one window to another. (See Book 2, Chapter 3 for information on using drag-and-drop to copy and move data entries.)

When you're finished working with workbook windows arranged in some manner in the Excel Work area, you can return to the normal full-screen view by clicking the Maximize button on one of the windows. As soon as you maximize one workbook window, all the rest of the arranged workbook windows are made full size as well. If you used the View Side by Side feature to set up the windows, you can do this by clicking the View Side by Side command button on the View tab again or by pressing Alt+WB.

Transferring sheets from one workbook to another

Instead of copying cell ranges from one workbook to another, you can move (or copy) entire worksheets between workbooks. You can do this with drag-and-drop or by choosing the Move or Copy Sheet option from the Format command button's drop-down menu on the Ribbon's Home tab.

To use drag-and-drop to move a sheet between open windows, you simply drag its sheet tab from its window to the place on the sheet tabs in the other window where the sheet is to be moved to. As soon as you release the mouse button, the entire worksheet is moved from one file to the other, and its sheet tab now appears among the others in that workbook. To copy a sheet rather than move it, you perform the same procedure, except that you hold down the Ctrl key as you drag the sheet tab from one window to the next.

To use the Move or Copy Sheet option on the Format command button's drop-down menu to move or copy entire worksheets, you follow these steps:

1. **Open both the workbook containing the sheets to be moved or copied and the workbook where the sheets will be moved or copied to.**

Both the source and destination workbooks must be open in order to copy or move sheets between them.

2. **Click the workbook window with sheets to be moved or copied.**

Doing this activates the source workbook so that you can select the sheet or sheets you want to move or copy.

3. **Select the sheet tab of the worksheet or worksheets to be moved or copied.**

To select more than one worksheet, hold down the Ctrl key as you click the individual sheet tabs.

4. **Click the Format button on the Home tab and then choose Move or Copy Sheet from the drop-down menu or press Alt+HOM.**

Doing this opens the Move or Copy dialog box, as shown in Figure 4-12.

5. **From the To Book drop-down menu, choose the filename of the workbook into which the selected sheets are to be moved or copied.**

If you want to move or copy the selected worksheets into a new workbook file, click the (New Book) item at the very top of this drop-down menu.

6. **In the Before Sheet list box, click the name of the sheet that should immediately follow the sheet(s) that you're about to move or copy into this workbook.**

If you want to move or copy the selected sheet(s) to the very end of the destination workbook, click (Move to End) at the bottom of this list box.

7. **If you want to copy the selected sheet(s) rather than move them, click the Create a Copy check box.**

If you don't click this check box, Excel automatically moves the selected sheet(s) from one workbook to the other instead of copying them.

8. **Click OK to close the Move or Copy dialog box and complete the move or copy operation.**

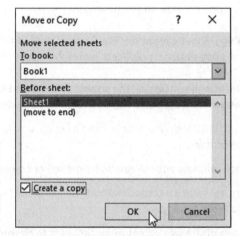

Consolidating Worksheets

Excel allows you to consolidate data from different worksheets into a single worksheet. Using the program's Consolidate command button on the Data tab of the Ribbon, you can easily combine data from multiple spreadsheets. For example, you can use the Consolidate command to total all budget spreadsheets prepared by each department in the company or to create summary totals for income statements for a period of several years. If you used a template to create each worksheet you're consolidating, or an identical layout, Excel can quickly consolidate the values by virtue of their common position in their respective worksheets. However, even when the data entries are laid out differently in each spreadsheet, Excel can still consolidate them provided that you've used the same labels to describe the data entries in their respective worksheets.

Most of the time, you want to total the data that you're consolidating from the various worksheets. By default, Excel uses the SUM function to total all the cells in the worksheets that share the same cell references (when you consolidate by position) or that use the same labels (when you consolidate by category). You can, however, have Excel use any of other following statistical functions when doing a consolidation: AVERAGE, COUNT, COUNTA, MAX, MIN, PRODUCT, STDEV, STDEVP, VAR, or VARP. (See Book 3, Chapter 5 for more information on these functions.)

To begin consolidating the sheets in the same workbook, you select a new worksheet to hold the consolidated data. (If need be, insert a new sheet in the workbook by clicking the Insert Worksheet button.) To begin consolidating sheets in different workbooks, open a new workbook. If the sheets in the various workbooks are generated from a template, open the new workbook for the consolidated data from that template.

Before you begin the consolidation process on the new worksheet, you choose the cell or cell range in this worksheet where the consolidated data is to appear. (This range is called the *destination area*.) If you select a single cell, Excel expands the destination area to columns to the right and rows below as needed to accommodate the consolidated data. If you select a single row, the program expands the destination area down subsequent rows of the worksheet, if required to accommodate the data. If you select a single column, Excel expands the destination area across columns to the right, if required to accommodate the data. If, however, you select a multi-cell range as the destination area, the program does not expand the destination area and restricts the consolidated data just to the cell selection.

TIP

If you want Excel to use a particular range in the worksheet for all consolidations you perform in a worksheet, assign the range name Consolidate_Area to this cell range. Excel then consolidates data into this range whenever you use the Consolidate command.

When consolidating data, you can select data in sheets in workbooks that you've opened in Excel or in sheets in unopened workbooks stored on disk. The cells that you specify for consolidation are referred to as the *source area*, and the worksheets that contain the source areas are known as the *source worksheets*.

If the source worksheets are open in Excel, you can specify the references of the source areas by pointing to the cell references (even when the Consolidate dialog box is open, Excel will allow you to activate different worksheets and scroll through them as you select the cell references for the source area). If the source worksheets are not open in Excel, you must type in the cell references as external references, following the same guidelines you use when typing a linking formula with an external reference (except that you don't type =). For example, to specify the data in range B4:R21 on Sheet1 in a workbook named `CG Music – 2014 Sales.xlsx` as a source area, you enter the following external reference:

```
'[CG Music – 2017 Sales.xlsx]Sheet1'!$b$4:$r$21
```

Note that if you want to consolidate the same data range in all the worksheets that use a similar filename (for example, `CG Music – 2015 Sales`, `CG Music – 2016 Sales`, `CG Music – 2017 Sales`, and so on), you can use the asterisk (*) or the question mark (?) as wildcard characters to stand for missing characters as in

```
'[CG Music – 20?? Sales.xlsx]Sheet1'!$B$4:$R$21
```

In this example, Excel consolidates the range A2:R21 in Sheet1 of all versions of the workbooks that use "CG - Music - 20" in the main file when this name is followed by another two characters (be they 15, 16, 17, 18, and so on).

When you consolidate data, Excel uses only the cells in the source areas that contain values. If the cells contain formulas, Excel uses their calculated values, but if the cells contain text, Excel ignores them and treats them as though they were blank (except in the case of category labels when you're consolidating your data by category as described later in this chapter).

Consolidating by position

You consolidate worksheets by position when they use the same layout (such as those created from a template). When you consolidate data by position, Excel does not copy the labels from the source areas to the destination area, only values. To consolidate worksheets by position, you follow these steps:

1. **Open all the workbooks with the worksheets you want to consolidate. If the sheets are all in one workbook, open it in Excel.**

    Now you need to activate a new worksheet to hold the consolidated data. If you're consolidating the data in a new workbook, you need to open it (File⇨New or Alt+FN). If you're consolidating worksheets generated from a template, use the template to create the new workbook in which you are to consolidate the spreadsheet data.

2. **Open a new worksheet to hold the consolidated data (Ctrl+N).**

    Next, you need to select the destination area in the new worksheet that is to hold the consolidated data.

3. **Click the cell at the beginning of the destination area in the consolidation worksheet, or select the cell range if you want to limit the destination area to a particular region.**

If you want Excel to expand the size of the destination area as needed to accommodate the source areas, just select the first cell of this range.

4. **Click the Consolidate command button on the Data tab of the Ribbon or press Alt+AN.**

Doing this opens the Consolidate dialog box similar to the one shown in Figure 4-13. By default, Excel uses the SUM function to total the values in the source areas. If you want to use another statistical function such as AVERAGE or COUNT, select the desired function from the Function drop-down list box.

5. **(Optional) Select the function you want to use from the Function drop-down list box if you don't want the values in the source areas summed together.**

Now, you need to specify the various source ranges to be consolidated and add them to the All References list box in the Consolidate dialog box. To do this, you specify each range to be used as the source data in the Reference text box and then click the Add button to add it to the All References list box.

6. **Select the cell range or type the cell references for the first source area in the Reference text box.**

When you select the cell range by pointing, Excel minimizes the Consolidate dialog box to the Reference text box so that you can see what you're selecting. If the workbook window is not visible, choose it from the Switch Windows button on the View tab or the Windows taskbar and then select the cell selection as you normally would. (Remember that you can move the Consolidate dialog box minimized to the Reference text box by dragging it by the title bar.)

If the source worksheets are not open, you can click the Browse command button to select the filename in the Browse dialog box to enter it (plus an exclamation point) into the Reference text box, and then you can type in the range name or cell references you want to use. If you prefer, you can type in the entire cell reference including the filename. Remember that you can use the asterisk (*) and question mark (?) wildcard characters when typing in the references for the source area.

7. **Click the Add command button to add this reference to the first source area to the All References list box.**

8. **Repeat Steps 6 and 7 until you have added all the references for all the source areas that you want to consolidate.**

9. **Click the OK button in the Consolidate dialog box.**

Excel closes the Consolidate dialog box and then consolidates all the values in the source areas in the place in the active worksheet designated as the destination area. Note that you can click the Undo button on the Quick Access toolbar or press Ctrl+Z to undo the effects of a consolidation if you find that you defined the destination and/or the source areas incorrectly.

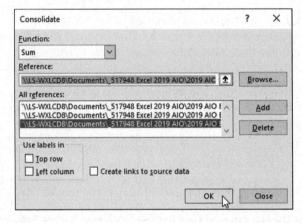

FIGURE 4-13:
Using the Consolidate dialog box to total sales data for three years stored on separate worksheets.

Figure 4-14 shows you the first part of a consolidation for three years (2015, 2016, and 2017) of record store sales in the newly created CG Music 2015 – 2017 Consolidated Sales.xlsx file in the workbook window in the upper-left corner. The Consolidated worksheet in this file totals the source area B4:R21 from the Sales worksheets in the CG Music – 2015 Sales.xlsx workbook with the 2015 annual sales, the CG Music – 2016 Sales.xlsx workbook with the 2016 annual sales, and the CG Music – 2017 Sales.xlsx workbook with the 2017 annual sales. These sales figures are consolidated in the destination area, B4:R21, in the Consolidated sheet in the CG Music 2015 – 2017 Consolidated Sales.xls workbook. (However, because all these worksheets use the same layout, only cell B4, the first cell in this range, was designated at the destination area.)

TIP

Excel allows only one consolidation per worksheet at one time. You can, however, add to or remove source areas and repeat a consolidation. To add new source areas, open the Consolidate dialog box and then specify the cell references in the Reference text box and click the Add button. To remove a source area, click its references in the All References list box and then click the Delete button. To perform the consolidation with the new source areas, click OK. To perform a second consolidation in the same worksheet, choose a new destination area, open the Consolidate dialog box, clear all the source areas you don't want to use in the All References list box with the Delete button, and then redefine all the new source areas in the Reference text box with the Add button before you perform the consolidation by clicking the OK button.

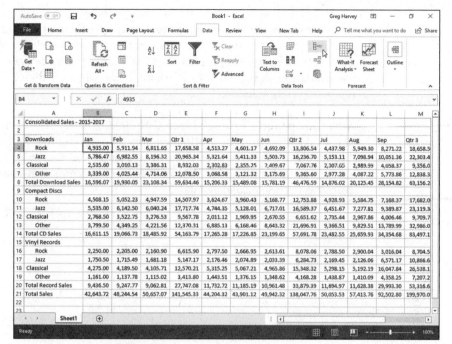

FIGURE 4-14:
The Consolidated worksheet after having Excel total sales from the last three years.

	A	B	C	D	E	F	G	H	I	J	K	L	M
1	Consolidated Sales - 2015-2017												
2													
3	Downloads	Jan	Feb	Mar	Qtr 1	Apr	May	Jun	Qtr 2	Jul	Aug	Sep	Qtr 3
4	Rock	4,935.00	5,911.94	6,811.65	17,658.58	4,513.27	4,601.17	4,692.09	13,806.54	4,437.98	5,949.30	8,271.22	18,658.5
5	Jazz	5,786.47	6,982.55	8,196.32	20,965.34	5,321.64	5,411.33	5,503.73	16,236.70	5,153.11	7,098.94	10,051.36	22,303.4
6	Classical	2,535.60	3,010.13	3,386.31	8,932.03	2,302.83	2,355.25	7,409.67	7,067.76	2,307.65	2,989.99	4,058.37	9,356.0
7	Other	3,339.00	4,025.44	4,714.06	12,078.50	3,068.58	3,121.32	3,175.69	9,365.60	2,977.28	4,087.22	5,773.86	12,838.3
8	Total Download Sales	16,596.07	19,930.05	23,108.34	59,634.46	15,206.33	15,489.08	15,781.19	46,476.59	14,876.02	20,125.45	28,154.82	63,156.2
9	Compact Discs												
10	Rock	4,508.15	5,052.23	4,947.59	14,507.97	3,624.67	3,960.43	5,168.77	12,753.88	4,928.93	5,584.75	7,168.37	17,682.0
11	Jazz	5,535.00	6,142.50	6,040.24	17,717.74	4,744.35	5,128.01	6,717.01	16,589.37	6,451.67	7,277.81	9,389.87	23,119.3
12	Classical	2,768.50	3,522.75	3,276.53	9,567.78	2,011.12	1,969.95	2,670.55	6,651.62	2,735.44	2,967.86	4,006.46	9,709.7
13	Other	3,799.50	4,349.25	4,221.56	12,370.31	6,885.13	6,168.46	8,643.32	21,696.91	9,366.51	9,829.51	13,789.99	32,986.0
14	Total CD Sales	16,611.15	19,066.73	18,485.92	54,163.79	17,265.28	17,226.85	23,199.65	57,691.78	23,482.55	25,659.93	34,354.68	83,497.1
15	Vinyl Records												
16	Rock	2,250.00	2,205.00	2,160.90	6,615.90	2,797.50	2,666.95	2,613.61	8,078.06	2,788.50	2,900.04	3,016.04	8,704.5
17	Jazz	1,750.50	1,715.49	1,681.18	5,147.17	2,176.46	2,074.89	2,033.39	6,284.73	2,169.45	2,126.06	6,571.17	10,866.6
18	Classical	4,275.00	4,189.50	4,105.71	12,570.21	5,315.25	5,067.21	4,965.86	15,348.32	5,298.15	5,192.19	16,047.84	26,538.1
19	Other	1,161.00	1,137.78	1,115.02	3,413.80	1,443.51	1,376.15	1,348.62	4,168.28	1,438.87	1,410.09	4,358.25	7,207.2
20	Total Record Sales	9,436.50	9,247.77	9,062.81	27,747.08	11,732.72	11,185.19	10,961.48	33,879.39	11,694.97	11,628.38	29,993.30	53,316.6
21	Total Sales	42,643.72	48,244.54	50,657.07	141,545.33	44,204.32	43,901.12	49,942.32	138,047.76	50,053.53	57,413.76	92,502.80	199,970.0
22													
23													

Consolidating by category

You consolidate worksheets by category when their source areas do not share the same cell coordinates in their respective worksheets, but their data entries do use common column and/or row labels. When you consolidate by category, you include these identifying labels as part of the source areas. Unlike when consolidating by position, Excel copies the row labels and/or column labels when you specify that they should be used in the consolidation.

When consolidating spreadsheet data by category, you must specify whether to use the top row of column labels and/or the left column of row labels in determining which data to consolidate. To use the top row of column labels, you click the Top Row check box in the Use Labels In section of the Consolidate dialog box. To use the left column of row labels, you click the Left Column check box in this area. Then, after you've specified all the source areas (including the cells that contain these column and row labels), you perform the consolidation in the destination area by clicking the Consolidate dialog box's OK button.

Linking consolidated data

Excel allows you to link the data in the source areas to the destination area during a consolidation. That way, any changes that you make to the values in the source area are automatically updated in the destination area of the consolidation worksheet. To create links between the source worksheets and the destination worksheet, you simply click the Create Links to Source Data check box in the Consolidate dialog box to put a check mark in it when defining the settings for the upcoming consolidation.

When you perform a consolidation with linking, Excel creates the links between the source areas and the destination area by outlining the destination area. (See "Outlining worksheets" earlier in this chapter for details.) Each outline level created in the destination area holds rows or columns that contain the linking formulas to the consolidated data.

Chapter **5**

Printing Worksheets

Printing the spreadsheet is one of the most important tasks that you do in Excel (maybe second only to saving your spreadsheet in the first place). Fortunately, Excel makes it easy to produce professional-looking reports from your worksheets. This chapter covers how to select the printer that you want to use; print all or just selected parts of the worksheet; change your page layout and print settings, including the orientation, paper size, print quality, number of copies, and range of pages, all from the Excel 2019 Backstage view. The chapter also enlightens you on how to use the Ribbon to set up reports using the correct margin settings, headers and footers, titles, and page breaks and use the Page Layout, Print Preview, and Page Break Preview features to make sure that the pages of your report are the way you want them to appear before you print them.

The printing techniques covered in this chapter focus primarily on printing the data in your spreadsheets. Of course, in Excel you can also print your charts in chart sheets. Not surprisingly, you will find that most of the printing techniques that you learn for printing worksheet data in this chapter also apply to printing charts in their respective sheets. (For specific information on printing charts, see Book 5, Chapter 1.)

Printing from the Excel 2019 Backstage View

The Excel 2019 Backstage view contains a Print screen (shown in Figure 5-1) opened by clicking File ⇨ Print or pressing Ctrl+P. This Print screen enables you to do any of the following:

» Change the number of spreadsheet report copies to be printed (1 copy is the default) by entering a new value in the Copies combo box.

» Click the name of a new printer to use in printing the spreadsheet report from the Printer drop-down list box. (See "Selecting the printer to use" that follows for details.)

» Change what part of the spreadsheet is printed in the report by selecting a new preset in the Active Sheets button's drop-down menu — you can choose between Print Active Sheets (the default), Print Entire Workbook, or Print Selection — or by entering a new value in the Pages combo boxes immediately below. Click the Ignore Print Area at the bottom of the Active Sheets button's drop-down menu when you want one of the other Print What options (Active Sheets, Entire Workbook, or Selection) that you selected to be used in the printing rather than the Print Area you previously defined. (See the "Setting and clearing the Print Area" section later in this chapter for details on how to set this area.)

» Print on both sides of the paper (assuming that your printer is capable of double-sided printing) by clicking either the Print on Both Sides, Flip Pages on Long Edge, or the Print on Both Sides, Flip Pages on Short Edge option from the Print One-Sided button's drop-down menu.

» Print multiple copies of the spreadsheet report without having your printer collate the pages of each copy (collating the copies is the default) by clicking the Uncollated option from the Collated button's drop-down menu.

» Change the orientation of the printing on the paper from the default portrait orientation to landscape (so that more columns of data and fewer rows are printed on each page of the report) by clicking the Landscape Orientation option from the Page Orientation button's drop-down menu.

» Change the paper size from Letter (8.5 x 11 in) to another paper size supported by your printer by clicking its option from the Page Size button's drop-down menu.

» Change the margins from the default Normal margins to Wide, Narrow, or the Last Custom Setting (representing the margin settings you last manually set for the report) by clicking one of these presets from the Margins button's drop-down menu. (See "Massaging the margins" later in this chapter for details.)

» Scale the worksheet so that all its columns or all its rows or all of its columns and rows fit onto a single printed page.

» Change the default settings used by your printer by using the options in the particular printer's Options dialog box. (These settings can include the print quality and color versus black and white or grayscale, depending upon the type of printer.) Open it by clicking the Printer Properties link right under the name of your printer in the Print screen.

» Preview the pages of the spreadsheet report on the right side of the Print screen. (See "Previewing the printout" later in this chapter for details.)

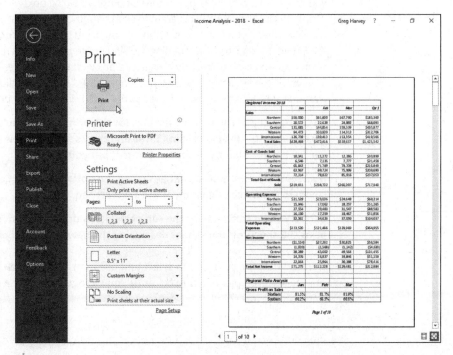

FIGURE 5-1:
Previewing your printout report and changing common print settings is a snap using the Print screen in the Excel 2019 Backstage view.

Selecting the printer to use

Windows allows you to install more than one printer for use with your applications. If you've installed multiple printers, the first one installed becomes the default printer, which is used by all Windows applications, including Excel 2019. If you get a new printer, you must first install it from the Windows 10 Control Panel before you can select and use the printer in Excel.

To select a new printer to use in printing the current worksheet, follow these steps:

1. Open the workbook with the worksheet that you want to print, activate that worksheet, and then click File ⇨ Print or simply press Ctrl+P.

The Print screen opens in the Backstage view (similar to the one shown in Figure 5-1). Be sure that you don't click the Quick Print button if you've added it to the Quick Access toolbar (as described later in this chapter), because doing so sends the active worksheet directly to the default printer (without giving you an opportunity to change the printer!).

2. Click the name of the new printer that you want to use from the Printer drop-down list box.

If the printer that you want to use isn't listed in the drop-down list, you can try to add the printer with the Add Printer link near the bottom of the list. When you click this button, Excel opens the Find Printers dialog box, where you specify the location for the program to search for the printer that you want to use. Note that if you don't have a printer connected to your computer, clicking the Find Printer button and opening the Find Printers dialog box results in opening a Find in the Directory alert dialog box with the message, "The Active Directory Domain Services is Currently Unavailable." When you click OK in this alert dialog box, Excel closes it as well as the Find Printers dialog box.

3. To change any of the default settings for the printer that you've selected, click the Printer Properties link Print and then select the new settings in the Properties dialog box for the printer that you selected.

4. Make any other required changes using the options (Pages, Collated, and so on) in the Settings section of the Print screen.

5. Click the Print button near the top of the left side of the Print screen to print the specified worksheet data using the newly selected printer.

Keep in mind that the printer you select and use in printing the current worksheet remains the selected printer in Excel until you change back to the original printer (or some other printer).

Previewing the printout

Excel 2019 gives you two ways to check the page layout before you send the report to the printer. In the worksheet, you can use the Page Layout view in the regular worksheet window that shows all the pages plus the margins along with the worksheet and row headings and rulers. Or, in the Excel Backstage view, you can use the old standby Print Preview on the right side of the Print screen, which shows you the pages of the report more or less as they appear on the printed page.

Checking the paging in Page Layout view

The Page Layout view — activated by clicking the Page Layout View button, the middle one of the three to the left of the Zoom slider on the Status bar or the Page Layout View command button on the View tab of the Ribbon — gives you instant access to the paging of the active worksheet.

As you can see in Figure 5-2, when you switch to Page Layout view, Excel adds horizontal and vertical rulers to the column letter and row number headings. In the Worksheet area, this view shows the margins for each printed page with any headers and footers defined for the report along with the breaks between each. (Often you have to use the Zoom slider to reduce the screen magnification to display the page breaks on the screen.)

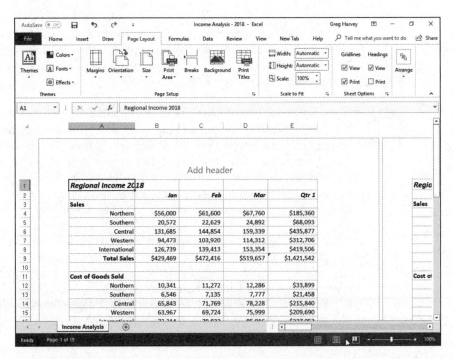

FIGURE 5-2:
Viewing a spreadsheet in Page Layout view.

TIP

To see all the pages required to print the active worksheet, drag the slider button in the Zoom slider on the Status bar to the left until you decrease the screen magnification sufficiently to display all the pages of data.

REMEMBER

Excel displays rulers using the default units for your computer (inches on a United States computer and centimeters on a European machine). To change the units, open the Advanced tab of the Excel Options dialog box (File ➪ Options ➪ Advanced or Alt+FTA) and then choose the appropriate unit from the Ruler Units drop-down menu (Inches, Centimeters, or Millimeters) in the Display section. Remember that you can turn the rulers off and back on in Page Layout view by deselecting the Ruler check box in the Show group on the View tab (Alt+WR) and then selecting it again (Alt+WR).

Previewing the pages of the report

Stop wasting paper and save your sanity by using the Print Preview feature before you print any worksheet, section of a worksheet, or entire workbook. Because of the peculiarities in paging worksheet data, check the page breaks for any report that requires more than one page. You can use Print Preview in the Print screen of the Excel Backstage view to see exactly how the worksheet data will be paged when printed. That way, you can return to the worksheet and make any necessary last-minute changes to the data or page settings before sending the report on to the printer.

To switch to the Print screen and preview the printout, choose File ➪ Print or simply press Ctrl+P. Excel displays the first page of the report on the right side of the Print screen. Look at Figure 5-3 to see the first preview page of a ten-page report as it initially appears in the Print screen.

TIP

If you use Print Preview frequently (as you should), you might want to add the Print Preview and Print button to the Quick Access toolbar and then open the Print screen in the Backstage view by clicking this button. To add a Print Preview and Print button, click the Customize Quick Access Toolbar button and then choose the Print Preview and Print option under Quick Print from its drop-down menu. (To remove the button, simply choose this same Print Preview option from the Customize Quick Access drop-down menu a second time.)

When Excel displays a full page in the Print Preview window, you sometimes can barely read its contents. In such a case, you can increase the view to actual size when you need to verify specific regions of the worksheet by clicking the Zoom to Page button at the bottom of the Print screen. Check out the difference in Figure 5-4 — here you can see what the first page of the ten-page report looks like after I zoom in by clicking the Zoom to Page button.

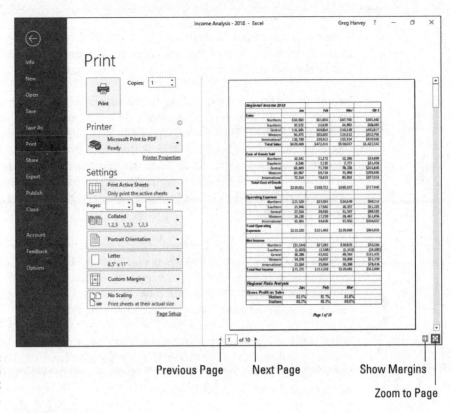

FIGURE 5-3:
Page 1 of a
ten-page report
in Print Preview.

Previous Page   Next Page   Show Margins

Zoom to Page

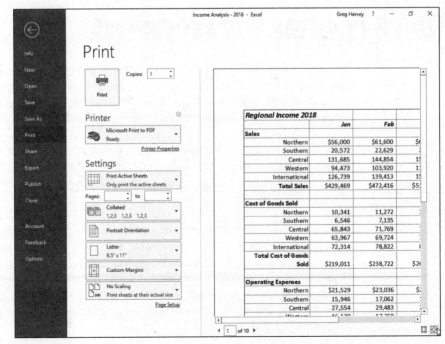

FIGURE 5-4:
Page 1 of a
ten-page report
after selecting
the Zoom to
Page button at
the bottom of
the Print screen.

Printing Worksheets

After you enlarge a page to actual size, use the scroll bars to bring new parts of the page into view in the Print Preview window. To return to the full-page view, you simply deselect the Zoom to Page button by clicking it a second time.

Excel indicates the number of pages in a report at the bottom left of the Print Preview area. If your report has more than one page, view pages that follow by clicking the Next Page button. To review a page you've already seen, back up a page by clicking the Previous Page button immediately below it. (The Previous Page button is grayed out if you're on the first page.) You can also advance to a particular page in the report by typing its page number into the text box to the immediate right of the Previous Page button that shows the current page and then pressing the Enter key.

If you want to display the current margin settings for the report in the print preview area, click the Show Margins button at the bottom of the Print screen to the immediate left of the Zoom to Page button. After the margins are displayed, you can then manually manipulate them by dragging them to new positions. (See "Massaging the margins" later in this chapter for details.)

When you finish previewing the report, you can print the spreadsheet report by clicking the Print button in the Print screen or you can exit the Backstage view and return to the worksheet by clicking the Back button at the very top of the File menu along the left side of the screen.

Quick Printing the Worksheet

As long as you want to use Excel's default print settings to print all the cells in the current worksheet, printing in Excel 2019 is a breeze. Simply add the Quick Print button to the Quick Access toolbar by clicking the Customize Quick Access Toolbar button and then choosing the Quick Print item from its drop-down menu.

After adding the Quick Print button to the Quick Access toolbar, you can use this button to print a single copy of all the information in the current worksheet, including any charts and graphics, everything but the comments you've added to cells.

When you click the Quick Print button, Excel routes the print job to the Windows print queue, which acts like a middleman and sends the job to the printer. While Excel sends the print job to the print queue, Excel displays a Printing dialog box to inform you of its progress (displaying such updates as *Printing Page 2 of 3*). After this dialog box disappears, you are free to go back to work in Excel. To stop the printing while the job is still being sent to the print queue, click the Cancel button in the Printing dialog box.

If you don't realize that you want to cancel the print job until after Excel finishes shipping it to the print queue (that is, while the Printing dialog box appears onscreen), you must take these steps:

1. **Right-click the printer icon in the notification area at the far right of the Windows 10 taskbar and then click the Open All Active Printers command from its shortcut menu.**

   This opens the dialog box for the printer with the Excel print job in its queue (as described under the Document Name heading in the list box).

2. **Select the Excel print job that you want to cancel in the list box of your printer's dialog box.**

3. **Click Document ⇨ Cancel from the menu and then click Yes to confirm you want to cancel the print job.**

4. **Wait for the print job to disappear from the queue in the printer's dialog box and then click the Close button to return to Excel.**

Working with the Page Setup Options

About the only thing the slightest bit complex in printing a worksheet is figuring out how to get the pages right. Fortunately, the command buttons in the Page Setup group on the Ribbon's Page Layout tab give you a great deal of control over what goes on which page.

There are two groups of buttons on the Page Layout tab that are helpful in getting your page settings exactly as you want them: the Page Setup group and the Scale to Fit group both described in upcoming sections.

TIP

To see the effect of changes you make to the page setup settings in the Worksheet area, put the worksheet into Page Layout view by clicking the Page Layout button on the Status bar as you work with the command buttons in Page Setup and Scale to Fit groups on the Page Layout tab.

Using the buttons in the Page Setup group

The Page Setup group of the Page Layout tab contains the following important command buttons:

» **Margins:** Select one of three preset margins for the report or to set custom margins on the Margins tab of the Page Setup dialog box. (See "Massaging the margins" later in this chapter.)

- » **Orientation:** Choose between Portrait and Landscape mode for the printing. (See "Getting the lay of the landscape" later in this chapter.)

- » **Size:** Select one of the preset paper sizes or to set a custom size or to change the printing resolution or page number on the Page tab of the Page Layout dialog box.

- » **Print Area:** Set and clear the Print Area. (See "Setting and clearing the Print Area" immediately following in this chapter.)

- » **Breaks:** Insert or remove page breaks. (See "Solving Page Break Problems" later in this chapter.)

- » **Background:** Open the Sheet Background dialog box, where you can select a new graphic image or photo to be used as a background for all the worksheets in the workbook. (Note that this button changes to Delete Background as soon as you select a background image.)

- » **Print Titles:** Open the Sheet tab of the Page Setup dialog box, where you can define rows of the worksheet to repeat at the top and columns at the left as print titles for the report. (See "Putting out the print titles" later in this chapter.)

Setting and clearing the Print Area

Excel includes a special printing feature called the Print Area. You click Print Area ⇨ Set Print Area on the Ribbon's Page Layout tab or press Alt+PRS to define any cell selection on a worksheet as the Print Area. After you define the Print Area, Excel then prints this cell selection anytime you print the worksheet (either with the Quick Print button on the Quick Access toolbar or by choosing File ⇨ Print and then clicking the Print button on the Print screen).

REMEMBER

Whenever you fool with the Print Area, you need to keep in mind that after you define it, its cell range is the only one you can print (regardless of what other print area options you select in the Print screen unless you click the Ignore Print Areas check box at the bottom of the very first drop-down menu in the Settings section of the Print screen and until you clear the Print Area).

To clear the Print Area (and therefore go back to the printing defaults Excel establishes in the Print screen), you just have to click Print Area ⇨ Clear Print Area on the Page Layout tab or simply press Alt+PRC.

REMEMBER

Keep in mind that you can also define and clear the Print Area from the Sheet tab of the Page Setup dialog box opened by clicking the Dialog Box launcher button in the Page Setup group on the Page Layout Ribbon tab (Alt+PSP). To define the Print Area from this dialog box, click the Print Area text box on the Sheet tab to insert the cursor and then select the cell range or ranges in the worksheet. (Remember that you can reduce the Page Setup dialog box to just this text box by clicking its minimize box.) To clear the Print Area from this dialog box, select the cell addresses in the Print Area text box and press the Delete key.

Massaging the margins

The Normal margin settings that Excel applies to a new report use standard top and bottom margins of 0.75 inch (¾ inch) and left and right margins of 0.7 inch with just over a ¼ inch separating the header and footer from the top and bottom margins, respectively.

In addition to the Normal margin settings, the program enables you to choose two other standard margins from the Margins button's drop-down menu in the Print screen (Ctrl+P):

>> **Wide** margins with 1-inch top, bottom, left, and right margins and ½ inch separating the header and footer from the top and bottom margins, respectively.

>> **Narrow** margins with top and bottom margins of ¾ inch, and left and right margins of ¼ inch with slightly more than ¼ inch separating the header and footer from the top and bottom margins, respectively.

Frequently, you find yourself with a report that takes up a full printed page and then just enough to spill over onto a second, mostly empty, page. To squeeze the last column or the last few rows of the worksheet data onto Page 1, try choosing Narrow from the Margins button's drop-down menu.

If that doesn't do it, you can try manually adjusting the margins for the report either from the Margins tab of the Page Setup dialog box or by dragging the margin markers in the print preview area on the Print screen in the Excel Backstage view. To get more columns on a page, try reducing the left and right margins. To get more rows on a page, try reducing the top and bottom margins.

To open the Margins tab of the Page Setup dialog box (shown in Figure 5-5), open the Page Setup dialog box (Alt+PSP) and then click the Margins tab. There, enter the new settings in the Top, Bottom, Left, and Right text boxes — or select the new margin settings with their respective spinner buttons.

TIP

Select one or both Center on Page options in the Margins tab of the Page Setup dialog box (refer to Figure 5-5) to center a selection of data (that takes up less than a full page) between the current margin settings. In the Center on Page section, click the Horizontally check box to center the data between the left and right margins. Click the Vertically check box to center the data between the top and bottom margins.

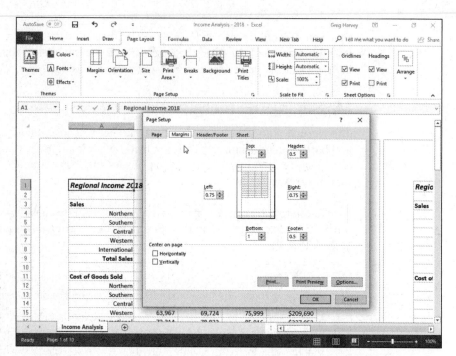

FIGURE 5-5:
Adjust your
report margins
from the Margins
tab in the Page
Setup dialog box.

If you click the Show Margins check box at the bottom of the Print screen in the Excel Backstage view (Ctrl+P) to change the margin settings, you can modify the column widths as well as the margins. (See Figure 5-6.) To change one of the margins, position the mouse pointer on the desired margin marker (the pointer shape changes to a double-headed arrow) and drag the marker with your mouse in the appropriate direction. When you release the mouse button, Excel redraws the page, using the new margin setting. You may gain or lose columns or rows, depending on what kind of adjustment you make. Changing the column width is the same story: Drag the column marker to the left or right to decrease or increase the width of a particular column.

Getting the lay of the landscape

The drop-down menu attached to the Orientation button in the Page Setup group of the Page Layout tab of the Ribbon contains two options:

>> **Portrait** (the default), where the printing runs parallel to the short edge of the paper

>> **Landscape,** where the printing runs parallel to the long edge of the paper

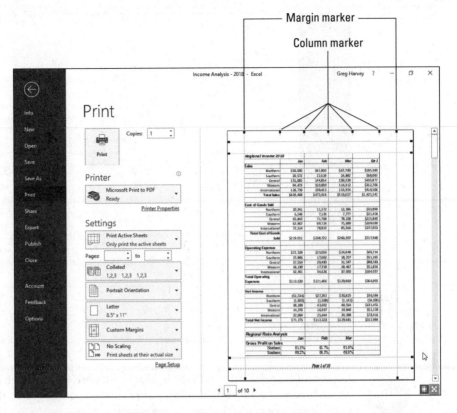

Margin marker

Column marker

FIGURE 5-6:
Drag a marker to adjust its margin in the Page Preview window when the Show Margins check box is selected.

Because many worksheets are far wider than they are tall (such as budgets or sales tables that track expenditures across all 12 months), you may find that their worksheets page better if you switch the orientation from the normal portrait mode (which accommodates fewer columns on a page because the printing runs parallel to the short edge of the page) to landscape mode.

In Figure 5-7, you can see the Print screen in the Backstage view with the first page of a report in landscape mode in the Page Layout view. For this report, Excel can fit three more columns of information on this page in landscape mode than it can in portrait mode. Therefore, the total page count for this report decreases from ten pages in portrait mode to six pages in landscape mode.

Putting out the print titles

Excel's Print Titles enable you to print particular row and column headings on each page of the report. Print titles are important in multi-page reports where the columns and rows of related data spill over to other pages that no longer show the row and column headings on the first page.

Printing Worksheets

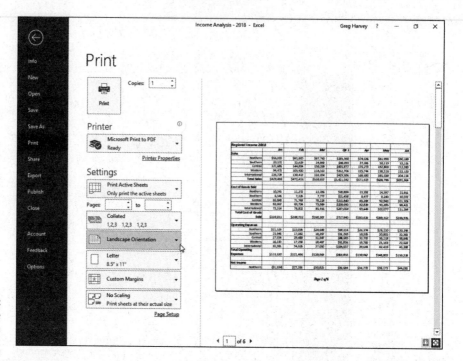

FIGURE 5-7:
A landscape
mode report in
Page Layout view.

REMEMBER

Don't confuse print titles with the header of a report. Even though both are printed on each page, header information prints in the top margin of the report; print titles always appear in the body of the report — at the top, in the case of rows used as print titles, and on the left, in the case of columns.

To designate rows and/or columns as the print titles for a report, follow these steps:

1. Click the Print Titles button on the Ribbon's Page Layout tab or press Alt+PI.

The Page Setup dialog box appears with the Sheet tab selected (similar to the one shown in Figure 5-8).

To designate worksheet rows as print titles, go to Step 2a. To designate worksheet columns as print titles, go to Step 2b.

2a. Select the Rows to Repeat at Top text box and then drag through the rows with information you want to appear at the top of each page in the worksheet below. If necessary, reduce the Page Setup dialog box to just the Rows to Repeat at Top text box by clicking the text box's Collapse/Expand button.

In the example I show you in Figure 5-8, I clicked the minimize button associated with the Rows to Repeat at Top text box and then dragged through rows 1 and 2 in column A of the Income Analysis worksheet, and the program entered the row range $1:$2 in the Rows to Repeat at Top text box.

Note that Excel indicates the print-title rows in the worksheet by placing a dotted line (that moves like a marquee) on the border between the titles and the information in the body of the report.

2b. **Select the Columns to Repeat at Left text box and then drag through the range of columns with the information you want to appear at the left edge of each page of the printed report in the worksheet below. If necessary, reduce the Page Setup dialog box to just the Columns to Repeat at Left text box by clicking its Collapse/Expand button.**

Note that Excel indicates the print-title columns in the worksheet by placing a dotted line (that moves like a marquee) on the border between the titles and the information in the body of the report.

3. **Click OK or press Enter to close the Page Setup dialog box or click the Print Preview button to preview the page titles in the Print Preview pane on the Print screen.**

After you close the Page Setup dialog box, the dotted line showing the border of the row and/or column titles disappears from the worksheet.

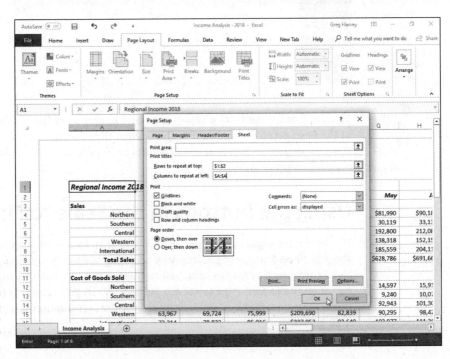

FIGURE 5-8: Specify the rows and columns to use as print titles on the Sheet tab of the Page Setup dialog box.

In Figure 5-8, rows 1 and 2 containing the worksheet title and column headings for the Income Analysis worksheet are designated as the print titles for the report. In Figure 5-9, you can see the Print Preview window with the second page of the report. Note how these print titles appear on all pages of the report.

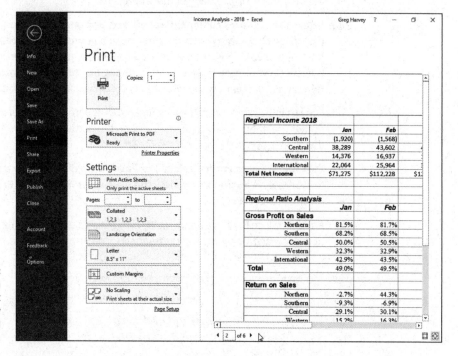

FIGURE 5-9:
Page 2 of a sample report in Print Preview with defined print titles.

REMEMBER

To clear print titles from a report if you no longer need them, open the Sheet tab of the Page Setup dialog box and then delete the row and column ranges from the Rows to Repeat at Top and the Columns to Repeat at Left text boxes before you click OK or press Enter.

Using the buttons in the Scale to Fit group

If your printer supports scaling options, you're in luck. You can always get a worksheet to fit on a single page simply by selecting the 1 Page option on the Width and Height drop-down menus attached to their command buttons in the Scale to Fit group on the Layout Page tab of the Ribbon. When you select these options, Excel figures out how much to reduce the size of the information you're printing to fit it all on one page.

If you preview this one page in the Print screen of the Backstage view (Ctrl+P) and find that the printing is just too small to read comfortably, return to the worksheet view. Then, reopen the Page tab of the Page Setup dialog box and try changing the number of pages in the Page(s) Wide and Tall text boxes (to the immediate right of the Fit To option button).

TIP

Instead of trying to stuff everything on one page, check out how your worksheet looks if you fit it on two pages across. Try this: Select 2 Pages from the Width button's drop-down list on the Page Layout tab and leave 1 Page selected in the Height drop-down list. Alternatively, see how the worksheet looks on two pages down: Select 1 Page from the Width button's drop-down list and 2 Pages from the Height button's drop-down list.

TIP

After using the Width and Height Scale to Fit options, you may find that you don't want to scale the printing. Cancel scaling by selecting Automatic on both the Width and Height drop-down lists and then entering **100** in the Scale text (or select 100 with its spinner buttons).

Using the Print Options on the Sheet tab of the Page Setup dialog box

The Print section of the Sheet tab of the Page Setup dialog box (Alt+PSP) contains some very useful Print check box options (none of which is automatically selected) and a couple of drop-down options of which you should be aware:

>> **Gridlines** check box to print the column and row gridlines on each page of the report

>> **Comments** drop-down to have all text notes added to the worksheet cells to be printed in the report either at the very end of the data in the report or on pages of the report as they are displayed in the worksheet (see Book 4, Chapter 3 for details on adding notes)

>> **Cell Errors As** drop-down to mask all the formula errors in the worksheet cells to be printed in the report with blank cell, double dashes, or #NA symbols (see Book 3, Chapter 2 for more information on error values in worksheet formulas)

>> **Black and White** check box to have Excel print the entire report in black ink, ignoring all color text enhancements and graphics in the report (useful when you only need a draft printout of the worksheet data and want to conserve your color ink cartridges)

>> **Draft Quality** check box to print a draft of the report at a lower resolution, thus saving on ink (note that not all printers support different printing at different resolutions so check the Quality option in your printer's Properties dialog box by clicking the Printer Properties link on the Print screen to be sure)

>> **Row and Column Headings** check box to print the row headings with the row numbers, and the column headings with the column letters on each page of the report

TIP

Click both Gridlines and Row and Column Headings check boxes when you want the printed version of your spreadsheet data to match as closely as possible their onscreen appearance. This is useful when you need to use the cell references on the printout to help you later locate the cells in the actual worksheet that needs editing. Note that you can select them without opening the Page Setup dialog box simply by clicking the Print check boxes in the Sheet Options group of the Layout Tab of the Ribbon. (The Gridline Print check box is located directly below Gridline label, and the Headings Print check box is directly below the Headings label in the Sheet Options group.) You can also do this by pressing Alt+PPG to select the Gridlines Print check box and Alt+PPH to select the Heading Print check box.

Headers and Footers

Headers and footers are simply standard text that appears on every page of the report. A header is printed in the top margin of the page, and a footer is printed — you guessed it — in the bottom margin. Both are centered vertically in the margins. Unless you specify otherwise, Excel does not automatically add either a header or footer to a new workbook.

TIP

Use headers and footers in a report to identify the document used to produce the report and display the page numbers and the date and time of printing.

The easiest way to add a header or footer to a report is to add it after putting the worksheet in Page Layout view by clicking the Page Layout View button on the Status bar (or by clicking the Page Layout View button on the Ribbon's View tab or by just pressing Alt+WP).

When the worksheet is displayed in Page Layout view, position the mouse pointer over the section in the top margin of the first page marked Add Header or in the bottom margin of the first page marked Add Footer.

REMEMBER

To create a centered header or footer, highlight the center section of this header/ footer area and then click the mouse pointer to set the insertion point in the middle of the section. To add a left-aligned header or footer, highlight and then click to set the insertion point flush with the left edge of the left section, or to add a right-aligned header or footer, highlight and click to set the insertion point flush with the right edge of the right section.

Immediately after setting the insertion point in the left, center, or right section of the header/footer area, Excel adds a Header & Footer Tools contextual tab with its own Design tab. (See Figure 5-10.) The Design tab is divided into Header & Footer, Header & Footer Elements, Navigation, and Options groups.

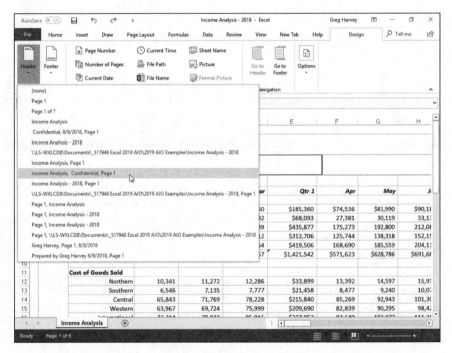

FIGURE 5-10:
Defining a new
header using the
Header drop-
down menu on
the Design tab of
the Header &
Footer Tools
contextual tab.

Adding a ready-made header or footer

The Header and Auto Footer buttons on the Design tab of the Header & Footer Tools contextual tab enable you to add stock headers and footers in an instant simply by clicking their examples from the drop-down menus that appear when you click them.

To create the centered header and footer for the report shown in Figure 5-11, I first chose

    Income Analysis, Confidential, Page 1

from the Header button's drop-down menu. (Income Analysis is the name of the worksheet; Confidential is stock text; and Page 1 is, of course, the current page number.)

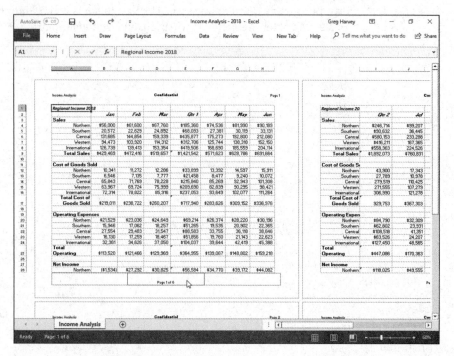

FIGURE 5-11:
The first page
of a report in
Page Layout view
shows you how
the header and
footer will print.

To set up the footer, I chose

    Page 1 of ?

from the Footer button's drop-down menu (which puts the current page number, along with the total number of pages, in the report). You can choose this paging option from either the Header or Footer drop-down menu.

Check out the results in Figure 5-11, which is the first page of the report in Page Layout view. Here you can see the header and footer as they will print. You can also see how choosing Page 1 of ? works in the footer: On the first page, you see the centered footer: Page 1 of 6; on the second page, you would see the centered footer Page 2 of 6.

If, after selecting a ready-made header or footer, you decide that you no longer need either the header or footer printed in your report, click the header or footer in Page Layout view and then choose the (none) option at the top of the Header button's or Footer button's drop-down menu. (The Design tab on the Header & Footer Tools contextual tab automatically appears and is selected on the Ribbon the moment you click the header or footer in Page Layout view.)

Creating a custom header or footer

Most of the time, the stock headers and footers available on the Header button's and Footer button's drop-down menus are sufficient for your report printing needs. Every once in a while, however, you may want to insert information not available in these list boxes or in an arrangement Excel doesn't offer in the ready-made headers and footers.

For those times, you need to use the command buttons that appear in the Header & Footer Elements group of the Design tab on the Header & Footer Tools contextual tab. These command buttons enable you to blend your own information with that generated by Excel into different sections of the custom header or footer you're creating.

The command buttons in the Header & Footer Elements group include the following:

- **Page Number:** Click this button to insert the &[Page] code that puts in the current page number.

- **Number of Pages:** Click this button to insert the &[Pages] code that puts in the total number of pages.

- **Current Date:** Click this button to insert the &[Date] code that puts in the current date.

- **Current Time:** Click this button to insert the &[Time] code that puts in the current time.

- **File Path:** Click this button to insert the &[Path]&[File] code that puts in the directory path along with the name of the workbook file.

- **File Name:** Click this button to insert the &[File] code that puts in the name of the workbook file.

- **Sheet Name:** Click this button to insert the &[Tab] code that puts in the name of the worksheet as shown on the sheet tab.

- **Picture:** Click this button to insert the &[Picture] code that inserts the image that you select from the Insert Pictures dialog box that enables you to get a graphics file on your computer or download one (see Book 5, Chapter 2 for more on inserting pictures).

>> **Format Picture:** Click this button to apply the formatting that you choose from the Format Picture dialog box to the &[Picture] code that you enter with the Insert Picture button without adding any code of its own.

To use these command buttons in the Header & Footer Elements group to create a custom header or footer, follow these steps:

1. **Put your worksheet into Page Layout view by clicking the Page Layout View button on the Status bar, or by choosing View⇨ Page Layout View on the Ribbon, or by pressing Alt+WP.**

   In Page Layout view, the text Add Header appears centered in the top margin of the first page, and the text Add Footer appears centered in the bottom margin.

2. **Position the mouse or Touch pointer in the top margin to create a custom header or in the bottom margin to create a custom footer, and then click the pointer in the left, center, or right section of the header or footer to set the insertion point and left-align, center, or right-align the text.**

   When Excel sets the insertion point, the text, Add Header and Add Footer, disappears, and the Design tab on the Header & Footer Tools contextual tab becomes active on the Ribbon.

3. **To add program-generated information to your custom header or footer such as the filename, worksheet name, current date, and so forth, click its command button in the Header & Footer Elements group.**

   Excel inserts the appropriate header/footer code preceded by an ampersand (&) in the header or footer. These codes are replaced by the actual information (filename, worksheet name, graphic image, and the like) as soon as you click another section of the header or footer or finish the header or footer by clicking the mouse pointer outside of it.

4. **(Optional) To add your own text to the custom header or footer, type it at the insertion point.**

   When joining program-generated information indicated by a header/footer code with your own text, be sure to insert the appropriate spaces and punctuation. For example, to have Excel display Page 1 of 4 in a custom header or footer, you do the following:

   a. **Type the word Page and press the spacebar.**

   b. **Click the Page Number command button and press the spacebar again.**

c. Type the word of and press the spacebar a third time.

d. Click the Number of Pages command button.

This inserts Page &[Page] of &[Pages] in the custom header (or footer).

5. **(Optional) To modify the font, font size, or some other font attribute of your custom header or footer, drag through its codes and text, click the Home tab, and then click the appropriate command button in the Font group.**

In addition to selecting a new font and font size for the custom header or footer, you can add bold, italics, underlining, and a new font color to its text with the Bold, Italic, Underline, and Font Color command buttons on the Home tab.

6. **After you finish defining and formatting the codes and text in your custom header or footer, click a cell in the Worksheet area to deselect the header or footer area.**

Excel replaces the header/footer codes in the custom header or footer with the actual information, while at the same time removing the Header & Footer Tools contextual tab from the Ribbon.

Figure 5-12 shows you a custom footer I added to a spreadsheet in Page Layout view. This custom footer blends my own text with program-generated page, date, and time information, and uses all three sections: left-aligned page information, a centered Preliminary warning, and right-aligned current date and time.

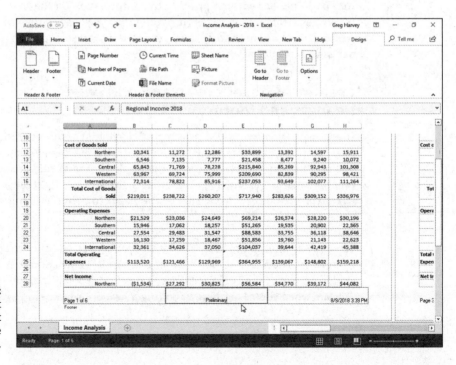

FIGURE 5-12:
A spreadsheet in Page Layout view showing the custom footer.

Creating unique first-page headers and footers

Excel 2019 enables you to define a header or footer for the first page that's different from all the rest of the pages. Simply click the Different First Page check box to put a check mark in it. (This check box is part of the Options group of the Design tab on the Header & Footer Tools contextual tab that appears when you're defining or editing a header or footer in Page Layout view.)

After selecting the Different First Page check box, go ahead and define the unique header and/or footer for just the first page (now marked First Page Header or First Page Footer). Then, on the second page of the report, define the header and/or footer (marked simply Header or Footer) for the remaining pages of the report. (See "Adding a ready-made header or footer" and "Creating a custom header or footer" earlier in the chapter for details.)

TIP

Use this feature when your spreadsheet report has a cover page that needs no header or footer. For example, say you have a report that needs the current page number and total pages centered at the bottom of all pages but the first, cover page. To do this, select the Different First Page check box on the Design tab of the Header & Footer Tools contextual tab on the Ribbon and then define a centered stock footer that displays the current page number and total pages (Page 1 of ?) on the second page of the report, leaving the Add Footer text intact on the first page.

Excel correctly numbers both the total number of pages in the report and the current page number without printing this information on the first page. So if your report has a total of six pages (including the cover page), the second page footer will read Page 2 of 6; the third page, Page 3 of 6; and so on, even if the first printed page has no footer at all.

Creating different even and odd page headers and footers

If you plan to do two-sided printing or copying of your spreadsheet report, you may want to define one header or footer for the even pages and another for the odd pages of the report. That way, the header or footer information (such as the report name or current page) alternates from being right-aligned on the odd pages (printed on the front side of the page) to being left-aligned on the even pages (printed on the back side of the page).

To create an alternating header or footer for a report, you click the Different Odd & Even Pages check box to put a check mark in it. (This check box is found in the Options group of the Design tab on the Header & Footer Tools contextual tab that appears when you're defining or editing a header or footer in Page Layout view.)

After that, create a header or footer on the first page of the report (now marked Odd Page Header or Odd Page Footer) in the third, right-aligned section header or footer area and then re-create this header or footer on the second page (now marked Even Page Header or Even Page Footer), this time in the first, left-aligned section.

Solving Page Break Problems

The Page Break Preview feature in Excel enables you to spot page break problems in an instant as well as fix them, such as when the program wants to split onto different pages information that you know should always appear on the same page.

Figure 5-13 shows a worksheet in Page Break Preview with an example of a bad vertical and horizontal page break that you can remedy by adjusting the location of the page break on Pages 1 and 3. Given the page size, orientation, and margin settings for this report, Excel inserts a vertical page break between columns H and I. This break separates the April, May, and June sales on Page 1 from the Qtr 2 subtotals on Page 3. It also inserts a horizontal page break between rows 28 and 29, splitting the Net Income heading from its data in the rows below.

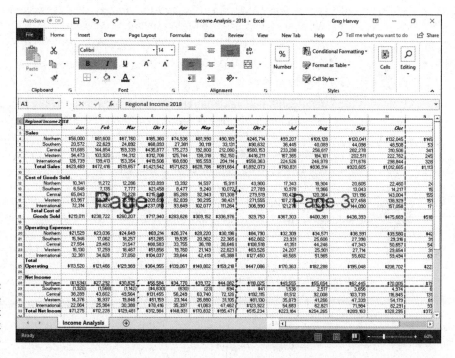

FIGURE 5-13: Preview page breaks in a report in Page Break Preview.

To correct the bad vertical page break, you need to move the page break to a column on the left several columns so that it occurs between columns E (with the Qtr 1 subtotals) and F (containing the April sales) so that the second quarter sales and subtotals are printed together on Page 3. To correct the bad horizontal page break, you need to move that break up one row so that the Net Income heading prints on the page with its data on Page 2.

Figure 5-13 illustrates how you can correct these two bad page breaks in Page Break Preview mode by following these steps:

1. **Click the Page Break Preview button (the third one in the cluster of three to the left of the Zoom slider) on the Status bar, or choose View ⇨ Page Break Preview on the Ribbon, or press Alt+WI.**

    This takes you into a Page Break Preview mode that shows your worksheet data at a reduced magnification (60 percent of normal in Figure 5-13) with the page numbers displayed in large, light type and the page breaks shown by heavy lines between the columns and rows of the worksheet.

2. **Position the mouse or Touch pointer somewhere on the page break indicator (one of the heavy lines surrounding the representation of the page) that you need to adjust; when the pointer changes to a double-headed arrow, drag the page indicator to the desired column or row and release the mouse button.**

    For the example shown in Figure 5-13, I dragged the page break indicator between Pages 1 and 3 to the left so that it's between columns E and F and the page indicator between Page 1 and 2 up so that its between row 26 and 27.

    In Figure 5-14, you can see Page 1 of the report as it then appears in the Print Preview window.

3. **After you finish adjusting the page breaks in Page Break Preview (and, presumably, printing the report), click the Normal button (the first one in the cluster of three to the left of the Zoom slider) on the Status bar, or click View ⇨ Normal on the Ribbon, or press Alt+WL to return the worksheet to its regular view of the data.**

TIP

You can also insert your own manual page breaks at the cell cursor's position by choosing Insert Page Break from the Breaks button's drop-down menu on the Page Layout tab (Alt+PBI), and you can remove them by choosing Remove Page Break from this menu (Alt+PBR). To remove all manual page breaks that you've inserted into a report, choose Reset All Page Breaks from the Breaks button's drop-down menu (Alt+PBA).

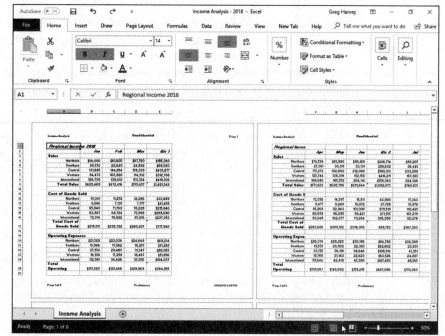

FIGURE 5-14:
Page 1 of the report in the Print Preview window after adjusting the page breaks in Page Break Preview mode.

Printing the Formulas in a Report

There's one more printing technique you may need every once in a while, and that's how to print the formulas in a worksheet in a report instead of printing the calculated results of the formulas. You can check over a printout of the formulas in your worksheet to make sure that you haven't done anything stupid (like replace a formula with a number or use the wrong cell references in a formula) before you distribute the worksheet company wide.

Before you can print a worksheet's formulas, you have to display the formulas, rather than their results, in the cells by clicking the Show Formulas button (the one that kind of looks like a page of a calendar with a tiny 15 above an *fx*) in the Formula Auditing group on the Formulas tab of the Ribbon (Alt+MH).

Excel then displays the contents of each cell in the worksheet as they normally appear only in the Formula bar or when you're editing them in the cell. Notice that value entries lose their number formatting, formulas appear in their cells (Excel widens the columns with best-fit so that the formulas appear in their entirety), and long text entries no longer spill over into neighboring blank cells.

Excel allows you to toggle between the normal cell display and the formula cell display by pressing Ctrl+`. (That is, press Ctrl and the key with the tilde on top.) This key — usually found in the upper-left corner of your keyboard — does double-duty as a tilde and as a weird backward accent mark: ` (Don't confuse that backward accent mark with the apostrophe that appears on the same key as the quotation mark!)

After Excel displays the formulas in the worksheet, you are ready to print it as you would any other report. You can include the worksheet column letters and row numbers as headings in the printout so that if you do spot an error, you can pinpoint the cell reference right away.

To include the row and column headings in the printout, put a check mark in the Print check box in the Headings column on the Sheet Options group of the Page Layout tab of the Ribbon before you send the report to the printer.

After you print the worksheet with the formulas, return the worksheet to normal by clicking the Show Formulas button on the Formulas tab of the Ribbon or by pressing Ctrl+`.

3

Formulas and Functions

Contents at a Glance

IN THIS CHAPTER

» **Summing data ranges with AutoSum**

» **Creating simple formulas with operators**

» **Understanding the operators and their priority in the formula**

» **Using the Insert Function button on the Formula bar**

» **Copying formulas and changing the type of cell references**

» **Building array formulas**

» **Using range names in formulas**

» **Creating linking formulas that bring values forward**

» **Controlling formula recalculation**

» **Dealing with circular references in formulas**

Chapter **1**

Building Basic Formulas

ormulas, to put it mildly, are the very "bread and butter" of the worksheet. Without formulas, the electronic spreadsheet would be little better than its green-sheet paper equivalent. Fortunately, Excel gives you the ability to do all your calculations right within the cells of the worksheet without any need for a separate calculator.

The formulas that you build in a spreadsheet can run the gamut from very simple to extremely complex. Formulas can rely totally upon the use of simple *operators* or the use of built-in *functions*, both of which describe the type of operation or calculation to perform and the order in which to perform it. Or they can blend the use of operators and functions together. When you use Excel functions in your formulas, you need to learn the particular type of information that a particular function uses in performing its calculations. The information that you supply a function and that it uses in its computation is referred to as the *argument(s)* of the function.

Formulas 101

From the simple addition formula to the most complex ANOVA statistical variation, all formulas in Excel have one thing in common: They all begin with the equal sign (=). This doesn't mean that you always have to type in the equal sign — although if you do, Excel expects that a formula of some type is to follow. When building a formula that uses a built-in function, oftentimes you use the Insert Function button on the Formula bar to select and insert the function, in which case, Excel adds the opening equal sign for you.

TIP

If you're an old Lotus 1-2-3 user and you still want to type the @ symbol to start a function, Excel accepts the at symbol and automatically converts it into an equal sign the moment that you complete the formula entry. It does mean, however, that each and every completed formula that appears on the Formula bar starts with the equal sign.

When building your formulas, you can use *constants* that actually contain the number that you want used in the calculation (such as "4.5%," "$25.00," or "-78.35"), or you can use cell addresses between the operators or as the arguments of functions. When you create a formula that uses cell addresses, Excel then uses the values that you've input in those cells in calculating the formula. Unlike when using constants in formulas, when you use cell addresses, Excel automatically updates the results calculated by a formula whenever you edit the values in the cells to which it refers.

Formula building methods

When building formulas manually, you can either type in the cell addresses or you can point to them in the worksheet. Using the Pointing method to supply the cell addresses for formulas is often easier and is always a much more foolproof method of formula building; when you type in a cell address, you are less apt to notice that you've just designated the wrong cell than when pointing directly to it. For this reason, stick to pointing when building original formulas and restrict typing cell addresses to the odd occasion when you need to edit a cell address in a formula and pointing to it is either not practical or just too much trouble.

TECHNICAL STUFF

FORMULAS AND FORMATTING

When defining a formula that uses operators or functions, Excel picks up the number formatting of the cells that are referenced in the formula. For example, if you add cell A2 to B3, as in =A2+B3, and cell B3 is formatted with the Currency Style format, the result will inherit this format and be displayed in its cell using the Currency Style.

When you use the Pointing method to build a simple formula that defines a sequence of operations, you stop and click the cell or drag through the cell range after typing each operator in the formula. When using the method to build a formula that uses a built-in function, you click the cell or drag through the cell range that you want used when defining the function's arguments in the Function Arguments dialog box.

WARNING

As with the other types of cell entries, you must take some action to complete a formula and enter it into the current cell (such as clicking the Enter button on the Formula bar, pressing the Enter key, or pressing an arrow key). Unlike when entering numeric or text entries, however, you will want to stay clear of clicking another cell to complete the data entry. This is because, when you click a cell when building or editing a formula on the Formula bar, more often than not, you end up not only selecting the new cell, but also adding its address to the otherwise complete formula.

As soon as you complete a formula entry, Excel calculates the result, which is then displayed inside the cell within the worksheet. (The contents of the formula, however, continue to be visible on the Formula bar anytime the cell is active.) If you make an error in the formula that prevents Excel from being able to calculate the formula at all, Excel displays an Alert dialog box suggesting how to fix the problem. If, however, you make an error that prevents Excel from being able to display a proper result when it calculates the formula, the program displays an Error value rather than the expected computed value. (See Book 3, Chapter 2 for details on dealing with both of these types of errors in formulas.)

Editing formulas

As with numeric and text entries, you can edit the contents of formulas either in their cells or on the Formula bar. To edit a formula in its cell, double-click the cell or press F2 to position the insertion pointer in that cell. (Double-clicking the cell positions the insertion pointer in the middle of the formula, whereas pressing F2 positions it at the end of the formula — you can also double-click at the beginning or end of the cell to position the insertion pointer there.) To edit a formula on the Formula bar, use the I-beam mouse to position the insertion point at the place in the formula that needs editing first.

As soon as you put the Excel program into Edit mode, Excel displays each of the cell references in the formula within the cell in a different color and uses this color to outline the cell or cell range in the worksheet itself. This coloration enables you to quickly identify the cells and their values that are referred to in your formula and, if necessary, modify them as well. You can use any of the four sizing handles that appear around the cell or cell range to modify the cell selection in the worksheet and consequently update the cell references in the formula.

When you AutoSum numbers in a spreadsheet

The easiest and often the most used formula that you will create is the one that totals rows and columns of numbers in your spreadsheet. Usually, to total a row or column of numbers, you can click the Sum command button (the one with the Σ on it) in the Editing group of the Home tab of the Ribbon. When you click this button, Excel inserts the built-in SUM function into the active cell and simultaneously selects what the program thinks is the most likely range of numbers that you want summed.

TIP

Instead of taking the time to click the Sum button on the Home tab, it's often faster and easier to simply press Alt+= (equal sign) to insert the SUM function in the current cell and have Excel select the range of cells most likely to be totaled.

Figure 1-1 demonstrates how this works. For this figure, I positioned the cell cursor in cell B7, which is the first cell where I need to build a formula that totals the various parts produced in April. I then clicked the Sum button on the Home tab of the Ribbon.

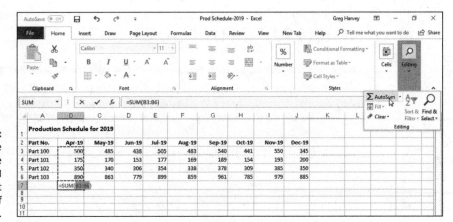

FIGURE 1-1:
Using the
AutoSum feature
to create a SUM
formula that
totals a column of
numbers.

As Figure 1-1 shows, Excel then inserted an equal sign followed by the SUM function and correctly suggested the cell range B3:B6 as the argument to this function (that is, the range to be summed). Because Excel correctly selected the range to be summed (leaving out the date value in cell B2), all I have to do is click the Enter button on the Formula bar to have the April total calculated.

Figure 1-2 shows another example of AutoSum to instantly build a SUM formula, this time to total the monthly production numbers for Part 100 in cell K3. Again, all I did to create the formula shown in Figure 1-2 was to select cell K3 and then click the Sum button on the Home tab. Again, Excel correctly selected B3:J3 as the range to be summed (rightly ignoring cell A3 with the row title) and input this range as the argument of the SUM function. All that remains to be done is to click the Enter button on the Formula bar to compute the monthly totals for Part 100.

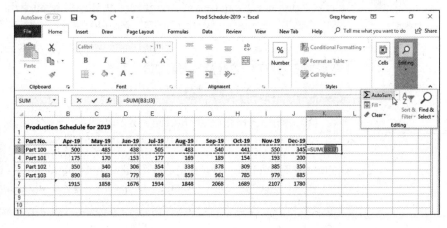

FIGURE 1-2:
Using the
AutoSum feature
to create a SUM
formula that
totals a row of
numbers.

WHEN AUTOSUM DOESN'T SUM

TIP

Although the Sum button's primary function is to build formulas with the SUM function that totals ranges of numbers, that's not its only function (pun intended). Indeed, you can have the AutoSum feature build formulas that compute the average value, count the number of values, or return the highest or lowest value in a range — all you have to do is click the drop-down button that's attached to the Sum command button on the Home tab and then click Average, Count Numbers, Max, or Min from its drop-down menu.

Also, don't forget about the Average, Count, and Sum indicator on the Status bar. This indicator automatically shows you the average value, the count of the numbers, and the total of all numbers in the current cell selection. You can use this feature to preview the total that's to be returned by the SUM formula that you create with the AutoSum button by selecting the cell range that contains the numbers to be summed.

If for some reason AutoSum doesn't select the entire or correct range that you want summed, you can adjust the range by dragging the cell cursor through the cell range or by clicking the marquee around the cell range, which turns the marching ants into a solid colored outline. Then position the mouse pointer on one of the sizing handles at the four corners. When it turns into a thick white arrowhead pointing to the center of a pair of black double-crossed arrows, drag the outline until it includes all the cells you want included in the total.

REMEMBER

Keep in mind that all Excel functions enclose their argument(s) in a closed pair of parentheses, as shown in the examples with the SUM function. Even those rare functions that don't require any arguments at all still require the use of a closed pair of parentheses (even when you don't put anything inside of them).

Totals and sums with the Quick Analysis tool

Instead of resorting to the Sum button and AutoFill to create totals for a worksheet table, you can use the Totals feature on the Quick Analysis tool to get the job done. The Quick Analysis tool offers a bevy of features for doing anything from adding conditional formatting, charts, pivot tables, and sparklines to your worksheet tables. And it turns out Quick Analysis is also a whiz at adding running totals and sums to the rows and columns of your new worksheet tables.

To use the Quick Analysis tool, all you have to do is select the worksheet table's cells and then click the Quick Analysis tool that automatically appears in the lower-right corner of the last selected cell. When you do this, a palette of options (from Formatting to Sparklines) appears right beneath the Quick Analysis tool. (See Figure 1-3.)

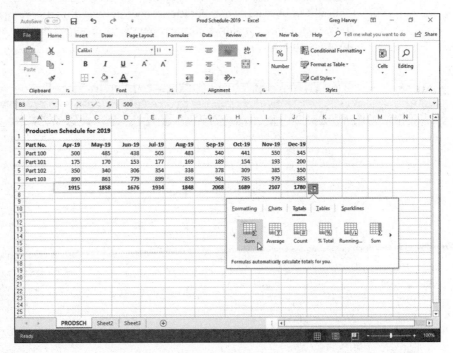

FIGURE 1-3:
Adding a row of totals with the Quick Analysis tool's Sum button.

To add totals to your selected table data, you first click the Totals tab. You can then use your mouse or Touch pointer to have Live Preview show you totals in a new row at the bottom by highlighting the Sum or Running Total button (with a spreadsheet containing a Sigma) or in a new column on the right by highlighting the second Sum button (with the spreadsheet with the last column highlighted). To actually add the SUM formulas with the totals to a new row or column, you simply click the Sum or Running Total button of choice.

TIP

If you have trouble selecting the Quick Analysis tool to open its palette for any reason, simply right-click the cell selection and click the Quick Analysis item on its shortcut menu.

Building formulas with computational operators

Many of the simpler formulas that you build require the sole use of Excel's operators, which are the symbols that indicate the type of calculation that is to take place between the cells and/or constants interspersed between them. Excel uses four different types of computational operators: arithmetic, comparison, text, and reference. Table 1-1 shows all these operators arranged by type and accompanied by an example.

TABLE 1-1   **The Different Types of Operators in Excel**

Type	Character	Operation	Example
Arithmetic	+ (plus sign)	Addition	=A2+B3
	– (minus sign)	Subtraction or negation	=A3–A2 or –C4
	* (asterisk)	Multiplication	=A2*B3
	/	Division	=B3/A2
	%	Percent (dividing by 100)	=B3%
	^	Exponentiation	=A2^3
Comparison	=	Equal to	=A2=B3
	>	Greater than	=B3>A2
	<	Less than	=A2<B3
	>=	Greater than or equal to	=B3>=A2
	<=	Less than or equal to	=A2<=B3
	<>	Not equal to	=A2<>B3
Text	&	Concatenates (connects) entries to produce one continuous entry	=A2&" "&B3t
Reference	: (colon)	Range operator that includes	=SUM(C4:D17)
	, (comma)	Union operator that combines multiple references into one reference	=SUM(A2,C4:D17,B3)
	(space)	Intersection operator that produces one reference to cells in common with two references	=SUM(C3:C6 C3:E6)

"Smooth operator"

Most of the time, you'll rely on the arithmetic operators when building formulas in your spreadsheets that don't require functions because these operators actually perform computations between the numbers in the various cell references and produce new mathematical results.

The comparison operators, on the other hand, produce only the logical value TRUE or the logical value FALSE, depending on whether the comparison is accurate. For example, say that you enter the following formula in cell A10:

```
=B10<>C10
```

If B10 contains the number 15 and C10 contains the number 20, the formula in A10 returns the logical value TRUE. If, however, both cell B10 and C10 contain the value 12, the formula returns the logical value FALSE.

The single text operator (the so-called ampersand) is used in formulas to join together two or more text entries (an operation with the highfalutin' name *concatenation*). For example, suppose that you enter the following formula in cell C2:

```
=A2&B2
```

If cell A2 contains John and cell B2 contains Smith, the formula returns the new (squashed together) text entry, JohnSmith. To have the formula insert a space between the first and last names, you have to include the space as part of the concatenation as follows:

```
=A2&" "&B2
```

TIP

You most often use the comparison operators with the IF function when building more complex formulas that perform one type of operation when the IF condition is TRUE and another when it is FALSE. You use the concatenating operator (&) when you need to join text entries that come to you entered in separate cells but that need to be entered in single cells (like the first and last names in separate columns). See Book 3, Chapter 2 for more on logical formulas, and Book 3, Chapter 6 for more on text formulas.

Order of operator precedence

When you build a formula that combines different computational operators, Excel follows the set order of operator precedence, as shown in Table 1-2. When you use operators that share the same level of precedence, Excel evaluates each element in the equation by using a strictly left-to-right order.

TABLE 1-2   **Natural Order of Operator Precedence in Formulas**

Precedence	Operator	Type/Function
1	–	Negation
2	%	Percent
3	^	Exponentiation
4	* and /	Multiplication and Division
5	+ and –	Addition and Subtraction
6	&	Concatenation
7	=, <, >, <=, >=, <>	All Comparison Operators

Suppose that you enter the following formula in cell A4:

```
=B4+C4/D4
```

Because division (like multiplication) has a higher level of precedence than addition (4 versus 5), Excel evaluates the division between cells C4 and D4 and then adds that result to the value in cell B4. If, for example, cell B4 contains 2, C4 contains 9, and D4 contains 3, Excel would essentially be evaluating this equation in cell A4:

```
=2+9/3
```

In this example, the calculated result displayed in cell A4 is 5 because the program first performs the division (9/3) that returns the result 3 and then adds it to the 2 to get the final result of 5.

If you had wanted Excel to evaluate this formula in a strictly left-to-right manner, you could get it to do so by enclosing the leftmost operation (the addition between B4 and C4) in a closed pair of parentheses. Parentheses alter the natural order of precedence so that any operation enclosed within a pair is performed before the other operations in the formula, regardless of level in the order. (After that, the natural order is once again used.)

To have Excel perform the addition between the first two terms (B4 and C4) and then divide the result by the third term (cell D4), you modify the original formula by enclosing the addition operation in parentheses as follows:

```
=(B4+C4)/D4
```

Assuming that cells B4, C4, and D4 still contain the same numbers (2, 9, and 3, respectively), the formula now calculates the result as 3.666667 and returns it to cell A4 (2+9=11 and 11/3=3.66667).

If necessary, you can *nest* parentheses in your formulas by putting one set of parentheses within another (within another, within another, and so on). When you nest parentheses, Excel performs the calculation in the innermost pair of parentheses first before anything else and then starts performing the operations in the outer parentheses.

Consider the following sample formula:

```
=B5+(C5–D5)/E5
```

In this formula, the parentheses around the subtraction (C5–D5) ensure that it is the first operation performed. After that, however, the natural order of precedence takes over. So the result of the subtraction is then divided by the value in E5, and that result is then added to the value in B5. If you want the addition to be performed before the division, you need to nest the first set of parentheses within another set as follows:

```
=(B5+(C5–D5))/E5
```

In this revised formula, Excel performs the subtraction between the values in C5 and D5, adds the result to the value in cell B5, and then divides that result by the value in cell E5.

WARNING

Of course, the biggest problem with parentheses is that you have to remember to enter them in pairs. If you forget to balance each set of nested parentheses by having a right parenthesis for every left parenthesis, Excel displays an Alert dialog box, informing you that it has located an error in the formula. It will also suggest a correction that would balance the parentheses used in the formula. Although the suggested correction corrects the imbalance in the formula, it unfortunately doesn't give you the calculation order that you wanted — and if accepted, the suggested correction would give you what you consider an incorrect result. For this reason, be very careful before you click the Yes button in this kind of Alert dialog box. Do so only when you're certain that the corrected parentheses give you the calculation order that you want. Otherwise, click No and balance the parentheses in the formula by adding the missing parenthesis or parentheses yourself.

Using the Insert Function button

Excel supports a wide variety of built-in functions that you can use when building formulas. Of course, the most popular built-in function is by far the SUM function, which is automatically inserted when you click the Sum command button on the Home tab of the Ribbon. (Keep in mind that you can also use this drop-down button attached to the Sum button to insert the AVERAGE, COUNT, MAX, and MIN functions — see the "When you AutoSum numbers in a spreadsheet" section previously in this chapter for details.) To use other Excel functions, you can use the Insert Function button on the Formula bar (the one with the *fx*).

When you click the Insert Function button, Excel displays the Insert Function dialog box, similar to the one shown in Figure 1-4. You can then use its options to find and select the function that you want to use and to define the argument or arguments that the function requires in order to perform its calculation.

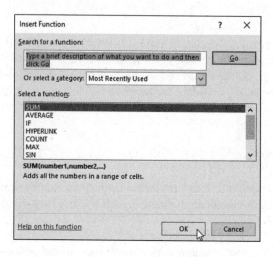

FIGURE 1-4:
Selecting a
function to
use in the
Insert Function
dialog box.

To select the function that you want to use, you can use any of the following methods:

>> Click the function name if it's one that you've used lately and is therefore already listed in the Select a Function list box.

>> Select the name of the category of the function that you want to use from the Or Select a Category drop-down list box (Most Recently Used is the default category) and then select the function that you want to use in that category from the Select a Function list box.

>> Replace the text "Type a brief description of what you want to do and then click Go" in the Search for a Function text box with keywords or a phrase about the type of calculation that you want to do (such as "return on invest-ment"). Click the Go button or press Enter and click the function that you want to use in the Recommended category displayed in the Select a Function list box.

When selecting the function to use in the Select a Function list box, click the function name to have Excel give you a short description of what the function does, displayed underneath the name of the function with its argument(s) shown in parentheses (referred to as the function's *syntax*). To get help on using the function, click the Help on This Function link displayed in the lower-left corner of the Insert Function dialog box to open the Help window in its own pane on the right. When you finish reading and/or printing this help topic, click the Close button to close the Help window and return to the Insert Function dialog box.

REMEMBER

You can select the most commonly used types of Excel functions and enter them simply by choosing their names from the drop-down menus attached to their command buttons in the Function Library group of the Formulas tab of the Ribbon. These command buttons include Financial, Logical, Text, Date & Time, Lookup & Reference, and Math & Trig. In addition, you can select functions in the Statistical, Engineering, Cube, Information, Compatibility, and Web categories from continuation menus that appear when you click the More Functions command button on the Formulas tab. And if you find you need to insert a function in the worksheet that you recently entered into the worksheet, chances are good that when you click the Recently Used command button, that function will be listed on its drop-down menu for you to select.

When you click OK after selecting the function that you want to use in the current cell, Excel inserts the function name followed by a closed set of parentheses on the Formula bar. At the same time, the program closes the Insert Function dialog box and then opens the Function Arguments dialog box, similar to the one shown in Figure 1-5. You then use the argument text box or boxes displayed in the Function Arguments dialog box to specify what numbers and other information are to be used when the function calculates its result.

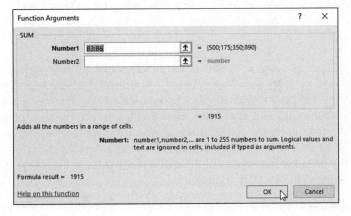

FIGURE 1-5:
Selecting the arguments for a function in the Function Arguments dialog box.

All functions — even those that don't take any arguments, such as the TODAY function — follow the function name by a closed set of parentheses, as in =TODAY( ). If the function requires arguments (and almost all require at least one), these arguments must appear within the parentheses following the function name. When a function requires multiple arguments, such as the DATE function, the various arguments are entered in the required order (as in *year, month, day* for the DATE function) within the parentheses separated by commas, as in DATE(20,7,23).

When you use the text boxes in the Function Arguments dialog box to input the arguments for a function, you can select the cell or cell range in the worksheet that contains the entries that you want used. Click the text box for the argument that you want to define and then either start dragging the cell cursor through the cells or, if the Function Arguments dialog box is obscuring the first cell in the range that you want to select, click the Collapse Dialog Box button located to the immediate right of the text box. Dragging or clicking this button reduces the Function Arguments dialog box to just the currently selected argument text box, thus enabling you to drag through the rest of the cells in the range.

If you started dragging without first clicking the Collapse Dialog Box button, Excel automatically expands the Function Arguments dialog box as soon as you release the mouse button. If you clicked the Collapse Dialog Box button, you have to click the Expand Dialog Box button (which replaces the Collapse Dialog Box button located to the right of the argument text box) in order to restore the Function Arguments dialog box to its original size.

As you define arguments for a function in the Function Arguments dialog box, Excel shows you the calculated result following the heading, "Formula result =" near the bottom of the Function Arguments dialog box. When you finish entering the required argument(s) for your function (and any optional arguments that may pertain to your particular calculation), click OK to have Excel close the Function Arguments dialog box and replace the formula in the current cell display with the calculated result.

You can also type the name of the function instead of selecting it from the Insert Function dialog box. When you begin typing a function name after typing an equal sign (=), Excel's AutoComplete feature kicks in by displaying a drop-down menu with the names of all the functions that begin with the character(s) you type. You can then enter the name of the function you want to use by double-clicking its name on this drop-down menu. Excel then enters the function name along with the open parenthesis as in =DATE(so that you can then begin selecting the cell range(s) for the first argument.

TIP

For details on how to use different types of built-in functions for your spreadsheets, refer to the following chapters in Book 3 that discuss the use of various categories: Refer to Chapter 2 for information on Logical functions; Chapter 3 for Date and Time functions; Chapter 4 for Financial functions; Chapter 5 for Math and Statistical functions; and Chapter 6 for Lookup, Information, and Text functions.

Copying Formulas

Copying formulas is one of the most common tasks that you do in a typical spreadsheet that relies primarily on formulas. When a formula uses cell references rather than constant values (as most should), Excel makes the task of copying an original formula to every place that requires a similar location a piece of cake. The program does this by automatically adjusting the cell references in the original formula to suit the position of the copies that you make. It does this through a system known as *relative cell addresses*, whereby the column references in the cell address in the formula change to suit their new column position and the row references change to suit their new row position.

Figures 1-6 and 1-7 illustrate how this works. For Figure 1-6, I used the AutoSum button in cell B7 to build the original formula that uses the SUM function that totals the April sales. The formula in cell B7 reads

    =SUM(B3:B6)

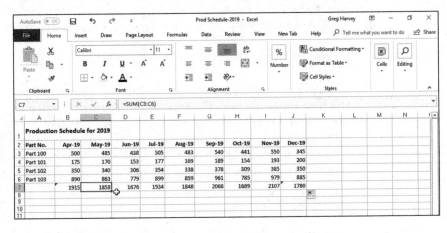

FIGURE 1-6:
An original formula copied with the Fill handle across the last row of the spreadsheet table.

CHAPTER 1 **Building Basic Formulas** 321

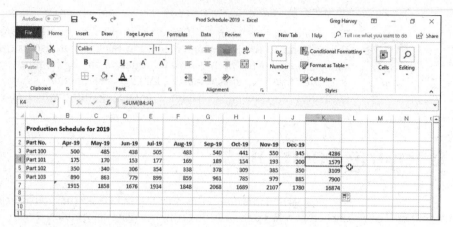

FIGURE 1-7:
An original
formula copied
with the Fill
handle down the
last column of the
data table.

I then used the AutoFill feature to copy this formula by dragging the Fill handle to include the cell range B7:J7. (Copying the formula with the cut-and-paste method would work just as well, although it's a little more work.) Note in the cell range C7:J7 that Excel did not copy the original formula to the other cells verbatim. (Otherwise, each of the copied formulas would return the same result, 1915, as the original in cell B7.) If you look at the Formula bar in Figure 1-5, you see that the copy of the original formula in cell C7 reads

```
=SUM(C3:C6)
```

In this copy, Excel adjusted the column reference of the range being summed from B to C to suit the new position of the copy. Figure 1-7 shows how this works when copying an original formula in the other direction, this time down a column. For this figure, I used the AutoSum button to create a SUM formula that totals all the monthly sales for Part 100 in row 3. The formula in cell K3 reads

```
=SUM(B3:J3)
```

You can then use the Fill handle to copy this formula down the last column of the table to include the cell range by positioning the cell cursor in K3 and then dragging the Fill handle down to select K3:K7. If you were to then position the cell cursor in cell K4, you would see on the Formula bar that when Excel copied the original formula in cell K3 down to cell K4, it automatically adjusted the row reference to suit its new position so that the formula in cell K4 reads

```
=SUM(B4:J4)
```

Although at first glance it appears that Excel isn't making exact copies of the original formula when it uses the relative cell addressing, that isn't technically true. Although the cell column references in the first example in Figure 1-6 and the row references in the second example in Figure 1-7 appear to be adjusted to suit the new column and row position when you view the worksheet by using the R1C1 cell notation system, you'd actually see that, in R1C1 notation (unlike the default A1 system), each and every copy of the original formula is *exactly* the same.

For example, the original formula that I input into cell B7 (known as cell R7C2 in the R1C1 system) to sum the April sales for all the different part numbers reads as follows when you switch to R1C1 notation:

```
=SUM(R[-4]C:R[-1]C)
```

In this notation, the SUM formula is more difficult to decipher, so I will explain and then translate it for you. In R1C1 notation, the cell range in the SUM argument is expressed in terms completely relative to the position of the cell containing the formula. The row portion of the cell range expresses how many rows above or below the one with the formula the rows are. (Negative integers indicate rows above, whereas positive integers indicate rows below.) The column portion of the cell range in the SUM argument expresses how many columns to the left or right of the one with the formula the columns are. (Positive integers indicate columns to the right, and negative integers indicate columns to the left.) When a column or row in the cell range is not followed by an integer in square brackets, this means that there is no change in the column or row.

Armed with this information, my translation R1C1 form of this formula may just make sense; it says, "sum the values in the range of the cells that is four rows (R[-4]) above the current cell in the same column (C) down through the cell that is just one row (R[-1]) above the current cell in the same column (C)." When this original formula is copied over to the columns in the rest of the table, it doesn't need to be changed because each copy of the formula performs this exact calculation (when expressed in such relative terms).

The original formula in Figure 1-7 that I entered into cell K3 and copied down to cell K6 appears as follows when you switch over to the R1C1 notation:

```
=SUM(RC[-9]:RC[-1])
```

It says, "sum the range of values in the cell nine columns to the left (C[-9]) in the same row through the cell that is one column to the left (C[-1]) in the same row." This is exactly what all the copies of this formula in the rows below it do, so that when Excel copies this formula it doesn't change.

TIP You can use the R1C1 notation to check that you've copied all the formulas in a spreadsheet table correctly. Just switch to the R1C1 system by clicking the R1C1 Reference Style check box in the Working with Formulas section on the Formulas tab of the Excel Options dialog box (File ➪ Options ➪ Formulas). Then move the cell cursor through all the cells with copied formulas in the table. When R1C1 notation is in effect, all copies of an original formula across an entire row or down an entire column of the table should be identical when displayed on the Formula bar as you make their cells current.

Absolute references

Most of the time, relative cell references are exactly what you need in the formulas that you build, thus allowing Excel to adjust the row and/or column references as required in the copies that you make. You will encounter some circumstances, however, where Excel should not adjust one or more parts of the cell reference in the copied formula. This occurs, for example, whenever you want to use a cell value as a constant in all the copies that you make of a formula.

Figure 1-8 illustrates just such a situation. In this situation, you want to build a formula in cell B9 that calculates what percentage April's part production total (B7) is of the total nine-month production (cell K7). Normally, you would create the following formula in cell B9 with all its relative cell references:

```
=B7/K7
```

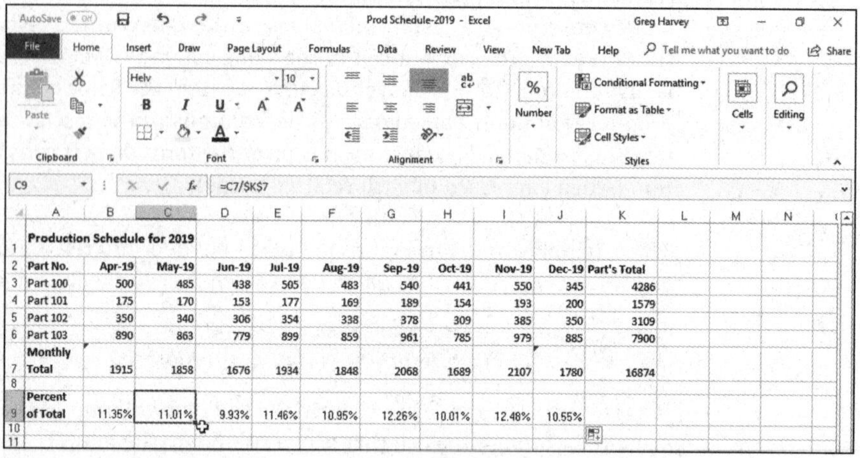

FIGURE 1-8:
Using an absolute address in the formula to calculate monthly percentage of the total.

However, because you want to copy this formula across to the range C9:J9 to calculate the percentages for the eight months (May through December), you need to alter the relative cell references in the last part of the formula in cell K7 so that this cell reference with the nine-month production total remains unchanged in all your copies.

You can start to understand the problem caused by adjusting a relative cell reference that should remain unchanged by just thinking about copying the original formula from cell B9 to C9 to calculate the percentage for May. In this cell, you want the following formula that divides the May production total in cell C7 by the nine-month total in cell K7:

```
=C7/K7
```

However, if you don't indicate otherwise, Excel adjusts both parts of the formula in the copies, so that C9 incorrectly contains the following formula:

```
=C7/L7
```

Because cell L7 is currently blank and blank cells have the equivalent of the value 0, this formula returns the #DIV/0! formula error as the result, thus indicating that Excel can't properly perform this arithmetic operation. (See Book 3, Chapter 2 for details on this error message.)

To indicate that you don't want a particular cell reference (such as cell K7 in the example) to be adjusted in the copies that you make of a formula, you change the cell reference from a relative cell reference to an *absolute cell reference.* In the A1 system of cell references, an absolute cell reference contains dollar signs before the column letter and the row number, as in $K$7. In the R1C1 notation, you simply list the actual row and column number in the cell reference, as in R7C11, without placing the row and column numbers in square brackets.

If you realize that you need to convert a relative cell reference to an absolute reference as you're building the original formula, you can convert the relative reference to absolute by selecting the cell and then pressing F4. To get an idea of how this works, follow along with these steps for creating the correct formula =B7/$K$7 in cell B9:

1. **Click cell B9 to make it active.**

2. **Type = to start the formula; then click cell B7 and type / (the sign for division).**

   The Formula bar now reads =B7/.

3. **Click K7 to select this cell and add it to the formula.**

   The Formula bar now reads =B7/K7.

4. **Press F4 once to change the cell reference from relative (K7) to absolute ($K$7).**

The Formula bar now reads =B7/$K$7. You're now ready to enter the formula and then make the copies.

5. **Click the Enter button on the Formula bar and then drag the Fill handle to cell J9 before you release the mouse button.**

Like it or not, you won't always anticipate the need for an absolute value until after you've built the formula and copied it to a range. When this happens, you have to edit the original formula, change the relative reference to absolute, and then make the copies again.

When editing the cell reference in the formula, you can change its reference by positioning the insertion point anywhere in its address and then pressing F4. You can also do this by inserting dollar signs in front of the column letter(s) and row number when editing the formula, although doing that isn't nearly as easy as pressing F4.

TIP

You can make an exact copy of a formula in another cell without using absolute references. To do this, make the cell with the formula that you want to copy the active one, use the I-beam pointer to select the entire formula in the Formula bar by dragging through it, and then click the Copy command button on the Home tab of the Ribbon (or press Ctrl+C). Next, click the Cancel button to deactivate the Formula bar, select the cell where you want the exact copy to appear, and then click the Paste command button on the Home tab (or press Ctrl+V). Excel then pastes an exact duplicate of the original formula into the active cell without adjusting any of its cell references (even if they are all relative cell references).

REMEMBER

Keep in mind when using the sum options on the Totals tab of the Quick Analysis tool's palette (see "Totals and sums with the Quick Analysis tool" earlier in this chapter for details) that all the cell references in the total and sum formulas that Excel creates are relative references.

TIP

If you're building the formula that requires an absolute or some sort of mixed cell reference (see the following section) on a touchscreen device and using the Touch keyboard with no access to function keys, you need to add the required dollar sign(s) into the formula on the Formula bar by using the dollar sign ($) key on the Touch keyboard. To access the dollar sign key, tap the Numeric key (&123) to switch the Touch keyboard out of the QWERTY letter arrangement.

A mixed bag of references

Some formulas don't require you to change the entire cell reference from relative to absolute in order to copy them correctly. In some situations, you need to indicate only that the column letter or the row number remains unchanged in all copies of the original formula. A cell reference that is part relative and part absolute is called a *mixed cell reference.*

In the A1 notation, a mixed cell reference has a dollar sign just in front of the column letter or row number that should not be adjusted in the copies. For example, $C10 adjusts row 10 in copies down the rows but leaves column C unchanged in all copies across columns to its right. Another example is C$10, which adjusts column C in copies to columns to the right but leaves row 10 unchanged in all copies down the rows. (For an example of using mixed cell references in a master formula, refer to the information on using the PMT Function in Book 3, Chapter 4.)

To change the cell reference that you select in a formula (by clicking the flashing insertion point somewhere in its column letter and row number) from relative to mixed, continue to press F4 until the type of mixed reference appears on the Formula bar. When the Formula bar is active and the insertion point is somewhere in the cell reference (either when building or editing the formula), pressing F4 cycles through each cell-reference possibility in the following order:

» The first time you press F4, Excel changes the relative cell reference to absolute (C10 to $C$10).

» The second time you press F4, Excel changes the absolute reference to a mixed reference where the column is relative and the row is absolute ($C$10 to C$10).

» The third time you select the Reference command, Excel changes the mixed reference where the column is relative and the row is absolute to a mixed reference where the row is relative and the column is absolute (C$10 to $C10).

» The fourth time you press F4, Excel changes the mixed reference where the row is relative and the column is absolute back to a relative reference ($C10 to C10).

If you bypass the type of cell reference that you want to use, you can return to it by continuing to press F4 until you cycle through the variations again to reach the one that you need.

Adding Array Formulas

As noted previously in this chapter, many spreadsheet tables use an original formula that you copy to adjacent cells by using relative cell references (sometimes referred to as a *one-to-many copy*). In some cases, you can build the original formula so that Excel performs the desired calculation not only in the active cell, but also in all the other cells to which you would normally copy the formula.

You do this by creating an *array formula*. An array formula is a special formula that operates on a range of values. If a cell range supplies this range (as is often the case), it is referred to as an *array range*. If this range is supplied by a list of numerical values, they are known as an *array constant*.

Although the array concept may seem foreign at first, you are really quite familiar with arrays because the column-and-row structure of the Excel worksheet grid naturally organizes your data ranges into one-dimensional and two-dimensional arrays. (1-D arrays take up a single row or column, whereas 2-D arrays take up multiple rows and columns.)

Figure 1-9 illustrates a couple of two-dimensional arrays with numerical entries of two different sizes. The first array is a 3 x 2 array in the cell range B2:C4. This array is a 3 x 2 array because it occupies three rows and two columns. The second array is a 2 x 3 array in the cell range F2:H3. This array is a 2 x 3 array because it uses two rows and three columns.

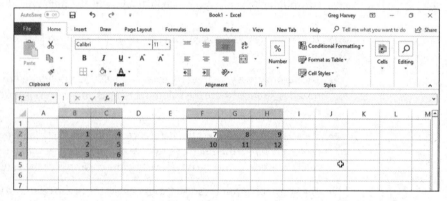

FIGURE 1-9:
Worksheet with
two different
sizes of arrays.

If you were to list the values in the first 3 x 2 array as an array constant in a formula, they would appear as follows:

```
{1,4;2,5;3,6}
```

Several things in this list are noteworthy. First, the array constant is enclosed in a pair of braces ({}). Second, columns within each row are separated by commas (,) and rows within the array are separated by semicolons (;). Third, the constants in the array are listed across each row and then down each column and *not* down each column and across each row.

The second 2 x 3 array expressed as an array constant appears as follows:

```
{7,8,9;10,11,12}
```

Note again that you list the values across each row and then down each column, separating the values in different columns with commas and the values in different rows with a semicolon.

The use of array formulas can significantly reduce the amount of formula copying that you have to do in a worksheet by producing multiple results throughout the array range in a single operation. In addition, array formulas use less computer memory than standard formulas copied in a range. This can be important when creating a large worksheet with many tables because it may mean the difference between fitting all your calculations on one worksheet and having to split your model into several worksheet files.

Building an array formula

To get an idea of how you build and use array formulas in a worksheet, consider the sample worksheet shown in Figure 1-10. This worksheet is designed to compute the biweekly wages for each employee. It will do this by multiplying each employee's hourly rate by the number of hours worked in each pay period. Instead of creating the following formula in cell R10 that you copy down the cells R11 through R13:

```
=A4*R4
```

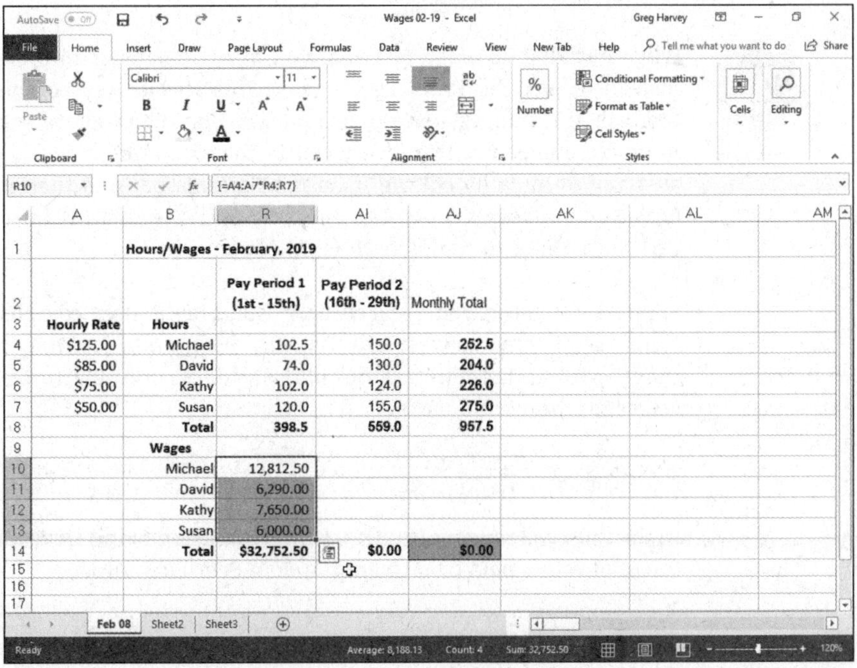

FIGURE 1-10:
Building an array formula to calculate hourly wages for the first pay period.

You can create the following array formula in the array range:

```
={A4:A7*R4:R7}
```

This array formula multiplies each of the hourly rates in the 4 x 1 array in the range A4:A7 with each of the hours worked in the 4 x 1 array in the range R4:R7. This same formula is entered into all cells of the array range (R10:R13) as soon as you complete the formula in the active cell R10. To see how this is done, follow along with the steps required to build this array formula:

1. **Make cell R10 the current cell, and then select the array range R10:R13 and type = (equal sign) to start the array formula.**

You always start an array formula by selecting the cell or cell range where the results are to appear. Note that array formulas, like standard formulas, begin with the equal sign.

2. **Select the range A4:A7 that contains the hourly rate for each employee as shown, type an * (asterisk for multiplication), and then select the range R4:R7 that contains the total number of hours worked during the first pay period.**

3. **Press Ctrl+Shift+Enter to insert an array formula in the array range.**

When you press Ctrl+Shift+Enter to complete the formula, Excel inserts braces around the formula and copies the array formula {=A4:A7*R4:R7} into each of the cells in the array range R10:R13.

WARNING

When entering an array formula, you must remember to press Ctrl+Shift+Enter instead of just the Enter key because this special key combination tells Excel that you are building an array formula, so that the program encloses the formula in braces and copies it to every cell in the array range. Also, don't try to create an array formula by editing it on the Formula bar and then insert curly braces because this doesn't cut it. The only way to create an array formula is by pressing Ctrl+Shift+Enter to complete the formula entry.

Figure 1-11 shows you the February wage table after completing all the array formulas in three ranges: R10:R13, AI10:AI13, and AJ10:AJ13. In the second cell range, AI10:AI13, I entered the following array formula to calculate the hourly wages for the second pay period in February:

```
{=A4:A7*AI4:AI7}
```

In the third cell range, AJ10:AJ13, I entered the following array formula to calculate the total wages paid to each employee in February 2016:

```
{=R10:R13+AI10:AI13}
```

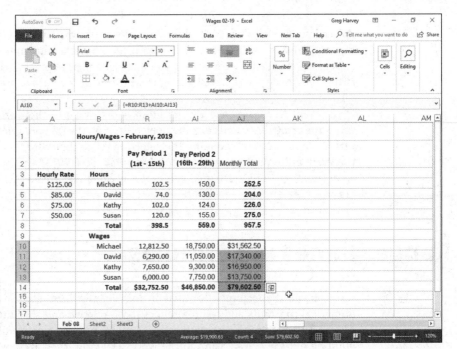

The following data is shown in the spreadsheet (Figure 1-11):

Hours/Wages - February, 2019

Hourly Rate	Hours	Pay Period 1 (1st - 15th)	Pay Period 2 (16th - 29th)	Monthly Total
$125.00	Michael	102.5	150.0	262.5
$85.00	David	74.0	130.0	204.0
$75.00	Kathy	102.0	124.0	226.0
$50.00	Susan	120.0	155.0	275.0
	Total	398.5	569.0	957.5
	Wages			
	Michael	12,812.50	18,750.00	$31,562.50
	David	6,290.00	11,050.00	$17,340.00
	Kathy	7,650.00	9,300.00	$16,950.00
	Susan	6,000.00	7,750.00	$13,750.00
	Total	$32,752.50	$46,850.00	$79,602.50

Formula bar: AJ10 = {=R10:R13+AI10:AI13}

WARNING

FIGURE 1-11:
The hourly wage spreadsheet after entering all three array formulas.

When you enter an array formula, the formula should produce an array with the same dimensions as the array range that you selected. If the resulting array returned by the formula is smaller than the array range, Excel expands the resulting array to fill the range. If the resulting array is larger than the array range, Excel doesn't display all the results. When expanding the results in an array range, Excel considers the dimensions of all the arrays used in the arguments of the operation. Each argument must have the same number of rows as the array with the most rows and the same number of columns as the array with the most columns.

Editing an array formula

Editing array formulas differs somewhat from editing normal formulas. In editing an array range, you must treat the range as a single unit and edit it in one operation (corresponding to the way in which the array formula was entered). This means that you can't edit, clear, move, insert, or delete individual cells in the array range. If you try, Excel will display an Alert dialog box stating "You cannot change part of an array."

To edit the contents of an array formula, select a cell in the array range and then activate Edit mode by clicking the formula or the Formula bar or pressing F2. When you do this, Excel displays the contents of the array formula without the customary braces. The program also outlines the ranges referred to in the array formula in

Building Basic Formulas

the cells of the worksheet in different colors that match those assigned to the range addresses in the edited formula on the Formula bar. After you make your changes to the formula contents, you must remember to press Ctrl+Shift+Enter to enter your changes and have Excel enclose the array formula in braces once again.

If you want to convert the results in an array range to their calculated values, select the array range and click the Copy button on the Ribbon's Home tab or press Ctrl+C. Then, without changing the selection, click the Paste Values option from the Paste button's drop-down menu (or press Alt+HVV). As soon as you convert an array range to its calculated values, Excel no longer treats the cell range as an array.

Range Names in Formulas

Thus far, all the example formulas in this chapter have used a combination of numerical constants and cell references (both relative and absolute and using the A1 and R1C1 notation). Although cell references provide a convenient method for pointing out the cell location in the worksheet grid, they are not at all descriptive of their function when used in formulas. Fortunately, Excel makes it easy to assign descriptive names to the cells, cell ranges, constants, and even formulas that make their function in the worksheet much more understandable.

To get an idea of how names can help to document the purpose of a formula, consider the following formula for computing the sale price of an item that uses standard cell references:

```
=B4*B2
```

Now consider the following formula that performs the same calculation but, this time, with the use of range names:

```
=Retail_Price*Discount_Rate
```

Obviously, the function of the second formula is much more comprehensible, not only to you as the creator of the worksheet but also to anyone else who has to use it.

TIP

Range names are extremely useful not only for documenting the function of the formulas in your worksheet, but also for finding and selecting cell ranges quickly and easily. This is especially helpful in a large worksheet that you aren't very familiar with or only use intermittently. After you assign a name to a cell range, you can locate and select all the cells in that range with the Go To dialog box.

Simply click the Go To option from the Find & Select button's drop-down menu on the Home tab of the Ribbon (or press Ctrl+G or F5). Then double-click the range name in the Go To list box, or click the range name and click OK or press Enter. Excel then selects the entire range and, if necessary, shifts the worksheet display so that you can see the first cell in that range on the screen.

TIP

If you're using Excel 2019 on a Windows device such as a tablet without the benefit of a keyboard or mouse, you will definitely find it to your advantage to assign range names to often-used cell ranges in your spreadsheets. That way, you can go to and select these ranges simply by tapping the Name box drop-down button followed by the range name. That's so much faster and easier than manually finding and selecting the range with your finger or stylus.

Defining range names

You can define a name for the selected cell range or nonadjacent selection by typing its range name into the Name box on the Formula bar and then pressing Enter. You can also name a cell, cell range, or nonadjacent selection by clicking the Define Name command button on the Ribbon's Formulas tab or by pressing Alt+MMD. Excel then opens the New Name dialog box, where you can input the selection's range name in the Name text box.

If Excel can identify a label in the cell immediately above or to the left of the active one, the program inserts this label as the suggested name in the Name text box. The program also displays the scope of the range name in the Scope drop-down list box and the cell reference of the active cell or the range address of the range or nonadjacent selection that is currently marked (by using absolute references) in the Refers To text box below. You can do the following:

>> To change the scope from the entire workbook to a particular worksheet in the workbook so that the range name is only recognized on that sheet, select the sheet's name from the Scope drop-down list.

>> To change the cell range the name refers to, select the cells in the worksheet. (Remember that you can collapse the New Name dialog box to the Refers To text box by clicking its Collapse button.)

>> To accept the suggested or edited name, scope, and cell selection, click the OK button, shown in Figure 1-12.

REMEMBER

When naming a range in the Name text box of the New Name dialog box, you need to follow the same naming conventions as when defining a name in the Name box on the Formula bar. Basically, this means that the name must begin with a letter rather than a number, contain no spaces, and not duplicate any other name in the workbook. (See Book 2, Chapter 2 for more on naming ranges.)

FIGURE 1-12:
Adding a new
range name in
the New Name
dialog box.

If you want to assign the same range name to similar ranges on different work-sheets in the workbook, preface the range name with the sheet name followed by an exclamation point and then the descriptive name. For example, if you want to give the name Costs to the cell range A2:A10 on both Sheet1 and Sheet2, you name the range Sheet1!Costs on Sheet1 and Sheet2!Costs on Sheet2. If you have renamed the worksheet to something more descriptive than Sheet1, you need to enclose the name in single quotes if it contains a space when you enter the range. For example, if you rename Sheet1 to Inc. Statement 19, you enter the range name including the worksheet reference for the Costs cell range as follows:

```
'Inc. Statement 19'!Costs
```

TIP

When you preface a range name with the sheet name as shown in this example, you don't have to use the sheet name part of the range name in the formulas that you create on the same worksheet. In other words, if you create a SUM formula that totals the values in the 'Inc. Statement 16'!Costs range somewhere on the Inc. Statement 16 worksheet, you can enter the formulas as follows:

```
=SUM(Costs)
```

However, if you were to create this formula on any other worksheet in the work-book, you would have to include the full range name in the formula, as in

```
=SUM('Inc. Statement 16'!Costs)
```

Naming constants and formulas

In addition to naming cells in your worksheet, you can also assign range names to the constants and formulas that you use often. For example, if you are creating a spreadsheet table that calculates sales prices, you can assign the discount percentage rate to the range name discount_rate. Then, you can supply this range name as a constant in any formula that calculates the sale discount used in determining the sale price for merchandise.

For example, to assign a constant value of 15% to the range name discount_rate, you open the New Name dialog box and then type **discount_rate** in the Name text box and **=15%** as the discount rate in the Refers To text box before clicking OK. After assigning this constant percentage rate to the range name discount_rate in this manner, you can apply it to any formula by typing or pasting in the name (see the "Using names in building formulas" section that follows in this chapter for details).

In addition to naming constants, you can also give a range name to a formula that you use repeatedly. When building a formula in the Refers To text box of the New Name dialog box (Alt+MMD), keep in mind that Excel automatically applies absolute references to any cells that you point to in the worksheet. If you want to create a formula with relative cell references that Excel adjusts when you enter or paste the range name in a new cell, you must press F4 to convert the current cell reference to relative or type in the cell address without dollar signs.

WARNING

When creating the constant in the New Name dialog box, don't change the Scope setting from Workbook to a particular sheet in the workbook unless you're positive that you'll never need to use that constant in a formula on any other worksheet. If you limit the scope to a particular worksheet, Excel 2019 does not let you use the range name in a formula on any other worksheet (you'll get the #NAME? error), and Scope is the one aspect you can't change when editing a range name via the Name Manager. (I discuss managing range names later in this chapter.)

Using names in building formulas

After you assign a name to a cell or cell range in your worksheet, you can then click the range name from the Use in Formula button's drop-down menu on the Ribbon's Formulas tab to paste it into the formulas that you build (Alt+MS).

For example, in the sample Autumn 2016 Furniture Sale table shown in Figure 1-13, after assigning the discount rate of 15% to the range name, discount_rate, you can create the formulas that calculate the amount of the sale discount. To do this, you multiply the retail price of each item by the discount_rate constant using the Use in Formula command button by following these steps:

1. **Make cell D3 active.**

2. **Type = (equal sign) to start the formula.**

3. **Click cell C3 to select the retail price for the first item and then type * (asterisk).**

   The formula on the Formula bar now reads, =C3*.

4. **Click the Use In Formula button on the FORMULAS tab or press Alt+MS.**

This action opens the drop-down menu on the Use in Formula button on which you can select the discount_rate range name.

5. **Choose the name discount_rate from the Use in Formula button's drop-down menu.**

The formula now reads =C3*discount_rate on the Formula bar.

6. **Click the Enter button on the Formula bar to input the formula in cell D3.**

Now, all that remains is to copy the original formula down column D.

7. **Drag the Fill handle in cell D3 down to cell D7 and release the mouse button to copy the formula and calculate the discount for the entire table.**

FIGURE 1-13: Pasting the range name for the discount_rate constant into a formula.

Creating names from column and row headings

You can use the Create from Selection command button on the Formulas tab of the Ribbon to assign existing column and row headings in a table of data to the cells in that table. When using this command button, you can have Excel assign the labels used as column headings in the top or bottom row of the table, the labels used as row headings in the leftmost or rightmost column, or even a combination of these headings.

For example, the sample worksheet in Figure 1-14 illustrates a typical table layout that uses column headings in the top row of the table and row headings in the first column of the table. You can assign these labels to the cells in the table by using the Create from Selection command button as follows:

1. Select the cells in the table, including those with the column and row labels that you want to use as range names.

For the example shown in Figure 1-14, you select the range B2:E7.

2. Click the Create from Selection command button on the Formulas tab or press Alt+MC.

This action opens the Create Names from Selection dialog box that contains four check boxes: Top Row, Left Column, Bottom Row, and Right Column. The program selects the check box or boxes in this dialog box based on the arrangement of the labels in your table. In the example shown in Figure 1-14, Excel selects both the Top Row and Left Column check boxes because the table contains both column headings in the top row and row headings in the left column.

3. After selecting (or deselecting) the appropriate Create Names In check boxes, click the OK button to assign the range names to your table.

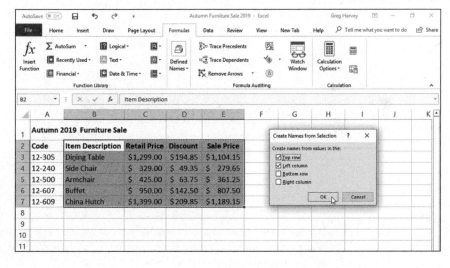

FIGURE 1-14: Creating range names from the row and column headings in a spreadsheet table.

Note that when you select both the Top Row and Left Column check boxes in the Create Names from Selection dialog box, Excel assigns the label in the cell in the upper-left corner of the table to the entire range of values in the table (one row down and one column to the right).

In the example illustrated in Figure 1-14, Excel assigns the name Item_Description (the heading for column B) to the cell range C3:E7. Similarly, the program assigns the column headings to the appropriate data in the table in the rows below, and assigns the row headings to the data in the appropriate columns to the right so that the name Retail_Price is assigned to the cell range C3:C7 and the name China_Hutch is assigned to the cell range C7:E7.

Managing range names

As you assign range names in your workbook, their names appear in the Name Manager dialog box. (See Figure 1-15.) You open this dialog box by clicking the Name Manager command button on the Formulas tab of the Ribbon or by pressing Alt+MN.

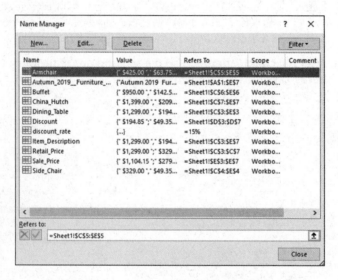

FIGURE 1-15:
The Name Manager lists all range names defined in the workbook.

The Name Manager enables you to do any of the following:

» Create new range names for the worksheet or workbook in the New Name dialog box opened by clicking the New button. (See "Defining range names" earlier in this chapter.)

» Edit existing range names in the Edit Name dialog box by clicking the name in the list box and then clicking the Edit button — you can change both the name and cell selection when editing a range name.

» Delete existing range names by clicking the name and then clicking the Delete button followed by the OK button in the Alert dialog box asking you to confirm its deletion.

>> Filter the range names in the list box of the Name Manager by clicking the Filter button and then clicking a filter option (Names Scoped to Worksheet, Names Scoped to Workbook, Names with Errors, Names without Errors, Defined Names, or Table Names) from its drop-down menu.

Be careful that you don't delete a range name that is already used in formulas in the worksheet. If you do, Excel will return the #NAME? error value to any formula that refers to the name you deleted!

Applying names to existing formulas

Excel doesn't automatically replace cell references with the descriptive names that you assign to them in the New Name or Create Names from Selection dialog boxes. To replace cell references with their names, you need to choose the Apply Names option from the Define Name button's drop-down menu or press Alt+MMA.

When you choose this command, Excel opens the Apply Names dialog box, where you select the range names that you want applied in formulas used in your worksheet by selecting the names in the Apply Names list box.

Note that when you first open this dialog box, it contains just two check boxes: Ignore Relative/Absolute and Use Row and Column Names (both of which are selected). You can click the Options button to expand the Apply Names dialog box and display other options that you can use when applying your range names, shown in Figure 1-16. The Apply Names options include the following:

>> **Ignore Relative/Absolute check box:** The program replaces cell references with the names that you've selected in the Apply Names list box, regardless of the type of reference used in their formulas. If you want Excel to replace only those cell references that use the same type of references as are used in your names (absolute for absolute, mixed for mixed, and relative for relative), deselect this check box. Most of the time, you'll want to leave this check box selected because Excel automatically assigns absolute cell references to the names that you define and relative cell references to the formulas that you build.

>> **Use Row and Column Names check box:** The names created from row and column headings with the Create Names command appear in your formulas. Deselect this option if you don't want these row and column names to appear in the formulas in your worksheet.

>> **Omit Column Name If Same Column check box:** This prevents Excel from repeating the column name when the formula is in the same column. Deselect this check box when you want the program to display the column name even in formulas in the same column as the heading used to create the column name.

>> **Omit Row Name If Same Row check box:** This prevents Excel from repeating the row name when the formula is in the same row. Deselect this check box when you want the program to display the row name even in formulas in the same row as the heading used to create the row name.

>> **Name Order:** Click the Row Column option button (the default) if you want the row name to precede the column name when both names are displayed in the formulas, or click the Column Row option button if you want the column name to precede the row name.

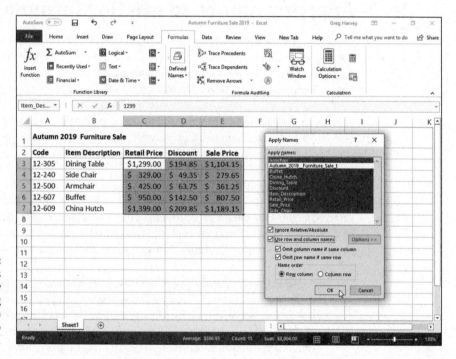

FIGURE 1-16:
Using the options in the Apply Names dialog box to assign range names to formulas.

After applying all the range names by using the default Apply Names options (that is, Ignore Relative/Absolute, Use Row and Column Names, Omit Column Name If Same Column, Omit Row Name If Same Row, and Name Order options selected), Excel replaces all the cell references in the formulas in the Sale Price table. In cell E3, for example, in place of the original formula, =C3–D3, the cell now contains the formula

```
=Retail_Price-Discount
```

Cell D3, to the immediate left, instead of =C3*discount_rate now contains:

```
=Retail_Price*discount_rate
```

Only one problem occurs with applying names by using the default settings. This problem begins to show up as soon as you select cell E4. Although this formula subtracts cell D4 from C4, its contents now also appear as

```
=Retail_Price-Discount
```

This is identical in appearance to the contents of cell E3 above (and, in fact, identical in appearance to cells E5, E6, and E7 in the cells below).

The reason that the formulas all appear identical (although they're really not) is because the Omit Row Name If Same Row check box was selected when I applied the range names to the formulas. With this setting selected, Excel doesn't bother to repeat the row name when the formula is in the same row.

When you deselect the Omit Row Name if Same Row check box while still selecting the Use Row and Column Name check box in the Apply Names dialog box, the formula in cell E3 would appear as follows:

```
=Dining_Table Retail_Price-Dining-Table Discount
```

If you were then to select cell E4 below, the formula would now appear quite differently in this form:

```
=Side_Chair Retail_Price-Side_Chair Discount
```

Now Excel displays both the row and column names separated by a space for each cell reference in the formulas in this column. Remember that the space between the row name and column name is called the *intersection operator*. (Refer to Table 1-1.) You can interpret the formula in E3 as saying, "Take the cell at the intersection of the Table row and Retail_Price column and subtract it from the cell at the intersection of the Table row and Discount column." The formula in E4 is similar, except that it says, "Take the cell at the intersection of the Side_chair row and Retail_Price column and subtract it from the cell at the intersection of the Side_chair row and Discount column."

Adding Linking Formulas

Linking formulas are formulas that transfer a constant or other formula to a new place in the same worksheet, same workbook, or even a different workbook without copying it to its new location. When you create a linking formula, it brings forward the constant or original formula to a new location so that the result in the linking formula remains dynamically tied to the original. If you change the original constant or any of the cells referred to in the original formula, the result in the cell containing the linking formula is updated at the same time as the cell containing the original constant or formula.

You can create a linking formula in one of two ways:

» Select the cell where you want the linking formula, type = (equal sign), and then click the cell with the constant (text or number) or the formula that you want to bring forward to that cell. Complete the cell entry by clicking the Enter button on the Formula bar or pressing the Enter key.

» Select the cell with the constant or formula that you want to bring forward to a new location and then click the Copy button in the Clipboard group on the Ribbon's Home tab or press Ctrl+C. Then click the cell where the linking formula is to appear before you choose the Paste Link option from the Paste button's drop-down menu.

When you use the first simple formula method to create a link, Excel uses a relative cell reference to refer to the cell containing the original value or formula (as in =A10 when referring to an entry in cell A10). However, when you use the second copy-and-paste link method, Excel uses an absolute cell reference to refer to the original cell (as in =$A$10 when referring to an entry in cell A10).

When you create a linking formula to a cell on a different sheet of the same workbook, Excel inserts the worksheet name (followed by an exclamation point) in front of the cell address. So, if you copy and paste a link to a formula in cell A10 on a different worksheet called Income 16, Excel inserts the following linking formula:

```
='Income 16'!$A$10
```

When you create a linking formula to a cell in a different workbook, Excel inserts the workbook filename enclosed in square brackets before the name of the worksheet, which precedes the cell address. So, if you bring forward a formula in cell A10 on a worksheet called Cost Analysis in the Projected Income 17 workbook, Excel inserts this linking formula:

```
='[Projected Income 17.xls]Cost Analysis'!$A$10
```

If you ever need to sever a link between the cell containing the original value or formula and the cell to which it's been brought forward, you can do so by editing the linking formula. Press F2, then immediately recalculate the formula by pressing F9, and then click the Enter button on the Formula bar or press Enter.

This replaces the linking formula with the currently calculated result. Because you've converted the dynamic formula into a constant, changes to the original cell no longer affect the one to which it was originally brought forward.

Controlling Formula Recalculation

Normally, Excel recalculates your worksheet automatically as soon you change any entries, formulas, or names on which your formulas depend. This system works fine as long as the worksheet is not too large or doesn't contain tables whose formulas depend on several values.

When Excel does calculate your worksheet, the program recalculates only those cells that are affected by the change that you've made. Nevertheless, in a complex worksheet that contains many formulas, recalculation may take several seconds (during which time, the pointer will change to an hourglass, and the word "Recalculation" followed by the number of cells left to be recalculated will appear on the left side of the Formula bar).

Because Excel recalculates dependent formulas in the background, you can always interrupt this process and make a cell entry or click a command even when the pointer assumes the hourglass shape during the recalculation process. As soon as you stop making entries or selecting commands, Excel resumes recalculating the worksheet.

To control when Excel calculates your worksheet, you click the Calculation Options button on the Formulas tab of the Ribbon and then click the Manual option button or press Alt+MXM. After switching to manual recalculation, when you make a change in a value, formula, or name that would usually cause Excel to recalculate the worksheet, the program displays the message "Calculate" on the Status bar.

When you're ready to have Excel recalculate the worksheet, you then click the Calculate Now (F9) command button (the one with a picture of the handheld calculator) on the Ribbon's FORMULAS tab or press F9 or Ctrl+=. This tells the program to recalculate all dependent formulas and open charts and makes the Calculate status indicator disappear from the Status bar.

REMEMBER

After switching to manual recalculation, Excel still automatically recalculates the worksheet whenever you save the file. When you are working with a really large and complex worksheet, recalculating the worksheet each time you want to save your changes can make this process quite time-consuming. If you want to save the worksheet without first updating dependent formulas and charts, you need to deselect the Recalculate Workbook before Saving check box in the Calculation Options section of the Formulas tab of the Excel Options dialog box (File⇨Options⇨Formulas or Alt+FTF).

TIP

If your worksheet contains data tables used to perform what-if analyses, switch from Automatic to Automatic except Data Tables recalculation by choosing Automatic Except Data Tables from the Options button's drop-down menu on the Formulas tab or pressing Alt+MXE. Doing so enables you to change a number of variables in the what-if formulas before having Excel recalculate the data table. (See Book 7, Chapter 1 for more on performing what-if analyses.)

Automatic, Automatic Except Data Tables, and Manual are by no means the only calculation options available in Excel. Table 1-3 explains each of the options that appear in the Calculation Options section of the Formulas tab of the Excel Options dialog box.

TABLE 1-3   ## The Calculation Options in Excel 2019

Option	Purpose
Automatic	Calculates all dependent formulas and updates open or embedded charts every time you make a change to a value, formula, or name. This is the default setting for each new worksheet that you start.
Automatic Except for Data Tables	Calculates all dependent formulas and updates open or embedded charts. Does not calculate data tables created with the Data Table feature. (See Book 7, Chapter 1, for information on creating data tables.) To recalculate data tables when this option button is selected, click the Calculate Now (F9) command button on the Formulas tab of the Ribbon or press F9 in the worksheet.
Manual	Calculates open worksheets and updates open or embedded charts only when you click the Calculate Now (F9) command button on the Formulas tab of the Ribbon or press F9 or Ctrl+= in the worksheet.
Recalculate Workbook before Saving	When this check box is selected, Excel calculates open worksheets and updates open or embedded charts when you save them even when the Manually option button is selected.
Enable Iterative Calculation	When this check box is selected, Excel sets the *iterations,* that is, the number of times that a worksheet is recalculated, when performing goal seeking (see Book 7, Chapter 1) or resolving circular references to the number displayed in the Maximum Iterations text box.
Maximum Iterations	Sets the maximum number of iterations (100 by default) when the Iteration check box is selected.
Maximum Change	Sets the maximum amount of change to the values during each iteration (0.001 by default) when the Iteration check box is selected.

Circular References

A *circular reference* in a formula is one that depends, directly or indirectly, on its own value. The most common type of circular reference occurs when you mistakenly refer in the formula to the cell in which you're building the formula itself. For example, suppose that cell B10 is active when you build this formula:

```
=A10+B10
```

As soon as you click the Enter button on the Formula bar or press Enter or an arrow key to insert this formula in cell B10 (assuming the program is in Automatic recalculation mode), Excel displays an Alert dialog box, stating that it cannot calculate the formula due to the circular reference.

If you then press Enter or click OK to close this Alert dialog box, an Excel Help window appears containing general information about circular references in two sections: Locate and Remove a Circular Reference and Make a Circular Reference Work by Changing the Number of Times Microsoft Excel Iterates Formulas.

When you close this Excel Help window by clicking its Close button, Excel inserts 0 in the cell with the circular reference, and the Circular Reference status indicator followed by the cell address with the circular reference appears on the Status bar.

Some circular references are solvable by increasing the number of times they are recalculated (each recalculation bringing you closer and closer to the desired result), whereas others are not (for no amount of recalculating brings them closer to any resolution) and need to be removed from the spreadsheet.

The formula in cell B10 is an example of a circular reference that Excel is unable to resolve because the formula's calculation depends directly on the formula's result. Each time the formula returns a new result, this result is fed into the formula, thus creating a new result to be fed back into the formula. Because this type of circular reference sets up an endless loop that continuously requires recalculating and can never be resolved, you need to fix the formula reference or remove the formula from the spreadsheet.

Figure 1-17 illustrates the classic example of a circular reference, which ultimately can be resolved. Here, you have an income statement that includes bonuses equal to 20 percent of the net earnings entered as an expense in cell B15 with the formula

```
=-B21*20%
```

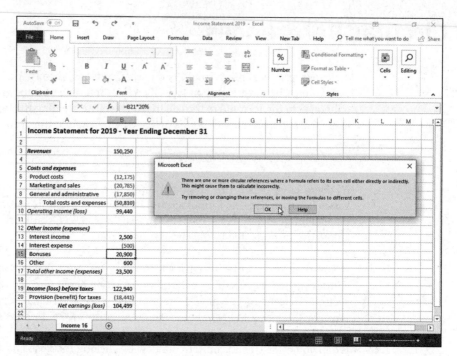

FIGURE 1-17:
Income statement with a resolvable circular reference.

This formula contains a circular reference because it refers to the value in B21, which itself indirectly depends on the amount of bonuses (the bonuses being accounted for as an expense in the very worksheet formulas that determine the amount of net earnings in cell B21).

To resolve the circular reference in cell B15 and calculate the bonuses based on net earnings in B21, you simply need to click the Enable Iterative Calculation check box in the Calculation Options section of the Formulas tab in the Excel Options dialog box (File⇨Options⇨Formulas or Alt+FTF). However, if manual recalculation is selected, you must click the Calculate Now (F9) command button on the Formulas tab of the Ribbon or press F9 or Ctrl+= as well.

Chapter **2**

Logical Functions and Error Trapping

Troubleshooting the formula errors in a worksheet is the main topic of this chapter. Here, you see how to locate the source of all those vexing formula errors so that you can shoot them down and set things right! The biggest problem with errors in your formulas — besides how ugly such values as #REF! and #DIV/0! are — is that they spread like wildfire through the workbook to other cells containing formulas that refer to their error-laden cells. If you're dealing with a large worksheet in a really big workbook, you may not be able to tell which cell actually contains the formula that's causing all the hubbub. And if you can't apprehend the cell that is the cause of all this unpleasantness, you really have no way of restoring law and order to your workbook.

Keeping in mind that the best defense is a good offense, you also find out in this chapter how to trap potential errors at their source and thereby keep them there. This technique, known affectionately as *error trapping* (just think of yourself as being on a spreadsheet safari), is easily accomplished by skillfully combining the IF function to combine with the workings of the original formula.

Understanding Error Values

If Excel can't properly calculate a formula that you enter in a cell, the program displays an *error value* in the cell as soon as you complete the formula entry. Excel uses several error values, all of which begin with the number sign (#). Table 2-1 shows you the error values in Excel along with the meanings and the most probable causes for their display. To remove an error value from a cell, you must discover what caused the value to appear and then edit the formula so that Excel can complete the desired calculation.

TABLE 2-1   **Error Values in Excel**

Error Value	Meaning	Causes
#DIV/0!	Division by zero	The division operation in your formula refers to a cell that contains the value 0 or is blank.
#N/A	No value available	Technically, this is not an error value but a special value that you can manually enter into a cell to indicate that you don't yet have a necessary value with the function, =NA().
#NAME?	Excel doesn't recognize a name	This error value appears when you incorrectly type the range name, refer to a deleted range name, or forget to put quotation marks around a text string in a formula (causing Excel to think that you're referring to a range name).
#NULL!	You specified an intersection of two cell ranges whose cells don't actually intersect	Because the space is the intersection, this error will occur if you insert a space instead of a comma (the union operator) between ranges used in function arguments.
#NUM!	Problem with a number in the formula	This error can be caused by an invalid argument in an Excel function or a formula that produces a number too large or too small to be represented in the worksheet.
#REF!	Invalid cell reference	This error occurs when you delete a cell referred to in the formula or if you paste cells over the ones referred to in the formula.
#VALUE!	Wrong type of argument in a function or wrong type of operator	This error is most often the result of specifying a mathematical operation with one or more cells that contain text.

If a formula in your worksheet contains a reference to a cell that returns an error value, that formula returns that error value as well. This can cause error values to appear throughout the worksheet, thus making it very difficult for you to discover which cell contains the formula that caused the original error value so that you can fix the problem.

Using Logical Functions

Excel uses the following logical functions, which appear on the Logical command button's drop-down menu on the Formulas tab of the Ribbon (Alt+ML). All the logical functions return either the logical TRUE or logical FALSE to their cells when their functions are evaluated. Here are the names of the functions along with their argument syntax:

» AND(*logical1,logical2,...*) — tests whether the *logical* arguments are TRUE or FALSE. If they are all TRUE, the AND function returns TRUE to the cell. If any are FALSE, the AND function returns FALSE.

» FALSE( ) — takes no argument and simply enters logical FALSE in its cell.

» IF(*logical_test,value_if_true,value_if_false*) — tests whether the *logical_test* expression is TRUE or FALSE. If TRUE, the IF function uses the *value_if_true* argument and returns it to the cell. If FALSE, the IF function uses the *value_if_false* argument and returns it to the cell.

» IFERROR(*value,value_if_error*) — returns the *value* argument when the cell referred to in another logical argument in which the IFERROR function is used doesn't contain an error value and the *value_if_error* argument when it does.

» IFNA(*value,value_if_na*) — returns the *value* argument when the cell referred to in another logical argument in which the IFNA function is used doesn't contain #NA and the *value_if_error* argument when it does.

» =IFS(*logical_test1,value_if_true1*) — tests whether or not one or more *logical_test* arguments are TRUE. The IFS function then returns the corresponding value argument (*value_if_true1* for *logical_test1*, *value_if_true2* for *logical_test2* and so on to *value_if_true127* for *logical_test127*), When no TRUE conditions are met, Excel returns the #NA error value.

» NOT(*logical*) — tests whether the *logical* argument is TRUE or FALSE. If TRUE, the NOT function returns FALSE to the cell. IF FALSE, the NOT function returns TRUE to the cell.

» OR(*logical1,logical2,...*) — tests whether the *logical* arguments are TRUE or FALSE. If any are TRUE, the OR function returns TRUE. If all are FALSE, the OR function returns FALSE.

» SWITCH(*expression,value1,result1,[default]*) — tests the value returned by the *expression* argument against a list of value arguments (*value1, value2,* and so on to *value126*) and returns the corresponding result (*result1* for *value1, result2* for *value2,* and so on to *result126* for *value126*) when a match is TRUE. Optional *default* argument is returned when none of the value arguments match the expression argument. When no *default* argument is specified, Excel returns the #NA error value when there is no match.

>> TRUE( ) — takes no argument and simply enters logical TRUE in its cell.

>> XOR(*logical1,logical2,. . .*) — tests whether the *logical* arguments (usually in an array) are predominantly TRUE or FALSE. When the number of TRUE inputs is odd, the XOR function returns TRUE. When the number of TRUE inputs is even, the XOR function returns FALSE.

The *logical_test* and *logical* arguments that you specify for these logical functions usually employ the comparison operators (=, <, >, <=, >=, or <>), which themselves return logical TRUE or logical FALSE values. For example, suppose that you enter the following formula in your worksheet:

```
=AND(B5=D10,C15>=500)
```

In this formula, Excel first evaluates the first *logical* argument to determine whether the contents in cell B5 and D10 are equal to each other. If they are, the first comparison returns TRUE. If they are not equal to each other, this comparison returns FALSE. The program then evaluates the second *logical* argument to determine whether the content of cell C15 is greater than or equal to 500. If it is, the second comparison returns TRUE. If it is not greater than or equal to 500, this comparison returns FALSE.

After evaluating the comparisons in the two *logical* arguments, the AND function compares the results: If *logical* argument 1 and *logical* argument 2 are both found to be TRUE, the AND function returns logical TRUE to the cell. If, however, either argument is found to be FALSE, the AND function returns FALSE to the cell.

When you use the IF function, you specify what's called a *logical_test* argument whose outcome determines whether the *value_if_true* or *value_if_false* argument is evaluated and returned to the cell. The *logical_test* argument normally uses comparison operators, which return either the logical TRUE or logical FALSE value. When the argument returns TRUE, the entry or expression in the *value_if_true* argument is used and returned to the cell. When the argument returns FALSE, the entry or expression in the *value_if_false* argument is used.

Consider the following formula that uses the IF function to determine whether to charge tax on an item:

```
=IF(E5="Yes",D5+D5*7.5%,D5)
```

If cell E5 (the first cell in the column where you indicate whether the item being sold is taxable or not) contains "Yes," the IF function uses the *value_if_true* argument that tells Excel to add the extended price entered in cell D5, multiply it by a tax rate of 7.5%, and then add the computed tax to the extended price. If, however, cell D5 is blank or contains anything other than the text "Yes," the IF function uses the *value_if_false* argument, which tells Excel to just return the extended price to cell D5 without adding any tax to it.

As you can see, the *value_if_true* and *value_if_false* arguments of the IF function can contain constants or expressions whose results are returned to the cell that holds the IF formula.

Evaluating the many talents of the IFS function

The IFS logical function enables you to test for multiple conditions (up to a maximum of 127) all in a single formula without having to go through the trouble and potential confusion of nesting multiple those IF functions within that formula.

The spreadsheet shown in Figure 2-1 illustrates how this nifty and powerful function works. Here, I want to test for three conditions:

>> "Weak" customer sales in an amount less than $5,000

>> "Moderate" customer sales in an amount between $5,000 and $10,000

>> "Strong" customer sales in an amount above $10,000

To do this with the IFS function, I create the following formula in cell C4 of my worksheet that evaluates the sales amount entered into cell B4:

```
=IFS(B4<5000,"Weak",AND(B4>=5000,B4<=10000),"Moderate",B4>10000,
   "Strong")
```

This IFS function contains three different *logical_test* arguments, using three different *value_if_true* resulting arguments:

>> If the value in cell B4 is less than 5000, then return the text entry *Weak* as the value in cell C4)

>> If the value in cell B4 is within the range of 5,000 and 10,000 (expressed with the nested AND logical function), then return the text entry *Moderate* as the value in cell C4)

>> IF the value in cell B4 is greater than 10,000, then return the text entry *Strong* as the value in cell C4)

Figure 2-1 shows you the result of copying the original IFS function formula entered into cell C4 down the range C5:C8 of the worksheet so that all of the values entered thus far in column B are evaluated as weak, moderate, or strong.

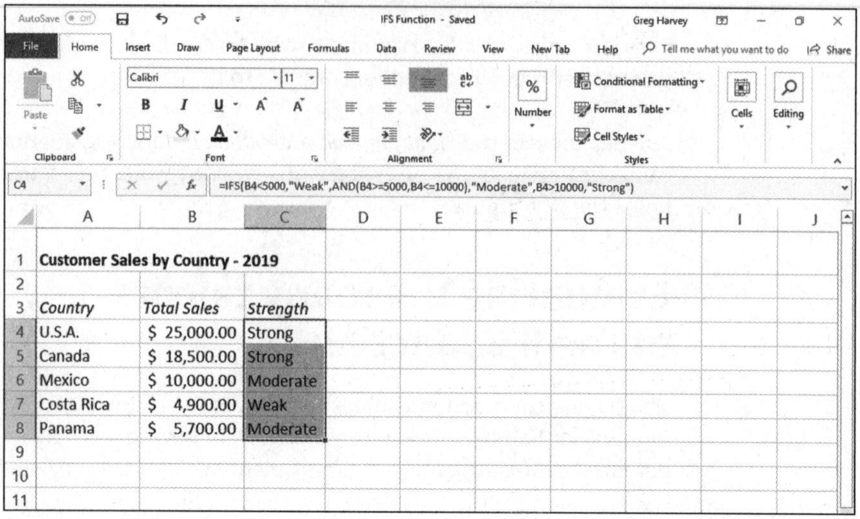

FIGURE 2-1:
Using the IFS
function to
test multiple
conditions in a
single formula.

SWITCH it out

The SWITCH logical function enables you to test a value returned by a single *expression* argument against a whole list of values (up to a 126) in the *value* arguments by returning resulting values specified by the corresponding *result* arguments.

To see how this works, consider the example shown in Figure 2-2. Here, I've entered the names of the days of the weeks in cell range A1:A7. In the cell range C2:C7, I've entered a rather random range of dates. In D2, I entered the original formula using the SWITCH logical function with a nested WEEKDAY function followed by a whole series of *value* and *result* arguments as follows:

```
=SWITCH(WEEKDAY(C2),1,$A$1,2,$A$2,3,$A$3,4,$A$4,5,$A$5,6,$A$6,
    7,$A$7)
```

The WEEKDAY function in this formula returns the day of week in any date as a number between 1 for Sunday and 7 for Saturday (see Book 3, Chapter 3 for more on using Date functions). This WEEKDAY function with cell C2 as its serial date number argument serves as the *expression* argument of the SWITCH function. Following this *expression* argument, you see a series of *value* and *result* arguments. When the WEEKDAY function returns one of the values (between 1 and 7), the SWITCH argument replaces it with the corresponding days of the week entered into the cell range A1:A7 as a vertical lookup table.

Note that when I entered the individual cell references from this days of the week lookup table into the appropriate *result* argument in the formula, I switched the cell reference from its default relative cell reference (as in A1, A2, and so forth) to its absolute cell reference ($A$1,$A$2, and so on). However, when I entered the cell reference C2 as the *serial_number* argument of the WEEKDAY function, I left it a relative reference. I did this so I could successfully copy the original formula created in cell D2 down to the range D3:D7 by having Excel adjust the C2 reference in the original formula in each formula copy to its appropriate row in column C, while at the same time preventing Excel from returning results for matches from any other cells outside the A1:A7 lookup table.

Figure 2-2 shows you the results. The original formula with the SWICH function in cell D2 has been copied down the column to the cell range D3:D7. These formulas all compare the day of the week number calculated by the WEEKDAY function on the dates entered into corresponding cells in the same row of column C. They then return the matching name of the day of the week from the cell range A1:A7 to their respective cells. Note that I also entered a column of WEEKDAY function formulas in the cell range E3:E7 so you can follow how the Excel went about matching the number of the day of the week against its name in A1:A7.

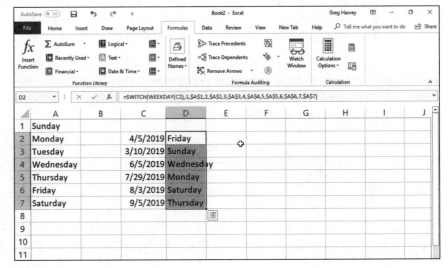

FIGURE 2-2:
Using the SWITCH function to match days of the week against a series of results returned by a WEEKDAY function

Error-Trapping Formulas

Sometimes, you know ahead of time that certain error values are unavoidable in a worksheet as long as it's missing certain data. The most common error value that gets you into this kind of trouble is our old friend, the #DIV/0! error value. Suppose, for example, that you're creating a new sales workbook from your sales template, and one of the rows in this template contains formulas that calculate the percentage that each monthly total is of the quarterly total. To work correctly, the formulas must divide the value in the cell that contains the monthly total by the value in the cell that contains the quarterly total. When you start a new sales workbook from its template, the cells that contain the formulas for determining the quarterly totals contain zeros, and these zeros put #DIV/0! errors in the cells with formulas that calculate the monthly/quarterly percentages.

These particular #DIV/0! error values in the new workbook don't really represent mistakes as such because they automatically disappear as soon as you enter some of the monthly sales for each quarter (so that the calculated quarterly totals are no longer 0). The problem that you may have is convincing your nonspreadsheet-savvy coworkers (especially the boss) that, despite the presence of all these error values in your worksheet, the formulas are hunky-dory. All that your coworkers see is a worksheet riddled with error values, and these error values undermine your coworkers' confidence in the correctness of your worksheet.

REMEMBER

Well, I have the answer for just such "perception" problems. Rather than risk having your manager upset over the display of a few little #DIV/0! errors here and there, you can set up these formulas so that, whenever they're tempted to return any type of error value (including #DIV/0!), they instead return zeros in their cells. Only when absolutely no danger exists of cooking up error values will Excel actually do the original calculations called for in the formulas.

This sleight of hand in an original formula not only effectively eliminates errors from the formula but also prevents their spread to any of its dependents. To create such a formula, you use the IF function, which operates one way when a certain condition exists and another when it doesn't.

To see how you can use the IF function in a formula that sometimes gives you a #DIV/0! error, consider the sample worksheet shown in Figure 2-3. This figure shows a blank Production Schedule worksheet for storing the 2019 production figures arranged by month and part number. Because I haven't yet had a chance to input any data into this table, the SUM formulas in the last row and column contain 0 values. Because cell K7 with the grand total currently also contains 0, all the percent-of-total formulas in the cell range B9:J9 contain #DIV/0! error values.

The first percent-of-total formula in cell B9 contains the following:

```
=B7/$K$7
```

Because cell K7 with the grand total contains 0, the formula returns the #DIV/0! error value. Now, let me show you how to set a trap for the error in the *logical_test* argument inside an IF function. After the *logical_test* argument, you enter the *value_if_true* argument (which is 0 in this example) and the *value_if_false* argument (which is the B7/$K$7). With the addition of the IF function, the final formula looks like this:

```
=IF($K$7=0,0,B7/$K$7)
```

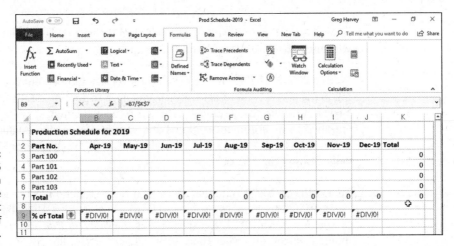

FIGURE 2-3:
Blank 2016
Production
Schedule
spreadsheet
that's full of
#DIV/0! errors.

This formula then inputs 0 into cell B9, as shown in Figure 2-4, when the formula actually returns the #DIV/0! error value (because cell K7 is still empty or has a 0 in it), and the formula returns the percentage of total production when the formula doesn't return the #DIV/0! error value (because cell K7 with the total production divisor is no longer empty or contains any other value besides 0). Next, all you have to do is copy this error-trapping formula in cell B9 over to J9 to remove all the #DIV/0! errors from this worksheet.

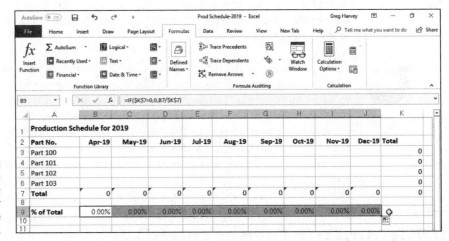

FIGURE 2-4:
2019 Production
Schedule
spreadsheet after
trapping all the
#DIV/0! errors.

The error-trapping formula created with the IF function in cell B9 works fine as long as you know that the grand total in cell K7 will contain either 0 or some other numerical value. It does not, however, trap any of the various error values, such as #REF! and #NAME?, nor does it account for the special #NA (Not Available) value. If, for some reason, one of the formulas feeding into the SUM formula in K8 returns one of these beauties, they will suddenly cascade throughout all the cells with the percent-of-total formulas (cell range B9:J9).

To trap all error values in the grand total cell K7 and prevent them from spreading to the percent-to-total formulas, you need to add the ISERROR function to the basic IF formula. The ISERROR function returns the logical value TRUE if the cell specified as its argument contains any type of error value, including the special #N/A value (if you use ISERR instead of ISERROR, it checks for all types of error values except for #N/A).

To add the ISERROR function, place it in the IF function as the *logical_test* argument. If, indeed, K7 does contain an error value or the #N/A value at the time the IF function is evaluated, you specify 0 as the *value_if_true* argument so that Excel inputs 0 in cell B9 rather than error value or #N/A. For the *value_if_false* argument, you specify the original IF function that inputs 0 if the cell K7 contains 0; otherwise, it performs the division that computes what percentage the April production figure is of the total production.

This amended formula with the ISERROR and two IF functions in cell B9 looks like this:

```
=IF(ISERROR($K$7),0,IF($K$7=0,0,B7/$K$7))
```

As soon as you copy this original formula to the cell range C9:J9, you've protected all the cells with the percent-of-total formulas from displaying and spreading any of those ugly error values.

TIP

Some people prefer to remove the display of zero values from any template that contains error-trapping formulas so that no one interprets the zeros as the correct value for the formula. To remove the display of zeros from a worksheet, deselect the Show a Zero in Cells That Have Zero Values check box in the Display Options for this Worksheet section of the Advanced tab of the Excel Options dialog box (File➪Options or Alt+FT). By this action, the cells with error-trapping formulas remain blank until you give them the data that they need to return the correct answers!

Whiting-Out Errors with Conditional Formatting

Instead of creating logical formulas to suppress the display of potential error values, you can use Conditional Formatting (see Book 2, Chapter 2 for details) to deal with them. All you have to do is create a new conditional formatting rule that displays all potential error values in a white font (essentially, rendering them invisible in the cells of your worksheet). I think of using conditional formatting in this manner to deal with possible error values in a worksheet as applying a kind of electronic white-out that masks rather than suppresses formula errors.

To create this conditional formatting white-out for cells containing formulas that could easily be populated with error values, you follow these steps:

1. **Select the ranges of cells with the formulas to which you want the new conditional formatting rule applied.**

2. **Click the Conditional Formatting button on the Home tab and then click New Rule from its drop-down menu (Alt+HLN).**

   Excel displays the New Formatting Rule dialog box.

3. **Click the Format Only Cells That Contain option in the Select a Rule Type section at the top of the New Formatting Rule dialog box.**

4. **Click the Errors item from the Cell Value drop-down menu under Format Only Cells With section of the New Formatting Rule dialog box.**

   The New Formatting Rule dialog box now contains an Edit the Rule Description section at the bottom of the dialog box with Errors displayed under the Format Only Cells With heading.

5. **Click the Format button to the immediate right of the Preview text box that now contains No Format Set.**

   Excel opens the Format Cells dialog box with the Font tab selected.

6. **Click the Color drop-down menu button, click the white swatch (the very first one on the color palette displayed under Theme Colors), and then click OK.**

   Excel closes the Format Cells dialog box and the Preview text box in the New Formatting Rule dialog box now appears empty (as the No Format Set text is now displayed in a white font).

7. **Click OK in the New Formatting Rule dialog box to close it and apply the new conditional formatting rule to your current cell selection.**

TIP

After applying the new conditional formatting rule to a cell range, you can test it out by deliberately entering an error value into one of the cells referenced in one of the formulas in that range now covered by the "white-out" conditional formatting. Entering the #NA error value in one of these cells with the =NA( ) function is perhaps the easiest to do. Instead of seeing #NA values spread throughout the cell range, the cells should now appear empty because of the white font applied to all the #N/As, rendering them, for all intents and purposes, invisible.

Formula Auditing

If you don't happen to trap those pesky error values before they get out into the spreadsheet, you end up having to track down the original cell that caused all the commotion and set it right. Fortunately, Excel offers some very effective formula-auditing tools for tracking down the cell that's causing your error woes by tracing the relationships between the formulas in the cells of your worksheet. By tracing the relationships, you can test formulas to see which cells, called *direct precedents* in spreadsheet jargon, directly feed the formulas and which cells, called *dependents* (nondeductible, of course), depend on the results of the formulas. Excel even offers a way to visually backtrack the potential sources of an error value in the formula of a particular cell.

The formula-auditing tools are found in the command buttons located in the Formula Auditing group on the Formulas tab of the Ribbon. These command buttons include the following:

- **Trace Precedents:** When you click this button, Excel draws arrows to the cells (the so-called *direct precedents*) that are referred to in the formula inside the selected cell. When you click this button again, Excel adds "tracer" arrows that show the cells (the so-called indirect precedents) that are referred to in the formulas in the direct precedents.

- **Trace Dependents:** When you click this button, Excel draws arrows from the selected cell to the cells (the so-called *direct dependents*) that use, or depend on, the results of the formula in the selected cell. When you click this button again, Excel adds tracer arrows identifying the cells (the so-called *indirect dependents*) that refer to formulas found in the direct dependents.

- **Remove Arrows:** Clicking this button removes all the arrows drawn, no matter what button or pull-down command you used to put them there. Click the drop-down button attached to this button to display a drop-down menu with three options: Remove Arrows to remove all arrows (just like clicking the Remove Arrows command button); Remove Precedent Arrows to get rid of the arrows that were drawn when you clicked the Trace Precedents button; and Remove Dependent Arrows to get rid of the arrows that were drawn when you clicked the Trace Dependents button.

- **Show Formulas:** To display all formulas in their cells in the worksheet instead of their calculated values — just like pressing Ctrl+` (tilde).

- **Error Checking:** When you click this button or click the Error Checking option on its drop-down menu, Excel displays the Error Checking dialog box, which describes the nature of the error in the current cell, gives you help on it, and enables you to trace its precedents. Click the Trace Error option from this button's drop-down menu to attempt to locate the cell that contains the original formula that has an error. Click the Circular References option from this button's drop-down menu to display a continuation menu with a list of all the cell addresses containing circular references in the active worksheet — click a cell address on this menu to select the cell with a circular reference formula in the worksheet. (See Book 3, Chapter 1 for more on circular references in formulas.)

>> **Evaluate Formula:** Clicking this button opens the Evaluate Formula dialog box, where you can have Excel evaluate each part of the formula in the current cell. The Evaluate Formula feature can be quite useful in formulas that nest many functions within them.

>> **Watch Window:** Clicking this button opens the Watch Window dialog box, which displays the workbook, sheet, cell location, range name, current value, and formula in any cells that you add to the watch list. To add a cell to the watch list, click the cell in the worksheet, click the Add Watch button in the Watch Window dialog box, and then click Add in the Add Watch dialog box that appears.

Clicking the Trace Precedents and Trace Dependents buttons in the Formula Auditing group of the Formulas tab on the Ribbon lets you see the relationship between a formula and the cells that directly and indirectly feed it, as well as those cells that directly and indirectly depend on its calculation. Excel establishes this relationship by drawing arrows from the precedent cells to the active cell and from the active cell to its dependent cells.

If these cells are on the same worksheet, Excel draws solid red or blue arrows extending from each of the precedent cells to the active cell and from the active cell to the dependent cells. If the cells are not located locally on the same worksheet (they may be on another sheet in the same workbook or even on a sheet in a different workbook), Excel draws a black dotted arrow. This arrow comes from or goes to an icon picturing a miniature worksheet that sits to one side, with the direction of the arrowheads indicating whether the cells on the other sheet feed the active formula or are fed by it.

Tracing precedents

You can click the Trace Precedents command button on the Formulas tab of the Ribbon or press Alt+MP to trace all the generations of cells that contribute to the formula in the selected cell (kinda like tracing all the ancestors in your family tree). Figures 2-5 and 2-6 illustrate how you can use the Trace Precedents command button or its hot key equivalent to quickly locate the cells that contribute, directly and indirectly, to the simple addition formula in cell B9.

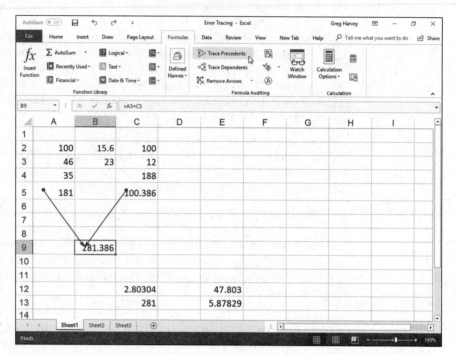

FIGURE 2-5:
Clicking the
Trace Precedents
command button
shows the direct
precedents of
the formula.

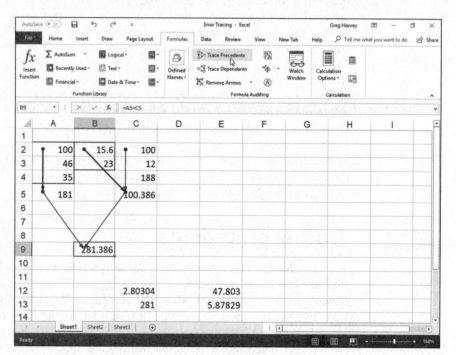

FIGURE 2-6:
Clicking the
Trace Precedents
command button
again shows
the indirect
precedents of
the formula.

Figure 2-5 shows the worksheet after I clicked the Trace Precedents command button the first time. As you can see, Excel draws trace arrows from cells A5 and C5 to indicate that they are the direct precedents of the addition formula in cell B9.

In Figure 2-6, you see what happened when I clicked this command button a second time to display the indirect precedents of this formula. (Think of them as being a generation earlier in the family tree.) The new tracer arrows show that cells A2, A3, and A4 are the direct precedents of the formula in cell A5 — indicated by a border around the three cells. (Remember that cell A5 is the first direct precedent of the formula in cell B9.) Likewise, cells B2 and B3 as well as cell C2 are the direct precedents of the formula in cell C5. (Cell C5 is the second direct precedent of the formula in cell B9.)

Each time you click the Trace Precedents command button, Excel displays another (earlier) set of precedents, until no more generations exist. If you are in a hurry (as most of us are most of the time), you can speed up the process and display both the direct and indirect precedents in one operation by double-clicking the Trace Precedents command button. To clear the worksheet of tracer arrows, click the Remove Arrows command button on the Formulas tab.

Figure 2-7 shows what happened after I clicked the Trace Precedents command button a third time (after clicking it twice before, as shown in Figures 2-5 and 2-6). Clicking the command button reveals both the indirect precedents for cell C5. The formulas in cells B2 and C2 are the direct precedents of the formula in cell C5. The direct precedent of the formula in cell C2 (and, consequently, the indirect precedent of the one in cell C5) is not located on this worksheet. This fact is indicated by the dotted tracer arrow coming from that cute miniature worksheet icon sitting on top of cell A3.

To find out exactly which workbook, worksheet, and cell(s) hold the direct precedents of cell C2, I double-clicked somewhere on the dotted arrow. (Clicking the icon with the worksheet miniature doesn't do a thing.) Double-clicking the dotted tracer arrow opens the Go To dialog box, which shows a list of all the precedents, including the workbook, worksheet, and cell references. To go to a precedent on another worksheet, double-click the reference in the Go To list box, or select it and click OK. (If the worksheet is in another workbook, this workbook file must already be open before you can go to it.)

The Go To dialog box, shown in Figure 2-8, displays the following direct precedent of cell C2, which is cell B4 on Sheet2 of the same workbook:

```
'[Error Tracing.xls]Sheet2'!$B$4
```

To jump directly to this cell, double-click the cell reference in the Go To dialog box.

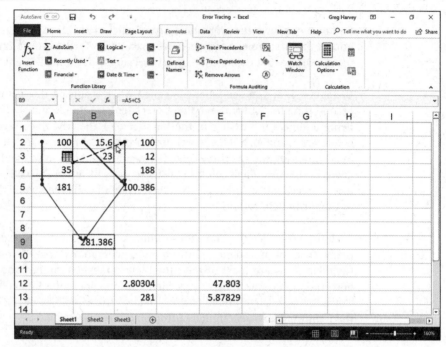

FIGURE 2-7:
Clicking the
Trace Precedents
command
button a third
time shows
a precedent
on another
worksheet.

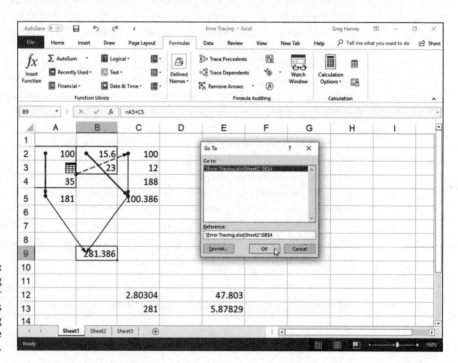

FIGURE 2-8:
Double-clicking
the dotted tracer
arrow opens
the Go To dialog
box showing the
location.

You can also select precedent cells that are on the same worksheet as the active cell by double-clicking somewhere on the cell's tracer arrow. Excel selects the precedent cell without bothering to open up the Go To dialog box.

TIP

You can use the Special button in the Go To dialog box (see Figure 2-8) to select all the direct or indirect precedents or the direct or indirect dependents that are on the same sheet as the formula in the selected cell. After opening the Go To dialog box (Ctrl+G or F5) and clicking the Special button, you simply click the Precedents or Dependents option button and then click between the Direct Only and All Levels option buttons before you click OK.

Tracing dependents

You can click the Trace Dependents command button in the Formula Auditing group of the Formulas tab on the Ribbon or press Alt+MD to trace all the generations of cells that either directly or indirectly utilize the formula in the selected cell (kind of like tracing the genealogy of all your ancestors). Tracing dependents with the Trace Dependents command button is much like tracing precedents with the Trace Precedents command button. Each time you click this button, Excel draws another set of arrows that show a generation of dependents further removed. To display both the direct and indirect dependents of a cell in one fell swoop, double-click the Trace Dependents command button.

Figure 2-9 shows what happened after I selected cell B9 and then double-clicked the Trace Dependents command button on the Formulas tab of the Ribbon to display both the direct and indirect dependents and then clicked it a third time to display the dependents on another worksheet.

As this figure shows, Excel first draws tracer arrows from cell B9 to cells C12 and C13, indicating that C12 and C13 are the direct dependents of cell B9. Then, it draws tracer arrows from cells C12 and C13 to E12 and E13, respectively, the direct dependents of C12 and C13 and the indirect dependents of B9. Finally, it draws a tracer arrow from cell E12 to another sheet in the workbook (indicated by the dotted tracer arrow pointing to the worksheet icon).

Error checking

Whenever a formula yields an error value other than #N/A (refer to Table 2-1 earlier in this chapter for a list of all the error values) in a cell, Excel displays a tiny error indicator (in the form of the triangle) in the upper-left corner of the cell, and an alert options button appears to the left of that cell when you make it active. If you position the mouse or Touch pointer on that options button, a drop-down button appears to its right that you can click to display a drop-down menu, and a ScreenTip appears below describing the nature of the error value.

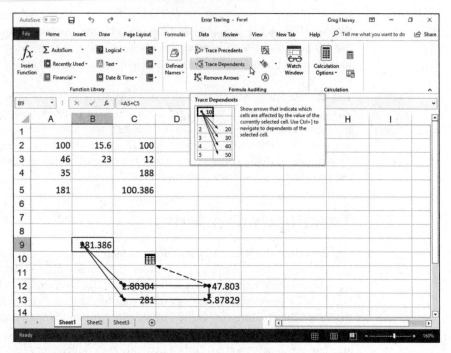

FIGURE 2-9:
Clicking the Trace
Dependents
command button
shows all the
dependents
of the formula
in cell B9.

When you click the drop-down button, a menu appears, containing an item with
the name of the error value followed by the following items:

>> **Help on This Error:** Opens an Excel Help window with information on the
type of error value in the active cell and how to correct it.

>> **Show Calculation Steps:** Opens the Evaluate Formula dialog box where you
can walk through each step in the calculation to see the result of each
computation.

>> **Ignore Error:** Bypasses error checking for this cell and removes the error alert
and Error options button from it.

>> **Edit in Formula Bar:** Activates Edit mode and puts the insertion point at the
end of the formula on the Formula bar.

>> **Error Checking Options:** Opens the Formulas tab of the Excel Options dialog
box where you can modify the options used in checking the worksheet for
formula errors. (See "Changing the Error Checking options" section that
immediately follows for details.)

If you're dealing with a worksheet that contains many error values, you can use
the Error Checking command button (the one with the check mark on top of a red
alert exclamation mark) in the Formula Auditing group on the Ribbon's Formulas
tab to locate each error.

When you click the Error Checking command button, Excel selects the cell with the first error value and opens the Error Checking dialog box (see Figure 2-10) that identifies the nature of the error value in the current cell.

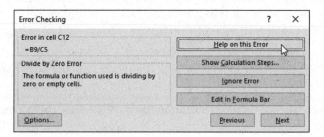

FIGURE 2-10:
Flagging an error value in a worksheet in the Error Checking dialog box.

The command buttons in the Error Checking dialog box directly correspond to the menu options that appear when you click the cell's alert options button (except that Error Checking Options on this drop-down menu is simply called the Options button in this dialog box).

In addition, the Error Checking dialog box contains Next and Previous buttons that you can click to have Excel select the cell with the next error value or return to the cell with the previously displayed error value.

REMEMBER

Note that when you click the Next or Previous button when Excel has flagged the very first or last error value in the worksheet, the program displays an alert dialog box letting you know that the error check for the worksheet is complete. When you click the OK button, Excel closes both the alert dialog box and the Error Checking dialog box. Also note that clicking the Ignore Error button is the equivalent of clicking the Next button.

Changing the Error Checking options

When you click Error Checking Options from the alert options drop-down menu attached to a cell with an error value or click the Options button in the Error Checking dialog box, Excel opens the Formulas tab of the Excel Options dialog box. This tab displays the Error Checking and Error Checking Rules options that are currently in effect in Excel. You can use these options on this Formulas tab to control when the worksheet is checked for errors and what cells are flagged:

>> **Enable Background Error Checking check box:** Has Excel check your worksheets for errors when the computer is idle. When this check box is selected, you can change the color of the error indicator that appears as a tiny triangle in the upper-left corner of the cell (normally this indicator is green) by clicking a new color on the Indicate Errors Using This Color's drop-down palette.

- >> **Indicate Errors Using This Color drop-down button:** Enables you to select a particular color for cells containing error values from the drop-down palette that appears when you click this button.

- >> **Reset Ignored Errors button:** Restores the error indicator and alert options button to all cells that you previously told Excel to ignore by clicking the Ignore Error item from the alert options drop-down menu attached to the cell.

- >> **Cells Containing Formulas That Result in an Error check box:** Has Excel insert the error indicator and adds the alert options button to all cells that return error values.

- >> **Inconsistent Calculated Column Formula in Tables check box:** Has Excel flag formulas in particular columns of cell ranges formatted as tables that vary in their computations from the other formulas in the column.

- >> **Cells Containing Years Represented as 2 Digits check box:** Has Excel flag all dates entered as text with just the last two digits of the year as errors by adding an error indicator and alert options button to their cells.

- >> **Numbers Formatted as Text or Preceded by an Apostrophe check box:** Has Excel flag all numbers entered as text as errors by adding an error indicator and alert options button to their cells.

- >> **Formulas Inconsistent with Other Formulas in Region check box:** Has Excel flag any formula that differs from the others in the same area of the worksheet as an error by adding an error indicator and alert options button to its cell.

- >> **Formulas Which Omit Cells in a Region check box:** Has Excel flag any formula that omits cells from the range that it refers to as an error by adding an error indicator and alert options button to its cell.

- >> **Unlocked Cells Containing Formulas check box:** Has Excel flag any formula whose cell is unlocked when the worksheet is protected as an error by adding an error indicator and alert options button to its cell. (See Book 4, Chapter 1 for information on protecting worksheets.)

- >> **Formulas Referring to Empty Cells check box:** Has Excel flag any formula that refers to blank cells as an error by adding an error indicator and alert options button to its cell.

- >> **Data Entered in a Table Is Invalid check box:** Has Excel flag any formulas for which you've set up Data Validation (see Book 2, Chapter 1 for details) and that contain values outside of those defined as valid.

Error tracing

Tracing a formula's family tree, so to speak, with the Trace Precedents and Trace Dependents command buttons on the Ribbon's Formulas tab is fine, as far as it goes. However, when it comes to a formula that returns a hideous error value, such as #VALUE! or #NAME!, you need to turn to Excel's trusty Trace Error option.

To select the Trace Error option in the current cell containing an untraced error value, click the Trace Error option from the Error Checking command button's drop-down menu or press Alt+MKE.

Selecting the Trace Error option is a lot like using both the Trace Precedents and the Trace Dependents command button options, except that the Trace Error option works only when the active cell contains some sort of error value returned by either a bogus formula or a reference to a bogus formula. In tracking down the actual cause of the error value in the active cell (remember that these error values spread to all direct and indirect dependents of a formula), Excel draws blue tracer arrows from the precedents for the original bogus formula and then draws red tracer arrows to all the dependents that contain error values as a result.

Figure 2-11 shows the sample worksheet after I made some damaging changes that left three cells — C12, E12, and E13 — with #DIV/0! errors (meaning that somewhere, somehow, I ended up creating a formula that is trying to divide by zero, which is a real no-no in the wonderful world of math). To find the origin of these error values and identify its cause, I clicked the Trace Error option on the Error Checking command button's drop-down menu while cell E12 was the active cell to engage the use of Excel's faithful old Trace Error feature.

You can see the results in Figure 2-11. Note that Excel has selected cell C12, although cell E12 was active when I selected the Trace Error option. To cell C12, Excel has drawn two blue tracer arrows that identify cells B5 and B9 as its direct precedents. From cell C12, the program has drawn a single red tracer arrow from cell C12 to cell E12 that identifies its direct dependent.

WHEN TRACE ERROR LOSES THE TRAIL

The Trace Error option finds errors along the path of a formula's precedents and dependents until it finds either the source of the error or one of the following problems:

- It encounters a branch point with more than one error source. In this case, Excel doesn't make a determination on its own as to which path to pursue.

- It encounters existing tracer arrows. Therefore, *always* click the Remove Arrows command button to get rid of trace arrows before you click the Trace Error option from the Error Checking button's drop-down menu.

- It encounters a formula with a circular reference. (See Book 3, Chapter 1 for more on circular references.)

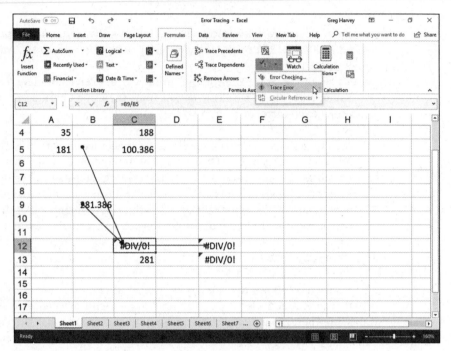

FIGURE 2-11:
Using the Trace
Error option
to show the
precedents and
dependents of
the formula.

As it turns out, Excel's Trace Error option is right on the money because the formula in cell C12 contains the bad apple rotting the whole barrel. I revised the formula in cell C12 so that it divided the value in cell B9 by the value in cell B5 without making sure that cell B5 first contained the SUM formula that totaled the values in the cell range B2:B4. The #DIV/0! error value showed up — remember that an empty cell contains a zero value as if you had actually entered 0 in the cell — and immediately spread to cells E12 and E13, which, in turn, use the value returned in C12 in their own calculations. Thus, these cells were infected with #DIV/0! error values as well.

As soon as you correct the problem in the original formula and thus get rid of all the error values in the other cells, Excel automatically converts the red tracer arrows (showing the proliferation trail of the original error) to regular blue tracer arrows, indicating merely that these restored cells are dependents of the formula that once contained the original sin. You can then remove all the tracer arrows from the sheet by clicking the Remove Arrows command button in the Formula Auditing group of the Ribbon's Formulas tab (or by pressing Alt+MAA).

Evaluating a formula

The Evaluate Formula command button in the Formula Auditing group of the Ribbon's Formulas tab (the one with *fx* inside a magnifying glass) opens the Evaluate Formula dialog box, where you can step through the calculation of a complicated formula to see the current value returned by each part of the calculation. This is often helpful in locating problems that prevent the formula from returning the hoped for or expected results.

To evaluate a formula step-by-step, position the cell pointer in that cell and then click the Evaluate Formula command button on the Formulas tab (or press Alt+MV). This action opens the Evaluate Formula dialog box with an Evaluation list box that displays the contents of the entire formula that's in the current cell.

To have Excel evaluate the first expression or term in the formula (shown underlined in the Evaluation list box) and replace it with the currently calculated value, click the Evaluate button. If this expression uses an argument or term that is itself a result of another calculation, you can display its expression or formula by clicking the Step In button (see Figure 2-12) and then calculate its result by clicking the Evaluate button. After that, you can return to the evaluation of the expression in the original formula by clicking the Step Out button.

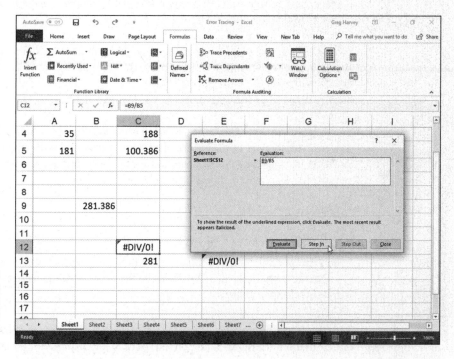

FIGURE 2-12: Calculating each part of a formula in the Evaluate Formula dialog box.

After you evaluate the first expression in the formula, Excel underlines the next expression or term in the formula (by using the natural order of precedence and a strict left-to-right order unless you have used parentheses to override this order), which you can then replace with its calculated value by clicking the Evaluate button. When you finish evaluating all the expressions and terms of the current formula, you can close the Evaluate Formula window by clicking its Close button in the upper-right corner of the window.

TIP

Instead of the Evaluate Formula dialog box, open the Watch Window dialog box by clicking the Watch Window button on the Formulas tab (Alt+MW) and add formulas to it when all you need to do is to keep an eye on the current value returned by a mixture of related formulas in the workbook. This enables you to see the effect that changing various input values has on their calculations (even when they're located on different sheets of the workbook).

Removing Errors from the Printout

What if you don't have the time to trap all the potential formula errors or track them down and eliminate them before you have to print out and distribute the spreadsheet? In that case, you may just have to remove the display of all the error values before you print the report.

To do this, click the Sheet tab in the Page Setup dialog box opened by clicking the Dialog Box launcher on the right side of the Page Setup group on the Page Layout tab. Click the Sheet tab in the Page Setup dialog box and then click the drop-down button attached to the Cell Errors As drop-down list box.

The default value for this drop-down list box is Displayed, meaning that all error values are displayed in the printout exactly as they currently appear in the worksheet. This drop-down list also contains the following items that you can click to remove the display of error values from the printed report:

>> Click the <blank> option to replace all error values with blank cells.

>> Click the -- option to replace all error values with two dashes.

>> Click the #N/A option to replace all error values (except for #N/A entries, of course) with the special #N/A value (which is considered an error value when you select the <blank> or — options).

REMEMBER

Blanking out error values or replacing them with dashes or #N/A values has no effect on them in the worksheet itself, only in any printout you make of the worksheet. You need to view the pages in the Print Preview area in the Print screen in the Backstage view (Ctrl+P) before you can see the effect of selecting an option besides the Displayed option in the Cell Errors As drop-down list box. Also, remember to reset the Cell Errors As option on the Sheet tab of the Page Setup dialog box back to the Displayed option when you want to print a version of the worksheet that shows the error values in all their cells in the worksheet printout.

Chapter **3**

Date and Time Formulas

C reating formulas that use dates and times can be a little confusing if you don't have a good understanding of how Excel treats these types of values. After you're equipped with this understanding, you can begin to make good use of the many Date and Time functions that the program offers.

This chapter begins with a quick overview of date and time numbers in Excel and how you can use them to build simple formulas that calculate differences between elapsed dates and times. The chapter goes on to survey Excel built-in Date and Time functions, including the Date functions that are available after you've installed and activated the Analysis ToolPak add-in.

Understanding Dates and Times

Excel doesn't treat the dates and times that you enter in the cells of your worksheet as simple text entries. (For more information on inputting numbers in a spreadsheet, see Book 2, Chapter 1.) Any entry with a format that resembles one of the date and time number formats utilized by Excel is automatically converted, behind the scenes, into a serial number. In the case of dates, this serial number represents the number of days that have elapsed since the beginning of the 20th century so that January 1, 1900, is serial number 1; January 2, 1900, is serial number 2; and so forth. In the case of times, this serial number is a fraction that represents the number of hours, minutes, and seconds that have elapsed since midnight, which is serial number 0.00000000, so that 12:00:00 p.m. (noon) is serial number 0.50000000; 11:00:00 p.m. is 0.95833333; and so forth.

As long as you format a numeric entry so that it conforms to a recognized date or time format, Excel enters it as a date or time serial number. Only when you enter a formatted date or time as a text entry (by prefacing it with an apostrophe) or import dates and times as text entries into a worksheet do you have to worry about converting them into date and time serial numbers, which enables you to build spreadsheet formulas that perform calculations on them.

Changing the Regional date settings

Excel isn't set up to automatically recognize European date formats in which the number of the day precedes the number of the month and year. For example, you may want 6/11/2019 to represent November 6, 2019, rather than June 11, 2019. If you're working with a spreadsheet that uses this type of European date system, you have to customize the Windows 10 Regional settings for the United States so that the Short Date format in Windows programs, such as Excel and Word 2019, use the D/m/yyyy (day, month, year) format rather than the default M/d/yyyy (month, day, year) format.

To make this change, you follow these steps:

1. **Click the Windows 10 Start button and then click the Settings button on the Start menu.**

   Windows 10 opens the Windows Settings dialog box.

2. **Click the Time & Language button on the Windows Settings screen.**

   The Date and Time settings appear in the Settings screen.

3. **Click the Change Date and Time formats link that appears under the Format examples that show you the current long and short date and time formatting.**

   The Change Date and Time Settings screen displays drop-down text boxes where you can select new formatting for the short and long dates.

4. **Click the Short Date drop-down button, click the dd-MMM-yy format at the bottom of the drop-down list, and then click the Close button.**

After changing the Short Date format in the Change Date and Time Formats Settings screen, the next time you launch Excel 2019, it automatically formats dates à la European — for example, 3/5/19 is interpreted as May 3, 2019, rather than March 5, 2019.

Don't forget to change the Short Date format back to its original M/d/yyyy Short Date format when working with spreadsheets that follow the "month-day-year" Short Date format preferred in the United States. Also, don't forget that you have to restart Excel to get it to pick up on the changes that you make to any of the Windows date and time format settings.

Building formulas that calculate elapsed dates

Most of the date formulas that you build are designed to calculate the number of days or years that have elapsed between two dates. To do this, you build a simple formula that subtracts the earlier date from the later date.

For example, if you input the date 4/25/95 in cell B4 and 6/3/14 in cell C4 and you want to calculate the number of days that have elapsed between April 25, 1995, and June 3, 2014, in cell D4, you would enter the following subtraction formula in that cell:

```
=C4-B4
```

Excel then inputs 6979 as the number of days between these dates in cell D5 using the General number format.

If you want the result between two dates expressed in the number of years rather than the number of days, divide the result of your subtraction by the number of days in a year. In this example, you can enter the formula =D4/365 in cell E4 to return the result 19.12055, which you can then round off to 19 by clicking the Decrease Decimal button in the Number group on the Home tab of the Ribbon or by pressing Alt+H9 until only 19 remains displayed in the cell.

Building formulas that calculate elapsed times

Some spreadsheets require that formulas calculate the amount of elapsed time between a starting and an ending time. For example, suppose that you keep a worksheet that records the starting and stopping times for your hourly employees, and you need to calculate the number of hours and minutes that elapse between these two times in order to figure their daily and monthly wages.

To build a formula that calculates how much time has elapsed between two different times of the day, subtract the starting time of day from the ending time of day. For example, suppose that you enter a person's starting time in cell B6 and ending time in C6. In cell D6, you would enter the following subtraction formula:

```
=C6-B6
```

Excel then returns the difference in cell D6 as a decimal value representing what fraction that difference represents of an entire day (that is, a 24-hour period). If, for example, cell B6 contains a starting time of 9:15 a.m. and cell C6 contains an ending time of 3:45 p.m., Excel returns the following decimal value to cell D6:

```
6:30 AM
```

To convert this time of day into its equivalent decimal number, you convert the time format automatically given to it to the General format (Ctrl+Shift+`), which displays the following result in cell D6:

```
0.270833
```

To convert this decimal number representing the fraction of an entire day into the number of hours that have elapsed, you simply multiply this result by 24 as in =D6*24, which gives you a result of 6.5 hours.

Using Date Functions

Excel contains a number of built-in Date functions that you can use in your spreadsheets. When you install and activate the Analysis ToolPak add-in (see Book 1, Chapter 2 for details), you have access to a number of additional Date functions — many of which are specially designed to deal with the normal Monday through Friday, five-day workweek (excluding, of course, your precious weekend days from the calculations).

TODAY

The easiest Date function has to be TODAY. This function takes no arguments and is always entered as follows:

```
=TODAY()
```

When you enter the TODAY function in a cell by clicking it on the Date & Time command button's drop-down list on the Ribbon's Formulas tab or by typing it, Excel returns the current date by using the following Date format:

9/15/2019

REMEMBER

Keep in mind that the date inserted into a cell with the TODAY function is not static. Whenever you open a worksheet that contains this function, Excel recalculates the function and updates its contents to the current date. This means that you don't usually use TODAY to input the current date when you're doing it for historical purposes (an invoice, for example) and never want it to change.

TIP

If you do use TODAY and then want to make the current date static in the spreadsheet, you need to convert the function into its serial number. You can do this for individual cells: First, select the cell, press F2 to activate Edit mode, press F9 to replace =TODAY() with today's serial number on the Formula bar, and click the Enter button to insert this serial number into the cell. You can do this conversion on a range of cells by selecting the range, copying it to the Clipboard by clicking the Copy button on the Home tab of the Ribbon (or pressing Ctrl+C), and then immediately pasting the calculated values into the same range by choosing the Paste Values option from the Paste command button's drop-down menu (or pressing Alt+HVV).

DATE and DATEVALUE

The DATE function on the Date & Time command button's drop-down menu returns a date serial number for the date specified by the *year, month,* and *day* argument. This function uses the following syntax:

DATE(*year,month,day*)

This function comes in handy when you have a worksheet that contains the different parts of the date in separate columns, similar to the one shown in Figure 3-1. You can use it to combine the three columns of date information into a single date cell that you can use in sorting and filtering. (See Book 6, Chapters 1 and 2 to find out how to sort and filter data.)

The DATEVALUE function on the Date & Time button's drop-down menu on the Formulas tab returns the date serial number for a date that's been entered into the spreadsheet as text so that you can use it in date calculations. This function takes a single argument:

DATEVALUE(*date_text*)

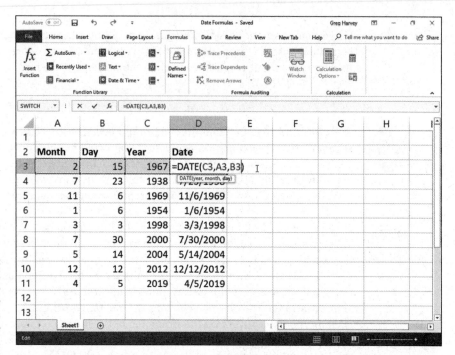

FIGURE 3-1:
Using the DATE
function to
combine separate
date information
into a single
entry.

Suppose, for example, that you've made the following text entry in cell B12:

```
'5/21/2019
```

(Remember that when you preface an entry with an apostrophe, Excel inserts that entry as text even if the program would otherwise put it in as a value.) You can then convert this text entry into a date serial number by entering the following formula in cell C12 next door:

```
=DATEVALUE(B12)
```

Excel then returns the date serial number, 43606, to cell C12, which you can convert into a more intelligible date by formatting it with one of Excel's Date number formats (Ctrl+1).

REMEMBER

You must convert the DATE and DATEVALUE functions into their calculated date serial numbers in order to sort and filter them. To convert these functions individually, select a cell, press F2 to activate Edit mode, and then press F9 to replace the function with the calculated date serial number; finally, click the Enter button on the Formula bar to insert this serial number into the cell. To do this conversion on a range of cells, select the range, copy it to the Clipboard by pressing Ctrl+C, and then immediately paste the calculated serial numbers into the same range by choosing the Paste Values option from the Paste command button's drop-down menu (or press Alt+HVV).

DAY, WEEKDAY, MONTH, and YEAR

The DAY, WEEKDAY, MONTH, and YEAR Date functions on the Date & Time command button's drop-down menu all return just parts of the date serial number that you specify as their argument:

>> DAY(*serial_number*) to return the day of the month in the date (as a number between 1 and 31).

>> WEEKDAY(*serial_number,[return_type]*) to return the day of the week (as a number between 1 and 7 or 0 and 6). The optional *return_type* argument is a number between 1 and 3; 1 (or no *return_type* argument) specifies the first type where 1 equals Sunday and 7 equals Saturday; 2 specifies the second type where 1 equals Monday and 7 equals Sunday; and 3 specifies the third type where 0 equals Monday and 6 equals Sunday.

>> MONTH(*serial_number*) to return the number of the month in the date serial number (from 1 to 12).

>> YEAR(*serial_number*) to return the number of the year (as an integer between 1900 and 9999) in the date serial number.

For example, if you enter the following DAY function in a cell as follows:

```
DAY(DATE(19,4,15))
```

Excel returns the value 15 to that cell. If, instead, you use the WEEKDAY function as follows:

```
WEEKDAY(DATE(19,4,15))
```

Excel returns the value 3, which represents Tuesday (using the first *return_type* where Sunday is 1 and Saturday is 7) because the optional *return_type* argument isn't specified. (See "Book 3, Chapter 3 for an example using the WEEKDAY function as the *expression* argument of the SWITCH function in order to replace the day numbers (1 – 7) with their corresponding names (Sunday – Saturday).

If you use the MONTH function on this date as in the following:

```
MONTH(DATE(19,4,15))
```

Excel returns 4 to the cell. If, however, you use the YEAR function on this date as in the following:

```
YEAR(DATE(19,4,15))
```

Excel returns 1919 to the cell (instead of 2019).

This means that if you want to enter a year in the 21st century as the *year* argument of the DATE function, you need to enter all four digits of the date, as in the following:

```
DATE(2019,4,15)
```

Note that you can use the YEAR function to calculate the difference in years between two dates. For example, if cell B6 contains 7/23/1978 and cell C6 contains 7/23/2019, you can enter the following formula using the YEAR function to determine the difference in years:

```
=YEAR(C6)-YEAR(B6)
```

Excel then returns 41 to the cell containing this formula.

Don't use these functions on dates entered as text entries. Always use the DATE-VALUE function to convert these text dates and then use the DAY, WEEKDAY, MONTH, or YEAR functions on the serial numbers returned by the DATEVALUE function to ensure accurate results.

DAYS360

The DAYS360 function on the Date & Time command button's drop-down menu returns the number of days between two dates based on a 360-day year (that is, one in which there are 12 equal months of 30 days each). The DAYS360 function takes the following arguments:

```
DAYS360(start_date,end_date,[method])
```

The *start_date* and *end_date* arguments are date serial numbers or references to cells that contain such serial numbers. The optional *method* argument is either TRUE or FALSE, where FALSE specifies the use of the U.S. calculation method and TRUE specifies the use of the European calculation method:

>> **U.S. (NASD) method (FALSE or *method* argument omitted):** In this method, if the starting date is equal to the 31st of the month, it becomes equal to the 30th of the same month; if the ending date is the 31st of a month and the starting date is earlier than the 30th of the month, the ending date becomes the 1st of the next month; otherwise, the ending date becomes equal to the 30th of the same month.

>> **European method (TRUE):** In this method, starting and ending dates that occur on the 31st of a month become equal to the 30th of the same month.

Other special Date functions

Excel includes other special Date functions in the Date and Time category in the Insert Function dialog box. These particular Date functions expand your abilities to do date calculations in the worksheet — especially those that work only with normal workdays, Monday through Friday.

EDATE

The EDATE (for Elapsed Date) function calculates a future or past date that is so many months ahead or behind the date that you specify as its *start_date* argument. You can use the EDATE function to quickly determine the particular date at a particular interval in the future or past (for example, three months ahead or one month ago).

The EDATE function takes two arguments:

```
EDATE(start_date,months)
```

The *start_date* argument is the date serial number that you want used as the base date. The *months* argument is a positive (for future dates) or negative (for past dates) integer that represents the number of months ahead or months past to calculate.

For example, suppose that you enter the following EDATE function in a cell:

```
=EDATE(DATE(2019,1, 31),1)
```

Excel returns the date serial number, 43524 which becomes 2/28/2019 when you apply the first Date format to its cell.

EOMONTH

The EOMONTH (for End of Month) function calculates the last day of the month that is so many months ahead or behind the date that you specify as its *start_date* argument. You can use the EOMONTH function to quickly determine the end of the month at a set interval in the future or past.

For example, suppose that you enter the following EOMONTH function in a cell:

```
=EOMONTH(DATE(2019,1,1),1)
```

Excel returns the date serial number, 43524, which becomes 2/28/2019 when you apply the first Date format to its cell.

NETWORKDAYS

The NETWORKDAYS function returns the number of workdays that exist between a starting date and ending date that you specify as arguments:

```
NETWORKDAYS(start_date,end_date,[holidays])
```

When using this function, you can also specify a cell range in the worksheet or array constant to use as an optional *holidays* argument that lists the state, federal, and floating holidays observed by your company. Excel then excludes any dates listed in the *holidays* argument when they occur in between *start_date* and *end_date* arguments.

Figure 3-2 illustrates how this function works. In this worksheet, I created a list in the cell range B3:B13 with all the observed holidays in the calendar year 2019 and named this range Days_Off. I then entered the following NETWORKDAYS function in cell E4:

```
NETWORKDAYS(DATE(2018,12,31),DATE(2019,12,31),Days_Off)
```

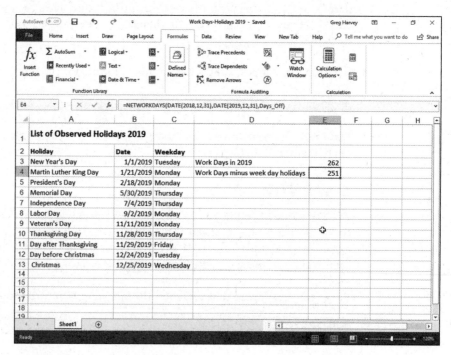

FIGURE 3-2: Using the NETWORKDAYS function to find the number of workdays between two dates.

The preceding function calculates the number of workdays between December 31, 2018, and December 31, 2019 (262 total work days), and then subtracts the dates listed in the cell range Days_Off (B3:B13) if they fall on a weekday. As all 11 holidays in the Days_Off range happen to fall on a weekday in the year 2019, the number of workdays between December 31, 2015, and December 31, 2019, is calculated as 251 in cell E4 (262−11=251).

WEEKNUM

The WEEKNUM function returns a number indicating where the week in a particular date falls within the year. This function takes the following arguments:

```
WEEKNUM(serial_number,[return_type])
```

In this function, the *serial_number* argument is the date whose week in the year you want to determine. The optional *return_type* argument is number 1 or 2, where number 1 (or omitted) indicates that the new week begins on Sunday and weekdays are numbered from 1 to 7. Number 2 indicates that the new week begins on Monday and that weekdays are also numbered from 1 to 7.

For example, if you enter the following WEEKNUM function in a cell:

```
=WEEKNUM(DATE(2019,1,20))
```

Excel returns the number 4, indicating that the week containing the date January 20, 2019, is the fourth week in the year when the Sunday is considered to be the first day of the week. (January 20, 2019, falls on a Sunday.) Note that if I had added 2 as the optional *return-type* argument, Excel would return 3 as the result because January 17, 2019, is deemed to fall on the last day of the third week of the year when Monday is considered the first day of the week.

WORKDAY

You can use the WORKDAY function to find out the date that is so many workdays before or after a particular date. This function takes the following arguments:

```
WORKDAY(start_date,days,[holidays])
```

The *start_date* argument is the initial date that you want used in calculating the date of the workday that falls so many days before or after it. The *days* argument is the number of workdays ahead (positive integer) or behind (negative integer) the *start_date*. The optional *holidays* argument is an array constant or cell range that contains the dates of the holidays that should be excluded (when they fall on a weekday) in calculating the new date.

For example, suppose that you want to determine a due date for a report that is 30 workdays after February 1, 2019, by using the same holiday schedule entered in the cell range named Days_Off (B3:B13) in the Work Days 2019 workbook, shown in Figure 3-2. To do this, you enter the following formula:

```
=WORKDAY(DATE(2019,2,1),30,Days_Off)
```

Excel then returns the serial number 43542 to the cell, which then appears as March 18, 2019 (a day after St. Patrick's Day), when you format it with the Short Date format.

YEARFRAC

The YEARFRAC (for Year Fraction) function enables you to calculate the fraction of the year, which is computed from the number of days between two dates. You can use the YEARFRAC function to determine the proportion of a whole year's benefits or obligations to assign to a specific period.

The YEARFRAC function uses the following arguments:

```
YEARFRAC(start_date,end_date,[basis])
```

The optional *basis* argument in the YEARFRAC function is a number between 0 and 4 that determines the day count basis to use in determining the fractional part of the year:

>> 0 (or omitted) to base it on the U.S. (NASD) method of 30/360 (see "DAYS360" earlier in the chapter for details on the U.S. method)

>> 1 to base the fraction on actual days/actual days

>> 2 to base the fraction on actual days/360

>> 3 to base the fraction on actual days/365

>> 4 to base the fraction on the European method of 30/360 (see "DAYS360" earlier in the chapter for details on the European method)

For example, if you enter the following YEARFRAC formula in a cell to find what percentage of the year remains as of October 15, 2019:

```
=YEARFRAC(DATE(2019,10,15),DATE(2019,12,31))
```

Excel returns the decimal value 0.2111111 to the cell, indicating that just over 21 percent of the year remains.

Using Time Functions

Excel offers far fewer Time functions when compared with the wide array of Date functions. Like the Date functions, however, the Time functions enable you to convert text entries representing times of day into time serial numbers so that you can use them in calculations. The Time functions also include functions for combining different parts of a time into a single serial time number, as well as those for extracting the hours, minutes, and seconds from a single time serial number.

NOW

The NOW function on the Date & Time command button's drop-down menu on the Formulas tab of the Ribbon (Alt+ME) gives you the current time and date based on your computer's internal clock. You can use the NOW function to date- and time-stamp the worksheet. Like the TODAY function, NOW takes no arguments and is automatically recalculated every time you open the spreadsheet:

```
=NOW( )
```

When you enter the NOW function in a cell, Excel puts the date before the current time. It also formats the date with the first Date format and the time with the 24-hour Time format. So, if the current date were August 19, 2019 and the current time was 12:57 p.m. at the moment when Excel calculates the NOW function, your cell would contain the following entry:

```
8/19/2019 12:57
```

TIP

Note that the combination Date/Time format that the NOW function uses is a custom number format. If you want to assign a different date/time to the date and time serial numbers returned by this function, you have to create your own custom number format and then assign it to the cell that contains the NOW function. (See Book 2, Chapter 2 for information on creating custom number formats.)

TIME and TIMEVALUE

The TIME function on the Date & Time command button's drop-down menu on the Formulas tab of the Ribbon (Alt+ME) enables you to create a decimal number representing a time serial number, ranging from 0 (zero) to 0.99999999, representing time 0:00:00 (12:00:00 AM) to 23:59:59 (11:59:59 PM). You can use the TIME function to combine the hours, minutes, and seconds of a time into a single time serial number when these parts are stored in separate cells.

The TIME function takes the following arguments:

```
TIME(hour,minute,second)
```

When specifying the *hour* argument, you use a number between 0 and 23. (Any number greater than 23 is divided by 24, and the remainder is used as the hour value.) When specifying the *minute* and *second* arguments, you use a number between 0 and 59. (Any *minute* argument greater than 59 is converted into hours and minutes, just as any *second* argument greater than 59 is converted into hours, minutes, and seconds.)

For example, if cell A3 contains 4, cell B3 contains 37, and cell C3 contains 0, and you enter the following TIME function in cell D3:

```
=TIME(A3,B3,C3)
```

Excel enters 4:37 AM in cell D3. If you then assign the General number format to this cell (Ctrl+Shift+` or Ctrl+~), it would then contain the time serial number, 0.192361.

The TIMEVALUE function converts a time entered or imported into the spreadsheet as a text entry into its equivalent time serial number so that you can use it in time calculations. The TIMEVALUE function uses a single *time_text* argument as follows:

```
TIMEVALUE(time_text)
```

So, for example, if you put the following TIMEVALUE function in a cell to determine the time serial number for 10:35:25:

```
=TIMEVALUE("10:35:25")
```

Excel returns the time serial number 0.441262 to the cell. If you then assign the first Time number format to this cell, the decimal number appears as 10:35:25 a.m. in the cell.

HOUR, MINUTE, and SECOND

The HOUR, MINUTE, and SECOND functions on the Date & Time command button's drop-down menu enable you to extract specific parts of a time value in the spreadsheet. Each of these three Time functions takes a single *serial_number* argument that contains the hour, minute, or second that you want to extract.

So, for example, if cell B5 contains the time 1:30:10 p.m. (otherwise known as serial number 0.5626157) and you enter the following HOUR function in cell C5:

```
=HOUR(B5)
```

Excel returns 13 as the hour to cell C5 (hours are always returned in 24-hour time). If you then enter the following MINUTE function in cell D5:

```
=MINUTE(B5)
```

Excel returns 30 as the number of minutes to cell D5. Finally, if you enter the following SECOND function in cell E5:

```
=SECOND(B5)
```

Excel returns 10 as the number of seconds to cell E5.

Chapter **4**

Financial Formulas

oney! There's nothing quite like it. You can't live with it, and you certainly can't live without it. Many of the spreadsheets that you work with exist only to let you know how much of it you can expect to come in or to pay out. Excel contains a fair number of sophisticated financial functions for determining such things as the present, future, or net present value of an investment; the payment, number of periods, or the principal or interest part of a payment on an amortized loan; the rate of return on an investment; or the depreciation of your favorite assets.

By activating the Analysis ToolPak add-in, you add more than 30 specialized financial functions that run the gamut from those that calculate the accrued interest for a security paying interest periodically and only at maturity, all the way to those that calculate the internal rate of return and the net present value for a schedule of nonperiodic cash flows.

Financial Functions 101

The key to using any of Excel's financial functions is to understand the terminology used by their arguments. Many of the most common financial functions, such as PV (Present Value), NPV (Net Present Value), FV (Future Value), PMT (Payment), and IPMT (Interest Payment) take similar arguments:

>> **PV** is the present value that is the principal amount of the annuity.

>> **FV** is the future value that represents the principal plus interest on the annuity.

>> **PMT** is the payment made each period in the annuity. Normally, the payment is set over the life of the annuity and includes principal plus interest without any other fees.

>> **RATE** is the interest rate per period. Normally, the rate is expressed as an annual percentage.

>> **NPER** is the total number of payment periods in the life of the annuity. You calculate this number by taking the Term (the amount of time that interest is paid) and multiplying it by the Period (the point in time when interest is paid or earned) so that a loan with a 3-year term with 12 monthly interest payments has 3 x 12, or 36 payment periods.

REMEMBER

When using financial functions, keep in mind that the *fv*, *pv*, and *pmt* arguments can be positive or negative, depending on whether you're receiving the money (as in the case of an investment) or paying out the money (as in the case of a loan). Also keep in mind that you want to express the *rate* argument in the same units as the *nper* argument, so that if you make monthly payments on a loan and you express the *nper* as the total number of monthly payments, as in 360 (30 x 12) for a 30-year mortgage, you need to express the annual interest rate in monthly terms as well. For example, if you pay an annual interest rate of 7.5 percent on the loan, you express the *rate* argument as 0.075/12 so that it is monthly as well.

The PV, NPV, and FV Functions

The PV (Present Value), NPV (Net Present Value), and FV (Future Value) functions all found on the Financial button's drop-down menu on the Ribbon's Formulas tab (Alt+MI) enable you to determine the profitability of an investment.

Calculating the Present Value

The PV, or Present Value, function returns the present value of an investment, which is the total amount that a series of future payments is worth presently. The syntax of the PV function is as follows:

```
=PV(rate,nper,pmt,[fv],[type])
```

The *fv* and *type* arguments are optional arguments in the function (indicated by the square brackets). The *fv* argument is the future value or cash balance that you want to have after making your last payment. If you omit the *fv* argument, Excel assumes a future value of zero (0). The *type* argument indicates whether the payment is made at the beginning or end of the period: Enter 0 (or omit the *type* argument) when the payment is made at the end of the period, and use 1 when it is made at the beginning of the period.

Figure 4-1 contains several examples using the PV function. All three PV functions use the same annual percentage rate of 1.25 percent and term of 10 years. Because payments are made monthly, each function converts these annual figures into monthly ones. For example, in the PV function in cell E3, the annual interest rate in cell A3 is converted into a monthly rate by dividing by 12 (A3/12). The annual term in cell B3 is converted into equivalent monthly periods by multiplying by 12 (B3 x 12).

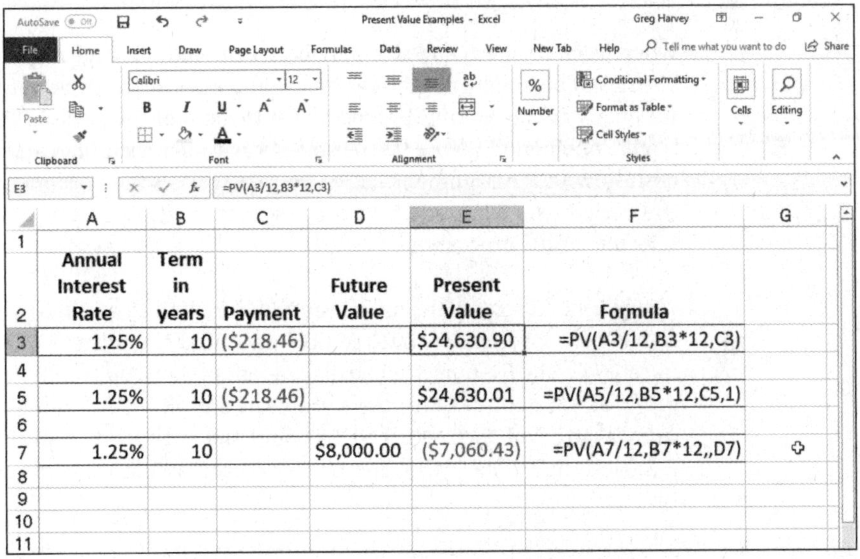

FIGURE 4-1: Using the PV function to calculate the present value of various investments.

Note that although the PV functions in cells E3 and E5 use the *rate, nper,* and *pmt* ($218.46) arguments, their results are slightly different. This is caused by the difference in the *type* argument in the two functions: the PV function in cell E3 assumes that each payment is made at the end of the period (the *type* argument is 0 whenever it is omitted), whereas the PV function in cell E5 assumes that each payment is made at the beginning of the period (indicated by a *type* argument of 1). When the payment is made at the beginning of the period, the present value of this investment is $0.89 higher than when the payment is made at the end of the period, reflecting the interest accrued during the last period.

The third example in cell E7 (shown in Figure 4-1) uses the PV function with an *fv* argument instead of the *pmt* argument. In this example, the PV function states that you would have to make monthly payments of $7,060.43 for a 10-year period to realize a cash balance of $8,000, assuming that the investment returned a constant annual interest rate of 1 1/4 percent. Note that when you use the PV function with the *fv* argument instead of the *pmt* argument, you must still indicate the position of the *pmt* argument in the function with a comma (thus the two commas in a row in the function) so that Excel doesn't mistake your *fv* argument for the *pmt* argument.

Calculating the Net Present Value

The NPV function calculates the net present value based on a series of cash flows. The syntax of this function is

```
=NPV(rate,value1,[value2],[...])
```

where *value1, value2,* and so on are between 1 and 13 value arguments representing a series of payments (negative values) and income (positive values), each of which is equally spaced in time and occurs at the end of the period. The NPV investment begins one period before the period of the *value1* cash flow and ends with the last cash flow in the argument list. If your first cash flow occurs at the beginning of the period, you must add it to the result of the NPV function rather than include it as one of the arguments.

Figure 4-2 illustrates the use of the NPV function to evaluate the attractiveness of a five-year investment that requires an initial investment of $30,000 (the value in cell G3). The first year, you expect a loss of $22,000 (cell B3); the second year, a profit of $15,000 (cell C3); the third year, a profit of $25,000 (cell D3); the fourth year, a profit of $32,000 (cell E3); and the fifth year, a profit of $38,000 (cell F3). Note that these cell references are used as the *value* arguments of the NPV function.

Unlike when using the PV function, the NPV function doesn't require an even stream of cash flows. The *rate* argument in the function is set at 2.25 percent. In this example, this represents the *discount rate* of the investment — that is, the interest rate that you may expect to get during the five-year period if you put your money into some other type of investment, such as a high-yield money-market account. This NPV function in cell A3 returns a net present value of $49,490.96, indicating that you can expect to realize a great deal more from investing your $30,000 in this investment than you possibly could from investing the money in a money-market account at the interest rate of 2.25 percent.

FIGURE 4-2:
Using the NPV function to calculate the net present value of an investment.

Calculating the Future Value

The FV function calculates the future value of an investment. The syntax of this function is

```
=FV(rate,nper,pmt,[pv],[type])
```

The *rate, nper, pmt,* and *type* arguments are the same as those used by the PV function. The *pv* argument is the present value or lump-sum amount for which you want to calculate the future value. As with the *fv* and *type* arguments in the PV function, both the *pv* and *type* arguments are optional in the FV function. If you omit these arguments, Excel assumes their values to be zero (0) in the function.

You can use the FV function to calculate the future value of an investment, such as an IRA (Individual Retirement Account). For example, suppose that you establish an IRA at age 43 and will retire 22 years from now at age 65 and that you plan to make annual payments into the IRA at the beginning of each year. If you assume a rate of return of 2.5 percent a year, you would enter the following FV function in your worksheet:

```
=FV(2.5%,22,-1500,,1)
```

Excel then indicates that you can expect a future value of $44,376.64 for your IRA when you retire at age 65. If you had established the IRA a year prior and the account already has a present value of $1,538, you would amend the FV function as follows:

```
=FV(2.5%,22,-1500,-1538,1)
```

In this case, Excel indicates that you can expect a future value of $47,024.42 for your IRA at retirement.

The PMT Function

The PMT function on the Financial button's drop-down menu on the Formulas tab of the Ribbon calculates the periodic payment for an annuity, assuming a stream of equal payments and a constant rate of interest. The PMT function uses the following syntax:

```
=PMT(rate,nper,pv,[fv],[type])
```

As with the other common financial functions, *rate* is the interest rate per period, *nper* is the number of periods, *pv* is the present value or the amount the future payments are worth presently, *fv* is the future value or cash balance that you want after the last payment is made (Excel assumes a future value of zero when you omit this optional argument as you would when calculating loan payments), and *type* is the value 0 for payments made at the end of the period or the value 1 for payments made at the beginning of the period. (If you omit the optional *type* argument, Excel assumes that the payment is made at the end of the period.)

The PMT function is often used to calculate the payment for mortgage loans that have a fixed rate of interest. Figure 4-3 shows you a sample worksheet that contains a table using the PMT function to calculate loan payments for a range of interest rates (from 2.75 percent to 4.00 percent) and principals ($150,000 to $159,000). The table uses the initial principal that you enter in cell B2, copies it to cell A7, and then increases it by $1,000 in the range A8:A16. The table uses the initial interest rate that you enter in cell B3, copies to cell B6, and then increases this initial rate by 1/4 of a percent in the range C6:G6. The term in years in cell B4 is a constant factor that is used in the entire loan payment table.

To get an idea of how easy it is to build this type of loan payment table with the PMT function, follow these steps for creating it in a new worksheet:

1. **Enter the titles** Loan Payments **in cell A1,** Principal **in cell A2,** Interest Rate **in cell A3,** and Term (in years) **in cell A4.**

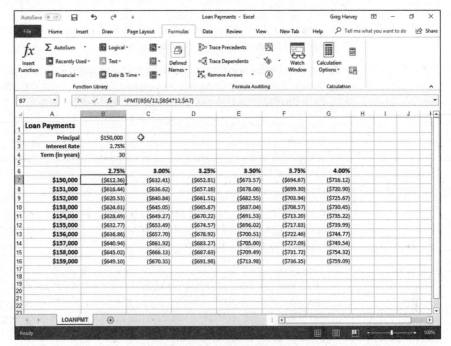

The spreadsheet shows the formula bar: B7, =PMT(B$6/12,$B$4*12,$A7)

	A	B	C	D	E	F	G
1	**Loan Payments**						
2	Principal	$150,000					
3	Interest Rate	2.75%					
4	Term (in years)	30					
5							
6		2.75%	3.00%	3.25%	3.50%	3.75%	4.00%
7	$150,000	($612.36)	($632.41)	($652.81)	($673.57)	($694.67)	($716.12)
8	$151,000	($616.44)	($636.62)	($657.16)	($678.06)	($699.30)	($720.90)
9	$152,000	($620.53)	($640.84)	($661.51)	($682.55)	($703.94)	($725.67)
10	$153,000	($624.61)	($645.05)	($665.87)	($687.04)	($708.57)	($730.45)
11	$154,000	($628.69)	($649.27)	($670.22)	($691.53)	($713.20)	($735.22)
12	$155,000	($632.77)	($653.49)	($674.57)	($696.02)	($717.83)	($739.99)
13	$156,000	($636.86)	($657.70)	($678.92)	($700.51)	($722.46)	($744.77)
14	$157,000	($640.94)	($661.92)	($683.27)	($705.00)	($727.09)	($749.54)
15	$158,000	($645.02)	($666.13)	($687.63)	($709.49)	($731.72)	($754.32)
16	$159,000	($649.10)	($670.35)	($691.98)	($713.98)	($736.35)	($759.09)

FIGURE 4-3:
Loan Payments table using the PMT function to calculate various loan payments.

2. **Enter $150,000 in cell B2, enter 2.75% in cell B3, and enter 30 in cell B4.**

   These are the starting values with which you build the Loan Payments table.

3. **Position the cell pointer in B6 and then build the formula =B3.**

   By creating a linking formula that brings forward the starting interest rate value in B3 with the formula, you ensure that the interest rate value in B6 will immediately reflect any change that you make in cell B3.

4. **Position the cell pointer in cell C6 and then build the formula =B6+.25%.**

   By adding 1/4 of a percent to the interest rate to the value in B6 with the formula =B6+0.25% in C6 rather than creating a series with the AutoFill handle, you ensure that the interest rate value in cell C6 will always be 1/4 of a percent larger than any interest rate value entered in cell B6.

5. **Drag the Fill handle in cell C6 to extend the selection to the right to cell G6.**

6. **Position the cell pointer in cell A7 and then build the formula =B2.**

   Again, by using the formula =B2 to bring the initial principal forward to cell A7, you ensure that cell A7 always has the same value as cell B2.

7. **Position the cell pointer in A8 active and then build the formula =A7+1000.**

   Here too, you use the formula =A7+1000 rather than create a series with the AutoFill feature so that the principal value in A8 will always be $1,000 greater than any value placed in cell A7.

Financial Formulas

CHAPTER 4 **Financial Formulas** 393

8. Drag the Fill handle in cell A8 down until you extend the selection to cell A16 and then release the mouse button.

9. In cell B7, click the Insert Function button on the Formula bar, select Financial from the Or Select a Category drop-down list, and then double-click the PMT function in the Select a Function list box.

The Function Arguments dialog box that opens allows you to specify the *rate, nper,* and *pv* arguments. Be sure to move the Function Arguments dialog box to the right so that no part of it obscures the data in columns A and B of your worksheet before proceeding with the following steps for filling in the arguments.

10. Click cell B6 to insert B6 in the Rate text box and then press F4 twice to convert the relative reference B6 to the mixed reference B$6 (column relative, row absolute) before you type /12.

You convert the relative cell reference B6 to the mixed reference B$6 so that Excel does *not* adjust the row number when you copy the PMT formula down each row of the table, but it *does* adjust the column letter when you copy the formula across its columns. Because the initial interest rate entered in B3 (and then brought forward to cell B6) is an *annual* interest rate, but you want to know the *monthly* loan payment, you need to convert the annual rate to a monthly rate by dividing the value in cell B6 by 12.

11. Click the Nper text box, click cell B4 to insert this cell reference in this text box, and then press F4 once to convert the relative reference B4 to the absolute reference $B$4 before you type *12.

You need to convert the relative cell reference B4 to the absolute reference $B$4 so that Excel adjusts neither the row number nor the column letter when you copy the PMT formula down the rows and across the columns of the table. Because the term is an *annual* period, but you want to know the *monthly* loan payment, you need to convert the yearly periods to monthly periods by multiplying the value in cell B4 by 12.

12. Click the Pv text box, click A7 to insert this cell reference in this text box, and then press F4 three times to convert the relative reference A7 to the mixed reference $A7 (column absolute, row relative).

You need to convert the relative cell reference A7 to the mixed reference $A7 so that Excel won't adjust the column letter when you copy the PMT formula across each column of the table, but will adjust the row number when you copy the formula down across its rows.

13. Click OK to insert the formula =PMT(B$6/12,$B$4*12,$A7) in cell B7.

Now you're ready to copy this original PMT formula down and then over to fill in the entire Loan Payments table.

14. Drag the Fill handle on cell B7 down until you extend the fill range to cell B16 and then release the mouse button.

After you've copied the original PMT formula down to cell B16, you're ready to copy it to the right to G16.

15. Drag the Fill handle to the right until you extend the fill range B7:B16 to cell G16 and then release the mouse button.

After copying the original formula with the Fill handle, be sure to widen columns B through G sufficiently to display their results. (You can do this in one step by dragging through the headers of these columns and then double-clicking the right border of column G.)

After you've created a loan table like this, you can then change the beginning principal or interest rate, as well as the term to see what the payments would be under various other scenarios. You can also turn on the Manual Recalculation so that you can control when the Loan Payments table is recalculated.

For information on how to switch to manual recalculation and use this mode to control when formulas are recalculated, see Book 3, Chapter 1. For information on how to protect the worksheet so that users can input new values only into the three input cells (B2, B3, and B4) to change the starting loan amount, interest rate, and the term of the loan, see Book 4, Chapter 1.

Depreciation Functions

Excel lets you choose from four different depreciation functions, each of which uses a slightly different method for depreciating an asset over time. These built-in depreciation functions found on the Financial button's drop-down menu on the Formulas tab of the Ribbon include the following:

» SLN(*cost,salvage,life*) to calculate straight-line depreciation

» SYD(*cost,salvage,life,per*) to calculate sum-of-years-digits depreciation

» DB(*cost,salvage,life,period,*[*month*]) to calculate declining balance depreciation

» DDB(*cost,salvage,life,period,*[*factor*]) to calculate double-declining balance depreciation

As you can see, with the exception of the optional *month* argument in the DB function and the optional *factor* argument in the DDB function, all the depreciation functions require the *cost*, *salvage*, and *life* arguments, and all but the SLN function require a *period* argument as well:

>> *Cost* is the initial cost of the asset that you're depreciating.

>> *Salvage* is the value of the asset at the end of the depreciation (also known as the salvage value of the asset).

>> *Life* is the number of periods over which the asset is depreciating (also known as the useful life of the asset).

>> *Per* or *period* is the period over which the asset is being depreciated. The units that you use in the *period* argument must be the same as those used in the *life* argument of the depreciation function so that if you express the life argument in years, you must also express the *period* argument in years.

Note that the DB function accepts an optional *month* argument. This argument is the number of months that the asset is in use in the first year. If you omit the *month* argument from your DB function, Excel assumes the number of months of service to be 12.

When using the DDB function to calculate the double-declining balance method of depreciation, you can add an optional *factor* argument. This argument is the rate at which the balance declines in the depreciation schedule. If you omit this optional *factor* argument, Excel assumes the rate to be 2 (thus, the name *double-declining balance*).

Figure 4-4 contains a Depreciation table that uses all four depreciation methods to calculate the depreciation of office furniture originally costing $50,000 to be depreciated over a 10-year period, assuming a salvage value of $1,000 at the end of this depreciation period.

The Formula bar shown in Figure 4-4 shows the SLN formula that I entered into cell B8:

```
=B7-SLN($C$3,$C$5,$C$4)
```

This formula subtracts the amount of straight-line depreciation to be taken in the first year of service from the original cost of $50,000. (This value is brought forward from cell C3 by the formula =C3.) After creating this original formula in cell B8, I then used the Fill handle to copy it down to cell B17, which contains the final salvage value of the asset in the 10th year of service.

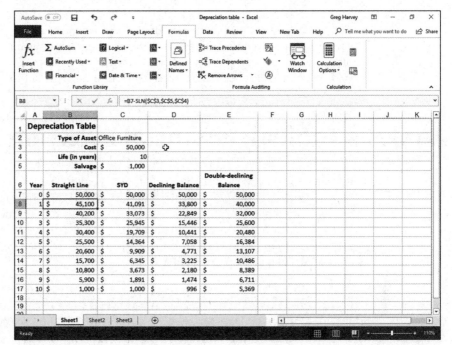

FIGURE 4-4:
A Depreciation table showing 10-year depreciation of an asset using various methods.

Cell C8 contains a similar formula for calculating the sum-of-years-digits depreciation for the office furniture. This cell contains the following formula:

```
=C7-SYD($C$3,$C$5,$C$4,$A8)
```

This formula subtracts the amount of sum-of-years-digits depreciation to be taken at the end of the first year from the original cost of $50,000 in cell C7 (also brought forward from cell C3 by the formula =C3). After creating this original formula in cell C8, I again used the Fill handle to copy it down to cell C17, which also contains the final salvage value of the asset in the 10th year of service.

I used the same basic procedure to create the formulas using the DB and DDB depreciation methods in the cell ranges D8:D17 and E8:E17, respectively. Cell D8 contains the following DB formula:

```
=D7-DB($C$3,$C$5,$C$4,$A8)
```

Cell E8 contains the following DDB formula:

```
=E7-DDB($C$3,$C$5,$C$4,$A8)
```

Financial Formulas

Note that, like the SYD function, both of these depreciation functions require the use of a *period* argument, which is supplied by the list of years in the cell range A8:A17. Note also that the value in cell C4, which supplies the *life* argument to the SYD, DB, and DDB functions, matches the year units used in this cell range.

Analysis ToolPak Financial Functions

By activating the Analysis ToolPak add-in (see Book 1, Chapter 2), you add a whole bunch of powerful financial functions to the Financial button's drop-down menu on the Formulas tab of the Ribbon. Table 4-1 shows all the financial functions that are added to the Insert Function dialog box when the Analysis ToolPak is activated. As you can see from this table, the Analysis ToolPak financial functions are varied and quite sophisticated.

TABLE 4-1 **Financial Functions in the Analysis ToolPak**

Function	What It Calculates
ACCRINT(issue,first_interest,settlement,rate, [par],frequency,[basis],[calc_methd])	Calculates the accrued interest for a security that pays periodic interest.
ACCRINTM(issue,maturity,rate,[par],[basis])	Calculates the accrued interest for a security that pays interest at maturity.
AMORDEGRC(cost,date_purchased,first_period, salvage,period,rate,[basis]) and AMORLINC(cost, date_purchased,first_period,salvage,period, rate,[basis])	Used in French accounting systems for calculating depreciation. AMORDEGRC and AMORLINC return the depreciation for each accounting period. AMORDEGRC works like AMORLINC except that it applies a depreciation coefficient in the calculation that depends upon the life of the assets.
COUPDAYBS(settlement,maturity, frequency,[basis])	Calculates the number of days from the beginning of a coupon period to the settlement date.
COUPDAYS(settlement,maturity, frequency,[basis])	Calculates the number of days in the coupon period.
COUPDAYSNC(settlement,maturity, frequency,[basis])	Calculates the number of days from the settlement date to the next coupon date.
COUPNCD(settlement,maturity, frequency,[basis])	Calculates a number that represents the next coupon date after a settlement date.
COUPNUM(settlement,maturity, frequency,[basis])	Calculates the number of coupons payable between the settlement date and maturity date, rounded up to the nearest whole coupon.
COUPPCD(settlement,maturity, frequency,[basis])	Calculates a number that represents the previous coupon date before the settlement date.

Function	What It Calculates
CUMIPMT(rate,nper,pv,start_period,end_period,type)	Calculates the cumulative interest paid on a loan between the start_period and end_period. The type argument is 0 when the payment is made at the end of the period and 1 when it's made at the beginning of the period.
CUMPRINC(rate,nper,pv,start_period,end_period,type)	Calculates the cumulative principal paid on a loan between the start_period and end_period. The type argument is 0 when the payment is made at the end of the period and 1 when it's made at the beginning of the period.
DISC(settlement,maturity,pr,redemption,[basis])	Calculates the discount rate for a security.
DOLLARDE(fractional_dollar,fraction)	Converts a dollar price expressed as a fraction into a dollar price expressed as a decimal number.
DOLLARFR(decimal_dollar,fraction)	Converts a dollar price expressed as a decimal number into a dollar price expressed as a fraction.
DURATION(settlement,maturity,coupon,yld,frequency,[basis])	Calculates the Macauley duration for an assumed par value of $100. (Duration is defined as the weighted average of the present value of the cash flows and is used as a measure of the response of a bond price to changes in yield.)
EFFECT(nominal_rate,npery)	Calculates the effective annual interest rate given the nominal interest rate and the number of compounding periods per year.
INTRATE(settlement,maturity,investment,redemption,[basis])	Calculates the interest rate for a fully invested security.
MDURATION(settlement,maturity,coupon,yld,frequency,[basis])	Calculates the modified Macauley duration for a security with an assumed part value of $100.
NOMINAL(effect_rate,npery)	Calculates the nominal annual interest rate given the effect rate and the number of compounding periods per year.
ODDFPRICE(settlement,maturity,issue,first_coupon,rate,yld,redemption,frequency,[basis])	Calculates the price per $100 face value of a security having an odd (short or long) first period.
ODDFYIELD(settlement,maturity,issue,first_coupon,rate,pr,redemption,frequency,[basis])	Calculates the yield of a security that has an odd (short or long) first period.
ODDLPRICE(settlement,maturity, last_interest,rate,yld,redemption,frequency,[basis])	Calculates the price per $100 face value of a security having an odd (short or long) last coupon period.
ODDLYIELD(settlement,maturity,last_interest,rate,pr,redemption,frequency,[basis])	Calculates the yield of a security that has an odd (short or long) last period.
PRICE(settlement,maturity,rate,yld,redemption,frequency,[basis])	Calculates the price per $100 face value of a security that pays periodic interest.
PRICEDISC(settlement,maturity,discount,redemption,[basis])	Calculates the price per $100 face value of a discounted security.

(continued)

TABLE 4-1 *(continued)*

Function	What It Calculates
PRICEMAT(settlement,maturity,issue,rate, yld,[basis])	Calculates the price per $100 face value of a security that pays interest at maturity.
RECEIVED(settlement,maturity,investment, discount,[basis])	Calculates the amount received at maturity for a fully invested security.
TBILLEQ(settlement,maturity,discount)	Calculates the bond-equivalent yield for a Treasury bill.
TBILLPRICE(settlement,maturity,discount)	Calculates the price per $100 face value for a Treasury bill.
TBILLYIELD(settlement,maturity,pr)	Calculates the yield for a Treasury bill.
XIRR(values,dates,[guess])	Calculates the internal rate of return for a schedule of cash flows that are not periodic.
XNPV(rate,values,dates)	Calculates the net present value for a schedule of cash flows that are not periodic.
YIELD(settlement,maturity,rate,pr,redemption, frequency,[basis])	Calculates the yield on a security that pays periodic interest (used to calculate bond yield).
YIELDDISC(settlement,maturity,pr,redemption, [basis])	Calculates the annual yield for a discounted security.
YIELDMAT(settlement,maturity,issue, rate,pr,[basis])	Calculates the annual yield of a security that pays interest at maturity.

You may note in Table 4-1 that many of the Analysis ToolPak financial functions make use of an optional *basis* argument. This optional *basis* argument is a number between 0 and 4 that determines the day count basis to use in determining the fractional part of the year:

» 0 (or omitted) to base it on the U.S. (NASD) method of 30/360 (see the coverage on the DAYS360 function in Book 3, Chapter 3 for details on the U.S. method)

» 1 to base the fraction on actual days/actual days

» 2 to base the fraction on actual days/360

» 3 to base the fraction on actual days/365

» 4 to base the fraction on the European method of 30/360 (see the DAYS360 coverage in Book 3, Chapter 3 for details on the European method)

REMEMBER

For detailed information on the other required arguments in the Analysis ToolPak financial functions shown in this table, select the function from the Financial button's drop-down list and then click the Help on This Function link in the lower-left corner of its Function Arguments dialog box.

IN THIS CHAPTER

» **Rounding off numbers**

» **Raising numbers to powers and finding square roots**

» **Conditional summing**

» **Using basic statistical functions, such as AVERAGE, MIN, and MAX**

» **Building formulas that count**

» **Using specialized statistical functions**

Chapter **5**

Math and Statistical Formulas

This chapter examines two larger categories of Excel functions: Math & Trig and statistical functions. The Math & Trig functions are found on the Math & Trig command button's drop-down menu on the Ribbon's Formulas tab (the button with the θ on the book cover). This category includes all the specialized trigonometric functions such as those that return the sine, cosine, or tangents of various angles and logarithmic functions (for finding the base-10 and natural logarithms of a number), along with the more common math functions for summing numbers, rounding numbers up or down, raising a number to a certain power, and finding the square root of numbers. Foremost among the more recently added Math & Trig functions in Excel 2019 is the Arabic function that converts any Roman numeral text in a worksheet range into Arabic numerals (xxi to 21, for example). This newer function compliments the older Roman function, which, you guessed it, converts Arabic numerals into Roman numeral text (16 into XVI, for instance).

The statistical functions are found on a continuation menu accessed from the More Functions command button's drop-down menu on the Formulas tab (the button with the ellipsis or three periods). Statistical functions include the more common functions that return the average, highest, and lowest values in a cell range all the way to the very sophisticated and specialized functions that calculate such things as the chi-squared distribution, binomial distribution probability, frequency, standard deviation, variance, and — my personal favorite — the skewness of a distribution in a particular population.

Math & Trig Functions

The mathematical functions are technically known as the Math & Trig category when you encounter them on the Math & Trig command button on the Ribbon's Formulas tab (Alt+MG) or in the Insert Function dialog box (opened by clicking the Insert Function button on the Formula bar).

This category groups together all the specialized trigonometric functions with the more common arithmetic functions. Although the trigonometric functions are primarily of use to engineers and scientists, the mathematical functions provide you with the ability to manipulate any type of values. This category of functions includes SUM, the most commonly used of all functions; functions such as INT, EVEN, ODD, ROUND, and TRUNC that round off the values in your worksheet; functions such as PRODUCT, SUMPRODUCT, and SUMSQ that you can use to calculate the products of various values in the worksheet; and the SQRT function that you can use to calculate the square root of a value.

Rounding off numbers

You use the ROUND function found on the Math & Trig command button's drop-down menu to round up or down fractional values in the worksheet as you might when working with financial spreadsheets that need to show monetary values only to the nearest dollar. Unlike when applying a number format to a cell, which affects only the number's display, the ROUND function actually changes the way Excel stores the number in the cell that contains the function. ROUND uses the following syntax:

```
ROUND(number,num_digits)
```

In this function, the *number* argument is the value that you want to round off, and *num_digits* is the number of digits to which you want the number rounded. If you enter 0 (zero) as the *num_digits* argument, Excel rounds the number to the nearest integer. If you make the *num_digits* argument a positive value, Excel rounds the number to the specified number of decimal places. If you enter the *num_digits* argument as a negative number, Excel rounds the number to the left of the decimal point.

Instead of the ROUND function, you can use the ROUNDUP or ROUNDDOWN function. Both ROUNDUP and ROUNDDOWN take the same *number* and *num_digits* arguments as the ROUND function. The difference is that the ROUNDUP function always rounds up the value specified by the number argument, whereas the ROUNDDOWN function always rounds the value down.

Figure 5-1 illustrates the use of the ROUND, ROUNDUP, and ROUNDDOWN functions in rounding off the value of the mathematical constant pi (π). In cell A3, I entered the value of this constant (with just nine places of nonrepeating fraction displayed when the column is widened) into this cell, using Excel's PI function in the following formula:

```
=PI()
```

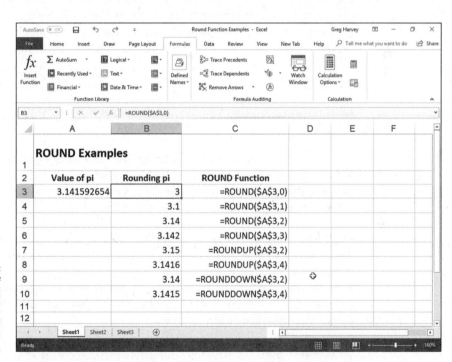

FIGURE 5-1:
Rounding off
the value of pi
with the ROUND,
ROUNDUP, and
ROUNDDOWN
functions.

I then used the ROUND, ROUNDUP, and ROUNDDOWN functions in the cell range B3 through B10 to round this number up and down to various decimal places.

Cell B3, the first cell that uses one of the ROUND functions to round off the value of pi, rounds this value to 3 because I used 0 (zero) as the *num_digits* argument of its ROUND function (causing Excel to round the value to the nearest whole number).

Math and Statistical Formulas

In Figure 5-1, note the difference between using the ROUND and ROUNDUP functions both with 2 as their *num_digits* arguments in cells B5 and B7, respectively. In cell B5, Excel rounds the value of pi off to 3.14, whereas in cell B7, the program rounds its value up to 3.15. Note that using the ROUNDDOWN function with 2 as its *num_digits* argument yields the same result, 3.14, as does using the ROUND function with 2 as its second argument.

The whole number and nothing but the whole number

You can also use the INT (for Integer) and TRUNC (for Truncate) functions on the Math & Trig command button's drop-down menu to round off values in your spreadsheets. You use these functions only when you don't care about all or part of the fractional portion of the value. When you use the INT function, which requires only a single *number* argument, Excel rounds the value down to the nearest integer (whole number). For example, cell A3 contains the value of pi, as shown in Figure 5-1, and you enter the following INT function formula in the worksheet:

```
=INT(A3)
```

Excel returns the value 3 to the cell, the same as when you use 0 (zero) as the *num_digits* argument of the ROUND function in cell B3.

The TRUNC function uses the same number and *num_digits* arguments as the ROUND, ROUNDUP, and ROUNDDOWN functions, except that in the TRUNC function, the *num_digits* argument is purely optional. This argument is required in the ROUND, ROUNDUP, and ROUNDDOWN functions.

The TRUNC function doesn't round off the number in question; it simply truncates the number to the nearest integer by removing the fractional part of the number. However, if you specify a *num_digits* argument, Excel uses that value to determine the precision of the truncation. So, going back to the example illustrated in Figure 5-1, if you enter the following TRUNC function, omitting the optional *num_digits* argument as in

```
=TRUNC($A$3)
```

Excel returns 3 to the cell just like the formula =ROUND($A$3,0) does in cell B3. However, if you modify this TRUNC function by using 2 as its *num_digits* argument, as in

```
=TRUNC($A$3,2)
```

Excel then returns 3.14 (by cutting the rest of the fraction) just as the formula =ROUND($A$3,2) does in cell B5.

The only time you notice a difference between the INT and TRUNC functions is when you use them with negative numbers. For example, if you use the TRUNC function to truncate the value −5.4 in the following formula:

```
=TRUNC(-5.4)
```

Excel returns −5 to the cell. If, however, you use the INT function with the same negative value, as in

```
=INT(-5.4)
```

Excel returns −6 to the cell. This is because the INT function rounds numbers down to the nearest integer using the fractional part of the number.

Let's call it even or odd

Excel's EVEN and ODD functions on the Math & Trig command button's drop-down menu also round off numbers. The EVEN function rounds the value specified as its *number* argument up to the nearest even integer. The ODD function, of course, does just the opposite: rounding the value up to the nearest odd integer. So, for example, if cell C18 in a worksheet contains the value 345.25 and you use the EVEN function in the following formula:

```
=EVEN(C18)
```

Excel rounds the value up to the next whole even number and returns 346 to the cell. If, however, you use the ODD function on this cell, as in

```
=ODD(C18)
```

Excel rounds the value up to the next odd whole number and returns 347 to the cell instead.

Building in a ceiling

The CEILING.MATH function on the Math & Trig command button's drop-down menu (Alt+MG) enables you to not only round up a number, but also set the multiple of significance to be used when doing the rounding. This function can be very useful when dealing with figures that need rounding to particular units.

For example, suppose that you're working on a worksheet that lists the retail prices for the various products that you sell, all based upon a particular markup over wholesale, and that many of these calculations result in many prices with cents below 50. If you don't want to have any prices in the list that aren't rounded to the nearest 50 cents or whole dollar, you can use the CEILING function to round up all these calculated retail prices to the nearest half dollar.

The CEILING.MATH function uses the following syntax:

```
CEILING.MATH(number,[significance],[mode])
```

The *number* argument specifies the number you want to round up and the optional *significance* argument specifies the multiple to which you want to round. (By default, the significance is +1 for positive numbers and −1 for negative numbers.) The optional *mode* argument comes into play only when dealing with negative numbers where the mode value indicates the direction toward (+1) or away (−1) from 0.

For the half-dollar example, suppose that you have the calculated number $12.35 in cell B3 and you enter the following formula in cell C3:

```
=CEILING.MATH(B3,0.5)
```

Excel then returns $12.50 to cell C3. Further, suppose that cell B4 contains the calculated value $13.67, and you copy this formula down to cell C4 so that it contains

```
=CEILING.MATH(B4,0.5)
```

Excel then returns $14.00 to that cell.

REMEMBER

CEILING.MATH in Excel 2019 replaces the CEILING function supported in older versions of Excel. You can still use the CEILING function to round your values; just be aware that this function is no longer available on the Math & Trig drop-down menu on the FORMULAS tab of the Ribbon or in the Insert Function dialog box. This means that you have to type **=cei** directly into the cell to have the CEILING function appear in the function drop-down menu immediately below CEILING.MATH.

POWER and SQRT

Although you can use the caret (^) operator to build a formula that raises a number to any power, you also need to be aware that Excel includes a math function called POWER found on the Math & Trig command button's drop-down menu that accomplishes the same thing. For example, to build a formula that raises 5.9 to the third power (that is, cubes the number), you can use the exponentiation operator, as in

```
=5.9^3
```

You can have Excel perform the same calculation with the POWER function by entering this formula:

```
=POWER(5.9,3)
```

In either case, Excel returns the same result, 205.379. The only difference between using the exponentiation operator and the POWER function occurs on that rare, rare occasion when you have to raise a number by a fractional power. In that case, you need to use the POWER function instead of the caret (^) operator to get the correct result. For example, suppose that you need to raise 20 by the fraction 3/4; to do this, you build the following formula with the POWER function:

```
=POWER(20,3/4)
```

To use the exponentiation operator to calculate the result of raising 20 by the fraction 3/4, you can convert the fraction into decimal form, as in

```
=20^0.75
```

The SQRT function on the Math & Trig command button's drop-down menu enables you to calculate the square root of any number that you specify as its sole *number* argument. For example, if you use the SQRT function to build the following formula in a cell:

```
=SQRT(144)
```

Excel returns 12 to that cell.

WARNING

The SQRT function can't deal with negative numbers, so if you try to find the square root of a negative value, Excel returns a nice #NUM! error value to that cell. To avoid such a nuisance, you need to use the ABS (for absolute) math function, which returns the absolute value of a number (that is, the number without a sign). For example, suppose that cell A15 contains ($49.00), a negative value formatted in parentheses with the Accounting Number format to show that it's something you owe, and you want to return the square root of this number in cell A16. To avoid the dreaded #NUM! error, you nest the ABS function inside the SQRT function. The ABS function returns the absolute value of the number you specify

Math and Statistical Formulas

as its sole argument (that is, the value without its sign). To nest this function inside the SQRT function, you create the following formula:

```
=SQRT(ABS(A15))
```

Excel then returns 7 instead of #NUM! to cell A16 because the ABS function removes the negative sign from the 49.00 before the SQRT function calculates its square root. (Remember that Excel always performs the calculations in the innermost pair of parentheses first.)

The SUM of the parts

No function in the entire galaxy of Excel functions comes anywhere close to the popularity of the SUM function in the spreadsheets that you build. So popular is this function, in fact, that Excel has its own Alt+= shortcut key as well as a Sum command button located on the HOME tab of the Ribbon (the one with the Σ on it) that you most often use to build your SUM formulas. You should, however, be aware of the workings of the basic SUM function that the AutoSum button enables you to use so easily.

For the record, the syntax of the SUM function is as follows:

```
SUM(number1,[number2],[...])
```

When using the SUM function, only the *number1* argument is required; this is the range of numbers in a cell range or array constant that you want added together. Be aware that you can enter up to a total of 29 other optional *number* arguments in a single SUM formula, all of which are separated by a comma (,). For example, you can build a SUM formula that totals numbers in several different ranges, as in

```
=SUM(B3:B10,Sheet2!B3:B10,Sheet3!B3:B10)
```

In this example, Excel sums the values in the cell range B3:B10 on Sheet1, Sheet2, and Sheet3 of the workbook, giving you the grand total of all these values in whatever cell you build this SUM formula.

Conditional summing

The SUM function is perfect when you want to get the totals for all the numbers in a particular range or set of ranges. But what about those times when you only want the total of certain items within a cell range? For those situations, you can use the SUMIF or SUMIFS function on the Math & Trig command button's drop-down menu.

The SUMIF function enables you to tell Excel to add together the numbers in a particular range *only* when those numbers meet the criteria that you specify. The syntax of the SUMIF function is as follows:

```
SUMIF(range,criteria,[sum_range])
```

In the SUMIF function, the *range* argument specifies the range of cells that you want Excel to evaluate when doing the summing; the *criteria* argument specifies the criteria to be used in evaluating whether to include certain values in the range in the summing; and finally, the optional *sum_range* argument is the range of all the cells to be summed together. If you omit the *sum_range* argument, Excel sums only the cells specified in the *range* argument (and, of course, only if they meet the criteria specified in the *criteria* argument).

The SUMIFS (that's ifs, plural) function works like SUMIF function except that it enables you to specify more than one criteria range that controls when a certain range of values are summed. Its syntax is a little bit different:

```
SUMIFS(sum_range,criteria_range,criteria,...)
```

For this function, the *sum_range* argument specifies all the possible values that can be summed, the *criteria_range* specifies the cells with all the entries that are to be evaluated by the if criteria, and the *criteria* argument contains the expression that is to be applied to the entries in the *criteria_range* to determine which of the values to total in the *sum_range*.

Summing certain cells with SUMIF

Figure 5-2 illustrates how you can use the SUMIF function to total sales by the items sold. This figure shows a Sales data list sorted by the store location and then the item sold. In this Daily Sales data list, there are three locations: Mission Street, Anderson Rd., and Curtis Way, of which only sales made at the Anderson Rd. location are visible in this figure.

To total the sales of Lemon tarts at all three locations in this data list, I created the following SUMIF formula in cell I3:

```
=SUMIF(item_sold,"=Lemon tarts",daily_sales)
```

In this example, item_sold is the range name given to the cell range C3:C62, which contains the list of each item that has been sold in the first five days of January, 2016 (Lemon tarts, Blueberry muffins, Lots of chips cookies, or Strawberry pie), and daily_sales is the range name assigned to the cell range G3:G62, which contains the extended sales made at each store for each item.

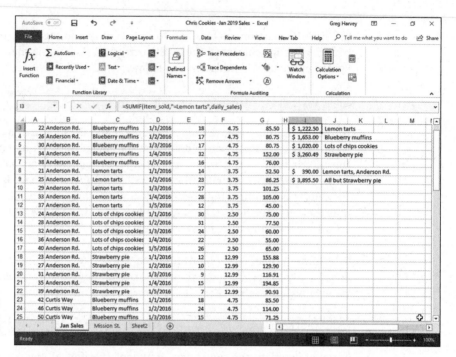

FIGURE 5-2:
Using SUMIF to total sales by items sold.

The SUMIF formula in cell I3 then looks for each occurrence of "Lemon tarts" in the item_sold range (the *criteria* argument for the SUMIF function) in the Item column of the Cookie Sales list and then adds its extended sales price from the daily_sales range in the Daily Sales column to the total.

The formulas in cells I4, I5, and I6 contain SUMIF functions very similar to the one in cell I3, except that they substitute the name of the dessert goodie in question in place of the =Lemon tarts *criteria* argument.

Summing on multiple criteria with SUMIFS

Figure 5-3 illustrates the use of the SUMIFS function to apply multiple criteria in the summing of the daily sales. Here, I want to know the total of the sales of one item (Lemon tarts) at one store location (Anderson Rd.).

In order to do this, I created the following formula in cell I8, using the SUMIFS function:

```
=SUMIFS(daily_sales,item_sold,"Lemon tarts",store,"Anderson
    Rd.")
```

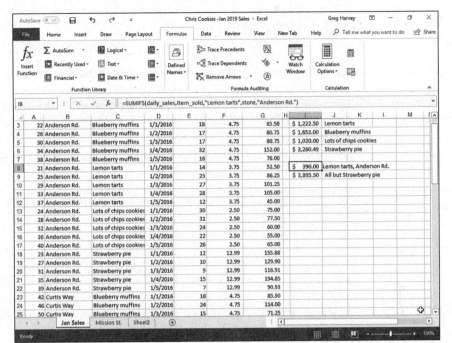

FIGURE 5-3:
Using SUMIFS to total sales by location as well as the items sold.

In this formula, the *sum_range* argument (specified first and not last as in SUMIF) is still the daily_sales cell range (G3:G62). The first *criteria_range* argument is item_sold (C3:C62) where the criteria is "Lemon tarts," and the second *criteria_range* argument is store (B3:B62) where the criteria is "Anderson Rd." When Excel evaluates the formula in cell I8, it applies both criteria so that the program ends up totaling only those daily sales where the item is Lemon tarts and the store location is Anderson Rd.

The formula in cell I9 immediately below in the worksheet shown in Figure 5-3 also uses the SUMIFS function, but this time applies just a single criteria in performing the summation. This formula sums the daily sales for any bakery item that is not a Strawberry pie:

```
=SUMIFS(daily_sales,item_sold,"<>Strawberry pie")
```

Because I prefaced the item Strawberry pie with the not (<>) operator (which can be placed before or after the open double quotation mark), Excel sums the sale of every item except for Strawberry pie.

Math and Statistical Formulas

Statistical Functions

Excel includes one of the most complete sets of statistical functions available outside a dedicated statistics software program. When you want to access these functions from the Ribbon's Formulas tab instead of using the Insert Function dialog box, you need to click the More Functions command button and then highlight the Statistical option at the very top of the drop-down menu (or press Alt+MQS). Doing this displays a continuation menu listing all the statistical functions in alphabetical order.

The statistical functions run the gamut from the more mundane AVERAGE, MAX, and MIN functions to the more exotic and much more specialized CHITEST, POISSON, and PERCENTILE statistical functions.

In addition to the more specialized statistical functions, Excel offers an assortment of counting functions that enable you to count the number of cells that contain values, count the number that are nonblank (and thus contain entries of any kind), or count the cells in a given range that meet the criteria that you specify.

AVERAGE, MAX, and MIN

The AVERAGE, MAX (for maximum), and MIN (for minimum) functions are the most commonly used of the statistical functions because they are of use to both the average number cruncher as well as the dedicated statistician. All three functions follow the same syntax as the good old SUM function. For example, the syntax of the AVERAGE function uses the following arguments just as the SUM, MAX, and MIN functions do:

```
AVERAGE(number1,[number2],[...])
```

Just as in the SUM function, the *number* arguments are between 1 and 30 numeric arguments for which you want the average. Figure 5-4 illustrates how you can use the AVERAGE, MAX, MIN, and MEDIAN functions in a worksheet. This example uses these functions to compute a few statistics on the selling prices of homes in a particular neighborhood. These statistics include the average, highest, lowest, and median selling price for the homes sold in April and May 2016. All the statistical functions in this worksheet use the same *number* argument; that is, the cell range named home_price in C3:C7.

The AVERAGE function computes the arithmetic mean of the values in this range by summing them and then dividing them by the number of values in the range. This AVERAGE function is equivalent to the following formula:

```
=SUM(home_price)/COUNT(home_price)
```

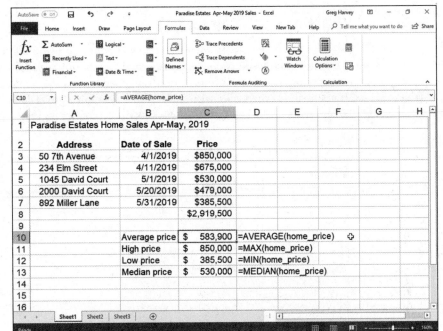

FIGURE 5-4:
Home sales spreadsheet using common statistical functions.

Note that this formula uses the SUM function to total the values and another statistical function called COUNT to determine the number of values in the list. The MAX and MIN functions simply compute the highest and lowest values in the cell range used as the *number* argument. The MEDIAN function computes the value that is in the middle of the range of values; that is, the one where half the values are greater and half are less. This is the reason that the median sales price (in cell C13) differs from the average sales price (in cell C10) in this worksheet.

Counting cells

Sometimes you need to know how many cells in a particular cell range, column or row, or even worksheet in your spreadsheet have cell entries and how many are still blank. Other times, you need to know just how many of the occupied cells have text entries and how many have numeric entries. Excel includes a number of counting functions that you can use in building formulas that calculate the number of cells in a particular region or worksheet that are occupied and can tell you what general type of entry they contain.

Building counting formulas

Figure 5-5 illustrates the different types of counting formulas that you can build to return such basic statistics as the total number of cells in a particular range, the number of occupied cells in that range, as well as the number of numeric and text entries in the occupied range. In this example spreadsheet, I gave the name sales_table to the cell range A1:C8 (shown selected in Figure 5-5).

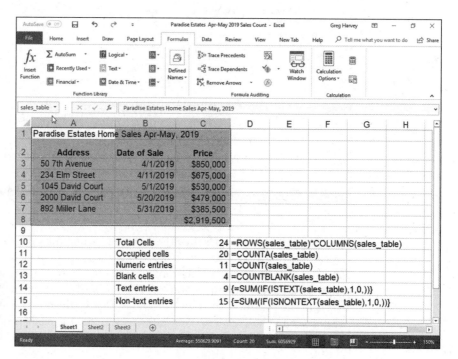

I then used the sales_table range name in a number of formulas that count its different aspects. The most basic formula is the one that returns the total number of cells in the sales_table range. To build this formula in cell C10, I used the ROWS and COLUMNS information functions (see Book 3, Chapter 6 for more on these types of functions) to return the number of rows and columns in the range, and then I created the following formula that multiplies these two values together:

```
=ROWS(sales_table)*COLUMNS(sales_table)
```

This formula, of course, returns 24 to cell C10. In the next formula, I calculated the number of these 24 cells that contain data entries (of whatever type) using the COUNTA function. This function counts the number of cells that are not empty in the ranges that you specify. The COUNTA function uses the following syntax:

```
COUNTA(value1,[value2],[...])
```

The *value* arguments (all of which are optional except for value1) are up to 30 different values or cell ranges that you want counted. Note that the COUNTA function counts a cell as long it has some entry, even if the entry is empty text set off by a single apostrophe ('). In the example shown in Figure 5-5, cell C11 contains the following COUNTA function:

```
=COUNTA(sales_table)
```

This formula returns 20 to cell C11. The next formula in the sample spreadsheet calculates the number of numeric entries in the cell range called sales_table. To do this, you use the COUNT function. The COUNT function takes the same arguments as COUNTA, the only difference being that COUNT counts a value or cell specified in its *value* arguments only if it contains a numeric entry.

Cell C12 contains the following formula for calculating the number of numeric entries in the Home Sales table range called sales_table:

```
=COUNT(sales_table)
```

Excel returns 11 to cell C12. Note that in calculating this result, Excel counts the five date entries (with the date of each sale) in the cell range B3:B7 as well as the six numeric data entries (with the selling prices of each home plus total) in the cell range C3:C8.

The next formula in the sample spreadsheet shown in Figure 5-5 uses the COUNTBLANK function to calculate the number of blank cells in the sales_table range. The COUNTBLANK function works just like the COUNTA and COUNT functions except that it returns the number of nonoccupied cells in the range. For this example, I entered the following COUNTBLANK function in cell C13:

```
=COUNTBLANK(sales_table)
```

Excel then returns 4 to cell C13 (which makes sense because you know that of the 24 total cells in this range, Excel already said that 20 of them have entries of some kind).

The last two counting formulas in the sample spreadsheet shown in Figure 5-5 return the number of text and nontext entries in the sales_table cell range. To do this, instead of counting functions, they use the ISTEXT and ISNONTEXT information functions as part of the IF conditions used in conjunction with the good old SUM function.

The first formula for returning the number of text entries in the sales_table range in cell C14 is

```
{=SUM(IF(ISTEXT(sales_table),1,0))}
```

The second formula for returning the number of nontext entries in the sales_table range in cell C15 is just like the one in cell C15 except that it uses the ISNONTEXT function instead of ISTEXT, as follows:

```
{=SUM(IF(ISNONTEXT(sales_table),1,0))}
```

The ISTEXT function in the formula in cell C14 returns logical TRUE when a cell in the sales_table range contains a text entry and FALSE when it does not. The ISNONTEXT function in the formula in cell C15 returns logical TRUE when a cell is blank or contains a numeric entry (in other words, anything but text) and FALSE when it contains text.

In both these formulas, the ISTEXT and ISNONTEXT functions are used as the *logical_test* arguments of an IF function with 1 as the *value_if_true* argument and 0 as the *value_if_false* argument (so that the cells are counted only when the ISTEXT or ISNONTEXT functions return the logical TRUE values). These IF functions are then nested within SUM functions, and these SUM functions, in turn, are entered as array formulas.

WARNING

Note that you must enter these formulas in the worksheet as array formulas (by pressing Ctrl+Shift+Enter) so that Excel performs its counting calculations on each and every cell in the sales_table cell range. If you just enter the SUM formula with the nested IF and ISTEXT and ISNONTEXT functions as regular formulas, they would return 0 as the count for both text and nontext entries in the sales_table cell range. (See Book 3, Chapter 1 for details on building array formulas.)

Counting occupied cells in entire rows, columns, and worksheets

You can use the COUNTA function to count the number of occupied cells in an entire row or column of a worksheet or even an entire worksheet in your workbook. For example, to count all the occupied cells in row 17 of a worksheet, you enter the following COUNTA formula:

```
=COUNTA(17:17)
```

If you want to find the number of nonblank cells in column B of the worksheet, you enter the following COUNTA formula:

```
=COUNTA(B:B)
```

To find out the number of occupied cells in the entire second worksheet of your workbook (assuming that it's still called Sheet2), you enter this COUNTA formula:

```
=COUNTA(Sheet2!1:1048576)
```

Note that you can also enter the argument for this COUNTA function by designating the entire range of column letters (rather than the range of row numbers) as in:

```
=COUNTA(Sheet2!A:XFD)
```

However, Excel automatically converts the argument that specifies the range of columns to rows, using absolute references ($1:$1048576) as soon as you enter the COUNTA function in its cell.

WARNING

When entering COUNTA functions that return the number of occupied cells in an entire row, column, or worksheet, you must be sure that you do *not* enter the formula in a cell within that row, column, or worksheet. If you do, Excel displays a Circular Reference Alert dialog box when you try to enter the formula in the worksheet. This happens because you are asking Excel to use the cell with the formula that does the counting in the count itself (definitely the type of circular logic that the program doesn't allow).

Conditional counting

Excel includes a COUNTIF function that you can use to count cells in a range only when they meet a certain condition. The COUNTIF function takes two arguments and uses the following syntax:

```
COUNTIF(range,criteria)
```

The *range* argument specifies the range of cells from which the conditional count is to be calculated. The *criteria* argument specifies the condition to use. You can express this argument as a number, expression, or text that indicates which cells to count. When specifying a number for the *criteria* argument, you don't have to enclose the number in quotes. For example, in a cell range named table_data, to count the number of entries that contain the number 5, you enter the following COUNTIF formula:

```
=COUNTIF(table_data,5)
```

However, when specifying an expression or text as the *criteria* argument, you must enclose the expression or text in closed quotes as in "=5", ">20", or "New York".

So, if you want to use COUNTIF to find out how many cells in the table_data range have values greater than 5, you enter this version of the COUNTIF function:

```
=COUNTIF(table_data,">5")
```

When you want to use the COUNTIF function to find out the number of cells whose contents are equal to the contents of a particular cell in the worksheet, you just add the cell reference as the function's *criteria* argument. For example, if you want to count the number of cells in the table_data range that are equal to the contents of cell B3 in the worksheet, you enter this formula:

```
=COUNTIF(table_data,B3)
```

However, when you want to specify an expression other than equality that refers to the contents of a cell in the worksheet, you must enclose the operator in a pair of double quotation marks and then add the ampersand (&) concatenation operator before the cell reference. For example, if you want to count how many cells in the table_data range have a value greater than the contents of cell B3, you enter this form of the COUNTIF function:

```
=COUNTIF(table_data,">"&B3)
```

Note that when specifying text as the condition, you can use the two wildcard characters: the asterisk (*) to represent an unspecified amount of characters and the question mark (?) to represent single characters in the COUNTIF function's *criteria* argument. For example, to count all the cells in the table_data range whose text entries end with the word *Street*, you use the asterisk in the COUNTIF *criteria* argument as follows:

```
=COUNTIF(table_data,"*Street")
```

To count the cells in the table_data range whose text entries contain the word *discount* anywhere in the entry, you sandwich *discount* between two asterisks in the COUNTIF *criteria* argument as follows:

```
=COUNTIF(table_data,"*discount*")
```

To count the cells in the table_data range whose cell entries consist of any two characters followed by the letter *y* (as in *day, say, pay,* and so on), you use two question marks to stand in for the nonspecific characters followed by a *y* in the COUNTIF *criteria* argument, as in

```
=COUNTIF(table_data,"??y")
```

When using the COUNTIF function to find the number of cells, you can include other statistical functions as the *criteria* argument. For example, suppose that you want to know the number of cells in the table_data range whose values are less than the average value in the range. To do this, you insert the AVERAGE function in the COUNTIF *criteria* argument as follows:

```
=COUNTIF(table_data,"<"&AVERAGE(table_data))
```

Using specialized statistical functions

You can use the built-in statistical functions found on the Statistical continuation menu or located in the Statistical category in the Insert Function dialog box, both of which I discuss earlier in this chapter. Excel also offers a complete set of special analysis tools as part of the Analysis ToolPak and Analysis ToolPak – VBA add-ins.

The tools included in the Analysis ToolPak enable you to analyze worksheet data by using such things as ANOVA, F-Test, rank and percentile, t-Test, and Fourier Analysis.

To load these tool packs so that you can use their functions, you need to open the Add-Ins dialog box by clicking File ⇨ Options ⇨ Add-Ins and then clicking the Go button at the bottom of the Excel Options dialog box (make sure that Excel Add-ins is displayed in the Manage drop-down list box before you click Go). In the Add-Ins dialog box, you then click the Analysis ToolPak and Analysis ToolPak – VBA check boxes before clicking OK.

After that, you simply click the Data Analysis button that's been added to the Analysis group on the Data tab of the Ribbon (Alt+AY2). Excel then opens the Data Analysis dialog box, as shown in Figure 5-6.

FIGURE 5-6: Selecting a statistical analysis tool added by the Analysis ToolPak.

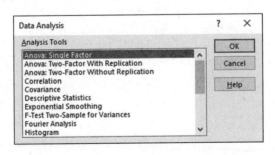

IN THIS CHAPTER

» Looking up data in a table and adding it to a list

» Transposing vertical cell ranges to horizontal and vice versa

» Getting information about a cell's contents

» Evaluating a cell's type with the IS information functions

» Using text functions to manipulate text entries

» Creating formulas that combine text entries

Chapter **6**

Lookup, Information, and Text Formulas

This chapter covers three categories of Excel functions: the lookup and reference functions that return values and cell addresses from the spreadsheet, the information functions that return particular types of information about cells in the spreadsheet, and the text functions that enable you to manipulate strings of text in the spreadsheet.

In these three different categories of Excel functions, perhaps none are as handy as the lookup functions that enable you to have Excel look up certain data in a table and then return other related data from that same table based on the results of that lookup.

Lookup and Reference

The lookup functions are located on the Lookup & Reference command button's drop-down menu (Alt+MO) on the Ribbon's Formulas tab. Excel makes it easy to perform table lookups that either return information about entries in the table or actually return related data to other data lists in the spreadsheet. By using Lookup tables to input information into a data list, you not only reduce the amount of data input that you have to do, but also eliminate the possibility of data entry errors. Using Lookup tables also makes it a snap to update your data lists: All you have to do is make the edits to the entries in the original Lookup table or schedule to have all their data entries in the list updated as well.

The reference functions in Excel enable you to return specific information about particular cells or parts of the worksheet; create hyperlinks to different documents on your computer, network, or the Internet; and transpose ranges of vertical cells so that they run horizontally and vice versa.

Looking up a single value with VLOOKUP and HLOOKUP

The most popular of the lookup functions are HLOOKUP (for Horizontal Lookup) and VLOOKUP (for Vertical Lookup) functions. These functions are located on the Lookup & Reference drop-down menu on the Formulas tab of the Ribbon (Alt+MO) as well as in the Lookup & Reference category in the Insert Function dialog box. They are part of a powerful group of functions that can return values by looking them up in data tables.

The VLOOKUP function searches vertically (from top to bottom) the leftmost column of a Lookup table until the program locates a value that matches or exceeds the one you are looking up. The HLOOKUP function searches horizontally (from left to right) the topmost row of a Lookup table until it locates a value that matches or exceeds the one that you're looking up.

The VLOOKUP function uses the following syntax:

```
VLOOKUP(lookup_value,table_array,col_index_num,[range_lookup])
```

The HLOOKUP function follows the nearly identical syntax:

```
HLOOKUP(lookup_value,table_array,row_index_num,[range_lookup])
```

In both functions, the *lookup_value* argument is the value that you want to look up in the Lookup table, and *table_array* is the cell range or name of the Lookup table that contains both the value to look up and the related value to return.

The *col_index_num* argument designates the column of the lookup table containing the values that are returned by the VLOOKUP function based on matching the value of the *lookup_value* argument against those in the table_array argument. You determine the *col_index_num* argument counting how many columns this column is over to the right from the first column of the vertical Lookup table, and you include the first column of the Lookup table in this count.

The *row_index_num* argument designates the row containing the values are returned by the HLOOKUP function in a horizontal table. You determine the *row_index_num* argument by counting how many rows down this row is from the top row of the horizontal Lookup table. Again, you include the top row of the Lookup table in this count.

When entering the *col_index_num* or *row_index_num* arguments in the VLOOKUP and HLOOKUP functions, the value you enter cannot exceed the total number of columns or rows in the Lookup table.

The optional *range_lookup* argument in both the VLOOKUP and the HLOOKUP functions is the logical TRUE or FALSE that specifies whether you want Excel to find an exact or approximate match for the *lookup_value* in the table_array. When you specify TRUE or omit the *range_lookup* argument in the VLOOKUP or HLOOKUP function, Excel finds an approximate match. When you specify FALSE as the *range_lookup* argument, Excel finds only exact matches.

Finding approximate matches pertains only when you're looking up numeric entries (rather than text) in the first column or row of the vertical or horizontal Lookup table. When Excel doesn't find an exact match in this Lookup column or row, it locates the next highest value that doesn't exceed the *lookup_value* argument and then returns the value in the column or row designated by the *col_index_num* or *row_index_num* arguments.

When using the VLOOKUP and HLOOKUP functions, the text or numeric entries in the Lookup column or row (that is, the leftmost column of a vertical Lookup table or the top row of a horizontal Lookup table) must be unique. These entries must also be arranged or sorted in ascending order; that is, alphabetical order for text entries, and lowest-to-highest order for numeric entries. (See Book 6, Chapter 1 for detailed information on sorting data in a spreadsheet.)

Figure 6-1 shows an example of using the VLOOKUP function to return either a 15% or 20% tip from a tip table, depending on the pretax total of the check. Cell F3 contains the VLOOKUP function:

```
=VLOOKUP(Pretax_Total,Tip_Table,IF(Tip_Percentage=0.15,2,3))
```

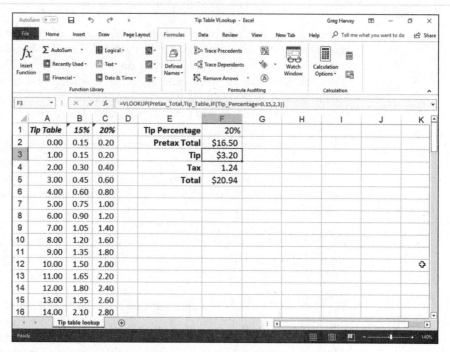

FIGURE 6-1:
Using the
VLOOKUP
function to return
the amount of
the tip to
add from a
Lookup table.

This formula returns the amount of the tip based on the tip percentage in cell F1 and the pretax amount of the check in cell F2.

To use this tip table, enter the percentage of the tip (15% or 20%) in cell F1 (named Tip_Percentage) and the amount of the check before tax in cell F2 (named Pretax_Total). Excel then looks up the value that you enter in the Pretax_Total cell in the first column of the Lookup table, which includes the cell range A2:C101 and is named Tip_Table.

Excel then moves down the values in the first column of Tip_Table until it finds a match, whereupon the program uses the *col_index_num* argument in the VLOOKUP function to determine which tip amount from that row of the table to return to cell F3. If Excel finds that the value entered in the Pretax_Total cell ($16.50 in this example) doesn't exactly match one of the values in the first column of Tip_Table, the program continues to search down the comparison range until it encounters the first value that exceeds the pretax total (17.00 in cell A19 in this example). Excel then moves back up to the previous row in the table and returns the value in the column that matches the *col_index_num* argument of the VLOOKUP function. (This is because the optional *range_lookup* argument has been omitted from the function.)

Note that the tip table example in Figure 6-1 uses an IF function to determine the *col_index_num* argument for the VLOOKUP function in cell F3. The IF function determines the column number to be used in the tip table by matching the percentage entered in Tip_Percentage (cell F1) with 0.15. If they match, the function returns 2 as the *col_index_num* argument, and the VLOOKUP function returns a value from the second column (the 15% column B) in the Tip_Table range. Otherwise, the IF function returns 3 as the *col_index_num* argument, and the VLOOKUP function returns a value from the third column (the 20% column C) in the Tip_Table range.

Figure 6-2 shows an example that uses the HLOOKUP function to look up the price of each bakery item stored in a separate price Lookup table and then to return that price to the Price/Doz column of the Daily Sales list. Cell F3 contains the original formula with the HLOOKUP function that is then copied down column F:

```
=HLOOKUP(item,Price_table,2,FALSE)
```

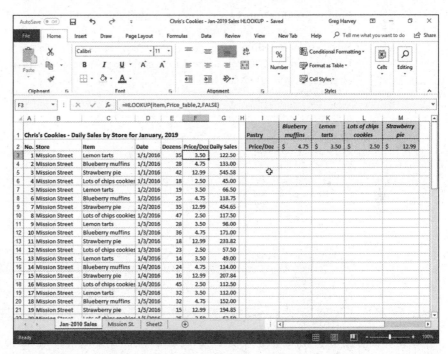

Lookup, Information, and Text Formulas

FIGURE 6-2:
Using the HLOOKUP function to return the price of a bakery item from a Lookup table.

In this HLOOKUP function, the range name Item that's given to the Item column in the range C3:C62 is defined as the *lookup_value* argument and the cell range name Price table that's given to the cell range I1:M2 is the *table_array* argument. The *row_index_num* argument is 2 because you want Excel to return the prices in the second row of the Prices Lookup table, and the optional *range_lookup* argument is FALSE because the item name in the Daily Sales list must match exactly the item name in the Prices Lookup table.

By having the HLOOKUP function use the Price table range to input the price per dozen for each bakery goods item in the Daily Sales list, you make it a very simple matter to update any of the sales in the list. All you have to do is change its Price/ Doz cost in this range, and the HLOOKUP function immediately updates the new price in the Daily Sales list wherever the item is sold.

Performing a two-way lookup

In both the VLOOKUP and HLOOKUP examples, Excel only compares a single value in the data list to a single value in the vertical or horizontal Lookup table. Some-times, however, you may have a table in which you need to perform a two-way lookup, whereby a piece of data is retrieved from the Lookup table based on look-ing up a value in the top row (with the table's column headings) and a value in the first column (with the table's row headings).

Figure 6-3 illustrates a situation in which you would use two values, the produc-tion date and the part number to look up the expected production. In the 2019 Production Schedule table, the production dates for each part form the column headings in the first row of the table, and the part numbers form the row headings in its first column of the table.

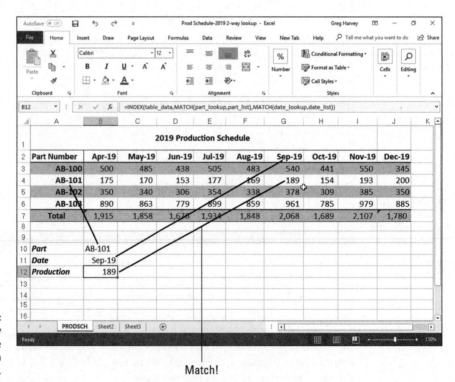

FIGURE 6-3:
Doing a two-way lookup in the Production Schedule table.

To look up the number of the part scheduled to be produced in a particular month, you need to the use the MATCH function, which returns the relative position of a particular value in a cell range or array. The syntax of the MATCH function is as follows:

```
MATCH(lookup_value,lookup_array,[match_type])
```

The *lookup_value* argument is, of course, the value whose position you want returned when a match is found, and the *lookup_array* is the cell range or array containing the values that you want to match. The optional *match_type* argument is the number 1, 0, or –1, which specifies how Excel matches the value specified by the *lookup_value* argument in the range specified by the *lookup_array* argument:

» Use *match_type 1* to find the largest value that is less than or equal to the *lookup_value*. Note that the values in the *lookup_array* must be placed in ascending order when you use the 1 *match_type* argument. (Excel uses this type of matching when the *match_type* argument is omitted from the MATCH function.)

» Use *match_type 0* to find the first value that is exactly equal to the *lookup_value*. Note that the values in the *lookup_array* can be in any order when you use the 0 *match_type* argument.

» Use *match_type –1* to find the smallest value that is greater than or equal to the *lookup_value*. Note that the values in the *lookup_array* must be placed in descending order when you use the –1 *match_type* argument.

In addition to looking up the position of the production date and part number in the column and row headings in the Production Schedule table, you need to use an INDEX function, which uses the relative row and column number position to return the number to be produced from the table itself. The INDEX function follows two different syntax forms: array and reference. You use the array form when you want a value returned from the table (as you do in this example), and you use the reference form when you want a reference returned from the table.

The syntax of the array form of the INDEX function is as follows:

```
INDEX(array,[row_num],[col_num])
```

The syntax of the reference form of the INDEX function is as follows:

```
INDEX(reference,[row_num],[col_num],[area_num])
```

The *array* argument of the array form of the INDEX function is a range of cells or an array constant that you want Excel to use in the lookup. If this range or constant contains only one row or column, the corresponding *row_num* or *col_num* arguments are optional. If the range or array constant has more than one row or more than one column, and you specify both the *row_num* and the *col_num* arguments, Excel returns the value in the *array* argument that is located at the intersection of the *row_num* argument and the *col_num* argument.

For the MATCH and INDEX functions in the example shown in Figure 6-3, I assigned the following range names to the following cell ranges:

» table_data to the cell range A2:J6 with the production data plus column and row headings

» part_list to the cell range A2:A6 with the row headings in the first column of the table

» date_list to the cell range A2:J2 with the column headings in the first row of the table

» part_lookup to cell B10 that contains the name of the part to look up in the table

» date_lookup to cell B11 that contains the name of the production date to look up in the table

As Figure 6-3 shows, cell B12 contains a rather long and — at first glance — complex formula using the range names outlined previously and combining the INDEX and MATCH functions:

```
=INDEX(table_data,MATCH(part_lookup,part_list),MATCH(date_
    lookup,date_list))
```

So you can better understand how this formula works, I break the formula down into its three major components: the first MATCH function that returns the *row_num* argument for the INDEX function, the second MATCH function that returns the *col_num* argument for the INDEX function, and the INDEX function itself that uses the values returned by the two MATCH functions to return the number of parts produced.

The first MATCH function that returns the *row_num* argument for the INDEX function is

```
MATCH(part_lookup,part_list)
```

This MATCH function uses the value input into cell B10 (named part_lookup) and looks up its position in the cell range A2:A6 (named part_list). It then returns this row number to the INDEX function as its *row_num* argument. In the case of the example shown in Figure 6-3 where part AB-101 is entered in the part_lookup cell in B10, Excel returns 3 as the *row_num* argument to the INDEX function.

The second MATCH function that returns the *col_num* argument for the INDEX function is

```
MATCH(date_lookup,date_list)
```

This second MATCH function uses the value input into cell B11 (named date_lookup) and looks up its position in the cell range A2:J2 (named date_list). It then returns this column number to the INDEX function as its *col_num* argument. In the case of the example shown in Figure 6-3 where September 1, 2016 (formatted as Sep-16), is entered in the date_lookup cell in B11, Excel returns 7 as the *col_num* argument to the INDEX function.

This means that for all its supposed complexity, the INDEX function shown on the Formula bar in Figure 6-3 contains the equivalent of the following formula:

```
=INDEX(table_data,3,7)
```

As Figure 6-3 shows, Excel returns 189 units as the planned production value for part AB-101 in September, 2016. You can verify that this is correct by manually counting the rows and the columns in the table_data range (cell range A2:J6). If you count down three rows (including row 2, the first row of this range), you come to Part 101 in column A. If you then count seven columns over (including column A with AB-101), you come to cell G4 in the Sep-16 column with the value 189.

Reference functions

The reference functions on the Lookup & Reference command button's drop-down list on the Formulas tab of the Ribbon (Alt+MO) are designed to deal specifically with different aspects of cell references in the worksheet. This group of functions includes:

>> ADDRESS to return a cell reference as a text entry in a cell of the worksheet

>> AREAS to return the number of areas in a list of values (*areas* are defined as a range of contiguous cells or a single cell in the cell reference)

>> COLUMN to return the number representing the column position of a cell reference

>> COLUMNS to return the number of columns in a reference

>> FORMULATEXT to return the formula referenced as a text string

>> GETPIVOTDATA to return data stored in an Excel pivot table (see Book 7, Chapter 2 for details)

>> HYPERLINK to create a link that opens another document stored on your computer, network, or the Internet (you can also do this with the Insert➪Hyperlink command — see Book 4, Chapter 2 for details)

>> INDIRECT to return a cell reference specified by a text string and bring the contents in the cell to which it refers to that cell

>> LOOKUP to return a value from an array

>> OFFSET to return a reference to a cell range that's specified by the number of rows and columns from a cell or a cell range

>> ROW to return the row number of a cell reference

>> ROWS to return the number of rows in a cell range or array

>> RTD to return real-time data from a server running a program that supports COM (Component Object Model) automation

>> TRANSPOSE to return a vertical array as a horizontal array and vice versa

Get the skinny on columns and rows

The COLUMNS and ROWS functions return the number of columns and rows in a particular cell range or array. For example, if you have a cell range in the spreadsheet named product_mix, you can find out how many columns it contains by entering this formula:

```
=COLUMNS(product_mix)
```

If you want to know how many rows this range uses, you then enter this formula:

```
=ROWS(product_mix)
```

As indicated in the previous chapter, you can use the COLUMNS and ROWS functions together to calculate the total number of cells in a particular range. For example, if you want to know the exact number of cells used in the product_mix cell range, you create the following simple multiplication formula by using the COLUMNS and ROWS functions:

```
=COLUMNS(product_mix)*ROWS(product_mix)
```

REMEMBER

Don't confuse the COLUMNS (plural) function with the COLUMN (singular) function and the ROWS (plural) function with the ROW (singular) function. The COLUMN function returns the number of the column (as though Excel were using the R1C1 reference system) for the cell reference that you specify as its sole argument. Likewise, the ROW function returns the number of the row for the cell reference that you specify as its argument.

Transposing cell ranges

The TRANSPOSE function enables you to change the orientation of a cell range (or an array — see the section on entering array formulas in Book 3, Chapter 1 for details). You can use this function to transpose a vertical cell range where the data runs down the rows of adjacent columns to one where the data runs across the columns of adjacent rows and vice versa. To successfully use the TRANSPOSE function, not only must you select a range that has an opposite number of columns and rows, but you must also enter it as an array formula.

For example, if you're using the TRANSPOSE function to transpose a 2 x 5 cell range (that is, a range that takes up two adjacent rows and five adjacent columns), you must select a blank 5 x 2 cell range (that is, a range that takes five adjacent rows and two adjacent columns) in the worksheet before you use the Insert Function button to insert the TRANSPOSE function in the first cell. Then, after selecting the 2 x 5 cell range that contains the data that you want to transpose in the Array text box of the Function Arguments dialog box, you need to press Ctrl+Shift+Enter to close this dialog box and enter the TRANSPOSE function into the entire selected cell range as an array formula (enclosed in curly braces).

Suppose that you want to transpose the data entered into the cell range A10:C11 (a 2 x 3 array) to the blank cell range E10:F12 (a 3 x 2 array) of the worksheet. When you press Ctrl+Shift+Enter to complete the array formula, after selecting the cell range A10:C11 as the *array* argument, Excel puts the following array formula in every cell of the range:

```
{=TRANSPOSE(A10:C11)}
```

Figure 6-4 illustrates the use of the TRANSPOSE function. The cell range B2:C4 contains the original 3 x 2 array that I showed earlier in Figure 1-9 in Book 3, Chapter 1 when discussing how you add array formulas to your worksheet. To convert this 3 x 2 array in the cell range B2:C4 to a 2 x 3 array in the range B6:D7, I followed these steps:

1. **Select the blank cell range B6:D7 in the worksheet.**

2. **Click the Lookup & Reference command button on the Ribbon's Formulas tab and then choose the TRANSPOSE option from the button's drop-down menu.**

Excel inserts =TRANSPOSE() on the Formula bar and opens the Function Arguments dialog box where the Array argument text box is selected.

3. **Drag through the cell range B2:C4 in the worksheet so that the Array argument text box contains B2:C4 and the formula on the Formula bar now reads =TRANSPOSE(B2:C4).**

4. **Press Ctrl+Shift+Enter to close the Insert Arguments dialog box (don't click OK) and to insert the TRANSPOSE array formula into the cell range B6:D7 as shown in Figure 6-4.**

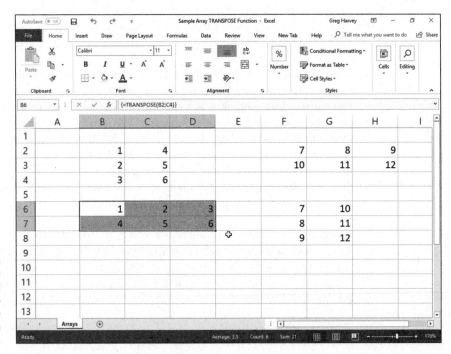

FIGURE 6-4:
Using the
TRANSPOSE
function to
change the
orientation of a
simple array.

WARNING

Clicking the OK button in the Function Arguments dialog box inserts the TRANS-POSE function into the active cell of the current cell selection. Doing this returns the #VALUE! error value to the cell. You must remember to press Ctrl+Shift+Enter to both close the dialog box and put the formula into the entire cell range.

TIP

If all you want to do is transpose row and column headings or a simple table of data, you don't have to go through the rigmarole of creating an array formula using the TRANSPOSE function. Simply copy the range of cells to be transposed with the Copy command button on the Home tab of the Ribbon. Position the cell cursor in the first empty cell where the transposed range is to be pasted before you click the Transpose option on the Paste command button's drop-down menu.

Information, Please . . .

The information functions on the continuation menu accessed by clicking the More Functions command button on the Formulas tab of the Ribbon and then highlighting the Information option (or by pressing Alt+MQI) consist of a number of functions designed to test the contents of a cell or cell range and give you information on its current contents.

These kinds of information functions are often combined with IF functions, which determine what type of calculation, if any, to perform. The information function then becomes the *logical_test* argument of the IF function, and the outcome of the test, expressed as the logical TRUE or logical FALSE value, decides whether its *value_if_true* or its *value_if_false* argument is executed. (See Book 3, Chapter 2 for information on using information functions that test for error values to trap errors in a spreadsheet.)

In addition to the many information functions that test whether the contents of a cell are of a certain type, Excel offers a smaller set of functions that return coded information about a cell's contents or formatting and about the current operating environment in which the workbook is functioning. The program also offers an N (for Number) function that returns the value in a cell and an NA (for Not Available) function that inserts the #N/A error value in the cell.

Getting specific information about a cell

The CELL function is the basic information function for getting all sorts of data about the current contents and formatting of a cell. The syntax of the CELL function is

```
CELL(info_type,[reference])
```

The *info_type* argument is a text value that specifies the type of cell information you want returned. The optional *reference* argument is the reference of the cell range for which you want information. When you omit this argument, Excel specifies the type of information specified by the *info_type* argument for the last cell that was changed in the worksheet. When you specify a cell range as the *reference* argument, Excel returns the type of information specified by the *info_type* argument for the first cell in the range (that is, the one in the upper-left corner, which may or may not be the active cell of the range).

Table 6-1 shows the various *info_type* arguments that you can specify when using the CELL function. Remember that you must enclose each *info_type* argument in the CELL function in double-quotes (to enter them as text values) to prevent Excel from returning the #NAME? error value to the cell containing the CELL function formula. So, for example, if you want to return the contents of the first cell in the range B10:E80, you enter the following formula:

```
=CELL("contents",B10:E80)
```

TABLE 6-1 The CELL Functions *info_type* Arguments

CELL Function info_type Argument	Returns This Information
"address"	Cell address of the first cell in the reference as text using absolute cell references
"col"	Column number of the first cell in the reference
"color"	1 when the cell is formatted in color for negative values; otherwise returns 0 (zero)
"contents"	Value of the upper-left cell in the reference
"filename"	Filename (including the full pathname) of the file containing the cell reference: returns empty text ("") when the workbook containing the reference has not yet been saved
"format"	Text value of the number format of the cell (see Table 6-2): Returns "-" at the end of the text value when the cell is formatted in color for negative values and "()" when the value is formatted with parentheses for positive values or for all values
"parentheses"	1 when the cell is formatted with parentheses for positive values or for all values
"prefix"	Text value of the label prefix used in the cell: Single quote (') when text is left-aligned; double quote (") when text is right-aligned; caret (^) when text is centered; backslash (\) when text is fill-aligned; and empty text ("") when the cell contains any other type of entry
"protect"	0 when the cell is unlocked and 1 when the cell is locked (see Book 4, Chapter 1 for details on protecting cells in a worksheet)
"row"	Row number of the first cell in the reference
"type"	Text value of the type of data in the cell: "b" for blank when cell is empty; "l" for label when cell contains text constant; and "v" for value when cell contains any other entry
"width"	Column width of the cell rounded off to the next highest integer (each unit of column width is equal to the width of one character in Excel's default font size)

Table 6-2 shows the different text values along with their number formats (codes) that can be returned when you specify "format" as the *info_type* argument in a CELL function. (Refer to Book 2, Chapter 3 for details on number formats and the meaning of the various number format codes.)

TABLE 6-2

Text Values Returned by the "format" *info_type*

Text Value	Number Formatting
"G"	General
"F0"	0
",0"	#,##0
"F2"	0.00
",2"	#,##0.00
"C0"	$#,##0_);($#,##0)
"C0-"	$#,##0_);[Red]($#,##0)
"C2"	$#,##0.00_);($#,##0.00)
"C2-"	$#,##0.00_);[Red]($#,##0.00)
"P0"	0%
"P2"	0.00%
"S2"	0.00E+00
"G"	# ?/? or # ??/??
"D4"	m/d/yy or m/d/yy h:mm or mm/dd/yy
"D1"	d-mmm-yy or dd-mmm-yy
"D2"	d-mmm or dd-mmm
"D3"	mmm-yy
"D5"	mm/dd
"D7"	h:mm AM/PM
"D6"	h:mm:ss AM/PM
"D9"	h:mm
"D8"	h:mm:ss

For example, if you use the CELL function that specifies "format" as the *info_type* argument on cell range A10:C28 (which you've formatted with the Comma style button on the Formula bar), as in the following formula

```
=CELL("format",A10:C28)
```

Excel returns the text value ",2-" (without the quotation marks) in the cell where you enter this formula signifying that the first cell uses the Comma style format with two decimal places and that negative values are displayed in color (red) and enclosed in parentheses.

Are you my type?

Excel provides another information function that returns the type of value in a cell. Aptly named, the TYPE function enables you to build formulas with the IF function that execute one type of behavior when the cell being tested contains a value and another when it contains text. The syntax of the TYPE function is

```
TYPE(value)
```

The *value* argument of the TYPE function can be any Excel entry: text, number, logical value, or even an Error value or a cell reference that contains such a value. The TYPE function returns the following values, indicating the type of contents:

>> 1 for numbers

>> 2 for text

>> 4 for logical value (TRUE or FALSE)

>> 16 for Error value

>> 64 for an array range or constant (see Book 3, Chapter 1)

The following formula combines the CELL and TYPE functions nested within an IF function. This formula returns the type of the number formatting used in cell D11 only when the cell contains a value. Otherwise, it assumes that D11 contains a text entry, and it evaluates the type of alignment assigned to the text in that cell:

```
=IF(TYPE(D11)=1,CELL("format",D11),CELL("prefix",D11))
```

Using the IS functions

The IS information functions (as in ISBLANK, ISERR, and so on) are a large group of functions that perform essentially the same task. They evaluate a value or cell reference and return the logical TRUE or FALSE, depending on whether the value is or isn't the type for which the IS function tests. For example, if you use the ISBLANK function to test the contents of cell A1 as in

```
=ISBLANK(A1)
```

Excel returns TRUE to the cell containing the formula when A1 is empty and FALSE when it's occupied by any type of entry.

Excel offers ten built-in IS information functions:

>> ISBLANK(*value*) to evaluate whether the value or cell reference is empty

>> ISERR(*value*) to evaluate whether the value or cell reference contains an Error value (except for #N/A)

>> ISERROR(*value*) to evaluate whether the value or cell reference contains an Error value (Including #N/A)

>> ISEVEN(*value*) to evaluate whether the value in the referenced cell is even (TRUE) or odd (FALSE)

>> ISLOGICAL(*value*) to evaluate whether the value or cell reference contains the logical TRUE or FALSE value

>> ISNA(*value*) to evaluate whether the value or cell reference contains the special #N/A Error value

>> ISNONTEXT(*value*) to evaluate whether the value or cell reference contains any type of entry other than text

>> ISNUMBER(*value*) to evaluate whether the value or cell reference contains a number

>> ISODD(*number*) to evaluate whether the value in the referenced cell is odd (TRUE) or even (FALSE)

>> ISREF(*value*) to evaluate whether the value or cell reference is itself a cell reference

>> ISTEXT(*value*) to evaluate whether the value or cell reference contains a text entry

For an example of how to use the ISERROR function, refer to the section on error trapping in Book 3, Chapter 2.

Much Ado about Text

Normally, when you think of doing calculations in a spreadsheet, you think of performing operations on its numeric entries. You can, however, use the text functions as well as the concatenation operator (&) to perform operations on its text entries as well (referred to collectively as *string operations*).

Using text functions

Text functions found on the Text command button's drop-down menu on the Ribbon's Formulas tab (Alt+MT) include two types of functions: functions such as VALUE, TEXT, and DOLLAR that convert numeric text entries into numbers and numeric entries into text, and functions such as UPPER, LOWER, and PROPER that manipulate the strings of text themselves.

Many times, you need to use the text functions when you work with data from other programs. For example, suppose that you purchase a target client list on disk, only to discover that all the information has been entered in all uppercase letters. In order to use this data with your word processor's mail merge feature, you would use Excel's PROPER function to convert the entries so that only the initial letter of each word is in uppercase.

Text functions such as the UPPER, LOWER, and PROPER functions all take a single *text* argument that indicates the text that should be manipulated. The UPPER function converts all letters in the *text* argument to uppercase. The LOWER function converts all letters in the *text* argument to lowercase. The PROPER function capitalizes the first letter of each word as well as any other letters in the *text* argument that don't follow another letter, and changes all other letters in the *text* argument to lowercase.

Figure 6-5 illustrates a situation in which you would use the PROPER function. Here, both last and first name text entries have been made in all uppercase letters. Follow these steps for using the PROPER function to convert text entries to the proper capitalization:

1. **Position the cell cursor in cell C3, click the Text command button on the Ribbon's Formulas tab (or press Alt+MT), and then choose PROPER from its drop-down menu.**

The Function Arguments dialog box for the PROPER function opens with the Text box selected.

2. **Click cell A3 in the worksheet to insert A3 in the Text box of the Function Arguments dialog box and then click OK to insert the PROPER function into cell C3.**

Excel closes the Insert Function dialog box and inserts the formula =PROPER(A3) in cell C3, which now contains the proper capitalization of the last name Aiken.

3. **Drag the Fill handle in the lower-right corner of cell C3 to the right to cell D3 and then release the mouse button to copy the formula with the PROPER function to this cell.**

Excel now copies the formula =PROPER(B3) to cell D3, which now contains the proper capitalization of the first name, Christopher. Now you're ready to copy these formulas with the PROPER function down to row 17.

4. **Drag the fill handle in the lower-right corner of cell D3 down to cell D17 and then release the mouse button to copy the formulas with the PROPER function down.**

The cell range C3:D17 now contains first and last name text entries with the proper capitalization. (See Figure 6-5.) Before replacing all the uppercase entries in A3:B17 with these proper entries, you convert them to their calculated values. This action replaces the formulas with the text as though you had typed each name in the worksheet.

5. **With the cell range C3:D17 still selected, click the Copy command button on the Home tab of the Ribbon.**

6. **Immediately choose the Paste Values option from the Paste command button's drop-down menu.**

You've now replaced the formulas with the appropriate text. Now you're ready to move this range on top of the original range with the all-uppercase entries. This action will replace the uppercase entries with the ones using the proper capitalization.

7. **With the cell range C3:D17 still selected, position the white-cross mouse or Touch pointer on the bottom of the range; when the pointer changes to an arrowhead, drag the cell range until its outline encloses the range A3:B17 and then release the mouse button or remove your finger or stylus from the touchscreen.**

Excel displays an alert box asking if you want the program to replace the contents of the destination's cells.

8. **Click OK in the Alert dialog box to replace the all-uppercase entries with the properly capitalized ones in the destination cells.**

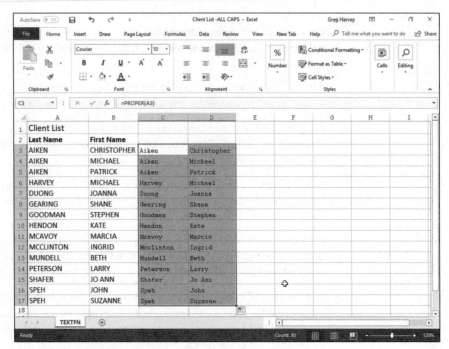

FIGURE 6-5:
Using the PROPER function to convert names in all uppercase letters to proper capitalization.

Your worksheet now looks like the one shown in Figure 6-6. Everything is fine in the worksheet with the exception of the two last names, Mcavoy and Mcclinton. You have to manually edit cells A11 and A12 to capitalize the *A* in McAvoy and the second *C* in McClinton.

The T function

The T text function enables you to test whether or not a cell entry somewhere else in the workbook contains text. It does this by testing the entry specified in its sole *value* argument as in

```
=T(C28)
```

If cell C28 in this example does currently contain a text entry, the T function brings that entry forward so that it appears in the cell containing the T function formula. If C28 currently contains anything else besides text, Excel puts empty text (with double quotes with nothing inside them) in the cell with the T function formula that makes it appear as though that cell is blank.

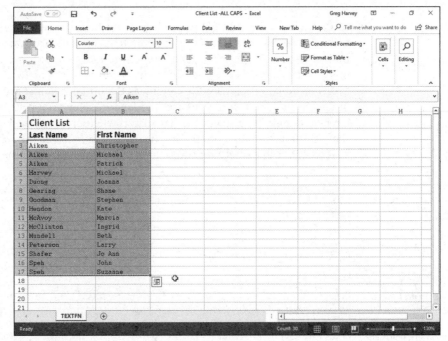

FIGURE 6-6:
Worksheet after replacing names in all uppercase letters with properly capitalized names.

TEXTJOIN function

The TEXTJOIN function gives you a new and easy to join together text entered into separate cells of a worksheet into one long text entry with each of its erstwhile individual text entries separated by whatever delimiting character you choose to use. This function is useful for those times when you have data lists that need to be exported to an external database program. The most common situation is when you need to convert to an Excel data list into a CSV (Comma Separated Value) text file that can be directly imported into an external database app. The TEXTJOIN function uses the following syntax:

```
=TEXTJOIN(delimiter,ignore_empty,text1,[text2],...)
```

To see how this might work, consider the example shown in Figure 6-7. Here, I have entered a data list into the cell range A1:F6 with clients names and addresses. To make it easy to sort and query this data, I have formatted this list as an Excel table. To save this data in a CSV text file ready for export to another program, I use the TEXTJOIN function, designating the comma (",") as the delimiter as follows:

```
=TEXTJOIN(",",FALSE,A2:F2)
```

In CSV files, individual fields (such as First Name, Last Name, and so on) are normally separated by commas (although spaces and Tabs are also used), and individual records (Amelia Adams, Jack Smith, and so on) are separated by link breaks (designated in a worksheet by the different rows). So for this original TEXTJOIN formula, I designate the comma as the initial *delimiter* argument (enclosed in double quotes). I then designate the *ignore_empty* argument as FALSE. This is a required logical argument that tells Excel whether or not to skip cells in the list that are blank. Finally, I designate the cell range A2:F2 as the sole text argument as it contains all name and address data that comprise Amelia Adams's record.

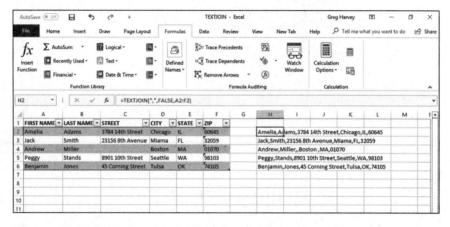

FIGURE 6-7:
Using the TEXTJOIN function to create a CSV file for export where fields are separated by commas and records by line breaks.

After entering the original TEXTJOIN formula in cell H2, I then use the Fill handle to copy the formula down to the cell range H3:H6. As a result, Excel combines each piece of name and address data into a single, long string of text separated by commas. In cell H4 in Figure 6-7, you can also see the result of setting the *ignore_empty* argument to FALSE the TEXTJOIN function. Because I've told Excel to not ignore empty fields, even though Andrew Miller's street address in cell C4 is missing, the TEXTJOIN function keeps a place for this data in the calculated result in H4 by placing a space followed by a comma immediately following Andrew Miller's name. This is important because the record of the exported CSV file needs to have the same amount of fields to prevent the external database program from putting the city of Chicago into the Street field and the state abbreviation of IL into the City field (and so on) in Andrew Miller's record in the resulting database.

All that's left to do after copying the TEXTJOIN formulas is to copy the values returned by these formulas to the worksheet of a new workbook and then save this new workbook as in the CSV file format. To do this, you follow these steps:

1. **Select the cell range H2:H6 with the TEXTJOIN formulas and press Ctrl+C.**

2. **Open a new workbook file by pressing Ctrl+N.**

3. **Click the Values options on the Paste button's drop-down menu to paste the long comma separated text entries into the cell range A1:A5 of in the new workbook (Book 1).**

4. **Save the new workbook file as a CSV file by pressing Ctrl+S, designating the new filename as well as the drive and folder where it's to be saved, clicking CSV (Comma Delimited) from the Save As Type drop-down menu, and clicking the Save button.**

After saving the joined comma separated client address data in the new CSV file, you're ready to send the file to whatever department needs it. (See Book 4, Chapter 4 for more on sharing files).

Concatenating text

You can use the ampersand (&) operator to concatenate (or join) separate text strings together. For example, in the Client list spreadsheet shown in Figure 6-6, you can use this operator to join together the first and last names currently entered in two side-by-side cells into a single entry, as shown in Figure 6-8.

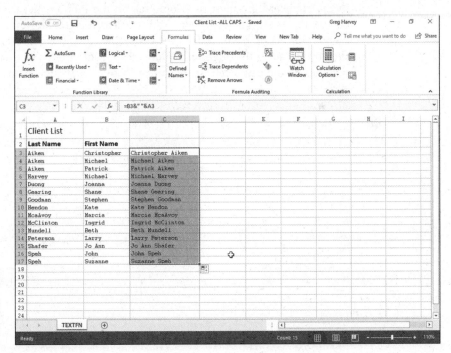

FIGURE 6-8: Spreadsheet after concatenating the first and last names in column C.

To join the first name entry in cell B3 with the last name entry in cell A3, I entered the following formula in cell C3:

```
=B3&" "&A3
```

Notice the use of the double quotes in this formula. They enclose a blank space that is placed between the first and last names joined to them with the two concatenation operators. If I didn't include this space in the formula and just joined the first and last names together with this formula

```
=B3&A3
```

Excel would return ChristopherAiken to cell C3, all as one word.

After entering the concatenation formula that joins the first and last names in cell C3 separated by a single space, I then drag the Fill handle in cell C3 down to C17 to join all the other client names in a single cell in column C.

After the original concatenation formula is copied down the rows of column C, I copy the selected cell range C3:C17 to the Clipboard by clicking the Copy button in the Clipboard group of the Home tab on the Ribbon, and then I immediately choose the Paste Values option from the Paste command button's drop-down menu. This action pastes calculated text values over the concatenation formulas, thereby replacing the original formulas. The result is a list of first and last names together in the same cell in the range C3:C17, as though I had manually input each one.

4

Worksheet Collaboration and Review

Contents at a Glance

IN THIS CHAPTER

» Assigning a password for opening a workbook

» Assigning a password for making editing changes in a workbook

» Using the Locked and Hidden protection formats

» Protecting a worksheet and selecting what actions are allowed

» Enabling cell range editing by particular users in a protected sheet

» Doing data entry solely in unlocked cells of a protected worksheet

» Protecting the workbook

Chapter **1**

Protecting Workbooks and Worksheet Data

Before you start sending out your spreadsheets for review (especially out of house), you need to make them secure. Security in Excel exists on two levels. The first is protecting the workbook file so that only people entrusted with the password can open the file to view, print, or edit the data. The second is protecting the worksheets in a workbook from unwarranted changes so that only people entrusted with that password can make modifications to its contents and design.

When it comes to securing the integrity of your spreadsheets, you can decide which aspects of the sheets in the workbook your users can and cannot change. For example, you might prevent changes to all formulas and headings in a spreadsheet, while still enabling users to make entries in the cells referenced in the formulas themselves.

Password-Protecting the File

By password-protecting the workbook, you can prevent unauthorized users from opening the workbook and/or editing the workbook. You set a password for opening the workbook file when you're dealing with a spreadsheet whose data is of a sufficiently sensitive nature that only a certain group of people in the company should have access to it (such as spreadsheets dealing with personal information and salaries). Of course, after you set the password required in order to open the workbook, you must supply this password to those people who need access in order to make it possible for them to open the workbook file.

You set a password for modifying the workbook when you're dealing with a spreadsheet whose data needs to be viewed and printed by different users, none of whom are authorized to make changes to any of the entries. For example, you might assign a password for modifying a workbook before distributing it companywide, after the workbook's been through a complete editing and review cycle and all the suggested changes have been merged. (See Book 4, Chapter 3 for details.)

Protecting the workbook when saving the file

If you're dealing with a spreadsheet whose data is of a sensitive nature and should not be modified by anyone who's not authorized to open it, you need to set both a password for opening and a password for modifying the workbook file. You assign either one or both of these types of passwords to a workbook file at the time you save it with the File ⇨ Save As command (Alt+FA).

When you choose this command (or click the Save button on the Quick Access toolbar or press Ctrl+S for a new file that's never been saved), Excel opens the Save As screen where you select the place where you want to save the file. (See Book 2, Chapter 1 for details.) After you select the place to save the file and assign its filename on the Save As screen, click the More Options link to have Excel open the Save As dialog box where you can then set the password to open and/or the password to modify the file by taking these steps:

1. **Click the Tools button in the Save As dialog box and then choose General Options from its drop-down menu.**

   Doing this opens the General Options dialog box, similar to the one shown in Figure 1-1, where you can enter a password to open and/or a password to modify in the File Sharing section. Your password can be as long as 255 characters, consisting of a combination of letters and numbers with spaces. When adding letters to your passwords, keep in mind that these passwords are case-sensitive. This means that opensesame and OpenSesame are not the same password because of the different use of upper- and lowercase letters.

REMEMBER

When entering a password, make sure that you don't enter something that you can't easily reproduce or, for heaven's sake, that you can't remember. You must be able to immediately reproduce the password in order to assign it, and you must be able to reproduce it later if you want to be able to open or change the darned workbook ever again.

2. **(Optional) If you want to assign a password to open the file, type the password (up to 255 characters maximum) in the Password to Open text box.**

As you type the password, Excel masks the actual characters you type by rendering them as dots in the text box.

If you decide to assign a password for opening and modifying the workbook at the same time, proceed to Step 3. Otherwise, skip to Step 4.

When entering the password for modifying the workbook, you want to assign a password that's different from the one you just assigned for opening the file (if you did assign a password for opening the file in this step).

3. **(Optional) If you want to assign a password for modifying the workbook, click the Password to Modify text box and then type the password for modifying the workbook there.**

Before you can assign a password to open the file and/or to modify the file, you must confirm the password by reproducing it in a Confirm Password dialog box exactly as you originally entered it.

4. **Click the OK button.**

Doing this closes the General Options dialog box and opens a Confirm Password dialog box, where you need to exactly reproduce the password. If you just entered a password in the Password to Open text box, you need to re-enter this password in the Confirm Password dialog box. If you just entered a password in the Password to Modify text box, you need only to reproduce this password in the Confirm Password dialog box.

However, if you entered a password in both the Password to Open text box and the Password to Modify text box, you must reproduce both passwords. In the first Confirm Password dialog box, enter the password you entered in the Password to Open text box. Immediately after you click OK in the first Confirm Password dialog box, the second Confirm Password dialog box appears, where you reproduce the password you entered in the Password to Modify text box.

5. **Type the password exactly as you entered it in the Password to Open text box (or Password to Modify text box, if you didn't use the Password to Open text box) and then click OK.**

If your password does not match exactly (in both characters and case) the one you originally entered, Excel displays an alert dialog box, indicating that the confirmation password is not identical. When you click OK in this alert dialog box, Excel returns you to the original General Options dialog box, where you can do one of two things:

- Reenter the password in the original text box.

- Click the OK button to redisplay the Confirm Password dialog box, where you can try again to reproduce the original. (Make sure that you've not engaged the Caps Lock key by accident.)

If you assigned both a password to open the workbook and one to modify it, Excel displays a second Confirm Password dialog box as soon as you click OK in the first one and successfully reproduce the password to open the file. You then repeat Step 5, this time exactly reproducing the password to modify the workbook before you click OK.

When you finish confirming the original password(s), you are ready to save the workbook in the Save As dialog box.

6. **(Optional) If you want to save the password-protected version under a new filename or in a different folder, edit the name in the File Name text box and then select the new folder from the Save In drop-down list.**

7. **Click the Save button to save the workbook with the password to open and/or password to modify.**

As soon as you do this, Excel saves the file if this is the first time you've saved it. If not, the program displays an alert dialog box indicating that the file you're saving already exists and asking you whether you want to replace the existing file.

8. **Click the Yes button if the alert dialog box that asks whether you want to replace the existing file appears.**

TIP

Select the Read-Only Recommended check box in the General Options dialog box instead of assigning a password for editing the workbook in the Password to Modify text box when you never want the user to be able to make and save changes in the same workbook file. When Excel marks a file as read-only, the user must save any modifications in a different file using the Save As command. (See "Entering a password to make editing changes" later in this chapter for more on working with a read-only workbook file.)

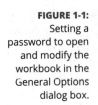

Assigning a password to open from the Info screen

Instead of assigning the password to open your workbook at the time you save changes to it, you can do this as well from Excel 2019's Info screen in the Backstage view by following these simple steps:

1. **Click File ➪ Info or press Alt+FI.**

   Excel opens the Info screen.

2. **Click the Protect Workbook button to open its drop-down menu and then choose Encrypt with Password.**

   Excel opens the Encrypt Document dialog box.

3. **Type the password exactly as you entered it in the Password text box and then click OK.**

   Excel opens the Confirm Password dialog box.

4. **Type the password in the Reenter Password text box exactly as you typed it into the Password text box in the Encrypt Document dialog box and then click OK.**

   Note that if you don't replicate the password exactly, Excel displays an alert dialog box indicating that the confirmation password is not identical. After you click OK to close this alert dialog box, you're returned to the Confirm Password dialog box.

   After successfully replicating the password, Excel closes the Confirm Password dialog box and returns you to the Info screen, where "A password is required to open this workbook" status message now appears under the Protect Workbook heading.

5. **Click the Save option on the Info screen.**

   Excel closes the Backstage and returns you to the regular worksheet window as the program saves your new password to open as part of the workbook file.

REMEMBER

Keep in mind that the drop-down menu attached to the Protect Workbook button in the Info screen in the Backstage does not contain an option for protecting the workbook from further modification after it's opened in Excel. Instead, it contains a Mark as Final option that assigns read-only status to the workbook file that prevents the user from saving changes to the file under the same filename.

Entering the password to gain access

After you save a workbook file to which you've assigned a password for opening it, you must thereafter be able to faithfully reproduce the password in order to open the file (at least until you change or delete the password). When you next try to open the workbook, Excel opens a Password dialog box like the one shown in Figure 1-2, where you must enter the password exactly as it was assigned to the file.

FIGURE 1-2:
Entering the password required to open a protected workbook file.

If you mess up and type the wrong password, Excel displays an alert dialog box letting you know that the password you entered is incorrect. When you click OK to clear the alert, you are returned to the original Excel window where you must repeat the entire file-opening procedure (hoping that this time you're able to enter the correct password). When you supply the correct password, Excel immediately opens the workbook for viewing and printing (and editing as well, unless you've also assigned a password for modifying the file). If you're unable to successfully reproduce the password, you are unable to open the file and put it to any use!

TIP

The last chance you have to chicken out of password-protecting the opening of the file is before you close the file during the work session in which you originally assign the password. If, for whatever reason, you decide that you don't want to go through the hassle of having to reproduce the password each and every time you open this file, you can get rid of it by clicking File⇨Save As or pressing Alt+FA, choosing General Options from the Tools drop-down menu, and then deleting the password in the Password to Open text box before clicking OK in the General Options dialog box and the Save button in the Save As dialog box. Doing this resaves the workbook file without a password to open it so that you don't have to worry about reproducing the password the next time you open the workbook for editing or printing.

A password-protected workbook file for which you can't reproduce the correct password can be a real nightmare (especially if you're talking about a really important spreadsheet with loads and loads of vital data). So, for heaven's sake, don't forget your password, or you'll be stuck. Excel does not provide any sort of command for overriding the password and opening a protected workbook, nor does Microsoft offer any such utility. If you think that you might forget the workbook's password, be sure to write it down somewhere and then keep that piece of paper in a secure place, preferably under lock and key. It's always better to be safe than sorry when it comes to passwords for opening files.

Entering the password to make changes

If you've protected your workbook from modifications with the Password to Modify option in the General Options dialog box, as soon as you attempt to open the workbook (and have entered the password to open the file, if one has been assigned), Excel immediately displays the Password dialog box where you must accurately reproduce the password assigned for modifying the file or click the Read Only button to open it as a read-only file.

As when supplying the password to open a protected file, if you type the wrong password, Excel displays the alert dialog box letting you know that the password you entered is incorrect. When you click OK to clear the alert, you are returned to the Password dialog box, where you can try re-entering the password in the Password text box.

When you supply the correct password, Excel immediately closes the Password dialog box, and you are free to edit the workbook in any way you wish (unless certain cell ranges or worksheets are protected). If you're unable to successfully reproduce the password, you can click the Read Only command button, which opens a copy of the workbook file into which you can't save your changes unless you use the File ⇨ Save As command and then rename the workbook and/or locate the copy in a different folder.

When you click the Read Only button, Excel opens the file with a [Read-Only] indicator appended to the filename as it appears on the Excel title bar. If you then try to save changes with the Save button on the Quick Access toolbar or File ⇨ Save command, the program displays an alert dialog box, indicating that the file is read-only and that you must save a copy by renaming the file in the Save As dialog box. As soon as you click OK to clear the alert dialog box, Excel displays the Save As dialog box, where you can save the copy under a new filename and/or location. Note that the program automatically removes the password for modifying from the copy so that you can modify its contents any way you like.

TIP

Because password-protecting a workbook against modification does not prevent you from opening the workbook and then saving an unprotected version under a new filename with the Save As command, you can assign passwords for modifying files without nearly as much trepidation as assigning them for opening files. Assigning a password for modifying the file assures you that you'll always have an intact original of the spreadsheet from which you can open and save a copy, even if you can never remember the password to modify the original itself.

Changing or deleting a password

Before you can change or delete a password for opening a workbook, you must first be able to supply the current password you want to change to get the darned thing open. Assuming you can do this, all you have to do to change or get rid of the password is open the Info screen in the Backstage view (Alt+FI) and then choose the Encrypt with Password option from the Protect Workbook button's drop-down menu.

Excel opens the Encrypt Document dialog box with your password in the Password text box masked by asterisks. To then delete the password, simply remove all the asterisks from this text box before you click OK.

To reassign the password, replace the current password with the new one you want to assign by typing it over the original one. Then, when you click OK in the Encrypt Document dialog box, re-enter the new password in the Confirm Password dialog box and then click its OK button. Finally, after closing the Encrypt Document dialog box, you simply click the Save option on the File menu in the Backstage view to save your changes and return to the regular worksheet window.

REMEMBER

To change or delete the password for modifying the workbook, you must do this from the General Options dialog box. Click File ➪ Save As (Alt+FA) and then, after indicating the place to save the file in the Save As screen, click the More Options link to open the Save As dialog box where you can choose the General Options item from the Tools drop-down menu. You then follow the same procedure for changing or deleting the password that's entered into the Password to Modify text box in the General Options dialog box.

Protecting the Worksheet

After you have the worksheet the way you want it, you often need the help of Excel's Protection feature to keep it that way. Nothing's worse than having an inexperienced data entry operator doing major damage to the formulas and functions that you've worked so hard to build and validate. To keep the formulas and standard text in a spreadsheet safe from any unwarranted changes, you need to protect the worksheet.

Before you start using the Protect Sheet and Protect Workbook command buttons on the Review tab of the Ribbon, you need to understand how protection works in Excel. All cells in the workbook are either locked or unlocked for editing and hidden or unhidden for viewing.

Whenever you begin a new spreadsheet, all the cells in the workbook have locked as their editing status and unhidden as their display status. However, this default editing and display status in and of itself does nothing until you turn on protection with the Protect Sheet and Protect Workbook command buttons on the Review tab. At that time, you are then prevented from making any editing changes to all cells with a locked status and from viewing the contents of all cells on the Formula bar when they contain the cell cursor with a hidden status.

What this means in practice is that, prior to turning on worksheet protection, you go through the spreadsheet removing the Locked Protection format from all the cell ranges where you or your users need to be able to do data entry and editing even when the worksheet is protected. You also assign the Hidden Protection format to all cell ranges in the spreadsheet where you don't want the contents of the cell to be displayed when protection is turned on in the worksheet. Then, when that formatting is done, you activate protection for all the remaining Locked cells and block the Formula bar display for all the Hidden cells in the sheet.

TIP

When setting up your own spreadsheet templates, you will want to unlock all the cells where users need to input new data and keep locked all the cells that contain headings and formulas that never change. You may also want to hide cells with formulas if you're concerned that their display might tempt the users to waste time trying to fiddle with or finesse them. Then, turn on worksheet protection prior to saving the file in the template file format. (See Book 2, Chapter 1, for details.) You are then assured that all spreadsheets generated from that template automatically inherit the same level and type of protection as you assigned in the original spreadsheet.

Changing a cell's Locked and Hidden Protection formatting

To change the status of cells from locked to unlocked or from unhidden to hidden, you use the Locked and Hidden check boxes found on the Protection tab of the Format Cells dialog box (Ctrl+1).

To remove the Locked protection status from a cell range or nonadjacent selection, you follow these two steps:

1. **Select the range or ranges to be unlocked.**

   To select multiple ranges to create a nonadjacent cell selection, hold down the Ctrl key as you drag through each range.

2. **Click the Format command button on the Ribbon's Home tab and then click the Lock option near the bottom of its drop-down menu or press Alt+HOL.**

Excel lets you know that the cells that contain formulas in the selected range are no longer locked by adding tiny green triangles to the upper-left corner of each cell in the range that, when clicked, display an alert drop-down button whose tool tip reads, "This cell contains a formula and is not locked to protect it from being changed inadvertently." When you click this alert button, a drop-down menu with Lock Cell as one of its menu items appears. Note that as soon as you turn on protection in the sheet, these indicators disappear.

You can also change the protection status of a selected range of cells with the Locked check box on the Protection tab of the Format Cells dialog box. Simply open the Format Cells dialog box (Ctrl+1), click the Protection tab, and then click the Locked check box to remove the check mark before you click OK.

To hide the display of the contents of the cells in the current selection, you click the Hidden check box instead of the Locked check box on the Protection tab of the Format Cells dialog box before you click OK.

REMEMBER

Remember that changing the protection formatting of cell ranges in the worksheet (as described above) does nothing in and of itself. It's not until you turn on the protection for your worksheet (as outlined in the next section) that your unlocked and hidden cells work or appear any differently from the locked and unhidden cells. At that time, only unlocked cells accept edits, and only unhidden cells display their contents on the Formula bar when they contain the cell cursor.

Protecting the worksheet

When you've gotten all cell ranges that you want unlocked and hidden correctly formatted in the worksheet, you're ready to turn on protection. To do this, you click the Protect Sheet command button on the Ribbon's Review tab or press Alt+RPS to open the Protect Sheet dialog box, shown in Figure 1-3.

FIGURE 1-3:
Selecting the
protection
options in the
Protect Sheet
dialog box.

When you first open this dialog box, only the Protect Worksheet and Contents of Locked Cells check box at the very top and the Select Locked Cells and Select Unlocked Cells check boxes in the Allow All Users of This Worksheet To list box are selected. All the other check box options (including some that are not visible without scrolling up the Allow All Users of This Worksheet To list box) are deselected.

This means that if you click OK at this point, the *only* things that you'll be permitted to do in the worksheet are edit *unlocked* cells and select cell ranges (of any type: both locked and unlocked alike).

TIP

If you really want to keep other users out of all the locked cells in a worksheet, clear the Select Locked Cells check box in the Allow All Users of This Worksheet To list box to remove its check mark. That way, your users are completely restricted to just those unlocked ranges where you permit data input and content editing.

WARNING

Don't, however, deselect the Select Unlocked Cells check box as well as the Select Locked Cells check box, because doing this makes the cell pointer disappear from the worksheet, making the cell address in the Name Box on the Formula bar the sole way for you and your users to keep track of their position in the worksheet (which is, believe me, the quickest way to drive you and your users stark-raving mad).

Selecting what actions are allowed in a protected sheet

In addition to enabling users to select locked and unlocked cells in the worksheet, you can enable the following actions in the protected worksheet by selecting their check boxes in the Allow All Users of This Worksheet To list box of the Protect Sheet dialog box:

>> **Format Cells:** Enables the formatting of cells (with the exception of changing the locked and hidden status on the Protection tab of the Format Cells dialog box).

>> **Format Columns:** Enables formatting so that users can modify the column widths and hide and unhide columns.

>> **Format Rows:** Enables formatting so that users can modify the row heights and hide and unhide rows.

>> **Insert Columns:** Enables the insertion of new columns in the worksheet.

>> **Insert Rows:** Enables the insertion of new rows in the worksheet.

>> **Insert Hyperlinks:** Enables the insertion of new hyperlinks to other documents, both local and on the web. (See Book 4, Chapter 2, for details.)

>> **Delete Columns:** Enables the deletion of columns in the worksheet.

>> **Delete Rows:** Enables the deletion of rows in the worksheet.

>> **Sort:** Enables the sorting of data in unlocked cells in the worksheet. (See Book 6, Chapter 1, for details.)

>> **Use AutoFilter:** Enables the filtering of data in the worksheet. (See Book 6, Chapter 2, for more information.)

>> **Use PivotTable & PivotChart:** Enables the manipulation of pivot tables and pivot charts in the worksheet. (For more about pivot tables, see Book 7, Chapter 2.)

>> **Edit Objects:** Enables the editing of graphic objects, such as text boxes, embedded images, and the like, in the worksheet. (See Book 5, Chapter 2, for details.)

>> **Edit Scenarios:** Enables the editing of what-if scenarios, including modifying and deleting them. (For details of what-if scenarios, see Book 7, Chapter 1.)

Assigning a password to unprotect the sheet

In addition to enabling particular actions in the protected worksheet, you can also assign a password that's required in order to remove the protections from the protected worksheet. When entering a password in the Password to Unprotect Sheet text box of the Protect Sheet dialog box, you observe the same guidelines as when assigning a password to open or to make changes in the workbook (255 characters maximum that can consist of a combination of letters, numbers, and spaces, with the letters being case-sensitive).

As with assigning a password to open or make changes to a workbook, when you enter a password (whose characters are masked with asterisks) in the Password to Unprotect Sheet text box and then click OK, Excel displays the Confirm Password dialog box. Here, you must accurately reproduce the password you just entered (including upper- and lowercase letters) before Excel turns on the sheet protection and assigns the password for removing protection.

If you don't successfully reproduce the password, when you click OK in the Confirm Password dialog box, Excel replaces it with an alert dialog box indicating that the confirmation password is not identical to the one you entered in the Protect Sheet dialog box. When you click OK to clear this alert dialog box, you are returned to the Protect Sheet dialog box, where you may modify the password in the Password to Unprotect Sheet text box before you click OK and try confirming the password again.

As soon as you accurately reproduce the password in the Confirm Password dialog box, Excel closes the Protect Sheet dialog box and enables protection for that sheet, using whatever settings you designated in that dialog box.

WARNING

If you don't assign a password to unprotect the sheet, any user with a modicum of Excel knowledge can lift the worksheet protection and make any manner of changes to its contents, including wreaking havoc on its computational capabilities by corrupting its formulas. Keep in mind that it makes little sense to turn on the protection in a worksheet if you're going to permit anybody to turn it off by simply clicking the Unprotect Sheet command button on the Review tab (which automatically replaces the Protect Sheet command button as soon as you turn on protection in the worksheet).

Removing protection from a worksheet

When you assign protection to a sheet, your input and editing are restricted solely to unlocked cells in the worksheet, and you can perform only those additional actions that you enabled in the Allow Users of this Worksheet To list box. If you try to replace, delete, or otherwise modify a locked cell in the protected worksheet, Excel displays an alert dialog box with the following message:

```
The cell or chart you're trying to change is on a protected
    sheet.
```

The message then goes on to tell you

```
To make a change, unprotect the sheet. You might be requested to
    enter a password.
```

If you've assigned a password to unprotect the sheet, when you click the Unprotect Sheet button, the program displays the Unprotect Sheet dialog box, where you must enter the password exactly as you assigned it. As soon as you remove the protection by entering the correct password in this dialog box and clicking OK, Excel turns off the protection in the sheet, and you can once again make any kinds of modifications to its structure and contents in both the locked and unlocked cells.

REMEMBER

Keep in mind that when you protect a worksheet, only the data and graphics on that particular worksheet are protected. This means that you can modify the data and graphics on other sheets of the same workbook without removing protection. If you have data or graphics on other sheets of the same workbook that also need protecting, you need to activate that sheet and then repeat the entire procedure for protecting it as well (including unlocking cells that need to be edited and selecting which other actions, if any, to enable in the worksheet, and whether to assign a password to unprotect the sheet) before distributing the workbook. When assigning passwords to unprotect the various sheets of the workbook, you may want to stick with a single password rather than have to worry about remembering a different password for each sheet, which is a bit much, don't you think?

Enabling cell range editing by certain users

You can use the Allow Users to Edit Ranges command button in the Protect group on the Review tab of the Ribbon to enable the editing of particular ranges in the protected worksheet by certain users. When you use this feature, you give certain users permission to edit particular cell ranges, provided that they can correctly provide the password you assign to that range.

To give access to particular ranges in a protected worksheet, you follow these steps:

1. **Click the Allow Users to Edit Ranges command button on the Ribbon's Review tab or press Alt+RU1.**

Note that the Allow Users to Edit Ranges command button is grayed out and unavailable if the worksheet is currently protected. In that case, you must remove protection by clicking the Unprotect Sheet command button on the Review tab before you retry Step 1.

Excel opens the Allow Users to Edit Ranges dialog box, where you can add the ranges you want to assign, as shown in Figure 1-4.

2. **Click the New button.**

Doing this opens the New Range dialog box where you give the range a title, define its cell selection, and provide the range password, as shown in Figure 1-5.

3. **If you wish, type a name for the range in the Title text box; otherwise, Excel assigns a name such as Range1, Range2, and so on.**

Next, you designate the cell range or nonadjacent cell selection to which access is restricted.

4. Click the Refers to Cells text box and then type in the address of the cell range (without removing the = sign) or select the range or ranges in the worksheet.

Next, you need to enter a password that's required to get access to the range. Like all other passwords in Excel, this one can be up to 255 characters long, mixing letters, numbers, and spaces. Pay attention to the use of upper- and lowercase letters because the range password is case-sensitive.

5. Type the password for accessing the range in the Range Password dialog box.

You need to use the Permissions button in the New Range dialog box to open the Permissions dialog box for the range you're setting.

6. Click the Permissions button in the Range Password dialog box.

Next, you need to add the users who are to have access to this range.

7. Click the Add button in the Permissions dialog box.

Doing this opens the Select Users or Groups dialog box, where you designate the names of the users to have access to the range.

8. Click the name of the user in the Enter the Object Names to Select list box at the bottom of the Select Users or Groups dialog box. To select multiple users from this list, hold down the Ctrl key as you click each username.

If this list box is empty, click the Advanced button to expand the Select Users or Groups dialog box and then click the Find Now button to locate all users for your location. You can then click the name or Ctrl+click the names you want to add from this list, and then when you click OK, Excel returns you to the original form of the Select Users or Groups dialog box and adds these names to its Enter the Object Names to Select list box.

9. Click OK in the Select Users or Groups dialog box.

Doing this returns you to the Permissions dialog box where the names you've selected are now listed in the Group or User Names list box. Now you need to set the permissions for each user. When you first add users, each one is permitted to edit the range without a password. To restrict the editing to only those who have the range password, you need to click each name and then select the Deny check box.

10. Click the name of the first user who must know the password and then select the Deny check box in the Permissions For list box.

You need to repeat this step for each person in the Group or User Names list box that you want to restrict in this manner. (See Figure 1-6.)

11. Repeat Step 10 for each user who must know the password and then click OK in the Permissions dialog box.

As soon as you click OK, Excel displays a warning alert dialog box, letting you know that you are setting a deny permission that takes precedence over any allowed entries, so that if the person is a member of two groups, one with an Allow entry and the other with a Deny entry, the deny entry permission rules (meaning that the person has to know the range password).

12. Click the Yes button in the Security alert dialog box.

Doing this closes this dialog box and returns you to the New Range dialog box.

13. Click OK in the New Range dialog box.

Doing this opens the Confirm Password dialog box where you must accurately reproduce the range password.

14. Type the range password in the Reenter Password to Proceed text box and then click the OK button.

Doing this returns you to the Allow Users to Edit Ranges dialog box where the title and cell reference of the new range are displayed in the Ranges Unlocked by a Password When Sheet Is Protected list box, as shown in Figure 1-7.

If you need to define other ranges available to other users in the worksheet, you can do so by repeating Steps 2 through 14.

When you finish adding ranges to the Allow Users to Edit Ranges dialog box, you're ready to protect the worksheet. If you want to retain a record of the ranges you've defined, go to Step 15. Otherwise, skip to Step 16.

15. (Optional) Select the Paste Permissions Information Into a New Workbook check box if you want to create a new workbook that contains all the permissions information.

When you select this check box, Excel creates a new workbook whose first worksheet lists all the ranges you've assigned, along with the users who may gain access by providing the range password. You can then save this workbook for your records. Note that the range password is not listed on this worksheet — if you want to add it, be sure that you password-protect the workbook so that only you can open it.

Now, you're ready to protect the worksheet. If you want to do this from within the Allow Users to Edit Ranges dialog box, you click the Protect Sheet button to open the Protect Sheet dialog box. If you want to protect the worksheet later on, you click OK to close the Allow Users to Edit Ranges dialog box and then click the Protect Sheet command button on the Review tab of the Ribbon (or press Alt+RPS) when you're ready to activate the worksheet protection.

16. Click the Protect Sheet button to protect the worksheet; otherwise, click the OK button to close the Allow Users to Edit Ranges dialog box.

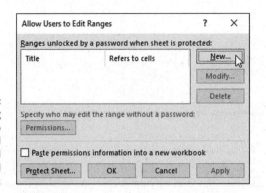

FIGURE 1-4:
Designating
the range to
be unlocked
by a password
in a protected
worksheet.

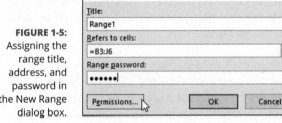

FIGURE 1-5:
Assigning the
range title,
address, and
password in
the New Range
dialog box.

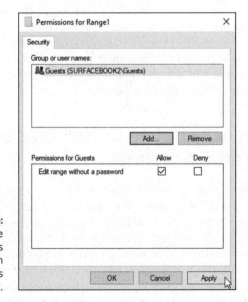

FIGURE 1-6:
Setting the
permissions
for each user in
the Permissions
dialog box.

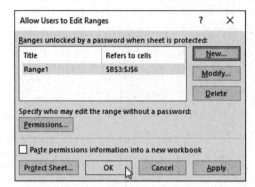

FIGURE 1-7:
Getting ready to
protect the sheet
in the Allow Users
to Edit Ranges
dialog box.

If you click the Protect Sheet button, Excel opens the Protect Sheet dialog box, where you can set a password to unprotect the sheet. This dialog box is also where you select the actions that you permit all users to perform in the protected worksheet (as outlined earlier in this chapter).

After you turn on protection in the worksheet, only the users you've designated are able to edit the cell range or ranges you've defined. Of course, you need to supply the range password to all the users allowed to do editing in the range or ranges at the time you distribute the workbook to them.

TIP

Be sure to assign a password to unprotect the worksheet at the time you protect the worksheet if you want to prevent unauthorized users from being able to make changes to the designated editing ranges in the worksheet. If you don't, any user can make changes by turning off the worksheet protection and thereby gaining access to the Allow Users to Edit Ranges command by clicking the Unprotect Sheet command button on the Review tab of the Ribbon.

Doing data entry in the unlocked cells of a protected worksheet

The best part of protecting a worksheet is that you and your users can jump right to unlocked cells and avoid even dealing with the locked ones (which you can't change, anyway) by using the Tab and Shift+Tab keys to navigate the worksheet. All you have to do is click the Select Locked Cells check box option to deselect it when you protect the worksheet. (See Protecting the worksheet" earlier in this chapter.) When you press the Tab key in a protected worksheet when the Select Locked Cells option is turned off, Excel jumps the cell cursor to the next unlocked cell to the right of the current one in that same row. When you reach the last unlocked cell in that row, the program then jumps to the first unlocked cell in the rows below. To move back to a previous unlocked cell, you press Shift+Tab. When Excel reaches the last unlocked cell in the spreadsheet, it automatically jumps back to the very first unlocked cell on the sheet.

Of course, provided that you haven't changed the behavior of the Enter key in the Editing Options section on the Advanced tab of the Excel Options dialog box (File⇨Options or Alt+FT), you can also use the Enter key to move down the columns instead of across the rows. However, pressing the Enter key to progress down a column selects locked cells in that column as well as the unlocked ones, whereas pressing the Tab key skips all those cells with the Locked protection format.

Figure 1-8 illustrates how you can put the Tab key to good use in filling out and navigating a protected worksheet. This figure shows a worksheet created from a Spa Holiday Hot Tubs invoice template. Because this invoice worksheet in the original template is protected, all worksheets generated from the template will be protected as well. The only cells that are unlocked in this sheet are the cells in the following ranges:

» F4:F6 with the invoice number, date, and customer ID fields

» C9:C13 with the name, company name, street address, city, state and zip, and phone number fields

» C16:D16 with the salesperson and job fields

» Cell G16 with the due date field

» C19:F38 with the quantity, description, and unit price fields

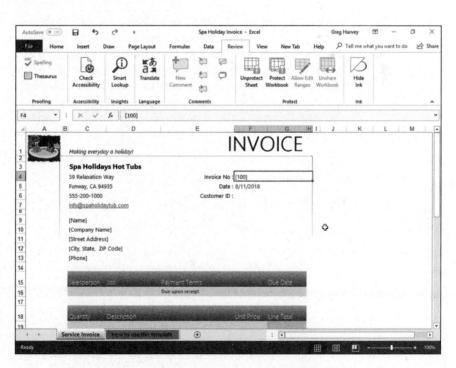

FIGURE 1-8:
Using the Tab key to move from unlocked cell to unlocked cell in a protected worksheet.

Protecting Workbooks and Worksheet Data

All the rest of the cells in this worksheet are locked and off limits.

To fill in the data for this new invoice, you can press the Tab key to complete the data entry in each field such as Invoice No., Date, Customer ID, Name, Company Name, Street Address, and so on. By pressing Tab, you don't have to waste time moving through the locked cells that contain headings that you can't modify anyway. If you need to back up and return to the previous field in the invoice, you just press Shift+Tab to go back to the previous unlocked cell.

TIP

To make it impossible for the user to select anything but the unlocked cells in the protected worksheet, you clear the Select Locked Cells check box in the Allow All Users of This Worksheet To list box of the Protect Sheet dialog box.

Protecting the workbook

There is one last level of protection that you can apply to your spreadsheet files, and that is protecting the entire workbook. When you protect the workbook, you ensure that its users can't change the structure of the file by adding, deleting, or even moving and renaming any of its worksheets. To protect your workbook, you click the Protect Workbook command button on the Ribbon's Review tab and then select the Protect Structure and Windows option from its drop-down menu (or press Alt+RPW).

Excel displays a Protect Structure and Windows dialog box like the one shown in Figure 1-9. This dialog box contains two check boxes: Structure (which is automatically selected) and Windows (which is not selected). This dialog box also contains a Password (Optional) text box where you can enter a password that must be supplied before you can unprotect the workbook. Like every other password in Excel, the password to unprotect the workbook can be up to 255 characters maximum, consisting of a combination of letters, numbers, and spaces, with all the letters being case-sensitive.

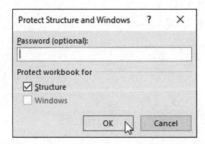

FIGURE 1-9:
Protecting a workbook in the Protect Structure and Windows dialog box.

When you protect a workbook with the Structure check box selected, Excel prevents you or your users from doing any of the following tasks to the file:

>> Inserting new worksheets

>> Deleting existing worksheets

>> Renaming worksheets

>> Hiding or viewing hidden worksheets

>> Moving or copying worksheets to another workbook

>> Displaying the source data for a cell in a pivot table or displaying a table's Report Filter fields on separate worksheets (see Book 7, Chapter 2, for details)

>> Creating a summary report with the Scenario Manager (see Book 7, Chapter 1, for details)

When you turn on protection for a workbook after selecting the Windows check box in the Protect Structure and Windows dialog box, Excel prevents you from changing the size or position of the workbook's windows (not usually something you need to control).

After you've enabled protection in a workbook, you can then turn it off by choosing the Protect Structure and Windows option on the Unprotect Workbook command button's drop-down menu or by pressing Alt+RPW again. If you've assigned a password to unprotect the workbook, you must accurately reproduce it in the Password text box in the Unprotect Workbook dialog box that then appears.

IN THIS CHAPTER

» Linking your spreadsheet to other Excel workbooks, Office documents, and web pages

» Linking to e-mail addresses

» Following the links that you create in the worksheet

» Editing hyperlinks in a worksheet

» Creating formulas that use the HYPERLINK function

Chapter **2**

Using Hyperlinks

The subject of this chapter is linking your worksheet with other documents through the use of *hyperlinks.* Hyperlinks are the kinds of links used on the web to take you immediately from one web page to another or from one website to another. Such links can be attached to text (thus the term, *hypertext*) or to graphics such as buttons or pictures. The most important aspect of a hyperlink is that it immediately takes you to its destination whenever you click the text or button to which it is attached.

In an Excel worksheet, you can create hyperlinks that take you to a different part of the same worksheet, to another worksheet in the same workbook, to another workbook or other type of document on your hard drive, or to a web page on your company's intranet or on the World Wide Web.

Hyperlinks 101

To add hyperlinks in an Excel worksheet, you must define two things:

» The object to which you want to anchor the link and then click to activate

» The destination to which the link takes you when activated

The objects to which you can attach hyperlinks include any text that you enter into a cell or any graphic object that you draw or import into the worksheet. (See Book 5, Chapter 2, for details on adding graphics to your worksheet.) The destinations that you can specify for links can be a new cell or range, the same workbook file, or another file outside the workbook.

The destinations that you can specify for hyperlinks that take you to another place in the same workbook file include

>> **The cell reference** of a cell on any of the worksheets in the workbook that you want to go to when you click the hyperlink.

>> **The range name** of the group of cells that you want to select when you click the hyperlink. The range name must already exist at the time you create the link.

The destinations that you can specify for hyperlinks that take you outside the current workbook include

>> **The filename** of an existing file that you want to open when you click the hyperlink. This file can be another workbook file or any other type of document that your computer can open.

>> **The URL address** of a web page that you want to visit when you click the hyperlink. This page can be on your company's intranet or on the World Wide Web and is opened in your web browser.

>> **An e-mail address** for a new message that you want to create in your e-mail program when you click the hyperlink. You must specify the recipient's e-mail address and the subject of the new message when you create the link.

Adding hyperlinks

The steps for creating a new hyperlink in the worksheet are very straightforward. The only thing you need to do beforehand is to add the jump text in the cell where you want the link or to draw or import the graphic object to which the link is to be attached (as described in Book 5, Chapter 2). Then, to add a hyperlink to the text in this cell or the graphic object, follow these steps:

1. **Position the cell pointer in the cell containing the text or click the graphic object to which you want to anchor the hyperlink.**

   After you have selected the cell with the text or the graphic object, you're ready to open the Insert Hyperlink dialog box.

2. **Click the Hyperlink command button on the Ribbon's Insert tab or press Alt+NI or Ctrl+K.**

The Insert Hyperlink dialog box opens (similar to the one shown in Figure 2-1). If you selected a graphic object or a cell that contains some entry besides text before opening this dialog box, you notice that the Text to Display text box contains <<Selection in Document>> and that this box is grayed out (because there isn't any text to edit when anchoring a link to a graphic). If you selected a cell with a text entry, that entry appears in the Text to Display text box. You can edit this text in this box; however, be aware that any change that you make to it here is reflected in the current cell when you close the Insert Hyperlink dialog box.

The ScreenTip button located to the immediate right of the Text to Display text box enables you to add text describing the function of the link when you position the mouse pointer over the cell or graphic object to which the link is attached. To add a ScreenTip for your link, follow Step 3. Note that if you don't add your own ScreenTip, Excel automatically creates its own ScreenTip that lists the destination of the new link when you position the mouse pointer on its anchor.

3. **(Optional) Click the ScreenTip button and then type the text that you want to appear next to the mouse pointer in the Set Hyperlink ScreenTip dialog box before you click OK.**

By default, Excel selects the Existing File or Web Page button in the Link To area on the left side of the Insert Hyperlink dialog box, thus enabling you to assign the link destination to a file on your hard drive or to a web page. To link to a cell or cell range in the current workbook, click the Place in This Document button. To link to a new document, click the Create New Document button. To link to a new e-mail message, click the E-Mail Address button.

4. **Select the type of destination for the new link by clicking its button in the Link To panel on the left side of the Insert Hyperlink dialog box.**

Now all that you need to do is to specify the destination for your link. How you do this depends on which type of link you're adding; see the following instructions for details.

- **Linking to a cell or named range in the current workbook:** After clicking the Place in This Document button in the Link To panel, enter the address of the cell to link to in the Type the Cell Reference text box and then click the name of the sheet that contains this cell listed under the Cell Reference range in the Or Select a Place in This Document list box. To link to a named range, simply click its name under Defined Names in the Or Select a Place in This Document list box.

- **Linking to an existing file:** After clicking the Existing File or Web Page button in the Link To panel, open its folder in the Look In drop-down list box and then click its file icon in the list box that appears immediately below this box. If you're linking to a web page, click the Address text box and enter the URL address (as in https:// and so on) there. If the file or web page that you select contains bookmarks (or range names, in the case of another Excel workbook) that name specific locations in the file to which you link, click the Bookmark button and then click the name of the location (bookmark) in the Select Place in Document dialog box before you click OK.

- **Creating a new e-mail message:** After clicking the E-Mail Address button in the Link To panel, enter the e-mail address (as in gharvey@mindovermedia.com) in the E-Mail Address text box and then click the Subject text box and enter the subject of the new e-mail message.

5. **Specify the destination for the new hyperlink by using the text boxes and list boxes that appear for the type of link destination that you selected.**

   Now you're ready to create the link.

6. **Click the OK button in the Insert Hyperlink dialog box.**

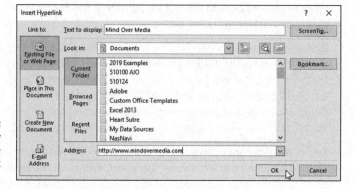

FIGURE 2-1:
Creating a new hyperlink in the Insert Hyperlink dialog box.

As soon as you click OK, Excel closes the Insert Hyperlink dialog box and returns you to the worksheet with the new link. If you anchored your new hyperlink to a graphic object, that object is still selected in the worksheet. (To deselect the object, click a cell outside its boundaries.) If you anchored your hyperlink to text in the current cell, the text now appears in blue and is underlined. (You may not be able to see the underlining until you move the cell cursor out of the cell.)

When you position the mouse pointer over the cell with the hypertext or the graphic object with the hyperlink, the mouse or Touch pointer changes from a thick, white cross to a hand with the index finger pointing upward. The ScreenTip that you assigned appears below and to the right of the hand mouse pointer.

If you didn't assign your own ScreenTip to the hyperlink when creating it, Excel adds its own message that shows the URL destination of the link. If the link is a hypertext link (that is, if it's anchored to a cell containing a text entry), the message in the ScreenTip also adds the following message:

```
Click once to follow. Click and hold to select this cell.
```

Follow that link!

To follow a hyperlink (assuming that your tablet or computer can connect to the Internet), click the link text or graphic object with the hand mouse or Touch pointer. Excel then takes you to the destination. If the destination is a cell in the workbook, Excel makes that cell current. If the destination is a cell range, Excel selects the range and makes the first cell of the range current. If this destination is a document created with another application program, Excel launches the application program (assuming that it's available on the current computer). If this destination is a web page on the World Wide Web, Excel launches your web browser, connects you to the Internet, and then opens the page in the browser.

After you follow a hypertext link to its destination, the color of its text changes from the traditional blue to a dark shade of purple (without affecting its underlining). This color change indicates that the hyperlink has been followed. (Note, however, that graphic hyperlinks don't show any change in color after you follow them.) Followed hypertext links regain their original blue color when you reopen their workbooks in Excel.

Editing hyperlinks

REMEMBER

Excel makes it easy to edit any hyperlink that you've added to your spreadsheet. The only trick to editing a link is that you have to be careful not to activate the link during the editing process. This means that you must always remember to right-click the link's hypertext or graphic to select the link that you want to edit because clicking results only in activating the link.

When you right-click a link, Excel displays its shortcut menu. If you want to modify the link's destination or ScreenTip, click Edit Hyperlink on this shortcut menu. This action opens the Edit Hyperlink dialog box with the same options as the Insert Hyperlink dialog box (shown previously in Figure 2-1). You can then use the Link To buttons on the left side of the dialog box to modify the link's destination or the ScreenTip button to add or change the ScreenTip text.

Removing a hyperlink

If you want to remove the hyperlink from a cell entry or graphic object without getting rid of the text entry or the graphic, right-click the cell or graphic and then click the Remove Hyperlink item on the cell's or object's shortcut menu.

If you want to clear the cell of both its link and text entry, click the Delete item on the cell's shortcut menu. To get rid of a graphic object along with its hyperlink, right-click the object (this action opens its shortcut menu) and then immediately click the object to remove the shortcut menu without either deselecting the graphic or activating the hyperlink. At this point, you can press the Delete key to delete both the graphic and the associated link.

Copying and moving a hyperlink

When you need to copy or move a hyperlink to a new place in the worksheet, you can use either the drag-and-drop or the cut-and-paste method. Again, the main challenge to using either method is selecting the link without activating it because clicking the cell or graphic object containing the link results in catapulting you over to the link's destination point.

To select a cell that contains hypertext, use the arrow keys to position the cell cursor in that cell or use the Go To feature (F5 or Ctrl+G) and enter the cell's address in the Go To dialog box to move the cell cursor there. To select a graphic object that contains a hyperlink, right-click the graphic to select it as well as to display its shortcut menu and then immediately click the graphic (with the left mouse button) to remove the shortcut menu while keeping the object selected.

After you have selected the cell or graphic with the hyperlink, you can move the link by clicking the Cut command button on the Home tab of the Ribbon (Ctrl+X) or copy it by clicking the Copy command button (Ctrl+C) and then paste it into its new position by clicking the Paste command button (Ctrl+V). When moving or copying hypertext from one cell to another, you can just click the cell where the link is to be moved or copied and then press the Enter key.

To move the selected link by using the drag-and-drop method, drag the cell or object with the mouse pointer (in the shape of a white arrowhead pointing to a black double-cross) and then release the mouse button to drop the hypertext or graphic into its new position. To copy the link, be sure to hold down the Ctrl key (which changes the pointer to a white arrowhead with a plus sign to its right) as you drag the outline of the cell or object.

REMEMBER

When attempting to move or copy a cell by using the drag-and-drop method, remember that you have to position the thick, white-cross mouse pointer on one of the borders of the cell before the pointer changes to a white arrowhead pointing to a black double-cross. If you position the pointer anywhere within the cell's borders, the mouse changes to the hand with the index finger pointing upward, indicating that the hyperlink is active.

Using the HYPERLINK Function

Instead of using the Hyperlink command button on the Insert tab of the Ribbon, you can use Excel's HYPERLINK function to create a hypertext link. (You can't use this function to attach a hyperlink to a graphic object.) The HYPERLINK function uses the following syntax:

```
HYPERLINK(link_location,[friendly_name])
```

The *link_location* argument specifies the name of the document to open on your local hard drive, on a network server (designated by a UNC address), or on the company's intranet or the World Wide Web (designated by the URL address — see the sidebar "How to tell a UNC from a URL address and when to care" for details). The optional *friendly_name* argument is the hyperlink text that appears in the cell where you enter the HYPERLINK function. If you omit this argument, Excel displays the text specified as the *link_location* argument in the cell.

When specifying the arguments for a HYPERLINK function that you type on the Formula bar (as opposed to one that you create by using the Insert Function feature by filling in the text boxes in the Function Arguments dialog box), you must remember to enclose both the *link_location* and *friendly_name* arguments in closed double quotes. For example, to enter a HYPERLINK function in a cell that takes you to the home page of the *For Dummies* website and displays the text "Dummies Home Page" in the cell, enter the following in the cell:

```
=HYPERLINK("http://www.dummies.com","Dummies Home Page")
```

TECHNICAL STUFF

HOW TO TELL A UNC FROM A URL ADDRESS AND WHEN TO CARE

The address that you use to specify a remote hyperlink destination comes in two basic flavors: UNC (Universal Naming Convention) and the more familiar URL (Universal Resource Locator). The type of address that you use depends on whether the destination file resides on a server on a network (in which case, you use a UNC address) or on a corporate intranet or the Internet (in which case, you use a URL address). Note that URLs also appear in many flavors, the most popular being those that use the Hypertext Transfer Protocol (HTTP) and begin with `http://` and those that use the File Transfer Protocol (FTP) and start with `ftp://`.

The UNC address for destination files on network servers start with two backslash characters (\\), following this format:

```
\\server\share\path\filename
```

In this format, the name of the file server containing the file replaces *server*, the name of the shared folder replaces *share*, the directory path specifying any subfolders of the shared folder replaces *path*, and the file's complete filename (including any filename extension, such as `.xls` for Excel worksheet) replaces *filename*.

The URL address for files published on websites follows this format:

```
internet service//internet address/path/filename
```

In this format, *internet service* is replaced with the Internet protocol to be used (either HTTP or FTP in most cases), *internet address* is replaced with the domain name (such as `www.dummies.com`) or the number assigned to the internet server, *path* is the directory path of the file, and *filename* is the complete name (including filename extensions such as `.htm` or `.html` for web pages).

Chapter **3**

Preparing a Workbook for Distribution

G iven Excel 2019's emphasis on saving your workbooks on your OneDrive in the cloud, it behooves you to be familiar not only with Excel's sharing capabilities (discussed at length in the following chapter), but also with its capabilities for checking compatibility and digitally signing the document before it goes out for review.

In this chapter, you discover how to check your workbook to prepare it for distribution. As part of this process, you may want to just comment on aspects of the spreadsheet and suggest possible changes rather than make these changes yourself or even mark up the spreadsheet with digital ink if your computer is equipped with a graphics tablet or running Excel 2019 on some sort of touchscreen device such as a Microsoft Surface Pro tablet. In this chapter, you find out how to get your two cents in by annotating a spreadsheet with text notes that indicate suggested improvements or corrections, as well as highlight potential change areas with ink.

Getting Your Workbook Ready for Review

The Info screen in the Excel 2019 Backstage view (Alt+FI) shown in Figure 3-1 enables you to prepare your workbook for distribution by inspecting the properties of your workbook. To do this, click the Check for Issues button in the Info screen and then select any of the following options:

>> **Inspect Document** to open the Document Inspector, which checks your documents for hidden content and metadata (data about the document). You can delete any such content that you find prior to distributing the file by clicking the Remove All button.

>> **Check Accessibility** to have Excel scan the workbook file for information that people with disabilities (particularly, some sort of sight impairment) might have difficulty with.

>> **Check Compatibility** to check a workbook file saved with the default Excel Workbook (*.xlsx) XML file format option for any loss in fidelity when it's saved in the older Excel 97–2003 Workbook (*.xls) binary file format.

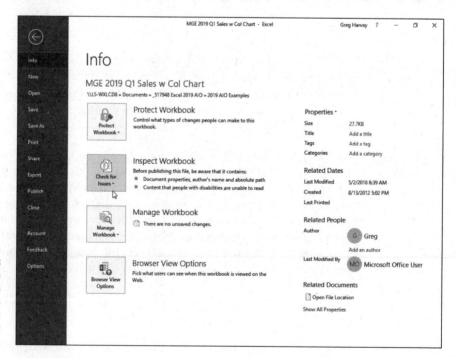

FIGURE 3-1:
Checking a workbook's properties in its Info screen in the Excel 2019 Backstage view.

Below the Check for Issues button, the Info screen contains a Manage Workbook button that, when clicked, gives you the following two options for recovering or clearing up draft versions of the workbook so that only the final version is available for sharing:

» **Check Out** to edit a private copy of the workbook and prevent others from making any changes to it

» **Recover Unsaved Versions** to enable you to browse all the versions of the current workbook that were closed without saving the final changes using Excel's AutoRecover feature (see Book 2, Chapter 1 for details)

At the very bottom of the Info screen, you find a Browser View Options button that, when clicked, opens the Browser View Options dialog box with a Show and Parameters tab. This tab enables you to control what parts of your workbook are displayed and can be edited when the file is shared online.

Adding properties to a workbook

You can add information about your workbook document (called metadata) in the Info panel in the Backstage view, using the various fields displayed in its right column (refer to Figure 3-1), which you open by clicking File ⇨ Info or pressing Alt+FI. You can then use the metadata that you enter into the Title, Tags, Categories, and Author fields in the Info panel in all the Windows quick searches or file searches you perform. Doing so enables you to quickly locate the file for opening in Excel for further editing and printing or distributing to others to review.

When entering more than one piece of data into a particular field such as Title, Tags, or Categories, separate each piece with a comma. When you're done adding metadata information to the fields, close the Info panel by clicking the File menu at the top of the panel or pressing Esc.

Click the Show All Properties link at the bottom of the right column of the Info screen containing the text boxes for particular document properties to add text boxes for additional document metadata fields including Comments, Template, Status, Subject, Hyperlink Base, Company, and Manager.

Digitally signing a document

Excel 2019 enables you to add digital signatures to the workbook files that you send out for review. After checking the spreadsheet and verifying its accuracy and readiness for distribution, you can (assuming that you have the authority within your company) digitally sign the workbook in one of two ways:

>> Add a visible signature line as a graphic object in the workbook that contains your name, the date of the signing, your title, and, if you have a digital tablet connected to your computer or are running Excel on a touchscreen device, your inked handwritten signature.

>> Add an invisible signature to the workbook indicated by the Digital Signature icon on the status bar and metadata added to the document that verifies the source of the workbook.

By adding a digital signature, you warrant the following three things about the Excel workbook you're about to distribute:

>> **Authenticity:** The person who signs the Excel workbook is the person he says he is (and not somebody else posing as the signer).

>> **Integrity:** The content of the file has not been modified in any way since the workbook was digitally signed.

>> **Nonrepudiation:** The signer stands behind the content of the workbook and vouches for its origin.

To make these assurances, the digital signature you add to the workbook must be valid in the following ways:

>> The certificate that is associated with the digital signature must be issued to the signing publisher by a reputable certificate authority.

>> The certificate must be current and valid.

>> The signing publisher must be deemed trustworthy.

REMEMBER

Microsoft partners such as Comodo, GlobalSign, and IdenTrust offer digital ID services to which you can subscribe. As reputable certificate authorities, their protection services vouch for your trustworthiness as a signing publisher and the currency of the certificates associated with your digital signatures. In addition, they enable you to set the permissions for the workbook that determine who can open the document and how they can use it. To sign up with one of these services, choose the Add Signature Services option from the Add a Signature Line button's drop-down menu and then follow the links on the Find Digital ID or Digital Signature Services web page.

To add a digital signature to your finalized workbook, you follow these steps:

1. **Inspect the worksheet data, save all final changes in the workbook file, and then position the cell pointer in a blank cell in the vicinity where you want the signature line graphic object to appear.**

   Excel adds the signature line graphic object in the area containing the cell pointer. If you don't move the cell cursor to a blank area, you may have to move the signature line graphic so that graphic's box doesn't obscure existing worksheet data or other graphics or embedded charts.

2. **Click Insert ➪ Add a Signature Line ➪ Microsoft Office Signature Line in the Text group on the Ribbon (Alt+NG).**

   Excel displays the Signature Setup dialog box similar to the one shown in Figure 3-2.

3. **Type the signer's name into the Suggested Signer text box and then press Tab.**

4. **Type the signer's title into the Suggested Signer's Title text box and then press Tab.**

5. **Type the signer's e-mail address into the Suggested Signer's E-Mail Address text box.**

6. **(Optional) Select the Allow the Signer to Add Comments in the Sign Dialog check box if you want to add your own comments.**

7. **(Optional) Deselect the Show Sign Date in Signature Line check box if you don't want the date displayed as part of the digital signature.**

8. **Click OK to close the Signature Setup dialog box.**

   Excel adds a signature line graphic object in the vicinity of the cell cursor with a big X that contains your name and title (shown in Figure 3-3).

9. **Double-click this signature line graphic object or right-click the object and then choose Sign from its shortcut menu.**

   If you don't have a digital ID with one of the subscription services or aren't a Windows Live subscriber, Excel opens a Get a Digital ID alert dialog box asking you if you want to get one now. Click Yes and then follow the links on the Available Digital IDs web page to subscribe to one.

   Otherwise, Excel opens the Sign dialog box similar to the one shown in Figure 3-3.

10. **Add your signature to the list box containing the insertion point.**

    To add your signature, click the Select Image link on the right, select a graphic file that contains a picture of your handwritten signature in the Select Signature Image dialog box, and then click Select. If you're using a touchscreen device or your computer has a digital tablet connected to it, you add this signature by physically signing your signature with digital ink.

11. Click the Commitment Type drop-down list box and choose one of the options from its drop-down menu: Created and Approved This Document, Approved This Document, or Created This Document.

If you selected the Allow the Signer to Add Comments in the Sign Dialog check box in Step 6, the Sign dialog box contains a Purpose for Signing This Document text box that you fill out in Step 12.

12. Click the Purpose for Signing This Document text box and then type the reason for digitally signing the workbook.

13. (Optional) Click the Details button to open the Additional Signing Information dialog box, where you can add the signer's role and title as well as information on the place where the document was created.

14. (Optional) Click the Change command button to open the Windows Securities dialog box, click the name of the person whose certificate you want to use in the list box, and then click OK.

By default, Excel issues a digital certificate for the person whose name is entered in the Suggested Signer text box back in Step 3. If you want to use a certificate issued to someone else in the organization, follow Step 12. Otherwise, proceed to Step 13.

15. Click the Sign button to close the Sign dialog box.

Excel closes the Sign dialog box.

Immediately after closing the Sign dialog box, Excel adds your name to the digital signature graphic object and displays the MARKED AS FINAL alert at the top of the worksheet as shown in Figure 3-4.

FIGURE 3-2:
Filling out the signing information in the Signature Setup dialog box.

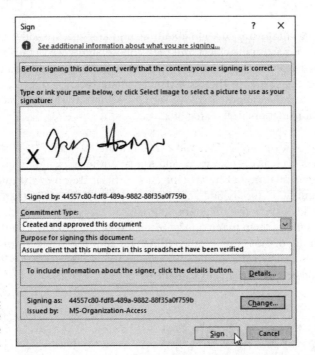

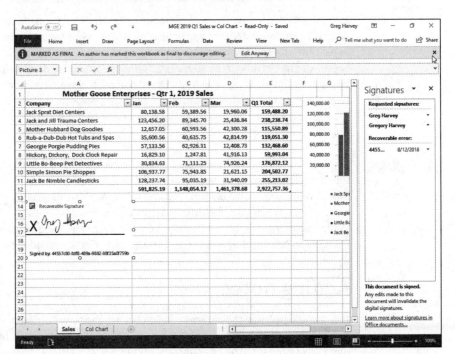

Preparing a Workbook
for Distribution

To display all the information about the digital signature added to the workbook, right-click its graphic object and then choose Signature Details from its shortcut menu. To delete a digital signature from a workbook (which you need to do if you discover the sheets in the book require modification), right-click the signature graphic and then choose Remove Signature from its shortcut menu and click OK in its confirmation alert dialog box.

In place of a signature line, you can add a digital stamp (traditionally, in Asian countries such as China, Japan, and Korea, authorities sign a document not with a written signature but by affixing their official stamp to the document, usually in red ink). To literally add your stamp of approval, rather than your signature, to a workbook, choose the Stamp Signature Line option from the Signature Line button's drop-down menu on the Insert tab of the Ribbon. You then follow steps very similar to those previously outlined for adding a digital signature line, except that you must select a graphic file that contains the image you want stamped in the workbook in lieu of your signature.

Annotating Workbooks

Even if you don't save your workbooks on a OneDrive or use Excel on a network, you still can annotate your worksheet by adding your notes to the cells of a workbook that ask for clarification or suggest changes, and then you can distribute copies of the workbook by e-mail to other people who need to review and, perhaps, respond to your remarks. Excel makes it easy to annotate the cells of a worksheet, and the Notes command button's options on the Review tab of the Ribbon make it easy to review these notes prior to e-mailing the workbook to others who have to review the notes, and even reply to suggested changes.

If you're running Excel 2019 on a computer equipped with a digital tablet or on a touchscreen device such as a Windows tablet, the Review tab of your Ribbon has a Start Inking command button (not included on this tab when running Excel on a regular PC). When you click the Start Inking command button, Excel adds an Ink Tools contextual tab to the Ribbon. You can then use the command buttons on its Pens tab to highlight and mark up various parts of the spreadsheet with digital ink.

Adding notes

You can add notes to the current cell by clicking the New Comment command button on the Ribbon's Review tab or by pressing Alt+RC. Excel responds by adding a Comment box (similar to the ones shown in Figure 3-5) with your name listed at the top (or the name of the person who shows up in the UserName text box on the Personalize tab of the Excel Options dialog box). You can then type the text of your note in this box. When you finish typing the text of the note, click the cell to which you're attaching the note or any other cell in the worksheet to close the Comment box.

WARNING

Don't confuse Notes with Comments on the Review tab. In earlier versions of Excel, notes were called comments. In Excel 2019, comments now refer to threaded comments that you can add to cells of a worksheet to promote a discussion of real or proposed editing changes with other team members with whom you've shared the workbook online (see Book 4, Chapter 4). As with online chats, the comments you post to a worksheet cell as well as responses made to them by other team members appear sequentially in a thread forming the conversation.

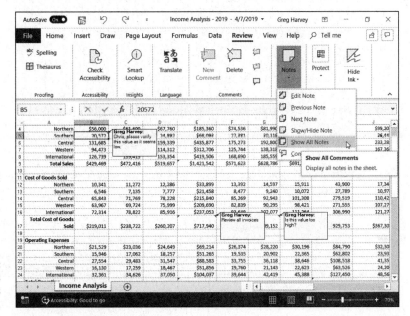

FIGURE 3-5:
Adding notes to various cells of a worksheet.

Displaying and hiding notes

Excel indicates that you've attached a note to a worksheet cell by adding a red triangle to the cell's upper-right corner. To display the Comment box with its text, you position the thick, white-cross mouse pointer on this red triangle, or you can click the Show All Notes command button on the Review tab (Alt+RA) to display all notes in the worksheet.

When you display a note by positioning the mouse pointer on the cell's red triangle, the note disappears as soon as you move the pointer outside the cell. When you display all the notes on the worksheet by clicking the Show All Notes command button on the Review tab, you must click the Show All Notes button a second time before Excel closes their Comment boxes (or press Alt+RA).

Editing and formatting notes

When you first add a note to a cell, its text box appears to the right of the cell with an arrow pointing to the red triangle in the cell's upper-right corner. If you need to, you can reposition a note's text box and/or resize it so that it doesn't obscure certain cells in the immediate region. You can also edit the text of a note and change the formatting of the text font.

To reposition or resize a note's text box or edit the note text or its font, you make the cell current by putting the cell cursor in it and then on the Review tab, click the Edit Note option on the Notes command button's drop-down menu, which replaces the New Note option, or press Alt+RTE. (You can also do this by right-clicking the cell and then choosing Edit Note from the cell's shortcut menu.)

Whichever method you use, Excel then displays the note's text box and positions the insertion point at the end of the note text. To reposition the text box, position the mouse pointer on the edge of the box (indicated with cross-hatching and open circles around the perimeter). When the mouse or Touch pointer assumes the shape of a white arrowhead pointing to a black double-cross, you can then drag the outline of the text box to a new position in the worksheet. After you release the mouse button, Excel draws a new line ending in an arrowhead from the repositioned note text box to the red triangle in the cell's upper-right corner.

When editing and formatting the notes you've added to the worksheet, you can do any of the following:

» To resize the note's text box, you position the mouse pointer on one of the open circles at the corners or in the middle of each edge on the box's perimeter. When the mouse pointer changes into a double-headed arrow, you drag the handle of the text box until its dotted outline is the size and shape you want. (Excel automatically reflows the note text to suit the new size and shape of the box.)

» To edit the text of the note (when the insertion point is positioned somewhere in it), drag the I-beam mouse pointer through text that needs to be replaced or press the Backspace key (to remove characters to the left of the insertion point) or Delete key (to remove characters to the right). You can insert new characters in the note to the right of the insertion point by simply typing them.

» To change the formatting of the note text, select the text by dragging the I-beam mouse pointer through it and then click the appropriate command button in the Font and Alignment groups on the Home tab of the Ribbon. (You can use Live Preview to see how a new font or font size, on its respective drop-down menu, looks in the comment, provided that these drop-down menus don't cover the Comment box in the worksheet.)

You can also right-click the text and choose Format Comment from the shortcut menu. Doing this opens the Format Comment dialog box (with the same options as the Font tab of the Format Cells dialog box) where you can change the font, font style, font size, font color, or add special effects including underlining, striketh-rough, as well as super- and subscripting.

When you finish making your changes to the note's text box and text, close the Format Comment box by clicking its cell or any of the other cells in the worksheet.

Deleting notes

When you no longer need a note, you can delete it by selecting its cell before you do either of the following:

>> Choose the Clear Comments and Notes option from the Clear button's drop-down menu on the Home tab of the Ribbon or press Alt+HZEEM.

>> Right-click the cell and then choose Delete Note from its shortcut menu.

If you delete a note in error, you can restore it to its cell by clicking the Undo command button on the Quick Access toolbar or pressing Ctrl+Z.

Marking up a worksheet with digital ink

If you're running Excel 2019 with a computer connected to a digital tablet or on a touchscreen, you can mark up your worksheets with digital ink using the commands on the new Draw tab of the Ribbon (the Draw tab is automatically added when running Excel on a device with a touch-sensitive display screen).

By default, Excel chooses the felt tip pen as the pen type for annotating the worksheet with digital ink. If you'd prefer to use a ballpoint pen or highlighter in marking up the worksheet, tap the Pen, Pencil, or Highlighter command button in the Pens group. If you don't have a stylus or digital pen available, tap the Draw with Touch command button on the Draw tab and then use your finger to make the pen, pencil, or highlighter ink annotations.

When using the highlighter or either of the two pen types (felt tip or ballpoint pen), you can select a nib from the Pens palette displayed in the middle of the Pens tab. You can also select a new line weight for the ink by choosing the point size (running from 3/4 all the way up to 6 points) from the Thickness command button's drop-down menu. You can also select a new ink color (yellow being the default color for the highlighter, red for the felt tip pen, and black for ballpoint pen) by selecting its color swatch on the Color command button's drop-down palette.

After you select the pen nib, color, and line weight, you can use your finger or the stylus that comes with your digital tablet to mark up the spreadsheet as follows:

» To highlight data in the spreadsheet with the highlighter, drag the highlight mouse pointer through the cells (just as though you had an actual yellow highlighter in your hand).

» To circle data in the spreadsheet with the felt tip pen, drag the pen tip mouse pointer around the cells in the worksheet.

» To add a note with the ballpoint pen, drag the pen tip mouse pointer to write out your text in the worksheet.

Figure 3-6 shows a copy of the Income Analysis worksheet after I used the Highlighter and Pen commands in the Pens group of the Draw tab to highlight cell B4 in the worksheet, circle it, and write the note text "verify" in digital ink.

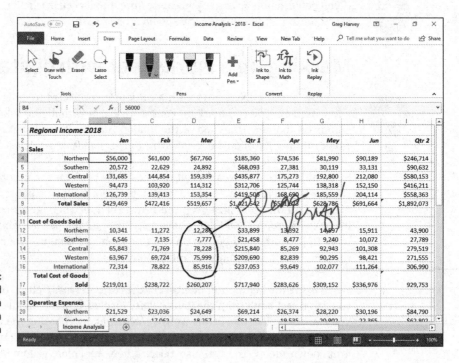

FIGURE 3-6: Adding inked notes to a worksheet with my finger on a Windows tablet.

If you make a mistake with ink, you need to remove it and start over again. To delete the ink, select the Eraser command button in the Tools group of the Draw tab and then tap somewhere on the highlighting, drawing, or handwriting you want to erase with the eraser mouse pointer. (Sometimes you have to drag through the ink to completely remove it.) Then, reselect the highlighter or felt tip or ball-point pen and reapply your ink annotation.

TIP

Tap the Hide Ink option on the Hide Ink command button on the Review tab (Alt+RH2H) to hide and redisplay the inked comments that you've added to your worksheet. The first time you tap this menu option when the inked comments you've added are displayed onscreen, Excel hides them. Tap the Hide Ink option again, when you want all your inked comments redisplayed in the worksheet.

TIP

Tap the Ink Replay command on the Draw tab (Alt+JIK) to have Excel play back the individual strokes of all the digital inking you've done to the current worksheet as a quick video. You can tap the Rewind and Forward buttons on the video playback controls that appear at the bottom of the Excel worksheet display when you select the Ink Replay button to remove and rebuild your ink strokes one at a time. You can even drag the Rewind/Forward button (the solid circle) in the playback controls to manually scrub through your ink strokes. When you're finished replaying the inked comments, tap the Ink Replay button again to remove the playback controls and deselect this command button.

WARNING

Note that in order for the Ink Replay command on the Draw tab to work, the inked notes you've added to the worksheet must be displayed in the Excel worksheet area at the time you tap it and not be hidden with the Hide Ink option on the Hide Ink command button's drop-down menu on the Review tab.

After marking a workbook up with your notes, you can then share it with clients or coworkers either by sending an e-mail message inviting them to review the workbook or actually sending them a copy as an e-mail attachment. (See Book 4, Chapter 4 for details.)

IN THIS CHAPTER

» **Co-authoring worksheets by sharing their workbooks with coworkers**

» **Sending worksheets as PDF files for review and comments**

» **Editing Excel worksheets with Excel Online**

» **Sharing Excel 2019 data with other Office programs**

» **Inserting Excel 2019 data into Word and PowerPoint documents**

» **Exporting workbooks as PDF, XPS, and HTML (web page) files**

Chapter **4**

Sharing Workbooks and Worksheet Data

Sharing data between Excel 2019 and other Windows programs that you use is the topic of this chapter. Perhaps the most straightforward way to share worksheet data is by sharing the Excel workbook saved in the cloud on your OneDrive, on your SharePoint team site, or in a folder in your Dropbox. This co-authoring sharing process enables you and those with whom you share your workbook to see all the editing changes made and saved (automatically with the AutoSave feature) to it in real time.

In other cases, data sharing simply involves getting the Excel data stored in tables, lists, and charts into other Office 2019 programs that you use, especially Microsoft Word documents and PowerPoint presentations. In other cases, data sharing involves getting data generated in other programs, such as in tables and lists created in Microsoft Word and contacts maintained in Microsoft Outlook, into an Excel worksheet.

In addition to data sharing that involves bringing data stored in different types of documents into Excel worksheets, the program supports data sharing in the form of *Actions* (formally known as SmartTags in Office versions prior to 2010) that can bring information into the spreadsheet that's related to a particular type of data entry, such as a date or a company's stock symbol. Information imported through the use of Actions can come from local sources, such as your Outlook Calendar, as well as from online sources, such as MSN MoneyCentral on the web. (For information on enabling Actions in Excel 2019, refer to Book 1, Chapter 2.)

Finally, you can give people access to worksheet data using programs other than Excel, including Acrobat Reader, the XML Paper Specification Viewer, and their own web browsers by saving the workbook in a special PDF, XPS, or HTML file format.

Sharing Your Workbooks Online

Excel 2019 makes it easy to share your spreadsheets with trusted clients and coworkers. Simply use the options on the Share screen in Backstage view to e-mail worksheets or send them by Skype Instant Message to others who have access to Excel on their computers. If you use Microsoft's Skype for Business online meeting software, you can present the worksheet to the other attendees as part of an online meeting.

And for workbook files saved on your OneDrive or SharePoint site, you can share the workbooks with coworkers so that both you and they can edit their contents at the same time with Excel on your own devices (or, if they don't have Excel, in their web browsers with the Excel Online web app). This process, referred to as co-authoring, enables you to see all the people with whom you've shared a workbook as well as all the editing changes they make to it as soon as the AutoSave feature saves these changes to the file.

Additionally, you yourself can edit the workbooks you save on your OneDrive when you're away from your office and the computer or device to which you have access doesn't have a compatible version of Excel installed on it. You simply use that device's Internet access to log on to the Documents folder of your OneDrive containing uploaded copies of your spreadsheets, and then you can use Excel Online, the web app version of Excel that runs on most modern web browsers to open and then review and edit them.

Sharing workbooks saved on your OneDrive

To share Excel workbooks from your OneDrive, you follow these steps:

1. **Open the workbook file you want to share in Excel 2019 and then click the Share button at the far right of the row with the Ribbon.**

   If you've not yet saved the workbook on your OneDrive, a Share dialog box appears inviting you to upload the workbook file to OneDrive. Once you have clicked the OneDrive button and the file is uploaded to the Cloud, the Share dialog box changes into the Send Link dialog box.

   Once the workbook has been saved to the Cloud, the Send Link dialog box (similar to the one shown in Figure 4-1) appears where you can invite coworkers and clients to share it.

2. **Begin typing the e-mail address of the first person with whom you want to share the workbook at the blinking insertion point. When Excel finds a match to the person's name in your Outlook address book or verifies the e-mail address that you have entered, click their button below the text box to add this recipient.**

   As you type, Excel matches the letters with the names and e-mail addresses entered in your Address book. When it finds possible matches, they are displayed below the input text box, and you can select the person's e-mail address by clicking the button with their name.

3. **(Optional) Click the Anyone with the Link Can Edit button to open the Link Settings dialog box. Here you can modify the people for whom the link works, deny editing privileges to those with whom you share the file, and/or set an expiration date after which the link is no longer operational before clicking the Apply button.**

   By default, Excel 2019 creates a sharing link that enables anyone who can access the workbook file online access to the file even when they are not logged into Office 365 or OneDrive. To restrict access to only coworkers in your company who are logged into Office 365, click the People in *<organization>* option (where *organization* is the name of your company as in People in Mind Over Media, the name of my company). To restrict the file sharing to only those to whom you've given prior access to the workbook file or its folder on your SharePoint site, click the People with Existing Access option. To create a sharing link that only particular people can use, click the Specific People option before you click the Apply button, Then, in the Send Link dialog box, click the ellipses (. . .) to the right of the Send Link title and click Manage Access on the drop-menu to open the Permissions dialog box where you select the names of the people with whom to share the workbook file before you click the back arrow button (←) to return to the Send Link dialog box.

By default, Excel allows the people with whom you share your workbooks to make editing changes to the workbook that are automatically saved on your OneDrive. If you want to restrict your recipients to reviewing the data without being able to make changes, be sure to click the Allow Editing check box to remove its check mark before you click Apply.

If you wish to set an expiration date after which the sharing link is no longer operational, click the Set Expiration Date button to open the pop-up calendar where you select an expiration date by clicking it in the calendar. After selecting the expiration date, click somewhere in the dialog box to close the pop-up calendar and enter the date in the Link Settings dialog box.

4. **(Optional) Click the Add a Message (Optional) text box and type any personal message that you want to incorporate as part of the e-mail with the generic invitation to share the file.**

By default, Excel creates a generic invitation.

5. **After adding all the recipients with whom you wish to share the workbook file in this manner, click the Share button in the Send Link pane.**

As soon as you click this Share button, Excel e-mails the invitation to share the workbook to each of the recipients entered in the Type Name or E-Mail Addresses text box. The program also adds the e-mail address and the editing status of each recipient (Can Edit or Can View) in the Share task pane.

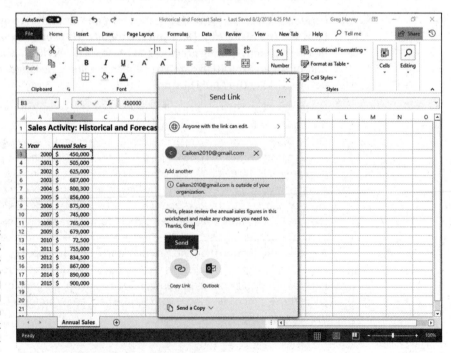

FIGURE 4-1: Inviting coworkers or clients to share an Excel workbook saved on OneDrive in the Share task pane.

All the people with whom you share a workbook receive an e-mail message containing a hyperlink to the workbook on your OneDrive. When they follow this link (and sign into the site if this is required), a copy of the workbook opens on a new page in their default web browser using the Excel Online web app. If you've given the user permission to edit the file, the web app contains an Edit Workbook drop-down button.

When the coworkers with whom you've shared the workbook click this button in Excel Online, they have a choice between choosing the Edit in Excel or Edit in Excel Online option from its drop-down menu. When the user chooses Edit in Excel, the workbook is downloaded and opened in his version of Excel. When the user chooses Edit in Excel Online, the browser opens the workbook in a new version of the Excel Online, containing Home, Insert, Data, Review, and View tabs, each with a more limited set of command options than Excel 2019, which you can use in making any necessary changes and which are automatically saved to workbook on the OneDrive when you close Excel Online.

While sharing a workbook with the default Anyone Can Edit option, all changes made by the people with whom you've shared the workbook are automatically saved by the AutoSave feature. If you happen to have the workbook open in Excel 2019 on your computer with the same worksheet displayed, their editing changes automatically appear in your worksheet (in as close to real time as the speed of your Internet access provides). Likewise, all the editing changes that you make to the workbook in Excel 2019 are automatically updated in their workbooks in Excel Online. Microsoft refers to this process as co-authoring.

TIP

If a questionable editing change appears in your worksheet when co-authoring with a coworker, add a comment to the cell containing the edit-in-question (Review⇨New Comment) that communicates your reservations about the change they made. A small balloon then appears above the cell where you made the comment in the user's worksheet in Excel Online. When the coworker clicks this balloon, Excel Online displays the text of your comment calling into question their edit in a Comments task pane. They can then reply to your reservations by typing their explanation for the change in the same comment in this task pane and then updating it in your workbook by clicking the Post button or they can just go ahead and make any necessary updates reflecting your reservations directly in the worksheet in Excel Online.

Getting Sharing links

Instead of sending e-mail invitations to individual recipients with links to the workbooks you want to co-author with them on your OneDrive, you can create hyperlinks to them that you can then make available to all the people who require online review and editing access.

To create a link to a workbook open in Excel 2019 that you've saved on your One-Drive, you click the Share button at the very right of the Ribbon and then click the hyperlink called Get a Sharing Link that appears at the very bottom of the Share task pane.

To create a view-only link that doesn't allow online editing, you then click the Create a View-Only Link button under the View-Only Link heading in the Share task pane. To create an edit-type link that enables online editing instead of a view-only link or in addition to it, you click the Create an Edit Link button by the Edit Link heading in this task pane.

Excel then displays the long and complex hyperlink for sharing your workbook under the View-Only Link or Edit Link heading (depending upon which Create Link button you selected).

REMEMBER

After creating a view link or an edit link for a workbook on your OneDrive, you can copy it to the Clipboard by clicking the Copy button that appears to the immediate right of the text box containing the edit or view-only link. After copying it to the Clipboard, you can insert it into a new e-mail message (Ctrl+V) that you send to all the people with whom you want to share the Excel workbook to which it refers.

E-mailing workbooks

To e-mail a copy of a workbook you have open in Excel to a client or coworker, click File ⇨ Share ⇨ E-mail (Alt+FY3E). When you do this, an E-Mail panel appears on the Share screen with the following five options:

>> **Send as Attachment** to create a new e-mail message using your default e-mail program with a copy of the workbook file as its attachment file.

>> **Send a Link** to create a new e-mail message using your default e-mail program that contains a hyperlink to the workbook file. (This option is available only when the workbook file is saved on your company's OneDrive or ISP's web server.)

>> **Send as Adobe PDF** to convert the Excel workbook to the Adobe PDF (Portable Document File) format and make this new PDF the attachment file in a new e-mail message. (Your e-mail recipient must have a copy of the Adobe Reader installed on his or her computer in order to open the attachment.)

>> **Send as XPS** to convert the Excel workbook to a Microsoft XPS (XML Paper Specification) file and make this new XPS file the attachment in a new e-mail message. (Your e-mail recipient must have an XPS Reader installed on his or her computer in order to open the attachment.)

>> **Send as Internet Fax** to send the workbook as a fax through an online fax service provider. You will need an account with a service provider as well as the Windows Fax and Scan feature installed.

After selecting the e-mail option you want to use, Windows opens a new e-mail message in your e-mail program with a link to the workbook file or the file attached to it. To send the link or file, fill in the recipient's e-mail address in the To text box and any comments you want to make about the spreadsheet in the body of the message before you click the Send button.

TIP

If you want to send a workbook or a PDF copy of it as an e-mail attachment when the Share task pane is open, you can do so by clicking the Send As Attachment link at the bottom of the task pane without having to bother with opening the Share screen in the Backstage view. When you click the Send As Attachment link, two new links, Send a Copy and Send a PDF, appear in the Share task pane. Select the Send a Copy link to attach a copy of the file in its native Excel file format to a new e-mail message in your e-mail program. Select the Send a PDF to convert the file into the more universal PDF file format before attaching it to a new message.

Sending Workbooks as Adobe PDF Files for Shared Commenting

Sometimes you may need to share workbooks with clients or coworkers who have no knowledge of using Excel but who, nonetheless, need to give you feedback about their worksheet data., For those situations, you can use Excel 2019's exciting new Send Adobe PDF For Shared Commenting command that converts the Excel workbook file into a PDF file that's either shared on the same internal server or sent as an e-mail attachment that they can review and comment on using a copy of the Adobe Acrobat software on their computer. After making their comments in the PDF file, they can share or send a copy of it in PDF format or even convert it into an Excel file so you can then accordingly make whatever changes are necessary in the Excel workbook itself.

To send your Excel workbook file as a PDF for comments, you follow these steps:

1. **Open the workbook file that contains the worksheet(s) you want converted to PDF and sent for comments in Excel 2019.**

2. **Click File ⇨ Save as Adobe PDF to open the Acrobat PDFMaker dialog box in the Backstage view (Alt+FY2).**

   The Acrobat PDFMaker dialog box (shown in Figure 4-2) contains Conversion Range options for selecting the Entire Workbook, a cell Selection, or individual Sheet(s) in it. When the default option Sheet(s) is selected, you can use the

<Add> option to select more than one worksheet in the workbook and then use the Move Up and Move Down options to arrange their order in the resulting PDF file.

Below this area, the dialog box contains a set of Conversion Options that enable you to convert the selected Conversion Range to other than Actual Size (the default) to either Fit the Paper Width or to Fit the Worksheet to a Single Page.

3. **After selecting your Conversion Range and Conversion Options in the Acrobat PDFMaker dialog box, click its Convert to PDF button.**

   Excel opens the Save Adobe PDF File As dialog box (very similar to the regular Save As dialog box except that the PDF Files is the only Save as Type option available and it is automatically selected). Right below the Save As Type drop-down list box, you see two check box options: View Result (selected by default) and Restrict Editing (deselected by default). If you don't feel you need to review the resulting PDF file before sending it out, you can deselect the View Result check box. If you don't want the people to whom you send the resulting PDF file to be able to edit the resulting PDF file, click the Restrict Editing button.

4. **Click the Save button in the Save Adobe PDF File As dialog box.**

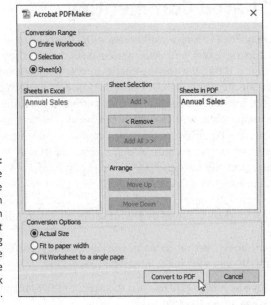

FIGURE 4-2:
Selecting the Conversion Range and Conversion Options in the Acrobat PDFMaker dialog box before converting the Excel workbook to a PDF file.

After converting the selected worksheet(s) to PDF with the View Result check box option selected, Windows 10 opens the resulting converted data file in the Adobe Acrobat software installed on your computer. You can then review the resulting PDF file in Acrobat and, if everything looks okay, decide how to share it with your coworkers:

» **Save File to Adobe Document Cloud** (Adobe Acrobat DC) where all coworkers with access to this service can open it for review and annotating

» **Attach as E-mail** to send the PDF file as a standard e-mail attachment to be sent in a new message using your default e-mail app (usually Outlook 2019)

» **Send & Track** to send your coworkers a link via your default e-mail app that, when clicked, enables them to preview the PDF file online in their web browser download onto their device for opening with Adobe Acrobat

After making their comments directly in the PDF file, your coworkers can save their edits and then either send them to you in a PDF file e-mail attachment or first convert the annotated PDF file into an Excel workbook file and send that file as am e-mail attachment that can open directly in Excel 2019.

REMEMBER

If you receive an e-mail message with an annotated PDF file attached to it, open it in your copy of Adobe Acrobat and then use its File ⇨ Export To ⇨ Spreadsheet ⇨ Microsoft Excel Workbook command (or equivalent) to convert the annotated PDF file into an Excel workbook file for opening in Excel 2019.

TIP

After you use the File ⇨ Save as Adobe PDF command, Excel adds an ACROBAT tab to end of your Excel Ribbon. This tab contains command buttons for setting PDF file preferences as well as opening the Acrobat PDFMaker dialog box directly in the worksheet area.

Editing worksheets in Excel Online

Microsoft offers several Office Online Web apps for Word, Excel, PowerPoint, and OneNote as part of your Windows account and OneDrive storage in the cloud. You can use Excel Online to edit worksheets saved on your OneDrive online right within your web browser.

This comes in real handy for those occasions when you need to make last-minute edits to an Excel worksheet but don't have access to a device on which Excel 2019 is installed. As long as the device has an Internet connection and runs a web browser that supports Excel Online (such as Internet Explorer on a Surface Pro tablet or even Safari on a MacBook Pro), you can make eleventh-hour edits to the data, formulas, and even charts that are automatically saved in the workbook file on your OneDrive.

REMEMBER

The great part about using Excel Online to edit a copy of your online workbook is that it runs successfully under the latest versions of Microsoft's Edge Explorer as well as under the latest versions of many other popular web browsers, including Mozilla Firefox for Windows, Mac, and Linux as well as Macintosh's Safari web browser on the iMac and iPad.

To edit a workbook saved on your OneDrive with the Excel Online, you follow these simple steps:

1. Launch the web browser on your device that supports the Excel web app and then go to `www.office.live.com` and sign in to your Windows account.

The Microsoft Office Home web page welcoming you to your Office 365 account appears. Under Apps on this page, you see a bunch of buttons for each of the online apps.

2. Click the Excel button under Apps.

Excel Online display a Welcome to Excel screen in your web browser. This screen is somewhat similar to the Open screen in Excel 2019 (see Figure 4-3). Across the top of this screen beneath the label New, a bunch of template thumbnails appear in a single row, starting with New Blank Workbook. Below the row of Excel templates, you see the following options for selecting the file you want to edit:

- **Recent** (the default) to list all the workbooks that have recently been uploaded to your OneDrive.

- **Pinned** to list just the workbook files that you've pinned (to pin a file, mouse over the name of the file in the Recent list and then click the push pin icon that appears after its filename).

- **Shared with Me** to list only those workbook files that have been shared with you.

- **Discover** to list shared workbooks that other are currently working on.

- **Upload and Open** to display a dialog box where you can select a local workbook file to upload and save on OneDrive for editing with Excel Online. Note that if the device on which you're using Excel Online has Excel installed on it, the Excel Open dialog box will appear. Otherwise, the file management dialog box for the device's operating system will appear (File Explorer on a Windows machine and Finder on a Mac).

If you can't locate the workbook file you want to edit using these options, click the Search Apps, Documents, People, and Sites text box at the top of the Welcome to Excel screen and start typing its filename here. As you type, Excel Online will display a list of results matching the characters that you've entered.

3. **Locate the Excel workbook file you want to edit and then click its filename.**

As soon as you select the name of the workbook file to edit, Excel Online opens the workbook in a new tab in your web browser, in the Editing view complete with a File button and the Home, Insert, Data, Review, and View Ribbon tabs (see Figure 4-4).

You can then use the option buttons on the Home and Insert tab (most of which are identical to those found on the Home and Insert tab on the Excel 2019 Ribbon) to modify the layout or formatting of the data and charts on any of its sheets. You can use the options on the Data tab to recalculate your workbook and sort data in ascending or descending order on its worksheets. You can also use the options on the Review add and display comments in the cells of the worksheets as well as options on the View tab to turn off Headings and Gridlines and switch back to Reading view. You can also add new data to the worksheets as well as edit existing data just as you do in Excel 2019.

WARNING

Note that if you open a workbook file in Excel Online that contains features that can't be displayed in your browser, the file will open in a new tab without the Ribbon, and a "There are some features in your workbook that we can't show in the browser" alert will appear above the worksheet area. To continue and edit a copy of the workbook file with Excel Online without the features that can't be displayed, click the Edit Workbook drop-down button and then click the Edit in Browser option on the drop-down menu (if Excel is installed on your device and you want access to all the workbook's features, click the Edit in Excel option instead). When you click the Edit in Browser option, an Edit a Copy dialog box appears. When you click the Edit a Copy button, a Save As dialog box with Editable appended to its original filename appears. After you click Save in this dialog box, the copy of the original workbook file opens in Excel Online in Editing view.

4. **When you're finished editing the workbook, click Close button on your web browser's tab to save your changes. If you want to save a copy under a new filename in the same folder on the OneDrive, click File⇨Save As and then click the Save As option to open a Save As dialog box where you can edit the filename that appears in the text box before you click its Save button. (Or click the Overwrite Existing Files check box if you want to save the changes under the same filename.)**

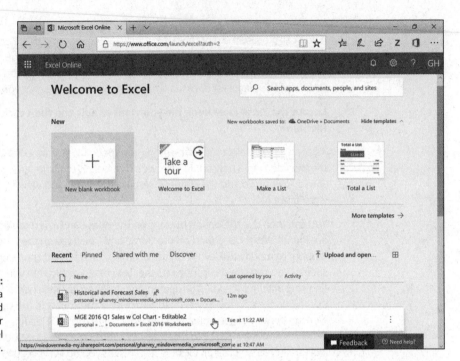

FIGURE 4-3:
Opening a workbook saved on OneDrive for editing in Excel Online.

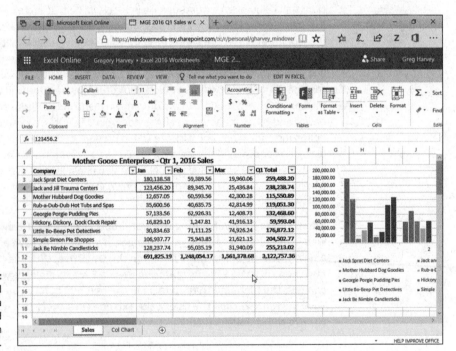

FIGURE 4-4:
Using Excel Online to edit a workbook saved on OneDrive in my web browser.

Excel 2019 Data Sharing Basics

You share information between Excel 2019 and other programs you use in two ways: You either copy or move discrete objects or blocks of data from one program's file to another, or you open an entire file created with one program in the other program.

The key to sharing blocks of data or discrete objects in Excel is the Windows Clipboard. Remember that Excel always gives you access to contents of the Clipboard in the form of the Clipboard task pane, which you can open by clicking the Dialog Box launcher in the lower-right corner of the Clipboard group at the beginning of the Home tab on the Ribbon. When the Clipboard task pane is open, you can then copy its objects or blocks of text into cells of the open worksheet simply by clicking the item in this task pane.

Because very few people purchase Excel 2019 as a separate program outside the Microsoft Office 2019 suite, it should be no surprise that most of the file sharing happens between Excel and one of the other major applications included in Microsoft Office (such as Word, PowerPoint, and Access).

However, before you rush off and start wildly throwing Excel 2019 worksheets into Word 2019 documents and Excel 2019 charts into PowerPoint 2019 presentations, you need to realize that Microsoft offers you a choice in the way that you exchange data between your various Office programs. You can either embed the worksheet or chart in the other program or set up a link between the Excel-generated object in the other program and Excel itself.

>> **Embedding** means that the Excel object (whether it's a worksheet or a chart) actually becomes part of the Word document or PowerPoint presentation. Any changes that you then need to make to the worksheet or chart must be made within the Word document or PowerPoint presentation. This presupposes, however, that you have Excel on the same device as Word or PowerPoint and that that device has sufficient memory to run them both.

>> **Linking** means that the Excel object (worksheet or chart) is only referred to in the Word document or PowerPoint presentation. Any changes that you make to the worksheet or chart must be made in Excel itself and then updated when you open the Word document or PowerPoint presentation to which it is linked.

Use the embedding method when the Excel object (worksheet or chart) is not apt to change very often, if at all. Use the linking method when the Excel object (worksheet or chart) changes fairly often, when you always need the latest-and-greatest version of the object to appear in your Word document or PowerPoint presentation, or when you don't want to make the Word or PowerPoint document any bigger by adding the Excel data to it.

REMEMBER

Be aware that when you link an Excel worksheet or chart to another Office document and you want to show or print that document on a different device, you must copy both the Excel workbook with the linked worksheet/chart and the Word or PowerPoint file to it. Also be aware that when you embed an Excel worksheet or a chart in another Office document and then want to edit it on another device, that device must have both Excel 2019 and the other Microsoft Office program (Word or PowerPoint 2019) installed on it.

Use the embedding or linking techniques only when you have a pretty good suspicion that the Excel stuff is far from final and that you want to be able to update the Excel data either manually (with embedding) or automatically (with linking). If your Excel stuff will remain unchanged, just use the old standby method of copying the Excel data to the Clipboard with the Copy command button on the Home tab (or pressing Ctrl+C) and then switching to the Word or PowerPoint document and pasting it in place with the Paste command button (or pressing Ctrl+V).

TIP

Excel maintains a very close relationship with Microsoft Access, thus making it easy to import data from any of the tables or queries set up for a database into your Excel worksheet. For details on how to bring in data from Access, see Book 6, Chapter 2.

Excel and Word 2019

Of all the Office programs (besides our beloved Excel), Microsoft Word 2019 is the one that you are most apt to use. You will probably find yourself using Word to type any memos, letters, and reports that you need in the course of your daily work (even if you really don't understand how the program works). From time to time, you may need to bring some worksheet data or charts that you've created in your Excel workbooks into a Word document that you're creating. When those occasions arise, check out the information in the next section.

Although Word has a Table feature that supports calculations through a kind of mini-spreadsheet operation, you probably will be more productive if you create the data (formulas, formatting, and all) in an Excel workbook and then bring that data into your Word document by following the steps outlined in the next section. Likewise, although you can keep, create, and manage the data records that you use in mail merge operations within Word, you probably will find it more expedient to create and maintain them in Excel — considering that you are already familiar with how to create, sort, and filter database records in Excel.

Getting Excel data into a Word document

As with all the other Office programs, you have two choices when bringing Excel data (worksheet cell data or charts) into a Word document: You can embed the data in the Word document, or you can link the data that you bring into Word to its original Excel worksheet. Embed the data or charts when you want to be able to edit right within Word. Link the data or charts when you want to be able to edit in Excel and have the changes automatically updated when you open the Word document.

Happily embedded after

The easiest way to embed a table of worksheet data or a chart is to use the good old drag-and-drop method: Simply drag the selected cells or chart between the Excel and Word program windows instead of to a new place in a worksheet. The only trick to dragging and dropping between programs is the sizing and maneuvering of the Excel and Word program windows themselves. Figures 4-5 and 4-6 illustrate the procedure for dragging a table of worksheet data with the 2005 to 2020 historical and forecasted annual sales activity from its worksheet (named Annual Sales) into a new Sales memo document in Word 2019.

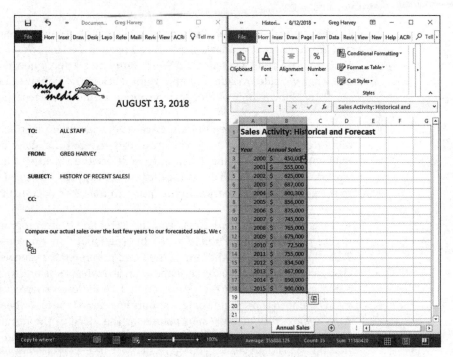

FIGURE 4-5:
Dragging the cell range A1:B18 from the Historical Sales worksheet to the Word memo.

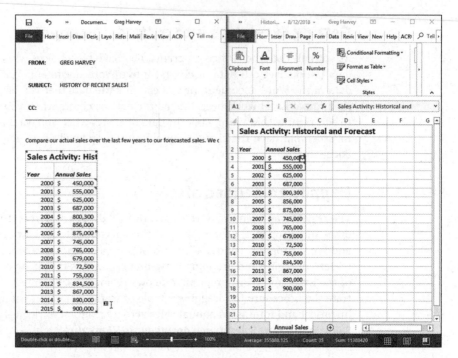

FIGURE 4-6:
Word memo
after copying the
worksheet data.

Before I could drag the selected worksheet data, I had to size and position the Excel and Word program windows. To do this, I opened the Historical Sales spreadsheet in Excel 2019 and then launched Word 2019 and started a new document. To tile the windows side by side, I simply right-clicked the Windows taskbar and then chose the Show Windows Side by Side option from its shortcut menu.

In Figure 4-5, you can see that the Excel 2019 window is positioned to the immediate right of the Word 2019 window after I selected the Show Windows Side by Side option. At that point, I had only to select the worksheet data in the Excel worksheet and then hold down the Ctrl key (to copy) as I dragged the outline over to the new paragraph marker in the memo in the Word document window.

As I passed over the border between the Excel and Word program windows, the mouse pointer changed shape to the international "oh-no-you-don't" symbol. When I reached the safe havens of the Word document area, however, the pointer changed again, this time to the shape of an arrowhead sticking up from a box with a plus sign. (How's that for a description?) To indicate where in the Word document to embed the selected data, I simply positioned the arrowhead-sticking-up-from-a-box-with-a-plus-sign pointer at the place in the document where the Excel stuff is to appear. Then I released the mouse button. Figure 4-6 shows you the embedded worksheet table that appeared after I released the mouse button.

You can also use the cut-and-paste method to embed worksheet data into a Word document. Simply select the cells in Excel and then copy them to the Clipboard by clicking the Copy button on the Home tab of the Ribbon (Ctrl+C). Then, open the Word document and position the cursor at the place where the spreadsheet table is to appear. Click the Paste Special option on the Paste button's drop-down menu on the Home tab of Word's Ribbon (or press Alt+HVS). Click Microsoft Excel Worksheet Object in Word's Paste Special dialog box and then click OK. Word then embeds the data in the body of the Word document just as though you had Ctrl+dragged the data from the Excel window over to the Word window.

Editing embedded stuff

The great thing about embedding Excel stuff (as opposed to linking, which I get to in a later section) is that you can edit the data right from within Word. Figure 4-7 shows the table after I centered it with the Center button on Word's Formatting toolbar. Notice what happens when I double-click the embedded table (or click the table once and then click Worksheet Object ⇨ Edit from the table's shortcut menu): A frame with columns and rows and scroll bars around two columns of sales data appears. Notice, too, that the tabs on the Word Ribbon have changed to ones on the Excel Ribbon. (It's like being at home when you're still on the road.) At this point, you can edit any of the table's contents by using the Excel commands that you already know.

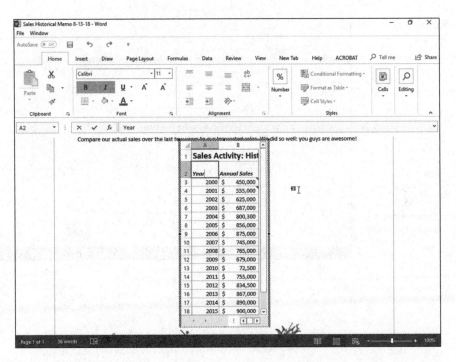

FIGURE 4-7:
Editing the embedded worksheet sales data from within the Word memo.

The links that bind

Of course, as nice as embedding is, you will encounter occasions when linking the Excel data to the Word document is the preferred method (and, in fact, even easier to do). First, I select a chart that I created in the worksheet by *single*-clicking it, not double-clicking it, as I would do to edit the chart in the worksheet.

Then, after copying the chart (or selected data) to the Clipboard by clicking the Copy command on the Excel Ribbon's Home tab, I switched over to Word and my memo to all account representatives. After positioning the insertion point at the beginning of the paragraph where the chart needs to be, I chose the Paste Special option from the Paste button's drop-down menu on the Home tab of Word's Ribbon. (You can also do this by pressing Alt+HVS.) Figure 4-8 shows the Paste Special dialog box that appears. In this dialog box, the crucial thing is to click the Paste Link option button and Microsoft Excel Chart Object in the list box before clicking OK. Figure 4-9 shows the Word memo after I clicked OK and pasted the Excel chart into place.

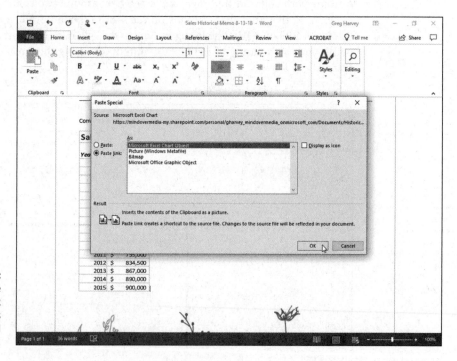

FIGURE 4-8:
Selecting the Paste Link option in Word's Paste Special dialog box.

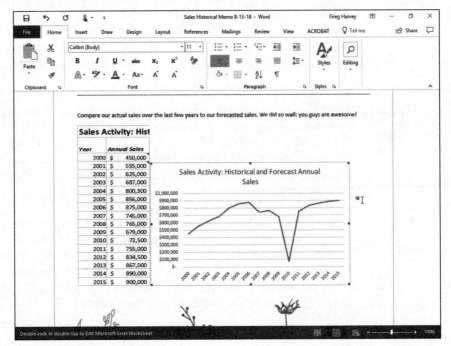

FIGURE 4-9:
Pasting the linked
chart into the
Word memo.

Editing linked data

Editing data linked to Excel (as a chart or cells) is not quite as delightful as editing embedded worksheet data. For one thing, you first have to go back to Excel and make your changes — although you can easily open Excel and its workbook just by double-clicking the linked chart. The nice thing, however is that any changes that you make to the original data or chart are immediately reflected in the Word document the moment you open it.

Excel and PowerPoint 2019

The process of embedding and linking worksheet data and charts in the slides of your Microsoft PowerPoint presentations is very similar to the techniques outlined for Word. To embed a cell selection or chart, drag the data or chart object from the Excel worksheet to the PowerPoint slide. If you prefer using the cut-and-paste method, copy the data or chart to the Clipboard (Ctrl+C), switch to PowerPoint, and choose the Paste Special option from the Paste button's drop-down menu on the Home tab of the PowerPoint Ribbon (or press Alt+HVS). Then, make sure that the Microsoft Excel Worksheet Object is selected in the As list box and the Paste option button is selected in PowerPoint's Paste Special dialog box before you click OK.

If you want to link Excel data or a chart that you pasted into a PowerPoint presentation slide to its source Excel workbook, the only thing you do differently is to click the Paste Link option button in the Paste Special dialog box before you click OK.

TIP

Sometimes, after making changes to the linked data or chart in Excel, you need to manually update the link in the PowerPoint presentation slide to ensure that your presentation has the latest-and-greatest version of the Excel data. To manually update a linked table of Excel spreadsheet data or a linked chart, go to the slide in question, right-click the table or chart, and then choose Update Link from its shortcut menu.

Figure 4-10 illustrates how easy it is to edit an Excel chart that is embedded in a PowerPoint 2019 slide. To edit the table from in PowerPoint, all I have to do is double-click the chart on the slide. The PowerPoint Ribbon then adds a Chart Tools contextual tab with its Design and Format tab command buttons so that I can use its command buttons to make all my editing changes (see Book 5, Chapter 1 to find out to create and edit Excel charts).

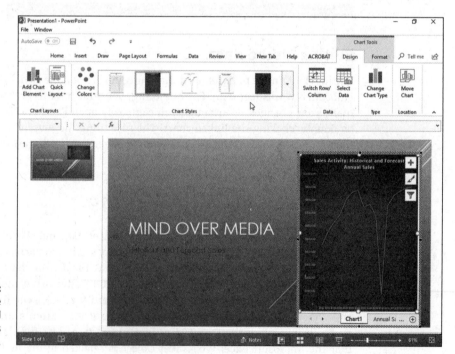

FIGURE 4-10:
Editing the embedded Excel Scatter chart in its PowerPoint slide.

Exporting Workbooks to Other Usable File Formats

Sometimes you may need to share worksheet data with coworkers and clients who do not have Excel installed on their computers. Therefore, they can't open up and print Excel workbook files saved either in the default XML file format (with the `.xlsx` filename extension) favored by Excel versions 2007 through 2016 or in the older binary file format (with the `.xls` filename extension) used in versions 97 through 2003.

It's hard to imagine a coworker or client getting by without Excel 2019, but it does happen. For those rare occasions, you can export your Excel workbook to one of three usable file formats for opening and printing with readily available software programs that support them:

>> **PDF files** for opening with Adobe Reader or Adobe Acrobat

>> **XPS files** for opening with the XML Paper Specification Viewer or newer web browser such as Internet Explorer 7 and up

>> **ODS files** for opening with open source spreadsheet program OpenOffice Calc

>> **HTML files** for opening with all types and versions of web browsers

When converting an Excel workbook to one of these other file formats, you can either change the file type in the Save As dialog box when using the File⇨Save As command, or you can export them from the Export screen in the Backstage view by using the File⇨Export command.

Saving and exporting worksheets as PDF files

The PDF (Portable Document File) file format, developed by Adobe Systems Incorporated, enables people to open and print documents without any access to the original programs with which the documents were created. All they then need installed in order to be able to open and print the worksheet-as-PDF file is a copy of Adobe Reader (a free download from www.adobe.com) or a copy of Adobe's Acrobat software.

Excel 2019 enables you to save your workbook files directly in this special PDF file format. To save a workbook as a PDF file, click File⇨Save As (Alt+FA), select the place where you want to save the new PDF file in the Save As screen, and then select PDF from the Save as Type drop-down list.

You can modify the filename and the drive and folder in which the new PDF file is saved and change any of the following options added to the bottom of the Save As dialog box:

» **Standard (Publishing Online and Printing)** following Optimize For (that is selected by default) or Minimum Size (Publishing Online) option buttons to compress the resulting PDF document for use on the web

» **Open File after Publishing** check box (selected by default) to have Excel automatically open the new workbook saved as PDF file in your copy of Adobe Reader or Acrobat

» **Options** button to open the Options dialog box where you can select the part of the workbook or worksheet to publish and choose to not have the document properties and accessibility tags included in the resulting PDF file

Note that if you need to restrict which parts of the current workbook are included in the new PDF file or you don't want nonprinting information included in the resulting file, click the Options button that appears immediately above the Publish button. Doing this opens the Options dialog box.

After you designate the filename and file location and select your PDF file options, click the Save button to have Excel save the workbook (or some part of it) in a new PDF file that automatically opens in your computer's Adobe Reader or Acrobat.

In addition to saving your workbook file in the PDF file format using the Save As dialog box, you can also accomplish the same thing from the Export screen. Click File ⇨ Export and then click the Create PDF/XPS button (or press Alt+FEPA) to open the Publish as PDF or XPS dialog box. In the Publish as PDF or XPS (which pretty much looks and acts like the Save As dialog box when PDF is selected as the file type), PDF is automatically selected as the file format type, and you can then use the Folder list box, Filename text box, and PDF options (in a slightly different order) as needed before clicking the Publish button to save the PDF file version of your Excel workbook.

TIP

If you create an Excel 2019 workbook that incorporates new features not supported in earlier versions of Excel, instead of saving the workbook as an .xls file, thereby losing all of its 2010 enhancements, consider saving it as a PDF file so that coworkers still using pre-2007 Excel versions can still have access to the data in all its glory via the Adobe Reader.

Saving worksheets as XPS files

The XPS (XML Paper Specification) file format also enables people to open and print Excel worksheets without access to the Excel program. In fact, spreadsheets saved in the XPS file format can be opened by anyone who uses Internet Explorer 10 on Windows 7 or 8 or uses Internet Explorer 6 or higher after installing Win FX Runtime Components or, barring that, a special XML Paper Specification Viewer (which is a free download from the Microsoft website at www.microsoft.com).

As with the PDF format, you can convert a workbook to an XPS file either in the Save As dialog box opened from the Save As screen (Alt+FA) or in the Publish as PDF or XPS dialog box opened from the Export screen by clicking the Create PDF/ XPS button (Alt+FEPA).

From either dialog box, you will need to choose XPS Document as the file format from the Save as Type drop-down menu. And in either dialog box, you have access (in a slightly different order) to Optimize For option buttons, Open File After Publishing check box, and the Options command button for controlling the file size and what to do after it's created.

After choosing XPS Document as the file type, if you don't need to edit the file-name (Excel automatically appends .xps to the current filename) or the folder location, simply click the Save button (in the Save As dialog box) or Publish button (in the Publish as PDF or XPS dialog box), and Excel saves the workbook in an XPS file.

If you want Excel to automatically open the new XPS file for your inspection in Internet Explorer or the XML Paper Specification Viewer, make sure that the Open File after Publishing check box is selected before you click the Publish button.

TIP

By default, the Standard (Publishing Online and Printing) option button is selected in the Optimize For section at the bottom of the Publish as PDF or XPS dialog box. If you want to make your XPS file version of the spreadsheet smaller for viewing online, click the Minimum Size (Publishing Online) option button before you click the Publish button. Also, if you need to restrict which parts of the current workbook are included in the new XPS file or don't want nonprinting information included in the resulting file, open the Options dialog box by clicking the Options button and select the part of the workbook or worksheet to publish and choose which nonprinting information to omit from the resulting XPS file.

Saving worksheets as ODS files

ODS (OpenDocument Spreadsheet) is the default spreadsheet file format that OpenOffice.org Calc, the spreadsheet program that comes with the open source and completely free OpenOffice suite, uses. To save your Excel workbook in this file format, you choose the OpenDocument Spreadsheet (*.ods) option at the very bottom of the Save as Type drop-down list in the Excel 2019 Save As dialog box.

REMEMBER

Keep in mind that OpenOffice.org Calc can open native Excel workbook files (either .xls or .xlsx) just as Excel 2019 can open .ods files with any prior conversion.

Saving worksheets as HTML files

If converting your worksheets to PDF or XPS files is way too complex for your needs, you can save your worksheets as good old HTML files for viewing and printing in anybody's web browser (as well as for publishing to your website). To save

1. **Click File ⇨ Save As or press Alt+FA to open the Save As screen in the Backstage view.**

    Here you select the place into which to save the HTML file.

2. **Select the drive and folder where you want the web version of the workbook saved.**

    Excel opens the Save As dialog box with the drive and folder you just designated open and selected.

3. **Choose Single File Web Page or Web Page from the Save as Type drop-down menu.**

    Select Single File Web Page as the file type when your workbook only has one worksheet or you want the data on all the worksheets to appear on a single page. Select Web Page when you want each worksheet in the workbook to appear on sequential web pages.

    When you select either web page option, Excel expands the Save As dialog box to include the Entire Workbook (selected by default) and Selection: Sheet option buttons along with the Page Title text box and Change Title command button.

    Next, you need to give a new filename to your web page in the File Name text box. Note that Excel automatically appends the filename extension .htm (for Hypertext Markup page) to whatever filename you enter here. When selecting a filename, keep in mind that some file servers (especially those running some flavor of UNIX) are sensitive to upper- and lowercase letters in the name.

4. Enter the filename for the new HTML file in the File Name text box.

By default, Excel selects the Entire Workbook option button, meaning that all the worksheets in the workbook that contain data will be included in the new HTML file. To save only the data on the current worksheet in the HTML file, you need to take Step 5.

5. (Optional) If you want only the current worksheet saved in the new HTML file, select the Selection: Sheet option button.

If you want, you can have Excel add a Page title to your new HTML file by taking Step 6. The page appears centered at the top of the page right above your worksheet data. Don't confuse the page title with the web page header that appears on the web browser's title bar — the only way to set the web page header is to edit this HTML tag after the HTML file is created.

6. (Optional) If you want to add a page title to your HTML file, click the Change Title button and then type the text in the Page Title text box in the Set Page Title dialog box before you click OK.

You're now ready to save your spreadsheet as an HTML file by clicking the Save button. If you want to see how this file looks in your web browser immediately upon saving it, click the Publish button to open the Publish as Web Page dialog box and save the file from there after selecting the Open Published Web Page in Browser check box. And if you want Excel to automatically save an HTML version of the worksheet each time you save the workbook, you select the AutoRepublish Every Time This Workbook Is Saved check box as well.

7. Click the Save button to save the file without opening it in your web browser. Otherwise, click the Publish button so that you can see the web page in your browser right after saving it.

If you click the Save button, Excel closes the Save As dialog box, saves the file to disk, and returns to the Excel window (that now contains the HTML version of your workbook or worksheet in place of the original .xls file).

If you click the Publish button to view the new HTML file in your browser, Excel opens the Publish as Web Page dialog box, where you select the Open Published Web Page in Browser check box before clicking the Publish button.

8. Click the Open Published Web Page in Browser check box and then click the Publish button.

When you click the Publish button, Excel closes the Publish As Web Page dialog box, saves the spreadsheet as an HTML file, and then immediately launches your default web browsing program while at the same time opening the new HTML file in the browser. After you finish looking over the new HTML file in your web browser, click its program window's Close button to close the browser and HTML file and to return to Excel and the original worksheet.

REMEMBER

Keep in mind that you can control which worksheets and named ranges (see Book 3, Chapter 1 for details) appear when a workbook is viewed in a web browser in the Browser View Options dialog box opened by clicking File ⇨ Export ⇨ Browser View Options and then clicking the Browser View Options button (Alt+FEBA).

TIP

If you add the Web Page Preview and Web Options commands as custom buttons to the Quick Access toolbar, you can use them to preview how a worksheet will appear as a web page locally in your web browser as well as control a whole variety of web page save options. To add these buttons, open the Customize the Quick Access Toolbar tab of the Excel Options dialog box (Alt+FTQ) and then add the Web Page Preview and Web Options from Commands Not in the Ribbon section. (See Book 1, Chapter 2 for details.)

5
Charts and Graphics

Contents at a Glance

IN THIS CHAPTER

» Understanding how to chart worksheet data

» Creating an embedded chart or one on its own chart sheet

» Editing an existing chart

» Formatting the elements in a chart

» Saving customized charts as templates and using these templates to create new charts

» Adding sparklines to worksheet data

» Printing a chart alone or with its supporting data

Chapter **1**

Charting Worksheet Data

C harts present the data from your worksheet visually by representing the data in rows and columns as bars on a chart, for example, or as pieces of a pie in a pie chart. For a long time, charts and graphs have gone hand-in-hand with spreadsheets because they allow you to see trends and patterns that you often can't readily visualize from the numbers alone. Which has more consistent sales, the Southeast region or the Northwest region? Monthly sales reports may contain the answer, but a bar chart based on the data shows it more clearly.

In this chapter, you first become familiar with the terminology that Excel uses as it refers to the parts of a chart — terms that may be new, such as *data marker* and *chart data series,* as well as terms that are probably familiar already, such as *axis.* After you get acquainted with the terms, you begin to put them to use going through the simple steps required to create the kind of chart that you want, either as part of the worksheet or a separate chart sheet.

The art of preparing a chart (and much of the fun) is matching a chart type to your purposes. To help you with this, I guide you through a tour of all the chart types available in Excel 2019, from old standbys, such as bar and column charts, and introduce you to new types added to Excel 2019 with which you may be less familiar, such as Treemap, Funnel, Waterfall, and Box and Whisker charts. Finally, you discover how to print charts, either alone or as part of the worksheet.

Worksheet Charting 101

The typical Excel chart is comprised of several distinct parts. Figure 1-1 shows an Excel clustered column chart added to a worksheet with labels identifying the parts of this chart. Table 1-1 summarizes the parts of the typical chart.

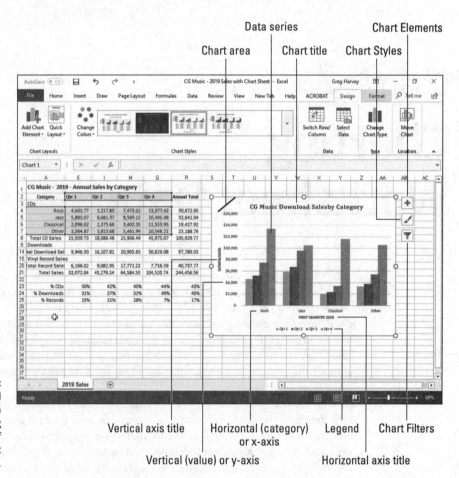

FIGURE 1-1:
A typical clustered column chart containing a variety of standard chart elements.

TABLE 1-1

Parts of a Typical Chart

Part	Description
Chart area	Everything inside the chart window, including all parts of the chart (labels, axes, data markers, tick marks, and other elements in this table).
Data marker	A symbol on the chart that represents a single value in the spreadsheet. A symbol may be a bar in a bar chart, a pie in a pie chart, or a line on a line chart. Data markers with the same shape or pattern represent a single data series in the chart.
Chart data series	A group of related values, such as all the values in a single row in the chart — all the quarterly sales for Rock CDs in the sample chart, for example. A chart can have just one data series (shown in a single bar or line), but it usually has several.
Series formula	A formula describing a given data series. The formula includes a reference to the cell that contains the data series name, references to worksheet cells containing the categories and values plotted in the chart, and the plot order of the series. The series formula can also have the actual data used to plot the chart. You can edit a series formula and control the plot order.
Axis	A line that serves as a major reference for plotting data in a chart. In two-dimensional charts, there are two axes: the x (horizontal/category) axis and the y (vertical/value) axis. In most two-dimensional charts (except, notably, column charts), Excel plots categories (labels) along the x-axis and values (numbers) along the y-axis. Bar charts reverse the scheme, plotting values along the y-axis. Pie charts have no axes. Three-dimensional charts have an x-axis, a y-axis, and a z-axis. The x- and y-axes delineate the horizontal surface of the chart. The z-axis is the vertical axis, showing the depth of the third dimension in the chart.
Tick mark	A small line intersecting an axis. A tick mark indicates a category, scale, or chart data series. A tick mark can have a label attached.
Plot area	The area where Excel plots your data, including the axes and all markers that represent data points.
Gridlines	Optional lines extending from the tick marks across the plot area, thus making it easier to view the data values represented by the tick marks.
Chart text	A label or title that you add to the chart. *Attached text* is a title or label linked to an axis such as the Chart Title, Vertical Axis Title, and Horizontal Axis Title that you can't move independently of the chart. *Unattached text* is text that you add such as a text box with the Text Box command button on the Insert tab of the Ribbon.
Legend	A key that identifies patterns, colors, or symbols associated with the markers of a chart data series. The legend shows the data series name corresponding to each data marker (such as the name of the red columns in a column chart).

Embedded charts versus charts on separate chart sheets

An *embedded chart* is a chart that appears right within the worksheet (like the one shown in Figure 1-1) so that when you save or print the worksheet, you save or print the chart along with it. Note that your charts don't have to be embedded. You can also choose to create a chart in its own chart sheet in the workbook at the time you create it. Embed a chart on the worksheet when you want to be able to print the chart along with its supporting worksheet data. Place a chart on its own sheet when you intend to print the charts of the worksheet data separately.

REMEMBER

Keep in mind that all charts (embedded or on their own sheets) are dynamically linked to the worksheet that they represent. This means that if you modify any of the values that are plotted in the chart, Excel immediately redraws the chart to reflect the change, assuming that the worksheet still uses automatic recalculation. When Manual recalculation is turned on, you must remember to press F9 or click the Calc Now (F9) command button on the Formulas tab of the Ribbon (Alt+MB) in order to get Excel to redraw the chart to reflect any changes to the worksheet values it represents.

TIP

You can print any chart that you've embedded in a worksheet by itself without any worksheet data (as though it were created on its own chart sheet) by selecting it before you open the Print dialog box.

Inserting recommended charts

My personal favorite way to create a new embedded chart from selected data in a worksheet in Excel 2019 is with the Recommended Charts command button on the Insert tab of the Ribbon (Alt+NR).

When you use this method, Excel opens the Insert Chart dialog box with the Recommended Charts tab selected similar to the one shown in Figure 1-2. Here, you can preview how the selected worksheet data will appear in different types of charts simply by clicking its thumbnail in the list box on the left. When you find the type of chart you want to create, you then simply click the OK button to have it embedded into the current worksheet.

MOVING AN EMBEDDED CHART ONTO ITS OWN CHART SHEET

If it's really important that the chart remain a separate element in the workbook, you can move the embedded chart onto its own chart sheet. Simply click the embedded chart if it's not already selected in the worksheet and then click the Move Chart command button in the Location group on the Design tab of the Chart Tools contextual tab on the Ribbon. Excel then opens the Move dialog box, where you then click the New Sheet option button and click OK to switch the embedded chart to a chart on a separate chart sheet.

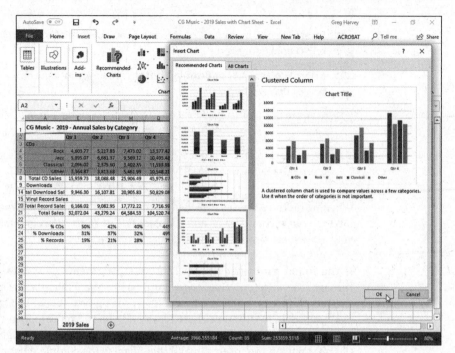

Inserting specific chart types from the Ribbon

To the right of the Recommended Charts button in the Charts group of the Ribbon's Insert tab, you find particular command buttons with galleries for creating the following particular types and styles of charts:

>> **Insert Column or Bar Chart** to preview your data as a 2-D or 3-D vertical column or horizontal bar chart

>> **Insert Hierarchy Chart** to preview your data in a Treemap or Sunburst hierarchy chart

>> **Insert Waterfall, Funnel, Stock, Surface, or Radar Chart** to preview your data as a 2-D waterfall, funnel, or stock chart (using typical stock symbols), 2-D or 3-D surface chart, or 3-D radar chart

>> **Insert Line or Area Chart** to preview your data as a 2-D or 3-D line or area chart

>> **Insert Statistic Chart** to preview a statistical analysis of your data as a 2-D histogram or box and whiskers chart

>> **Insert Combo Chart** to preview your data as a 2-D combo clustered column and line chart or clustered column and stacked area chart

» **Insert Pie or Doughnut Chart** to preview your data as a 2-D or 3-D pie chart or 2-D doughnut chart

» **Insert Scatter (X,Y) or Bubble Chart** to preview your data as a 2-D scatter (X,Y) or bubble chart

» **Maps** to preview categories across regions in your data as a 2-D filled map chart

» **PivotChart** to preview your data as a PivotChart (see Book 7, Chapter 2 for more on creating this special type of interactive summary chart)

When using the galleries attached to these chart command buttons on the Insert tab to preview your data as a particular style of chart, you can embed the chart in your worksheet simply by clicking its chart icon.

If you're not sure what type of chart best represents your data, rather than go through the different chart type buttons on the Ribbon's Insert tab, you can use the All Charts tab of the Insert Chart dialog box shown in Figure 1-3 to "try out" your data in different chart types and styles. You can open the Insert Chart dialog box by clicking the Dialog Box launcher in the lower-right corner of the Charts group on the Insert tab and then display the complete list of chart types by clicking the All Charts tab in this dialog box.

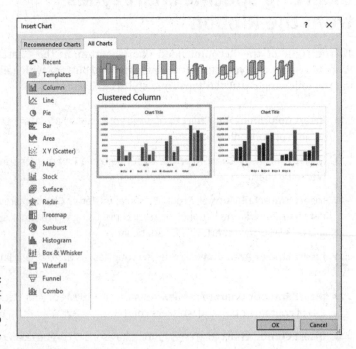

FIGURE 1-3:
Insert Chart dialog box with the All Charts tab selected.

Excel 2019 includes some exciting new chart types that you can only preview and select from the All Charts tab in the Insert Chart dialog box. These new chart types include

» **Treemap** to show hierarchical data in a tree-like structure using nested rectangles of different colors representing the branches and sub-branches within related data. Treemap charts provide a great way to represent very large amounts of hierarchical data in a very compact space.

» **Box & Whisker** to show the spread and skew within an ordered data set or within two sets of data compared to one other. The Box and Whisker chart depicts five variables within the groups of data: maximum, upper quartile, median, lower quartile, and minimum. The maximum and minimum values are represented as thin vertical and horizontal lines (the whiskers) above and below a rectangle (the box) depicting the upper and lower quartiles with a horizontal dividing line that represents the median.

» **Waterfall** to show the effect of sequential intermediate values that increase or decrease on initial values in the data set. The intermediate values showing the increase or decrease can either be based on time or on different categories. Values in the data are represented by floating columns of various sizes and colors.

» **Funnel** to show the progressive reduction within an ordered data set as a percentage of the whole represented as different colored slices within an inverted triangle (creating a funnel shape). Funnel charts, like Pie charts, do not have an X- and Y-axis.

Inserting charts with the Quick Analysis tool

For those times when you need to select a subset of a data table as the range to be charted (as opposed to selecting a single cell within a data table), you can use the Quick Analysis tool to create your chart. Just follow these steps:

1. **Click the Quick Analysis tool that appears at the lower-right corner of the current cell selection.**

   Doing this opens the palette of Quick Analysis options with the initial Formatting tab selected and its various conditional formatting options displayed.

2. **Click the Charts tab at the top of the Quick Analysis options palette.**

   Excel selects the Charts tab and displays buttons for different types of charts that suit the selected data, such as Column, Stacked Bar, and Clustered Bar, followed by a More Charts option buttons. The different types of chart buttons preview the selected data in that kind of chart. The final More Charts button opens the Insert Chart dialog box with the Recommended Charts tab selected. Here you can preview and select a chart from an even wider range of chart types.

3. **In order to preview each type of chart that Excel 2019 can create using the selected data, highlight its chart type button in the Quick Analysis palette.**

As you highlight each chart type button in the options palette, Excel's Live Preview feature displays a large thumbnail of the chart that will be created from your table data. (See Figure 1-4.) This thumbnail appears above the Quick Analysis options palette for as long as the mouse or Touch pointer is over its corresponding button.

4. **When a preview of the chart you actually want to create appears, click its button in the Quick Analysis options palette to create it.**

Excel 2019 then creates and inserts an embedded chart of the selected type in the current worksheet. This embedded chart is active so that you can immediately move it and edit it as you wish.

FIGURE 1-4:
Previewing the embedded chart to insert from the Quick Analysis tool.

Creating a chart on a separate chart sheet

Sometimes you know you want your new chart to appear on its own separate sheet in the workbook and you don't have time to fool around with moving an embedded chart created with the Quick Analysis tool or the various chart command buttons on the Insert tab of the Ribbon to its own sheet. In such a situation, simply position the cell pointer somewhere in the table of data to be graphed (or select the specific cell range in a larger table) and then just press F11.

Excel then creates a clustered column chart using the table's data or cell selection on its own chart sheet (Chart1) that precedes all the other sheets in the workbook as shown in Figure 1-5. You can then customize the chart on the new chart sheet as you would an embedded chart that's described later in the chapter.

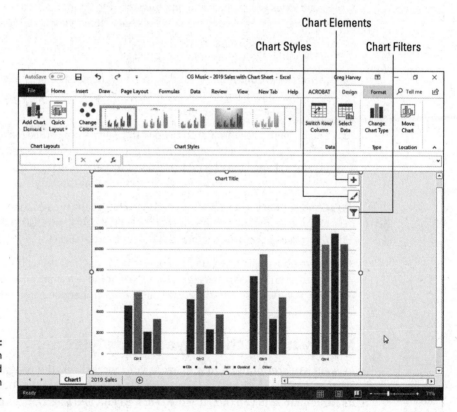

FIGURE 1-5:
Clustered column chart created on its own chart sheet.

Refining the chart from the Design tab

You can use the command buttons on the Design tab of the Chart Tools contextual tab to make all kinds of changes to your new chart. This tab contains the following command buttons:

» **Chart Layouts:** Click the Add Chart Element button to select the type of chart element you want to add. (You can also do this by selecting the Chart Elements button in the upper-right corner of the chart itself.) Click the Quick Layout button and then click the thumbnail of the new layout style you want applied to the selected chart on the drop-down gallery.

» **Chart Styles:** Click the Change Colors button to open a drop-down gallery and then select a new color scheme for the data series in the selected chart. In the Chart Styles gallery, highlight and then click the thumbnail of the new chart style you want applied to the selected chart. Note that you can select a new color and chart style in the opened galleries by clicking the Chart Styles button in the upper-right corner of the chart itself.

» **Switch Row/Column:** Click this button to immediately interchange the worksheet data used for the Legend Entries (series) with that used for the Axis Labels (Categories) in the selected chart.

» **Select Data:** Click this button to open the Select Data Source dialog box, where you can not only modify which data is used in the selected chart but also interchange the Legend Entries (series) with the Axis Labels (Categories), but also edit out or add particular entries to either category.

» **Change Chart Type:** Click this button to change the type of chart and then click the thumbnail of the new chart type on the All Charts tab in the Change Chart dialog box, which shows all kinds of charts in Excel.

» **Move Chart:** Click this button to open the Move Chart dialog box, where you move an embedded chart to its own chart or move a chart on its own sheet to one of the worksheets in the workbook as an embedded chart.

Modifying the chart layout and style

As soon as Excel draws a new chart in your worksheet, the program selects your chart and adds the Chart Tools contextual tab to the end of the Ribbon and selects its Design tab. You can then use the Quick Layout and Chart Styles galleries to further refine the new chart.

Figure 1-6 shows the original clustered column chart (created in Figure 1-5) after selecting Layout 9 on the Quick Layout button's drop-down gallery and then selecting the Style 8 thumbnail on the Chart Styles drop-down gallery. Selecting Layout 9 adds Axis Titles to both the vertical and horizontal axes as well as creating the Legend on the right side of the graph. Selecting Style 8 gives the clustered column chart its dark background and contoured edges on the clustered columns themselves.

Switching the rows and columns in a chart

Normally when Excel creates a new chart, it automatically graphs the data by rows in the cell selection so that the column headings appear along the horizontal (category) axis at the bottom of the chart and the row headings appear in the legend (assuming that you're dealing with a chart type that utilizes an *x*- and *y*-axis).

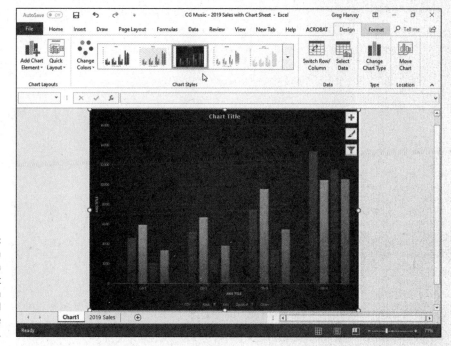

FIGURE 1-6:
Clustered column chart on its own chart sheet after selecting a new layout and style from the Design tab.

TRYING ON ALL YOUR CHOICES IN THE CHART STYLES GALLERY

TIP

When selecting a new style for your chart, you can display all the style choices by clicking that gallery's More button (the one with the horizontal bar directly over a triangle pointing downward). Doing this displays the thumbnails of all your layout and style choices for the new chart. You can also scroll through the rows of style choices by clicking the Previous Row or Next Row buttons immediately above it with the respective upward- or downward-pointing triangles.

You can click the Switch Row/Column command button on the Design tab of the Chart Tools contextual tab to switch the chart so that row headings appear on the horizontal (category) axis and the column headings appear in the legend (or you can press Alt+JCW).

Figure 1-7 demonstrates how this works. This figure shows the same clustered column chart after selecting the Switch Row/Column command button on the Design tab. Now, column headings (Qtr 1, Qtr 2, Qtr 3, and Qtr 4) are used in the legend on the right and the row headings (Genre, Rock, Jazz, Classical, and Other) appear along the horizontal (category) axis.

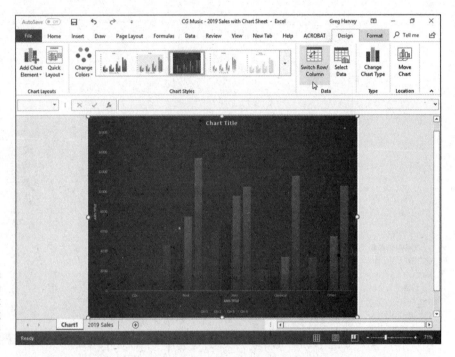

Editing the source of the data graphed in the chart

When you click the Select Data command button on the Design tab of the Chart Tools contextual tab (or press Alt+JCE), Excel opens a Select Data Source dialog box similar to the one shown in Figure 1-8. The controls in this dialog box enable you to make the following changes to the source data:

>> Modify the range of data being graphed in the chart by clicking the Chart Data Range text box and then making a new cell selection in the worksheet or typing in its range address.

>> Switch the row and column headings back and forth by clicking its Switch Row/Column button.

>> Edit the labels used to identify the data series in the legend or on the horizontal (category) by clicking the Edit button on the Legend Entries (Series) or Horizontal (Categories) Axis Labels side and then selecting the cell range with appropriate row or column headings in the worksheet.

>> Add additional data series to the chart by clicking the Add button on the Legend Entries (Series) side and then selecting the cell containing the heading for that series in the Series Name text box and the cells containing the values to be graphed in that series in the Series Values text box.

>> Delete a label from the legend by clicking its name in the Legend Entries (Series) list box and then clicking the Remove button.

>> Modify the order of the data series in the chart by clicking the series name in the Legend Entries (Series) list box and then clicking the Move Up button (the one with the arrow pointing upward) or the Move Down button (the one with the arrow pointing downward) until the data series appears in the desired position in the chart.

>> Indicate how to deal with empty cells in the data range being graphed by clicking the Hidden and Empty Cells button and then selecting the appropriate Show Empty Cells As option button (Gaps, the default; Zero and Connect Data Points with Line, for line charts). Click the Show Data in Hidden Rows and Columns check box to have Excel graph data in the hidden rows and columns within the selected chart data range.

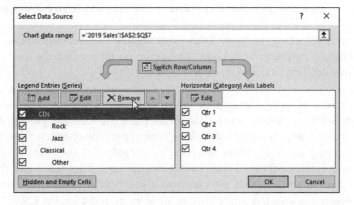

FIGURE 1-8: Using the Select Data Source dialog box to remove the empty Genre label from the legend of the clustered column chart.

The example clustered column chart in Figures 1-6 and 1-7 illustrates a common situation where you need to use the options in the Source Data Source dialog box. The worksheet data range for this chart, A2:Q7, includes the Genre row heading in cell A3 that is essentially a heading for an empty row (E3:Q3). As a result, Excel includes this empty row as the first data series in the clustered column chart. However, because this row has no values in it (the heading is intended only to identify the type of music download recorded in that column of the sales data table), its cluster has no data bars (columns) in it — a fact that becomes quite apparent when you switch the column and row headings, as shown earlier in Figure 1-7.

To remove this empty data series from the clustered column chart, you follow these steps:

1. **Click the Chart1 sheet tab and then click somewhere in the chart area to select the clustered column chart; click the Design tab under Chart Tools on the Ribbon and then click the Select Data command button on the Design tab of the Chart Tools contextual tab.**

   Excel opens the Select Data Source dialog box in the 2016 Sales worksheet similar to the one shown in Figure 1-8.

2. **Click the Switch Row/Column button in the Select Data Source dialog box to place the row headings (Genre, Rock, Jazz, Classical, and Other) in the Legend Entries (Series) list box.**

3. **Click Genre at the top of the Legend Entries (Series) list box and then click the Remove button.**

   Excel removes the empty Genre data series from the clustered column chart as well as removing the Genre label from the Legend Entries (Series) list box in the Select Data Source dialog box.

4. **Click the Switch Row/Column button in the Select Data Source dialog box again to exchange the row and column headings in the chart and then click the Close button to close the Select Data Source dialog box.**

After you close the Select Data Source dialog box, you will notice that the various colored outlines in the chart data range no longer include row 3 with the Genre row heading (A3) and its empty cells (E3:Q3).

TIP

Instead of going through all those steps in the Select Data Source dialog box to remove the empty Genre data series from the example clustered column chart, you can simply remove the Genre series from the chart on the Chart Filters button pop-up menu. When the chart's selected, click the Chart Filters button in the upper-right corner of the chart (with the cone filter icon) and then deselect the Genre check box that appears under the SERIES heading on the pop-up menu before clicking the Apply button. As soon as you click the Chart Filters button to close its menu, you see that Excel has removed the empty data series from the redrawn clustered column chart.

ADDING HIDDEN ROWS AND COLUMNS OF DATA TO A CHART

The sales data graphed in the sample clustered column chart shown in Figures 1-6, 1-7, and 1-8 only includes the quarterly download totals in each music category. To do this, I outlined the data in this entire table and then collapsed the outlined columns down to their second level so that only the quarterly subtotals and yearly grand totals were displayed (see Book 2, Chapter 4 for details) before selecting the range A2:Q7 as the clustered column chart's data range. Because all the columns with the monthly download data in each quarter were hidden at the time I originally created the chart (as a result of collapsing the outlined columns to the second level), Excel didn't include their data as part of it.

If I decide that I do want to see the monthly downloads represented in the clustered column chart, to accomplish this, all I have to do is open the Select Data Source dialog box (by clicking the Select Data button on the Chart Tools Design tab) and then click its Hidden and Empty Cells command button. Excel then opens a Hidden and Empty Cell Settings dialog box, where I click the Show Data in Hidden Rows and Columns check box and then click OK. Excel then immediately redraws the chart adding columns representing the monthly sales to those for the quarterly subtotals in all four of its clusters.

Customizing chart elements from the Format tab

The command buttons on the Format tab on the Chart Tools contextual tab make it easy to customize particular parts of your chart. Table 1-2 shows you the options that appear on the Format tab. Note that depending on the type of chart that's selected at the time, some of these options may be unavailable.

TABLE 1-2 **Format Tab Options**

Tab Group	Option Name	Purpose
Current Selection	Chart Elements	Click this command button to select a new chart element by choosing its name from the button's drop-down menu.
	Format Selection	Click this command button to open a Format dialog box for the currently selected chart element as displayed on the Chart Elements drop-down list button.
	Reset to Match Style	Click this command button to remove all custom formatting from the selected chart and to return it to the original formatting bestowed by the style selected for the chart.

(continued)

TABLE 1-2 *(continued)*

Tab Group	Option Name	Purpose
Insert Shapes		Click the thumbnail of the shape you want to add to your chart on the drop-down gallery with a whole bunch of preset graphic shapes. (See Book 5, Chapter 2 for details.)
Shape Styles	Shape Styles	Click the Shape Styles' More button to display a drop-down gallery in which you can preview and select new colors and shapes for the currently selected chart element as displayed on the Chart Elements drop-down list button.
	Shape Fill	Click this command button to display a drop-down color palette in which you can preview and select a new fill color for the currently selected chart element as displayed on the Chart Elements drop-down list button.
	Shape Outline	Click this command button to display a drop-down color palette in which you can preview and select an outline color for the currently selected chart element as displayed on the Chart Elements drop-down list button.
	Shape Effects	Click this command button to display a drop-down menu containing a variety of graphics effect options (including Shadow, Glow, Soft Edges, Bevel, and 3-D Rotation), many of which have their own pop-up palettes that allow you to preview their special effects, where you can select a new graphics effect for the currently selected chart element as displayed on the Chart Elements drop-down list button.
WordArt Styles	WordArt Styles	Click the WordArt Styles More button to display a drop-down WordArt gallery in which you can preview and select a new WordArt text style for the titles selected in the chart. If the Chart Area is the currently selected chart element as displayed on the Chart Elements drop-down list button, the program applies the WordArt style you preview or select to all titles in the chart.
	Text Fill	Click this command button to display a drop-down color palette in which you can preview and select a new text fill color for the titles selected in the chart. If the Chart Area is the currently selected chart element as displayed on the Chart Elements drop-down list button, the program applies the WordArt style you preview or select to all titles in the chart. You can also select an image to be used as the text fill rather than a color by selecting the Picture option below the color palette.
	Text Outline	Click this command button to display a drop-down color palette in which you can preview and select a new text outline color for the titles selected in the chart. If the Chart Area is the currently selected chart element as displayed on the Chart Elements drop-down list button, the program applies the WordArt style you preview or select to all titles in the chart.
	Text Effects	Click this command button to display a drop-down menu with the Shadow, Reflection, Glow, Bevel, 3-D Rotation, and Transform graphics effect options active, each of which have their own pop-up palettes that you can use to preview and select special effects for the titles selected in the chart. If the Chart Area is the currently selected chart element as displayed on the Chart Elements drop-down list button, the program applies the WordArt style you preview or select to all titles in the chart.

Tab Group	Option Name	Purpose
Arrange	Bring Forward	Click this button to move the object to a higher layer in the stack or choose the Bring to Front option from the button's drop-down menu to bring the selected embedded chart or other graphic object to the top of its stack. (See Book 5, Chapter 2 for details.)
	Send Backward	Click this button to move the object to a lower level in the stack or choose the Send to Back option from the button's drop-down menu to send the selected embedded chart or other graphic object to the bottom of its stack. (See Book 5, Chapter 2 for details.) Note that this command button and its options are available only when more than one embedded chart or other graphic object is selected in the worksheet.
	Selection Pane	Click this command button to display and hide the Selection and Visibility task pane that shows all the graphic objects in the worksheet and enables you to hide and redisplay them as well as promote or demote them to different layers. (See Book 5, Chapter 2 for details.) Note that this command button and its options are available only when more than one embedded chart or other graphic object is selected in the worksheet.
	Align	Click this button to display a drop-down menu that enables you to snap the selected chart to an invisible grid on another graphic object as well as to choose between a number of different alignment options when multiple graphic objects are selected. (See Book 5, Chapter 2 for details.)
	Group	Click this button to display a drop-down menu that enables you to group the selected embedded chart with other graphic objects (such as text boxes or predefined shapes) for purposes of positioning and formatting. (See Book 5, Chapter 2 for details.) Note that this command button and its options are available only when more than one embedded chart or other graphic object is selected in the worksheet.
	Rotate	Click this button to display a drop-down menu with options that enable you to rotate or flip a selected graphic object. Note that this command button and its options are available only when graphic objects other than embedded charts are selected in the worksheet.
Size	Shape Height	Use this text box to modify the height of the selected embedded chart by typing a new value in it or selecting one with the spinner buttons.
	Shape Width	Use this text box to modify the width of the selected embedded chart by typing a new value in it or selecting one with the spinner buttons.

Customizing the elements of a chart

The Chart Elements button (with the plus sign icon) that appears in the upper-right corner of your chart when it's selected contains a list of the major chart elements that you can add to your chart. To add a particular element missing from the chart, select the element's check box in the list to put a check mark in it.

To remove a particular element currently displayed in the chart, deselect the element's check box to remove its check mark.

To add or remove just part of a particular chart element or, in some cases as with the Chart Title, Data Labels, Data Table, Error Bars, Legend, and Trendline, to also specify its layout, you select the desired option on the element's continuation menu. (See Figure 1-9.)

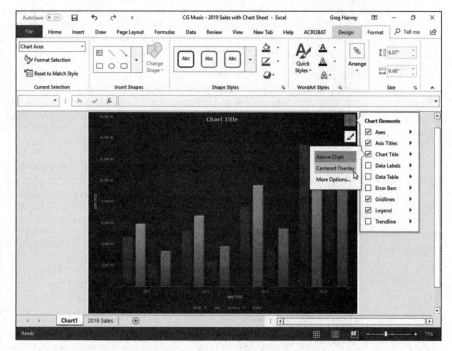

FIGURE 1-9:
Repositioning the chart title in the example clustered column using the Chart Element button's menus.

So, for example, to reposition a chart's title, you click the continuation button attached to Chart Title on the Chart Elements menu to display and select from among the following options on its continuation menu:

» **Above Chart** to add or reposition the chart title so that it appears centered above the plot area

» **Centered Overlay** to add or reposition the chart title so that it appears centered at the top of the plot area

» **More Options** to open the Format Chart Title task pane on the right side of the Excel window so you can use the options that appear when you select the Fill & Line, Effects, and Size and Properties buttons under Title Options and the Text Fill & Outline, Text Effects, and the Textbox buttons under Title Options in this task pane to modify almost any aspect of the title's formatting

Adding data labels to the series in a chart

Data labels identify the data points in your chart (that is, the columns, lines, and so forth used to graph your data) by displaying values from the cells of the worksheet represented next to them. To add data labels to your selected chart and position them, click the Chart Elements button next to the chart and then select the Data Labels check box before you select one of the following options on its continuation menu:

>> **Center** to position the data labels in the middle of each data point

>> **Inside End** to position the data labels inside each data point near the end

>> **Inside Base** to position the data labels at the base of each data point

>> **Outside End** to position the data labels outside of the end of each data point

>> **Data Callout** to add text labels as well as values that appear within text boxes that point to each data point

>> **More Options** to open the Format Data Labels task pane on the right side where you can use the options that appear when you select the Fill & Line, Effects, Size & Properties, and Label Options buttons under Label Options and the Text Fill & Outline, Text Effects, and Textbox buttons under Text Options in the task pane to customize almost any aspect of the appearance and position of the data labels

REMEMBER

To remove all data labels from the data points in a selected chart, clear the Data Labels check box on the Chart Elements menu.

Adding a data table to a chart

Sometimes, instead of data labels that can easily obscure the data points in the chart, you'll want Excel to draw a data table beneath the chart showing the worksheet data it represents in graphic form.

To add a data table to your selected chart and position and format it, click the Chart Elements button next to the chart and then select the Data Table check box before you select one of the following options on its continuation menu:

>> **With Legend Keys** to have Excel draw the table at the bottom of the chart, including the color keys used in the legend to differentiate the data series in the first column

>> **No Legend Keys** to have Excel draw the table at the bottom of the chart without any legend

>> **More Options** to open the Format Data Table task pane on the right side where you can use the options that appear when you select the Fill & Line, Effects, Size & Properties, and Table Options buttons under Table Options and the Text Fill & Outline, Text Effects, and Textbox buttons under Text Options in the task pane to customize almost any aspect of the data table

Figure 1-10 illustrates how the sample clustered column chart (introduced in Figure 1-6) looks with a data table added to it. This data table includes the legend keys as its first column.

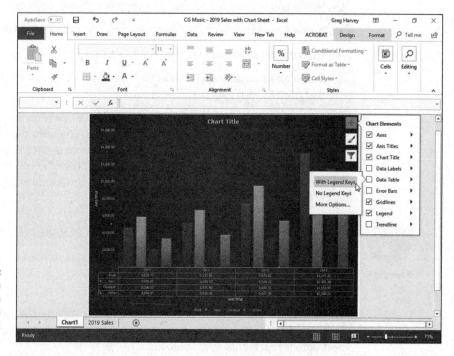

If you decide that having the worksheet data displayed in a table at the bottom of the chart is no longer necessary, simply click to deselect the Data Table check box on the Chart Elements menu.

REMEMBER

Editing the chart titles

When Excel first adds any title to a new chart, the program gives it a generic name, such as Chart Title or AXIS TITLE (for both the x- and y-axis title). To replace such generic titles with the actual chart titles, click the title in the chart or click the name of the title on the Chart Elements drop-down list. (Chart Elements is the first drop-down button in the Current Selection group on the Format tab under Chart Tools. Its text box displays the name of the element currently selected in the chart.) Excel lets you know that a particular chart title is selected by placing selection handles around its perimeter.

After you select a title, you can click the insertion point in the text and then edit as you would any worksheet text, or you can click to select the title, type the new title, and press Enter to completely replace it with the text you type. To force part of the title onto a new line, click the insertion point at the place in the text where the line break is to occur. After the insertion point is positioned in the title, press Enter to start a new line.

After selecting a title, you can then click the insertion point in the text and then edit as you would any worksheet text, or you can triple-click to select the entire title and completely replace it with the text you type. To force part of the title onto a new line, click the insertion point at the place in the text where the line break is to occur. After the insertion point is positioned in the title, press Enter to start a new line. After you finish editing the title, click somewhere else on the chart area to deselect it (or a worksheet cell, if you've finished formatting and editing the chart).

Double-click anywhere in a word in the chart title to completely select that word. Triple-click anywhere in the title text to completely select that chart title. When you double- or triple-click a chart title, a mini-bar appears above the title with buttons for modifying the selected text's font, font size, and alignment, as well as for adding text enhancements such as bold, italic, and underlining.

TIP

If you want, you can instantly create a title for your chart by linking it to a heading that's been entered into one of the cells in your worksheet. That way, if you update the heading in the worksheet, it's automatically updated in your chart. To link a chart title to a heading in a worksheet cell, click the title in the chart to select it, then type = on the Formula bar, click the cell in the worksheet that contains the text you want to use as the chart title, and press Enter. Excel shows that the chart title is now dynamically linked to the contents of the cell by displaying its absolute cell reference whenever that title is selected in the chart.

Formatting elements of a chart

Excel 2019 offers you several methods for formatting particular elements of any chart that you create. The most direct way is to right-click the chart element (title, plot area, legend, data series, and so forth) in the chart itself. Doing so displays a mini-bar with options such as Fill, Outline, and (in the case of chart titles), Style. You can then use the drop-down galleries and menus attached to these buttons to connect the selected chart element.

If the mini-bar formatting options aren't sufficient for the kind of changes you want to make to a particular chart element, you can open a task bar for the element. The easiest way to do this is by right-clicking the element in the chart and then selecting the Format option at the bottom of the shortcut menu that appears. This Format option, like the task pane that opens on the right side of the worksheet window, is followed by the name of the element selected so that when the Chart Title is selected, this menu option is called Format Chart Title, and the task pane that opens when you select this option is labeled Format Chart Title. (See Figure 1-11.)

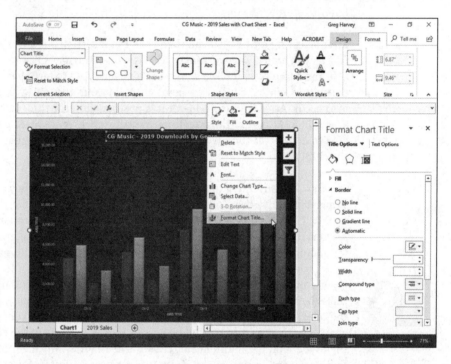

FIGURE 1-11:
Formatting the Chart Title with the options in the Format Chart Title task pane.

The element's task pane contains groups of options, often divided into two categories: Options for the selected element on the left — such as Title Options in the Format Chart Title task pane or Legend Options in the Format Legend task pane — and Text Options on the right. Each group, when selected, then displays its own cluster of buttons and each button, when selected has its own collection of formatting options, often displayed only when expanded by clicking the option name.

TIP

You can click the drop-down button found to the immediate right of any Options group in any Format task pane to display a drop-down menu with a complete list of all the elements in that chart. To select another element for formatting, simply select its name from this drop-down list. Excel then selects that element in the chart and switches to its Format task pane so that you have access to all its groups of formatting options.

REMEMBER

Keep in mind that the Format tab on the Chart Tools contextual tab also contains a Shape Styles and WordArt Styles group of command buttons that you can sometimes use to format the element you've selected in the chart. Table 1-2, shown earlier in this chapter, gives you the lowdown on the command buttons in these groups on the Format tab.

Formatting chart titles with the Format Chart Title task pane

When you choose the Format Chart Title option from a chart title's shortcut menu, Excel displays a Format Chart Title task pane similar to the one shown in Figure 1-11. The Title Options group is automatically selected as is the Fill & Line button (with the paint can icon).

As you can see in Figure 1-11, there are two groups of Fill & Line options: Fill and Border (neither of whose particular options are initially displayed when you first open the Format Chart Title task pane — in this figure, I clicked both Fill and Border so that you could see all of the Fill options and the first part of the Border options). Next to the Line & Fill button is the Effects button (with the pentagon icon). This button has four groups of options associated with it: Shadow, Glow, Soft Edges, and 3-D Format.

You would use the formatting options associated with the Fill & Line and Effects buttons in the Title Options group when you want to change the look of the text box that contains the select chart title. More likely when formatting most chart titles, you will want to use the commands found in the Text Options group to actually change the look of the title text.

When you click Text Options in the Format Chart Title task pane, you find three buttons with associated options:

>> **Text Fill & Outline** (with a filled A with an outlined underline at the bottom icon): When selected, it displays a Text Fill and Text Outline group of options in the task pane for changing the type and color of the text fill and the type of outline.

>> **Text Effects** (with the outlined A with a circle at the bottom icon): When selected, it displays a Shadow, Reflection, Glow, Soft Edges, and 3-D Format and 3-D Rotation group of options in the task pane for adding shadows to the title text or other special effects.

>> **Textbox** (with the A in the upper-left corner of a text box icon): When selected, it displays a list of Text Box options for controlling the vertical alignment, text direction (especially useful when formatting the Vertical [Value]Axis title), and angle of the text box containing the chart title. It also includes options for resizing the shape to fit the text and how to control any text that overflows the text box shape.

Formatting chart axes with the Format Axis task pane

The axis is the scale used to plot the data for your chart. Most chart types will have axes. All 2-D and 3-D charts have an x-axis known as the horizontal axis and a y-axis known as the vertical axis with the exception of pie charts and radar charts. The horizontal x-axis is also referred to as the category axis and the vertical y-axis as the value axis except in the case of XY (Scatter) charts, where the horizontal x-axis is also a value axis just like the vertical y-axis because this type of chart plots two sets of values against each other.

When you create a chart, Excel sets up the category and values axes for you automatically, based on the data you are plotting, which you can then adjust in various ways. The most common ways you will want to modify the category axis of a chart is to modify the interval between its tick marks and where it crosses the value axis in the chart. The most common ways you will want to modify a value axis of a chart is to change the scale that it uses and assign a new number formatting to its units.

To make such changes to a chart axis in the Format Axis task pane, right-click the axis in the chart and then select the Format Axis option at the very bottom of its shortcut menu. Excel opens the Format Axis task pane with the Axis Options group selected, displaying its four command buttons: Fill & Line, Effects, Size & Properties, and Axis Options. You then select the Axis Options button (with the clustered column data series icon) to display its four groups of options: Axis Options, Tick Marks, Labels, and Number.

Then, click Axis Options to expand and display its formatting options for the particular type of axis selected in the chart. Figure 1-12 shows the formatting options available when you expand this and the vertical (value) or y-axis is selected in the sample chart.

The Axis Options for formatting the Vertical (Value) Axis include:

>> **Bounds** to determine minimum and maximum points of the axis scale. Use the Minimum option to reset the point where the axis begins — perhaps $4,000 instead of the default of $0 — by clicking its Fixed option button and then entering a value higher than 0.0 in its text box. Use the Maximum to determine the highest point displayed on the vertical axis by clicking its Fixed option button and then entering the new maximum value in its text box — note that data values in the chart greater than the value you specify here simply aren't displayed in the chart.

>> **Units** to change the units used in separating the tick marks on the axis. Use the Major option to modify the distance between major horizontal tick marks (assuming they're displayed) in the chart by clicking its Fixed option button

and then entering the number of the new distance in its text box. Use the Minor option to modify the distance between minor horizontal tick marks (assuming they're displayed) in the chart by clicking its Fixed option button and then entering the number of the new distance in its text box.

» **Horizontal Axis Crosses** to reposition the point at which the horizontal axis crosses the vertical axis by clicking the Axis Value option button and then entering the value in the chart at which the horizontal axis is to cross or by clicking the Maximum Axis Value option button to have the horizontal axis cross after the highest value, putting the category axis labels at the top of the chart's frame.

» **Logarithmic Scale** to base the value axis scale upon powers of ten and recalculate the Minimum, Maximum, Major Unit, and Minor Unit accordingly by selecting its check box to put a check mark in it. Enter a new number in its text box if you want the logarithmic scale to use a base other than 10.

» **Values in Reverse Order** to place the lowest value on the chart at the top of the scale and the highest value at the bottom (as you might want to do in a chart to emphasize the negative effect of the larger values) by selecting its check box to put a check mark in it.

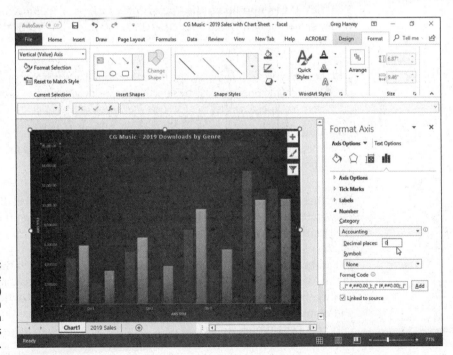

FIGURE 1-12:
Formatting the Vertical (Value) Axis with the options in the Format Axis task pane.

The Axis Options for formatting the Horizontal (Category) Axis include

>> **Axis Type** to indicate for formatting purposes that the axis labels are text entries by clicking the Text Axis option button, or indicate that they are dates by clicking the Date Axis option button.

>> **Vertical Axis Crosses** to reposition the point at which the vertical axis crosses the horizontal axis by clicking the At Category Number option button. Then enter the number of the category in the chart (with 1 indicating the leftmost category) after which the vertical axis is to cross or by clicking the At Maximum option button to have the vertical axis cross after the very last category on the right edge of the chart's frame.

>> **Axis Position** to reposition the horizontal axis so that its first category is located at the vertical axis on the left edge of the chart's frame and the last category is on the right edge of the chart's frame by selecting the On Tick Marks option button rather than between the tick marks (the default setting).

>> **Categories in Reverse Order** to reverse the order in which the data markers and their categories appear on the horizontal axis by clicking its check box to put a check mark in it.

The Tick Marks options in the Format Axis task pane include the following two options whether the Horizontal (Category) Axis or the Vertical (Value) Axis is selected:

>> **Major Type** to change how the major horizontal or vertical tick marks intersect the opposite axis by selecting the Inside, Outside, or Cross option from its drop-down list.

>> **Minor Type** to change how the minor horizontal or vertical tick marks intersect the opposite axis by selecting the Inside, Outside, or Cross option from its drop-down list.

Note that when modifying the Horizontal (Category) Axis, Excel offers an Interval Between Marks Tick Marks option that enables you to change the span between the tick marks that appear on this x-axis.

In addition to changing y- and x-axis formatting settings with the options found in the Axis Options and Tick Marks sections in the Format Axis task pane, you can modify the position of the axis labels with the Label Position option under Labels and number formatting assigned to the values displayed in the axis with Category option under Number.

To reposition the axis labels, click Labels in the Format Axis task pane to expand and display its options. When the Vertical (Value) Axis is the selected chart element, you can use the Label Position option to change the position to beneath the horizontal axis by selecting the Low option, to above the chart's frame by selecting the High option, or to completely remove their display in the chart by selecting the None option on its drop-down list.

When the Horizontal (Category) Axis is selected, you can also specify the Interval between the Labels on this axis, specify their Distance from the Axis (in pixels), and even modify the Label Position with the same High, Low, and None options.

To assign a new number format to a value scale (General being the default), click Number in the Format Axis task pane to display its formatting options. Then, select the number format from the Category drop-down list and specify the number of decimal places and symbols (where applicable) as well as negative number formatting that you want applied to the selected axis in the chart.

Saving a customized chart as a template

After going through extensive editing and formatting of one of Excel's basic chart types, you may want to save your work of art as a custom chart type that you can then use again with different data without having to go through all the painstaking steps to get the chart looking just the way you want it. Excel makes it easy to save any modified chart that you want to use again as a custom chart type.

To convert a chart on which you've done extensive editing and formatting into a custom chart type, you take these steps:

1. **Right-click the customized chart in the worksheet or on its chart sheet to select its chart area and display its shortcut menu.**

   You can tell that the chart area (as opposed to any specific element in the chart) is selected because the Format Chart Area option appears near the bottom of the displayed shortcut menu.

2. **Choose the Save As Template option from the shortcut menu.**

   Excel opens the Save Chart Template dialog box. The program automatically suggests Chart1.crtx as the filename, Chart Template Files (*.crtx) as the file type, and the Charts folder in the Microsoft Templates folder as the location.

3. **Edit the generic chart template filename in the File Name text box to give the chart template file a descriptive name without removing the .crtx filename extension.**

4. **Click the Save button to close the Save Chart Template dialog box.**

After creating a custom chart template in this manner, you can then use the template anytime you need to create a new chart that requires similar formatting by following these steps:

1. **Select the data in the worksheet to be graphed in a new chart using your chart template.**

2. **Click the Dialog Box launcher in the lower-right corner of the Charts group on the Insert tab of the Ribbon.**

   The Insert Chart dialog box appears with the Recommended Charts tab selected.

3. **Click the All Charts tab and then select the Templates option in the Navigation pane of the Insert Chart dialog box.**

   Excel then displays thumbnails for all the chart templates you've saved in the main section of the Create Chart dialog box. To identify these thumbnails by filename, position the mouse pointer over the thumbnail image.

4. **Click the thumbnail for the chart template you want to use to select it and then click OK.**

As soon as you click OK, Excel applies the layout and all the formatting saved as part of the template file to the new embedded chart created with the data in the current cell selection.

Adding Sparkline Graphics to a Worksheet

Excel 2019 supports a type of information graphic called sparklines that represents trends or variations in collected data. *Sparklines* — invented by Edward Tufte — are tiny graphs (generally about the size of text that surrounds them). In Excel 2019, sparklines are the height of the worksheet cells whose data they represent and can be any one of following three chart types:

>> **Line** that represents the selected worksheet data as a connected line showing whose vectors display their relative value

>> **Column** that represents the selected worksheet data as tiny columns

» **Win/Loss** that represents the selected worksheet data as a win/loss chart whereby wins are represented by blue squares that appear above the red squares representing the losses

To add sparklines to the cells of your worksheet, you follow these general steps:

1. **Select the cells in the worksheet with the data you want represented by a sparkline.**

2. **Click the type of chart you want for your sparkline (Line, Column, or Win/Loss) in the Sparklines group of the Insert tab or press Alt+NSL for Line, Alt+NSO for Column, or Alt+NSW for Win/Loss.**

   Excel opens the Create Sparklines dialog box, which contains two text boxes: Data Range, which shows the cells you selected with the data you want graphed, and Location Range, where you designate the cell or cell range where you want the sparkline graphic to appear.

3. **Select the cell or range of cells where you want your sparkline to appear in the Location Range text box and then click OK.**

   When creating a sparkline that spans more than a single cell, the Location Range must match the Data Range in terms of the same amount of rows and columns. (In other words, they need to be arrays of equal size and shape.)

TIP

Because sparklines are so small, you can easily add them to the cells in the final column of a table of data. That way, the sparklines can depict the data visually and enhance their meaning while remaining an integral part of the table whose data they epitomize.

Figure 1-13 shows you a worksheet data table after adding sparklines to the table's final column. These sparklines depict the variation in the sales over four quarters as tiny line graphs. As you can see in this figure, when you add sparklines to your worksheet, Excel 2016 adds a Design tab to the Ribbon under Sparkline Tools.

This Design tab contains buttons that you can use to edit the type, style, and format of the sparklines. The final group (called Group) on this Design tab enables you to band together a range of sparklines into a single group that can share the same axis and/or minimum or maximum values (selected using the options on its Axis drop-down button). This is very useful when you want a collection of different sparklines to all share the same charting parameters so that they equally represent the trends in the data.

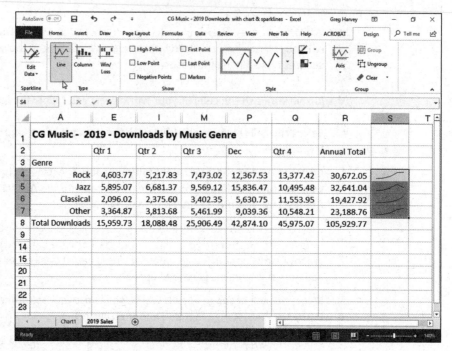

FIGURE 1-13:
Sparklines
graphics
representing
the variation
in the data in
a worksheet
table as tiny Line
charts.

Adding Infographics to a Worksheet

Excel 2019 enables you to easily add basic infographics to your worksheets from the Insert tab of the Ribbon with the addition of Bing Maps and People Graph to the drop-down menu on its Add-Ins button, and the Filled Map option in its Maps button. These infographics enhancements enable you to create visual representations of regionally related worksheet data that can point out trends and quickly convey their most pertinent information.

All you need in order to add great-looking infographics to a worksheet is some geographically related data. The geographic regions that Excel automatically recognizes and can work with when creating infographics include

>> Names of Countries, such USA, Russia, Canada, and so forth

>> Names of Provinces, such as Manitoba, Ontario, British Columbia, and so forth

>> Names of States, such as Maine, Connecticut, Florida, and so forth

>> Two-letter state abbreviations, such CA, NY, IA, and so forth

>> Postal codes, such as 94107, 78641, or SN13 9NH, WC2N 5DU, and the like

To see just how easy it is to use Excel 2019's infographics, I created a simple worksheet that contains two columns of data. The first column contains four country names (China, India, USA, and Brazil) and the second contains associated population figures (from 2018 data). Figure 1-14 shows the infographic that I created with the Bing Maps add-in for this data.

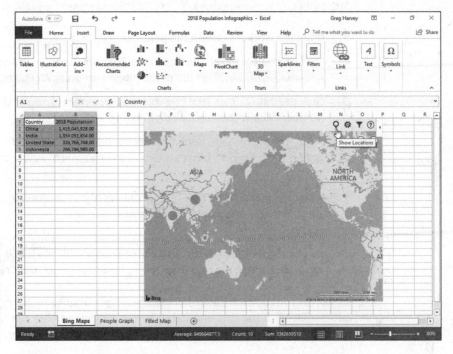

FIGURE 1-14:
Adding a Bing
Maps infographic
to the illustrate
the 2018
population by
country data in a
worksheet.

To create this Bing Maps infographic, I followed these steps:

1. **Position the cell cursor in one of the cells of the table with the population data (A1:B5).**

2. **Click the Bing Maps button on the drop-down menu attached to the Add-ins button on Insert tab of the Ribbon (or press Alt+NZ1A1).**

3. **Click the Show Locations button (the leftmost one in the top row) of the Welcome to Bing Maps graphic.**

That's all there is to it. Bing Maps automatically draws a 2-D map of the world including the four named countries and draws blue circles in each of them, representing the relative size of their populations (according to the values in the

B column of the Excel data table). If I wanted to, I could then use the Settings button (the second one on the top row with the cog icon) to change the default formatting of the population infographic or even filter its data with the Filters button (the third one on the top row).

Figure 1-15 shows the People Graph infographic created from the same population data table an Excel worksheet. To create this infographic, I followed these steps:

1. **Open the worksheet with the population data table.**

2. **Click the People Graph button on the drop-down menu attached to the Add-ins button on Insert tab of the Ribbon (or press Alt+NZ1A2).**

3. **Click the Data button (the one with tiny worksheet icon) at the top of the Numbers About the App default infographic.**

    When you click the Data button, a Data panel appears in the default infographic where you can select the data to be represented as well as change the title.

4. **Select the placeholder title text (Numbers About the App) in the Title text box and then replace it by entering your own title.**

5. **Click the Select Your Data button in the Data panel right above the Title text box and then drag through the cell range with the labels and values you want used in the new infographic before you click the Create button.**

As soon as you click the Create button, the People Graph add-in replaces its default infographic with the title and Excel data you specified. You can then use its Settings button (the one with the cog icon) to modify its formatting if you so choose.

Figure 1-16 shows the Filled Map chart created using the same population worksheet data as for the Bing Maps and People Graph infographics shown in Figures 1-14 and 1-15, respectively. This is the easiest of the three to create. All I had to do is position the cell cursor in one of the cells with the population data before clicking the Maps button on the Insert tab of the Ribbon.

Excel immediately created the Filled Map chart shown in Figure 1-16. All I then had to do was replace the Chart Title placeholder with the Population (2018) chart title shown in this figure.

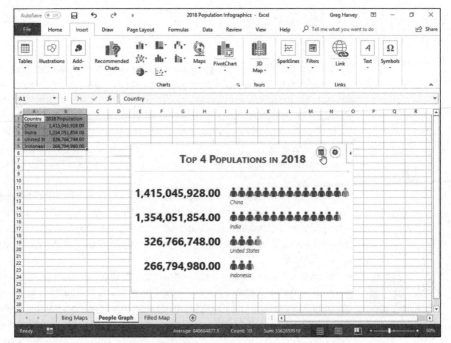

FIGURE 1-15:
Adding a
People Graph
infographic to the
illustrate the 2018
population by
country data in a
worksheet.

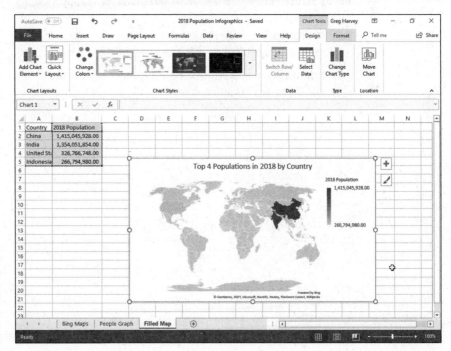

FIGURE 1-16:
Adding a Filled
Map chart
infographic to the
illustrate the 2018
population by
country data in a
worksheet.

Printing Charts

To print an embedded chart as part of the data on the worksheet, you simply print the worksheet from the Print Settings screen in the Backstage view by pressing Ctrl+P. To print an embedded chart by itself without the supporting worksheet data, click the chart to select it before you press Ctrl+P to open the Print screen in the Backstage view. In the Print screen, the Print Selected Chart appears as the default selection in the very first drop-down list box under the Settings heading and a preview of the embedded chart appears in the Preview pane on the right.

To print a chart that's on a separate chart sheet in the workbook file, activate the chart sheet by clicking its sheet tab and then press Ctrl+P to open the Print panel, where Print Active Sheet(s) appears in as the default selection for the Settings drop-down list box and the chart itself appears in the Preview pane on the right.

REMEMBER

When you want to print an embedded chart alone — that is, without its supporting data or in its own chart sheet — you may want to select the print quality options on the Chart tab of the Page Setup dialog box (which you can open by clicking the Page Setup link in the Print screen in the Backstage view or by clicking the Dialog Box launcher on the Page Layout tab) before sending the chart to the printer. The Print Quality options on the Chart tab include the following:

>> **Draft Quality:** Select this check box to print the chart using your printer's draft-quality setting.

>> **Print in Black and White:** Select this check box to have your color printer print the chart in black and white.

IN THIS CHAPTER

» **Understanding what graphic objects are and how Excel treats them**

» **Managing graphic objects on the worksheet**

» **Adding online images to the spreadsheet**

» **Adding text boxes with arrows**

» **Inserting 2-D line art, icons, pictures, and 3-D model graphics in the worksheet**

» **Adding WordArt text and SmartArt diagrams to the worksheet**

» **Capturing screenshots of the Windows desktop as Excel graphics**

» **Applying graphic themes to the worksheet**

Chapter **2**

Adding Graphic Objects

Just as charts can really help to clarify trends and implications that aren't readily apparent in your worksheet data, graphics that you add to a worksheet can really spruce up your charts and make them read even better. Although you may often look at Excel graphic objects as chart enhancements, you can also use them to enhance regular spreadsheet data. Depending on the type of spreadsheet, you may even end up using graphic elements not simply as a way to embellish the data, but also as a superior way to actually present it in the worksheet, especially when the data requires diagrammatic presentation.

Excel supports two types of graphic objects: those that you create yourself from the Shapes gallery or with the 3D Models, SmartArt, Text Box, and WordArt or the Screenshot command buttons on the Insert tab of the Ribbon, and those created by others that you import with the Pictures and Online Pictures command buttons. This chapter covers how to create graphics with text and text as graphics, as well as basic graphic shapes. It also covers how to import two different types of graphic images: Online graphic images downloaded from the Internet along with local pictures and digital photos stored in a variety of different graphics file formats that Excel can read.

Graphic Objects 101

It is important to understand that all graphic objects (including embedded charts as covered in Book 5, Chapter 1), whether you create them or import them, are discrete objects in the worksheet that you can select and manipulate. To select a graphic object, you simply click it. Excel lets you know that the object is selected by placing white circular sizing handles around the perimeter. In the case of 2-D images, the program also adds a circular 2-D rotation handle that appears directly above and connected to the sizing handle of the graphic's perimeter (the handle is on the top edge, in the middle) if the graphic can be rotated. In the case of 3-D models, Excel also adds a central rotation handle that enables you to manipulate the object in space around its x-, y-, and z- axes. On some drawn objects (especially 3-D ones), yellow shaping handles also appear at the places where you can manipulate some part of the object's shape, as shown in Figure 2-1.

To select multiple graphic objects in the worksheet, hold down the Shift or Ctrl key as you click each object. When you select more than one object, any manipulations that you perform affect all the selected objects.

To deselect a graphic object, just click the thick, white cross pointer in any cell in the worksheet that it doesn't cover. To deselect an object when you have several graphics selected at one time, click an unobstructed cell or another graphic.

Manipulating graphics

When you position the mouse pointer on a graphic object's sizing handle, the mouse pointer becomes a double-headed arrow that you can then drag to increase or decrease the overall size and shape of the object. To constrain a graphic while resizing it, click the sizing handle and then press and hold down the Shift key as you drag. Holding down the Shift key restricts your dragging so that the graphic retains its original proportions as you make it bigger or smaller. To constrain the proportions of an object in two dimensions, hold down the Shift key as you drag one of the corner sizing handles.

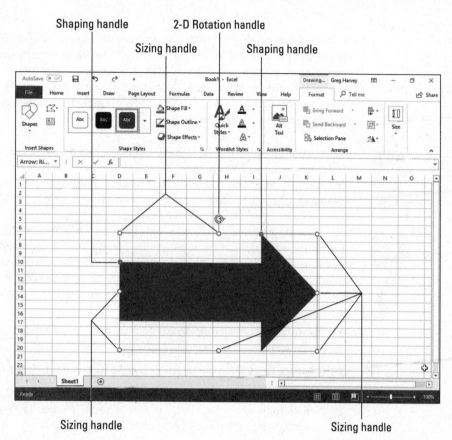

Shaping handle   2-D Rotation handle

Sizing handle   Shaping handle

FIGURE 2-1:
When you click
a graphic object
to select it, the
rotation and
circular sizing
handles appear.

Sizing handle   Sizing handle

Adding Graphic Objects

When you position the pointer on a graphic object's 2-D or 3-D rotation handle, the pointer becomes a curved arrow pointing clockwise. As you prepare to drag a 2-D rotation handle, the pointer becomes four curved arrows in a circle pointing in the clockwise direction. You can then rotate the graphic to any degree in a circle that pivots around the rotation handle.

When you position the pointer on an object's 3-D rotation handle, the pointer becomes a circular arrow that's also pointing clockwise. You can then rotate the object in a 3-dimensional space as the handle pivots around the image so that the object can be displayed from any angle above or below as well as in front, on either side, or in back.

When you position the pointer on a graphic's shaping handle (if it has one), the pointer becomes an arrowhead without any handle. You can then drag this pointer to reshape the side or section of the graphic. In the case of some 3-D graphic shapes, dragging the shaping handle rotates a part of the graphic in such a way that it alters the object's perspective, thus changing the way it's viewed.

To move the selected graphic object, position the mouse pointer somewhere inside the object's perimeter. Then, when the pointer becomes an arrowhead with a black double-cross at its point, drag the object to its new position within the worksheet. To copy the selected object, hold down the Ctrl key as you drag the graphic. (When you press the Ctrl key, a plus sign, indicating that the object is being copied, appears above the arrowhead pointer.)

REMEMBER

When working with graphic objects on a touchscreen, you can use your finger or stylus on the various handles to rotate, reshape, and resize your image. In addition, you can pinch and open your fingers (forefinger and thumb) to resize a selected graphic object, making it smaller and larger, respectively.

TIP

When moving graphics in a worksheet, you can make use of an invisible grid to help you position them. This is especially helpful when you're trying to align one graphic with another (for example, when aligning two charts side by side in a worksheet). To turn on the grid, you choose the Snap to Grid option in the Arrange group of the Format under the following contextual tab:

>> **Drawing Tools** when the selected graphic object is a drawn graphic, such as a predefined shape, text box, or WordArt

>> **Graphics Tools** when the selected object is an icon downloaded from the extensive online Icon library

>> **Picture Tools** when the selected graphic object is an imported line art image or digital photo, or a screenshot created with the Take a Screenshot command

>> **SmartArt Tools** when the graphic object is a piece of SmartArt

After the Snap to Grid feature is turned on, whenever you position an object very close to an invisible horizontal or vertical gridline, it snaps to this line as soon as you release the mouse button.

TIP

You can "nudge" a selected graphic object into its desired position with a keyboard by pressing the arrow keys. When you press an arrow key, Excel moves the object just a very little bit in that direction. Nudging is very useful when you have an object that's almost in place and requires very little handling to get it into just the right position.

If you no longer need a graphic object, you can get rid of it by clicking it to select the object and then pressing the Delete key to remove it.

Moving graphic objects to new layers

All graphic objects that you add to a worksheet lay on different invisible layers that reside on top of the worksheet and over the worksheet data in the cells below. This means that if you move a graphic object over a cell that contains an entry, the graphic hides the data beneath it. Likewise, if you draw a shape or add an image and then position it on top of another graphic object (such as an embedded chart or other shape or picture), it also covers up the graphic below.

Figure 2-2 illustrates this situation. In this figure, you see a thumbs-up icon (named Graphic 20 in the Selection task pane) partially covering a photo of a hundred dollar bill (Picture 16) and its caption (TextBox 17) and a 3-D model of a Microsoft Surface Pro (3D Model 18). The distinct layers of the four graphic images are illustrated by their order in the list in the Selection task pane, and the currently selected layer is shown by the green highlight.

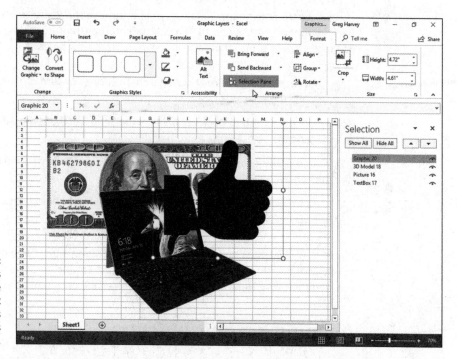

FIGURE 2-2:
Graphic objects on top obscure any worksheet data and parts of other graphics below.

REMEMBER

You display the Selection task pane by clicking the Selection Pane command button on the Format tab on the Graphics Tools, Drawing Tools, or Picture Tools contextual tab, depending on the type of graphic object selected.

Excel makes it easy to move the graphic objects on the same worksheet to other layers using the Selection task pane. Simply click the name of the object in this task pane that you want to move and then drag the object up or down in the Select task pane, or you can click the Bring Forward button (the one with the arrow pointing upward at the top of the task pane to the immediate right of the Hide All button) or the Send Backward button (the one with the arrow pointing downward right next to it) to move the object. Clicking the Bring Forward button moves the selected object up a level in the Selection task pane just as clicking the Send Backward button moves the object down a level.

REMEMBER

Note that any graphic object that appears above others in the list in the Selection task pane obscures all the objects below it, provided that the objects' check boxes in the task pane are not empty but contain eye icons (meaning that they're visible in the worksheet) *and* that the objects overlap each other in whole or part in their placement on the worksheet.

TIP

If the Selection task pane is not open, you can use the Bring to Front and Send to Back command buttons on the Format tab on the Graphics Tools, Drawing Tools, or Picture Tools contextual tabs to move them to new layers:

>> Choose the **Bring to Front** option from the Bring Forward drop-down menu to bring the selected graphic object to the top of the stack.

>> Choose the **Send to Back** option from the Send Backward drop-down menu to send the object to the bottom of the stack.

>> Click the **Bring Forward** button to bring the selected object up to the next higher layer.

>> Click the **Send Backward** button to send the selected object down to the next layer.

Figure 2-3 illustrates how easy it is to move a graphic object to a different level in the Selection task pane. For this figure, I clicked Explosion 14 in the list and then selected the Bring to Front option to put this shape on top of all the others.

Aligning graphic objects

When you're dealing with two graphic objects, one on top of the other, and you want to align them with each other, you can use the options on the Align command button's drop-down menu on the Format tab of the Drawing Tools or Picture Tools contextual menu after selecting both of them in the worksheet.

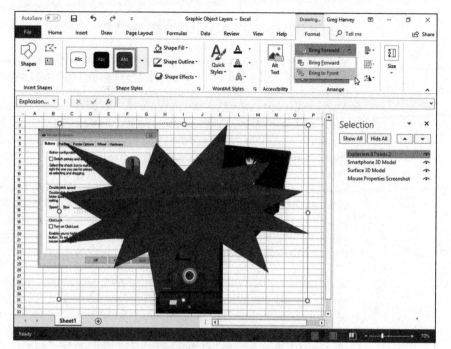

FIGURE 2-3:
Worksheet after
moving the
Explosion graphic
to the top layer
with the Bring to
Front option.

The alignment options on this button's drop-down menu include

>> **Align Left** to left align the graphic on the top layer with the one underneath

>> **Align Center** to center the graphic on the top layer with the one underneath

>> **Align Right** to right align the graphic on the top layer with the one underneath

>> **Align Top** to top align the graphic on the top layer with the one underneath

>> **Align Middle** to center vertically the graphic on the top layer with the one underneath

>> **Align Bottom** to bottom align the graphic on the top layer with the one underneath

>> **Distribute Horizontally** to equally distribute the selected graphic objects (three or more) horizontally

>> **Distribute Vertically** to equally distribute the selected graphic objects (three or more) vertically

Grouping graphic objects

Sometimes you need to work with more than one graphic object. For example, the hundred dollar bill photo (Picture 16) and its caption (TextBox 17) shown in Figures 2-3 would naturally be grouped together (see Figure 2-4). If you find that you're constantly selecting two or more objects at the same time in order to move them or rotate them together, you can make life a lot simpler by grouping the graphics. When you group selected graphic objects, Excel then makes them into a single graphic object, which you can then manipulate.

To group a bunch of graphics together, select them all (either by Shift+clicking or Ctrl+clicking each one). After they are selected, right-click the object on the top layer and then click Group⇨Group from the object's shortcut menu or click the Group option from the Group Objects command button's drop-down menu on the Format tab of the object's particular Tools contextual menu.

Excel indicates that the selected graphics are now grouped in the worksheet (and for all intents and purposes, are a single graphic object) by placing a single set of sizing handles around the perimeter formed by all the former separate graphics and by giving them a group number in the Selection task pane. You can then manipulate the grouped graphic as a single entity by moving it, sizing it, rotating it, and so forth, as you would any other object. In the Selection task pane, Excel create a new number Group that encompasses the erstwhile separate graphic objects, which are now indented in the list beneath the Group heading.

The great thing about grouping a bunch of different objects is that Excel never forgets that they were once separate objects that you could independently manipulate. This means that you can always turn them back into separate graphics by ungrouping them. To do this, right-click the composite graphic object and then click Group⇨Ungroup from its shortcut menu or choose the Ungroup option from the Group Objects command button's drop-down menu on the object's particular Tools Format tab.

Excel shows that the composite object is once again separated into many different objects by displaying sizing handles around each object's perimeter. You can then deselect them all and manipulate each one once again independently by selecting it alone before moving, resizing, or rotating it. If you decide that you want the now-independent objects to be joined as a group once again, you can do this by right-clicking any one of the graphics in the erstwhile group and then clicking Group⇨Regroup from its shortcut menu or choosing the Regroup option from the Group Objects command button's drop-down menu's Format contextual tab.

Figure 2-4 illustrates grouping in action. For this figure, I selected both the hundred dollar photo (Picture 16) and its caption (TextBox 17) and then chose Group from the Group Objects button's drop-down menu. As you can see, in grouping the two objects together into one, Excel created a new Group 21 object in the Selection task pane that consists of Textbox 17 caption and the Picture 16 photo. After grouping the two graphics, not only will the caption whenever I reposition the hundred dollar bill, but they would also both resize when I modify any of the sizing handles, and it would rotate together if I were to manipulate the grouped graphics' rotation handle.

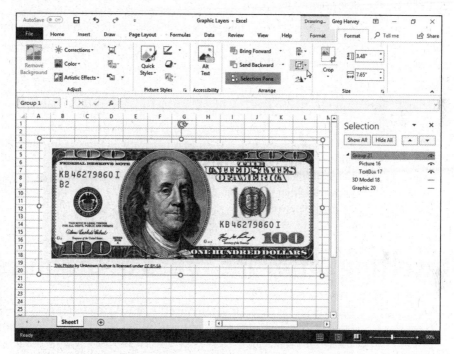

Adding Graphic Objects

Managing graphic objects in the Selection task pane

As previously discussed in the "Moving graphic objects to new layers" section earlier in this chapter, the Selection task pane that you display by clicking the Selection Pane button on the Format tab of the Graphics, Drawing, Picture Tools, or SmartArt Tools contextual tab on the Ribbon makes it easy to move graphic objects that overlap one another in some manner to different layers in the stack.

In addition to rearranging graphic objects on different layers, you can use this task pane to select particular graphic objects for editing or formatting as well as to temporarily hide their display in the worksheet:

>> To select a graphic object in the worksheet, click its name in the list in the Selection task pane — to select multiple graphics, press Ctrl as you click their names in the list.

>> To hide a particular graphic object in the worksheet, click the eye icon after its name (to close the eye), and to redisplay it, click this eye icon a second time to reopen its eye.

>> To hide all the graphic objects (including embedded charts) on the worksheet, click the Hide All button at the top of the task pane, and to redisplay them, click the Show All button.

TIP

Click the graphic object's name in the Selection task pane to select it for editing or formatting whenever the object is difficult to select directly in the worksheet by clicking its shape or image, which is often the case when the object's part of a stack of graphics. If you want to rename the graphic from the generic name Excel gives it (Picture 10, TextBox 12, Right Arrow 11, Group 21, and so forth), click the name in the Selection task pane and then edit or replace it in the text box that then appears. When you finish editing the graphic's name, click outside the text box to apply the new name.

Inserting Different Types of Graphics

Excel makes it easy for you to insert many different types of graphic images into your worksheets using the options on the Illustrations button's menu on the Insert tab:

>> **Pictures** to import photos and other types of digital artwork saved locally on your computer, often in the Pictures library

>> **Online Pictures** to download and insert photos and other types of graphic images saved online — these online images include clip art saved on the Office.com website, web images that you locate using the Bing search engine, or images that you've saved in the cloud on your OneDrive

>> **Shapes** to draw predefined and free-form graphic shapes using any of the shape thumbnails displayed on the drop-down gallery attached to the Shapes option

- **Icons** to download predefined black-and-white icons in a whole host of categories from the Insert Icons gallery

- **3D Models** to download 3-D graphics in several categories from the Microsoft Remix 3D online community website

- **SmartArt** to generate complex graphical lists and relationship charts (like organizational charts) using the gallery opened by selecting the SmartArt option

- **Screenshot** to take a snapshot of all or part of your Windows desktop and insert it as a graphic object in your worksheet

Inserting 2-D online images

Excel 2019 makes its easy to download pictures from the web using the Bing Image search engine and insert them into your worksheets. To download an image, open the Online Pictures dialog box (Alt+NF) and then select one of the predefined categories displayed or select the Search Bing text box, where you type the keyword for the types of images you want to locate. When conducting a search, after you press Enter or click the Search button (with the magnifying glass icon), the Online Pictures dialog box displays a scrollable list of thumbnails for images matching your keyword. (See Figure 2-5.) You can then position the mouse pointer over any of the thumbnails to display a short description plus the size (in pixels) of the image in the lower-left corner of the Insert Pictures dialog box.

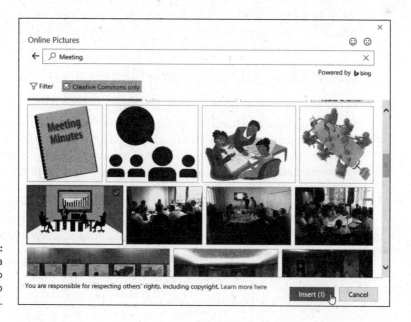

FIGURE 2-5: Selecting a web image to download into your worksheet.

Below the display of thumbnail images, the Online Pictures dialog box also displays a disclaimer informing you that the online images that Bing has returned in the search use what's called Creative Commons. This licensing grants free distribution of what is otherwise copyrighted material under certain conditions (often noncommercial or educational use). The disclaimer then goes on to urge you to review the license for any image you insert into your worksheet so that you may be certain that you are in compliance with these conditions (always a good idea). After reading this disclaimer, you can close its text box by clicking its Close button with the x in it.

When you click a predefined graphics category or do a Bing image search, Excel then displays a row of drop-down buttons (Size, Type, Color, and Layout) beneath the Search text box in the Search Results dialog box. You can use the options on these drop-down buttons to refine the image search. For example, if you click the Car category in the Online Pictures dialog box and then want to restrict the thumbnail display to photographs of cars, you would click the Photograph option on the Type drop-down button.

To select an image for downloading, click the tiny check box in the upper-left corner of its displayed thumbnail. To select more than one image, hold down the Ctrl key as you click each thumbnail's check box. To insert the selected web image(s) into the current worksheet, click the Insert button.

TIP

To download photos and pictures saved in folders on your OneDrive, click the Browse button to the right of the Bing heading and then click OneDrive on the drop-down button near the top of the Online Pictures dialog box. Excel then displays a list of folders (including the Pictures folder) that you can open and peruse for the image you want to import into your Excel worksheet.

Inserting 3-D online images

Excel 2019 also supports the use of 3-D images downloaded from the Microsoft Remix 3D online community website using the From Online Sources option on drop-down menu of the 3D Models command button located in the Illustrations group on the Insert tab (Alt+NS3O). When you insert one of these 3-D image into your worksheet, you can rotate it so that it can be viewed from any angle you want.

To insert a 3-D model, open the Online 3D Models dialog box (as shown in Figure 2-6) and select a thumbnail of the model from one of its displayed categories or from a search you perform of the 3-D images uploaded to the Microsoft Remix 3D website.

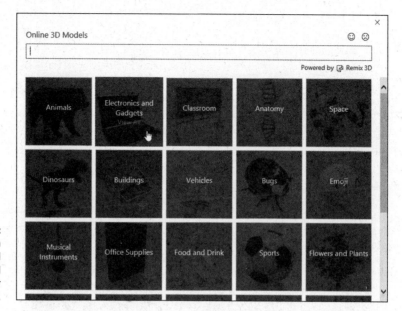

FIGURE 2-6:
Selecting an
online 3-D model
to download
insert into your
worksheet.

Inserting local pictures

If you want to bring in an image such as a digital photo or a scanned image saved locally on your computer in one of its local or network drives, choose the Pictures option from the Illustrations button's drop-down menu on the Ribbon's Insert tab or just press Alt+NP. Just be aware that even though Excel does compress pictures by default, depending upon the size of the photo or digital image, inserting such a graphic can dramatically increase the size of your Excel workbook file.

This opens the Insert Picture dialog box similar to the one shown in Figure 2-7. Selecting a graphics file to insert into your worksheet in this dialog box works very much like selecting an Excel workbook file to open in the Open dialog box: Select the drive and folder containing the graphics file in the Navigation pane on the left. Next, select the file to insert by clicking the thumbnail of graphics image before clicking the Insert button to open it and insert its image into your open worksheet.

TIP

If you want to bring in a graphic image created in another graphics program that's not saved in its own file, you select the graphic in that program and then copy it to the Clipboard. (Press Ctrl+C.) When you get back to your worksheet, place the cursor where you want the picture to go and then paste the image in place. (Press Ctrl+V or click the Paste command button at the very beginning of the Home tab.)

REMEMBER

When you insert a picture from a graphics file into the worksheet, it's automatically selected (indicated by the sizing handles around its perimeter and its rotation handle at the top). To deselect the graphic image and set it in the worksheet, click anywhere in the worksheet outside of the image.

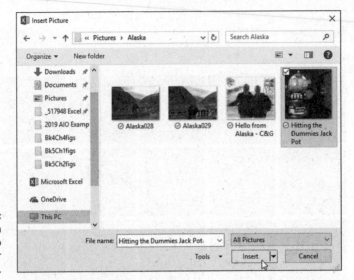

FIGURE 2-7:
Selecting a
local image to
insert into your
worksheet.

Editing pictures

As long as a photo or other graphics image is selected in your worksheet (indicated by the sizing handles around its perimeter and a rotation handle at the top), you can make any of the following editing changes to it:

» Move the selected image to a new location in the chart by dragging it.

» Resize the selected image by dragging the appropriate sizing handle.

» Rotate the selected 2-D or 3-D image by dragging its rotation handle (the green circle at the top) in a clockwise or counterclockwise direction. Rotate a 3-D model in space by dragging its 3-D rotation handle at the center of the image around the graphic

» Delete the selected image by pressing the Delete key.

Formatting photos and line art pictures

When an inserted two-dimensional graphics image is selected, Excel adds the Picture Tools contextual tab to the Ribbon and automatically selects its sole Format tab.

The Format tab's command buttons are arranged into several groups: Adjust, Picture Styles, Arrange, and Size. The Adjust group contains the following important command buttons:

- **»** **Remove Background** to remove the background from the selected clip art image.

- **»** **Corrections** to increase or decrease the picture's sharpness or brightness and contrast by selecting a new preset thumbnail image or by clicking Picture Corrections Options to open the Format Picture dialog box, where you can adjust these settings with its Sharpen and Soften or Brightness and Contrast sliders.

- **»** **Color** to open a drop-down menu, where you can select a new color thumbnail for the image or select a transparent color that drops out of the picture.

- **»** **Artistic Effects** to apply a special effect filter to the image by selecting one of the preset thumbnail images or by clicking Artistic Effects Options to open the Artistic Effects tab of the Format Picture dialog box, where you can select another filter to apply or reset the image by removing all previously applied filters.

- **»** **Compress Pictures** to open the Compress Pictures dialog box, where you can compress all images in the worksheet or just the selected graphic image to make them more compact and thus make the Excel workbook somewhat smaller when you save the images as part of its file.

- **»** **Change Picture** to open the Insert Picture dialog box, where you can select an image in a new graphics file to replace the picture. When replacing the currently selected picture with the new image, Excel automatically sizes and formats the new image with the settings applied to the old.

- **»** **Reset Picture** button to remove all formatting changes made and return the picture to the state it was in when you originally inserted it into the worksheet.

REMEMBER

You can also format a picture by opening the Format Picture task pane opened by selecting the image and then pressing Ctrl+1. Then, click the appropriate button — Fill & Line, Effects, Size & Properties, or Picture — to access the appropriate formatting options.

You can also use the command buttons in the Picture Styles group to format the selected graphic image. Click a thumbnail on the Picture Styles drop-down gallery to select a new orientation and style for the selected picture or select a new border shape on the Picture Shape button's drop-down palette, a new border color on the Picture Border button's drop-down color palette, or a new shadow or 3-D rotation effect from the Picture Effects button's drop-down menu.

Figure 2-8 shows an imported photo I took of my partner at a *Winning For Dummies* slot machine as the image is being formatted in Live Preview with Double Frame, Black on the Picture Styles drop-down gallery. Note that in this style, Excel places the image in an inner light black frame surrounded by a much heavier outer frame.

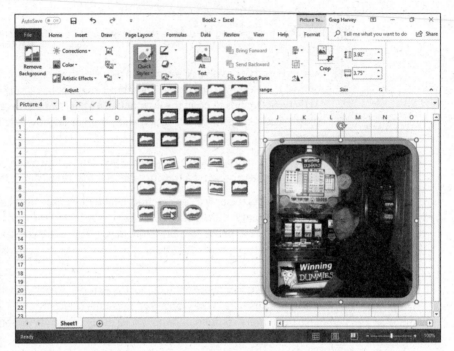

FIGURE 2-8:
Live Preview in
the Picture Styles
gallery enables
you to see how a
style affects your
picture before
you apply it.

REMEMBER

Keep in mind that you can remove a uniform background in a selected picture by clicking the Remove Background button in the Format tab's Adjust group. Excel then adds a Background Removal contextual tab to the Ribbon and applies a violet filter to the identified background of the selected picture. You can then adjust the violet filter to indicate the extent of the image background to be removed. Then, you click the Keep Changes button on the Background Removal contextual tab to close it and to remove the image's background.

Formatting 3-D model images

When you select a 3-D image that you've inserted into your worksheet, Excel adds a 3D Model Tools contextual tab to the ribbon with its own Format tab. This Format tab is divided into the following groups:

» **Adjust** to replace the selected image with another online or local 3-D model or to reset the image to its original rotation and/or size

» **3D Model Views** to select a preset three-dimensional rotation

» **Accessibility** with its sole Alt Text button to open the Alt Text task pane where you can enter a description of the graphic that the computer can read aloud to a visually-impaired user

>> **Arrange** to modify the selected image's layer or to group or align it with other images (see "Aligning graphic objects" earlier in this chapter for details)

>> **Size** to enter a new width or height (in inches, if that is the default unit in Excel) for the selected image

TIP

You can also format a selected 3-D image with the options in the Format 3D Model task pane opened by pressing Ctrl+1 or clicking the Format 3D Model button on the right side of the 3D Model Views group or the Size and Position button on the right side of the Size group on the Format tab under the 3D Model Tools contextual tab. This task pane contains four buttons, Fill & Line, Effects, Size & Options, and 3D Model, with all sorts of options for formatting the appearance of the selected 3-D image.

Drawing Graphics

The Shapes gallery along with the SmartArt, Text Box, and WordArt command buttons found on the on the Ribbon's Insert tab enable you to draw a wide variety of graphic objects. Some of these graphic objects, including the callout graphics on the Shapes gallery and all the SmartArt, Text Box, and WordArt graphics, enable you to combine text and graphics.

Drawing predefined shapes

The Shapes gallery, opened by clicking the Shapes command button in the Illustrations group on the Ribbon's Insert tab (Alt+NSH), contains a wide variety of predefined shapes that you can draw in your worksheet simply by dragging the mouse pointer.

When you open the Shapes gallery, you see that the gallery is divided into nine sections: Recently Used Shapes, Lines, Rectangles, Basic Shapes, Block Arrows, Equation Shapes, Flowchart, Stars and Banners, and Callouts.

After you click the thumbnail of one of the preset shapes in this drop-down gallery, the pointer becomes a crosshair, and you use it to draw the graphic by dragging it until it's approximately the size you want.

REMEMBER

After you release the mouse button or remove your finger or stylus from the touchscreen, the shape you've drawn in the worksheet is still selected. This is indicated by the sizing handles around its perimeter and the rotation handle at the top, which you can use to reposition and resize it, if need be. In addition, the program activates the Format tab on the Drawing Tools contextual tab, and you can use the Shape Styles gallery or other command buttons to further format the shape until it's exactly the way you want it. To set the shape and remove the sizing and rotation handles, click anywhere in the worksheet outside of the shape.

TIP

When drawing a rectangle or an oval, you can constrain the tool to draw a square or circle by holding down the Shift key as you drag the mouse. Note that when drawing a two-dimensional shape, such as a rectangle, square, oval, or circle, Excel automatically draws the shape with a blue fill that obscures any data or graphic objects that are beneath the shape on layers below.

REMEMBER

In addition to drawing your own basic shapes, lines, and arrows from the gallery, you can draw block arrows, equation symbols, flow chart symbols, banners, and callouts by selecting them from their respective areas on the Shapes gallery. Note that, when you draw one of the callouts, Excel positions the insertion point within the selected callout shape, thus enabling you to then enter the text of the callout. After you finish entering the text, click somewhere outside the shape to deselect the callout. (See the "Adding text boxes" section that follows for information on how to edit and format the callout text.)

Adding text boxes

Text boxes are special graphic objects that combine text with a rectangular graphic object. They're great for calling attention to significant trends or special features in the charts that you create. (See Book 5, Chapter 1, for details.)

To create a text box, click the Text Box command button in the Text group on the Ribbon's Insert tab (or press Alt+NX). Your pointer's cursor then appears as a thin vertical line with a short horizontal line crossing near the bottom. You can then drag this pointer to draw the outline of the new text box. As soon as you release the mouse button or remove your finger or stylus from the touchscreen, Excel draws the text box and places the standard insertion point in the upper-left corner of the box.

You can then start typing the text that you want displayed in the text box. When the text that you type reaches the right edge of the text box, Excel automatically starts a new line. If you reach the end of the text box and keep typing, Excel then scrolls the text up, and you then have to resize the text box to display all the text that you've entered. If you want to break a line before it reaches the right edge of the text box, press the Enter key. When you finish entering the text, click anywhere on the screen outside the text box to deselect it.

Keep in mind that although text boxes are similar to cell Comments in that they also display the text that you enter in a rectangular box, they do differ from Comments in that text boxes are *not* attached to particular cells and *are* always displayed in the worksheet. (Comments show only when you position the mouse pointer over the cell or select the comment with the Reviewing toolbar — see Book 4, Chapter 3 for details.)

Note that text boxes differ somewhat from other graphic objects that you add to the worksheet. Unlike other graphic objects in Excel, text boxes display two different border patterns when you select them: A dotted-line pattern is displayed when you click inside the text box, thus enabling you to format and edit the text, and a solid-line pattern is displayed when you click the border of the text box or start dragging the box to reposition it, thus indicating that you can format and edit the box itself.

Formatting a text box

After you've added a text box, you can format its text by changing the font, font size, font style, and alignment of the text (including its orientation); you can also format the text box by changing its background color and line style, object positioning properties, and — perhaps most important of all — its text margins.

To change the formatting of all the text entered in a text box, click its TextBox name in the Selection task pane or click its graphic object in the worksheet until the solid outline appears around the box, and then click the appropriate command buttons in the Font and Alignment groups on the Ribbon's Home tab. Choose from the following options:

» **Font** or **Font Size** drop-down list buttons and the **Increase Font Size** and **Decrease Font Size** command buttons to change the font or font size of the text. Use Live Preview to see how the new font and font size looks in the text box.

» **Bold, Italic,** or **Underline** command buttons to add these attributes to the text in the text box.

» **Font Color** drop-down list button to apply a new color to the text in the text box.

» **Align Text Left, Center,** or **Align Text Right** command buttons to change the horizontal alignment of the text in regard to the left and right edges of the text box.

» **Top Align, Middle Align,** or **Bottom Align** command buttons to change the vertical alignment of the text in regard to the top and bottom edges of the text box.

- » **Increase Indent** or **Decrease Indent** command buttons to indent text within the box's borders or remove previous indenting.

- » **Orientation** command button to modify the orientation of the text in the text box by selecting the Vertical Text, Rotate Text Up, or the Rotate Text Down option.

To change the formatting of some of the text in a text box, click the insertion point in the text box and select the text before you use one of these command buttons to modify its appearance.

To change the formatting of the text box itself, click its TextBox name in the Selection task pane (opened by clicking the Selection Pane button on the Drawing Tools Format tab) or click its graphic object in the worksheet until the solid outline appears around the box, then click the Drawing Tools Format tab on the Ribbon, and then choose among the following formatting options:

- » **Edit Shape** drop-down list button (the one with the dots around the graphic object in the Insert Shapes group) to change the text box shape or edit the wrap points

- » **Shape Styles** gallery to select a new outline, fill, and text color all at one time by clicking one of the gallery's thumbnails (after using Live Preview to see how the new color scheme looks)

- » **Shape Fill** drop-down list button to select a new color, gradient, picture, or texture for the text box fill or to remove any existing fill (by selecting the No Fill option)

- » **Shape Outline** drop-down list button to select a new color, line weight, or line style for the outline of the text box or to remove its outline (by selecting the No Outline option)

- » **Shape Effects** drop-down list button to select a new special effect such as a shadow, glow, or other 3-D effect using the options and palettes available from its drop-down menu

- » **WordArt Styles** drop-down palette to apply a new WordArt style for the text in the text box by clicking one of the gallery's thumbnails (after using Live Preview to see how the new WordArt text style looks)

- » **Text Fill** drop-down list button (the one with the A with a line drawn under it) to select a new fill color, gradient, picture, or texture for the text in the text box or to remove any existing fill color (by selecting the No Fill option)

>> **Text Outline** drop-down list button (the one with the pencil added to the A with the line drawn under it) to select a new color, line weight, or line style for the text in the text box or to remove its current outline (by selecting the No Outline option)

>> **Text Effects** drop-down list button to select a new special effect such as a shadow, glow, or other 3-D effect for the text in the text box using the options and palettes available from its drop-down menu

TIP

When you first enter the text in a text box, Excel sets pretty scanty internal margins so that there's not a lot of white space between the text characters and the edge of the text box. If you're anything like me, one of the first things that you'll want to do is add decent margins to the text box.

To do this, open the Format Shape task pane while the text box is selected by right-clicking the text box and then choosing Format Shape from its shortcut menu. Then, click the Size & Properties tab (the one third to the right under the Shape Options | Text Options labels) followed by the TextBox button and enter the new values (in fractions of an inch) that you want to use in the Top Margin, Bottom Margin, Left Margin, and Right Margin text boxes. Also, select the Resize Shape to Fit Text check box to put a check mark in it if you want Excel to automatically resize the text box to suit any formatting changes you make to its text (such as increasing the font size, adding bold, or selecting a new text alignment).

Editing the text in a text box

You can edit the text in a text box as you would in any cell of the worksheet. To insert new text, click the insertion point at the appropriate place and start typing. To delete text, press the Backspace key to delete characters to the left of the insertion point or the Delete key to delete characters to its right. To delete an entire section of text, select it with the I-beam mouse pointer and then press the Delete key.

To spell check some or all of the text in the text box, select the text by dragging the I-beam mouse or Touch pointer through it and then click the Spelling button on the Review tab of the Ribbon (or just press F7).

To delete a text box from the worksheet, click its border to select the box (indicated by the solid as opposed to dotted outline) and then press the Delete key. Be sure that you don't click inside the box because this selects only the text (indicated by the dotted outline), in which case, pressing the Delete key doesn't get rid of anything but characters of text at the cursor's position.

Adding an arrow to a text box

When creating a text box, you may want to add an arrow to point directly to another graphic object or to the part of an embedded chart to which you're referencing. To add an arrow, follow these steps:

1. **Click the text box to which you want to attach the arrow in the chart or worksheet to select it.**

Sizing handles appear around the text box, and the Format tab on the Drawing Tools contextual tab is selected on the Ribbon.

2. **Click the Arrow command button in the Insert Shapes drop-down gallery at the very beginning of the Format tab.**

The Arrow command button is the second from the left in the Lines section of Shapes gallery (with the picture of an arrow). When you click this button, it becomes selected in the gallery palette (indicated by the button's green shading) and the mouse or Touch pointer assumes the crosshair shape.

3. **Drag the crosshair pointer from the place on the text box where the end of the arrow (the one *without* the arrowhead) is to appear to the place where the arrow starts (and the arrowhead will appear) and release the mouse button.**

As soon as you release the mouse button or remove your finger or stylus from the touchscreen, Excel draws two points, one at the base of the arrow (attached to the text box) and another at the arrowhead. At the same time, the contents of the Shape Styles drop-down gallery changes to line styles.

4. **Click the More button in the lower-right corner of the Shapes Styles drop-down gallery to display the thumbnails of all its line styles and then highlight individual thumbnails to see how the arrow would look in each.**

As you highlight the different line styles in this gallery, Excel draws the arrow between the two selected points in the text box using the highlighted style.

5. **Click the thumbnail of the line style you want the new arrow to use in the Shape Styles gallery.**

Excel then draws a new arrow using the selected shape style, which remains selected (with sizing handles at the beginning and end of the arrow). You can then edit the arrow as follows:

» Move the arrow by dragging its outline into position.

» Change the length of the arrow by dragging the sizing handle at the arrowhead.

>> Change the direction of the arrow by pivoting the mouse or Touch pointer around a stationary selection handle.

>> Change the shape of the arrowhead or the thickness of the arrow's shaft by clicking a thumbnail on the Shape Styles drop-down gallery or clicking a new option on the Shape Fill, Shape Outline, and Shape Effects button on the Format tab of the Drawing Tools contextual tab. Alternatively, open the Format Shape task pane (Ctrl+1) and then select the appropriate options after selecting the Fill & Line, Effects, Size & Properties, or Picture button.

>> Delete the arrow by pressing the Delete key.

Inserting WordArt

The WordArt gallery, opened by clicking the WordArt command button in the Text group of the Insert tab of the Ribbon, makes it a snap to add really artsy text to the worksheet. The only thing to keep in mind when adding WordArt is that, just as its name implies, this text is really a graphic (art) object that behaves just like any other Excel graphic object although it contains only text!

You can easily add this type of "graphic" text to your worksheet by following these steps:

1. **Click the WordArt command button on the Insert tab of the Ribbon or press Alt+NW.**

   Excel displays the WordArt drop-down gallery, as shown in Figure 2-9.

2. **Click the A thumbnail in the WordArt style you want to use in the WordArt drop-down gallery.**

   Excel inserts a selected text box containing Your Text Here in the center of the worksheet with this text in the WordArt style you selected in the gallery.

3. **Type the text you want to display in the worksheet in the Text text box.**

   As soon as you start typing, Excel replaces the Your Text Here text in the selected text box with the characters you enter.

4. **(Optional) To format the background of the text box, use Live Preview in the Shape Styles drop-down gallery on the Format tab to find the style to use and then set it by clicking its thumbnail.**

   The Format tab on the Drawing Tools contextual tab is automatically added and activated whenever WordArt text is selected in the worksheet.

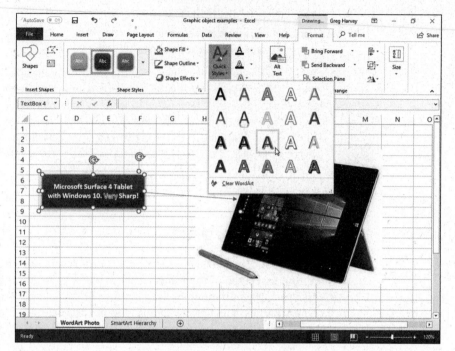

FIGURE 2-9:
Selecting the text
style for the new
WordArt text
from its drop-
down gallery.

5. **After making any final adjustments to the size, shape, or orientation of the WordArt text with the sizing and rotation handles, click a cell somewhere outside of the text to deselect the graphic.**

Note that Excel automatically compresses the text to fill the shape and size of its text box. To put more space between the words and the characters in each word, make the text box wider by dragging the sizing handle on either side of the text box.

When you click outside of the WordArt text, Excel deselects the graphic, and the Drawing Tools contextual tab disappears from the Ribbon. (If you ever want this tab to reappear, all you have to do is click somewhere on the WordArt text to select the graphic.)

Figure 2-10 shows the WordArt label for the web image of the downloaded slot machine photo introduced earlier after creating the text in the WordArt style called Fill – Blue, Accent Color 1, Shadow in the WordArt gallery with the Arch: Down Transform Text Effect on the Drawing Tools Format tab.

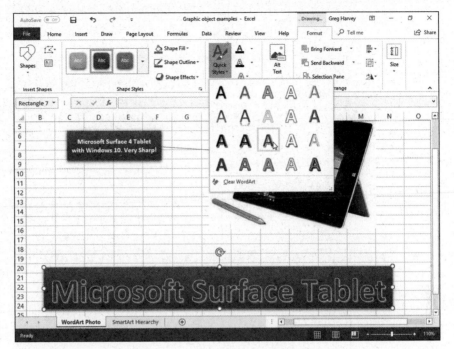

FIGURE 2-10:
Formatted
WordArt graphic
added as a label
for a downloaded
photo.

Inserting SmartArt graphics

SmartArt graphics give you the ability to quickly and easily construct fancy graphical lists, diagrams, and captioned pictures in your worksheet. SmartArt lists, diagrams, and pictures come in a wide array of configurations that include a variety of organizational charts and flow diagrams that enable you to add your own text to predefined graphic shapes.

To insert a SmartArt graphic into the worksheet, click the Insert a SmartArt command button in the Illustrations group on the Ribbon's Insert tab (or press Alt+M1). Excel then opens the Choose a SmartArt Graphic dialog box (shown in Figure 2-11), where you select a category in the navigation pane on the left followed by the list's or diagram's thumbnail in the center section before you click OK.

Excel then inserts the basic structure of the list, diagram, or picture into your worksheet with [Text] placeholders (as shown in Figure 2-12) showing where you can enter titles, descriptions, captions, and, in the case of, SmartArt pictures, picture icons showing where you can insert your own pictures into the SmartArt graphic. At the same time, the Design tab of the SmartArt Tools contextual tab appears on the Ribbon with Layouts and SmartArt Styles galleries for the particular type of SmartArt list or diagram you originally selected.

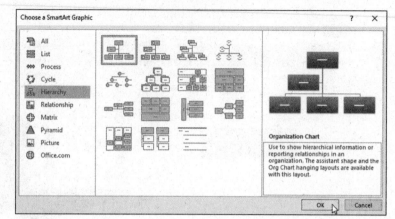

FIGURE 2-11:
Select the
SmartArt list,
diagram, or
picture to insert
in the worksheet
in this dialog box.

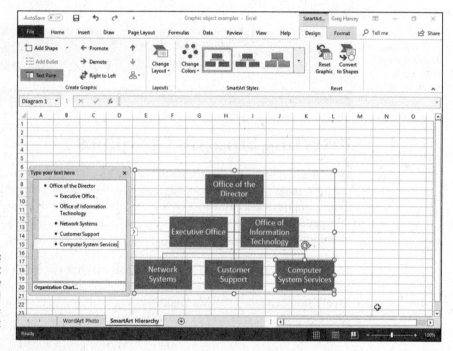

FIGURE 2-12:
Adding text
for a new
organizational
chart in the
SmartArt
text pane.

Filling in the text for a new SmartArt graphic

To fill in the text for the first for your new SmartArt graphic, click its [Text] place-holder and then simply type the text.

When you finish entering the text for your new diagram, click outside the graphic to deselect it.

If the style of the SmartArt list or diagram you select comes with more sections than you need, you can delete the unused graphics by clicking them to select them (indicated by the selection and rotation handles around it) and then pressing the Delete key.

Adding images to a SmartArt picture

If the SmartArt graphic object you've added to your worksheet is one of those from the Picture group of the Choose a SmartArt Graphic dialog box, your selected SmartArt graphic contains an Insert Picture button (marked only by a small picture icon) along with the [Text] indicators. To add a graphic image to the SmartArt object, click this picture icon to open an Insert Pictures dialog box with the following three options:

>> **From a File** to open the Insert Picture dialog box where you can select a local photo or other graphic image saved in a local or networked drive on your computer (see "Inserting local pictures" earlier in this chapter)

>> **Online Pictures** to open the Online Pictures dialog box where you can download a photo or other graphic image from online source such as Flickr or your OneDrive (see "Inserting 2-D online images" earlier in this chapter)

>> **From Icons** to open the Insert Icons dialog box where you can select one of the many categories of black and white images to insert

Formatting a SmartArt graphic

After you deselect your SmartArt graphic, you can still format its text and format. To format the text, select all the graphic objects in the SmartArt list or diagram that need the same type of text formatting — remember you can select several objects in the list or diagram by holding down Ctrl as you click them — and then clicking the appropriate command buttons in the Font group on the Home tab of the Ribbon.

To refine or change the default formatting the SmartArt graphic, you can use the Layouts, Change Colors, and SmartArt Styles drop-down galleries available on the Design tab of the SmartArt Tools contextual tab:

>> Click the More button in the Layouts group and then click a thumbnail on the Layouts drop-down gallery to select an entirely new layout for your SmartArt graphic.

>> Click the Change Colors button in the SmartArt Styles group and then click a thumbnail in the drop-down Theme Colors gallery to change the color scheme for the current layout.

>> Click the More button in the SmartArt Styles group and then click a thumbnail on the SmartArt Styles drop-down gallery to select a new style for the current layout, using the selected color scheme.

Adding Screenshots of the Windows 10 Desktop

The Screenshot command button in the Illustrations group of the Insert tab enables you to capture Windows desktop graphics and insert them directly into your worksheet. Before clicking this button, you need to open up the other application window whose document you want to capture as an Excel graphic object or set up the Windows desktop icons that you want to capture.

Then, switch back to the Excel 2019 program window and click the Screenshot button on the Insert tab or press Alt+NSC. Excel then opens a Screenshot drop-down menu similar to the one shown in Figure 2-13.

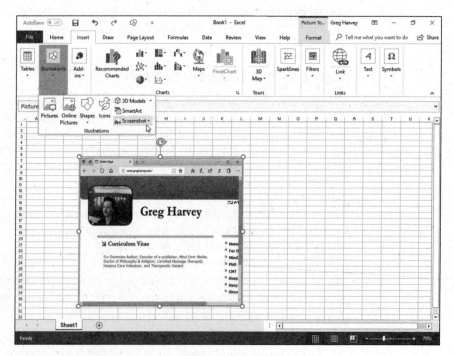

FIGURE 2-13:
Inserting a Windows screenshot of a web page into your worksheet.

If you have application windows open on the Windows desktop, a thumbnail of each window appears on this Screenshot drop-down menu under the heading Available Screen Shots. To capture one of the open window's information as a graphic object in the current Excel worksheet, you simply click its thumbnail on this drop-down menu and Excel adds the window as a selected graphic in your sheet.

If you don't want to capture any of the discrete application windows as graphics, you can use the Screen Clipping option that appears at the bottom of the Screen-shot drop-down menu to select the section of the desktop to capture as a graphic. When you click the Screen Clipping option, Windows minimizes the Excel applica-tion window and displays the desktop with all of its windows and icons displayed but in a gauzy, hazy transparent mode. You then drag the black-cross pointer to select the section of the desktop you want captured as a worksheet graphic object. (As you drag, Windows removes the gauzy effect from the area you select.) When you release the mouse button, Windows immediately reopens the Excel program window with the section of the desktop added as a selected worksheet graphic.

Using Themes

With themes, Excel 2019 enables you to uniformly format all the graphics that you add to a worksheet. You can select a new theme for the active worksheet simply by clicking the thumbnail of the theme you want to use in the Themes drop-down gallery opened by clicking the Themes command button on the Ribbon's Page Layout tab (or by pressing Alt+PTH).

REMEMBER

Use Live Preview to see how the graphics you've added to your worksheet appear in the new theme before you click its thumbnail.

Excel Themes combines three default elements: the color scheme applied to the graphics, the font (body and heading) used in the graphics, and the graphic effects applied. If you prefer, you can change any or all of these three elements in the worksheet by clicking their individual command buttons in the Themes group at the start of the Page Layout tab:

>> **Colors** to select a new color scheme by clicking its thumbnail of its color swatches on the drop-down palette. Click Customize Colors at the bottom of this palette to open the Create New Theme Colors dialog box where you can customize each element of the color scheme and save it with a new descriptive name.

>> **Fonts** to select a new font by clicking its thumbnail on the drop-down list. Click Customize Fonts at the bottom of this list to open the Create New Theme Fonts dialog box, where you can customize the heading and body fonts for both Latin and East Asian text and save it with a new descriptive name.

>> **Effects** to select a new set of graphics effects by clicking its thumbnail in the drop-down gallery.

TIP

To save your newly selected color scheme, font, and graphic effects as a custom theme that you can reuse in other workbooks, click the Themes command button and then click Save Current Theme at the bottom of the gallery to open the Save Current Theme dialog box. Edit the generic Theme1 name in the File Name text box (without deleting the .thmx filename extension) and then click the Save button. Excel then adds the custom theme to a Custom Themes section in the Themes drop-down gallery that you can apply to any active worksheet simply by clicking its thumbnail.

6

Data Management

Contents at a Glance

IN THIS CHAPTER

» Setting up a data list

» Adding data to a data list

» Editing records in a data list

» Finding records in a data list

» Sorting records on values in a data list

» Sorting a list on font color, fill color, or cell icons

» Subtotaling data in a data list

Chapter **1**

Building and Maintaining Data Lists

I n addition to its considerable computational capabilities, Excel is also very accomplished at maintaining vast collections of related data in what are referred to as *database tables* or, more often, *data lists* (which is a little more accurate). This chapter covers all the basic procedures for creating and then maintaining different types of data lists in the Excel worksheet.

This basic information includes how to design the basic data list and then format it as a table so that you can add new data to the list without having to redefine it and can sort its data so that it's arranged the way you like to see the information. For data lists that contain numerical data, you also find out how to subtotal and total the data. For information on how to find data in the data list and produce subsets of the list with just the data you need, refer to Book 6, Chapter 2.

Data List Basics

In Excel, a data list, or database table, is a table of worksheet data that utilizes a special structure. Unlike the other types of data tables that you might create in an Excel spreadsheet, a data list uses *only* column headings (technically known as *field names*) to identify the different kinds of items that the data list tracks. Each column in the data list contains information for each item you track in the database, such as the client's company name or telephone number (technically known as a *field* of the data list). Each row in the data list contains complete information about each entity that you track in the data list, such as ABC Corporation or National Industries (technically known as a *record* of the data list).

After you've organized your data into a data list that follows this structure, you can then use a variety of commands on the Ribbon's Data tab to maintain the data, as well as to reorder the information it contains. In data lists with numerical fields, you can also use the Subtotal command button to calculate subtotals and totals in the list when a certain field changes.

Designing the basic data list

All you have to do to start a new data list in a worksheet is to enter the names of the fields that you want to track in the top row of the worksheet, enter the first record of data beneath, and then format the two rows of data as a table. (See Book 2, Chapter 1 for details.) When entering the field names (as column headings), be sure each field name in the data list is unique and, whenever possible, keep the field name short. When naming fields, you can align the field name in the cell so that its text wraps to a new line by clicking the Wrap Text command button on the Ribbon's Home tab after entering the name in its cell (Alt+HW). Also, you should not use numbers or formulas that return values as field names. (You can, however, use formulas that return text, such as a formula that concatenates labels entered in different cells.)

When deciding on what fields you need to create, you need to think of how you'll be using the data that you store in your data list. For example, in a client data list, you split the client's name into separate title, first name, and last name fields if you intend to use this information in generating form letters and mailing labels with your word processor. That way, you are able to address the person by his or her first name (as in *Dear Jane*) in the opening of the form letter you create, as well as by his or her full name and title (as in *Dr. Jane Jackson*) in the mailing label you generate.

Likewise, you split up the client's address into separate street address, city, state, and zip code fields when you intend to use the client data list in generating form letters, and you also want to be able to sort the records in descending order by zip code and/or send letters only to clients located in the states of New York, New Jersey, or Connecticut. By keeping discrete pieces of information in separate fields, you are assured that you will be able to use that field in finding particular records and retrieving information from the data list, such as finding all the records where the state is California or the zip code is between 94105 and 95101.

To set up a new data list in a worksheet, you follow these steps:

1. **Click the blank cell where you want to start the new data list and then enter the column headings (field names) that identify the different kinds of items you need to keep track of.**

   After creating the fields of the data list by entering their headings, you're ready to enter the first row of data.

2. **Make the first entries in the appropriate columns of the row immediately below the one containing the field names.**

   These entries in the first row beneath the one with the field names constitute the first *record* of the data list.

3. **Click the Format as Table button on the Ribbon's Home tab and then click a thumbnail of one of the table styles in the drop-down gallery.**

   As soon as you click the Format as Table button, a marquee appears around all the cells in the new data list including the top row of field names. As soon as you click a table style in the drop-down gallery, the Format As Table dialog box appears, listing the address of the cell range enclosed in the marquee in the Where Is the Data for Your Table text box, and the My Table Has Headers check box is selected.

4. **Click the OK button to close the Format As Table dialog box.**

Excel formats your new data list in the selected table format and adds AutoFilter (drop-down buttons) to each of the field names in the top row.

Figure 1-1 shows you a brand new employee data list after formatting the first row with the field names and second row with the first data record as a table using Table Style Light 1. This new data list begins in row 1 of this worksheet, which contains the column headings with the names for the ten fields in this data list (ID No through Profit Sharing) all with AutoFilter buttons (thanks to the formatting as a table). Note that employees' names are divided into separate First Name and Last Name fields in this list (columns B and C, respectively). Note too, that the first actual record of the data list is entered in row 2 of the worksheet, directly under the row with the field names. When entering your records for a new data list, you don't skip rows but keep entering each record one above the other going down successive rows of the worksheet.

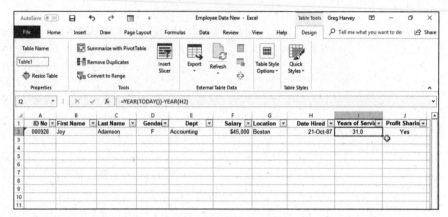

FIGURE 1-1:
Creating an employee data list with the row of field names and first data record.

When you're entering the row with the first data record, be sure to format all the cells the way you want the entries in that field to appear in all the subsequent data records in the data list. For example, if you have a Salary field in the data list, and you want the salaries formatted with the Currency style number format without any decimal places, be sure to format the salary entry in the first record in this manner. If you have a Zip Code field, format it with the Special Zip Code format or as Text so that Excel doesn't drop the initial zeros from codes that begin with them such as 00234. That way, all subsequent records will pick up that same formatting for their respective fields when you enter them with Excel's data form.

Creating calculated fields

When creating a new data list, you can make full use of Excel's calculating capabilities by defining fields whose entries are returned by formula rather than entered manually. The sample employee list introduced in Figure 1-1 contains just such a calculated field (shown on the Formula bar) in cell I2 that contains the first entry in the Years of Service field.

The original formula for calculating years of service in cell I2 is as follows:

```
=YEAR(TODAY())-YEAR(H2)
```

This formula uses the YEAR Date function to subtract the serial number of the year in which the employee was hired (entered into the Date Hired field) in cell H2 from the serial number of the current year (returned by the TODAY function). After entering and formatting this original formula in cell I2, the data table picks up this formula and automatically copies it and applies it to any new record you add to the data list.

Modifying the structure of the data list

You may find after creating your data list that you need to modify its structure by adding or deleting some fields. To add a new field, you select the column (by clicking the column letter) where you want the field inserted, and then click the Insert command button on the Ribbon's Home tab to insert a new column. Replace the generic Column1 field name given to the new field in the top row with a descriptive name and then enter the entries for that field for each record in the data list. To delete an entire field from the data list (field name and entries), select its column and then click the Delete command button on the Home tab.

TIP

To avoid losing data or disturbing the layout of data located outside of the data list caused by adding or deleting its fields, don't place any data tables or other entries in rows beneath the last row of the data list. In other words, always keep the rows used by the columns of the data list free for new records by locating all related data in columns to the right of the last field.

Add new records to a data list

After creating the field names and one record of the data list and formatting them as a table, you're ready to start entering the rest of the records in subsequent rows of the list. The most direct way to do this is to press the Tab key when the cell cursor is in the last cell of the first record. Doing this causes Excel to add an extra row to the data list, where you can enter the appropriate information for the next record.

TIP

When doing data entry directly in a data list table, press the Tab key to proceed to the next field in the new record rather than the → key. That way, when you complete the entry in the last field of the record, you automatically extend the data list, add a new record, and position the cell cursor in the first field of that record — if you press → to complete the entry, Excel simply moves the cell cursor to the next cell outside of the data list table.

Adding the Form button to the Quick Access toolbar

Instead of entering the records of a data list directly in the table, you can use Excel's data form to make the entries. The only problem with using the data form is that its command button is not found anywhere on the Ribbon: The only way to access the data form is by adding its command button as a custom Ribbon tab or to the Quick Access toolbar.

To add the Form button to the Quick Access toolbar, you follow these steps:

1. **Click the Customize Quick Access Toolbar button at the end of the toolbar and then click the More Commands option on its drop-down menu.**

   Excel opens the Excel Options dialog box with the Quick Access Toolbar tab selected. The Form command button you want to add is available only when you select Commands Not in the Ribbon on All Commands from the Choose Commands From drop-down list.

2. **Select Commands Not in the Ribbon from the Choose Commands From drop-down list and then click the Form button to select it.**

3. **Click the Add button to add the Form button to the end of the Quick Access toolbar.**

4. **Click OK to close the Excel Options dialog box and return to the work-sheet with the data list.**

Using the data form

The first time you click the custom Form button you've added to the Quick Access toolbar, Excel analyzes the row of field names and entries for the first record and creates a data form that lists the field names down the left side of the form, with the entries for the first record in the appropriate text boxes next to them.

Figure 1-2 shows you the data form that Excel creates for the sample Employee data list shown earlier in Figure 1-1. As you can see in this figure, the data form consists of a dialog box (whose title bar contains the name of the current worksheet file, which just happens to be Employee Data List) that contains a vertical listing of each field defined for the data list.

When you click the custom Form button on the Quick Access toolbar to display the data form, Excel automatically displays the field entries for the first record entered (which just happens to be the only record in the list at this point). On the right side of the dialog box, the data form indicates the current record number out of the total number of records in the data list (1 of 1 in this case). This part of the form also contains a number of command buttons that enable you to add a new record, find a particular record for editing, or delete a record from the data list.

When the data form is displayed in the active document, you can use the scroll bar to the right of the fields to move through the records in the data list, or you can use various direction keys. Table 1-1 summarizes the use of the scroll bar and these keys. For example, to move to the next record in the data list, you can press the ↓ or the Enter key or click the scroll arrow at the bottom of the scroll bar. To move to the previous record in the data list (assuming that there's more than one), you can press the ↑ key or Shift+Enter key or click the scroll arrow at the top of the scroll bar. To select a field in the current record for editing, you can click that field's text box or press the Tab key (next field) or press Shift+Tab (previous field) until you select the field (and its current entry).

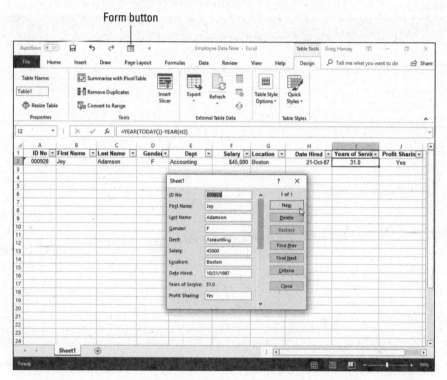

Form button

FIGURE 1-2:
Opening the data form in the new data list to add a new record.

Note that the data form does not allow you to select and edit calculated fields (such as the Years of Service field shown earlier in Figure 1-2). Although calculated fields and their current entries are listed in the data form, the form doesn't bother to provide a text box for the fields for making editing changes. To modify the contents of a calculated field, you would need to modify the original formula in the appropriate field in the first record and recopy the edited formula down to the other existing records in the list.

Adding new records with the data form

To add a new record to the data list, you can either move to the end of the data list (by dragging the scroll box to the very bottom of the scroll bar or by pressing Ctrl+↓ or Ctrl+PgDn) or simply click the New command button. Any way you do it,

Building and
Maintaining Data Lists

Excel displays a blank data form (marked New Record at the right side the dialog box), which you can then fill out. After entering the information for a field, press the Tab key to advance to the next field in the record. (Be careful not to press the Enter key because doing so inserts the new record into the data list.)

TABLE 1-1   ## Techniques for Navigating the Data Form

Movement	Keystrokes or Scroll Bar Technique
Next record, same field in the data list	Press the ↓ or the Enter key, click the downward-pointing scroll arrow, or click the Find Next command button.
Previous record, same field in the data list	Press ↑ or Shift+Enter, click the upward-pointing scroll arrow, or click the Find Prev command button.
Next field in the data form	Press Tab.
Previous field in the data form	Press Shift+Tab.
Move 10 records forward in the data list	Press PgDn.
Move 10 records backward in the data list	Press PgUp.
Move to the first record in the data list	Press Ctrl+↑ or Ctrl+PgUp or drag the scroll box to the top of the scroll bar.
Move to the last record in the data list	Press Ctrl+↓ or Ctrl+PgDn or drag the scroll box to the bottom of the scroll bar.
Move within a field	Press ← or → to move one character at a time, press Home to move to the first character, and press End to move to the last character.

When you're making an entry in a new field, you can copy the entry from the same field in the previous record into the current field by pressing Ctrl+" (double quotation mark). You can use this keystroke shortcut, for example, to carry forward entries in the text box for the State field when you are entering a series of records that all use the same state.

When you've entered all the information you have for the new record, press the ↓ or the Enter key or click the New button again. Excel then inserts the new record as the last record in the data list and displays a blank data form where you can enter the next record. When you finish adding records to the data list, press the Esc key or click the Close button to close the Data Form dialog box.

Editing records in the data form

The data form makes it easy to edit records in your data list. In a smaller data list, you can use the navigation keys or the scroll bar in the data form to locate the record that requires editing. In a larger data list, you can use the Criteria command button to quickly locate the record you need to change, as described in the next section.

When you've displayed the data form for the record that needs editing, you can then perform your editing changes by selecting the text boxes of the necessary fields and making your changes, just as you would edit the entry in its cell in the worksheet.

Finding records with the data form

You can use the Criteria button in the data form to find the records in your data list that you need to edit (or delete as described in the next section). When you click the Criteria button in the data form, Excel clears all the field text boxes so that you can enter the criteria to search for. For example, assume that you need to edit Sherry Caulfield's profit sharing status. You don't have her paperwork in front of you, so you can't look up her employee number. You do know, however, that she works in the Boston office and, although you don't remember exactly how she spells her last name, you do know that it begins with a C instead of a K.

To locate her record, you can at least narrow the search down to all the records where the Location field contains Boston and the employee's Last Name begins with the letter C. To do this, you open the data form for the Employee data list, click the Criteria command button, and then enter the following in the Last Name field:

```
C*
```

Then, in the Location field, you enter

```
Boston
```

When entering the criteria for locating matching records in the data form, you can use the question mark (?) and the asterisk (*) wildcard characters, just as you do when using the Excel Find feature to locate cells with particular entries. (See Book 2, Chapter 3, for a review of using these wildcard characters.)

When you click the Find Next button or press the Enter key, Excel locates the first record in the data list where the last name begins with the letter C and the location is Boston. This is William Cobb's record. Then, to locate the next record that matches your criteria, you click the Find Next button or press Enter, which brings you to Sherry Caulfield's record. Having located Sherry's record, you can then change her profit sharing status by selecting the Profit Sharing text box and replacing No with Yes. Excel inserts the editing change that you make in the record's data form into the data list itself as soon as you close the Data Form dialog box by clicking the Close button.

When using the Criteria button in the data form to find records, you can use the following logical operators when entering search criteria in fields that use numbers or dates:

>> **Equal to (=):** Finds records with the same text, value, or date you enter.

>> **Greater than (>):** Finds records after the text characters (in the alphabet) or the date, or larger than the value you enter.

>> **Greater than or equal to (>=):** Finds records the same as the text characters, date, or value you enter or after the characters (in the alphabet), after the date, or larger than the value.

>> **Less than (<):** Finds records before the text characters (in the alphabet) or date or smaller than the value you enter.

>> **Less than or equal to (<=):** Finds records the same as the text characters, date, or value you enter or before the characters (in the alphabet) or the date, or larger than the value.

>> **Not equal to (<>):** Finds records not the same as the text, value, or date you enter.

For example, to find all the records where the employee's annual salary is $50,000, you can enter **=50000** or simply **50000** in the Salary field text box. However, to find all the records for employees whose annual salaries are less than or equal to $35,000, you enter **<=35000** in the Salary field text box. To find all the records for employees with salaries greater than $45,000, you would enter **>45000** in the Salary field text box instead. If you wanted to find all of the records where the employees are female *and* make more than $35,000, you would enter **F** in the Gender field text box and **>35000** in the Salary field text box in the same Criteria data form.

When specifying search criteria that fit a number of records, you may have to click the Find Next or Find Prev button several times to locate the record you want to work with. If no record fits the search criteria you enter in the Criteria data form, your computer will beep at you when you click the Find Next or Find Prev button.

To change your search criteria, select the appropriate text box(es) and delete the old criteria and then enter the new criteria. To switch back to the current record without using the search criteria you enter, click the Form button. (This button replaces the Criteria button as soon you click the Criteria button.)

Deleting records with the data form

In addition to adding and editing records with the data form, you can also delete them. To delete a record, you simply display its data form and then click the Delete button. Be very careful when deleting records, however, because you cannot restore the records you delete with Excel's Undo feature. For this reason, Excel displays an alert dialog box whenever you click the Delete button, indicating that the record displayed in the data form is about to be permanently deleted. To continue and remove the record, you need to click OK or press Enter. To save the current record, press the Esc key or click the Cancel button instead.

REMEMBER

Keep in mind that although you can use the Criteria data form to locate a group of records that you want to delete, you can remove only one record at a time with the Delete button.

Eliminating records with duplicate fields

You can use Excel's Eliminate Duplicates feature to quickly find and remove duplicate records from a list (or rows from a table). This is a great feature especially when you're dealing with a really large data list in which several different people do the data entry and which should not have any duplicate records (such as client lists, personnel files, and the like).

To have Excel remove all duplicate records from a data list or table, you follow these simple steps:

1. Position the cell cursor in one of the cells of the data list or table.

2. Click the Remove Duplicates command button on the Ribbon's Data tab or press Alt+AM.

Excel selects all the cells in the data list while at the same time displaying the Remove Duplicates dialog box similar to the one shown in Figure 1-3.

When this dialog box first opens, Excel automatically selects all the fields in the list (by placing check marks in the check boxes in front of their names in the Columns list box). When all the fields are selected and you click OK in this dialog box, Excel deletes only complete duplicates (in other words, copies) of the records in the list.

If you want the program to remove records where there's any duplication of entries in particular fields (such as the ID No field), you remove the check marks from all the columns except for those whose duplication are sufficient reason for deleting the entire record (as described in Step 3). Otherwise, you proceed directly to Step 4.

3. **(Optional) Remove the check marks from all fields in the Columns list box except for those whose duplicates are reason for deleting the record.**

If only one or two fields out of many need to be selected in the Columns list box, click the Unselect All button to remove the check marks from all field check boxes and then individually click the fields that can't have duplicate entries.

4. **Click OK to have Excel close the Remove Duplicates dialog box and remove the duplicate records (rows) from the selected data list.**

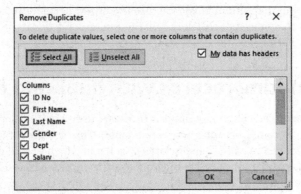

FIGURE 1-3:
Using the Remove Duplicates dialog box to remove duplicate records from a data list.

Sorting Data

You can use the Sort & Filter Data command button on the Ribbon's Home tab and the AutoFilter buttons on the field names to quickly sort data. You can sort the records in your data list by sorting its rows, and you can sort the fields in the data list by sorting its columns.

REMEMBER

In sorting, you can specify either ascending or descending sort order for your data. When you specify ascending order (which is the default), Excel arranges text in A-to-Z order and values from smallest to largest. When you specify descending order, Excel reverses this order and arranges text in Z-to-A order and values range from largest to smallest. When sorting on a date field, keep in mind that ascending order puts the records in oldest to newest order, while descending order gives you the records in newest to oldest date order.

REMEMBER

Keep in mind that, although sorting is most often applied to rearranging and maintaining data list records and fields, you can use the Sort & Filter command button to reorder data in any worksheet table, whether or not the table follows the strict data list structure.

MORE ABOUT ASCENDING AND DESCENDING SORT ORDERS

When you use the ascending sort order on a field in a data list that contains many different kinds of entries, Excel places numbers (from smallest to largest) before text entries (in alphabetical order), followed by any logical values (FALSE and TRUE), error values, and finally, blank cells. When you use the descending sort order, Excel arranges the different entries in reverse: numbers are still first, arranged from largest to smallest; text entries go from Z to A; and the TRUE logical value precedes the FALSE logical value.

Sorting records on a single field

When you need to sort the data list only on one particular field (such as the ID No, Last Name, or Location field), you simply click that field's AutoFilter button and then select the appropriate sort option from its drop-down list:

>> **Sort A to Z** or **Sort Z to A** in a text field

>> **Sort Smallest to Largest** or **Sort Largest to Smallest** in a number field

>> **Sort Oldest to Newest** or **Sort Newest to Oldest** in a date field

Excel then reorders all the records in the data list in accordance with the new ascending or descending order in the selected field. If you find that you've sorted the list in error, simply click the Undo button on the Quick Access toolbar or press Ctrl+Z right away to return the list to its previous order.

Excel 2019 shows when a field has been used in sorting the data list by adding an up or down arrow to its filter button. An arrow pointing up indicates that the ascending sort order was used and one pointing down indicates that the descending sort order was used.

Sorting records on multiple fields

When you need to sort a data list on more than one field, you use the Sort dialog box (shown in Figure 1-4). And you need to sort on more than one field when the first field contains duplicate values and you want to determine how the records with duplicates are arranged. (If you don't specify another field to sort on, Excel just puts the records in the order in which you entered them.)

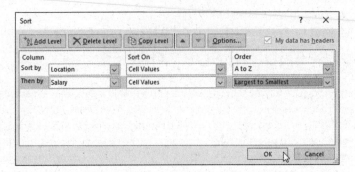

The best and most common example of when you need more than one field is when sorting a large database alphabetically in last-name order. Say that you have a database that contains several people with the last name Smith, Jones, or Zastrow (as is the case when you work at Zastrow and Sons). If you specify the Last Name field as the only field to sort on (using the default ascending order), all the duplicate Smiths, Joneses, and Zastrows are placed in the order in which their records were originally entered. To better sort these duplicates, you can specify the First Name field as the second field to sort on (again using the default ascending order), making the second field the tie-breaker, so that Ian Smith's record precedes that of Sandra Smith, and Vladimir Zastrow's record comes after that of Mikhail Zastrow.

To sort records in a data list using the Sort dialog box, follow these steps:

1. **Position the cell cursor in one of the cells in the data list table.**

2. **Click the Sort button in the Sort & Filter group on the Data tab or press Alt+ASS.**

   Excel selects all the records of the database (without including the first row of field names) and opens the Sort dialog box, as shown in Figure 1-4. Note that you can also open the Sort dialog box by selecting the Custom Sort option on the Sort & Filter drop-down button's menu or by pressing Alt+HSU.

3. **Select the name of the field you first want the records sorted by from the Sort By drop-down list.**

   If you want the records arranged in descending order, remember also to select the descending sort option (Z to A, Smallest to Largest, or Oldest to Newest) from the Order drop-down list to the right.

4. **(Optional) If the first field contains duplicates and you want to specify how the records in this field are sorted, click the Add Level button to insert another sort level, select a second field to sort on from the Then By drop-down list, and select either the ascending or descending option from its Order drop-down list to its right.**

5. **(Optional) If necessary, repeat Step 4, adding as many additional sort levels as required.**

6. **Click OK or press Enter.**

Excel closes the Sort dialog box and sorts the records in the data list using the sorting fields in the order of their levels in this dialog box. If you see that you sorted the database on the wrong fields or in the wrong order, click the Undo button on the Quick Access toolbar or press Ctrl+Z to immediately restore the data list records to their previous order.

TIP

By default, when you perform a sort operation, Excel assumes that you're sorting a data list that has a header row (with the field names) that is not to be reordered with the rest of the records in doing the sort. You can, however, use the Sort feature to sort a cell selection that doesn't have such a header row. In that case, you need to specify the sorting keys by column letter, and you need to be sure to deselect the My Data Has Headers check box to remove its check mark in the Sort dialog box.

Also, the Sort dialog box contains an Options button that, when clicked, opens a Sort Options dialog box, which contains options for doing a case-sensitive sort on fields that contain text. This dialog box also contains options for changing the orientation of the sort from the normal top-to-bottom order to left-to-right order when you want to sort columns in a list.

Figure 1-5 illustrates sorting the employee data list first in ascending order by location and then in descending order by salary. For this sort, the Location field is designated as the field (column) to sort on in the first level and the Salary field as the other field (column) as the second level. Also, to have the records within each location sorted from highest to lowest salary, I selected Largest to Smallest from the Order drop-down list to the right of the first Then By combo box.

After clicking OK in the Sort dialog box, you will note in Figure 1-5 how the records are now organized first in ascending order by the city listed in the Location field (Atlanta, Boston, Chicago, and so on) and within each city in descending order by Salary (38,900, 32,200, 29,200, and so on).

Sometimes, you may need to sort on a whole bunch of fields to get the desired order. For example, suppose that you are working with a personnel data list like the one shown in Figure 1-6, and you want to organize the records in alphabetical order, first by department, then by supervisor, and finally by last name, first name, and middle name. To sort the records in this data list on these five fields, you have to define each of the columns as a separate level in the Sort dialog box as follows:

» First by Department field in A to Z order

» Then by Supervisor field in A to Z order

» Then by Last Name field in A to Z order

» Then by First Name field in A to Z order

» Then by Middle Name field in A to Z order

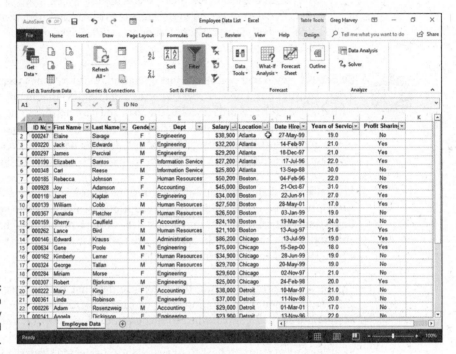

FIGURE 1-5:
Employee data list sorted by location and salary.

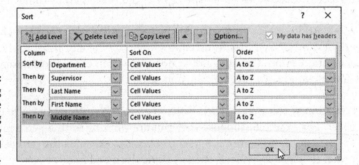

FIGURE 1-6:
The Sort dialog box with five levels of sorting keys for sorting the Personnel data list.

Figure 1-6 shows you the Sort dialog box after defining these as the columns on five separate levels on which to sort the personnel data list. Figure 1-7 shows you the result. As you can see after performing this sort operation, the records are now arranged in ascending order by department, then by supervisor within department, and finally by the last name, first name, and middle name under each supervisor.

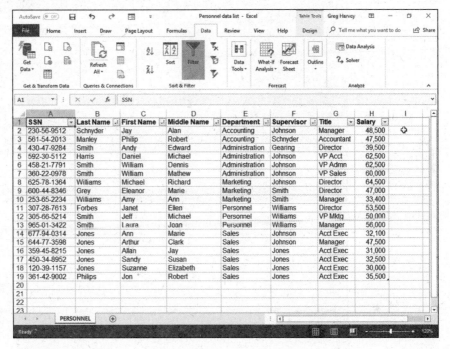

FIGURE 1-7:
The Personnel data list after sorting by department, supervisor, last, first, and finally middle names.

Sorting the columns of a data list

You can use Excel's column sorting capability to change the order of the fields in a data list without having to resort to cutting and pasting various columns. When you sort the fields in a data list, you add a row at the top of the list that you define as the primary sorting level. The cells in this row contain numbers (from 1 to the number of the last field in the data list) that indicate the new order of the fields.

Figures 1-8 and 1-9 illustrate how you can use column sorting to modify the field order of a data list in the sample Personnel data list. As you see in Figure 1-8, I began this process by inserting a new row (row 1) above the row with the field names for this data list. The cells in this row contain numbers that indicate the new field order. After the fields are sorted using the values in this row, the SSN field remains first (indicated by 1), the Department field becomes second (2), Supervisor field third (3), followed by First Name (4), Middle Name (5), Last Name (6), Title (7), and Salary (8).

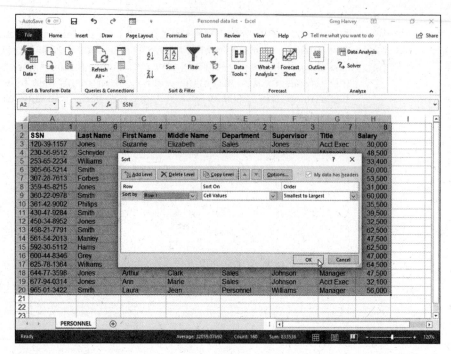

FIGURE 1-8:
Setting up the Personnel data list to sort by columns by adding a primary sort order row.

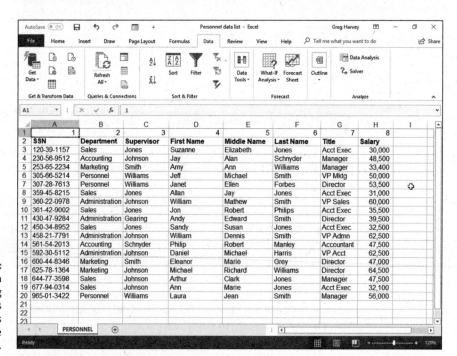

FIGURE 1-9:
Personnel data list after sorting the columns using the values entered in the first row.

WARNING

You can't sort data you've formally formatted as a data table in this manner until you convert the table back into a normal cell range because the program won't recognize the row containing the column's new order numbers as part of the table on which you can perform a sort. In this example, to get around the problem, you take the following steps:

1. **Click a cell in the data table and then click the Convert to Range command button on the Design tab of the Table Tools contextual tab.**

    Excel displays an alert dialog box asking you if you want to convert the table to a range.

2. **Click the Yes button in the alert dialog box to do the conversion.**

3. **Select all the records in the Personnel data list along with the top row containing the numbers on which to sort the columns of the list as the cell selection.**

    In this case, you select the cell range A1:H20 as the cell selection.

4. **Click the Sort command button on the Data tab (or press Alt+ASS).**

    Excel opens the Sort dialog box. You can also open the Sort dialog box by selecting Custom Sort from the Sort & Filter button's drop-down list or by pressing Alt+HSU.

5. **Click the Options button in the Sort dialog box.**

    Excel opens the Sort Options dialog box.

6. **Select the Sort Left to Right option button and then click OK.**

7. **Click Row 1 in the Row drop-down list in the Sort dialog box.**

    The Sort On drop-down list box should read Values, and the Order drop-down list box should read Smallest to Largest, as shown in Figure 1-8.

8. **Click OK to sort the data list using the values in the top row of the current cell selection.**

    Excel sorts the columns of the Personnel data list according to the numerical order of the entries in the top row (which are now in a 1-to-8 order) as shown in Figure 1-9. Now, you can get rid of the top row with these numbers.

9. **Select the cell range A1:H1 and then click the Delete button on the Home tab.**

    Excel deletes the row of numbers and pulls up the Personnel data list so that its row of field names is now in row 1 of the worksheet. Now, all that's left to do is to reformat the Personnel data list as a table again so that Excel adds AutoFilter buttons to its field names and the program dynamically keeps track of the data list's cell range as it expands and contracts.

10. Click the Format as Table command button on the Home tab (or press Alt+HT) and then click a table style from the Light, Medium, or Dark section of its gallery.

Excel opens the Format As Table dialog box and places a marquee around all the cells in the data list.

11. Make sure that the My Table Has Headers check box has a check mark in it and that all the cells in the data list are included in the cell range displayed in the Where Is the Data for Your Table text box before you click OK.

Figure 1-9 shows the personnel data list after sorting its fields according to the values in the first row. After sorting the data list, you then delete this row and modify the widths of the columns to suit the new arrangement and reformat the list as a table before you save the worksheet.

WARNING

When sorting the columns in a data list, you must remember to click the Options button and select the Sort Left to Right option button in the Orientation section of the Sort Options dialog box. Otherwise, Excel sorts your records instead of your columns, and in the process, the row of field names becomes sorted in with the other data records in your list!

Sorting a data list on font and fill colors and cell icons

Although you normally sort the records of a data list or rows of a table on the values (entries) contained in one or more columns of the list or table, Excel 2019 also enables you to sort on the font or fill color or cell icons that you assign to them as well. These colors and icons are assigned by using the Conditional Formatting feature to mark those values in the columns of a data list or table that are within or outside certain parameters with a distinctive font or fill colors or cell icon. (See the section on the Conditional Formatting feature in Book 2, Chapter 2 for details.)

To sort a data list on a font color, fill color, or cell icon in a single field of the table, you click its AutoFilter button and then choose the Sort by Color option from the drop-down menu. Excel then displays a continuation menu on which you click the font color, fill color, or cell icon to use in the sort:

>> To sort the records so that those with a particular font color in the selected column — assigned with the Conditional Formatting Highlight Cell Rules or Top/Bottom Rules options — appear at the top of the data list, click its color swatch in the Sort by Font Color section on the continuation menu.

>> To sort the records so that those with a particular fill color in the selected column — assigned with the Conditional Formatting Highlight Cell Rules, Top/Bottom Rules, Data Bars, or Color Scales options — appear at the top of the data list, click its color swatch in the Sort by Font Color section on the continuation menu.

>> To sort the records so that those with a particular cell icon in the selected column — assigned with the Conditional Formatting Icon Sets options — appear at the top of the data list, click the icon in the Sort by Cell Icon section of the continuation menu.

You can also sort the data list on more than one color or cell icon in the Sort dialog box opened by selecting the Custom Sort option from the Sort & Filter button's drop-down list on the Ribbon's Home tab or on the Sort by Color continuation menu.

When you want to sort the records in a data list on more than one font or fill color or cell icon, you select the field with the color or icon from the Column drop-down list; select Font Color, Fill Color, or Cell Icon in the Sort On drop-down list; and then click the color swatch or icon to use in the first level of the sort in the Order drop-down list.

If you need to add another sort level, you click the Add Level button and then repeat this procedure of selecting the field in the Column drop-down list, selecting the Font Color, Fill Color, or Cell Icon in the Sort On drop-down list, and selecting the specific color or icon in the Order drop-down list. When you finish defining all the levels for the sort, click OK to have Excel go ahead and sort the list's records.

REMEMBER

You can sort the records in the data list order by all the fill colors or cell icons assigned by applying the Conditional Formatting Color Scales and Cell Icons options. For each of three or five sorting levels you define in the Sort dialog box, the name of the field in the Column drop-down list button remains the same in all levels along with the Fill Color or Cell Icon option in the Sort On drop-down list button. Only the actual color or icon selected in the Order drop-down list button changes, reflecting the order in which you want to see the records appear in the sorted data list.

Subtotaling Data

You can use Excel's Subtotals feature to subtotal data in a *sorted* data list. You sort the list on the field for which you want subtotals shown before you designate the field that contains the values you want subtotaled — these are almost always not the same fields in the data list.

For example, to subtotal the salaries within each department in my sample Employee data list, you first sort the list in A-to-Z order on the Dept column. Then, you designate this Dept field as the one for which you want the subtotals calculated (so that a subtotal appears at each change in department) and the Salary field as to be subtotaled so that Excel uses the SUM function on its data entries.

Keep in mind when you use the Subtotals feature, you aren't restricted to having the values in the designated field added together with the SUM function. You can instead have Excel return the number of entries with the COUNT function, the average of the entries with the AVERAGE function, the highest entry with the MAXIMUM function, the lowest entry with the MINIMUM function, or even the product of the entries with the PRODUCT function.

Excel does not allow you to subtotal a data list formatted as a table. Before you can use the Subtotal command button, you must first convert your table into a normal range of cells. To do this, click a cell in the table and then click the Design tab on the Table Tools contextual tab on the Ribbon. Finally, click the Convert to Range command button in the Tools group followed by the Yes button in the alert dialog box asking you to confirm this action. Excel then removes the filter buttons from the columns at the top of the data list while still retaining the original table formatting.

Figures 1-10 and 1-11 illustrate how easy it is to use the Subtotals feature to obtain totals in a data list. In Figure 1-10, I sorted the sample Employee data list first by the Dept field in ascending order and then by the Salary field in descending order (Largest to Smallest) and converted the data list to a range. I then clicked the Subtotal command button in the Outline group on the Ribbon's Data tab to open the Subtotal dialog box shown in Figure 1-10.

Here, I selected the Dept field as the field for which the subtotals are to be calculated in the At Each Change In drop-down list box, Sum as the function to use in the Use Function drop-down list box, and the Salary check box as the field whose values are to be summed in the Add Subtotal To list box.

Figure 1-11 shows the results I obtained after clicking OK in the Subtotal dialog box. Here, you see the bottom of the data list showing the salary subtotals for the Administration, Engineering, Human Resources, and Information Services departments along with the grand total of the salaries for all the departments. The grand total is displayed at the bottom of the data list because I left the Summary below Data check box selected in the Subtotal dialog box — if I hadn't wanted a grand total, I would have removed the check mark from this check box.

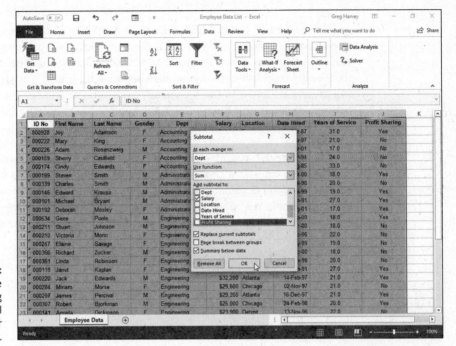

FIGURE 1-10:
Using the
Subtotal dialog
box to subtotal
the salaries for
each department.

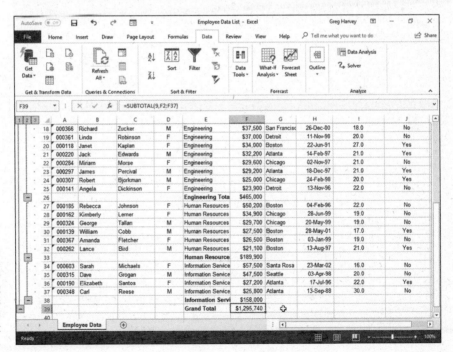

FIGURE 1-11:
Bottom of the
data list showing
the subtotals
and grand total
for department
salaries.

As you can see in Figure 1-11, when you use the Subtotals command, Excel outlines the data at the same time that it adds the rows with the departmental salary totals and the grand total. This means that you can collapse the data list down to just its departmental subtotal rows or even just the grand total row simply by collapsing the outline down to the second or first level. (Remember that you can toggle between showing and hiding the outline symbols at the left edge of the data list by pressing Ctrl+8.)

TIP

In a large data list, you may want Excel to insert page breaks (often referred to as *breaks*) every time data changes in the field on which the list is being subtotaled (that is, the field designated in the At Each Change In drop-down list box). To do this, you simply select the Page Break between Groups check box in the Subtotal dialog box to put a check mark in it before you click OK to subtotal the list.

IN THIS CHAPTER

» Understanding how to filter and query a data list

» Using AutoFilter to filter out unwanted data

» Filtering a list with custom criteria

» Filtering a list on font color, fill color, or cell icons

» Using Database functions to compute statistics from records that match your filter criteria

» Performing external data queries with text files, web pages, and data files kept in other database sources

Chapter **2**

Filtering and Querying a Data List

t's one thing to set up a data list and load it with tons of data and quite another to get just the information that you need out of the list. How you go about extracting the data that's important to you is the subject of this chapter. The procedure for specifying the data that you want displayed in an Excel data list is called *filtering* the data list or database. The procedure for extracting only the data that you want from the database or data list is called *querying* the database.

In addition to helping you with filtering and querying the data in your list, this chapter explains how you can use Excel's Database functions to perform calculations on particular numerical fields for only the records that meet the criteria that you specify. These calculations can include getting totals (DSUM), averages (DAVERAGE), the count of the records (DCOUNT and DCOUNTA), and the like.

Finally, this chapter introduces you to querying external data sources in order to bring all or just some of their data into the more familiar worksheet setting. These can be in the form of external databases in other Windows database programs, such as Microsoft Access 2019 or in even more sophisticated, server-based database-management systems, such as those provided by SQL Analysis Services, Microsoft Windows Azure Marketplace, and OData Data connections. They can also be in the form of data tables stored on web pages and in text files, whose data needs to be parsed into separate cells of an Excel worksheet.

Data List Filtering 101

If you ever have the good fortune to attend my class on database management, you'll hear my spiel on the difference between data and information in the tables in a database (or *data list*, in Excel-speak). In case you're the least little bit interested, it goes like this: A data list or the tables that make up a database consist of a vast quantity of raw data, which simply represents all the stuff that everybody in the company wants stored on a given subject (employees, sales, clients, you name it). For example, suppose that you keep a data list on the sales transactions made by your customers. This data list can very well track such stuff as the customers' identification numbers, names, addresses, telephone numbers, whether they have a charge account with the store, the maximum amount that they can charge, the purchases that they've made (including the dates and amounts), and whether their accounts are due (or overdue).

However, this vast quantity of *data* stored in the customer data list is not to be confused with the *information* that particular people in the office want out of the data. For example, suppose that you're working in the marketing department and you're about to introduce a line of expensive household items that you want to advertise. You want to limit the advertising to those customers who have a charge account with the store and have purchased at least $5,000 of merchandise in the last six months. Use the *data* provided in the data list to supply that *information* by selecting only those customers out of the entire data list.

On the other hand, suppose that you work in the accounting department and you need to send out nasty notices to all the customers who have charge accounts that are more than 90 days past due. In this case, you want only the data identifying those customers whose accounts are overdue. You couldn't care less about what was actually purchased. All you care about is reaching these folks and convincing them to pay up. You again use the *data* provided in the data list to supply the *information* to select only those customers that you need from the data list.

From these simple examples, it should be clear that the data that supplies information to one group in the company at a particular time is often not the same data that supplies information to another group. In other words, for most people, the data list dispenses information only when you are able to filter out the stuff that you currently don't want to see, and leaves behind just the stuff that interests you.

Filtering Data

Filtering the data list to leave behind only the information that you want to work with is exactly the procedure that you follow in Excel. At the most basic level, you use the AutoFilter feature to temporarily hide the display of unwanted records and leave behind only the records that you want to see. Much of the time, the capabilities of the AutoFilter feature are all that you need, especially when your main concern is simply displaying just the information of interest in the data list.

You will encounter situations, however, in which the AutoFilter feature is not sufficient, and you must do what Microsoft refers to as *advanced filtering* in your data list. You need to use advanced filtering to filter the data list when you use computed criteria (such as when you want to see all the records where the entry in the Sales column is twice the amount in the Owed column) and when you need to save a copy of the filtered data in a different part of the worksheet (Excel's version of querying the data in a data list).

Using AutoFilter

Excel's AutoFilter feature makes filtering out unwanted data in a data list as easy as clicking the AutoFilter button on the column on which you want to filter the data and then choosing the appropriate filtering criteria from that column's drop-down menu.

TIP

If you open a worksheet with a data list and you don't find AutoFilter buttons attached to each of the field names at the top of the list, you can display them simply by positioning the cell pointer in one of the cells with the field names and then clicking the Filter command button on the Ribbon's Data tab or pressing Ctrl+Shift+L or Alt+AT.

The filter options on a column's AutoFilter drop-down menu depend on the type of entries in the field. On the drop-down menu in a column that contains only date entries, the menu contains a Date Filters option to which a submenu of the actual filters is attached. On the drop-down menu in a column that contains only numeric entries (besides dates) or a mixture of dates with other types of numeric entries, the menu contains a Number Filters option. On the drop-down menu in a column that contains only text entries or a mixture of text, date, and other numeric entries, the menu contains a Text Filters option.

Doing basic filtering by selecting specific field entries

In addition to the Date Filters, Text Filters, or Number Filters options (depending on the type of field), the AutoFilter drop-down menu for each field in the data list contains a list box with a complete listing of all entries made in that column, each with its own check box. At the most basic level, you can filter the data list by clearing the check box for all the entries whose records you don't want to see in the list.

TIP

This kind of basic filtering works best in fields such as City, State, or Country, which contain many duplicates, so you can see a subset of the data list that contains only the cities, states, or countries you want to work with at the time.

The easiest way to perform this basic type of filtering on a field is to first deselect the check box in front of the (Select All) option at the top of the field's list box to clear the check boxes, and then select each of the check boxes containing the entries for the records you do want displayed in the filtered data list. After you finish selecting the check boxes for all the entries you want to keep, you click OK to close the AutoFilter drop-down menu.

Excel then hides rows in the data list for all records except for those that contain the entries you just selected. The program also lets you know which field or fields have been used in the filtering operation by adding a cone filter icon to the column's AutoFilter button. To restore all the records to the data list, you can remove the filtering by clicking the Clear command button in the Sort & Filter group of the Data tab of the Ribbon or by pressing Alt+AC.

When doing this basic kind of list filtering, you can select specific entries from more than one field in this list. Figure 2-1 illustrates this kind of situation. Here, I want only the employees in the company who work in the Engineering and Information Services departments in the Chicago and Seattle offices. To do this, I selected only the Engineering and Information Services entries in the list box on the Dept field's AutoFilter drop-down menu and only the Chicago and Seattle entries in the list box on the Location field's AutoFilter drop-down menu.

As you can see in Figure 2-1, after filtering the Employee data list so that only the records for employees in either the Engineering or Information Services department in either the Chicago or Seattle office locations are listed, Excel adds the cone filter icon to the AutoFilter buttons on both the Dept and Location fields in the top row, indicating that the list is filtered using criteria involving both fields.

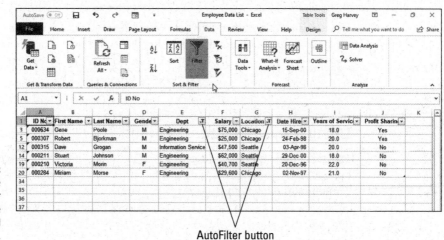

FIGURE 2-1:
The employee data list after filtering the Dept and Location fields.

AutoFilter button

REMEMBER

Keep in mind that after filtering the data list in this manner, you can then copy remaining records that make up the desired subset of the data list to a new area in the same worksheet or to a new sheet in the workbook. You can then sort the data (by adding AutoFilter buttons with the Filter command button on the Data tab), chart the data (see Book 5, Chapter 1), analyze the data (see "Using the Database Functions" later in this chapter), or summarize the data in a pivot table (covered in Book 7, Chapter 2).

Using the Text Filters options

The AutoFilter drop-down menu for a field that contains only text or a combination of text, date, and numeric entries contains a Text Filters option that when you click or highlight displays its submenu containing the following options:

» **Equals:** Opens the Custom AutoFilter dialog box with the Equals operator selected in the first condition.

» **Does Not Equal:** Opens the Custom AutoFilter dialog box with the Does Not Equal operator selected in the first condition.

» **Begins With:** Opens the Custom AutoFilter dialog box with the Begins With operator selected in the first condition.

» **Ends With:** Opens the Custom AutoFilter dialog box with the Ends With operator selected in the first condition.

» **Contains:** Opens the Custom AutoFilter dialog box with the Contains operator selected in the first condition.

>> **Does Not Contain:** Opens the Custom AutoFilter dialog box with the Does Not Contain operator selected in the first condition.

>> **Custom Filter:** Opens the Custom AutoFilter dialog box where you can select your own criteria for applying more complex AND or conditions.

Using the Date Filters options

The AutoFilter drop-down menu for a field that contains only date entries contains a Date Filters option that when you click or highlight displays its submenu containing the following options:

>> **Equals:** Opens the Custom AutoFilter dialog box with the Equals operator selected in the first condition.

>> **Before:** Opens the Custom AutoFilter dialog box with the Is Before operator selected in the first condition.

>> **After:** Opens the Custom AutoFilter dialog box with the Is After operator selected in the first condition.

>> **Between:** Opens the Custom AutoFilter dialog box with the Is After or Equal To operator selected in the first condition and the Is Before or Equal To operator selected in the second AND condition.

>> **Tomorrow:** Filters the data list so that only records with tomorrow's date in this field are displayed in the worksheet.

>> **Today:** Filters the data list so that only records with the current date in this field are displayed in the worksheet.

>> **Yesterday:** Filters the data list so that only records with yesterday's date in this field are displayed in the worksheet.

>> **Next Week:** Filters the data list so that only records with date entries in the week ahead in this field are displayed in the worksheet.

>> **This Week:** Filters the data list so that only records with date entries in the current week in this field are displayed in the worksheet.

>> **Last Week:** Filters the data list so that only records with date entries in the previous week in this field are displayed in the worksheet.

>> **Next Month:** Filters the data list so that only records with date entries in the month ahead in this field are displayed in the worksheet.

>> **This Month:** Filters the data list so that only records with date entries in the current month in this field are displayed in the worksheet.

- **Last Month:** Filters the data list so that only records with date entries in the previous month in this field are displayed in the worksheet.

- **Next Quarter:** Filters the data list so that only records with date entries in the three-month quarterly period ahead in this field are displayed in the worksheet.

- **This Quarter:** Filters the data list so that only records with date entries in the current three-month quarterly period in this field are displayed in the worksheet.

- **Last Quarter:** Filters the data list so that only records with date entries in the previous three-month quarterly period in this field are displayed in the worksheet.

- **Next Year:** Filters the data list so that only records with date entries in the calendar year ahead in this field are displayed in the worksheet.

- **This Year:** Filters the data list so that only records with date entries in the current calendar year in this field are displayed in the worksheet.

- **Last Year:** Filters the data list so that only records with date entries in the previous calendar year in this field are displayed in the worksheet.

- **Year to Date:** Filters the data list so that only records with date entries in the current year up to the current date in this field are displayed in the worksheet.

- **All Dates in the Period:** Filters the data list so that only records with date entries in the quarter (Quarter 1 through Quarter 4) or month (January through December) that you choose from its submenu are displayed in the worksheet.

- **Custom Filter:** Opens the Custom AutoFilter dialog box where you can select your own criteria for more complex AND or conditions.

TIP

When selecting dates for conditions using the Equals, Is Before, Is After, Is Before or Equal To, or Is After or Equal To operator in the Custom AutoFilter dialog box, you can select the date by clicking the Date Picker button (the one with the calendar icon) and then clicking the specific date on the drop-down date palette. When you open the date palette, it shows the current month and the current date selected. To select a date in an earlier month, click the Previous button (the one with the triangle pointing left) until its month is displayed in the palette. To select a date in a later month, click the Next button (the one with the triangle pointing right) until its month is displayed in the palette.

Using the Number Filters options

The AutoFilter drop-down menu for a field that contains only number entries besides dates or a combination of dates and other numeric entries contains a

Number Filters option that when you click or highlight it displays its submenu containing the following options:

>> **Equals:** Opens the Custom AutoFilter dialog box with the Equals operator selected in the first condition.

>> **Does Not Equal:** Opens the Custom AutoFilter dialog box with the Does Not Equal operator selected in the first condition.

>> **Greater Than:** Opens the Custom AutoFilter dialog box with the Is Greater Than operator selected in the first condition.

>> **Greater Than or Equal To:** Opens the Custom AutoFilter dialog box with the Is Greater Than or Equal To operator selected in the first condition.

>> **Less Than:** Opens the Custom AutoFilter dialog box with the Is Less Than operator selected in the first condition.

>> **Less Than or Equal To:** Opens the Custom AutoFilter dialog box with the Is Less Than or Equal to operator selected in the first condition.

>> **Between:** Opens the Custom AutoFilter dialog box with the Is Greater Than or Equal To operator selected in the first condition and the Is Less Than or Equal To operator selected in the second AND condition.

>> **Top 10:** Opens the Top 10 AutoFilter dialog box so that you can filter the list to just the ten or so top or bottom values or percentages in the field. (See "Making it to the Top Ten!" that follows in this chapter for details.)

>> **Above Average:** Filters the data list to display only records where the values in the field are greater than the average of the values in this field.

>> **Below Average:** Filters the data list to display only records where the values in the field are less than the average of the values in this field.

>> **Custom Filter:** Opens the Custom AutoFilter dialog box where you can select your own criteria for more complex AND or conditions.

Making it to the Top Ten!

The Top Ten option on the Number Filters option's submenu enables you to filter out all records except those whose entries in that field are at the top or bottom of the list by a certain number (10 by default) or in a certain top or bottom percent (10 by default). Of course, you can only use the Top Ten item in numerical fields and date fields; this kind of filtering doesn't make any sense when you're dealing with entries in a text field.

When you click the Top Ten option on the Number Filters option's submenu, Excel opens the Top 10 AutoFilter dialog box where you can specify your filtering criteria. By default, the Top 10 AutoFilter dialog box is set to filter out all records except those whose entries are among the top ten items in the field by selecting Top in the drop-down list box on the left, 10 in the middle combo box, and Items in the drop-down list box on the right. If you want to use these default criteria, you simply click OK in the Top 10 AutoFilter dialog box.

Figure 2-2 shows you the sample employee data list after using the Top 10 Items AutoFilter to display only the records with the top ten salaries in the data list.

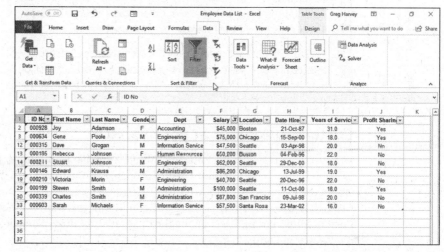

FIGURE 2-2:
Using the Top 10 Items AutoFilter to filter out all records except for those with the top ten salaries.

You can also change the filtering criteria in the Top 10 AutoFilter dialog box before you filter the data. You can choose between Top and Bottom in the leftmost drop-down list box and between Items and Percent in the rightmost one. You can also change the number in the middle combo box by clicking it and entering a new value or using the spinner buttons to select one.

Filtering a data list on a field's font and fill colors or cell icons

Just as you can sort a data list using the font or fill color or cell icons that you've assigned with the Conditional Formatting feature to values in the field that are within or outside of certain parameters (see the section on the Conditional Formatting feature in Book 2, Chapter 2 for details), you can also filter the list.

To filter a data list on a font color, fill color, or cell icon used in a field, you click its AutoFilter button and then select the Filter by Color option from the drop-down menu. Excel then displays a submenu from which you choose the font color, fill color, or cell icon to use in the sort:

>> To filter the data list so that only the records with a particular font color in the selected field — assigned with the Conditional Formatting Highlight Cell Rules or Top/Bottom Rules options — appear in the list, click its color swatch in the Filter by Font Color submenu.

>> To filter the data list so that only the records with a particular fill color in the selected field — assigned with the Conditional Formatting Highlight Cell Rules, Top/Bottom Rules, Data Bars, or Color Scales options — appear in the list, click its color swatch in the Filter by Font Color submenu.

>> To filter the data list so that only the records with a particular cell icon in the selected field — assigned with the Conditional Formatting Icon Sets options — appear in the list, click the icon in the Filter by Cell Icon submenu.

Custom AutoFilter at your service

You can click the Custom Filter option on a field's Text Filters, Date Filters, or Number Filters continuation menu to open the Custom AutoFilter dialog box, where you can specify your own filtering criteria by using conditions with the AND OR logical operators (called AND OR conditions for short). When you click the Custom Filter option, Excel opens the Custom AutoFilter dialog box, similar to the one shown in Figure 2-3.

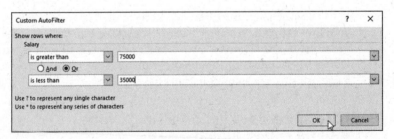

FIGURE 2-3: Using Custom AutoFilter to filter out records except for those within a range of salaries.

Here, you select the type of operator to use in evaluating the first and second conditions in the top and bottom drop-down list boxes and the values to be evaluated in the first and second conditions in the associated combo boxes. You also specify the type of relationship between the two conditions with the And or option button. (The And option button is selected by default.)

When selecting the operator for the first and second condition in the leftmost drop-down list boxes at the top and bottom of the Custom AutoFilter dialog box, you have the following choices, depending on the types of entries in the selected field:

» **Equals:** Matches records where the entry in the field is identical to the text, date, or number you enter in the associated combo box.

» **Does Not Equal:** Matches records where the entry in the field is anything other than the text, date, or number you enter in the associated combo box.

» **Is After:** Matches records where the entry in the date field comes after the date you enter or select in the associated combo box.

» **Is After or Equal To:** Matches records where the entry in the date field comes after or is the same as the date you enter or select in the associated combo box.

» **Is Before:** Matches records where the entry in the date field precedes the date you enter or select in the associated combo box.

» **Is Before or Equal To:** Matches records where the entry in the date field precedes or is the same as the date you enter or select in the associated combo box.

» **Is Greater Than:** Matches records where the entry in the field follows the text in the alphabet, comes after the date, or is larger than the number you enter in the associated combo box.

» **Is Greater Than or Equal To:** Matches records where the entry in the field follows the text in the alphabet or is identical, the date comes after or is identical, or the number is larger than or equal to the one you enter in the associated combo box.

» **Is Less Than:** Matches records where the entry in the field comes before the text in the alphabet, comes before the date, or is less than the number you enter in the associated combo box.

» **Is Less Than or Equal To:** Matches records where the entry in the field comes before the text in the alphabet or is identical, the date comes before or is identical, or the number is less than or equal to the one you enter in the associated combo box.

» **Begins With:** Matches records where the entry in the field starts with the text, the part of the date, or the number you enter in the associated combo box.

» **Does Not Begin With:** Matches records where the entry in the field starts with anything other than the text, the part of the date, or the number you enter in the associated combo box.

» **Ends With:** Matches records where the entry in the field ends with the text, the part of the date, or the number you enter in the associated combo box.

>> **Does Not End With:** Matches records where the entry in the field ends with anything other than the text, the part of the date, or the number you enter in the associated combo box.

>> **Contains:** Matches records where the entry in the field contains the text, the part of the date, or the number you enter in the associated combo box.

>> **Does Not Contain:** Matches records where the entry in the field contains anything other than the text, the part of the date, or the number you enter in the associated combo box.

REMEMBER

Note that you can use the Begins With, Ends With, and Contains operators and their negative counterparts when filtering a text field — you can also use the question mark (?) and asterisk (*) wildcard characters when entering the values for use with these operators. (The question mark wildcard stands for individual characters, and the asterisk stands for one or more characters.) You use the other logical operators when dealing with numeric and date fields.

When specifying the values to evaluate in the associated combo boxes on the right side of the Custom AutoFilter dialog box, you can type in the text, number, or date, or you can select an existing field entry by clicking the box's drop-down list button and then clicking the entry on the drop-down menu. In date fields, you can select the dates directly from the date drop-down palette opened by clicking the box's Date Picker button (the one with the calendar icon).

Figure 2-3 illustrates setting up filtering criteria in the Custom AutoFilter dialog box that selects records whose Salary values fall within two separate ranges of values. In this example, I'm using an OR condition to filter out all records where the salaries fall below $35,000 or are greater than $75,000 by entering the following complex condition:

```
Salary Is Greater Than 75000 OR Is Less Than 35000
```

Using the Advanced Filter

When you use advanced filtering, you don't use the field's AutoFilter buttons and associated drop-down menu options. Instead, you create a so-called Criteria Range somewhere on the worksheet containing the data list to be filtered before opening the Advanced Filter dialog box.

If you use the Advanced Filter feature to do a query, you extract copies of the records that match your criteria by creating a subset of the data list. You can locate the Criteria Range in the top rows of columns to the right of the data list and then specify the Copy To range underneath the Criteria Range, similar to the arrangement shown in Figure 2-4.

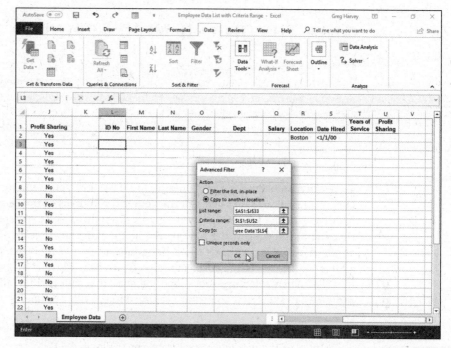

FIGURE 2-4:
Using Advanced
Filter to copy
records that meet
the criteria in the
Criteria Range.

To create a Criteria Range, you copy the names of the fields in the data list to a new part of the worksheet and then enter the values (text, numbers, or formulas) that are to be used as the criteria in filtering the list in rows underneath. When setting up the criteria for filtering the data list, you can create either comparison criteria or calculated criteria.

After you've set up your criteria range with all the field names and the criteria that you want used, you click the Advanced command button on the Ribbon's Data tab (or press Alt+AQ) to open the Advanced Filter dialog box similar to the one shown in Figure 2-4. Here, you specify whether you just want to filter the records in the list (by hiding the rows of all those that don't meet your criteria) or you want to copy the records that meet your criteria to a new area in the worksheet (by creating a subset of the data list).

To just filter the data in the list, leave the Filter the List, In-Place option button selected. To query the list and copy the data to a new place in the same worksheet (note that the Advanced Filter feature doesn't let you copy the data to another sheet or workbook), you select the Copy to Another Location option button. When you select this option button, the Copy To text box becomes available, along with the List Range and Criteria Range text boxes.

ONLY THE UNIQUE NEED APPLY!

To filter out duplicate rows or records that match your criteria, select the Unique Records Only check box in the Advanced Filter dialog box before you start the filtering operation. You can remove the display of all duplicate records from a data list by selecting this check box and removing all cell references from the Criteria Range text box before you click OK or press Enter.

To specify the data list that contains the data that you want to filter or query, click the List Range text box and then enter the address of the cell range or select it directly in the worksheet by dragging through its cells. To specify the range that contains a copy of the field names along with the criteria entered under the appropriate fields, you click the Criteria Range text box and then enter the range address of this cell range or select it directly in the worksheet by dragging through its cells. When selecting this range, be sure that you include all the rows that contain the values that you want evaluated in the filter or query.

If you're querying the data list by copying the records that meet your criteria to a new part of the worksheet (indicated by clicking the Copy to Another Location option button), you also click the Copy To text box and then enter the address of the cell that is to form the upper-left corner of the copied and filtered records or click this cell directly in the worksheet.

After specifying whether to filter or query the data and designating the ranges to be used in this operation, click OK to have Excel apply the criteria that you've specified in the Criteria Range in either filtering or copying the records.

After filtering a data list, you may feel that you haven't received the expected results — for example, no records are listed under the field names that you thought should have several. You can bring back all the records in the list by clicking the Clear command button on the Data tab of the Ribbon or by pressing Alt+AC. Now you can fiddle with the criteria in the Criteria Range text box and try the whole advanced filtering thing all over again.

Specifying comparison criteria

Entering selection criteria in the Criteria Range for advanced filtering is very similar to entering criteria in the data form after selecting the Criteria button. However, you need to be aware of some differences. For example, if you are searching for the last name *Paul* and enter the label **Paul** in the criteria range under the cell containing the field name Last Name, Excel will match any last name that begins with *P-a-u-l* such as Pauley, Paulson, and so on. To avoid having Excel match any other last name beside Paul, you would have to enter a formula in the cell below the one with the Last Name field name, as in

```
="Paul"
```

When entering criteria for advanced filtering, you can also use the question mark (?) or the asterisk (*) wildcard character in your selection criteria just like you do when using the data form to find records. If, for example, you enter **J*n** under the cell with the First Name field name, Excel will consider any characters between *J* and *n* in the First Name field to be a match including Joan, Jon, or John as well as Jane or Joanna. To restrict the matches to just those names with characters between *J* and *n* and to prevent matches with names that have trailing characters, you need to enter the following formula in the cell:

```
="J*n"
```

When you use a selection formula like this, Excel will match names such as Joan, Jon, and John but not names such as Jane or Joanna that have a character after the *n*.

When setting up selection criteria, you can also use the other comparative operators, including >, >=, <, <=, and <>, in the selection criteria. See Table 2-1 for descriptions and examples of usage in selection criteria for each of these logical operators.

TIP

To find all the records where a particular field is blank in the database, enter = and press the spacebar to enter a space in the cell beneath the appropriate field name. To find all the records where a particular field is *not* blank in the database, enter <> and press the spacebar to enter a space in the cell beneath the appropriate field name.

TABLE 2-1   ## The Comparative Operators in the Selection Criteria

Operator	Meaning	Example	Locates
=	Equal to	="CA"	Records where the state is *CA*
>	Greater than	>m	Records where the name starts with a letter after *M* (that is, N through Z)
>=	Greater than	>=3/4/02	Records where the date is on or after or equal to *March 4, 2002*
<	Less than	<d	Records where the name begins with a letter before *D* (that is, A, B, or *C*)
<=	Less than	<=12/12/04	Records where the date is on or before or equal to *December 12, 2004*
<>	Not equal to	<>"CA"	Records where the state is not equal to *CA*

Setting up logical AND logical OR conditions

When you enter two or more criteria in the same row beneath different field names in the Criteria Range, Excel treats the criteria as a logical AND condition and selects only those records that meet both of the criteria. Figure 2-5 shows an example of the results of a query that uses an AND condition. Here, Excel has copied only those records where the location is Boston *and* the date hired is before January 1, 2000, because both the criteria Boston and <1/1/00 are placed in the same row (row 2) under their respective field names, Location and Date Hired.

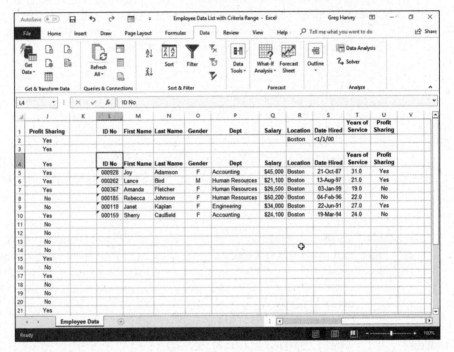

FIGURE 2-5:
Copied records where the location is Boston and the date hired is prior to January 1, 2000.

When you enter two or more criteria in different rows of the Criteria Range, Excel treats the criteria as a logical OR and selects records that meet any one of the criteria they contain. Figure 2-6 shows you an example of the results of a query using an OR condition. In this example, Excel has copied records where the location is either Boston or San Francisco because Boston is entered under the Location field name in the second row (row 2) of the Criteria Range above San Francisco entered in the third row (row 3).

When creating OR conditions, you need to remember to redefine the Criteria Range to include all the rows that contain criteria, which in this case is the cell range L2:U3. (If you forget, Excel uses only the criteria in the rows included in the Criteria range.)

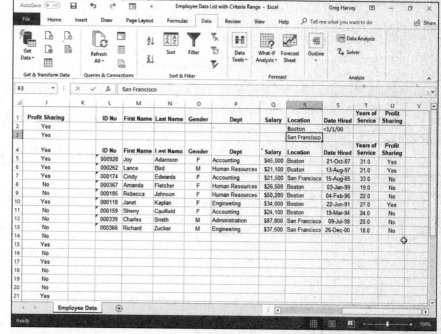

FIGURE 2-6:
Copied records
where the
location is Boston
and the date
hired prior to
January 1, 2000
or the location
is San Francisco
location for any
date hired.

When setting up your criteria, you can combine logical AND logical OR conditions (again, assuming that you expand the Criteria Range sufficiently to include all the rows containing criteria). For example, if you enter **Boston** in cell R2 (under Location) and **<1/1/00** in cell S2 (under Date Hired) in row 2 and enter **San Francisco** in cell R3 and then repeat the query, Excel copies the records where the location is Boston and the date hired is before January 1, 2000, as well as the records where the location is San Francisco (regardless of the date hired).

Setting up calculated criteria

You can use calculated criteria when filtering or querying your data list. All you need to do is enter a logical formula that Excel can evaluate as either TRUE or FALSE in the Criteria Range under a made-up name that is *not* any field name used in the data list (I repeat, is *not* a field name in the data list). Calculated criteria enable you to filter or query records based on a comparison of entries in a particular field with entries in other fields of the list or based on a comparison with entries in the worksheet that lie outside the data list itself.

Figure 2-7 shows an example of using a calculated criterion that compares values in a field to a calculated value that isn't actually entered in the data list. Here, you want to perform a query that copies all the records from the Employee data list where the employee's salary is above the average salary. In this figure, cell V2 contains the formula that uses the AVERAGE function to compute average employee salary and then compares the first salary entry in cell F2 of the data list to that average with the following formula:

```
=F2>AVERAGE($F$2:$F$33)
```

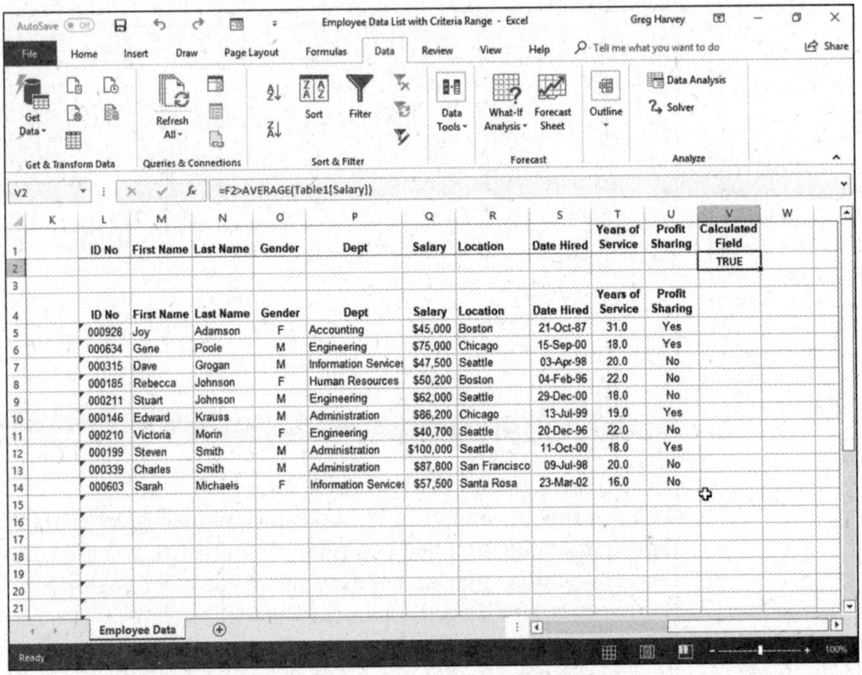

FIGURE 2-7:
Copied records extracted from the data list for employees whose salaries are above the salary average.

Note that this logical formula is placed under the label Calculated Criteria in cell V2, which has been added to the end of the Criteria Range. Cell F2 is the first cell in the data list that contains a salary entry. The cell range, $F$2:$F$33, used as the argument of the AVERAGE function, is the range in the Salary field that contains all the salary entries.

To use this calculated criterion, you must remember to place the logical formula under a name that isn't used as a field name in the data list itself. (In this example, the label Calculated Criteria does not appear anywhere in the row of field names.) You must include this label and formula in the Criteria Range. (For this query example, the Criteria Range is defined as the cell range L2:V2.)

When you then perform the query by using the Advanced Filter feature, Excel applies this calculated criterion to every record in the database. Excel does this by adjusting the first Salary field cell reference F2 (entered as a relative reference) as the program examines the rest of the records below. Note, however, that the range reference specified as the argument of the AVERAGE function is entered as an absolute reference ($F$2:$F$33) in the criterion formula so that Excel won't adjust this reference but compare the Salary entry for each record to AVERAGE computed for this entire range (which just happens to be 40,161). Note in Figure 2-7 how Excel 2019 automatically converts the cell references ($F$2:$F$33) in the AVERAGE function's argument to the range name equivalent, (Table2[Salary]).

REMEMBER

When entering formulas for calculated criteria that compare values outside the data list to values in a particular field, you should always reference the cell containing the very first entry for that field in order to ensure that Excel applies your criteria to every record in the data list.

You can also set up calculated criteria that compare entries in one or more fields to other entries in the data list. For example, to extract the records where the Years of Service entry is at least two years greater than the record above it (assuming that you have sorted the data list in ascending order by years of service), you would enter the following logical formula under the cell labeled Calculated Criteria:

```
=I3>I2+2
```

Most often, when referencing cells within the data list itself, you want to leave the cell references relative so that they can be adjusted, because each record is examined, and the references to the cells outside the database are absolute so that these won't be changed when making the comparison with the rest of the records.

When you enter the logical formula for a calculated criterion, Excel returns the logical value TRUE or FALSE. This logical value applies to the field entry for the first record in the data list that you refer to in the logical formula. By inspecting this field entry in the database and seeing whether it does indeed meet your intended selection criteria, you can usually tell whether your logical formula is correct.

Using the AND OR functions in calculated criteria

You can also use Excel's AND, OR, and NOT functions with the logical operators in calculated criteria to find records that fall within a range. For example, to find all the records in the employee database where the salaries range between $55,000 and $75,000, you would enter the following logical formula with the AND function under the cell with the label Calculated Criteria:

```
=AND(F2>=55000,F2<=75000)
```

To find all the records in the Employee data list where the salary is either below $29,000 or above $45,000, you would enter the following logical formula with the OR function under the cell with the label Calculated Criteria:

```
=OR(F2<29000,F2>45000)
```

Using the Database Functions

Excel includes a number of database functions that you can use to calculate statistics, such as the total, average, maximum, minimum, and count in a particular field of the data list only when the criteria that you specify are met. For example, you could use the DSUM function in the sample Employee data list to compute the sum of all the salaries for employees who were hired after January 1, 2000, or you could use the DCOUNT function to compute the number of records in the data list for the Human Resources department.

The database functions, regardless of the difference in names (and they all begin with the letter *D*) and the computations that they perform, all take the same three arguments as illustrated by the DAVERAGE function:

```
DAVERAGE(database,field,criteria)
```

The arguments for the database functions require the following information:

» *database* is the argument that specifies the range containing the list and it must include the row of field names in the top row.

» *field* is the argument that specifies the field whose values are to be calculated by the database function (averaged in the case of the DAVERAGE function). You can specify this argument by enclosing the name of the field in double quotes (as in "Salary" or "Date Hired"), or you can do this by entering the number of the column in the data list (counting from left to right with the first field counted as 1).

» *criteria* is the argument that specifies the address of the range that contains the criteria that you're using to determine which values are calculated. This range must include at least one field name that indicates the field whose values are to be evaluated and one cell with the values or expression to be used in the evaluation.

Note that in specifying the *field* argument, you must refer to a column in the data list that contains numeric or date data for all the database functions with the exception of DGET. All the rest of the database functions can't perform computations on text fields. If you mistakenly specify a column with text entries as the field argument for these database functions, Excel returns an error value or 0 as the result. Table 2-2 lists the various database functions available in Excel along with an explanation of what each one calculates. (You already know what arguments each one takes.)

TABLE 2-2   **The Database Functions in Excel**

Database Function	What It Calculates
DAVERAGE	Averages all the values in a field of the data list that match the criteria you specify.
DCOUNT	Counts the number of cells with numeric entries in a field of the data list that match the criteria you specify.
DCOUNTA	Counts the number of nonblank cells in a field of the data list that match the criteria you specify.
DGET	Extracts a single value from a record in the data list that matches the criteria you specify. If no record matches, the function returns the #VALUE! error value. If multiple records match, the function returns the #NUM! error value.
DMAX	Returns the highest value in a field of the data list that matches the criteria you specify.
DMIN	Returns the lowest value in a field of the data list that matches the criteria you specify.
DPRODUCT	Multiplies all the values in a field of the data list that match the criteria you specify.
DSTDEV	Estimates the standard deviation based on the sample of values in a field of the data list that match the criteria you specify.
DSTDEVP	Calculates the standard deviation based on the population of values in a field of the data list that match the criteria you specify.
DSUM	Sums all the values in a field of the data list that match the criteria you specify.
DVAR	Estimates the variance based on the sample of values in a field of the data list that match the criteria you specify.
DVARP	Calculates the variance based on the population of values in a field of the data list that match the criteria you specify.

REMEMBER

The Database functions are too rarely used to rate their own command button on the Ribbon's Formulas tab. As a result, to use them in a worksheet, you must click the Insert Function (*fx*) button on the Formula bar, select Database from the Select a Category drop-down list box, and then click the function to use or type the Database function directly into the cell.

Figure 2-8 illustrates the use of the Database function, DSUM. Cell C2 in the worksheet shown in this figure contains the following formula:

```
=DSUM(Table1[#All],"Salary",F1:F2)
```

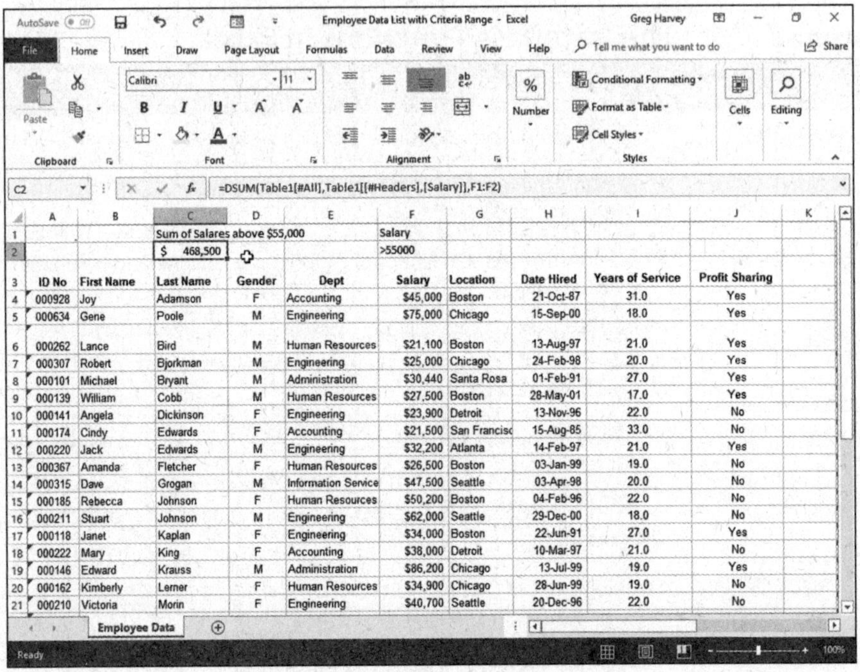

FIGURE 2-8: Using the DSUM to total the salaries over $55,000 in the Employee data list.

This DSUM function computes the total of all the salaries in the data list that are above $55,000. This total is $468,500, as shown in cell C2, which contains the formula.

To perform this calculation, I specified the range A3:J35, which contains the entire data list. This range includes the top row of field names as the *database* argument (which Excel 2019 automatically converted to its range name equivalent, Table1[#All]). I then specified "Salary" as the field argument of the DSUM function because this is the name of the field that contains the values that I want totaled. Finally, I specified the range F1:F2 as the *criteria* argument of the DSUM function because these two cells contain the criteria range that designate that only the values exceeding 55000 in the Salary field are to be summed.

External Data Query

Excel 2019 makes it super easy to query data lists (tables) stored in external databases to which you have access and then extract the data that interests you into your worksheet for further manipulation and analysis. These data sources can include Microsoft Access database files, web pages on the Internet, text files, and other data sources, such as database tables on SQL Servers and Analysis Services, XML data files, and data tables from online connections to Microsoft Windows Azure DataMarket and OData Data feeds.

When importing data from such external sources into your Excel worksheets, you may well be dealing with data stored in multiple related tables all stored in the database (what is referred to in Excel 2019 as a *Data Model*). The relationship between different tables in the same database is based on a common field (column) that occurs in each related data table, which is officially known as a *key field,* but in Excel is generally known as a *lookup column.* When relating tables on a common key field, in at least one table, the records for that field must all be unique with no duplicates, such as Clients data table where the Customer ID field is unique and assigned only once (where it's known as the *primary key*). In the other related data table, the common field (known as the *foreign key*) may or may not be unique as in an Orders data table where entries in its Customer ID may not all be unique, as it's quite permissible (even desirable) to have the same client purchasing multiple products multiple times.

There's only one other thing to keep in mind when working with related data tables and that is the type of relationship that exists between the two tables. There are two types of relationships supported in an Excel Data Model:

>> **One-to-one relationship** where the entries in both the primary and foreign key fields are totally unique such as a relationship between a Clients data list and Discount data list where the Customer ID field occurs only once in each table (as each client has only one discount percentage assigned)

>> **One-to-many relationship** where duplicate entries in the foreign key field are allowed and even expected as in a relationship between a Clients data list and an Orders data list where the Customer ID field may occur multiple times (as the client makes multiple purchases)

TIP

Most of the time Excel 2019 is able to figure out the relationship between the data tables you import. However, if Excel should ever get it wrong or your tables contain more than one common field that could possibly serve as the key, you can manually define the proper relationship. Simply select the Relationships button in the Data Tools group on the Ribbon's Data tab (Alt+AZDA) to open the Manage Relationships dialog box. There you click New to open the Create Relationship dialog box, where you define the common field in each of the two related data tables. After creating this relationship, you can use any of the fields in either of the two related tables in reports that you prepare or pivot tables that you create. (See Book 7, Chapter 2 for details on creating and using pivot tables.)

To import data from external database files and tables, you select the Get Data command button on the Ribbon's Data tab (Alt+APN). When you do this, Excel displays a menu with the following choices:

>> **From File** to import data from a file saved on a local or network drive in various file formats, including Excel workbook, text or CSV (Comma Delimited Value), XML (Extensible Markup Language), and JSON (JavaScript Object Notation) file formats

>> **From Database** to import data from data tables in a specific type of database file, including SQL Server Database, Microsoft Access, Analysis Services, and SQL Analysis Server Database

>> **From Azure** to import data from an Azure SQL database or one of the various storage spaces available on this standalone Microsoft cloud service (visit https://azure.microsoft.com for more information)

>> **From Online Services** to import data saved on an online service to which you already subscribe, such as Facebook or LinkedIn

>> **From Other Sources** to import data from a variety of sources, including Table/Range (data tables in the existing workbook) or From Web (data tables on a web page) or using existing queries from Microsoft Query, OData Feed, ODBC (Open Database Connectivity), OLEDB (Object Linking and Embedded Database), and Blank Query to create a new query with Excel's Power Query Editor add-in

>> **Combine Queries** to merge two existing data tables in the current workbook or append one data table to another

>> **Launch Power Query Editor** to open Excel 2019's Query Editor add-in that enables you to create advanced data queries that connect various data sources and perform complex analysis (called Get & Transform in Excel 2016)

>> **Data Catalog Search** to launch Power BI (Business Intelligence), a Microsoft standalone visual data analytics program, and import data into Excel from the Power BI Data Catalog (see https://powerbi.microsoft.com for more information)

>> **My Data Catalog Queries** to reuse a query that you have previously sent to the Power BI Data Catalog

>> **Data Source Settings** to open the Data Source Settings dialog box where you can manage permissions for the external data sources that Excel can use in data queries

>> **Query Options** to open the Query Options dialog box where you manage the global and current workbook load and privacy settings

Retrieving data from Access database tables

To make an external data query to an Microsoft Access database table, you click Data⇨Get Data⇨From Database⇨From Microsoft Access Database on the Ribbon or press Alt+APNDC. Excel opens the Import Data dialog box, where you select the name of the Access database (using an *.mdb file extension) and then click the Import button.

After Excel establishes a connection with the Access database file you select in the Import Data dialog box, the Navigator dialog box opens (similar to the one shown in Figure 2-9). The Navigator dialog box is divided into two panes: Selection on the left and Preview on the right. When you click the name of a data table or query in the Selection Pane, Excel displays a portion of the Access data in the Preview pane on the right. To import multiple (related) data tables from the selected Access database, select the Enable Multiple Items check box. Excel then displays check boxes before the name of each table in the database. After you select the check boxes for all the tables you want to import, you have a choice of options:

>> **Load** button to import the Access file data from the item(s) selected in the Navigator directly into the current worksheet starting at the cell cursor's current position

>> **Load To** option on the Load button's drop-down menu to open the Import Data dialog box where you can how you want to view the imported Access data (as a worksheet data Table, PivotTable, PivotChart, or just data connection without importing any data) and where to import the Access data (existing or new worksheet) as well as whether or not to add the Access data to the worksheet's Data Model

>> **Transform Data** button to display the Access data table(s) in the Excel Power Query Editor where you can further query and transform the data before importing into the current Excel worksheet with its Close & Load or Close & Load To option

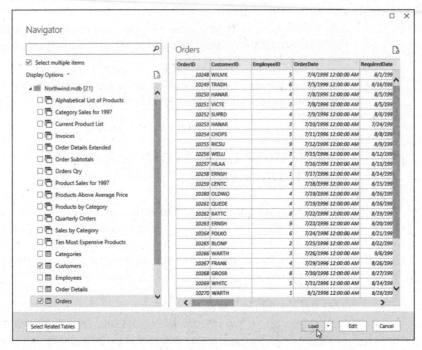

FIGURE 2-9:
Using the Navigator to select which data tables and queries from the Northwind Access database to import into the current Excel worksheet.

When you select the Load To option to specify how and where to import the Access data, the Import Data dialog box contains the following option buttons:

>> **Table** option button to have the data in the Access data table(s) imported into an Excel data table in either the current or new worksheet — see the "Existing Worksheet" and "New Worksheet" bullets that follow. Note that when you import more than one data table, the Existing Worksheet option is no longer available, and the data from each imported data table will be imported to a separate new worksheet in the current workbook.

>> **PivotTable Report** option button (the default) to have the data in the Access data table(s) imported into a new pivot table (see Book 7, Chapter 2) that you can construct with the Access data.

>> **PivotChart** option button to have the data in the Access data table(s) imported into a new pivot table (see Book 7, Chapter 2) with an embedded pivot chart that you can construct with the Access data.

>> **Only Create Connection** option button to create a connection to the Access database table(s) that you can use later to actually import its data.

>> **Existing Worksheet** option button to have the data in the Access data table(s) imported into the current worksheet starting at the current cell address listed in the text box below.

» **New Worksheet** option button to have the data in the Access data table(s) imported into new sheet(s) that's added to the end of the sheets already in the workbook.

» **Add This Data to the Data Model** check box to add the imported data in the Access data table(s) to the Data Model already defined in the Excel workbook using relatable, key fields.

» **Properties** drop-down button to open the drop-down menu with the Import Relationships Between Tables check box (selected by default) and Properties item. Deselect the check box to prevent Excel from recognizing the relationship established between the data tables in Access. Click the Properties button to open the Connection Properties dialog box, where you can modify all sorts of connection properties, including when the Access data's refreshed in the Excel worksheet and how the connection is made.

Figure 2-10 shows you a new Northwind Customer Orders workbook after importing both the Customers and Orders data tables from the sample Northwind Access database as new data tables on separate worksheets. When I imported the two data tables, Excel automatically added two new worksheets (Sheet2 and Sheet3) to the workbook, while at the same time importing the Customers data table to Sheet2 (which I renamed Customers) and the Orders data table to Sheet3 (renamed Orders). I then deleted Sheet1 (which was blank) prior to taking the screenshot for Figure 2-10.

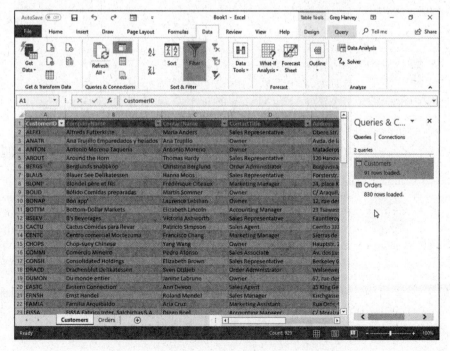

FIGURE 2-10: Customers worksheet with the data imported from the Access Customers data table in the sample Northwind database.

Figure 2-11 shows same new workbook, this time with the Orders worksheet selected and the Manage Relationships dialog box open (by clicking the Relationships button on the Data tab or pressing Alt+AA). When Excel imported these two data tables, it automatically picked up on and retained the original relationship between them in the Northwind database, where the CustomerID field is the primary key field in the Customers data table and a foreign key field in the Orders data table.

After importing the external data into one of your Excel worksheets, you can then use the Filter buttons attached to the various fields to sort the data (as described in Book 6, Chapter 1) and filter the data (as described earlier in this chapter).

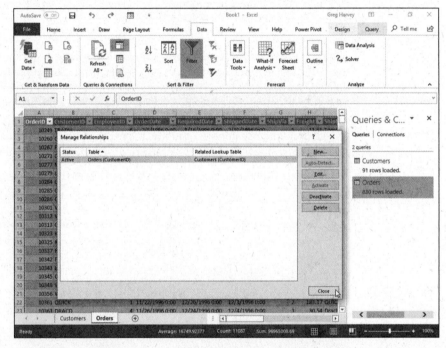

FIGURE 2-11:
Orders worksheet with the data imported from the Orders data table in the sample Northwind database showing the relationship with the Customers table.

REMEMBER

After you import data from an external source, such as a Microsoft Access database, into a worksheet, Excel automatically displays a Queries & Connections task pane with two tabs: Queries, which displays the source(s) of the data imported into the current workbook, and Connections, which displays their connection to the workbook Data Model (and to each other if there are multiple sources and they are related to each other). If this task pane is not currently displayed in the current worksheet, click Data⇨Queries & Connections (or press Alt+AO) to redisplay it.

TIP

Excel keeps a list of all the external data sources and data queries you make to the current workbook so that you can reuse them to import updated data from another database or web page. To quickly reconnect with a data source, click the Recent Sources button on the Data tab (Alt+PR) to open the Recent Sources dialog box where you click the name of the external file before you select the Connect button. To reuse a query, click the Existing Connections button on the Data tab (Alt+AX) to open the Existing Connections dialog box to access this list and then click the name of the query to repeat before you click the Open button.

Retrieving data from the web

To make a web page query, you click the From Web command button on the Ribbon's Data tab or press Alt+AFW. Excel then opens the From Web Query dialog box containing an URL text box where you specify the address of the web page containing the data you want to import into Excel as in

www.nasdaq.com

After you click OK in the From Web dialog box, Excel establishes a connection with the web page before opening the Navigator dialog box (similar to the one shown in Figure 2-12). When you select a table in the list in the Selection pane on the left, Excel displays a preview of the data in the Table View tab of the Preview pane on the right (to display the data more or less as it appears on the web page itself, you click the Web View tab in this pane). To import more than one table of data from a web page, click the Select Multiple Items check box and then click the check boxes in front of the name (Table 1, Table 2, and so on) you want imported.

After you finish checking the table or tables you want to import on the page, you can select one of the following three import options:

» **Load** button to import the web data in the tables selected in the Navigator directly into the current worksheet starting at the cell cursor's current position

» **Load To** option on the Load button's drop-down menu to open the Import Data dialog box where you can choose how you want to view the imported Access data (as a worksheet data Table, PivotTable, PivotChart, or just data connection without importing any data) and where to import the web data (into an existing or new worksheet) as well as whether or not to add the web data to the worksheet's Data Model

» **Transform Data** button to display the web data table(s) in the Excel Power Query Editor where you can further query and transform the data before importing into the current Excel worksheet with its Close & Load or Close & Load To option

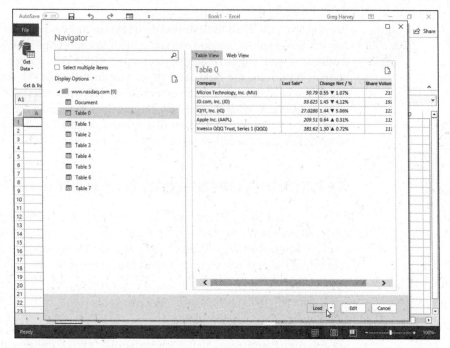

FIGURE 2-12:
Selecting a stock
market table in
the Navigator
dialog box to
import from the
NASDAQ home
page into a new
Excel worksheet.

After importing your web data into a new or existing worksheet, you can then manipulate the data as would any other worksheet table, including filtering it and sorting with the AutoFilter buttons.

TIP

When working with tables of stock quotes imported from financial websites, such as NASDAQ and MSN Money, during periods when the markets are still open and active, you can use the Refresh All command on the Data tab of the Ribbon (Alt+ARA) to keep the stock prices and trading volume entries in your worksheet up to date.

WARNING

You can only make web queries when your computer has Internet access. So, if you're using Excel on a device that can't connect to the web at the moment, you won't be able to perform a new web query until you get to a place where you can get online.

Retrieving data from text files

If you have a text file containing data you need to bring into your worksheet, you can import it by clicking the From Text/CSV command button on the Ribbon's Data tab (Alt+AFT) and then selecting the file to use in the Import Data dialog box. After you select the text file containing the data you need to retrieve in this dialog box and click its Import button, Excel opens the Navigator dialog box with the name of the text or CSV (Comma Separated Value) file as its title.

This version of the Navigator (as shown in Figure 2-13) automatically scans and analyzes the data in the text or CSV file and attempts to correctly split up (or *parse*) its data into separate cells of the worksheet based on what Excel character the program determines is the standard character used to separate each data item (such as a comma or tab) in every line, just as it uses the character for the Enter key to mark the separation of each line of data within the file.

REMEMBER

Text files that use the comma to separate data items are known as *CSV files* (for Comma Separated Values). Those that use tabs to separate the individual data items are known as *Tab delimited* files. Note that some programs use the generic term, *delimited files,* to refer to any text file that uses a standard character, such as a comma or tab, to separate its individual data items.

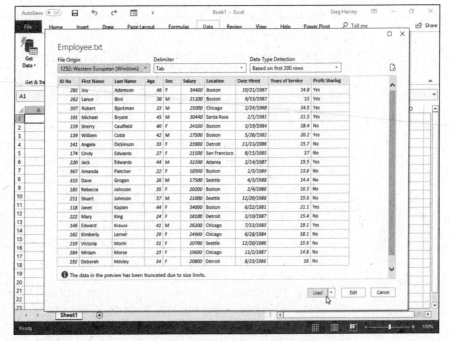

FIGURE 2-13:
Importing the data in a tab-delimited text file into a worksheet using the options in Navigator dialog box.

If Excel has correctly parsed the data in your text or CSV file as shown in the preview in the Navigator, you can then select one of the following three import options to bring the data into your worksheet:

>> **Load** button to import the parsed text data previewed in the Navigator directly into the current worksheet starting at the cell cursor's current position

>> **Load To** option on the Load button's drop-down menu to open the Import Data dialog box where you can choose how you want to view the imported

text data (as a worksheet data Table, PivoTable, PivotChart, or just data connection without importing any data) and where to import the web data (into an existing or new worksheet) as well as whether or not to add the web data to the worksheet's Data Model

» **Transform Data** button to display the parsed text data in the Excel Power Query Editor where you can further query and transform the data before importing into the current Excel worksheet with its Close & Load or Close & Load To option

If Excel has not correctly parsed the data in your text or CSV file in the preview in the Navigator, you can try changing one of the three settings used in determining how the data is parsed before proceeding with any kind of import:

» **File Origin** to select a new text file type based on its country code on the File Origin drop-down menu

» **Delimiter** to select a new delimiting character on the Delimiter drop-down menu to be used in parsing the data into separate cells

» **Data Type Detection** to change the number of rows used in trying to determine whether the parsed data is a number, date, or text value either by selecting the Based on Entire Dataset option on the Data Type Detection drop-down menu to use all the rows in the file or select Do Not Detect Data Types option to prevent Excel from trying to differentiate the data types

If Excel still can't correctly parse your text or CSV file in the preview and insists on importing each row of text data into a single column, all is not lost. You can still go ahead with the import and then after bringing the data of the text file into a new or existing worksheet, use the Convert to Text Wizard to correctly parse it into separate columns.

To do this, select the cells with the imported text data as a range before you click the Test to Columns command button on the Data tab of the Ribbon (Alt+AE). Excel then opens the Convert Text to Columns Wizard – Step 1 of 3 dialog box. Here, you choose between the Delimited and Fixed Width option as determining how the data is to be separated before clicking the Next button to open the Convert Text to Columns Wizard – Step 2 of 3 dialog box.

In the Step 2 of 3 dialog box when you previously selected the Delimited option in the Step 1 of 3 dialog box, you need to select the delimiting character in the event that the wizard selects the wrong character in the Delimiters section before clicking the Next button. If your text file uses a custom delimiting character, you need to select the Other check box and then enter that character in its text box.

If your file uses two consecutive characters (such as a comma and a space), you need to select their check boxes as well as the Treat Consecutive Delimiters As One check box.

By default, the Convert Text to Columns Wizard treats any characters enclosed in a pair of double quotes as text entries (as opposed to numbers). If your text file uses a single quote, click the single quote (') character in the Text Qualifier drop-down list box.

If, instead, you selected the Fixed Width option in the Step 1 of 3 dialog box, the Step 2 of 3 dialog box previews the column breaks that indicate how the text data will appear when split apart into separate columns of the worksheet. You can then modify the column breaks in the preview with your mouse. Click in the sample data shown in the Data Preview area to create new column breaks and modify the extent of the breaks by dragging their borders. When the column breaks in the data preview appear correct, click the Next button to open the Convert Text to Columns Wizard - Step 3 of 3 dialog box.

In the Step 3 of 3 dialog box, you get to assign a data type to the various columns of text data or indicate that a particular column of data should be skipped and therefore not imported into your Excel worksheet.

When setting data formats for the columns of the text file, you can choose among the following three data types:

» **General** (the default) to convert all numeric values to numbers, entries recognized as date values to dates, and everything else in the column to text

» **Text** to convert all the entries in the column to text

» **Date** to convert all the entries to dates by using the date format shown in the associated drop-down list box

To assign one of the three data types to a column, click its column in the Data Preview section and then click the appropriate radio button (General, Text, or Date) in the Column Data Format section in the upper-right corner.

In determining values when using the General data format, Excel uses the period (.) as the decimal separator and the comma (,) as the thousands separator. If you're dealing with data that uses these two symbols in just the opposite way (the comma for the decimal and the period for the thousands separator), as is the case in many European countries, click the Advanced button in the Step 3 of 3 dialog box to open the Advanced Text Import Settings dialog box. There, select the comma (,) in the Decimal Separator drop-down list box and the period (.) in the Thousands Separator drop-down list box before you click OK. If your text file uses trailing minus signs (as in 100–) to represent negative numbers (as in –100), make sure that the Trailing Minus for Negative Numbers check box contains a check mark.

If you want to change the date format for a column to which you've assigned the Date data format, click its M-D-Y code in the Date drop-down list box (where *M* stands for the month, *D* for the day, and *Y* for the year).

REMEMBER

To skip the importing of a particular column, click it in the Data Preview and then select the Do Not Import Column (Skip) option button at the bottom of the Column Data Format section.

After you have all the columns formatted as you want, click the Finish button in the Convert Text to Columns – Step 3 of 3 dialog box. Excel then splits the entries in the imported text file into separate columns of the current worksheet, and all that's left for you to do is, perhaps, adjust the column widths to suit.

Querying data from other data sources

Database tables created and maintained with Microsoft Office Access are not, of course, the only external database sources on which you can perform external data queries. To import data from other sources, you click the From Database button on the Get Data button's drop-down menu on the Data tab or press Alt+APND to open a drop-down menu with other database options including:

>> **From SQL Server Database** to import data from an SQL server database.

>> **From Analysis Services** to import data from an SQL Server Analysis cube.

>> **From SQL Server Analysis Services Database (Import)** to import data from an SQL server database using an optional MDX or DAX query.

In addition, the From Other Sources option on the Get Data drop-down menu offers you the following querying choices:

>> **From Table/Range** to create a new query in the Power Query Editor using the selected Excel data table or named cell range in the current worksheet (same as clicking the From Table/Range command button on the Ribbon's Data tab).

>> **From Web** to import data from a web page (same as clicking the From Web command button on the Ribbon's Data tab).

- **From Microsoft Query** to import data from a database table using Microsoft Query that follows the ODBC (Open DataBase Connectivity) standards.

- **From SharePoint List** to import data from a Microsoft SharePoint website.

- **From OData Data Feed** to import data any database table following the Open Data Protocol (shortened to OData) — note that you must provide the file location (usually a URL address) and user ID and password to access the OData data feed before you can import any of its data into Excel.

- **From Hadoop File (HDFS)** to import data from a Hadoop Distributed File System.

- **From Active Directory** to import data from the Microsoft Active Directory service for Windows domain networks.

- **From Microsoft Exchange** to import data from a Microsoft Exchange Server.

- **From ODBC** to import data from a database that follows Microsoft's ODBC (Open Database Connectivity) standards.

- **From OLEDB** to import data from a database that follows the OLEDB (Object Linked Embedded Database) standards.

- **Blank Query** to create a brand new database query in the Power Query Editor.

Transforming a data query in the Power Query Editor

Whenever you do a data query in Excel 2019 using the Get Data, From Text/CSV, From Web, or From Table/Range command buttons on the Ribbon's Data tab, you have the option of transforming that query in the Power Query Editor. When you do an external query with the Get Data, From Text/CSV, or From Web options, you open the Power Query Editor after specifying the data table(s) to import into Excel by clicking Transform Data button in the Navigator dialog box. However, whenever you use the Table/Range command to designate a selected cell range in the current worksheet as a data table, Excel automatically opens the data table in a new Power Query Editor window so that you can create or transform an existing query.

Although the subject of using the Power Query Editor to perform advanced queries is well beyond the scope of this book, basic use of the Power Query Editor should prove to be no problem as the Power Query Editor's interface and essential features are very similar to those of Excel 2019.

Figure 2-14 shows the Power Query Editor window after opening it to create a new query with the Bo-Peep Client list data table entered into the current Excel worksheet (in the cell range, A1:I34 and named, Client_List). To create the new query, all I had to do was select the range before clicking the From Table/Range command button on the Data table of the Ribbon.

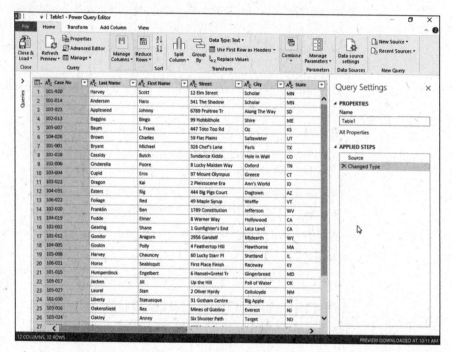

As you see in this figure, in the Power Query Editor, the imported Excel client data table retains its worksheet row and column arrangement with the column headings complete with Auto-Filter drop-down buttons intact. Above the data table, the Power Query Editor sports a Ribbon type command structure with a File menu followed by four tabs: Home, Transform, Add Column, and View. To the right of the imported data table, a Query Settings task pane appears that not only displays the source of the data (a worksheet cell range named Client_List) but also all the steps applied in building this new query.

Once the Bo-Peep data records are loaded into the Power Query Editor, I can use its commands to query the data before returning the subset of records to a new worksheet in Excel. For this query, I am interested in creating a subset of records where the status of the file is still active and the account is marked unpaid (in other words, all the clients who still owe the company money). To do this, I use the AutoFill buttons on the Status and Paid fields (see Figure 2-15) to filter the records to display just those with Active in the Status field and No in the Paid field. Then, I sort the records by from the highest to lowest amount owed by sorting on the Total Due field in descending order. After that, I'm ready to select the Close & Load To option on the Close & Load command button on the Home tab to save my query and load it into a new worksheet in the current workbook. To do this, I simply accept the default settings of Table and New Worksheet in the Import Data dialog box that appears after selecting the Close & Load To option prior to click OK.

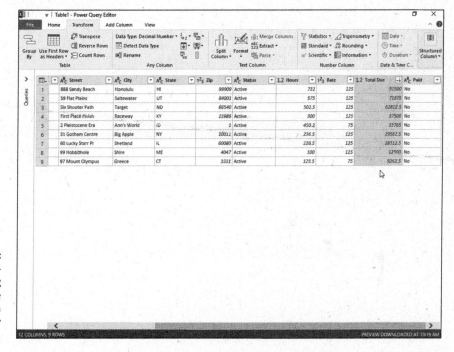

FIGURE 2-15:
Setting the filtering and sorting criteria for the new data query in the Power Query Editor.

Figure 2-16 shows you the results. Here you see the new Excel worksheet that the Editor created (Sheet 1 in front of the Client List sheet) before it copied the filtered and sorted subset of the Bo-Peep records into a new data table in cell range A1: L10. When the Power Query Editor imported this new data table, the program also assigned it a table style, added AutoFilter buttons, and opened a Queries & Connections task pane. Now all that's left to do is a bit of formatting, renaming the worksheet, and sending past due notices to all the delinquent clients listed in this table!

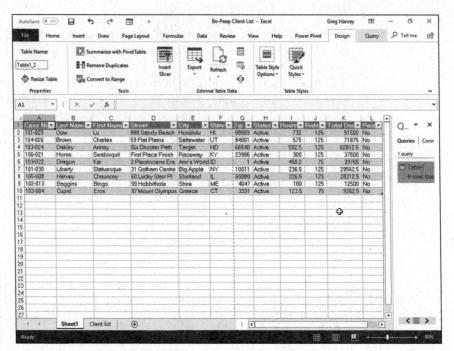

FIGURE 2-16:
The Bo-Peep data queried in the Power Query Editor after loading it into a new Excel worksheet.

7

Data Analysis

Contents at a Glance

Chapter **1**

Performing What-If Scenarios

ecause electronic spreadsheet formulas are so good at automatically updating their results based on new input, they have long been used (and sometimes, misused) to create financial projections based on all sorts of assumptions. Under the guise of what-if analysis, you will often find the number crunchers of the company using Excel as their crystal ball for projecting the results of all sorts of harebrained schemes designed to make the company a fast million bucks.

As you start dabbling in this form of electronic fortune-telling, keep in mind that the projections you get back from this type of analysis are only as good as your assumptions. So when the results of what-if analysis tell you that you're going to be richer than King Midas after undertaking this new business venture, you still need to ask yourself whether the original assumptions on which these glowing projections are based fit in with real-world marketing conditions. In other words, when the worksheet tells you that you can make a million bucks of pure profit by selling lead-lined boxer shorts, you still have to question how many men really need that kind of protection and are willing to pay for it.

In Excel, what-if analysis comes in a fairly wide variety of flavors (some of which are more complicated than others). In this chapter, I introduce you to three simple and straightforward methods:

>> **Data tables** enable you to see how changing one or two variables affects the bottom line. (For example, you may want to know what happens to the net profit if you fall into a 45 percent tax bracket, a 60 percent tax bracket, and so on.)

>> **Goal seeking** enables you to find out what it takes to reach a predetermined objective, such as how much you have to sell to make a $20 million profit this year.

>> **Scenarios** let you set up and test a wide variety of cases, all the way from the best-case scenario (profits grow by 20 percent) to the worst-case scenario (in which you don't make any profit).

At the end of the chapter, I introduce you to the Solver add-in utility, which enables you to find solutions to more complex what-if problems involving multiple variables. You can use the Solver to help you with classic resource problems, such as finding the correct product mix in order to maximize your profits, staffing to minimize your general costs, and routing to minimize transportation costs.

Using Data Tables

In an Excel spreadsheet, you can see the effect of changing an input value on the result returned by a formula as soon as you enter a new input value in the cell that feeds into the formula. Each time you change this input value, Excel automatically recalculates the formula and shows you the new result based on the new value. This method is of limited use, however, when you are performing what-if analysis and need to be able to see the range of results produced by using a series of different input values in the same worksheet so that you can compare them to each other.

To perform this type of what-if analysis, you can use Excel's Data Table command. When creating a data table, you enter a series of input values in the worksheet, and Excel uses each value in the formula that you specify. When Excel is finished computing the data table, you see the results produced by each change in the input values in a single range of the worksheet. You can then save the data table as part of the worksheet if you need to keep a record of the results of a series of input values.

When creating data tables, you can create a one-variable or a two-variable data table. In a one-variable data table, Excel substitutes a series of different values for a single input value in a formula. In a two-variable data table, Excel substitutes a series of different values for two input values in a formula.

Creating a one-variable data table

To create a one-variable data table, you need to set up the master formula in your worksheet and then, in a different range of the worksheet, enter the series of different values that you want substituted for a single input value in that formula. Figures 1-1 and 1-2 demonstrate how this is done.

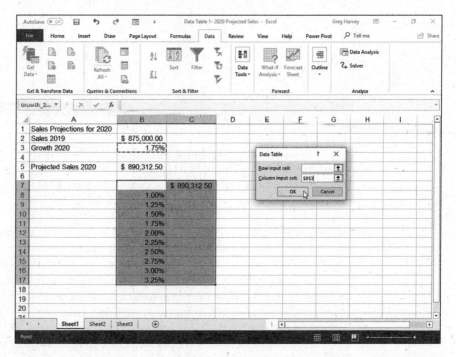

FIGURE 1-1:
Creating a one-variable data table.

In Figure 1-1, cell B5 contains a simple formula for computing the projected sales for 2020, assuming an annual growth rate of 1.75% over the annual sales in 2019. The 2020 projected sales in this cell are calculated with the following formula:

```
=Sales_2019+(Sales_2019*Growth_2020)
```

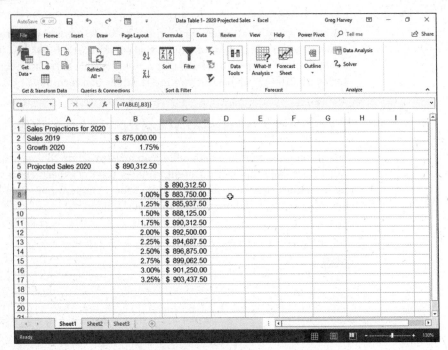

FIGURE 1-2:
The completed
one-variable
data table.

This formula adds cell B2 (named Sales_2019) to the contents of B2 multiplied by the growth rate of 1.75% in cell B3 (named Growth_2020). Cell B5 shows you that, assuming an annual growth rate of 1.75% in the year 2020, you can project total sales of $890,312.50.

But what if the growth rate in 2020 is not as low as 1.75%, or what if the growth rate is even (heaven forbid) lower than anticipated? To create the one-variable table to answer these questions, you first bring forward the master formula in cell B5 to cell C7 with the formula =B5 (which appears as =Projected_Sales_2020 on the Formula bar as this is the range name given to the cell). Then, you enter the series of different growth rates as the input values in column B, starting in cell B8. (Cell B7, at the intersection of the row with the master formula and the column with the input values, must be left blank in a one-variable data table.) This series of input values for the data table can be created with the AutoFill feature. (See Book 2, Chapter 1 for details.) In this example, a data series that increments each succeeding value by 0.25% percent is created in the cell range B8:B17, starting at 1.00 percent and ending at 3.25% percent.

After bringing the formula in cell B5 forward to cell C7 with the linking formula =B5 and generating the growth rate series in the cell range B8:B17, you then select the cell range B7:C17 and click the What-If Analysis command button in the Data Tools group on the Data tab and then click Data Table on its drop-down menu (or press Alt+AWT) to open the Data Table dialog box shown in Figure 1-1.

In this dialog box, you specify the row input cell in the Row Input Cell text box and/or the column input cell in the Column Input Cell text box. The cell that you designate as the row or column input cell in the Table dialog box must correspond to the cell in the worksheet that contains the original input value that is fed into the master formula.

In the data table in this example, you need to designate only B3 as the column input cell. (In the case of Figure 1-1, when you click this cell or use an arrow key to select this cell, Excel enters the absolute cell reference, as in $B$3.) You choose cell B3 because this is the cell that contains the growth rate value used in the master formula.

After indicating the row or column input cells, Excel computes the data table when you click the OK button. In this example, the program creates the data table by substituting each input value in the data series in the range B8:B17 into the column input cell B3. The value of cell B3 is then used in the master formula to calculate a new result, which is entered in the corresponding cell in the cell range C8:C17. After the program has finished calculating the data table, Excel returns the original value to the row or column input cell (in this case, 1.75% in cell B3).

Figure 1-2 shows the completed data table. Here, you can see at a glance how changing a quarter percentage point for the growth rate affects the projected sales for 2020. After creating the data table, you can then format the results and save the table as part of the worksheet.

REMEMBER

If you want to see how using a different range of variables affects the results in the table, you only need to enter the new input values in the existing range. By default, Excel automatically recalculates the results in the output range of a data table whenever you change any of its input values. If you want to control when each data table is recalculated while still allowing the formulas in the worksheet to be automatically recalculated, click the Automatic Except Data Tables option on the Options command button on the Formulas tab (Alt+MXE).

Excel computes the results in a data table by creating an array formula that uses the TABLE function. (See Book 3, Chapter 1, for more information on array formulas.) In this example, the array formula entered into the cell range C8:C17 is as follows:

```
{=TABLE(,B3)}
```

The TABLE function can take two arguments, *row_ref* and/or *column_ref*, which represent the row input cell and column input cell for the data table, respectively.

In this example, the data table uses only a column input cell, so B3 is the second and only argument of the TABLE function. Because Excel enters the results in a data table by using an array formula, Excel won't allow you to clear individual result cells in its output range. If you try to delete a single result in the data table, Excel displays an Alert dialog box, stating that you can't change part of a table.

TIP

If you want to delete just the results in the output range of a data table, you must select all the cells in the output range (cell range C8:C17, in the current example) before you press the Delete key or choose the Clear All option from the Clear button's drop-down menu (or press Alt+HEA).

Creating a two-variable data table

When you have a master formula in a worksheet in which you want to see the effect of changing two of its input values, you create a two-variable data table. When you create a two-variable data table, you enter two ranges of input values to be substituted in the master formula: a single-row range in the first row of the table and a single-column range in the first column of the data table. When you create a two-variable data table, you place a copy of the master formula in the cell at the intersection of this row and column of input values.

Figure 1-3 shows the typical setup for a two-variable data table. This figure uses the projected sales worksheet shown previously in the section on a one-variable data table. Here, however, a second variable has been added to projecting the total sales in 2020. This worksheet contains a value in cell B4 (named Expenses_2020) that shows the projected percentage of expenses to sales, which is used, in turn, in the master formula in cell B5 as follows:

```
=Sales_2019+(Sales_2019*Growth_2020)-(Sales_2019*Expenses_2020)
```

Note that when you factor in the expenses of 10% of the annual sales, the projected sales at an annual growth rate of 1.75% falls in cell B5 from $890,312.50 to $802,812.50.

To determine how changing both the growth rate and the percentage of expenses to sales will affect the projected sales for 2020, you create a two-variable data table. In setting up this table, you still enter the variable growth rates down column B in the cell range B8:B17. Then, you enter the variable expense rates across row 7 in the range C7:F7. This time, you bring forward the master formula by entering the formula =B5 in cell B7, the cell at the intersection of the row and column containing the two input variables.

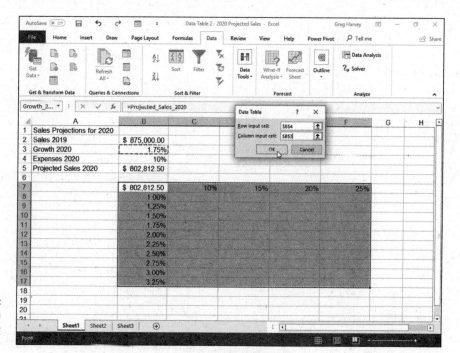

FIGURE 1-3:
Creating a
two-variable
data table.

After setting up the two series of variables in this manner, you are ready to create the table by selecting the cell range B7:F17 and opening the Table dialog box, as shown in Figure 1-3. For a two-variable data table, you must designate both a row input and column cell in the worksheet. In this example, the row input cell is B4, which contains the original expense-to-sales percentage, and the column input cell remains B3, which contains the original growth rate. After these two input cells are entered in the Table dialog box, you are ready to generate the data table by clicking the OK button.

Figure 1-4 shows the completed two-variable data table with the results of changing both the projected growth rate and the projected expenses. As with a one-variable data table, you can save this two-variable data table as part of your worksheet. You can also update the table by changing any of the (two types) input variables.

The array formula entered in the output range (C8:F17) to create this two-variable data table is very similar to the one created previously for the one-variable data table, only this time the TABLE function uses both a *row_ref* and *column_ref* argument as follows:

```
{=TABLE(B4,B3)}
```

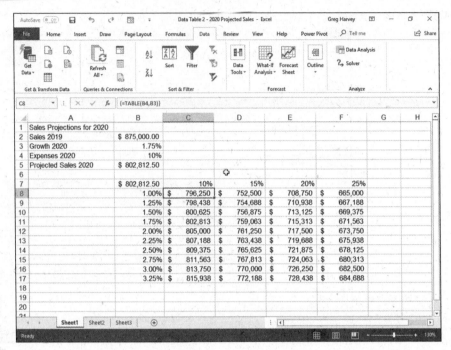

A	B	C	D	E	F	G	H
1 Sales Projections for 2020							
2 Sales 2019	$ 875,000.00						
3 Growth 2020	1.75%						
4 Expenses 2020	10%						
5 Projected Sales 2020	$ 802,812.50						
6							
7	$ 802,812.50	10%	15%	20%	25%		
8	1.00%	$ 796,250	$ 752,500	$ 708,750	$ 665,000		
9	1.25%	$ 798,438	$ 754,688	$ 710,938	$ 667,188		
10	1.50%	$ 800,625	$ 756,875	$ 713,125	$ 669,375		
11	1.75%	$ 802,813	$ 759,063	$ 715,313	$ 671,563		
12	2.00%	$ 805,000	$ 761,250	$ 717,500	$ 673,750		
13	2.25%	$ 807,188	$ 763,438	$ 719,688	$ 675,938		
14	2.50%	$ 809,375	$ 765,625	$ 721,875	$ 678,125		
15	2.75%	$ 811,563	$ 767,813	$ 724,063	$ 680,313		
16	3.00%	$ 813,750	$ 770,000	$ 726,250	$ 682,500		
17	3.25%	$ 815,938	$ 772,188	$ 728,438	$ 684,688		

FIGURE 1-4:
The completed
two-variable
data table.

REMEMBER

Remember that because this data table used an array formula, you must select all the cells in the output range if you want to delete them.

Exploring Different Scenarios

Excel enables you to create and save sets of input values that produce different results as *scenarios* with the Scenario Manager option on the What-If Analysis button's drop-down menu on the Data tab of the Ribbon. A scenario consists of a group of input values in a worksheet to which you assign a name, such as *Best Case, Worst Case, Most Likely Case,* and so on. Then, to reuse the input data and view the results that they produce in the worksheet, you simply select the name of the scenario that you want to use, and Excel applies the input values stored in that scenario to the appropriate cells in the worksheet. After creating your different scenarios for a worksheet, you can also use the Scenario Manager to create a summary report showing both the input values stored in each scenario and the key results produced by each.

Creating new scenarios

When creating a scenario for your worksheet, you create a spreadsheet that uses certain cells that change in each scenario (appropriately enough, called *changing cells*). To make it easier to identify the changing cells in each scenario that you create (especially in any scenario summary reports that you generate), you should assign range names to the variables in the spreadsheet with the Name a Range or Create from Selection command buttons on the Formulas tab of the Ribbon before you create your scenarios.

To create your scenarios with the Scenario Manager, follow these steps:

1. Select the changing cells in the spreadsheet — that is, the cells whose values vary in each of your scenarios.

Remember that you can select nonadjacent cells in the worksheet by holding down the Ctrl key as you click them.

2. Click the What-If Analysis command button on the Ribbon's Data tab and then click Scenario Manager on its drop-down menu or press Alt+AWS.

This action opens the Scenario Manager dialog box.

3. Click the Add button in the Scenario Manager dialog box.

This action opens the Add Scenario dialog box, similar to the one shown in Figure 1-5. The Add Scenario dialog box contains a Scenario Name text box, where you give the new scenario a descriptive name such as *Best Case, Most Likely Case,* and so on. This dialog box also contains a Changing Cells text box that contains the addresses of the variable cells that you selected in the worksheet, a Comment box that contains a note with your name and the current date, so you'll always know when you created the particular scenario, and Protection check boxes that prevent users from making changes and/or enable you to hide the scenario when the worksheet is protected.

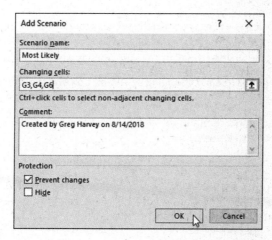

FIGURE 1-5:
Adding a new
Most Likely
scenario for the
sales forecast.

4. **Type a descriptive name for the new scenario in the Scenario Name text box.**

Now, you should check over the cell references in the Changing Cells text box to make sure that they're correct. You can modify them if necessary by clicking the Changing Cells text box and then by clicking the cells in the worksheet while holding down the Ctrl key. You can also edit the note in the Comment box if you want to add more information about your assumptions as part of the new scenario.

By default, Excel protects a scenario from changes when you turn on protection for the worksheet (see Book 4, Chapter 1, for details) so that you can't edit or delete the scenario in any way. If you want Excel to hide the scenario as well when worksheet protection is turned on, click the Hide check box. If you don't want to protect or hide the scenario when worksheet protection is turned on, click the Prevent Changes check box to remove its check mark and leave the Hide check box as it is.

5. **In the Protection section of the Add Scenario dialog box, choose what kind of scenario protection that you need, if any, with the Prevent Changes and Hide check boxes.**

Now you're ready to specify the changing values for the new scenario.

6. **Click OK in the Add Scenario dialog box.**

This action closes the Add Scenario dialog box and then opens the Scenario Values dialog box, similar to the one shown in Figure 1-6. The Scenario Values dialog box numbers and shows the range name (assuming that you named each of the cells), followed by the current value for each of the changing values that you selected in the worksheet before starting to define different scenarios for your spreadsheet.

You can accept the values shown in the text box for each changing cell if it suits the current scenario that you're defining, or you can increase or decrease any or all of them as needed to reflect the scenario's assumptions.

7. **Check the values in each changing cell's text box and modify the values as needed.**

Now you're ready to close the Scenario Values dialog box, which completes the definition of the new scenario.

8. **Click the Add button in the Scenario Values dialog box.**

This action closes the Scenario Values dialog box and returns you to the Add Scenario dialog box, where you can define a new scenario name for the changing cells.

9. Repeat Steps 4 to 7 to add all the other scenarios that you want to create.

After you finish defining all the different scenarios you want to apply to the changing values in the spreadsheet, you can close the Scenario Values dialog box and then return to the Scenario Manager dialog box, where you can use the Show button to see how using different sets of changing values affects your spreadsheet.

10. Click OK in the Add Values dialog box and then click the Close button in the Scenario Manager dialog box.

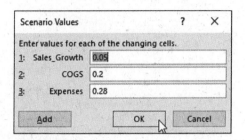

FIGURE 1-6: Specifying the changing values in the Scenario Values dialog box.

When you return to the Scenario Manager dialog box, the names of all the scenarios that you added appear in the Scenarios list box. For example, in Figure 1-7, you see that three scenarios — Most Likely, Best Case, and Worst Case — are now listed in the Scenarios list box.

To show a particular scenario in the worksheet that uses the values you entered for the changing cells, you simply double-click the scenario name in this list box or click the name and then click the Show command button. Figure 1-7 shows the results in the sample forecast worksheet after showing the Worst Case scenario.

If, after creating the scenarios for your worksheet, you find that you need to use different input values or you want to add or remove scenarios, you can edit the scenarios in the Scenario Manager dialog box. To modify the scenario's name and/or the input values assigned to the changing cells of that scenario, click the scenario name in the Scenarios list box and then click the Edit button so that you can make the appropriate changes in the Edit Scenario dialog box. To remove a scenario from a worksheet, select the scenario's name in the Scenarios list box and then click the Delete button. Note, however, that if you delete a scenario in error, you can't restore it with the Undo command. Instead, you must re-create the scenario by using the Add command button as outlined previously.

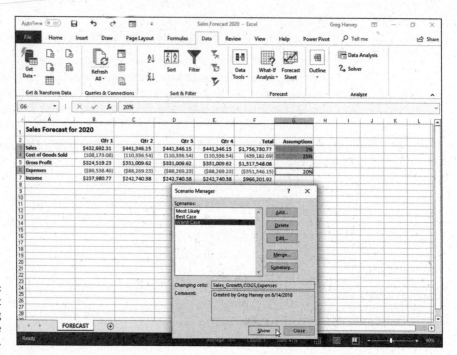

FIGURE 1-7:
Spreadsheet
after showing
the Worst Case
scenario.

You can also merge scenarios from other Excel workbook files that are open. (Of course, the workbooks must share the same spreadsheet layout and changing cells.) To merge a scenario into the current worksheet from another workbook, click the Merge button in the Scenario Manager dialog box and then select the workbook from the Book drop-down list box and the worksheet from the Sheet drop-down list box before you click OK. Excel then copies all the scenarios defined for that worksheet and merges them with any scenarios that you've defined for the current worksheet.

Producing a summary report

After creating the different scenarios for your worksheet, you can use the Summary button in the Scenario Manager dialog box to create a summary report that shows the changing values used in each scenario and, if you want, key resulting values that each produces. When you click the Summary button, Excel opens a Scenario Summary dialog box, similar to the one shown in Figure 1-8, where you may designate a cell selection of result cells in the Result Cells text box to be included in the report. After selecting the result cells for the report, click OK to have Excel generate the summary report and display it in a new worksheet window.

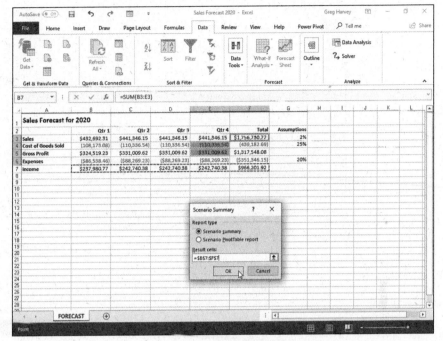

FIGURE 1-8:
Designating the result cells in the Scenario Summary dialog box.

In the example shown in Figure 1-8, the cell range C7:G7, containing the projected income figures for the sales forecast, are designated as the result cells to be included in the summary report. Figure 1-9 shows the actual summary report generated for this sample worksheet in a new document window. Note that because all the changing and result cells in this worksheet are named, the summary report uses their range names in place of their cell references. Also, when the Scenario Manager generates a summary report, it automatically outlines the summary data, thus creating two vertical levels — one for the changing cells and another for the result cells.

After generating a summary report, you can save it by clicking the Save command button on the Quick Access toolbar (Ctrl+S) and/or print it by clicking the Quick Print command button (Ctrl+P).

TIP

Note that the Scenario Summary dialog box contains an option, Scenario Pivot-Table Report, which enables you to view the scenario results as a pivot table. See Book 7, Chapter 2 for details on the uses of pivot tables.

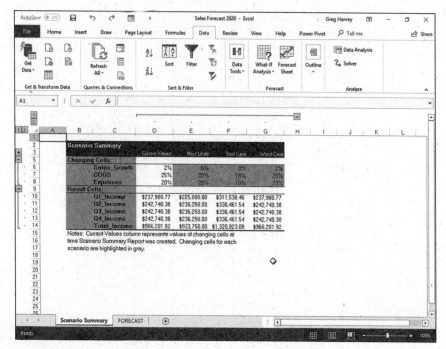

Hide and Goal Seeking

Sometimes, you know the outcome that you want to realize in a worksheet, and you need Excel to help you find the input values necessary to achieve those results. This procedure, which is just the opposite of the what-if analysis that I've been examining in this chapter, is referred to as *goal seeking*.

When you simply need to find the value for a single variable that will give the desired result in a particular formula, you can perform this simple type of goal seeking with the Goal Seek command. If you have charted the data and created a two-dimensional column, bar, or line chart, you can also perform the goal seeking by directly manipulating the appropriate marker on the chart. And when you need to perform more complex goal seeking, such as that which involves changing multiple input values to realize a result or constraining the values to a specific range, you can use the Solver command.

To use the Goal Seek command, simply select the cell containing the formula that will return the result that you are seeking (referred to as the *set cell*), indicate what value you want this formula to return, and then indicate the location of the input value that Excel can change to return the desired result. Figures 1-10 and 1-11 illustrate how you can use the Goal Seek command to find how much sales must increase to realize first quarter income of $475,000 (given certain growth, cost of goods sold, and expense assumptions).

FIGURE 1-10:
Using goal
seeking to find
out how much
sales must
increase to reach
a target income.

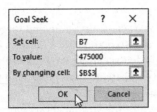

FIGURE 1-11:
A spreadsheet
showing a goal-
seeking solution
and the Goal Seek
Status dialog box.

To find out how much sales must increase to return a net income of $475,000 in the first quarter, you first select cell B7, which contains the formula that calculates the first quarter income before you choose Goal Seek from the What-If Analysis button's drop-down menu on the Ribbon's Data tab or press Alt+AWG. This action opens the Goal Seek dialog box, similar to the one shown in Figure 1-10. Because cell B7 is the active cell when you open this dialog box, the Set Cell text box already contains the cell reference B7. You then select the To Value text box and enter **475000** as the goal. Then, you select the By Changing Cell text box and select cell B3 in the worksheet (the cell that contains the first quarter sales).

Figure 1-11 shows you the Goal Seek Status dialog box that appears when you click OK in the Goal Seek dialog box to have Excel go ahead and adjust the sales figure to reach your desired income figure. As this figure shows, Excel increases the sales in cell B3 from $432,692.31 to $1,817,500.00 which, in turn, returns $475,000.00 as the income in cell B7. The Goal Seek Status dialog box informs you that goal

Performing What-If Scenarios

seeking has found a solution and that the current value and target value are now the same. (If this were not the case, the Step and Pause buttons in the dialog box would become active, and you could have Excel perform further iterations to try to narrow and ultimately eliminate the gap between the target and current values.)

If you want to keep the values entered in the worksheet as a result of goal seeking, click OK to close the Goal Seek Status dialog box. If you want to return to the original values, click the Cancel button instead. If you change the value by clicking OK, remember that you can still switch between the "before" and "after" input values and results by clicking the Undo button on the Quick Access toolbar or by pressing Ctrl+Z.

TIP

To flip back and forth between the "after" and "before" values when you've closed the Goal Seek Status dialog box, press Ctrl+Z to display the original values before goal seeking and then Ctrl+Y to display the values engendered by the goal-seeking solution.

Using the Solver

Although the Data Table and Goal Seek commands work just fine for simple problems that require determining the direct relationship between the inputs and results in a formula, you need to use the Solver add-in when dealing with more complex problems. For example, use the Solver to find the best solution when you need to change multiple input values in your model and you need to impose constraints on these values and/or the output value.

The Solver add-in works by applying iterative methods to find the "best" solution given the inputs, desired solution, and the constraints that you impose. With each iteration, the program applies a trial-and-error method (based on the use of linear or nonlinear equations and inequalities) that attempts to get closer to the optimum solution.

When using the Solver add-in, keep in mind that many problems, especially the more complicated ones, have many solutions. Although the Solver returns the optimum solution, given the starting values, the variables that can change, and the constraints that you define, this solution is often not the only one possible and, in fact, may not be the best solution for you. To be sure that you are finding the best solution, you may want to run the Solver more than once, adjusting the initial values each time you solve the problem.

When setting up the problem for the Solver add-in in your worksheet, define the following items:

>> **Objective cell:** The target cell in your worksheet whose value is to be maximized, minimized, or made to reach a particular value. Note that this cell must contain a formula.

>> **Variable cells:** The changing cells in your worksheet whose values are to be adjusted until the answer is found.

>> **Constraint cells:** The cells that contain the limits that you impose on the changing values in the variable cells and/or the target cell in the objective cell.

After you finish defining the problem with these parameters and have the Solver add-in solve the problem, the program returns the optimum solution by modifying the values in your worksheet. At this point, you can choose to retain the changes in the worksheet or restore the original values to the worksheet. You can also save the solution as a scenario to view later before you restore the original values.

TIP

You can use the Solver add-in with the Scenario Manager to help set up a problem to solve or to save a solution so that you can view it at a later date. The changing cells that you define for the Scenario Manager are automatically picked up and used by the Solver when you select this command, and vice versa. Also, you can save the Solver's solution to a problem as a scenario (by clicking the Save Scenario button in the Solver dialog box) that you can then view with the Scenario Manager.

Setting up and defining the problem

The first step in setting up a problem for the Solver to work on is to create the worksheet model for which you will define the objective cell, variables cells, and the constraint cells.

REMEMBER

Keep in mind that the Solver is an add-in utility. This means that, before you can use it, you need to make sure that the Solver add-in program is still loaded, as indicated by the appearance of the Solver button in the Analysis group at the end of the Data tab on the Ribbon. If this button is missing, you can load Solver by opening the Add-Ins tab of the Excel Options dialog box (Alt+FTAA) and then clicking the Go button after making sure that Excel Add-Ins is displayed in the Manage drop-down list box to its immediate left. Then, select the Solver Add-in check box in the Add-Ins dialog box to put a check mark in it before you click OK to close the dialog box and reload the add-in.

To define and solve a problem with the Solver add-in after you've loaded the add-in and have created your worksheet model, you follow these steps:

1. **Click the Solver command button in the Analyze group at the end of the Ribbon's Data tab.**

   Excel opens the Solver Parameters dialog box, which is similar to the one shown in Figure 1-12.

2. **Click the target cell in the worksheet or enter its cell reference or range name in the Set Objective text box.**

   Next, you need to select the To setting. Click the Max option button when you want the target cell's value to be as large as possible. Click the Min option button when you want the target cell's value to be as small as possible. Click the Value Of option button and then enter a value in the associated text box when you want the target cell's value to reach a particular value.

3. **Click the appropriate option button option in the To section of the dialog box. If you select the Value Of option button, enter the value to match in the associated text box.**

   Next, designate the variable cells — that is, the ones Solver can change to reach your Equal To goal.

4. **Click the By Changing Variable Cells text box and then select the cells to change in the worksheet or enter their cell references or range name in the text box.**

   Remember that to select nonadjacent cells in the worksheet, you need to hold down the Ctrl key as you click each cell in the selection. To have Excel choose the changing cells for you based on the target cell that you selected, click the Guess button to the right of this text box.

   Before having Solver adjust your model, you may add constraints for the target cell or any of the changing cells that determine its limits when adjusting the values.

5. **(Optional) Click the Add button to the right of the Subject to the Constraints list box in the Solver Parameters dialog box.**

   This action opens the Add Constraint dialog box. When defining a constraint, choose the cell whose value you want to constrain or select the cell in the worksheet or enter its cell reference in the Cell Reference text box. Then select the relationship (=, <=, >=, or *int* for integer or *bin* for binary) from the drop-down list box to the right and (unless you chose *int* or *bin*) enter the appropriate value or cell reference in the Constraint text box.

   To continue adding constraints for other cells used by the Solver, click the Add button to add the constraint and clear the text boxes in the Add Constraint dialog box. Then, repeat Step 5 to add a new constraint. After you finish defining constraints for the target cell and changing values in the model, click OK to close the Add Constraint dialog box and return to the Solver Parameters dialog box (which now lists your constraints in the Subject to the Constraints list box).

6. **(Optional) Deselect the Make Unconstrained Variables Non-Negative check box if you want to allow negative values when the variable cells are not subject to constraints.**

   By default, the Solver Add-in employs the GRG (Generalized Reduced Gradient) Nonlinear method in solving the model whose parameters you're setting known as a very efficient way to solve smooth nonlinear problems. To use the LP Simplex method (for Linear Programming following the Simplex algorithm) or Evolutionary engine for solving non-smooth problems, you need to follow Step 7.

7. **(Optional) Select LP Simplex or Evolutionary from the Select a Solving Method drop-down list to use either one of these methods solving nonsmooth problems.**

8. **Click the Solve button to have the Solver solve the problem as you've defined it in the Solver Parameters dialog box.**

FIGURE 1-12: Specifying the parameters to apply to the model in the Solver Parameters dialog box.

Solving the problem

When you click the Solve button, the Solver Parameters dialog box disappears, and the status bar indicates that the Solver is setting up the problem and then keeps you informed of the progress in solving the problem by showing the number of the intermediate (or trial) solutions as they are tried. To interrupt the solution process at any time before Excel calculates the last iteration, press the Esc key. Excel then displays the Show Trial Solution dialog box, informing you that the solution process has been paused. To continue the solution process, click the Continue button. To abort the solution process, click the Stop button.

When Excel finishes the solution process, the Solver Results dialog box appears, similar to the one shown in Figure 1-13. This dialog box informs you whether the Solver was able to find a solution, given the target cell, changing cells, and constraints defined for the problem. To retain the changes that the Solver makes in your worksheet model, leave the Keep Solver Solution option button selected and click OK to close the Solver Results dialog box. To return the original values to the worksheet, click the Restore Original Values option button instead. To save the changes as a scenario before you restore the original values, click the Save Scenario button and assign a name to the current scenario before you click the Restore Original Values option and OK button.

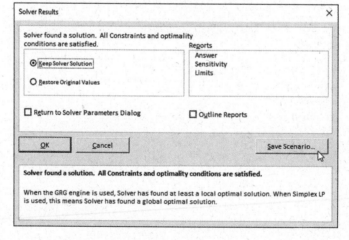

FIGURE 1-13: The Solver Results dialog box showing that Solver found a solution to the problem.

WARNING

Unlike when using the Goal Seek command, after clicking the Keep Solver Solution option button in the Solver Results dialog box, you can't use the Undo command button on the Quick Access toolbar to restore the original values to your worksheet. If you want to be able to switch between the "before" and "after" views of your worksheet, you must save the changes with the Save Scenario button and then select the Restore Original Values option button. That way, you can retain the "before" view in the original worksheet and use the Scenario Manager to display the "after" view created by the Solver.

Changing the Solver options

For most of the problems, the default options used by the Solver are adequate. In some situations, however, you may want to change some of the Solver options before you begin the solution process. To change the solution options, click the Options button in the Solver Parameters dialog box. Excel then opens the Options dialog box with the All Methods tab selected, shown in Figure 1-14, where you can make all necessary changes. (See Table 1-1 for information on each option.)

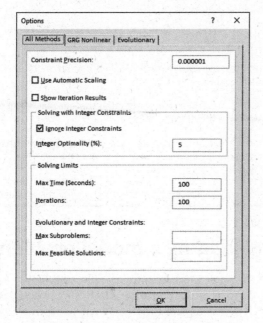

FIGURE 1-14:
Modifying the solution options in the Options dialog box.

After changing the options, click OK to return to the Solver Parameters dialog box; from here, you can then click the Solve button to begin the solution process with the new solution settings that you just changed.

TIP

When you use the default GRG (Generalized Reduced Gradient) Nonlinear or Evolutionary method, you can set additional Solver settings using the options on the GRG Nonlinear and Evolutionary tabs of the Options dialog box. These options include changing the Converge, Population Size, and Random Seed settings for either of these particular methods.

TABLE 1-1 **The Solver Option Settings**

Option	Function
Constraint Precision	Specifies the precision of the constraints. The number that you enter in this text box determines whether the value in a constraint cell meets the specified value or the upper or lower limit you have set. Specify a lower number (between 0 and 1) to reduce the time it takes the Solver to return a solution to your problem.
Use Automatic Scaling	Select this check box to have the Solver automatically scale the results when solving the problem.
Show Iteration Results	Select this check box to have the Solver show the results for the iterations followed in solving the problem.
Ignore Integer Constraints	Select this check box to have the Solver ignore any constraints you specify that use integers.
Integer Optimality (%)	Specifies the percentage of integer optimality criteria that the Solver applies in solving the problem.
Max Time (seconds)	Specifies the maximum number of seconds that the Solver will spend on finding the solution.
Iterations	Specifies the maximum number of times that the Solver will recalculate the worksheet when finding the solution.
Max Subproblems	Specifies the maximum number of subproblems that the Solver takes on when using the Evolutionary method to solve the problem.
Max Feasible Solutions	Specifies the maximum number of feasible solutions that the Solver will pursue when you select the Evolutionary method for solving the problem.

Saving and loading a model problem

The objective cell, variable cells, constraint cells, and Solver options that you most recently used are saved as part of the worksheet when you click the Save button on the Quick Access toolbar (Ctrl+S). When you define other problems for the same worksheet that you want to save, you must click the Save Model button in the Solver Options dialog box and indicate the cell reference or name of the range in the active worksheet where you want the problem's parameters to be inserted.

When you click the Load/Save button, Excel opens the Load/Save Model dialog box, containing a Select Model Area text box. This text box contains the cell references for a range large enough to hold all the problem's parameters, starting with the active cell. To save the problem's parameters in this range, click OK. If this range includes cells with existing data, you need to modify the cell reference in this text box before you click OK to prevent Excel from replacing the existing data.

After you click OK, Excel copies the problem's parameters in the specified range. These values are then saved as part of the worksheet the next time you save the workbook. To reuse these problem parameters when solving a problem, you simply need to open the Solver Options dialog box, click the Load/Save button to open the Load/Save Model dialog box, click the Load button, and then select the range containing the saved problem parameters. When you click OK in the Load Model dialog box, Excel loads the parameters from this cell range into the appropriate text boxes in the Solver Parameters dialog box. You can then close the Solver Options dialog box by clicking OK, and you can solve the problem by using these parameters by clicking the Solve command button.

REMEMBER

Remember that you can use the Reset All button whenever you want to clear all the parameters defined for the previous problem and return the Solver options to their defaults.

Creating Solver reports

You can create three different types of reports with the Solver:

>> **Answer report:** Lists the target cell and changing cells with their original and final values, along with the constraints used in solving the problem.

>> **Sensitivity report:** Indicates how sensitive an optimal solution is to changes in the formulas that calculate the target cell and constraints. The report shows the changing cells with their final values and the *reduced gradient* for each cell. (The reduced gradient measures the objective per unit increase in the changing cell.) If you defined constraints, the Sensitivity report lists them with their final values and the *Lagrange multiplier* for each constraint. (The Lagrange multiplier measures the objective per unit increase that appears in the right side of the constraint equation.)

>> **Limits report:** Shows the target cell and the changing cells with their values, lower and upper limits, and target results. The lower limit represents the lowest value that a changing cell can have while fixing the values of all other cells and still satisfying the constraints. The upper limit represents the highest value that will do this.

Excel places each report that you generate for a Solver problem in a separate worksheet in the workbook. To generate one (or all) of these reports, select the report type (Answer, Sensitivity, or Limits) from the Reports list box of the Solver Results dialog box (as shown previously in Figure 1-13). To select more than one report, just click the name of the report.

When you click OK to close the Solver Results dialog box (after choosing between the Keep Solver Solution and Restore Original Values options), Excel generates the report (or reports) that you selected in a new worksheet that it adds to the beginning of the workbook. (Report sheet tabs are named by report type, as in *Answer Report 1*, *Sensitivity Report 1*, and *Limits Report 1*.)

Chapter 2

Performing Large-Scale Data Analysis

The subject of this chapter is performing data analysis on a larger scale in Excel 2019 worksheets, often with visual components that enable you and your users to immediately spot developing trends. The primary Excel tool for performing such large-scale analysis on your worksheet data is the *pivot table* and its visual counterpart, the pivot chart. Pivot tables enable you to quickly summarize large amounts of data revealing inherent relationships and trends, whereas pivot charts enable you to easily visualize these connections.

In addition, you have access to Excel's Power Pivot add-in when you need to perform analysis on really large data models whose tables contain really huge amounts of data. Finally, Excel 2019 offers you visual data analysis features designed to help you quickly identify significant indicators of your business's health and well-being: 3D Maps, which produces stunning, interactive, 3-D maps animating data over time, and Forecast Sheet, which generates worksheets showing developing trends in your data.

Creating Pivot Tables

Pivot table is the name given to a special type of data summary table that you can use to analyze and reveal the relationships inherent in the data lists that you maintain in Excel. Pivot tables are great for summarizing particular values in a data list or database because they do their magic without making you create formulas to perform the calculations. Unlike the Subtotals feature, which is another summarizing feature (see Book 6, Chapter 1 for more information), pivot tables let you play around with the arrangement of the summarized data — even after you generate the table. (The Subtotals feature only lets you hide and display different levels of totals in the list.) This capability to change the arrangement of the summarized data by rotating row and column headings gives the pivot table its name.

Pivot tables are also versatile because they enable you to summarize data by using a variety of summary functions (although totals created with the SUM function will probably remain your old standby). You can also use pivot tables to cross-tabulate one set of data in your data list with another. For example, you can use this feature to create a pivot table from an employee database that totals the salaries for each job category cross-tabulated (arranged) by department or job site. Moreover, Excel 2019 makes it easy to create pivot tables that summarize data from more than one related data list entered in the worksheet or retrieved from external data in what's known as a Data Model. (See Book 6, Chapter 2 for more on relating data lists and retrieving external data.)

Excel 2019 offers several methods for creating new pivot tables in your worksheets:

>> **Quick Analysis tool:** With all the cells in the data list selected, click the Quick Analysis tool and then select your pivot table on the Tables tab of its drop-down palette.

>> **Recommended PivotTables button:** With the cell pointer in one of the cells of a data list, click the Recommended PivotTables button on the Insert tab and then select your pivot table in the Recommended PivotTables dialog box.

>> **PivotTable button:** With the cell pointer in one of the cells of a data list, click the PivotTable button on the Insert tab and then use the Create PivotTable dialog box to specify the contents and location of your new table before you manually select the fields in the data source to use.

Pivot tables with the Quick Analysis tool

Excel 2019 makes it simple to create a new pivot table using a data list selected in your worksheet with its new Quick Analysis tool. To preview various types of pivot tables that Excel can create for you on the spot using the entries in a data list that you have open in an Excel worksheet, simply follow these steps:

1. **Select all the data (including the column headings) in your data list as a cell range in the worksheet.**

   If you've assigned a range name to the data list, you can select the column headings and all the data records in one operation simply by choosing the data list's name from the Name box drop-down menu.

REMEMBER

2. **Click the Quick Analysis tool that appears right below the lower-right corner of the current cell selection.**

   Doing this opens the palette of Quick Analysis options with the initial Formatting tab selected and its various conditional formatting options displayed.

3. **Click the Tables tab at the top of the Quick Analysis options palette.**

   Excel selects the Tables tab and displays its Table and PivotTable option buttons. The Table button previews how the selected data would appear formatted as a table. The other PivotTable buttons preview the various types of pivot tables that can be created from the selected data.

4. **To preview each pivot table that Excel 2019 can create for your data, highlight its PivotTable button in the Quick Analysis palette.**

   As you highlight each PivotTable button in the options palette, Excel's Live Preview feature displays a thumbnail of a pivot table that can be created using your table data. This thumbnail appears above the Quick Analysis options palette for as long as the mouse or Touch pointer is over its corresponding button.

5. **When a preview of the pivot table you want to create appears, click its button in the Quick Analysis options palette to create it.**

   Excel 2019 then creates the previewed pivot table on a new worksheet that is inserted at the beginning of the current workbook. This new worksheet containing the pivot table is active so that you can immediately rename and relocate the sheet as well as edit the new pivot table, if you wish.

Figures 2-1 and 2-2 show you how this procedure works. In Figure 2-1, I've highlighted the fourth suggested PivotTable button in the Quick Analysis tool's option palette. The previewed table in the thumbnail displayed above the palette shows the salaries subtotals and grand totals in the Employee Data list organized whether or not the employees participate in profit sharing (Yes or No).

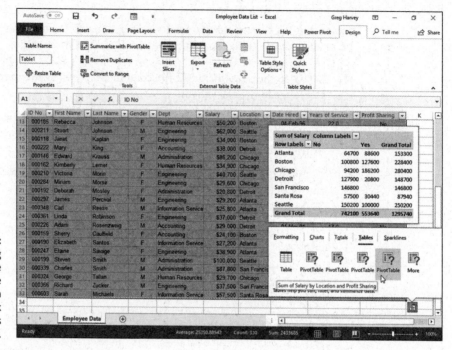

FIGURE 2-1:
Previewing the pivot table created from the selected data in the Quick Analysis options palette.

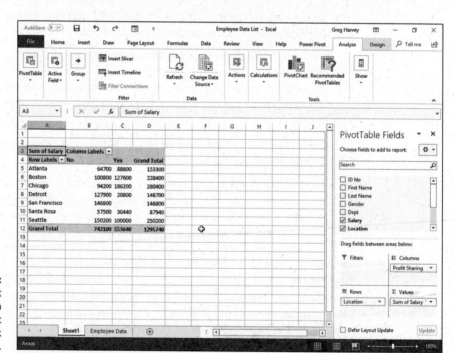

FIGURE 2-2:
Previewed pivot table created on a new worksheet with the Quick Analysis tool.

Figure 2-2 shows you the pivot table that Excel created when I clicked the highlighted button in the options palette in Figure 2-1. Note this pivot table is selected on its own worksheet (Sheet1) that's been inserted in front of the Employee Data worksheet. Because the new pivot table is selected, the PivotTable Fields task pane is displayed on the right side of the Excel worksheet window and the PivotTable Tools context tab is displayed on the Ribbon. You can use the options on this task pane and contextual tab to then customize your new pivot table as described in the "Formatting a Pivot Table" section later in this chapter.

REMEMBER

Note that if Excel can't suggest various pivot tables to create from the selected data in the worksheet, a single Blank PivotTable button is displayed after the Table button in the Quick Analysis tool's options on the Tables tab. You can select this button to manually create a new pivot table for the data as described later in this chapter.

Recommended pivot tables

If creating a new pivot table with the Quick Analysis tool (described in the previous section) is too much work for you, you can quickly generate a pivot table with the new Recommended Pivot Tables command button. To use this method, follow these three easy steps:

1. **Select a cell in the data list for which you want to create the new pivot table.**

   Provided that the data list has a row of column headings with contiguous rows of data as described in Book 6, Chapter 1, this can be any cell in the table.

2. **Click the Recommended PivotTables command button on Insert tab of the Ribbon or press Alt+NSP.**

   Excel displays a Recommended PivotTables dialog box similar to the one shown in Figure 2-3. This dialog box contains a list box on the left side that shows samples of all the suggested pivot tables that Excel 2019 can create from the data in your list.

3. **Select the sample of the pivot table you want to create in the list box on the left and then click OK.**

As soon as you click OK, Excel creates a new pivot table following the selected sample on its own worksheet inserted in front of the others in your workbook. This pivot table is selected on the new sheet so that the Pivot Table Fields task pane is displayed on the right side of the Excel worksheet window and the PivotTable Tools contextual tab is displayed on the Ribbon. You can use the options on this task pane and contextual tab to then customize your new pivot table as described in the "Formatting a Pivot Table" section later in this chapter.

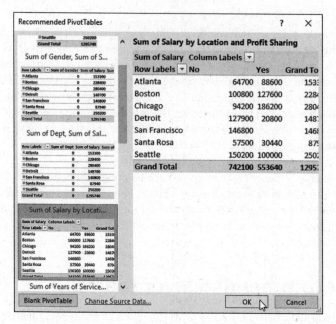

FIGURE 2-3:
Creating a new
pivot table from
the sample
pivot tables
displayed in the
Recommended
PivotTables
dialog box.

Manually created pivot tables

Creating pivot tables with the Quick Analysis tool or the Recommended Pivot-Tables button on the Insert tab is fine provided that you're only summarizing the data stored in a single data list that's stored in your Excel worksheet.

When you want your pivot table to work with data from fields in more than one (related) data table or with data stored in a data table that doesn't reside in your worksheet as when connecting with an external data source (see Book 6, Chapter 2), you need to manually create the pivot table.

Creating a pivot table with local data

To manually create a new pivot table using a data list stored in your Excel work-book, simply open the worksheet that contains that list (see Book 6, Chapter 1) you want summarized by the pivot table, position the cell pointer somewhere in the cells of this list, and then click the PivotTable command button on the Ribbon's Insert tab or press Alt+NVT.

Excel then selects all the data in the list indicated by a marquee around the cell range before it opens a Create PivotTable dialog box similar to the one shown in Figure 2-4, where the Select a Table or Range option is selected. You can then adjust the cell range in the Table/Range text box under the Select a Table or Range option button if the marquee does not include all the data to be summarized in the pivot table.

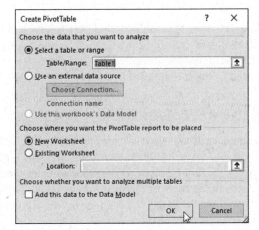

FIGURE 2-4:
Indicate the
data source
and pivot table
location in the
Create PivotTable
dialog box.

By default, Excel builds the new pivot table on a new worksheet it adds to the workbook. If you want the pivot table to appear on the same worksheet, select the Existing Worksheet option button and then indicate the location of the first cell of the new table in the Location text box. (Just be sure that this new pivot table isn't going to overlap any existing tables of data.)

REMEMBER

If the list you've selected in the Table/Range text box is related to another data list in your workbook and you want to be able to analyze and summarize data from both, be sure to select the Add This Data to the Data Model check box at the bottom of the Create PivotTable dialog box before you click OK. (See Book 6, Chapter 2 for details on creating relationships between data lists using key fields.)

Creating a pivot table from external data

If you're creating a pivot table using external data not stored in your workbook, you want to locate the cell pointer in the first cell of the worksheet where you want the pivot table before opening the Create PivotTable dialog box by selecting the PivotTable button on the Insert tab.

When the cell pointer's in a blank cell when you open the Create PivotTable dialog box, Excel automatically selects the Use an External Data Source option as the data source and the Existing Worksheet option as the location for the new pivot table. To specify the external data table to use, you then click the Choose Connections button to open the Existing Connections dialog box, where you select the name of the connection you want to use before you click the Open button. (See Book 6, Chapter 2 for information on establishing connections with external database tables.)

Excel then returns you to the Create PivotTable dialog box, where the name of the selected external data connection is displayed after the Connection Name heading. You can then modify the location settings, if need be, before creating the new pivot table by clicking OK. Note that the Add This Data to the Data Model check box is automatically selected (and cannot be deselected) — the relationships between the data tables in the source database specified by the external data connection are automatically reflected in fields displayed in the Field list for the new pivot table.

Constructing the new pivot table

After you indicate the source and location for the new pivot table in the Create PivotTable dialog box and click its OK button, the program adds a placeholder graphic (with the text, "To build a report, choose fields from the PivotTable Field List") indicating where the new pivot table will go in the worksheet while at the same time displaying a PivotTable Fields task pane on the right side of the Worksheet area. (See Figure 2-5.)

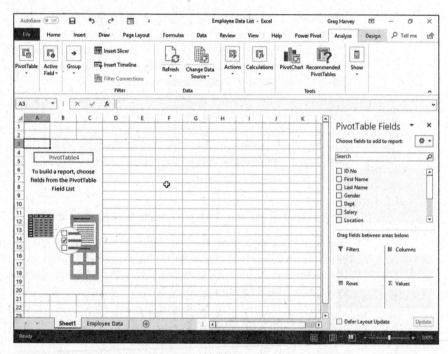

FIGURE 2-5:
A new pivot table displaying the blank table grid and the PivotTable Fields List task pane.

This PivotTable Fields task pane is divided into two areas: the Choose Fields to Add to Report list box with the names of all the fields in the data list you selected as the source of the table preceded by an empty check box at the top, and an area identified by the heading, Drag Fields Between Areas Below, which is divided into four drop zones (FILTERS, COLUMNS, ROWS, and VALUES) at the bottom.

To complete the new pivot table, all you have to do is assign the fields in the PivotTable Fields task pane to the various parts of the table. You do this by dragging a field name from the Choose Fields to Add to Report list box to one of the four areas (or drop zones) in the Drag Fields Between Areas Below section at the bottom of the task pane:

>> **FILTERS** for the fields that enable you to page through the data summaries shown in the actual pivot table by filtering out sets of data — they act as the filters for the report. So, for example, if you designate the Year Field from a data list as a report filter, you can display data summaries in the pivot table for individual years or for all years represented in the data list. They appear at the top of the report above the columns and rows of the pivot table.

>> **COLUMNS** for the fields that determine the arrangement of data shown in the columns of the pivot table — their entries appear in the table's column headings.

>> **ROWS** for the fields that determine the arrangement of data shown in the rows of the pivot table — their entries appear in the table's row headings.

>> **VALUES** for the fields whose data are presented in the cells in the body of the pivot table — they are the values that are summarized in the last row and column of the table (totaled by default).

REMEMBER

You can also add fields to the new pivot table simply by selecting the check box in front of the field name. Keep in mind when you use this method to build your pivot table that if Excel identifies the field as text, it automatically adds it to the ROWS area and when it identifies the field as numeric, the program adds it to the VALUES area. To remove a field from the pivot table, simply clear its check box in the PivotTable Fields task pane.

To better understand how you can use these various areas in a pivot table, look at a completed pivot table in Figure 2-6. For this pivot table, I dragged these fields in the employee data list to the following areas in the PivotTable Fields task pane:

>> **Gender** field contains F (for female) or M (for male) to indicate the employee's gender — to the FILTERS area.

>> **Location** field contains the names of the various cities with corporate offices — to the COLUMNS area.

>> **Dept** field contains the names of the various departments in the company — to the ROWS area.

>> **Salary** field contains the annual salary for each employee — to the VALUES area.

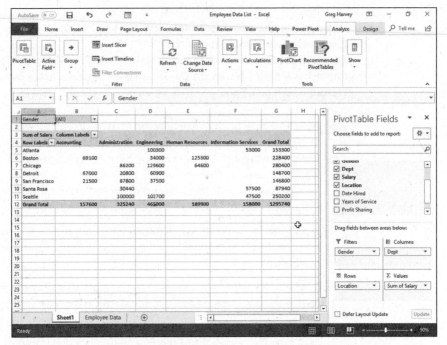

FIGURE 2-6:
A completed
pivot table after
adding the
fields from the
employee data
list to its various
sections.

As a result, this pivot table now displays the sum of the salaries for both the men and women employees in each location (across the columns) and then presents these sums by their department (in each row).

As soon as you create a new pivot table (or select the cell of an existing table in a worksheet), Excel selects the Analyze tab of the PivotTable Tools contextual tab added to the end of the Ribbon. Among the many groups on this tab, you find the Active Field group, which contains the following useful command buttons:

>> **Active Field** text box indicating the pivot table field that is active in the worksheet

>> **Field Settings** button to open the Field Settings dialog box, where you can change various settings for the pivot table field that's active in the worksheet

>> **Drill Down** and **Drill Up** buttons to display lower levels with detail data (Drill Down) or higher levels with summary data (Drill Up) in a chart or matrix

>> **Expand Field** and **Collapse Field** buttons to hide and redisplay the expand (+) and collapse (–) buttons in front of particular Column Fields or Row Fields that enable you to temporarily remove and then redisplay their particular summarized values in the pivot table

CHANGING THE PIVOTTABLE FIELDS TASK PANE DISPLAY

REMEMBER

By default, Excel displays the list of fields stacked on top of the four areas — FILTERS, COLUMNS, ROWS, and VALUES — in the PivotTable Fields task pane. You can change this arrangement by clicking the Tools drop-down button (to the immediate right of the Choose Fields to Add to Report heading) and then choosing one of the following options from its drop-down menu: Fields Section and Areas Section Side-by-Side to place the list of fields in a column to the left of the four areas, Fields Section Only to list only the fields, Areas Section Zones Only (2 by 2) to list only the areas in two columns, or Areas Section Zones Only (1 by 4) to list only the areas in one column.

When you display only the four areas in the PivotTable Fields task pane, you can click the drop-down buttons that appear to the right of the name of each field you add to the four areas to manipulate the fields: Move to Report Filter to move the field to the FILTERS area, Move to Row Labels to move the field to the ROWS area, Move to Column Labels to move the field to the COLUMNS area, Move to Values to move the field to the VALUES area, Remove Field to remove the field from its current drop zone, or Field Settings to open the Fields Settings dialog box, where you can adjust the subtotals, filter, layout, and print settings for the field.

Formatting a Pivot Table

Excel 2019 makes formatting a new pivot table you've added to a worksheet as quick and easy as formatting any other table of data or list of data. All you need to do is click a cell of the pivot table to add the PivotTable Tools contextual tab to the end of the Ribbon and then click its Design tab to display its command buttons.

The Design tab on the PivotTable Tools contextual tab is divided into three groups:

>> **Layout** group to add subtotals and grand totals to the pivot table and modify its basic layout

>> **PivotTable Style Options** group to refine the pivot table style you select for the table using the PivotTable Styles gallery to the immediate right

>> **PivotTable Styles** group containing the gallery of styles you can apply to the active pivot table by clicking the desired style thumbnail

Performing Large-Scale Data Analysis

Refining the pivot table layout and style

After selecting a style from the PivotTable Styles gallery on the Design tab on the PivotTable Tools contextual tab, you can then refine the style using the command buttons in the Layout group and the check boxes in the PivotTable Style Options group.

The Layout group on the Design tab contains the following four command buttons:

- **Subtotals** to hide the display of subtotals in the summary report or have them displayed at the top or bottom of their groups in the report

- **Grand Totals** to turn on or off the display of grand totals in the last row or column of the report

- **Report Layout** to modify the display of the report by selecting between the default Compact Form and the much more spread-out Outline Form (which connects the subtotals across the columns of the table with lines or shading depending on the table style selected) and Tabular Form (which connects the row items in the first column and the subtotals across the columns of the table with gridlines or shading depending on the table style selected)

- **Blank Rows** to insert or remove a blank row after each item in the table

The PivotTable Style Options group contains the following four check boxes:

- **Row Headers** to remove and then re-add the font and color formatting from the row headers of the table in the first column of the table applied by the currently selected pivot table style

- **Column Headers** to remove and then re-add the font and color formatting from the column headers at the top of the table applied by the currently selected pivot table style

- **Banded Rows** to add and remove banding in the form of gridlines or shading (depending on the currently selected pivot table style) from the rows of the pivot table

- **Banded Columns** to add and remove banding in the form of gridlines or shading (depending on the currently selected pivot table style) from the columns of the pivot table

Figure 2-7 shows the original pivot table created from the employee data list after making the following changes:

- Adding the Years of Service field as a second row field and then closing the PivotTable Fields task pane

>> Selecting the Banded Rows check box in the PivotTable Style Options group on the Design contextual tab

>> Choosing the Show in Outline Form option from the Report Layout command button's drop-down menu in the Layout group of the Design tab

>> Choosing the Insert Blank Line after Each Item option from the Blank Rows command button's drop-down menu in the Layout group of the Design tab

>> Choosing the Show All Subtotals as Bottom of Group option from the Subtotals command button's drop-down menu in the Layout group of the Design tab

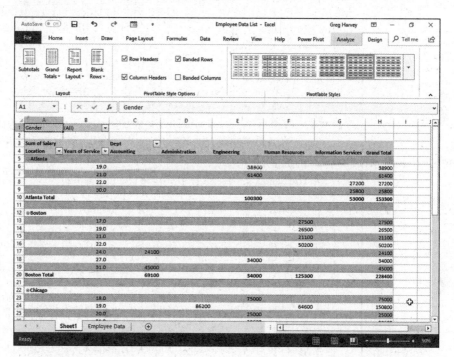

FIGURE 2-7:
Revised pivot table in the Outline Form with an extra blank row between each item in the pivot table.

Formatting the parts of the pivot table

Even after applying a table style to your new pivot table, you may still want to make some individual adjustments to its formatting, such as selecting a new font, font size, or cell alignment for the text of the table and a new number format for the values in the table's data cells.

You can make these types of formatting changes to a pivot table by selecting the part of the table to which the formatting is to be applied and then selecting the new formatting from the appropriate command buttons in the Font, Alignment, and Number groups on the Home tab of the Ribbon.

Applying a new font, font size, or alignment to the pivot table

You can modify the text in a pivot table by selecting a new font, font size, or horizontal alignment. To make these formatting changes to the text in the entire table, select the entire table before you use the appropriate command buttons in the Font and/or Alignment group on the Home tab. To apply these changes only to the headings in the pivot table, select only its labels before using the commands on the Home tab. To apply these changes only to the data in the body of the pivot table, select only its cells.

To help you select the cells you want to format in a pivot table, use the following Select items on the Actions command button's drop-down list:

1. **Click a cell in the pivot table in the worksheet and then click the Select drop-down button in the Actions group on the Analyze tab under the PivotTable Tools contextual tab (Alt+JTW).**

2. **On the Select submenu, you can do the following:**

   - Click the Label and Values option to select the cells with the row and column headings and those with the values in the table.

   - Click the Values option to select only the cells with values in the table.

   - Click the Labels option to select only the cells with the rows and column headings in the table.

   - Click the Entire PivotTable option on the Select submenu to select all the pivot table cells, including the Report Filter cells.

   - Click the Enable Selection option to be able to select single rows or columns of the pivot table by clicking it with the mouse or Touch pointer.

You can also use the following hot keys to select all or part of your pivot table:

>> **Alt+JTWA** to select the label cells with the row and column headings as well as the data cells with the values in the body of the pivot table

>> **Alt+JTWV** to select only the data cells with the values in the body of the pivot table

>> **Alt+JTWL** to select only the label cells with the row and column headings in the pivot table

>> **Alt+JTWT** to select the entire table, that is, all the cells of the pivot table including those with the Report Filter

REMEMBER

You can use the Label and Values, Values, and Labels options on the Select button's drop-down menu and their hot key equivalents only *after* you have selected the Entire Table option to select all the cells.

TIP

Use Live Preview to preview the look of a new font or font size on the Font or Font Size drop-down menu in the Font group on the Ribbon's Home tab.

Applying a number format to the data cells

When you first create a pivot table, Excel does not format the data cells in the table that contain the values corresponding to the field or fields you add to the VALUES area in the PivotTable Fields task pane and the subtotals and grand totals that Excel adds to the table. You can, however, assign any of the Excel number formats to the values in the pivot table in one of two manners.

In the first method, you select the entire table (Alt+JTWT), then select only its data cells in the body of the pivot table (Alt+JTWV), and then apply the desired number format using the command buttons in the Number group of the Home tab of the Ribbon. For example, to format the data cells with the Accounting number format with no decimal places, you click the Accounting Number Format command button and then click the Decrease Decimal command button twice.

You can also apply a number format to the data cells in the body of the pivot table by following these steps:

1. Click the name of the field in the pivot table that contains the words "Sum of" and then click the Field Settings button in the Active Field group of Analyze tab to open the Summarize Values By tab of the Value Field Settings dialog box.

In my Employee example pivot table, this field is called Sum of Salary because the Salary field is summarized. Note that this field is located at the intersection of the Column and Row Label fields in the table.

2. Click the Number Format command button in the Value Field Settings dialog box to open the Number tab of the Format Cells dialog box.

3. Click the type of number format you want to assign to the values in the pivot table on the Category list box of the Number tab.

Performing Large-Scale Data Analysis

4. (Optional) Modify any other options for the selected number format such as Decimal Places, Symbol, and Negative Numbers that are available for that format.

5. Click OK twice — the first time to close the Format Cells dialog box and the second to close the Value Field Settings dialog box.

Sorting and Filtering the Pivot Table Data

When you create a new pivot table, you'll notice that Excel automatically adds AutoFilter buttons to the Report Filter field as well as the labels for the Column and Row fields. These AutoFilter buttons enable you to filter out all but certain entries in any of these fields, and in the case of the Column and Row fields, to sort their entries in the table.

When you add more than one Column or Row field to your pivot table, Excel adds collapse buttons (–) that you can use to temporarily hide subtotal values for a particular secondary field. After clicking a collapse button in the table, it immediately becomes an expand button (+) that you can click to redisplay the subtotals for that one secondary field.

Filtering the report

Perhaps the most important AutoFilter buttons in a pivot table are the ones added to the Report Filter field(s). By selecting a particular option on the drop-down lists attached to one of these AutoFilter buttons, only the summary data for that subset you select is then displayed in the pivot table itself.

For example, in the example pivot table (refer to Figure 2-6) that uses the Gender field from the employee data list as the Report Filter field, you can display the sum of just the men's salaries by location and department in the body of the pivot table simply by clicking the Gender field's filter button and then selecting M from the drop-down list before you click OK. Likewise, you can view the summary of the women's salaries by selecting F from this filter button's drop-down list. To later redisplay the summary of the salaries for all the employees, you then reselect the (All) option from this list before you click OK.

Excel then displays M in the Gender Report Filter field instead of the default (All) and replaces the standard drop-down button icon with a cone-shaped filter icon, indicating that the field is currently being filtered to show only some of the values in the data source.

Filtering individual Column and Row fields

The AutoFilter buttons on the Column and Row fields enable you to filter particular groups and, in some cases, individual entries in the data source. To filter the summary data in the columns or rows of a pivot table, click the Column or Row field's filter button and start by deselecting the check box for the (Select All) option at the top of the drop-down list to clear its check mark. Then, select the check boxes for all the groups or individual entries whose summed values you still want displayed in the pivot table to put check marks back in each of their check boxes before you click OK.

As when filtering a Report Filter field in the table, Excel replaces the standard drop-down button icon displayed in the particular Column or Report field with a cone-shaped filter icon. This icon indicates that the field is currently being filtered and only some of its summary values are now displayed in the pivot table. To redisplay all the values for a filtered Column or Report field, you need to click its filter button and then select the (Select All) option at the top of its drop-down list before you click OK.

Figure 2-8 shows the original sample pivot table after formatting the values (with a number format that uses a comma as a thousands separator and displays zero decimal places) and then filtering its Gender Filter Report Field to women by selecting F (for Female) and its Dept Row Field to Accounting, Administration, and Human Resources.

TIP

Notice in Figure 2-8 that after filtering the pivot table by selecting F in the Gender Filter Report field and selecting Accounting, Administration, and Human Resources departments as the only Dept Row fields, the filtered pivot table no longer displays salary summaries for all of the company's locations. (Santa Rosa, Seattle, and Atlanta locations are missing.) You can tell that the table is missing these locations because there are no women employees in the three selected departments and not as a result of filtering the Location Column Labels field because its drop-down button still uses the standard icon and not the cone filter icon now shown to the right of the Gender Filter Report and Dept Row Labels fields.

Slicing the pivot table data

Excel 2019 supports *slicers*, a graphic tool for filtering the data in your pivot table. Instead of having to filter the data using the check boxes attached to an item list on the drop-down menus on a field's AutoFilter button, you can use slicers instead. Slicers, which float as graphic objects over the worksheet, not only enable you to quickly filter the data in particular fields of a pivot table, but also enable you to connect slicers to multiple pivot tables or to a pivot table and a pivot chart you've created.

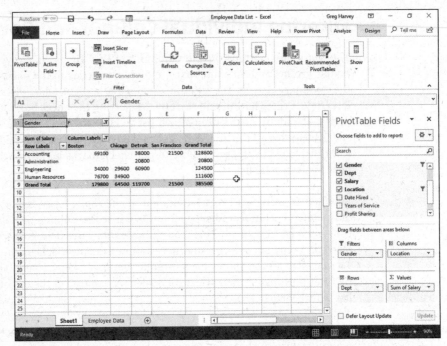

FIGURE 2-8:
The pivot table after filtering the Gender Filter Report field and the Dept Row field.

To use slicers on a pivot table, click one of the table's cells and then click the Insert Slicer button in the Filter group of the table's Analyze tab. Excel then displays an Insert Slicers dialog box containing a list of all the fields in the current pivot table. You then select the check boxes for all the fields you want to filter the pivot table for before you select OK.

Excel then displays a slicer for each field you select in the Insert Slicers dialog box. Each slicer appears as a rectangular graphic object that contains buttons for each entry in the particular pivot table field. You can then filter the data in the pivot table simply by clicking the individual entries in the slicer for all the values you still want displayed in the table. To display values for multiple, nonconsecutive entries in a particular field, you hold down the Ctrl key as you click entries in its slicer. To display values of multiple consecutive values, you click the first entry in its slicer and then hold the Shift key as you click the last entry you want included.

Figure 2-9 shows you the pivot table for the employee data list after I used three slicers to filter it. The first slicer is for the Gender field, where I selected M so that only the records for the men are displayed in the pivot table. The second slicer is for the Dept field, where I clicked the Engineering item to display only the men's salaries in Engineering. The third and final slicer is for the Location field, where I selected the Chicago, San Francisco, and Seattle locations (by holding down the Ctrl key as I clicked their buttons in the Location slicer). As a result, the employee data pivot table is now filtered so that you see only the salary totals for the men in the Engineering departments at the Chicago, San Francisco, and Seattle offices.

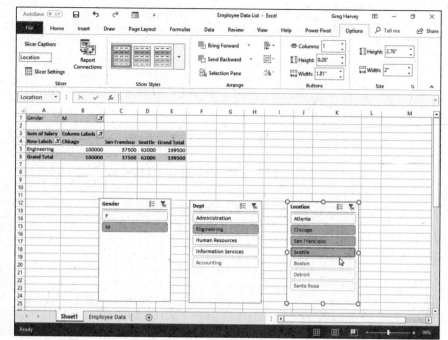

FIGURE 2-9:
Employee pivot table showing the men's salaries in the Engineering department in Chicago, San Francisco, and Seattle.

REMEMBER

Because slicers are graphic objects, when you add them to your worksheet, the program automatically adds an Options tab under a Slicer Tools contextual tab to the Ribbon. This Options tab contains many of the same graphic controls that you're used to when dealing with standard graphic objects such as shapes and text boxes, including a Slicer Styles drop-down gallery and Bring Forward, Send Back, and Selection Pane that you can use to format the currently selected slicer. You can also use the Height and Width options in the Buttons and Size groups to modify the dimensions of the slicer and the buttons it contains. Finally, you can use the Report Connections command button to open the Report Connections dialog box, where you can connect additional pivot tables to the currently selected slicer.

To move a slicer, you click it to select it and then drag it from somewhere on its border using the black-cross pointer with an arrowhead. To deselect the items you've selected in a slicer, click the button in the upper-right corner of the slicer with a red *x* through the filter icon. To get rid of a slicer (and automatically redisplay the PivotTable Fields task pane), select the slicer and then press the Delete key.

Using timeline filters

Excel 2019 also enables you to filter your data with its timeline feature. You can think of timelines as slicers designed specifically for date fields that enable you to filter data out of your pivot table that doesn't fall within a particular period, thereby allowing you to see timing of trends in your data.

To create a timeline for your pivot table, select a cell in your pivot table and then select the Insert Timeline button in the Filter group on the Analyze contextual tab under the PivotTable Tools tab on the Ribbon. Excel then displays an Insert Time-lines dialog box displaying a list of pivot table fields that you can use in creating the new timeline. After selecting the check box for the date field you want to use in this dialog box, click OK.

Figure 2-10 shows you the timeline I created for the sample Employee Data list by selecting its Date Hired field in the Insert Timelines dialog box. As you can see, Excel created a floating Date Hired timeline with the years and months demar-cated and a bar that indicates the time period selected. By default, the timeline uses months as its units, but you can change this to years, quarters, or even days by clicking the time units' drop-down button immediately below the filter icon in the upper-right corner of the timeline and then selecting the desired time unit.

For Figure 2-10, I selected the Years option as the timeline's unit and then selected the period 1995 through 1999 so that the pivot table shows the salaries by depart-ment and location for only employees hired during this four-year period. I did this simply by dragging the timeline bar in the Date Hired timeline graphic so that it begins at 1995 and extends just up to 2000. And should I need to filter the pivot table salary data for other hiring periods, I would simply modify the start and stop times by dragging the timeline bar in the Date Hired timeline.

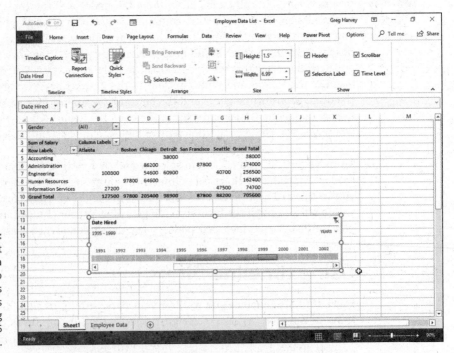

FIGURE 2-10:
Employee pivot table using a timeline filter to show the salaries for employees hired during the period 1995 through 1999.

Sorting the pivot table

You can instantly reorder the summary values in a pivot table by sorting the table on one or more of its Column or Row fields. To re-sort a pivot table, click the AutoFilter button for the Column or Row field you want to use in the sort and then click either the Sort A to Z option or the Sort Z to A option at the top of the field's drop-down list.

Click the Sort A to Z option when you want the table reordered by sorting the labels in the selected field alphabetically, or, in the case of values, from the smallest to largest value, or, in the case of dates, from the oldest to newest date. Click the Sort Z to A option when you want the table reordered by sorting the labels in reverse alphabetical order (Z to A), values from the highest to smallest, and dates from the newest to oldest.

Modifying the Pivot Table

As the term *pivot* implies, the fun of pivot tables is being able to rotate the data fields by using the rows and columns of the table, as well as to change what fields are used on the fly. For example, suppose that after making the data list's Location field the pivot table's Column Labels Field, and its Dept field the Row Labels Field, you now want to see what the table looks like with the Dept field as the Column Labels Field and the Location field as the Row Labels Field.

No problem: All you have to do is open the PivotTable Fields task pane (Alt+JTL) and then drag Location from the COLUMNS area to the ROWS area and then drag Dept from the ROWS to COLUMNS. *Voilà* — Excel rearranges the totaled salaries so that the rows of the pivot table show the location grand totals, and the columns now show the departmental grand totals. Figure 2-11 shows this new arrangement for the pivot table.

In fact, when pivoting a pivot table, not only can you rotate existing fields, but you can also add new fields to the pivot table or assign more fields to the table's COLUMNS and ROWS areas.

Figure 2-12 illustrates this situation. This figure shows the same pivot table after making a couple of key changes to the table structure. First, I added the Profit Sharing field as a second Report Filter field by dragging it to the FILTERS area in the PivotTable Fields task pane. Then, I made Location a second Row Labels Field by dragging it from the COLUMNS area to the ROWS area. Finally, for this figure, I changed the setting in the Gender Report Filter from the default of All to M and changed the Profit Sharing Report Filter to Yes.

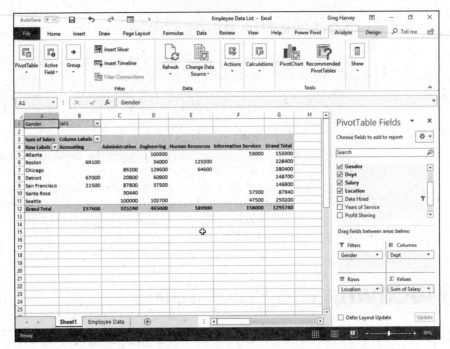

FIGURE 2-11:
Pivoting the table so that Dept is now the Column Labels Field and Location the Row Labels Field.

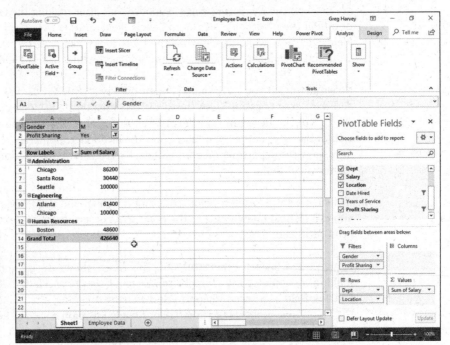

FIGURE 2-12:
The pivot table after adding Profit Sharing as another Report Filter and making both the Dept and Location Row Fields.

As a result, the modified pivot table shown in Figure 2-12 now shows the salary totals for all the men in the corporation arranged first by their department and then by their location. Because I added Profit Sharing as a second Report Filter, I can see the totals for just the men or just the women who are or aren't currently enrolled in the profit sharing plan simply by selecting the appropriate Report Filter settings.

Changing the summary functions

By default, Excel uses the good old SUM function to total the values in the numeric field(s) that you add to the VALUES area, thereby assigning them to the data cells in the body of the pivot table. Some data summaries require the use of another summary function, such as the AVERAGE or COUNT function.

To change the summary function that Excel uses, you open the Field Settings dialog box for one of the fields that you use as the data items in the pivot table. You can do this either by clicking the Value Field Settings option on the field's drop-down menu in the VALUES area in the PivotTable Fields task pane (Alt+JTL) or by right-clicking the field's label and then selecting Value Field Settings on its shortcut menu.

After you open the Value Field Settings dialog box for the field, you can change its summary function from the default Sum to any of the following functions by selecting it on the Summarize By tab:

>> **Count** to show the count of the records for a particular category (note that COUNT is the default setting for any text fields that you use as Data Items in a pivot table)

>> **Average** to calculate the average (that is, the arithmetic mean) for the values in the field for the current category and page filter

>> **Max** to display the largest numeric value in that field for the current category and page filter

>> **Min** to display the smallest numeric value in that field for the current category and page filter

>> **Product** to display the product of the numeric values in that field for the current category and page filter (all nonnumeric entries are ignored)

>> **Count Numbers** to display the number of numeric values in that field for the current category and page filter (all nonnumeric entries are ignored)

>> **StdDev** to display the standard deviation for the sample in that field for the current category and page filter

>> **StdDevp** to display the standard deviation for the population in that field for the current category and page filter

>> **Var** to display the variance for the sample in that field for the current category and page filter

>> **Varp** to display the variance for the population in that field for the current category and page filter

After you select the new summary function to use on the Summarize By tab of the Value Field Settings dialog box, click the OK button to have Excel apply the new function to the data presented in the body of the pivot table.

Adding Calculated Fields

In addition to using various summary functions on the data presented in your pivot table, you can create your own Calculated Fields for the pivot table. Calculated Fields are computed by a formula that you create by using existing numeric fields in the data source. To create a Calculated Field for your pivot table, follow these steps:

1. **Click any of the cells in the pivot table and then select the Calculated Field option from the Fields, Items, & Sets button's drop-down list on the Analyze tab or press Alt+JTJF.**

The Fields, Items, & Sets command button is found in the Calculations group on Analyze tab on the PivotTable Tools contextual tab.

Excel opens the Insert Calculated Field dialog box similar to the one shown in Figure 2-13.

2. **Enter the name for the new field in the Name text box.**

Next, you create the formula in the Formula text box by using one or more of the existing fields displayed in the Fields list box.

3. **Click the Formula text box and then delete the zero (0) after the equal sign and position the insertion point immediately following the equal sign (=).**

Now you're ready to type in the formula that performs the calculation. To do this, insert numeric fields from the Fields list box and indicate the operation to perform on them with the appropriate arithmetic operators (+, -, *, or /).

4. **Enter the formula to perform the new field's calculation in the Formula text box, inserting whatever fields you need by clicking the name in the Fields list box and then clicking the Insert Field button.**

For example, in Figure 2-13, I created a formula for the new calculated field called Bonus that multiplies the values in the Salary Field by 2.5 percent (0.025) to compute the total amount of annual bonuses to be paid. To do this, I selected the Salary field in the Fields list box and then clicked the Insert Field button to add Salary to the formula in the Formula text box (as in =Salary). Then, I typed *0.025 to complete the formula (=Salary*0.025).

When you finish entering the formula for your calculated field, you can add the calculated field to the PivotTable Fields task pane by clicking the Add button. After you click the Add button, it changes to a grayed-out Modify button. If you start editing the formula in the Formula text box, the Modify button becomes active so that you can click it to update the definition.

5. **Click OK in the Insert Calculated Field dialog box.**

This action closes the Insert Calculated Field dialog box and adds the summary of the data in the calculated field to your pivot table.

FIGURE 2-13:
Creating a
calculated field
for a pivot table.

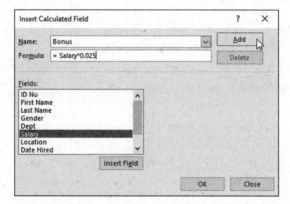

After you finish defining a calculated field to a pivot table, Excel automatically adds its name to the field list in the PivotTable Fields task pane and to the VALUES area thereby assigning the calculated field as another Data item in the body of the pivot table.

REMEMBER If you want to temporarily hide a calculated field from the body of the pivot table, click the name of the calculated field in the field list in the PivotTable Fields task pane (Alt+JTL) to remove the check mark from its check box in the field list. Then, when you're ready to redisplay the calculated field, you can do so by clicking its check box in the field list in the PivotTable Fields task pane again to put a check mark back into it.

Changing the pivot table options

You can use the PivotTable Options dialog box (shown in Figure 2-14) to change the settings applied to any and all pivot tables that you create in a workbook. You open this dialog box by clicking the PivotTable command button on the PivotTable Tools tab's Analyze tab followed by the Options menu item on the Options drop-down button or by simply pressing Alt+JTTT.

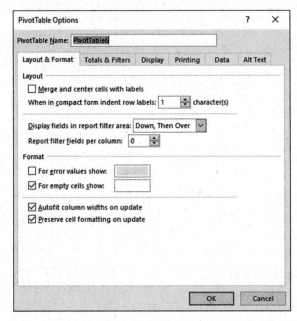

FIGURE 2-14:
Modifying the pivot table options in the PivotTable Options dialog box.

The PivotTable Options dialog box contains the following six tabs:

» **Layout & Format** with options for controlling the various aspects of the layout and formatting of the cells in the pivot table

» **Totals & Filters** with options for controlling the display of the subtotals and grand totals in the report, and filtering and sorting the table's fields

» **Display** with options for controlling the display items in the table and the sorting of the fields in the PivotTable

» **Printing** with options for controlling print expand and collapse buttons when displayed in the pivot table, and print titles with the row and column labels on each page of the printout

>> **Data** with options for controlling how the data that supports the pivot table is stored and refreshed

>> **Alt Text** with options for adding alternate, text-based titles and descriptions of the information in the pivot table for those with vision impairments who then hear the title and description read aloud

TIP

Perhaps the most important pivot table option is the Classic PivotTable Layout (Enables Dragging of Fields in the Grid) check box option on the Display tab. When you select this check box, Excel lets you rearrange the fields within the pivot table simply by dragging their icons onto the desired part of the table (Table Filter, Column Labels, or Row Labels). The program also lets you add fields to the pivot table by dragging them from the field list in the PivotTable Fields task pane and dropping them on the part of the table to which they are to be added.

Creating Pivot Charts

Instead of generating just a plain old boring pivot table, you can spice up your data summaries quite a bit by generating a pivot chart to go along with a supporting pivot table. To create a pivot chart from your pivot table, simply follow these two steps:

1. **Click the PivotChart command button in the Tools group on the Analyze tab under the PivotTable Tools contextual tab or press Alt+JTC.**

Excel opens the Insert Chart dialog box where you can select the type and subtype of the pivot chart you want to create. (See Book 5, Chapter 1.)

2. **Click the thumbnail of the subtype of chart you want to create in the Insert Chart dialog box and then click OK.**

As soon as you click OK after selecting the chart subtype, Excel inserts an embedded pivot chart into the worksheet containing the original pivot table. This new pivot chart contains drop-down buttons for each of the four different types of fields used in the pivot chart (Report Filter, Legend Fields, Axis Fields, and Values). You can use these drop-down buttons to sort and filter the data represented in the chart. (See "Filtering a pivot chart" later in this chapter for details.)

In addition, Excel replaces the PivotTable Tools on the Ribbon with a PivotChart Tools contextual tab. This PivotChart Tools tab is then further subdivided into three tabs: Analyze, Design, and Format, which is automatically selected.

Performing Large-Scale Data Analysis

Moving a pivot chart to its own sheet

Although Excel automatically creates all new pivot charts on the same worksheet as the pivot table, you may find customizing and working with the pivot chart easier if you move the chart to its own chart sheet in the workbook. To move a new pivot chart to its own chart sheet in the workbook, follow these steps:

1. **Click the Analyze tab under the PivotChart Tools contextual tab to bring its tools to the Ribbon and then click the Move Chart command button or press Alt+JTV.**

   Excel opens the Move Chart dialog box.

2. **Click the New Sheet option button in the Move Chart dialog box.**

3. **(Optional) Rename the generic Chart1 sheet name in the accompanying text box by entering a more descriptive name there.**

4. **Click OK to close the Move Chart dialog box and open the new chart sheet with your pivot chart.**

Figure 2-15 shows a clustered column pivot chart after moving the chart to its own chart sheet in the workbook.

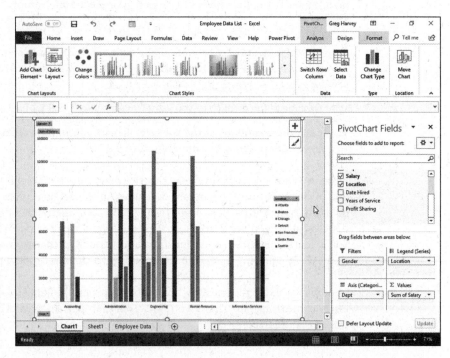

FIGURE 2-15: Clustered column pivot chart moved to its own Pivot Chart sheet.

Filtering a pivot chart

When you graph the data in a pivot table using a typical chart type such as column, bar, or line that uses both an x- and y-axis, the Row labels in the pivot table appear along the x- or category-axis at the bottom of the chart and the Column labels in the pivot table become the data series that are delineated in the chart's legend. The numbers in the Values field are represented on the y- or value-axis that goes up the left side of the chart.

When you generate a new pivot chart, Excel adds drop-down list buttons to each of the types of fields represented. You can then use these drop-down buttons in the pivot chart itself to filter the charted data represented in this fashion like you do the values in the pivot table. Remove the check mark from the (Select All) or (All) option and then add a check mark to each of the fields you still want represented in the filtered pivot chart.

Click the following drop-down buttons to filter a different part of the pivot chart:

» **Report Filter** to filter which data series are represented in the pivot chart

» **Axis Fields (Categories)** to filter the categories that are charted along the x-axis at the bottom of the chart

» **Legend Fields (Series)** to filter the data series shown in columns, bars, or lines in the chart body and identified by the chart's legend

Formatting a pivot chart

The command buttons on the Design and Format tabs attached to the PivotChart Tools contextual tab make it easy to further format and customize your pivot chart. Use the Design tab buttons to select a new chart style for your pivot chart or even a brand-new chart type and further refine your pivot chart by adding chart titles, text boxes, and gridlines. Use the Format tab's buttons to refine the look of any graphics you've added to the chart as well as select a new background color for your chart.

REMEMBER

To get specific information on using the buttons on these tabs, see Book 5, Chapter 1, which covers creating charts from regular worksheet data. The Chart Tools contextual tab that appears when you select a chart you've created contains the same Design and Format tabs with comparable command buttons.

Using the Power Pivot Add-in

The Power Pivot add-in, first introduced in Excel 2010, enables you to efficiently work with and analyze large datasets (such as those with hundreds of thousands or even millions of records) has been made a much more integral part of Excel 2019. In fact, the Power Pivot technology that makes it possible for Excel to easily manage massive amounts of data from many related data tables is now part and parcel of Excel 2019 in the form of its Data Model feature. This means that you don't even have to trot out and use the Power Pivot add-in in order to be able to create Excel pivot tables that utilize tons of data records stored in multiple, related data tables. (See Book 6, Chapter 2 for details.)

If you do decide that you want to use Power Pivot in managing large datasets and doing advanced data modeling in your Excel pivot tables, instead of having to download the add-in from the Microsoft Office website, you can start using Power Pivot simply by activating the add-in as follows:

1. **Click File⇨Options⇨Add-Ins or press Alt+FTAA.**

    Excel opens the Add-Ins tab of the Excel Options dialog box with Excel Add-Ins selected in the Manage drop-down list.

2. **Click the Manage drop-down list button and then select COM Add-Ins from the drop-down list before you select the Go button.**

    Excel displays the COM Add-Ins dialog box that contains (as of this writing) the following COM (Component Object Model) add-ins: Acrobat PDFMaker COM Addin, Microsoft Power Map for Excel, and Microsoft Power Pivot for Excel.

3. **Click the check box in front of Microsoft Office Power Pivot for Excel to select it and then click OK.**

    Excel closes the COM Add-Ins dialog box and returns you to the Excel 2019 worksheet window that now contains a Power Pivot tab at the end of the Ribbon.

TIP

If the Power Pivot tab doesn't appear at the end of the Excel 2019 Ribbon after loading the Microsoft Power Pivot for Excel Com Add-in as outlined in these steps, open the Customize Ribbon tab of the Options dialog box (Alt+FTC). Chances are that the Power Pivot check box under the Main tabs list box on the right hand side is not checked, and all you have to do is to click this check box to put a check mark in it. After you do this and click OK to close the Options dialog box, you should see the Power Pivot tab immediately to the right of the View tab on the Ribbon.

Data modeling with Power Pivot

Power Pivot makes it easy to perform sophisticated modeling with the data in your Excel pivot tables. To open the Power Pivot for Excel window, you click the Manage button in the Data Model group on the Power Pivot tab shown in Figure 2-16.

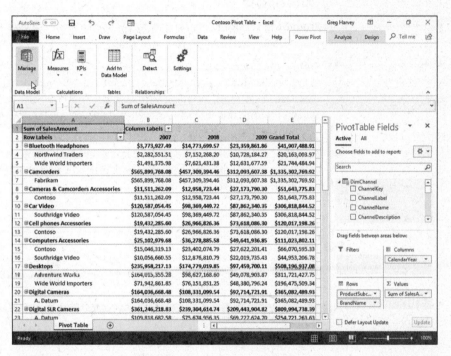

FIGURE 2-16:
Opening the Power Pivot for Excel window with the Manage button on the Power Pivot Ribbon tab.

If your workbook already contains a pivot table that uses a Data Model created with external data already imported in the worksheet (see Book 6, Chapter 2 for details) when you select the Manage button, Excel opens a Power Pivot for Excel window similar to the one shown in Figure 2-17. This window contains tabs at the bottom for all the data tables that you imported for use in the pivot table. You can then review, filter, and sort the records in the data in these tables by selecting their respective tabs followed by the appropriate AutoFilter or Sort command button. (See Book 6, Chapter 1 for details.)

If you open the Power Pivot for Excel window before importing the external data and creating your pivot table in the current Excel workbook, the Power Pivot window is empty of everything except the Ribbon with its three tabs: Home, Design, and Advanced. You can then use the From Database, From Data Service, or From Other Services buttons in the Get External Data group on the Home tab to import the data tables that make your Data Model:

>> **From Database** to import data tables from a Microsoft SQL Server, Microsoft Access database, or from a database on a SQL Server Analysis cube to which you have access

>> **From Data Service** to import data tables from a database via an OData (Open Data) Feed to which you have access

>> **From Other Sources** to open the Table Import Wizard that enables you to import data tables from databases saved in a wide variety of popular database file formats, including Microsoft SQL Azure, Oracle, Teradata, Sybase, Informx, and IBM DB2, as well as data saved in flat files, such as another Excel workbook file or even a text file

>> **Existing Connections** to import the data tables specified by a data query that you've already set up with an existing connection to an external data source (see Book 6, Chapter 2 for details)

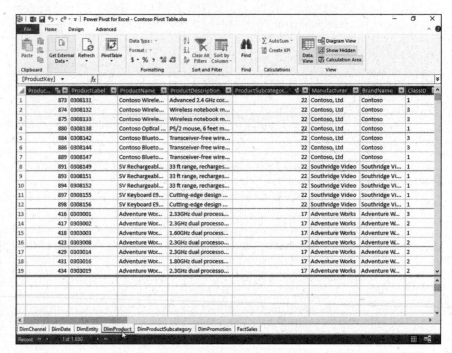

FIGURE 2-17:
The Power Pivot window with tabs for all the data tables imported into Excel when creating the workbook's pivot table.

After you select the source of your external data using one of the command button options available from the Power Pivot window in the Get External Data group, Excel opens a Table Import Wizard with options appropriate for defining the database file or server (or both) that contains the tables you want imported. Be aware that, when creating a connection to import data from most external sources (except for other Excel workbooks and text files), you're required to provide both a recognized username and password.

TIP

If you don't have a username and password but know you have access to the database containing the data you want to use in your new pivot table, import the tables and create the pivot table in the Excel window using the Get Data button's drop-down menus found on the Data tab of its Ribbon and then open the Power Pivot window to use its features in doing your advanced data modeling.

WARNING

You cannot import data tables from the Windows Azure Marketplace or using an OData data feed using the Get External Data command button in the Power Pivot window if Microsoft.NET Full Framework 4.0 or higher is not already installed on the device running Excel 2019. If you don't want to or can't install this very large library of software code describing network communications on your device, you must import the data for your pivot tables from these two sources in the Excel program window, using the appropriate options on its Get Data button's drop-down menu found on the Data tab of its Ribbon.

Switching between the Data View and Diagram View

Diagram View is among the most useful features for data modeling offered by the Excel 2019 PowerPivot add-in. When you switch from the default Data View to Diagram View either by clicking the Diagram View button on the Ribbon or the Diagram button in the lower-right corner to the right of the Display button, all the data tables used in the Data Model are graphically displayed in the PowerPivot window. (See Figure 2-18.)

Each data table graphic object is labeled by name on its title bar and displays within it a list of all its fields. To see all the fields within a particular table, you may have to resize it by dragging the mouse or Touch pointer at its corners or midpoints. To avoid obscuring a data table below when enlarging a table located above it to display more of its fields, you can move either the upper or lower data table out of the way by dragging it by its title bar.

In addition to graphic representations of all data tables in the current Data Model, the Diagram View shows all existing relationships between them. It does this by drawing connecting lines between each of the related tables. The data table containing the primary key field is indicated by a dot at the end of its connecting line and the table containing the foreign key by an arrowhead at the end of its line. To see the name of the key field in each related table, simply click the connecting line: Power Pivot then selects the fields in both tables indicated by surrounding them with blue outlines.

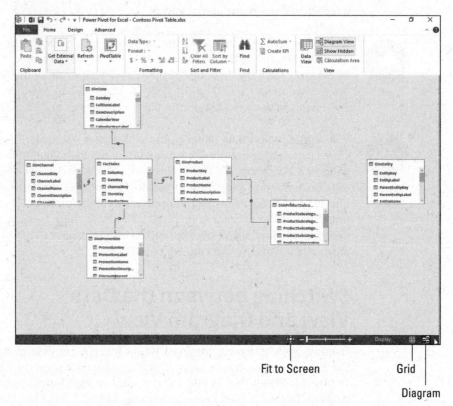

FIGURE 2-18:
Switching from
Data View to
Diagram View in
the Power Pivot
for Excel window.

Not only can you easily review the relationships between data tables in Diagram View, but you can also modify them. The most usual way is to create relationships between unrelated tables by locating their key fields and then literally drawing a line between the tables. To locate fields shared by two data tables in the Power Pivot diagram in either a one-to-one or one-to-many relationship, you can expand the data table graphics to display the entire list of their fields as well as use the Zoom slider at the top of the window beneath the Ribbon to zoom in and out on the tables. (To see all the tables at once, click the Fit to Screen button to the immediate left of the Zoom slider.)

FOR MORE ON DATA MODELING WITH POWER PIVOT FOR EXCEL

Being able to establish relationships between data tables in Diagram View represents just a small part of Power Pivot's data modeling capabilities. To find out more about data modeling with Power Pivot for Excel 2019, be sure to review the online help topics by selecting its Help button in the Power Pivot for Excel window.

In addition to visually locating shared fields, you can also use PowerPivot's search feature (by clicking the Find button on the Home tab) to search for particular field names. When you locate two tables that share a field that might work as a key field, you can relate them simply by dragging a line from the potential key field in one table to the key field in the other. When you release the mouse button or remove your finger or stylus on a touchscreen device, Excel draws a blue outline between the tables indicating the new relationship based on the two shared fields.

WARNING

If the shared fields don't represent a one-to-one or one-to-many relationship (see Book 6, Chapter 2 for details) because the values in one or both are not unique, Excel displays an alert dialog box indicating that the PowerPivot is not able to establish a relationship between your tables. In such a case, you are forced to find another data table in the Data Model that contains the same field, but this time with unique values (that is, no duplicates). If no such field exists, you'll be unable to add to the table in question to the Data Model and, as a result, your Excel pivot table won't be able to summarize its data.

TIP

To make it easier to draw the line that creates the relationship between two data tables with a shared key field, you should position the tables near one another in the Diagram View. Remember that you can move the data table graphic objects around in the Power Pivot for Excel window simply by dragging them by their title bars.

Adding calculated columns courtesy of DAX

DAX stands for Data Analysis Expression and is the name of the language that Power Pivot for Excel uses to create calculations between the columns (fields) in your Excel Data Model. Fortunately, creating a calculation with DAX is more like creating an Excel formula that uses a built-in function than it is like using a programming language such as VBA or HTML.

This similarity is underscored by the fact that all DAX expressions start with an equal sign just like all standard Excel formulas and that as soon as you start typing the first letters of the name of a DAX function you want to use in the expression you're building, an Insert Function–like drop-down menu with all the DAX functions whose names start with those same letters appears. And as soon as you select the DAX function you want to use from this menu, PowerPivot not only inserts the name of the DAX function on the PowerPivot Formula bar (which has the same Cancel, Enter, and Insert Function buttons as the Excel Formula bar), but also displays the complete syntax of the function, showing all the required and optional arguments of that function immediately below the Formula bar.

In addition to using DAX functions in the expressions you create for calculated columns in your Data Model, you can also create simpler expressions using the good old arithmetic operators that you know so well from your Excel formulas (+ for addition, – for subtraction, * for multiplication, / for division, and so on).

To create a calculated column for your Data Model, PowerPivot must be in Data View. (If you're in Diagram View, you can switch back by clicking the Data View command button on the Power Pivot window's Home tab or by clicking the Grid button in the lower right corner of the PowerPivot window.) When Power Pivot for Excel is in Data View, you can create a new calculated field by following these steps:

1. **Click the tab of the data table in the Power Pivot window to which you want to add the calculated column.**

2. **Click the Add button on the Design tab of the Power Pivot Ribbon.**

   Power Pivot adds a new column at the end of the current data table with the generic field name, *Add Column.*

3. **Type = (equal sign) to begin building your DAX expression.**

   PowerPivot activates its Formula bar where it inserts the equal to sign.

4. **Build your DAX expression on the Power Pivot Formula bar more or less as you build an Excel formula in a cell of one of its worksheets.**

   To use a DAX function in the expression, click the Insert Function button on the Power Pivot Formula bar and select the function to use in the Insert Function dialog box (which is very similar to the standard Excel Insert Function dialog box except that it contains only DAX functions). To define an arithmetic or text calculation between columns in the current data table, you select the columns to use by clicking them in the data table interspersed with the appropriate operator. (See Table 1-1 in Book 3, Chapter 1 for a complete list of operators.)

   To select a field to use in a calculation or as an argument in a DAX function, click its field name at the top of its column to add it to the expression on the

Power Pivot Formula bar. Note that Power Pivot automatically encloses all field names used in DAX expressions in a pair of square brackets as in

```
=[UnitPrice]*[Quantity]
```

where you're building an expression in an extended price calculated column that multiplies the values in the UnitPrice field by those in the Quantity field of the active data table.

5. **Click the Enter button on the Power Pivot Formula bar to complete the expression and have it calculated.**

As soon as you click the Enter button, Power Pivot performs the calculations specified by the expression you just created, returning the results to the new column. (This may take several moments depending upon the number of records in the data table.) As soon as Power Pivot completes the calculations, the results appear in the cells of the Add Column field. You can then rename the column by double-clicking its *Add Column* generic name, typing in the new field name, and pressing Enter.

After creating a calculated column to your data table, you can view its DAX expression simply by clicking its field name at the top of its column in the Power Pivot Data View. If you ever need to edit its expression, you can do so simply by clicking the field name to select the entire column and then click the insertion point in the DAX expression displayed on the PowerPivot Formula bar. If you no longer need the calculated column in the pivot table for its Data Model, you can remove it by right-clicking the column and then selecting Delete Columns on its shortcut menu. If you simply want to hide the column from the Data View, you select the Hide from Client Tools item on this shortcut menu.

REMEMBER

Keep in mind that DAX expressions using arithmetic and logical operators follow the same order of operator precedence as in regular Excel formulas. If you ever need to alter this natural order, you must use nested parentheses in the DAX expression to alter the order as you do in Excel formulas. (See Book 3, Chapter 1 for details.) Just be careful when adding these parentheses that you don't disturb any of the square brackets that always enclose the name of any data table field referred to in the DAX expression.

Using the 3D Map feature

3D Map is the new name of an exciting visual analysis feature formerly known as Power Map in Excel 2016. 3D Map enables you to use geographical, financial, and other types of data along with date and time fields in your Excel data model to create animated 3-D map tours.

To create a new animation for the first tour in 3D Map, you follow these general steps:

1. **Open the worksheet that contains the data for which you want to create the new Power Map animation.**

2. **Position the cell cursor in one of the cells in the data list and then click Insert⇨3D Map⇨Open Power Map (Alt+NSMO) on the Excel Ribbon.**

   Excel opens a 3D Map window with a new Tour (named Tour 1) with its own Ribbon with a single Home tab similar to the one shown in Figure 2-21. This window is divided into three panes. The Layer pane on the right contains an outline of the default Layer 1 with three areas: Data, Filters, and Layer Options. The Data area in the Layer Pane is automatically expanded to display a Location, Height, Category, and Time list box. The central pane contains a 3-D globe on which your data will be mapped. A floating Field List containing fields in the selected Excel data model initially appears over this 3-D globe. The left Tour Editor pane contains thumbnails of all the tours and their scenes animated for your data model in 3D Map (by default, there is just one scene marked Scene 1 when you create your first tour).

3. **Drag fields from the floating Field List to the Location, Height, Category, and Time list boxes in the Layer Pane to build your map.**

   Drag the geographical fields whose location data are to be represented visually on the globe map and drop them into the Location list box in the Layer Pane. 3D Map displays data points for each location field for your animation on the 3-D globe as you drop it into the Location list box. The program associates the selected location field with a geographical type in the drop-down list box to the right of the field name in the Location list box in the Layer pane. You can modify the type by selecting its drop-down button, if necessary. Just keep in mind that each location field needs to have a unique geographical type.

   You also add fields from the floating Field List that you want depicted in the animation to the Height, Size, or Value list boxes (depending upon the type of visualization selected) as follows:

   - Add values you want represented in the type of chart displayed on the 3-D map to the Height list box. By default, Excel uses the Sum function for value fields, but you can change this function to Average, Count, Maximum, Minimum, or No Aggregation by clicking its drop-down button in the Location list box.

   - Add data fields that you want to appear as categories in the legend for the 3D Map animation to Category list box. The items in this field are automatically added to a floating legend in the 3-D map if your chart type has a legend.

- Add date and time fields to the Time list box to set the time element for your 3D Map animation. By default, 3D Map does not associate the fields you add here to any time unit. You can specify the time unit by selecting Second, Minute, Hour, Day, Month, Quarter, or Year from the field's drop-down list button in the Time list box.

4. **Select the type of visualization by clicking its icon under the Data heading in the Layer Pane: Stacked Column (default), Clustered Column, Bubble, Heat Map, or Region.**

   3D Map now displays data points for your Height, Size, or Value data on the 3-D globe appropriate to the type of visualization selected along with a floating legend for the data values (organized by any fields used as categories) in the center pane of the 3D Map window. At the bottom of the map, you see a Time Line control with a play button that enables you to play and control the animation (see Figure 2-19).

5. **(Optional) Click the Map Labels button on the Ribbon to add country and city names to the maps on your 3-D globe.**

6. **(Optional) Click the Close the Layer Pane button and Close the Tour Editor button to hide the display of Layer and Tour Editor panes, respectively.**

   Now, your 3-D globe with the Layer 1 legend on the right side and animation timeline below fill the entire window below the 3D Map Ribbon. Note that you can redisplay the Layer pane and the Tour Editor pane in the 3D Map window at any time by clicking the Layer Pane or Tour Editor Ribbon buttons, respectively.

7. **(Optional) Drag the Layer 1 legend so that it's not obstructing your 3-D globe. You can also resize the legend by selecting it and then dragging its sizing handles. If the Time Line animation control is obstructing key areas of the globe, you can hide it by clicking its Close button.**

   You can redisplay the Time Line control at any time by clicking the Time Line button in the Time group on the 3D Map Ribbon. Note that you can't reposition or resize the Time Line control when it is displayed and that you can play your animation by clicking the Play Tour button on the Ribbon when the Time Line control is hidden.

8. **(Optional) Drag the globe to display the area of the world with the locations you want to watch when you play your animation or use the Rotate Left (Shift+@--left), Rotate Right (Shift+@--right), Tilt Up (Shift+@--up), or Tilt Down (Shift+@--down) buttons to bring this area into view. Then, click the Zoom In (Shift+ +) or Zoom Out (Shift + -) to bring the area closer into view or further away.**

   Once you have the viewing window beneath the 3D Map Ribbon positioned the way you want it when viewing your animation, you are ready to play the 3-D map tour you've created.

9. Click the Play Tour button on the Ribbon or the Play button on the Time Line control (if it's still visible).

When you click the Play Tour button on the Ribbon, 3D Map automatically hides the Tour Editor and Layer pane along with the Time Line control if they are still visible at that time. You can pause the animation by clicking the Pause button that appears in a cluster of controllers in a bar at the bottom of the screen or by pressing the spacebar on your keyboard. When you're finished watching the animation, return to the regular Editing view of 3D Map by clicking the Go Back to Edit View button (the one with the arrow pointing left at the very beginning of the bar at the bottom of the screen) or press the Esc key on your keyboard.

10. Click the Close button in the far right corner of the 3D Map title bar to close 3D Map and return to your Excel worksheet and then save the workbook (Ctrl+S) to save your 3D Map tour as part of the workbook file.

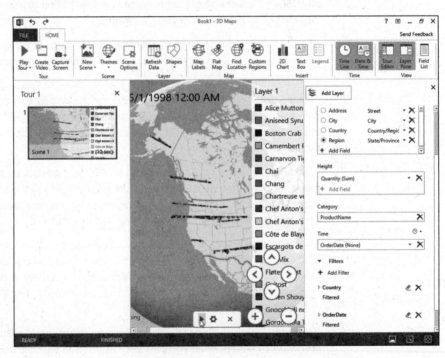

FIGURE 2-19:
3D Map window with new Clustered Column 3-D animation for visualizing the quantities ordered of various Northwind items between July 1996 and May 1998 at various locations in western Canada and United States.

After you create your initial animation tour for the data model in your Excel workbook, you can always replay it simply by reopening it in 3D Map and clicking Play Tour on its Ribbon. To reopen the tour when the workbook with the data model is open in Excel, select Insert⇨3D Map⇨Open Power Map on the Excel Ribbon (Alt+NSMO) and then click the Tour 1 button at the top of the Launch Power Map dialog box.

Once the tour is open in 3D Map, you can also edit it. You can change the appearance of the 3-D globe in your animation by selecting a new theme by clicking the Themes button in Scene group of the 3D Map Ribbon and then selecting a thumbnail on this button's drop-down palette. You can flatten 3-D globe to make it two-dimensional by clicking the Flat Map button in the Map group of the Ribbon.

You can also add new layers to your original scene that animate a different data set over the same or a different set of date and time values. To add a new layer, click the Add Layer button in the Layer group of the 3D Map Ribbon and then define the type of visualization and the fields to use in your data model for the location, analysis, and time (following the same steps as outlined earlier for creating the initial layer of the first scene of a new tour). After you add a new layer (automatically named Layer 1) to your original scene, 3D Map shows the legends for both Layer 1 and 2 (which often overlap and need to be separated manually). 3D Map also shows the data points for each layer's location, analysis, category, and time fields when you play the animation.

If you want to see the animation for just one of the layers in your scene, you hide all the other layers before you play the animation. To do this, click the Layer Manager button at far left on the top of the Layer Pane and then click the Show or Hide Layer button (the one with the CBS eyeball icon) in front of the name of all layers you don't want to view in the animation.

In addition to adding new layers to a scene, you can also add entirely new scenes to your tour that use a copy of the active scene, a new 3-D globe world, or a custom map with an entirely new background. To create a new scene, click the New Scene button in the Scene group of the 3D Map Ribbon and then click Copy Scene, World Map, or New Custom Map options on its drop-down menu. After you select the type of scene, you then define the animation for the new scene using the steps you followed earlier in creating the opening animation for the first layer in the first scene of the tour. To play the animations you add to the layers of any new scene you add to your 3D Map tour, you simply click the Scene thumbnail in the Tour Editor pane before you click the Play Tour button on the Ribbon or the Play button on its Time Line controller.

TIP

Use the Create Video and Capture Screen buttons in the Tour group of the 3D Map Ribbon to share completed animations with your colleagues and clients. Click Capture Screen to take a static picture of the visualization displayed on your 3-D globe that Excel saves in the Office Clipboard. Once in the Clipboard, you can use the Paste feature (Ctrl+V) to paste the graphic into a worksheet after you close 3D Map and return to Excel.

Click the Create Video button to create a video of the animation for the currently selected scene and layer(s) in your tour. When you click this button, 3D Map opens a Create Video dialog box where you choose the quality of the video selecting one of the following option buttons: Presentation & HD Displays (largest size and best quality at 1080 pixels), Computers and Tablets (medium size and quality at 720 pixels), or Quick Export & Mobile (lowest quality and smallest size at 320 pixels). If you want an existing music or narration file to accompany the animation, click the Soundtrack Options button and then select the sound file and the playback options followed by Apply before you click the Create button to make the video. 3D Map then generates a video of the currently selected animation saved as .mp4 video file in your device's default Video folder. You can then save this video file to a folder on your OneDrive or Dropbox to share with colleagues or clients. You can also play the video on your device using its default video player.

Creating Forecast Worksheets

The Forecast Sheet feature in Excel 2019 makes it super easy to turn a worksheet containing historical financial data into a remarkable visual forecast worksheet. All you do is open the worksheet with your historical data, position the cell cursor in one of its cells, and then click the Forecast Sheet button on the Data Tab of the Ribbon (Alt+AFC).

Excel then selects all the historical data in the surrounding worksheet table (which typically includes a column for dates as well as one for the related financial data) while at the same time opening the Create Forecast Worksheet dialog box (similar to the one shown in Figure 2-20).

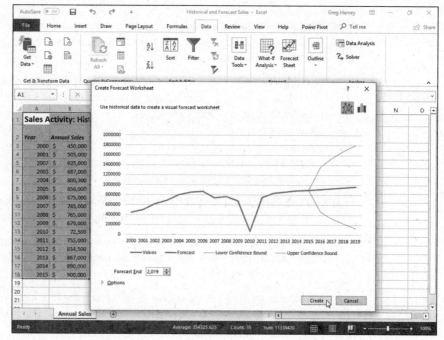

FIGURE 2-20:
Defining the options for a new line chart that shows historical and projected sales in the Create a Forecast Worksheet dialog box.

By default, Excel selects a line chart to visually depict the trends in its forecast, but, if you wish, you can have the program use a column chart instead. Simply click the Column Chart icon to the immediate right of the Line Chart icon at the top of the Create Forecast Worksheet dialog box.

In addition to selecting the type of chart to be used in the forecast worksheet, you can also control the date at which the forecast chart ends. You do this by selecting a new date in the Forecast End text box that appears below the preview of the embedded line or column chart. For example, in Figure 2-21, my historical data table includes annual sales for the years 2000 through 2015, and Excel automatically uses this data to extend the forecast end date out four years to 2019. If I wanted to extend the forecast beyond this end date, I would simply enter the new year into the Forecast End text box (or select one with the spinner buttons).

Beneath the Forecast End text box in the Create Forecast Worksheet dialog box, you find an Options button that when clicked (as shown in Figure 2-21) expands the dialog box to include the following options:

>> **Forecast Start** enables you to select a starting date in the historical data later than the one Excel automatically selects (which is the first date in the worksheet table).

>> **Confidence Interval** allows you to select a new degree confidence that Excel uses to set the Lower- and Upper Confidence Bound line in the forecast when using the default line chart.

>> **Seasonally** changes from the Detect Automatically to Set Manually option where you can enter or select a new value indicating the number of points in the values range of your data table that are part of a recurring seasonal pattern. When Excel can't automatically detect seasonality in your worksheet data, a warning appears (shown in Figure 2-21) that so advises you and suggests that you select the Set Manually option button (and leave the default setting at zero) to get better results in the forecast.

>> **Include Forecast Statistics** has Excel include a table of forecast accuracy metrics and smoothing factors in the resulting forecast worksheet.

>> **Timeline Range** modifies the cell range containing the date values in your historical data (by default, Excel selects all these values it identifies in the current worksheet table).

>> **Values Range** modifies the cell range containing the financial values in your historical data (by default, Excel selects all these values it identifies in the current worksheet table).

>> **Fill Missing Points Using** to have Excel automatically fill in any missing data points it finds in the worksheet table in the forecast chart using either interpolation or zeros.

>> **Aggregate Duplicates Using** modifies the statistical function.

After selecting all the desired options in the Create Forecast Worksheet dialog box, you have only to click the Create button to have Excel create a new forecast worksheet. This new sheet contains a formatted data table that combines your historical data with the forecast values as well as an embedded line or column chart (depending upon your selection) depicting the trend in both the historical and forecast values.

Figure 2-21 shows the brand new forecast worksheet that the Excel Forecast Sheet feature created for me using the original historical sales data shown in Figure 2-21 after I selected Set Manually option button with the setting at zero and selected the Include Forecast Statistics check box before clicking Create in the Create Forecast Worksheet dialog box. As you can see, Excel placed this new forecast worksheet (named Sheet1) before the worksheet containing my historical data (named Annual Sales).

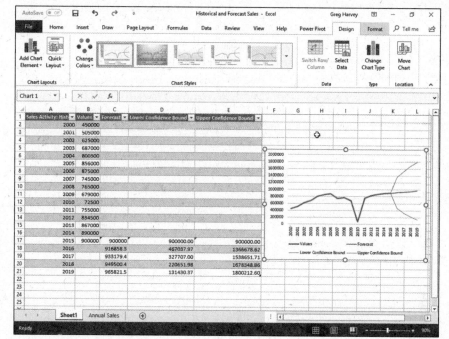

FIGURE 2-21:
Worksheet with
embedded line
chart depicting
historical and
forecast sales
created with the
Forecast Sheet
feature.

Note that in order to display all the forecast values in the new formatted data table in Figure 2-21, I repositioned and resized the embedded line chart so that it fits nicely in the lower-right corner before taking the screenshot. If I wanted, I could move this chart to its own chart sheet before saving the new forecast table and chart as part of the Historical and Forecast Sales workbook.

8

Macros and VBA

Contents at a Glance

IN THIS CHAPTER

» **Understanding how macros do what they do**

» **Recording macros for instant playback**

» **Using the relative option when recording macros**

» **Running the macros you've recorded**

» **Changing the macro security settings**

» **Assigning your macros to the Ribbon and Quick Access toolbar**

Chapter **1**

Recording and Running Macros

M acros enable you to automate almost any task that you can undertake in Excel 2019. By using Excel's macro recorder to record tasks that you perform routinely, you not only speed up the procedure considerably (because Excel can play back your keystrokes and mouse actions much faster than you can perform them manually), but you are also assured that each step in the task is carried out the same way each and every time you perform the task.

Excel's macro recorder records all the commands and keystrokes that you make in a language called Visual Basic for Applications (VBA), which is a special version of the BASIC programming language developed and refined by the good folks at Microsoft for use with all their Office application programs. You can then use Excel's Visual Basic Editor to display and make changes to the macro's VBA code.

In this chapter, you find out how to use Excel's macro recorder to record, test, and play back macros that you use to automate repetitive tasks required when building and using your Excel worksheets and charts. In the next chapter, you find out how to use Excel's Visual Basic Editor to debug and edit the macros that you record, as well as to create complex macros that run custom functions and set up and run custom Excel applications, complete with their own pull-down menus and dialog boxes.

Macro Basics

You can create macros in one of two ways:

>> Use Excel's macro recorder to record your actions as you undertake them in a worksheet.

>> Enter the instructions that you want followed in VBA code in the Visual Basic Editor.

Either way, Excel creates a special *module* sheet that holds the actions and instructions in your macro. The macro instructions in a macro module (whether recorded by Excel or written by you) are stored in the Visual Basic for Applications programming language.

You can then study the VBA code that the macro recorder creates and edit this code in the Visual Basic Editor, which you open by clicking the Visual Basic command button on the Developer tab (when this optional tab is displayed on the Ribbon) or by pressing Alt+F11.

Recording macros

With Excel's macro recorder, you can create many of the utility-type macros that help you to perform the repetitive tasks necessary for creating and editing your worksheets and charts. When you turn on the macro recorder, the macro recorder records all your actions in the active worksheet or chart sheet as you make them. Note that the macro recorder doesn't record the keystrokes or mouse actions that you take to accomplish an action — only the VBA code required to perform the action itself. This means that mistakes that you make while taking an action that you rectify won't be recorded as part of the macro; for example, if you make a typing error and then edit it while the macro recorder is on, only the corrected entry shows up in the macro without the original mistakes and steps taken to remedy them.

The macros that you create with the macro recorder can be stored either as part of the current workbook, in a new workbook, or in a special, globally available Personal Macro Workbook named PERSONAL.XLSB that's stored in a folder called XLSTART on your hard disk. When you record a macro as part of your Personal Macro Workbook, you can run that macro from any workbook that you have open. (This is because the PERSONAL.XLSB workbook is secretly opened whenever you launch Excel, and although it remains hidden, its macros are always available.) When you record macros as part of the current workbook or a new workbook, you can run those macros only when the workbook in which they were recorded is open in Excel.

When you create a macro with the macro recorder, you decide not only the workbook in which to store the macro but also what name and shortcut keystrokes to assign to the macro that you are creating. When assigning a name for your macro, use the same guidelines that you use when you assign a standard range name to a cell range in your worksheet. When assigning a shortcut keystroke to run the macro, you can assign

>> The Ctrl key plus a letter from A to Z, as in Ctrl+Q

>> Ctrl+Shift and a letter from A to Z, as in Ctrl+Shift+Q

You can't, however, assign the Ctrl key plus a punctuation or number key (such as Ctrl+1 or Ctrl+/) to your macro.

The Ribbon's View tab contains a Macros command button to which a drop-down menu containing the following three options is attached:

>> **View Macros:** Opens the Macro dialog box where you can select a macro to run or edit (Alt+WMV).

>> **Record Macro:** Opens the Record Macro dialog box where you define the settings for your new macro and then start the macro recorder; this is the same as clicking the Record Macro button on the Status bar (Alt+WMR).

>> **Use Relative References:** Uses relative cell addresses when recording a macro, making the macro more versatile by enabling you to run it in areas of a worksheet other than the ones originally used in the macro's recording (Alt+WMU).

Excel 2019 also enables you to add a Developer tab to the Ribbon. This tab contains a Record Macro and Use Relative References button that you can use in recording your macros. To add the Developer tab to the Excel 2019 Ribbon, you follow these two steps:

1. **Click File⇨Options and then click the Customize Ribbon tab or press Alt+FTC.**

    Excel opens the Customize the Ribbon pane within the Excel Options dialog box.

2. **Click the Developer check box in the Main Tabs list on the right side of the Customize the Ribbon pane in the Excel Options dialog box and then click OK.**

You can then turn on the macro recorder by doing any of the following:

>> Click the Record Macro button on the Excel Status bar (to the immediate right of the Ready indicator)

>> Click the Record Macro option on the Macros drop-down button on the View tab (Alt+WMR)

>> Click the Record Macro command button on the Developer tab (Alt+LR)

No matter how you turn on the macro recorder, once you do, it records all your actions in the active worksheet or chart sheet as you make them.

To see how easy it is to create a macro with the macro recorder, follow along with these steps for creating a macro that enters the company name in 12-point, bold type and centers the company name across rows A through E with the Merge and Center feature:

1. **Open the Excel workbook that contains the worksheet data or chart you want your macro to work with.**

   If you're building a macro that adds new data to a worksheet (as in this example), open a worksheet with plenty of blank cells in which to add the data. If you're building a macro that needs to be in a particular cell when its steps are played back, put the cell cursor in that cell.

2. **Click the Record Macro button on the Status bar or select the Record Macro option on the Macros command button on the View tab or press Alt+WMR.**

   The Record Macro dialog box opens, similar to the one shown in Figure 1-1, where you enter the macro name, define any keystroke shortcut, select the workbook in which to store the macro, and enter a description of the macro's function.

3. **Replace the Macro1 temporary macro name by entering your name for the macro in the Macro Name text box.**

   When naming a macro, you must not use spaces in the macro name and it must begin with a letter and not some number or punctuation symbol. For this example macro, you replace Macro1 in the Macro Name text box with the name Company_Name.

   REMEMBER

   Next, you can enter a letter between A and Z that acts like a shortcut key for running the macro when you press Ctrl followed by that letter key. Just remember that Excel has already assigned a number of Ctrl+letter keystroke shortcuts for doing common tasks, such as Ctrl+C for copying an item to the Clipboard and Ctrl+V for pasting an item from the Clipboard into the worksheet. If you assign the same keystrokes to the macro that you're building, your macro's shortcut keys override and, therefore, disable Excel's ready-made shortcut keystrokes.

4. **(Optional) Click the Shortcut Key text box and then press the letter of the alphabet that you want to assign to the Ctrl key combination that can run the macro.**

For this example macro, you simply press Shift+C to assign Ctrl+Shift+C as the shortcut keystroke (so as not to disable the ready-made Ctrl+C shortcut).

Next, you need to decide where to save the new macro that you're building. Select Personal Macro Workbook from the Store Macro In drop-down list box to be able to run the macro anytime you like. Select This Workbook (the default) when you need to run the macro only when the current workbook is open. Select New Workbook if you want to open a new workbook in which to record and save the new macro.

5. **Select the Personal Macro Workbook, New Workbook, or This Workbook item from the Store Macro In drop-down list to indicate where to store the new macro.**

For this example macro, select the Personal Macro Workbook so that you can use it to enter the company name in any Excel workbook that you create or edit.

TIP

Next, you should document the purpose and functioning of your macro in the Description list box. Although this step is purely optional, it is a good idea to get in the habit of recording this information every time you build a new macro so that you and your coworkers can always know what to expect from the macro when any of you run it.

6. **(Optional) Click the Description list box and then insert a brief description of the macro's purpose in front of the information indicating the date and who recorded the macro.**

Now you're ready to close the Record Macro dialog box and start recording your macro.

7. **Click OK to close the Record Macro dialog box.**

When you do this, the Record Macro dialog box closes. Click the Use Relative References option on the Macros command button on the View tab or the Use Relative References command button on the Developer tab (when it's displayed) when you want the macro recorder to record the macro relative to the position of the current cell. Doing this often makes a macro more versatile as it enables you to run the macro in areas in the worksheet other than the cells used in its original recording.

8. (Optional) Click the Use Relative References option on the Macros command button on the View tab (Alt+WMU) or click the Use Relative References command button on the Developer tab (Alt+LU) if you want to be able to play back the macro anywhere in the worksheet.

9. Select the cells, enter the data, and click the Excel commands required to perform the tasks that you want recorded just as you normally would in creating or editing the current worksheet, using either the keyboard or the mouse or a combination of the two.

For the example macro, all you do is type the company name and click the Enter button on the Formula bar to complete the entry in the current cell. Next, click the Bold button and then click 12 on the Font Size drop-down list on the Formatting toolbar. Finally, drag through cells A1:E1 to select this range and then click the Merge and Center button, again on the Formatting toolbar.

After you finish taking all the actions in Excel that you want recorded, you're ready to shut off the macro recorder.

10. Click the Stop Recording button on the Excel Status bar or Stop Recording option on the Macros button's drop-down menu on the View tab or the Stop Recording button in the Code group of the Developer tab.

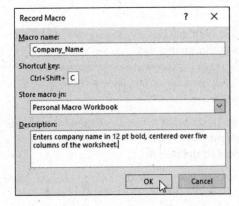

FIGURE 1-1:
Getting ready to record the Company_Name macro in the Record Macro dialog box.

TIP

The Record Macro/Stop Recording button to the Status bar (to the immediate right of the Ready status indicator) is by far the most direct and easiest way to turn the macro recorder on and off. When using it to record a new macro, as soon as you click OK in the Record Macro dialog box to actually start recording your actions, this Record Macro button on the Status bar changes to a Stop Recording button, and you can click it when you are done recording all the actions to be included in the macro.

Running a macro

After recording a macro, you can run it by doing any of the following:

>> Click the View Macros option on the Macros command button on the View tab or press Alt+WMV.

>> Click the Macros command button on the Developer tab of the Ribbon when it's displayed or press Alt+LPM.

>> Press Alt+F8.

Excel then opens the Macro dialog box, which is similar to the one shown in Figure 1-2. As this figure shows, Excel lists the names of all the macros in the current workbook and in your Personal Macro Workbook (provided you've created one) in the Macro Name list box. Click the name of the macro that you want to play and click the Run button or press Enter.

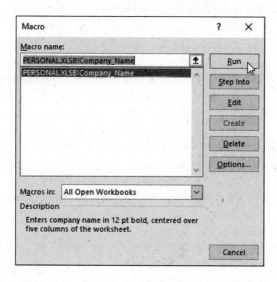

FIGURE 1-2:
Selecting the macro to run in the Macro dialog box.

If you assigned a shortcut keystroke to the macro, you don't have to bother opening the Macro dialog box to play the macro: Simply press Ctrl plus the letter key or Ctrl+Shift plus the letter key that you assigned and Excel immediately plays back all of the commands that you recorded.

REMEMBER

Before testing a new macro, you may need to select a new worksheet or at least a new cell range within the active worksheet. When recording cell references in a macro, the macro recorder always inserts absolute references in the macro sheet unless you click the Relative Reference button on the Stop Recording toolbar before you start choosing the commands and taking the actions in the spreadsheet that you want recorded as part of the macro. This means that your macro enters its data entries or performs its formatting in the same area of the active worksheet (unless the code in the macro itself causes the macro to first select a new area or select a new sheet in the active workbook).

If you run your macro in a worksheet that already contains data in the cells that the macro uses, you run the risk of having existing data and/or formatting over-written during the macro's execution. Keep in mind that, although you can use the Undo feature to reverse the very last action performed by your macro, most macros perform a series of actions, so you may end up using multiple levels of Undo before you are able to successfully reconstruct your spreadsheet.

Assigning Macros to the Ribbon and the Quick Access Toolbar

Instead of running a macro by selecting it in the Macro dialog box or by pressing shortcut keys you assign to it, you can assign the macro to a custom tab on the Ribbon or a custom button on the Quick Access toolbar and then run it by clicking that custom button.

Adding your macros to a custom tab on the Ribbon

To assign a macro to a custom tab on the Excel 2019 Ribbon, you follow these steps:

1. **Click File⇨Options and then click the Custom Ribbon button in the Excel Options dialog box (or press Alt+FTC).**

   Excel displays the Customize the Ribbon pane in the Excel Options dialog box.

2. **Click Macros in the Choose Commands From drop-down list box on the left.**

   Excel lists the names of the all the macros created in the current workbook and saved in the PERSONAL.XLSB workbook in the Choose Commands From list box.

3. **Click the name of the custom group on the custom tab to which you want to add the macro in the Main Tabs list box on the right.**

   If you haven't already created a custom tab and group for the macro or need to create a new one, you then need to follow these steps:

a. *Click the New Tab button at the bottom of the Main Tabs list.*

Excel adds both a New Tab (Custom) and New Group (Custom) item to the Main Tabs list while at the same time selecting the New Group (Custom) item.

b. *Click the New Tab (Custom) item you just added to the Main Tabs.*

c. *Click the Rename button at the bottom of the Main Tabs list box and then type a display name for the new custom tab before you click OK.*

d. *Click the New Group (Custom) item right below the custom tab you just renamed.*

e. *Click the Rename button and then type a display name for the new custom group before you click OK.*

4. **In the Choose Commands From list box on the left, click the name of the macro you want to add to the custom group now selected in the Main Tabs list box on the right.**

5. **Click the Add button to add the selected macro to the selected custom group on your custom tab and then click the OK button to close the Excel options dialog box.**

After you add a macro to the custom group of a custom Ribbon tab, the name of the macro then appears on a button sporting a generic icon (a programming diagram chart) when you select the custom tab on the Ribbon. All you have to do to run the macro is to click this macro command button.

Adding your macros to custom buttons on the Quick Access toolbar

To assign a macro to a custom button on the Quick Access toolbar, you follow these steps:

1. **Click the Customize Quick Access Toolbar button at the end of the Quick Access toolbar and then click More Commands from the drop-down menu to open the Quick Access Toolbar tab of the Excel Options dialog box.**

2. **Select Macros from the Choose Commands From drop-down list box.**

Excel lists the names of the all the macros created in the current workbook and saved in the PERSONAL.XLSB workbook in the Choose Commands From list box.

3. **Click the name of the macro to add to a custom button on the Quick Access toolbar in the Choose Commands From list box and then click the Add button.**

4. **Click OK to close the Excel Options dialog box.**

After you close the Excel Options dialog box, a custom button with a generic macro icon (picturing a standard command flowchart icon) appears on the Quick Access toolbar. To see the name of the macro assigned to this custom macro button as a ScreenTip, position the mouse pointer over the button. To run the macro, click the button.

REMEMBER

Keep in mind that you can also assign macros to the graphic objects you add to your worksheet, including shapes you draw, clip art, and pictures you import. To assign a macro to a graphic object, right-click it and then click the Assign Macro option from its shortcut menu. Then click the name of the recorded macro to run in the list box of the Assign Macro dialog box and click OK. Thereafter, when you position the mouse pointer over the graphic object, the pointer becomes a hand with a pointing index finger (just like when you assign a hyperlink to a graphic — see Book 4, Chapter 2), indicating that you can click it to run the macro.

Macro Security

Excel 2019 uses a system called Microsoft Authenticode that enables developers to authenticate their macro projects or add-ins created with Visual Basic for Applications by a process referred to as *digital signing.* When you run a macro in your worksheet that's not saved in the trusted locations on your computer, such as the Templates and XLSTART folder in your user area on the computer, Excel checks to see whether the macro is digitally signed and that the signature is both valid and current. The macro's developer must have a certificate issued by a reputable authority or a trusted publisher.

If the program cannot verify a macro's digital signature (perhaps because it doesn't have one) or the trustworthiness of its macro publisher, the program then displays a security alert on the message bar underneath the Excel Ribbon. This alert area contains an Enable Content and a Trust Center command button. You can then click the Enable Content button to ignore the alert and go ahead and run the macro, assuming that you can vouch for the macro's publisher and are sure that running the macro poses no security risk to your computer. You click the Trust Center command button in the security alert on the message bar to open the Trust Center dialog box, where you can add to the trusted locations on your computer system and change the macro security settings.

REMEMBER

You can also open the Macro Settings tab of the Trust Center dialog box by clicking the Macro Security command button on the Developer tab (Alt+LAS) or clicking the Trust Center Settings button on the Trust Center tab of the Excel Options dialog box (Alt+FTT).

By default, Excel selects the Disable All Macros with Notification option button on the Macro Settings tab of the Trust Center dialog box. When this setting is selected, all macros that are not saved in one of the trusted locations are automatically disabled in the worksheet, but you do get a security alert each time you try to run one of these macros that enables you to ignore the alert and go ahead and run the macro by clicking the Enable Content button.

The Macro Settings tab of the Trust Center dialog box also contains these other option you can select:

>> **Disable All Macros without Notification** to disable all macros not saved in one of your computer's trusted locations and all security alerts so that you and the other users of the worksheet have no way to ignore the alert and run the macro. Select this option when you don't trust someone else's macros and want to make it impossible to run a macro carrying a computer virus.

>> **Disable All Macros with Notification** (the default) to control the disabling of macros not saved in one of your computer's trusted locations and security alerts. When you select this setting, worksheet users can't ignore the alert and run the macro. Select this option when you want to maintain control over running potentially untrustworthy macros.

>> **Disable All Macros except Digitally Signed Macros** to automatically enable digitally signed macros from a publisher that you've indicated is trustworthy and to disable all macros that are not digitally signed without notification. When you select this option and try to run a digitally signed macro that's not from a publisher you've indicated is trustworthy, Excel displays an alert in the message bar with a Trust All Documents from this Publisher button that you can select, thereby adding the publisher to the trusted list.

WARNING

>> **Enable All Macros (Not Recommended; Potentially Dangerous Code Can Run)** to throw all caution to the wind and allow all macros to run in any worksheet you open — this is one option you never ever want to select, because it could cause serious damage to your machine!

>> **Trust Access to the VBA Project Object Model** to grant access to Visual Basic for Applications object model (see Book 8, Chapter 2) from an automation client.

To change the trusted locations on your computer, you need to click the Trusted Locations tab in the Trust Center dialog box. You can then use these options to change the location settings:

>> **Add New Location:** Use this command button to open the Microsoft Office Trusted Location dialog box, where you select a new folder on your computer as a trusted location either by entering its directory pathname in the Path text

box or selecting it with the Browse button. Click the Subfolders of This Location Are Also Trusted check box if you want all subfolders within the designated folder to be included as trusted locations.

>> **Allow Trusted Locations on My Network (Not Recommended):** Click this check box so that you can designate folders to which you have access on your local network as trusted locations using the Add New Location command button (as described in the immediately preceding bullet point).

>> **Disable All Trusted Locations:** Click this check box to immediately disable all the folders currently designated as trusted locations and allow only macros from publishers designated as trustworthy to run in Excel.

IN THIS CHAPTER

» Getting familiar with Visual Basic for Applications and the Visual Basic Editor

» Editing a macro in the Visual Basic Editor

» Creating a dialog box that prompts you for input for your macro

» Writing new macros in the Visual Basic Editor

» Using VBA to create user-defined functions

» Using your user-defined functions in your spreadsheets

» Saving user-defined functions as Excel Add-ins

Chapter **2**

VBA Programming

The subject of this chapter is Visual Basic for Applications (usually known simply as VBA), which is the official programming language of Excel, and how you can use it to edit the macros that you record (as described in Book 8, Chapter 1) as well as to write new macros. The key to editing and writing macros in VBA is its editing program, the Visual Basic Editor (often abbreviated as VBE). The Visual Basic Editor offers a rich environment for coding and debugging VBA code with an interface that rivals Excel itself in terms of features and complexity.

VBA is a huge subject, well beyond the scope of this book. In this chapter, I simply introduce you to the Visual Basic Editor, and I explain how to use it to do basic macro editing. I also show you how to use the Visual Basic Editor to create custom Excel functions that you can then use when building formulas in your Excel spreadsheets. Custom functions (also known as *user-defined functions* or UDFs) work just like built-in functions except that they perform only the calculations that you define, by using just the arguments that you specify.

If this basic introduction to Visual Basic for Applications and using the Visual Basic Editor inspires you to go on and try your hand at real VBA project development in Excel, I recommend *VBA For Dummies*, 5th Edition by John Paul Mueller as an excellent next step. Their book gives you the lowdown on all the ins and outs of VBA programming in that old, familiar, down-home *For Dummies* style that you've come to know and love.

Using the Visual Basic Editor

The first question that you may have is where the heck did they stick this Visual Basic Editor that you've heard so much about? Actually, the Visual Basic Editor is always ready to step forward whenever you press Alt+F11 or click the Visual Basic command button on the Developer tab or press Alt+LV when this optional tab is displayed on the Ribbon.

REMEMBER

The Developer tab is not one of the permanent tabs on the Excel Ribbon. If your Ribbon doesn't have a Developer tab, this just means that you haven't yet added it to the Ribbon, something you definitely want to do when working with macros. To add the Developer tab, click the Developer check box in the Main Tabs list box on the Customize Ribbon tab of the Excel Options dialog box (Alt+FTC) to select it.

Figure 2-1 shows the arrangement of the typical components in the Visual Basic Editor after you first open its window and open a new module sheet. As you can see, this window contains its own menu bar (with a few more menus than the regular Excel window uses). Beneath the menu bar, you find a Visual Basic Editor Standard toolbar. This toolbar, shown in Figure 2-2, contains a number of buttons that you may use when creating and editing VBA code.

Beneath the Standard toolbar in the Visual Basic Editor, you find a number of tiled windows of various sizes and shapes. Keep in mind that these are the default windows. They aren't the only windows that you can have open in the Visual Basic Editor (as though it weren't crowded and confusing enough), nor is this the only way that they can be arranged.

The two most important windows (at least, when you're first starting out using the Visual Basic Editor) are the Project Explorer window and the Code window. The Project Explorer window, which is located to the immediate left of the Code window (refer to Figure 2-1), shows you all the projects that you have open in the Visual Basic Editor and enables you to easily navigate their various parts. Note that in VBA, a *project* consists of all the code and user forms that belong to a particular workbook along with the sheets of the workbook itself.

Properties window   Code window

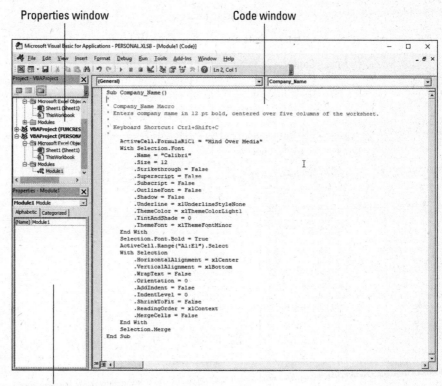

FIGURE 2-1:
The Visual Basic
Editor window
as it normally
appears when
editing a macro.   Project Explorer window

The macros that you record in the workbook, as well as any that you write for it in the Visual Basic Editor, are recorded on module sheets to which generic names are assigned, such as Module1, Module2, and so forth. The actual lines of VBA programming code for the macro that are stored on a particular module sheet appear in the Code window when you select its module in the Project Explorer window. (The Code window appears to the immediate right of the Project Explorer window.)

To open a module in the Code window, double-click its module icon in the Project Explorer or right-click the module icon and then click View Code at the top of its shortcut menu.

TIP

If you want to rename a module in your VBA project to something a little more descriptive than Module1, Module2, and so on, you can do this in the Properties window that appears immediately below the Project Explorer. Simply click and drag through the name (such as Module1 or Module2) that appears after the label (Name) on the Alphabetic tab in the Properties window and replace it with a more descriptive name before you press Enter. When renaming a module, remember that you must use the same naming guidelines as when naming a range name in a worksheet: Begin the module name with a letter of the alphabet and don't put any spaces between words. (Use underlines instead.)

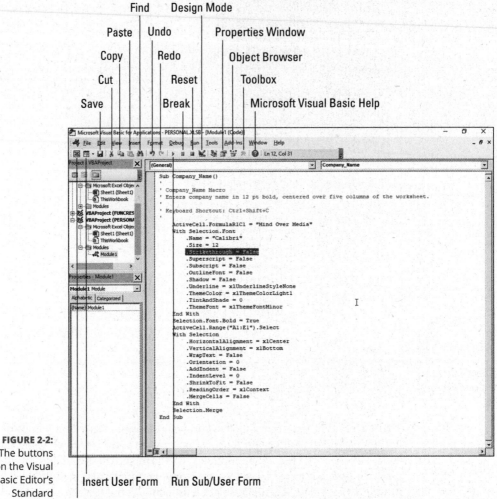

Find   Design Mode

Paste   Undo   Properties Window

Copy   Redo   Object Browser

Cut   Reset   Toolbox

Save   Break   Microsoft Visual Basic Help

FIGURE 2-2:
The buttons
on the Visual
Basic Editor's
Standard
toolbar.

Insert User Form   Run Sub/User Form

View Microsoft Excel

Editing recorded macros

After you've created a macro, you don't necessarily have to re-record it to change the way it behaves. In many cases, you will find it more expedient to change its behavior by simply editing its contents in the Visual Basic Editor. Note that if the macro you want to edit is stored in your Personal Macro Workbook (that personal.xlsb file in the XLSTART folder — see Book 8, Chapter 1 for details), you *must* unhide this workbook before you edit it in the Visual Basic Editor.

To unhide the Personal Macro Workbook, follow these steps:

1. **Click the Unhide command button on the Ribbon's View tab or press Alt+WU.**

Excel opens the Unhide dialog box showing the workbook, PERSONAL.XLSB, in its Unhide Workbook list box.

2. **Click PERSONAL.XLSB in the Unhide Workbook list box and then press Enter.**

This action makes the Personal Macro Workbook visible and activates it so that you can now edit its macros in the Visual Basic Editor.

To open a macro for editing in the Visual Basic Editor, follow these steps:

1. **Click the View Macros option on the Macros command button on the View tab or press Alt+WMV or Alt+F8.**

This action opens the Macro dialog box showing all the names of the macros that you've defined in the workbook and in your Personal Macro Workbook.

2. **Click the name of the macro that you want to edit in the Macro Name list box and then click the Edit button.**

This action opens the Visual Basic Editor with the code for your macro displayed in the Code window unless you select the name of a macro saved in the Personal Macro Workbook and this workbook is still hidden. In that case, Excel displays an Alert dialog box telling you that you can't edit a hidden macro and informing you that you need to unhide this workbook. You then need to click OK in the Alert dialog box, press Escape to close the Macro dialog box, and then follow the steps for unhiding the Personal Macro Workbook immediately preceding these steps before you repeat these first two macro editing steps.

After you have the lines of code for the macro displayed in the Code window in the Visual Basic Editor, you can edit any of its statements as needed. If you want to obtain a printout of the lines of code in your macro before you begin making changes, click File ⇨ Print on the Visual Basic Editor menu bar or press Ctrl+P. This action opens a Print – VBAProject dialog box with the Current Module option button selected in the Range section and the Code check box selected in the Print What section so that you can go ahead and click OK to have Excel print all the statements in the macro.

When editing the macro's commands, remember that you can use the Edit ⇨ Undo (Ctrl+Z) command to undo any deletion that you make by mistake.

3. **Edit the statements in the Code window of the Visual Basic Editor as needed.**

After you finish editing the macro, you're ready to return to your spreadsheet, where you can test out the modified macro and make sure that you haven't added some wacky, unwanted command to the macro or, even worse, crippled it so that it no longer runs at all.

4. **Click the View Microsoft Excel button at the beginning of the Standard toolbar or click the workbook's minimized button on the Windows taskbar.**

Select an appropriate or safe place in which to test your modified macro and then run it, either by pressing its shortcut keys or by pressing Alt+F8, clicking it in the Macro list box, and then clicking the Run button.

If something doesn't work as intended or if the macro doesn't work at all, you need to return to the Visual Basic Editor and find and correct your error(s). Click the Visual Basic command button on the Developer tab of the Ribbon (Alt+LV) to return to the Visual Basic Editor and have a try at editing the code one more time.

If everything checks out and runs as planned, you need to save your changes as outlined in Step 5.

5. **Click the Save button on the Quick Access toolbar to save the changes to the modified macro if it's stored as part of the current workbook.**

If you modified a global macro saved as part of the Personal Macro Workbook, you have to exit Excel in order to save your changes to the macro. When you click the Excel program window's Close button or press Alt+FX or Alt+F4, Excel displays an alert dialog box asking whether you want to save the changes you made to the personal.xlsb file. Click the Yes button to save your macro modifications as you close down Excel.

REMEMBER

Keep in mind that Excel automatically hides the Personal Macro Workbook when you exit Excel if you don't click the Hide command button on the View tab or press Alt+WH when the PERSONAL.XLSB workbook is active sometime before exiting the program. This means that you must remember to click the Unhide command button on the View tab (Alt+WU) and select this personal macro workbook in the Unhide dialog box to make it visible before the next time you launch Excel and need to edit any of its macros during any subsequent editing session.

Finding and replacing code in the macro

You can use the Find feature in the Visual Basic Editor to quickly locate the statements or properties that need editing in your macro. You open the Find dialog box, shown in Figure 2-3, by clicking Edit ⇨ Find on the menu bar, clicking the

Find button on the Standard toolbar, or by pressing Ctrl+F. This dialog box is very similar to the one you use when finding entries in your Excel spreadsheet. The main difference is that the Find dialog box gives you different choices for what to search for (in addition to the familiar options for finding whole words only and matching case):

>> **Current Procedure** option button to search only the current programming procedure in the Code window

>> **Current Module** option button to search only the macros in the current module (the default)

>> **Current Project** option button to search all the macros in all modules within the current project

>> **Selected Text** option button to search only the text that you've selected in the Code window (this option is not available unless you've selected a block of text in the current code)

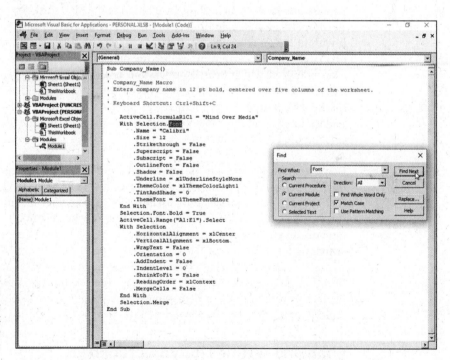

FIGURE 2-3:
Using the Find feature to locate the code to edit in the Code window.

After you enter the Visual Basic property or statement as your search string in the Find What text box, select the search options, and click the Find Next button, Excel attempts to locate its first occurrence in the code. When it does, the program highlights that occurrence in the current procedure, module, VBA project, or selected text block (depending on which Search option you use). To find the next occurrence, you can click the Find Next button in the Find dialog box again or, if you close this dialog box, press F3.

If you have a number of occurrences throughout the macro that require the same type of updating, you can use the Replace feature to both find and replace them in the macro code. This is particularly useful when you decide to change a particular value throughout a macro (such as selecting the cell range named "income_08" for processing instead of the range "income_07"), and you want to make sure that you don't miss any occurrences.

To open the Replace dialog box, click Edit⇨Replace on the Visual Basic Editor menu bar or press Ctrl+H. Note that you can open the Replace dialog box from within the Find dialog box by clicking its Replace button.

The Replace dialog box that appears is just like the Find dialog box, except that it contains a Replace With text box along with the Find What text box and has Replace and Replace All buttons in addition to the Find Next button. After entering the property or statement to find in the Find What text box and the one to replace it with in the Replace With text box, click the Find Next button to locate the first occurrence in the current procedure, module, VBA project, or selected text block (depending on which Search option you use). After this occurrence is selected in the Code window, you have it replaced with the replacement text by clicking the Replace button. Excel then locates the next occurrence, which you can then replace by clicking the Replace button or pass over to find the next occurrence by clicking the Find Next button.

WARNING

Don't use the Replace All button to replace all the occurrences in your macro unless you're 100 percent sure that you won't be globally replacing something that shouldn't be replaced and possibly screwing up your macro big time. I once typed "selection.font.bold = ture" into the Replace With text box when I intended to enter "selection.font.bold = true" as the replacement text when searching for the property "Selection.Font.Bold = False" in the macro. I then clicked the Replace All button only to discover to my dismay that I introduced this error throughout the code! Of course, I then had to turn around and use the Replace feature to find all the instances of "selection.font.bold = ture" and replace them with "Selection.Font.Bold = true".

Changing settings for VBA properties

Even when you don't know anything about programming in VBA (and even if you aim to keep it that way), you can still get the gist of some of the more obvious properties in a macro that change certain settings, such as number format or font attribute, by experimenting with assigning them new values.

In the Company_Name macro shown previously in Figure 2-3, for example, you can tell that the section of VBA commands between the line

```
With Selection.Font
```

and the line

```
End With
```

contains the procedure for assigning various font attributes for the current cell selection.

Going a step further, you probably can figure out that most of these attributes are being reset by making the attribute equal to a new entry or value, such as

```
.Name = "Calibri"
```

or

```
.Size = 14
```

or an attribute is being reset by turning it on or off by setting it equal to True or False, such as

```
Selection.Font.Bold = True
```

to make the text in the current cell selection bold.

Now, it doesn't require a programming degree (at least, not the last time I checked) to get the bright idea that you can make your macro behave differently just by — carefully — editing these settings. For example, suppose that you want the final font size to be 24 points instead of 14. All you have to do is change

```
.Size = 14
```

to

```
.Size = 24
```

Likewise, you can have the macro apply single underlining to the cell selection by changing

```
.Underline = xlUnderlineStyleNone
```

to

```
.Underline = xlUnderlineStyleSingle
```

Getting macro input by adding a dialog box

One of the biggest problems with recording macros is that any text or values that
you have the macro enter for you in a worksheet or chart sheet can never vary
thereafter. If you create a macro that enters the heading "Bob's Barbecue Pit"
in the current cell of your worksheet, this is the only heading you'll ever get out of
that macro. However, you can get around this inflexibility by using the InputBox
function. When you run the macro, this Visual Basic function causes Excel to display an Input dialog box where you can enter whatever title makes sense for the
new worksheet. The macro then puts that text into the current cell and formats
this text, if that's what you've trained your macro to do next.

To see how easy it is to use the InputBox function to add interactivity to an otherwise staid macro, follow the steps for converting the Company_Name macro that
currently inputs the text "Mind Over Media" to one that actually prompts you for
the name that you want entered. The InputBox function uses the following syntax:

```
InputBox(prompt[,title][,default][,xpos][,ypos]
    [,helpfile,context])
```

In this function, only the *prompt* argument is required with the rest of the arguments being optional. The *prompt* argument specifies the message that appears
inside the Input dialog box, prompting the user to enter a new value (or in this
case, a new company name). The *prompt* argument can be up to a maximum of
1,024 characters. If you want the prompt message to appear on different lines
inside the dialog box, you enter the functions Chr(13) and Chr(10) in the text (to
insert a carriage return and a linefeed in the message, respectively).

The optional *title* argument specifies what text to display in the title bar of the
Input dialog box. If you don't specify a *title* argument, Excel displays the name of
the application on the title bar. The optional *default* argument specifies the default
response that automatically appears in the text box at the bottom of the Input
dialog box. If you don't specify a default argument, the text box is empty in the
Input dialog box.

The *xpos* and *ypos* optional arguments specify the horizontal distance from the left
edge of the screen to the left edge of the dialog box and the vertical distance from
the top edge of the screen to the top edge of the dialog box. If you don't specify
these arguments, Excel centers the input dialog box horizontally and positions it
approximately one-third of the way down the screen vertically.

The *helpfile* and *context* optional arguments specify the name of the custom Help file that you make available to the user to explain the workings of the Input dialog box as well as the type of data that it accepts. As part of the process of creating a custom help file for use in the Excel Help system, you assign the topic a context number appropriate to its content, which is then specified as the *context* argument for the InputBox function. When you specify a help file and *context* argument for this function, Excel adds a Help button to the custom Input dialog box that users can click to access the custom help file in the Help window.

Before you can add the line of code to the macro with the InputBox function, you need to find the place in the Visual Basic commands where the line should go. To enter the Mind Over Media text into the active cell, the Company_Name macro uses the following Visual Basic command on Line 9:

```
ActiveCell.FormulaR1C1 = "Mind Over Media"
```

To add interactivity to the macro, you need to insert the InputBox function on a line in the Code window right above this `ActiveCell.FormulaR1C1` statement, as follows:

1. **Position the insertion point in the Code window at the beginning of the `ActiveCell.FormulaR1C1` statement and press Enter to insert a new line.**

   Now that you've added a new line, you need to move the insertion point up to it.

2. **Press the ↑ key to position the insertion point at the beginning of the new line.**

   On this line, you want to create a variable that supplies the *prompt* argument to the InputBox function. To do this, you state the name of the variable (InputMsg in this case) followed by its current entry. Be sure to enclose the message text on the right side of the equal sign in a closed pair of double quotation marks.

3. **Type the following code to create the InputMsg variable on line 9 and then press the Enter key to start a new line 10:**

   ```
   InputMsg = "Enter the company name or title for this
       worksheet in the text box below and then click OK:"
   ```

   Next, you create a variable named InputTitle that supplies the optional *title* argument for the InputBox function. This variable makes the text "Spreadsheet Title" appear as the title of the Input dialog box. Again, be sure to enclose the name for the dialog box title bar in quotation marks.

4. **Type the following code to create the InputTitle variable on line 10 and then press Enter to insert a new line 11:**

   ```
   InputTitle = "Spreadsheet Title"
   ```

Next, you create a variable name DefaultText that supplied the optional *default* argument to the InputBox function. This variable makes the text, "Mind Over Media," appear as the default entry on the text box at the bottom of the custom Company Name Input dialog box.

5. **Type the following code to create the DefaultText variable on line 11 and then press Enter to insert a new line 12:**

```
DefaultText = "Mind Over Media"
```

Next, you create a final variable named CompanyName that specifies the InputBox function as its entry (using the InputMsg, InputTitle, and DefaultText variables that you just created) and stores the results of this function.

6. **Type the following code to create the SpreadsheetTitle variable that uses the InputBox function on line 1:**

```
SpreadsheetTitle = InputBox(InputMsg, InputTitle,
    DefaultText)
```

Finally, you replace the value, "Mind Over Media", in the ActiveCell. FormulaR1C1 property with the SpreadsheetTitle variable (whose value is determined by whatever is input into the Spreadsheet Title Input dialog box), thus effectively replacing this constant in the macro with the means for making this input truly interactive.

7. **Select "Mind Over Media" on line 1 and replace it with** SpreadsheetTitle **(with *no* quotation marks).**

8. **Save the edited macro by clicking the Save button on the Visual Basic toolbar and then return to the worksheet by clicking the View Microsoft Excel button or pressing Alt+F11. Then, click the Hide button in the Window group of the VIEW tab.**

Now, you're ready to open a new workbook and run the edited macro by pressing Ctrl+N.

Figure 2-4 shows the Code window with the edited Company_Name macro after adding the statements that make it interactive. Figure 2-5 shows the Spreadsheet Title dialog box in action in the worksheet. This input dialog box now automatically appears and prompts you for input whenever you run the edited and now fully interactive version of the Company_Name macro.

To go ahead and enter Mind Over Media into the current cell and then format it by using the rest of the macro commands, you just click OK in this custom dialog box. To enter and format the name of another company, you simply type the name of the company (which automatically replaces Mind Over Media in the text box) before you click OK.

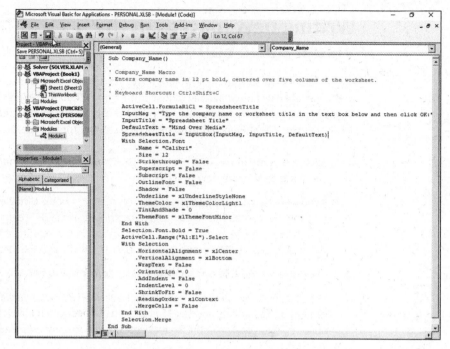

FIGURE 2-4:
The Company_
Name Code
window after
adding variables
and the InputBox
function.

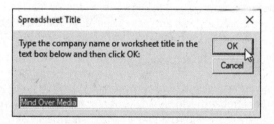

FIGURE 2-5:
The Spreadsheet
Title dialog box
that appears
when you run the
Company_Name
macro.

TECHNICAL
STUFF

WHY NOT SIMPLY TYPE IN THE ARGUMENTS OF THE INPUTBOX FUNCTION?

The biggest reason for using the variables InputMsg, InputTitle, and DefaultText to supply the *prompt, title,* and *default* arguments of the InputBox function — rather than just typing them into the function — is their length. If you typed in all three pieces of text within the parentheses of the InputBox function, you would end up with one of the longest (and hardest to read) lines of code in history. When you use variables to do the job, as in the example shown previously, you end up with lines of code that fit on one screen, thus making the lines of code easier to read and also making it possible to print them on a normal piece of paper. If you use the variables on other procedures in the macro, declaring them all together at the beginning of the code also makes it easy to update their values.

Writing new macros in the Visual Basic Editor

After you have the skill in the VBA language, you can write new macros from scratch in the Visual Basic Editor instead of just editing ones that you've previously recorded in your spreadsheet by using Excel's macro recorder. When creating a macro from scratch in the Visual Basic Editor, you need to follow these general steps:

1. **Click the name of the VBA project in the Project Explorer window where you want to add the new macro.**

If you want to write a macro just for the current workbook, click the VBAProject function that contains its filename in parentheses, as in VBAProject (My Spreadsheet). If you want to write a global macro in the Personal Macro Workbook, click VBAProject (PERSONAL.XLSB) in the Project Explorer window.

2. **Click Insert⇨Module on the Visual Basic Editor menu bar.**

Excel responds by opening a new, blank Code window in the Visual Basic Editor window and by adding another Module icon (named with the next available number) in the outline in the Project Explorer window under the appropriate VBA Project.

Next, you begin your macro by creating a subroutine (all macros, even the ones you record in the spreadsheet, are really Visual Basic subroutines). To do this, you just type sub (for subroutine).

3. **Type** sub **and then press the spacebar.**

Now, you need to name your new macro, which you do by naming your subroutine. Remember that in naming your new macro (or a subroutine), you follow the same rules as when naming a range name (begin with a letter and no spaces).

4. **Type the name of your macro and then press the Enter key.**

As soon as you press the Enter key, the Visual Basic Editor inserts a closed pair of parentheses after the macro's name, a blank line, and an End Sub statement on its own line below that. It then positions the insertion point at the beginning of the blank line between the lines with the Sub and End Sub statements. It's here that you enter the lines of code for the macro that you're writing.

5. **Enter the lines of VBA code for the macro in between the Sub and End Sub statements.**

Before you begin writing the VBA statements that your macro is to execute, you should first document the purpose and functioning of this macro. To do this, type an apostrophe (') at the beginning of each line of this text to enter it as a comment. (Excel knows not to try to execute any line of code that's prefaced with an apostrophe.) When you press the Enter key to start a new line that begins with an apostrophe, the line of text turns green, indicating that the Visual Basic Editor considers it to be a comment that's not to be executed when the macro runs.

After you document the purpose of the macro with your comments, you begin entering the statements that you want the macro to execute (which must not be prefaced by apostrophes). To indent lines of code to make them easier to read, press Tab. If you need to outdent the line, press Shift+Tab. For help on writing VBA code, refer to the VBA online help. When you finish writing the code for your macro, you need to save it before you test it.

6. **Click File ⇨ Save on the Visual Basic Editor menu bar or press Ctrl+S.**

After you save your new macro, you can click the View Microsoft Excel button on the Standard toolbar to return to your worksheet where you can try it. To run the new macro that you've written, click View ⇨ Macros on the Ribbon or press Alt+F8 to open the Macro dialog box and then click the name of the macro that you just wrote before you click OK.

If Excel encounters an error when running the macro, it returns you to the Visual Basic Editor, and an Alert Microsoft Visual Basic dialog box appears, indicating (in very cryptic form) the nature of the error. Click the Debug button in this dialog box to have the Visual Basic Editor highlight the line of code that it can't execute. You can then attempt to find the mistake and edit it in the line of code. If you do eliminate the cause of the error, the Visual Basic Editor removes the highlighting from that line of code, and you can then click the Continue button (which automatically replaces the Run button when the Editor goes into debug mode) with the blue triangle pointing to the right on the Standard toolbar to continue running the macro.

Creating Custom Excel Functions

One of the best uses of VBA in Excel is to create custom spreadsheet functions also known as *user-defined functions* (UDFs for short). User-defined functions are great because you don't have to access the Macro dialog box to run them. In fact, you enter them into your spreadsheets just like you do any of the other built-in spreadsheet functions, either with the Insert Function button on the Formula bar or by typing them directly into a cell.

To create a user-defined function, you must do four little things:

>> Create a new module sheet where the custom function is to be defined in the Visual Basic Editor by selecting its project in the Project Explorer window and then clicking Insert ➪ Module on the Visual Basic Editor menu bar.

>> Enter the name of the custom function and specify the names of the arguments that this function takes on in the first line in the Code window — note that you can't duplicate any built-in function names, such as SUM or AVERAGE functions, and so on, and you must list argument names in the order in which they are processed and enclosed in parentheses.

>> Enter the formula, or set of formulas, that tells Excel how to calculate the custom function's result by using the argument names listed in the Function command with whatever arithmetic operators or built-in functions are required to get the calculation made on the line or lines below.

>> Indicate that you've finished defining the user-defined function by entering the End Function command on the last line.

To see how this procedure works in action, consider this scenario: Suppose that you want to create a custom function that calculates the sales commissions for your salespeople based on the number of sales they make in a month as well as the total amount of their monthly sales. (They sell big-ticket items, such as RVs.) Your custom Commission function will then have two arguments — *TotalSales* and *ItemsSold* — so that the first line of code on the module sheet in the Code window is

```
Function Commission(TotalSales,ItemsSold)
```

In determining how the commissions are actually calculated, suppose that you base the commission percentage on the number of sales made during the month. For five sales or fewer in a month, you pay a commission rate of 4.5 percent of the salesperson's total monthly sales; for sales of six or more, you pay a commission rate of 5 percent.

To define the formula section of the Commission custom function, you need to set up an IF construction. This IF construction is similar to the IF function that you enter into a worksheet cell except that you use different lines in the macro code for the construction in the custom function. An ELSE command separates the command that is performed if the expression is True from the command that is performed if the expression is False. The macro code is terminated by an END IF command. To set the custom function so that your salespeople get 4.5 percent of total sales for five or fewer items sold and 5 percent of total sales for more than five items sold, you enter the following lines of code underneath the line with the Function command:

```
If ItemsSold <= 5 Then
    Commission = TotalSales * 0.045
Else
    Commission = TotalSales * 0.05
End If
```

Figure 2-6 shows you how the code for this user-defined function appears in the Code window for its module sheets. The indents for the IF...END IF statements are made with the Tab key and make differentiating the parts of the IF construction easy. The first formula, Commission = TotalSales * 0.045 is used when the IF expression ItemsSold <= 5 is found to be True. Otherwise, the second formula underneath the Else command, Commission = TotalSales * 0.05 is used.

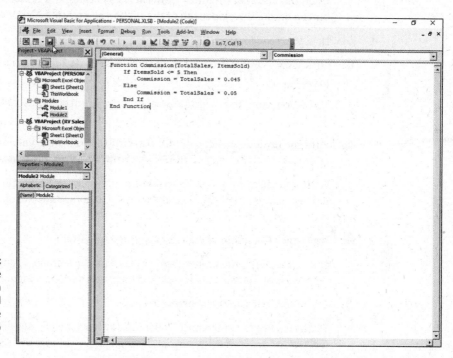

FIGURE 2-6: Entering the Commission user-defined function in the Personal Macro Workbook.

After entering the definition for your user-defined function, you are ready to save it by clicking File ⇨ Save on the Visual Basic Editor menu bar or by pressing Ctrl+S. Then, you can click the View Microsoft Excel button on the Standard toolbar to return to the worksheet where you can try out your new custom function.

TIP

If you want to be able to use your user-defined function in any spreadsheet you create, be sure that you select VBAProject (personal.xlsb) in the Project Explorer window before you open a new module and define the custom function there.

Adding a description to a user-defined function

To help your user understand the purpose of your custom functions, you can add descriptions that appear in Insert Function and Function Arguments dialog boxes that help explain what the function does. To add this kind of description to your user–defined function, you use the Object Browser, a special window in the Visual Basic Editor that enables you to get information about particular objects available to the project that you have open.

To add a description for your user–defined function, follow these steps:

1. **Open the Visual Basic Editor from Excel by clicking the Visual Basic button on the Developer tab of the Ribbon or pressing Alt+LV or Alt+F11.**

Now, you need to open the Object Browser.

2. **Click View⇨Object Browser from the Visual Basic Editor menu bar or press F2.**

This action opens the Object Browser window, which obscures the Code window.

3. **Click the drop-down list box that currently contains the value <All Libraries> and then select VBAProject from the drop-down list.**

When you select VBAProject from this drop-down list, the Object Browser then displays your user-defined function as one of the objects in one of the Classes in the pane on the left.

4. **Right-click the name of your user-defined function.**

This action selects the function and displays it in the Members pane on the right, while at the same time displaying the object's shortcut menu.

5. **Click Properties on the shortcut menu.**

This action opens the Member Options dialog box for your user-defined function, where you can enter your description of this function, as shown in Figure 2-7.

6. **Type the text that you want to appear in the Insert Function and Function Arguments dialog box for the user-defined function in the Description text box and then click OK.**

Now, you can close the Object Browser and save your changes.

7. **Click the Close Window button to close the Object Browser and then click File⇨Save.**

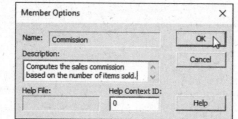

Using a custom function in your spreadsheet

The great thing about custom functions is that they can be inserted into your worksheets with the Insert Function button on the Formula bar. Figures 2-8, 2-9, and 2–10 illustrate how easy it is to enter the custom Commission function in a worksheet with this button.

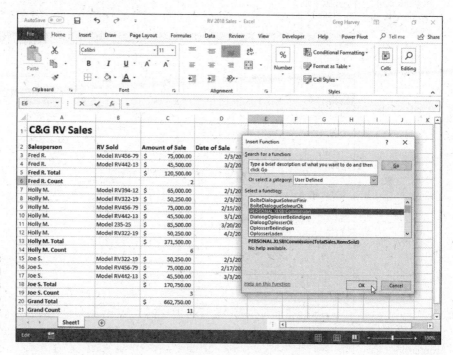

FIGURE 2-8:
Selecting a cell in the RV Sales spreadsheet into which to enter the Commission function.

Figure 2-8 shows a worksheet that contains a table with the April 2018 RV sales for three salespeople: Fred, Holly, and Jack. As you can see, the Automatic Sub-totals feature (covered in Book 6, Chapter 1) has been used to compute both the monthly total sales (with the SUM function) and the number of sales (with the COUNT function) for each of these three salespeople.

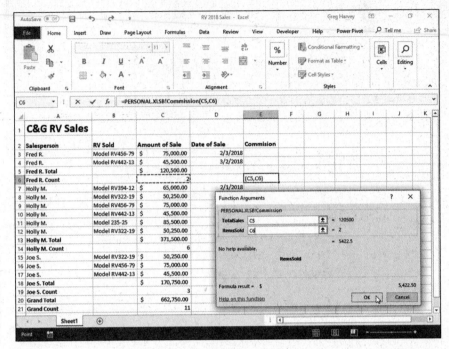

FIGURE 2-9:
Specifying the TotalSales and ItemsSold arguments in the RV Sales spreadsheet.

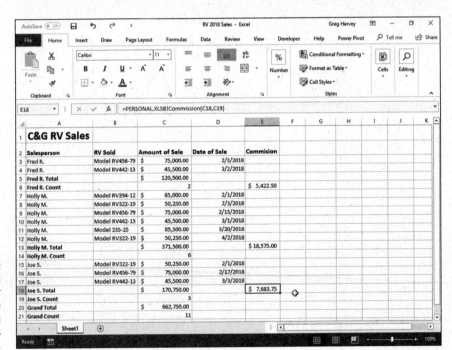

FIGURE 2-10:
Completed spreadsheet for all salespeople computed with the Commissions function.

To calculate the April monthly commissions for each salesperson in this table, you select the cell where you want the first commission to be calculated (Fred's commission in cell E5). Click the Insert Function button on the Formula bar and then click User Defined at the very bottom of the Or Select a Category drop-down list. Doing this displays the PERSONAL.XLSB!Commission custom function in the Select a Function list box.

When you click OK after selecting the PERSONAL.XLSB!Commission function in the Insert Function dialog box, the Function Arguments dialog box appears, as shown in Figure 2-9. Here, you select cell C4 with Fred's total sales amount for April as the TotalSales argument and cell C5 with the number of sales made in that month as the ItemsSold argument.

When you click OK in the Function Arguments dialog box, Excel calculates Fred's commission by using the 4.5 percent commission rate because his two sales made in April are well below the five sales necessary to bump him up to the 5 percent commission rate used by the custom Commission function. Figure 2-10 shows the completed April sales table after calculating the monthly commissions for Fred, Holly, and Jack. In using the custom Commission function, both Fred and Holly fall into the 4.5 percent commission rate. Only Jack, the April RV sales king, gets paid the higher 5 percent commission rate for his six sales during this month.

Saving custom functions in add-in files

The only limitation to the user-defined functions that you save as part of a regular workbook file or the Personal Macro Workbook file is that when you enter them directly into a cell (without the use of the Insert Function dialog box), you must preface their function names with their filenames. For example, if you want to type in the custom Commission function that's saved in the Personal Macro Workbook, you enter the following formula:

```
=Commission(C9,C10)
```

Assuming that cell C9 contains the total sales and cell C10 contains the number of items sold, Excel returns the #NAME? error value to the cell. If you then edit the function to include the Personal Macro Workbook's filename as follows

```
=PERSONAL.XLSB!Commission(C9,C10)
```

Excel calculates the sales commission based on the *TotalSales* in C9 and the *Items-Sold* in C10, returning this calculated value to the cell containing this user-defined function.

To be able to omit the filename from the custom functions that you create when you enter them directly into a cell, you need to save the workbook file that contains them as a special add-in file. (For details on using add-ins in Excel, see Book 1, Chapter 2.) Then, after you've saved the workbook with your user-defined functions as an add-in file, you can start entering them into any worksheet sans their filename qualifier by activating the add-in in the Add-Ins dialog box. (Press Alt+FTAA and then click the Go command button when Excel Add-Ins is displayed on the Manage drop-down list button.)

To convert a workbook containing the user-defined functions that you want to be able to enter into worksheets without their filenames, follow these steps:

1. **Unhide the PERSONAL workbook in which you've saved your user-defined functions in Excel by clicking the Unhide button on the View tab and then selecting PERSONAL followed by OK.**

2. **Press Alt+F11 or click the Visual Basic command button on the Developer tab or press Alt+LV.**

   This action opens the Visual Basic Editor window with the workbook file containing the user-defined functions selected in the Project Explorer window. Now you want to set up protection for this workbook so that no one but you can modify its contents.

3. **Click Tools⇨VBAProject Properties from the Visual Basic Editor's menu bar.**

   This action opens the VBAProject — Project Properties dialog box with a General and a Protection tab, shown in Figure 2-11.

4. **Click the Protection tab and then click the Lock Project for Viewing check box.**

   Putting a check mark in this check box prevents other users from viewing the custom functions so that they can't make any changes to them. Next, you add a password that prevents them from removing the view protection status.

5. **Click the Password text box, enter the password there, and then click the Confirm Password text box and re-enter the password exactly as you entered it in the text box above before you click OK.**

   Now you're ready to return to the worksheet where you need to add a title and description for the new add-in file.

6. **Click the View Microsoft Excel button at the beginning of the Standard toolbar.**

   This action returns you to the worksheet in Excel. Before saving the workbook as an add-in, you should add a title for the user-defined functions that it contains. (This information then appears in the Add-Ins dialog box whenever you select the add-in file.)

7. **Click File ⇨ Info.**

Excel 2019 displays the Info screen about the workbook in the Backstage view. Here you enter a brief name for the add-in in the Title field and a longer description of its custom functions.

8. **Click the Title text box and enter a descriptive title for the add-in, and then click the Save As option on the menu in the Backstage view.**

This action opens the Save As screen where the XLSTART folder is currently selected.

9. **Click XSTART under Current Folder in the right-hand panel.**

Excel opens the Save As dialog box, where you need to change the file type to Excel Add-In (*.xlam) and then specify the filename (to which Excel automatically appends the `.xlam` filename extension) under which to save it.

10. **Click the Save as Type pop-up button and then select Excel Add-In (*.xlam) as the type.**

11. **Click the File Name combo box and make any necessary changes to the filename (without changing the `.xlam` filename extension) before you click the Save button.**

After saving your workbook as an add-in file, you're ready to activate the add-in so that you can enter its user-defined functions in any worksheet.

12. **Click File ⇨ Options ⇨ Add-Ins or press Alt+FTAA.**

13. **Click the Go button near the bottom of the Add-Ins tab after checking to make sure that Excel Add-Ins is displayed on the Manage drop-down list button.**

This action opens the Add-Ins dialog box showing the names of all the available add-ins. You must now add the name of your new add-in to this list.

14. **Click the name of your new add-in file in the Browse list box and then click OK.**

This action closes the Browse dialog box and returns you to the Add-Ins dialog box that now lists your new add-in file. Now all you have to do is make sure that the check box in front of the name of the new add-in (which displays the title and description you gave the add-in at the bottom of the Add-Ins dialog box) is selected before you click OK. (See Figure 2-12.)

15. **Click the check box in front of the name of the new add-in and then click OK.**

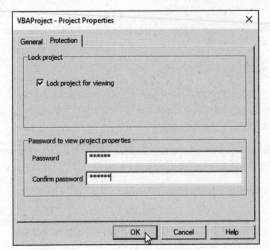

FIGURE 2-11:
Protecting the
VBA project
so that its
user-defined
functions can't be
changed.

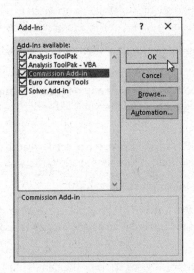

FIGURE 2-12:
Activating the
new add-in file
in the Add-Ins
dialog box.

As soon as you click OK, Excel closes the Add-Ins dialog box and returns you to the VBA Editor window. You can then select the Save button (Ctrl+S) followed by the View Microsoft Excel button (Alt+F11) on the VBA standard toolbar. When you're back in the PERSONAL workbook, you can then hide it again by clicking the Hide button on the View tab (Alt+WH).

REMEMBER

After that, you can start entering the custom functions that this add-in file contains directly into the cells of any spreadsheet without having to open the Insert Function dialog box.

Index

D

dash (-), 96

data analysis

  3D Map feature

    adding layers, 713

    adding scenes, 713

    creating animations, 709–712

    editing animations, 713

    general discussion, 709

    replaying animations, 712–713

    sharing animations, 713–714

  forecast worksheets, 714–717

  general discussion, 673

  pivot charts

    creating, 699

    filtering, 701

    formatting, 701

    moving to own sheet, 700

  pivot tables

    adding fields, 693–694

    calculated fields, 696–697

    changing settings, 698–699

    changing summary function, 695–696

    creating manually, 674, 678–683

    creating recommended, 677–678

    creating with Quick Analysis tool, 674–677

    defined, 674

    filtering, 688–692

    formatting, 683–688

    pivoting, 693–694

    sorting, 693

    versatility of, 674

  Power Pivot add-in

    adding calculated columns, 707–709

    data modeling with, 703–705

    loading, 702

    online help topics, 707

    switching between Data View and Diagram View, 705–707

  what-if analysis

    data tables, 650–656

    general discussion, 649

    goal seeking, 650, 662–664

    scenarios, 650, 656–662

    Solver add-in, 664–672

Data Analysis Expression (DAX), 707–709

data entry

  AutoComplete feature

    disabling temporarily, 105–106

    overriding, 105

    overview, 104–105

  AutoCorrect feature

    adding automated replacements to, 106–107

    capitalization errors, 106

    typo errors, 106

  AutoFill feature

    custom lists, 115–117

    Fill button, 112–113

    Fill handle, 109–110

    formulas, 112

    overriding, 111

    overview, 109

    reverse order, 111

    ScreenTip indicator, 110

    series with increments other than one, 113–115

    on touchscreen devices, 112

  AutoRecover feature

    abandoning recovered version, 131

    opening recovered version, 130

    retaining original version, 131

    retaining recovered version for later viewing, 131

    saving recovered version, 131

    setting time interval, 130

  in cell ranges, 101

  completing entries, 99–101

  constraining to cell ranges, 107–108

  in corresponding cells of selected worksheets, 101

  Data Validation feature

    applying to similarly formatted cells, 121–122

    drop-down menus, 122

    error alert message, 120–121, 123

    identifying cells with data validation, 123

    input message, 120–121, 123

    list of restrictions, 121

    overview, 119

DGET database function, 629

digital ink
  deleting, 489
  digital stamps, 484
  hiding/redisplaying, 489
  highlighting, 488
  ink color, 487–488
  line weight, 487
  pen type, 487
  playback, 489
  writing, 488

digital signatures
  adding, 480–483
  digital stamps, 484
  displaying, 484
  general discussion, 479–480
  invisible, 480
  purpose of, 480
  validity of, 480
  visible, 480

DISC financial function, 399

#DIV/0! error value, 325, 348, 353–354

DMAX database function, 629

DMIN database function, 629

document recovery, 130–131

dollar sign ($), 96, 162, 325, 327

DOLLAR text function, 438

DOLLARDE financial function, 399

DOLLARFR financial function, 399

double-clicking, defined, 28

doughnut charts, 524

DPRODUCT database function, 629

dragging and dropping
  copying by, 218–219
  editing cells, 216–219
  general discussion, 216–217
  process for, 217–218
  sharing data between programs, 505–506
  to unseen part of worksheet, 217–218

dragging through cell selections, defined, 28

DSTDEV database function, 629

DSTDEVP database function, 629

DSUM database function, 628–630

DURATION financial function, 399

DVAR database function, 629

DVARP database function, 629

E

editing worksheets
  clearing comments, 205
  clearing data, 205
  clearing hyperlinks, 205
  completing entries, 202
  cutting, copying, and pasting, 216–217, 219–226
  deleting cells, 205–207
  deleting data, 202
  deleting hyperlinks, 205
  dragging and dropping, 216–219
  editing in Formula bar vs. in cell, 204
  finding and replacing data, 230–232
  finding data, 227–230
  general discussion, 193–194
  groups of worksheets, 262–263
  inserting cells, 207–209
  inserting data, 202
  moving, 216–218
  redoing edits, 203–204
  replacing data, 201–202
  undoing edits, 202–204

EFFECT financial function, 399

e-mail
  hyperlinks to addresses, 470, 472
  sharing workbooks online
    as attachments, 496
    as hyperlinks, 496
    as Internet fax, 497
    as PDF files, 496–497
    as XPS files, 496

embedded charts. *See also* charts
  defined, 521
  moving onto separate chart sheets, 522
  printing, 552
  separate chart sheets vs., 521–522

equal sign (=), 94–95, 308, 314, 316, 623

error trapping
  with conditional formatting, 356–357
  defined, 347

MIN (minimum) statistical function, 412, 606

Mini Calendar add-in, 74

mini-toolbar
  cell formatting, 156–158
  disabling/enabling, 50

minus sign (–), 314, 316

Mueller, John Paul, 734

Multipurpose Internet Mail Extension Hypertext
    Markup Language (MIME HTML), 127

N

#N/A error value, 348, 355

#NAME? error value, 348, 355

1900 date system, 67, 96–97

1904 date system, 67, 96–97

NOMINAL financial function, 399

not equal to sign (<>), 314, 316, 623

NOT logical function, 349

NOW() function, 164–165

#NULL! error value, 348

#NUM! error value, 348

number formats
  Accounting number format, 156
  affecting display vs. value, 159
  assigning, 158–159, 179–180
  assigning colors to, 163, 165
  Comma Style Number format, 156, 179
  creating, 163–165, 181
  Currency Style Number format, 179
  custom, 161
  Date number formats, 163, 371–372
  defining by example, 180
  General number format, 158–159
  identifying format applied to active cell, 155
  for masking display of data, 165–166
  merging into other workbooks, 182
  Percent Style Number format, 156, 179
  predefined, 159–161
  Time number formats, 163, 371–372

numbers (values; numeric entries)
  categories of, 93–94
  dates and times, 93–94, 96–99
  defined, 92

  entering as text, 93–94
  fractions, 94
  inputting numbers, 95–96
  numeric formulas, 99

O

Object Linking and Embedded Database (OLEDB),
    632

OData Data connections, 610, 631–632

ODBC (Open Database Connectivity), 632

ODD math function, 405

ODDFPRICE financial function, 399

ODDFYIELD financial function, 399

ODDLPRICE financial function, 399

ODDLYIELD financial function, 399

ODF (OpenDocument Format), 128

ODS files, 128, 511, 514

Office 2019
  changing background pattern, 22
  look and feel of, 14
  subscription information, 22

Office 365, 1, 493

Office add-ins
  closing, 74
  deleting, 74
  inserting into worksheets, 74
  installing, 72–73
  overview, 72

OFFSET reference function, 430

OLEDB (Object Linking and Embedded Database),
    632

OneDrive (formerly: SkyDrive)
  AutoSaving to by default, 21
  displaying contents of, 199
  overview, 125
  preventing Excel from asking for password when
    saving, 128
  sharing workbooks online
    editing changes, 495
    editing via Excel Online, 499–502
    expiration dates, 494
    hyperlinks, 495–496
    process for, 493–495

About the Author

Greg Harvey has authored tons of computer books, the most recent being *Excel 2019 For Dummies.* He started out training business users on how to use IBM personal computers and their attendant computer software in the rough-and-tumble days of DOS, WordStar, and Lotus 1-2-3 in the mid-80s of the last century. After working for a number of independent training firms, he went on to teach semester-long courses in spreadsheet and database management software at Golden Gate University in San Francisco.

His love of teaching has translated into an equal love of writing. *For Dummies* books are, of course, his all-time favorites to write because they enable him to write to his favorite audience, the beginner. They also enable him to use humor (a key element to success in the training room) and, most delightful of all, to express an opinion or two about the subject matter at hand.

Dedication

To all the students in my different computer classes who taught me so much about what's really important and what's not when it comes to using computer software.

Author's Acknowledgments

I am always so grateful to the many people who work so hard to bring my book projects into being, and this one is no exception. If anything, I am even more thankful for their talents, given the size and complexity of an All-in-One.

This time, special thanks are in order to Katie Mohr for giving me this opportunity to write (and write and write) about Excel in this great All-in-One format. Next, I want to express great thanks to my project editor, Kelly Ewing. Thanks also go to Russ Mullen for the great technical edit, to Mohammed Zafar for coordinating the book's production, and to everybody at Wiley Publishing.

Publisher's Acknowledgments

Associate Publisher: Katie Mohr

Project Editor: Kelly Ewing

Technical Editor: Russ Mullen

Editorial Assistant: Matthew Lowe

Sr. Editorial Assistant: Cherie Case

Production Editor: Mohammed Zafar Ali

Cover Image: © Jojje/Shutterstock